CAMBRIDGE LIBRAI

Books of enduring scholarly value

Linguistics

From the earliest surviving glossaries and translations to nineteenth-century academic philology and the growth of linguistics during the twentieth century, language has been the subject both of scholarly investigation and of practical handbooks produced for the upwardly mobile, as well as for travellers, traders, soldiers, missionaries and explorers. This collection will reissue a wide range of texts pertaining to language, including the work of Latin grammarians, groundbreaking early publications in Indo-European studies, accounts of indigenous languages, many of them now extinct, and texts by pioneering figures such as Jacob Grimm, Wilhelm von Humboldt and Ferdinand de Saussure.

Coptic Etymological Dictionary

Coptic was the language spoken in Egypt from late ancient times to the seventeenth century, when it was overtaken by Arabic as the national language. Derived from ancient Egyptian, the language of the hieroglyphs, it was written in an adapted form of Greek script. This dictionary lists about 2,000 Coptic words whose etymology has been established from ancient Egyptian and Greek sources, covering two-thirds of the known Coptic vocabulary and complementing W. E. Crum's 1939 *Coptic Dictionary*, still the standard in the field. The Egyptian forms are quoted in hieroglyphic and/or demotic forms. An appendix lists the etymologies of Coptic place-names. The final work of Czech Egyptologist Jaroslav Černý (1898–1970), Professor of Egyptology at Oxford, the Dictionary was brought through to publication by colleagues after his death.

Cambridge University Press has long been a pioneer in the reissuing of out-of-print titles from its own backlist, producing digital reprints of books that are still sought after by scholars and students but could not be reprinted economically using traditional technology. The Cambridge Library Collection extends this activity to a wider range of books which are still of importance to researchers and professionals, either for the source material they contain, or as landmarks in the history of their academic discipline.

Drawing from the world-renowned collections in the Cambridge University Library, and guided by the advice of experts in each subject area, Cambridge University Press is using state-of-the-art scanning machines in its own Printing House to capture the content of each book selected for inclusion. The files are processed to give a consistently clear, crisp image, and the books finished to the high quality standard for which the Press is recognised around the world. The latest print-on-demand technology ensures that the books will remain available indefinitely, and that orders for single or multiple copies can quickly be supplied.

The Cambridge Library Collection will bring back to life books of enduring scholarly value (including out-of-copyright works originally issued by other publishers) across a wide range of disciplines in the humanities and social sciences and in science and technology.

Coptic Etymological Dictionary

EDITED BY JAROSLAV ČERNÝ

CAMBRIDGE
UNIVERSITY PRESS

CAMBRIDGE UNIVERSITY PRESS

Cambridge, New York, Melbourne, Madrid, Cape Town, Singapore,
São Paolo, Delhi, Dubai, Tokyo, Mexico City

Published in the United States of America by Cambridge University Press, New York

www.cambridge.org
Information on this title: www.cambridge.org/9781108013994

This edition first published 1976
This digitally printed version 2010

ISBN 978-1-108-01399-4 Paperback

COPTIC ETYMOLOGICAL DICTIONARY

Et igitur qui hoc lexico contentus non fuerit, et opportunitas erit et materies ad aliud lexicon conficiendum.

An old lexicographer

COPTIC ETYMOLOGICAL DICTIONARY

COMPILED BY

J. ČERNÝ

Sometime Professor of Egyptology in the University of Oxford

CAMBRIDGE UNIVERSITY PRESS

CAMBRIDGE

LONDON · NEW YORK · MELBOURNE

Published by the Syndics of the Cambridge University Press
The Pitt Building, Trumpington Street, Cambridge CB2 1RP
Bentley House, 200 Euston Road, London NW1 2DB
32 East 57th Street, New York, NY10022, USA
296 Beaconsfield Parade, Middle Park, Melbourne 3206, Australia

Library of Congress Catalogue Card Number: 69–10192

ISBN 0 521 07228 X

First published 1976

Printed in Great Britain
at the University Printing House, Cambridge
(Euan Phillips, University Printer)

CONTENTS

PUBLISHERS' NOTE

Professor Černý died at an early stage in the printing of this book. The heavy task of seeing through the press the larger part of the proofs was undertaken by Professor A. F. Shore, Dr I. E. S. Edwards and Mr T. G. H. James of the Department of Egyptian Antiquities, British Museum. To these three scholars the Press owes a deep debt of gratitude. In addition, the Press is obliged to the Reverend Professor J. M. Plumley for advice in the setting of the hieroglyphic passages in Professor Černý's manuscript, and to Dr A. Alcock for compiling the index of Coptic words whose etymology is still unknown.

Thanks are also due to the British Academy and to the Allocators of the Sir Alan Gardiner Settlement for Egyptological Purposes for generous subventions towards production costs.

PREFACE

Students of the Egyptian language will be aware that, whereas the *Wörterbuch der aegyptischen Sprache* and W. Erichsen's *Demotisches Glossar* include Coptic equivalents of ancient Egyptian and Demotic words, W. E. Crum, for reasons which he explains in his Preface, does not give etymologies of Coptic words in his *Coptic Dictionary*. Instead, he refers his readers to the first edition of W. Spiegelberg's *Koptisches Handwörterbuch* for this information, but it must be said that Spiegelberg's book lacks some etymologies which were already known fifty years ago when it was published. In the meantime further progress has been made in this field of study and the present dictionary is an attempt to assemble in as concise a form as possible all the results now available.

A similar, though less detailed, work was being prepared by the late Eugène Dévaud as early as 1922. Students will find appended to his *Études d'étymologie copte* the scheme and a specimen page of the intended publication. He lists a series of Coptic words whose etymologies could be considered as certain, together with their ancient Egyptian and Demotic antecedents, the authority being quoted in each case. Dévaud's death in 1929, however, prevented its completion. But his labours were not wasted, for his widow gave the catalogue-slips to Crum who bequeathed them for the use of students to the Griffith Institute, Oxford, with the remainder of his scientific papers.

My own interest in the study of Coptic etymologies led me, more than twenty-five years ago, to begin compiling a slip-index which was never intended for publication. Exploring the countless works of early Egyptologists in order to find out who had first succeeded in identifying the ancient Egyptian or the Demotic ancestor of a Coptic word would have required more time than I could spare. It was only after I went to Oxford in 1951 that I discovered how much of this laborious research had already been done by Dévaud and I drew freely on his results when putting together my material for this dictionary. Even with this most valuable assistance I found it necessary to re-examine his evidence and to check his references. Moreover, works which were inaccessible to him had to be scrutinized and etymologies which had been discovered since his death had to be incorporated. In fairness to Dévaud I must add that I discarded some of the etymologies which he had accepted and reinstated others which he had rejected.

My guiding principle in compiling this dictionary has been to adopt only etymologies which I considered certain, probable or at least possible. Nevertheless, in a few instances, I have included etymologies which have been generally accepted even though they seem to me suspect. If two or more etymologies have been proposed by previous writers for one word I have usually relied on my own judgment in choosing the one which appeared to me preferable, without recording those which I have rejected. Many Coptic words can be traced back through Demotic to ancient Egyptian and thus the continuity throughout each phase of the language is demonstrable, but there are also many words for which the Demotic link is missing and I do not regard the proposed derivation from ancient Egyptian as necessarily weakened by its absence.

The experience of other lexicographers in languages which are better known than Egyptian and Coptic has shown how easy it is to be misled and I have no illusions about my own fallibility in this respect. I hope, however, that the present work will prove useful to scholars, and I also hope it will encourage others to take up the study. There is still much to be done in this field, as will be apparent to anyone who refers to the index of Coptic words for which no etymology has yet been suggested.

Oxford, 1970 J. ČERNÝ

ABBREVIATIONS

Achmîmic dialect

A_2 Subachmîmic dialect

abn. abnormal

abs. absolute

Adelung, *Mithradates* J. C. Adelung, *Mithradates oder allgemeine Sprachenkunde mit dem Vater Unser als Sprachprobe in bey nahe fünfhundert Sprachen und Mundarten*, Berlin 1806–17

Aeg. *Aegyptus. Rivista italiana di egittologia e di papirologia*, Milan

Aeth. hieroglyphic texts of Dynasty XXV (Ethiopian Period)

Äg. Denkm. in Miramar *Die aegyptischen Denkmaeler in Miramar*, Beschrieben, erläutert und hrsg. von S. Reinisch, Vienna 1865

Åkerblad, *Lettre* Åkerblad, *Lettre sur l'inscription égyptienne de Rosette adressée au citoyen Silvestre de Sacy*, Paris 1802

Akhm. Akhmîmic

Allberry, *Psalm-Book* C. R. C. Allberry, *A Manichaean Psalmbook*, pt. II, Stuttgart 1938

Am. E. A. Amélineau, *La géographie de l'Égypte à l'époque copte*, Paris 1893

Anc. Egypt
Ancient Egypt } *Ancient Egypt* (British School of Archaeology in Egypt), London 1914–35

Ankhsh. S. R. K. Glanville, *Catalogue of Demotic Papyri in the British Museum*, Vol. II. *The Instructions of 'Onchsheshonqy*, London 1955

Anm. Anmerkung

Ann. du Service
Ann. Serv. } *Annales du Service des Antiquités de l'Égypte*, Cairo

Apisritual Demotic Papyrus Vienna no. 27, published in facsimile Ernst Ritter von Bergmann, *Hieratische und hieratisch-demotische Texte der Sammlung aegyptischer Alterthümer des Allerhöchsten Kaiserhauses*, plates X–XVIII, Vienna 1886

AR
Ar. } Arabic

Aram. Aramaic

ASAE *Annales du Service des Antiquités de l'Égypte*, Cairo

B Bohairic dialect

B. of D. Book of the Dead

bab. Talm. babylonian Talmudic

Berlin med. P. unpublished demotic medical papyrus, Berlin

Bibl. ég. *Bibliothèque égyptologique publiée sous la direction de G. Maspero*, Paris 1893–1918

BIFAO *Bulletin de l'Institut français d'archéologie orientale*, Cairo

Birch, *Harris* *Facsimile of an Egyptian hieratic papyrus of the reign of Rameses III, now in the British Museum*, British Museum 1876

BKU *Aegyptische Urkunden aus den Koeniglichen Museen zu Berlin, Koptische Urkunden*, Berlin

Boeser, *Pap. Insinger* P. A. A. Boeser, *Transkription und Übersetzung des Papyrus Insinger*, Leiden (Rijksmuseum van Oudheden. Oudheidkundige mededeelingen) 1922

Boh. Bohairic dialect

Böhlig–Labib Alexander Böhlig and Pahor Labib, *Die Koptisch-Gnostische Schrift ohne Titel aus Codex II von Nag Hammadi* (Deutsche Akademie der Wissenschaften zu Berlin. Institut für Orientforschung) 1962

Borchardt, *Sahurēʿ* Ludwig Borchardt, *Das Grabdenkmal des Königs Saḥu-reʿ* (Ausgrabungen der Deutschen Orient-Gesellschaft in Abusir 1902–8) 1910

Brockelmann, *Lex.* C. Brockelmann, *Lexicon Syriacum*, Second edition, Halis Saxonum 1928

Brugsch, *De natura* H. Brugsch, *De natura et indole linguae popularis Aegyptiorum*, Berlin 1850

Brugsch, *Dict. géogr.* H. Brugsch, *Dictionnaire géographique de l'ancienne Égypte*, Leipzig 1879

Brugsch, *Gr. dém.* H. Brugsch, *Grammaire démotique*, Berlin 1855

Brugsch, *Gr. hier.* H. Brugsch, *Grammaire hiéroglyphique*, Leipzig 1872

Brugsch, *Mat. cal.* / *Matér. cal.* H. Brugsch, *Matériaux pour servir à la reconstruction du calendrier des anciens Égyptiens*, Leipzig 1864

Brugsch, *Nouv. rech.* H. Brugsch, *Nouvelles recherches sur la division de l'année des anciens Égyptiens*, Berlin 1856

Brugsch, *Pamonth.* H. Brugsch, *Die Inschrift von Rosette. Theil I. Sammlung demotischer Urkunden*, Tafel V–VII, pp. 22–8, 40–2, Berlin 1850 (Demotic Book of The Dead of Pamonthes)

Brugsch, *Rec. de mon.* H. Brugsch, *Recueil de monuments égyptiens dessinés sur lieux*, 7 vols. Leipzig 1862–85

Brugsch, *Rhind* H. Brugsch, *A. Henry Rhind's zwei bilingue Papyri*, Berlin 1865

Brugsch, *Rosettana* H. Brugsch, *Inscriptio Rosettana hieroglyphica*, Berlin 1851

Brugsch, *Scriptura Aeg. dem.* / *Scriptura Aeg. demotica* H. Brugsch, *Scriptura Aegyptiorum demotica ex papyris et inscriptionibus explanata*, Berlin 1848

Brugsch, *Thes.* / *Thesaurus* H. Brugsch, *Thesaurus Inscriptionum Aegyptiacarum*, 6 vols., Leipzig 1883–91

Bull. Soc. arch. copte *Sociéte d'archéologie copte. Bulletin*, Cairo

Bull. Soc. Ling. *Société de linguistique de Paris. Bulletin*, Paris

Bunsen, *Geschichte* C. Bunsen, *Aegyptens Stelle in der Weltgeschichte. Geschichtliche Untersuchung in fünf Büchern*, Hamburg 1845–57

Burchardt, *Die altkanaan. Fremdworte* M. Burchardt, *Die altkanaanäischen Fremdworte und Eigennamen im Ägyptischen*, Leipzig 1909–10

Caminos, *Chronicle* R. Caminos, *The Chronicle of Prince Osorkon*, Rome 1958

Canopus W. Spiegelberg, *Der demotische Text der Priesterdekrete von Kanopus und Memphis (Rosettana)*, Heidelberg 1922

CdE *Chronique d'Égypte*, Brussels

CGC *Catalogue général des antiquités égyptiennes du musée du Caire*, Cairo

Chabas, *Mél. ég.*
Mél. égypt. } F. J. Chabas, *Mélanges egyptologiques. Série 3, tome 1–2*, Châlon-sur-Saône 1873

Chabas, *Pap. mag. Harris* F. J. Chabas, *Le papyrus magique Harris*, Châlon-sur-Saône 1860

Chabas, *Voyage* F. J. Chabas, *Voyage d'un Égyptien en Syrie, en Phénicie, en Palestine, &c*, Châlon-sur-Sâone 1866

Champollion, *Dict.* Jean-François Champollion, *Dictionnaire égyptien en écriture hiéroglyphique*, Paris 1841

Champollion, *Gr.*
Gr. ég. } [Jean-François] Champollion le Jeune, *Grammaire égyptienne, ou Principes généraux de l'écriture sacrée égyptienne appliquée à la représentation de la langue parlée*, Paris 1836

Champollion, *Précis* Jean-François Champollion, *Précis du Système Hiéroglyphique des anciens Egyptiens*, Paris 1824

Chassinat, *Ms. mag. copte* É. Chassinat, *Le Manuscrit magique copte No. 42573 du Musée Égyptien du Caire*, Cairo 1955

Chassinat, *Pap. méd.* É. Chassinat, *Un papyrus médical copte*, Cairo 1921

CMSS W. E. Crum, *Coptic manuscripts brought from the Fayyum by W. M. Flinders Petrie*, London 1893

CO W. E. Crum, *Coptic ostraca from the collections of the Egypt Exploration Fund, the Cairo Museum and others*, London 1902

Coffin Texts A. De Buck, *The Egyptian Coffin Texts*, 7 vols., Chicago 1935–61

comm. communication

constr. construct

corr. correction

Couyat-Montet, *Hammâmât* J. Couyat and P. Montet, *Les Inscriptions Hiéroglyphiques et Hiératiques du Ouâdi Hammâmât*, 2 vols., Cairo 1912–13

Crum W. E. Crum, *A Coptic Dictionary*, Oxford 1939 (Issued in six parts 1929–39)

Crum, Add. Additions and Corrections in Crum, *A Coptic Dictionary*, pp. xiv–xxiv

Crum, *Dict.* W. E. Crum, *A Coptic Dictionary*, Oxford 1939 (Issued in six parts 1929–39)

Crum, *Epiphanius* W. E. Crum and H. G. Evelyn White, *The Monastery of Epiphanius at Thebes*, Part II, New York (Metropolitan Museum of Art) 1926

CT A. De Buck, *The Egyptian Coffin Texts*, 7 vols., Chicago 1935–61

D Demotic

Dalman G. H. Dalman, *Aramäisch-neuhebräisches Wörterbuch*, Frankfurt a. Main 1922

Davies, *El Amarna* N. de. G. Davies, *The Rock Tombs of El Amarna*, 6 vols., London (Egypt Exploration Fund) 1903–8

Davis, *Rekhmire* N. de G. Davies, *The Tomb of Rekh-mi-re' at Thebes*, 2 vols., New York (Metropolitan Museum of Art) 1943

Dawson, *Ch. W. Goodwin* W. R. Dawson, *Charles Wycliffe Goodwin, 1817–1878; a pioneer of Egyptology*, Oxford 1934

Dem. demotic

Dem. mag. Pap. F. Ll. Griffith and H. Thompson, *The demotic magical papyrus of London and Leiden*, 3 vols., London 1904–9
Dem. Ostr. Strassburg unpublished demotic ostraca in Strassburg
det. determinative
Deut. Deuteronomy
Dévaud, *Études* E. Dévaud, *Études d'etymologie copte*, Fribourg 1922
Devéria, *Mém. et fragments* Th. Devéria, *Mémoires et fragments publiés par G. Maspero* (Bibliothèque égyptologique tome 4–5), Paris 1896–7
Dioscorides, *De mat. med.* Dioscorides, *de Materia Medica*, ed. M. Wellmann, Berlin 1906–14
Dozy, *Suppl.* R. Dozy, *Supplément aux Dictionnaires Arabes*, Leiden 1881
Drioton, *Médamoud* É. Drioton, *Médamoud (1925), Les inscriptions* (Fouilles de l'Institut français d'archéologie orientale III, ii), Cairo 1926
Dümichen, *Rec.* H. Brugsch and J. Duemichen, *Recueil de monuments égyptiens. Partie 3–6. Geographische Inschriften altägyptischer Denkmäler...von Johannes Duemichen Abtheilung 1–4*, Leipzig 1865–85

Edfou De Rochemonteix and É. Chassinat, *Le Temple d'Edfou*, 14 vols. (Mission archéologique française au Caire, Mémoires), Cairo 1892–1934
Edgerton, *Griffith Studies* W. F. Edgerton in *Studies presented to F. Ll. Griffith*, edited by S. R. K. Glanville, London (Egypt Exploration Society) 1932.
Edinburgh stone 912 Royal Scottish Museum 1956–316, edited by Černý in *Oriens Antiquus* 6 (1967), 47–50 [= Botti Memorial Volume]
Egn. Egyptian
Er. W. Erichsen, *Demotisches Glossar*, Copenhagen 1954
Erichsen, *Dem. Glossar.* W. Erichsen, *Demotisches Glossar*, Copenhagen 1954
Erichsen, *Dem. Lesest.* / *Dem. Lesestücke* W. Erichsen, *Demotische Lesestücke*, Leipzig 1940
Erichsen–Schott, *Fragmente memph. Théologie* W. Erichsen and S. Schott, *Fragmente memphitischer Theologie in demotischer Schrift (Pap. demot. Berlin 13603)*, Wiesbaden 1954
Erman, *Äg. Glossar* A. Erman, *Aegyptisches Glossar. Die häufigeren Worte der aegyptischen Sprache*, Berlin 1904
Erman, *Äg. Gr.*³ / *Aeg. Gr.* A. Erman, *Ägyptische Grammatik*, Berlin 1894. Third edition 1911
Erman, *Lebensmüde* A. Erman, *Gespräch eines Lebensmüden mit seiner Seele*, Berlin 1896
Erman, *Näg. Gr.*² / *Neuäg. Gr.* A. Erman, *Neuägyptische Grammatik*, Leipzig 1880. Second edition 1933
Erman, *Pluralbildung* A. Erman, *Die Pluralbildung des Aegyptischen*, Leipzig 1878
Erman, *Westcar* / *Spr. Westcar* A. Erman, *Die Sprache des Papyrus Westcar*, Göttingen 1889
Erman–Grapow, *Äg. Handwb.* A. Erman and H. Grapow, *Aegyptisches Handwörterbuch*, Berlin 1921
Erman–Grapow, *Wb.* A. Erman and H. Grapow, *Wörterbuch der ägyptischen Sprache*, 5 vols., Berlin 1926–31

Erman–Lange, *Pap. Lansing* A. Erman and H. O. Lange, *Papyrus Lansing: Eine ägyptische Schulhandschrift der 20 Dynastie*, Copenhagen 1925
Ernout–Meillet A. Ernout and A. Meillet, *Dictionnaire étymologique de la langue latine*, Third edition, Paris 1951
Eskhons The decree of Amonrasonther for Neskhons, quoted from G. Maspero, *Les Momies royales de Déir el-Baharî, Mission archéologique française au Caire* 1, Paris 1889, plates xxv–xxvii
Eth. Ethiopic
Ev. Ver. M. Malinine, H. Puech and G. Quispel, *Evangelium Veritatis*, Munich 1956
Ex. Exodus

F Fayyûmic and related dialects

G Greek
Gardiner, *Admonitions* A. H. Gardiner, *The Admonitions of an Egyptian Sage*, Leipzig 1909
Gardiner, *Eg. gr.* A. H. Gardiner, *Egyptian Grammar*, Oxford 1926. Second edition, fully revised 1950
Gardiner, *Gr.*[3] A. H. Gardiner, *Egyptian Grammar*, Third edition, revised, Oxford 1957
Gardiner, *Hierat. Texts* A. H. Gardiner, *Egyptian Hieratic Texts*, Leipzig 1911
Gardiner, *Late Eg. Stories* A. H. Gardiner, *Late-Egyptian Stories*, Brussels (Bibliotheca Aegyptiaca 1) 1932
Gardiner, *Onom.* A. H. Gardiner, *Ancient Egyptian Onomastica*, 2 vols., Oxford 1947
Gardiner, *Sinuhe* A. H. Gardiner, *Notes on the Story of Sinuhe*, Paris 1916
Gauthier H. Gauthier, *Dictionnaire des noms géographiques contenus dans les textes hiéroglyphiques*, 7 vols., Cairo 1925–31
Ge. Genesis
Gesenius–Buhl, *Hebr. und aram. Wörterbuch*[14] F. Buhl, *Wilhelm Gesenius' hebraisches und aramaisches Handwörterbuch über das Alte Testament*, 14 edition, Leipzig 1921
Glanville, *Griffith Studies* *Studies presented to F. Ll. Griffith*, edited by S. R. K. Glanville, London (Egypt Exploration Society) 1932
Gött. gel. Anz. *Göttingische gelehrte Anzeigen*
GR }
Gr.-R. } hieroglyphic texts of the Graeco-Roman period
Griffith, *Pap. Rylands* }
Ryl. } F. Ll. Griffith, *Catalogue of the Demotic Papyri in the John Rylands Library in Manchester*, 3 vols., Manchester 1909
Griffith, *Stories* F. Ll. Griffith, *Stories of the High Priests of Memphis*, Oxford 1900
Griffith–Thompson F. Ll. Griffith and H. Thompson, *The demotic magical papyrus of London and Leiden*, 3 vols., London 1904–9
Groff, *Décr. Canope* W. N. Groff, 'Le décret de Canope', in *Revue égyptologique* 6 (1891), 13–21
Groff, *Les deux versions* W. N. Groff, *Les deux versions démotiques du décret de Canope*, Paris 1888

Harpist
Harpiste } E. Revillout, 'La vie d'artiste ou de bohème en Égypte', in *Revue égyptologique* 3 (1885), 98ff.
H hieroglyphic
HAM Hamitic
W. Hatch W. H. P. Hatch, 'Three hitherto unpublished leaves from a manuscript of the *Acta Apostolarum Apocrypha* in Bohairic', in *Coptic Studies in honor of Walter Ewing Crum* (= *Bulletin of the Byzantine Institute* 2), Boston 1950
Hebr. Hebrews
Helck, *Die Beziehungen* W. Helck, *Die Beziehungen Ägyptens zu Vorderasiens im 3. und 2. Jahrtausend v. Chr.*, Wiesbaden 1962
Hess, *Gnost. Pap.* J. J. Hess, *Der gnostische Papyrus von London*, Freiburg 1892
Hess, *Rosette* J. J. Hess, *Der demotische Teil der dreisprachigen Inschrift von Rosette*, Freiburg 1902
Hess, *Stne* J. J. Hess, *Der demotische Roman von Stne Ḫa-m-us*, Leipzig 1888
Hierat. Ostr. Nat. Library, Vienna unpublished hieratic ostraca in the Nationalbibliothek, Vienna
Hincks, *An Attempt* etc. E. Hincks, 'An attempt to ascertain the number, names and powers of the letters of the hieroglyphic, or ancient Egyptian alphabet', in *Transactions of the Royal Irish Academy*, 21 (Dublin 1848), pt 2, 132–232
H.O. J. Černý and A. H. Gardiner, *Hieratic Ostraca*, I, Oxford 1957
Hom. H. J. Polotsky, *Manichäische Homilien* (*Manichäischen Handschriften der Sammlung A. Chester Beatty*), Vol. I, Stuttgart 1934
Hor. The Old Coptic Horoscope. See J. Černý, P. E. Kahle and R. A. Parker, in *Journal of Egyptian Archaeology* 43 (1957), 86ff.
Horus and Seth 'The Contendings of Horus and Seth', transcribed text in A. H. Gardiner, *Late-Egyptian Stories*, Brussels 1932

Is. Isaiah
Israel Stela Stela of Year 5 of Merneptah, see Kitchen, *Ramesside Inscriptions* IV, 1 (Oxford 1968), 13ff.

JA *Journal asiatique*, Paris
James, *Ḥeḳanakhte* T. G. H. James, *The Ḥeḳanakhte Papers and other early Middle Kingdom Documents*, New York 1962
JAOS *Journal of the American Oriental Society*, Baltimore
J.E. Journal d'entrée (the register of accessions in the Cairo Museum)
JEA *Journal of Egyptian Archaeology*, London
Jer. Jeremiah
JNES *Journal of Near Eastern Studies*, Chicago
Jos. Joshua
Journal as. *Journal asiatique*, Paris
Junker, *Pap. Lonsdorfer I* H. Junker, *Papyrus Lonsdorfer I* (Sitzungsberichte, Akademie der Wissenschaften in Wien. Philosophisch-historische Klasse. Vol. 197, 2), Vienna 1921

K 197 A. Kircher, the *Scalae* in *Lingua Aegyptiaca Restituta*, Rome 1643
Kahle, *Bal.*
Bala'izah } P. E. Kahle, *Bala'izah. Coptic Texts from Deir-el-Bala'izah in Upper Egypt*, 2 vols., Oxford 1954

Kasser, *P. Bodmer XXI* R. Kasser, *P. Bodmer XXI*, Geneva 1964
Keimer, *Gartenpflanzen* L. Keimer, *Die Gartenpflanzen im Alten Ägypten*, Hamburg–Berlin 1924
Kêmi *Kêmi. Revue de philologie et d'archéologie égyptiennes et coptes*, Paris
Kh. Tales of Khamwese; see F. Ll. Griffith, *Stories of the High Priests of Memphis*, London 1900
Kircher A. Kircher, *Lingua Aegyptiaca Restituta*, Rome 1643
Krall, *Kopt. Texte* J. Krall, *Koptische Texte = Corpus papyrorum Raineri archiducis Austriae*, Vienna 1895

La Croze, *Lexicon* M. V. de La Croze, *Lexicon Aegyptiaco-Latinum*... Oxford 1775
Lagarde, *Ges. Abh.*
Ges. Abhandlungen } P. de Lagarde, *Gesammelte Abhandlungen*, Leipzig 1866
Lagarde, *Mitt.* P. de Lagarde, *Mitteilungen*, I–IV, Göttingen 1884–9
Lagarde, *Übersicht* P. de Lagarde, *Übersicht über die in Aramäischen, Arabischen und Hebräischen übliche Bildung der Nomina = Abhandlung der Königliche Gesellschaft der Wissenschaften zu Göttingen*, vol. 35, Göttingen 1889
Lange, *Amenemope* H. O. Lange, *Das Weisheitsbuch des Amenemope*, Copenhagen 1925
Late Aeth. Late Aethiopic
Lauth, *Manetho* F. J. Lauth, *Manetho und der Turiner Königs-Papyrus*, Munich, 1865
L. Cypr. O. von Lemm, 'Sahidische Bruchstücke der Legende von Cyprian von Antiochien', in *Memoires de l'Académie impériale des Sciences de St.-Pétersbourg*, VIIIe Série, Tome IV, no. 6, St Petersburg 1899
LD R. Lepsius, *Denkmäler aus Ägypten und Nubien*, 6 vols., Berlin 1849–58
Lefebvre, *Petosiris* G. Lefebvre, *Le tombeau de Petosiris*, 3 parts, Cairo 1923–4
L.E.
L.Eg. } Late Egyptian
L.Egn.
LEM A. H. Gardiner, *Late-Egyptian Miscellanies*, Brussels 1937
Lemm, *Kopt. Misc.* O. von Lemm, *Koptische Miscellen*, St Petersburg 1907
Le Page Renouf, *Lifework* P. Le Page Renouf, *The Lifework of Sir Peter Le Page Renouf*, 4 vols., Paris 1902–7
Lepsius, *Chronologie* R. Lepsius, *Die Chronologie der Ägypter*, Berlin 1849
Lepsius, *Lettre à Rosellini* R. Lepsius, *Lettre à Mr. le Professeur H. Rosellini sur l'alphabet hiéroglyphique*, Rome, 1837. From *Annali dell'instituto archeologico, Roma*, vol. 9, 1837
LES A. H. Gardiner, *Late-Egyptian Stories*, Brussels 1932
Lev. Leviticus
Lexa, *Beiträge* F. Lexa, *Beiträge zum demotischen Wörterbuche aus dem Papyrus Insinger*, Prague 1916 (author's edition)
Lexa, *Dem. Totb.*
Totb. } F. Lexa, *Das demotische Totenbuch der Pariser Nationalbibliothek* (*Demotische Studien*, by W. Spiegelberg, vol. 4), Leipzig 1910
Lichtheim, *Dem. Ostraca* M. Lichtheim, *Demotic Ostraca from Medinet Habu*, Chicago 1957

Liddell–Scott H. G. Liddell and R. Scott, *A Greek–English Lexicon*, 9th ed., Oxford 1940

Lovesongs Beatty In A. H. Gardiner, *The Library of A. Chester Beatty. The Chester Beatty Papyri, No. 1*, Oxford 1931

LRL J. Černý, *Late Ramesside Letters*, Brussels 1939

M. MSS in the Pierpont Morgan Library, New York, as reproduced and numbered in 56 vols. of photographs

Macadam, *Kawa* M. F. L. Macadam, *The Temples of Kawa*, 2 vols., Oxford 1949, 1955

Mag.P. F. Ll. Griffith and H. Thompson, *The Demotic Magical Papyrus of London and Leiden*, 3 vols., London 1904–9

Mal. Malachi

Mani H
  Hom. H. J. Polotsky, *Manichäische Homilien*, Stuttgart 1934

Mani Keph. H. J. Polotsky and A. Böhlig, *Manichäische Handschriften der Staatlichen Museen Berlin*, I, *Kephalaia*, Stuttgart 1935

Mani Ps. C. R. C. Allberry, *A Manichaean Psalm-book*, Stuttgart 1938

Margolis M. L. Margolis, *A Manual of the Aramaic Language of the Babylonian Talmud*, Munich 1910

Mariette, *Dendérah* A. Mariette, *Dendérah, description générale du grand temple de cette ville*, 5 vols., 1870–80

Mattha, *Dem. Ostraka* G. Mattha, *Demotic Ostraka from the Collections at Oxford, Paris, Berlin, Vienna and Cairo*, Cairo 1945

W. Max Müller, *Liebespoesie* W. Max Müller, *Die Liebespoesie der Alten Ägypter*, Leipzig 1899

MDAIK *Mitteilungen des Deutschen archäologischen Instituts Abteilung Kairo*, Mainz

M.Eg. Middle Egyptian

Mélanges Charles Moeller *Mélanges d'histoire offerts à Charles Moeller*, Louvain 1914

Mém. et fragm. T. Devéria, *Memoires et fragments*, 2 vols., *Bibliothéque égyptologique concernant les œuvres des égyptologues français*, Vols. 4 and 5, Paris 1896, 1897

Mém. mission arch. franç. *Mission archéologique française au Caire. Mémoires*

Mic. Micah

Mitt. Erzh. Rainer *Mittheilungen aus der Sammlung der Papyrus Erzherzog Rainer*, Vienna

Mitt. Kairo *Mitteilungen des Deutschen archäologischen Instituts Abteilung Kairo*, Mainz

M.K. Middle Kingdom

Möller, *Pap. Rhind*
  Rhind G. Möller, *Die beiden Totenpapyrus Rhind des Museums zu Edinburg*, Leipzig 1913

Mond–Myers, *The Bucheum* Sir R. Mond and O. H. Myers, *The Bucheum*, 3 vols., London 1934

Mor. MSS in the Pierpont Morgan Library, New York, as reproduced and numbered in 56 vols. of photographs

Mus. crit. *Museum criticum, or Cambridge Classical Researches*, Cambridge

Nachr. Ges. Wiss. Gött.
Nachrichten der K. Ges. d. Wiss. zu Göttingen, phil.-hist. Kl. *Nachrichten von der*

(königliche) Gesellschaft des Wissenschaften zu Göttingen, Philologische-historische Klasse, Göttingen

N.K. New Kingdom

O Old Coptic

O.Berlin Ostraca in the Berlin Museum

Obs. Observation

O.Cairo Ostraca in the Egyptian Museum, Cairo

O.Campbell Ostraca formerly owned by Colin Campbell, now in Hunterian Museum, Glasgow

O.DM J. Černý, *Catalogue des Ostraca hiératiques non litteraires de Deir el-Médineh*, 5 vols., Cairo 1935–51

O.F. Ll. Griffith Ostraca formerly in the possession of F. Ll. Griffith, now in the Ashmolean Museum, Oxford

O.IFAO Unpublished ostraca in the Institut français d'archéologie orientale du Caire

O.K. Old Kingdom

O.Louvre Ostraca in the Musée du Louvre, Paris

OLZ *Orientalistische Literaturzeitung*, Berlin

O.Michaelides Ostraca in the possession of G. Michaelides, some published in H. Goedicke and E. Wente, *Ostraka Michaelides*, Wiesbaden 1962

O.Murray Ostracon Murray; unpublished demotic ostracon

d'Orb. Papyrus d'Orbiney = Papyrus B.M. 10183 (for text, see A. H. Gardiner, *Late-Egyptian Stories*, Brussels 1932)

Orientalia *Orientalia Commentarii periodici Pontificii Instituti Biblici*, Rome

Ostr. Turin Ostraca in the Egyptian Museum, Turin

Oudh. Med.
Oudh. Meded. } *Oudheidkundige Mededelingen uit het Rijksmuseum van Oudheden te Leiden*, Leiden

P Coptic MSS in the Bibliothèque Nationale, Paris (Crum's copies)

P. Anast. 4 Papyrus Anastasi 4 = Papyrus B.M. 10249 (for text see A. H. Gardiner, *Late-Egyptian Miscellanies*, Brussels 1937)

Pap. Ebers Papyrus Ebers. (For text see G. Ebers, *Papyros Ebers*, 2 vols., Leipzig 1875)

Pap. jud. 'Papyrus judiciaire' in the Egyptian Museum, Turin

Pap. Krall Papyrus Krall in Vienna, cited from W. Speigelberg, *Der Sagenkreis des Königs Petubastis*, Leipzig 1910

Parker, *Dem. Math. Pap.* R. A. Parker, *Demotic Mathematical Papyri*, Providence 1972

part. coni. participium coniunctum

Pauly–Wissowa Pauly–Wissowa–(Kroll–Mittelhaus), *Real-Encyclopädie der classischen Altertumswissenschaft*, Stuttgart

Payne-Smith R. Payne Smith, *A Compendious Syriac Dictionary*, Oxford 1907 (reprint of 1903 ed.)

P.Berlin Papyrus Berlin (no. 3108 published in W. Spiegelberg, *Demotische Papyrus aus den Königlichen Museen zu Berlin*, Leipzig 1902)

P.BM
P. Brit. Mus. } Papyrus in the British Museum

P.Bodmer Papyrus in the Bodmer Library, Coligny–Geneva
p.c. participium coniunctum
P.Cairo Papyrus in the Egyptian Museum, Cairo
P.Chester Beatty Papyrus in the Chester Beatty Library, Dublin, or formerly in the possession of Sir A. Chester Beatty (the latter, now in British Museum, published by A. H. Gardiner, *Hieratic Papyri in the British Museum, Third Series*, London 1935)
P.Dodgson Papyrus formerly in the possession of the Rev. A. Dodgson, now in the Ashmolean Museum, Oxford (published by F. Ll. Griffith in *PSBA* 31 (1909), 100)
PER Persian
Petrie, *Gizeh and Rifeh* W. M. F. Petrie, *Gizeh and Rifeh*, London 1907
Petrie, *Medum* W. M. F. Petrie, *Medum*, London 1892
Petub. Petubastis. See W. Spiegelberg, *Der Sagenkreis des königs Petubastis*, Leipzig 1910
Peyron, Peyron, *Lex* V. A. Peyron, *Lexicon linguae copticae*, Turin 1835
P.Fay Papyrus from the Fayyûm (cited from Sir H. Thompson's notes)
PGM K. Preisendanz (ed.), *Papyri Graeci Magicae*, 3 vols., Leipzig–Berlin 1928, 1931, 1941
P.Harris Papyrus Harris I = B.M. 9999, published by W. Erichsen, *Papyrus Harris I*, Brussels 1933
P.Hauswaldt W. Speigelberg, *Die demotischen Papyri Hauswaldt*, Leipzig 1913
P.Kasan Papyrus Kasan (unpublished)
Piehl, *Inscr. hiér.* K. Piehl, *Inscriptions hiéroglyphiques recueillies en Europe et en Egypte*, Leipzig and Stockholm 1886–1903
Pierret, *Voc. hiér* P. Pierret, *Vocabulaire hiéroglyphique*, Paris 1875
Pl. Plate/Plural
P.Lansing Papyrus Lansing. See A. H. Gardiner, *Late-Egyptian Miscellanies* (Bibliotheca Aegyptiaca, VII), Brussels 1937
Pleyte, *Ét. ég.* W. Pleyte, *Études égyptologiques*, Leiden 1866–9
Pleyte, *Pap. Rollin* W. Pleyte, *Les papyrus Rollin de la Bibliotheque imperiale de Paris*, Leiden 1868
Pleyte–Boeser, *Suten-χeft.* W. Pleyte and P. A. A. Boeser, *Suten-χeft, Le livre royal* (*Papyrus Insinger*), Leiden 1899
P.Lille H. Sottas, *Papyrus démotiques de Lille*, Tome 1, Paris 1921
Pliny, *Hist. nat.* *Historia naturalis*
Pliny, *Nat. hist.* *A Natural History*
Plumley J. M. Plumley, *An Introductory Coptic Grammar* (*Sahidic Dialect*), London 1948
P. mag. Salt Papyrus Magical Salt (P. Derchain, *Le Papyrus Salt* 825, Brussels 1965)
P.Mallet Papyrus Mallet (G. Maspero, *Recueil de travaux relatifs à la philologie et à l'archéologie égyptiennes et assyriennes*, Vol. 1, 47–79, Paris 1870)
P.Millingen The Millingen Papyrus (Fr. Ll. Griffith, *The Milligen Papyrus* (*teaching of Amenemhat*)), in *Z.Ä.S.* 34 (1896), 35–51
Polotsky, *Études* H. J. Polotsky, *Études de syntaxe copte*, Cairo 1944
Polotsky, *Manich. Homilien* H. J. Polotsky, *Manichäische Homilien* (*Manichäische Handschriften den Sammlung A. Chester Beatty*), Vol. 1, Stuttgart 1934

P.Reinach   Th. Reinach, *Papyrus grecs et démotiques*, Paris 1905
Preisigke   F. Preisigke, *Namenbuch*, Amsterdam 1967
Ps.   Psalm-book (See C. R. C. Allberry)
P.Sallier I   Papyrus Sallier I (A. H. Gardiner, *Late-Egyptian Miscellanies*, *Bibliotheca Aegyptiaca* VII, Brussels 1937)
PSBA   *Proceedings of the Society of Biblical Archaeology*, London 1878–1917

Qual.   Qualitative

Ranke   H. Ranke, *Die ägyptische Personennamen*, Vol. I, Glückstadt, 1935
Rec. Champollion   *Recueil d'études égyptologiques dediées à la mémoire de Jean-François Champollion*, Paris 1922
Rec. trav.   *Recueil de travaux relatifs à la philologie et à l'archéologie égyptiennes et assyriennes*, Paris 1870–1923
Renouf, *Egypt. Ess.*   P. Le Page Renouf, *Egyptological and Philological Essays* (G. Maspero and W. H. Rylands, *The Life-work of Sir Peter Le Page Renouf*, Vol. I, Paris 1902)
Revillout, *Nouv. chrest. dém.*   E. Revillout, *Nouvelle chrestomathie démotique*, Paris 1878
Revillout, *Pap. mor.*
Pap. moral.
Pap. mor. de Leide   E. Revillout, 'Le papyrus moral de Leide', in *Journal asiatique*, série 10, vol. 5, 193–249; vol. 6, 275–332; vol. 8, 83–148; vol. 9, 429–508, Paris 1905–8
Revillout, *Poème*   E. Revillout, *Un poème satyrique*, Paris 1885
Revillout, *Setna*   E. Revillout, *Le roman de Setna, étude philologique et critique avec traduction mot à mot du texte démotique*, Paris 1877
Revue d'ég.   *Revue d'égypte*
Rochemonteix, *Edfou*   M. de C. Rochemonteix, *Le temple d'Edfou*, Vols. I and II fasc.
Rösch, *Vorbem.*
Vorbemerkungen   F. Rösch, *Vorbemerkungen zu einen Grammatik der achmimischen Mundart*, Strassburg 1909
Rosetta   Rosetta Stone (see J. J. Hess, *Der demotische Teil der dreisprachigen Inschrift von Rosette, übersetzt und erklärt*, Freiburg 1902)
Rossi, *Etym. aeg.*
Etym. aegypt.   I. Rossi, *Etymologiae Aegyptiacae*, Rome 1808
de Rougé, *Chrest.*
Chrest. ég.   E. de Rougé, *Chrestomathie égyptienne*, Paris 1867–76
de Rougé, *I.H.*   E. de Rougé, *Inscriptions hiéroglyphiques copiées en Egypte*, Paris 1877
de Rougé, *Oeuvres div.*   E. de Rougé, *Oeuvres diverses*, Paris 1907–8

S   Sa'idic (Sahidic) dialect
S^A Sa'idic with Achmîmic tendency
Sa.   Wisdom of Solomon
de Sacy, *Abdellatif*   S. de Sacy, *Relation de l'Egypte par Abd-Allatif, médecin arabe de Baghdad*, Paris 1810
Saite   Saite Period

Salvolini, *Analyse gramm.* F. Salvolini, *Analyse grammaticale raisonnée de différents textes anciens Egyptiens*, Paris 1836

Salvolini, *Obél. Paris* F. Salvolini, *Traduction et analyse gammaticale des inscriptions sculptées sur l'obélisque égyptien de Paris, suivie d'une notice relative à la lecture des noms de rois qui y sont mentionnés*, Paris 1837

Saulcy, *Anal. gram.* L. F. J. C. de Saulcy, *Analyse grammaticale du texte démotique du décret de Rosette*, Paris 1845

S: BMar Sa'idic: E. A. Wallis Budge, *Coptic Martyrdoms etc. in the Dialect of Upper Egypt*, London 1914

Schäfer, *Nastesen* H. Schäfer, *Die aethiopische Königsinschrift des Berliner Museums, Regierungsbericht des Königs Nastesen des Gegners des Kambyses*, Leipzig 1901

Schiaparelli, *Relazione* E. Schiaparelli, *Relazione sui lavori della missione archeologica Italiana in Egitto*, 2 vols, Turin 1924, 1927

Schmidt, *Kephalaia* C. Schmidt, *Manichäische Handschriften der staatlichen Museen Berlin*, Band 1, *Kephalaia*, Stuttgart 1935

Sethe, *Bürgschaftsurk.* K. Sethe and J. Partsch, *Demotische Urkunden zum ägyptischen Bürgschaftsrechte vorzügleich der Ptolemäerzeit*, Leipzig 1920

Sethe, *Nominalsatz* K. Sethe, *Der Nominalsatz im Ägyptischen und Koptischen*, Leipzig 1916

Sethe, *Verbum* K. Sethe, *Das aegyptische Verbum im Altaegyptischen, Neuaegyptischen und Koptischen*, Leipzig 1902

Sf Sa'idic dialect with Fayyûmic tendency

ShP. Shenoute, MSS in the Bibliothèque Nationale, Paris

Si. Ecclesiasticus, according to Lagarde's numeration

sic l. *sic legendum*

Sinai A. H. Gardiner, T. E. Peet and J. Černý, *The Inscriptions of Sinai* (2nd edition), London 1955

Sottas, *Pap. de Lille* H. Sottas, *Papyrus démotiques de Lille*, Tome 1, Paris 1921

Spiegelberg, *Chronik*
Dem. Chron.
Dem. Chronik } W. Spiegelberg, *Die sogenannte demotische Chronik des Pap. 215 der Bibliothèque Nationale zu Paris*, Leipzig 1914

Spiegelberg, *Dem. Denkmäler* W. Spiegelberg, *Catalogue général des antiquités égyptiennes du Musée du Caire. Die demotischen Denkmäler*, 2 vols., Leipzig 1904–8

Spiegelberg, *Dem. Pap. Strassburg* W. Spiegelberg, *Die demotischen Papyrus der Strassburger Bibliothek*, Strassburg 1902

Spiegelberg, *Die dem. Pap. Loeb* W. Spiegelberg, *Die demotischen Papyri Loeb*, Munich 1931

Spiegelberg, *Eigennamen* W. Spiegelberg, *Aegyptische und griechische Eigennamen aus Mumienetiketten der römischen Kaiserzeit*, Leipzig 1901

Spiegelberg, *Hauswaldt* W. Spiegelberg, *Die demotischen Papyri Hauswaldt*, Leipzig 1913

Spiegelberg, *Kopt. Handwb.* W. Spiegelberg, *Koptisches Handwörterbuch*, Heidelberg 1921

Spiegelberg, *Krüge* W. Spiegelberg, *Demotische Texte auf Krügen* (*Demotische Studien*, Heft 5), Leipzig 1912

Spiegelberg, *Mythus* W. Spiegelberg, *Der ägyptische Mythus vom Sonnenauge*, Strassburg 1917

Spiegelberg, *Rechnungen*
Sethosrechnungen } W. Spiegelberg, *Rechnungen aus der Zeit Setis I (circa 1350 v. Chr.) mit anderen Rechnungen des neuen Reiches*, Strassburg 1896
Spiegelberg–Ricci, *Pap. Reinach* W. Spiegelberg and S. de Ricci, *Papyrus Grecs et Demotiques recueillis en Égypte et publiés par Théodore Reinach*, Paris 1905
Spr. Westcar A. Erman, *Die Sprache des Papyrus Westcar*, Göttingen 1890
St. constr. *Status constructus*
Ste Fare Garnot, *Mél Maspero* J. Sainte Fare Garnot, 'Etat présent des études linguistiques relatives à l'ancien égyptien', in *Mélanges Maspero*, I, Cairo 1961
Steindorff, *Lehrbuch* G. Steindorff, *Lehrbuch der koptischen Grammatik*, Chicago 1951
Steindorff, *Prolegomena* G. Steindorff, *Prolegomena zu einer koptischen Nominalclasse*, Berlin 1884
Stern, *Kopt. Gr.* L. Stern, *Koptische Grammatik*, Leipzig 1880
Suppl. Supplement
Synaxarium J. Forget, *Synaxarium Alexandrinum.* Excudebat Karolus de Luigi (*Corpus scriptorum christianorum orientalium, Arabic Series*), Rome 1905–
Syr. Syriac
Syria Syria, *Revue d'art oriental et d'archéologie*, Paris 1920–

Targ. Targum
Tableau gén. Tableau général. In J. F. Champollion, *Précis du système hiéroglyphique des anciens Égyptiens*, Paris 1824
Tattam, *Lexicon* H. Tattam, *Lexicon Ægyptiaco-Latinum*, Oxford 1835
Temple of Esna S. Sauneron, *Le temple d'Esna* (Vol. II, texts 1–193; Vol. III, texts 194–398; Vol. IV, texts 399–642), Cairo 1963–9
Theban Ostraca A. H. Gardiner and Sir Herbert Thompson, *Theban Ostraca*, London 1913
Till
Till, *Kopt. Gr.* } W. C. Till, *Koptische Grammatik* (*Saïdischer Dialekt*), Leipzig 1955
Till, *Achm.-kopt. Gr.* W. C. Till, *Achmîmisch-Koptische Grammatik*, Leipzig 1928
Till, *Arz.* W. C. Till, *Die Arzneikunde der Kopten*, Berlin 1951
Till, *Coptica* W. C. Till, 'Die Coptica der Wiener papyrussammlung', in *ZDMG.* 95 (1941), 165–218
Till, *CPR* Papyri in the Rainer Collection, Staatsbibliothek Vienna (Till's copies)
Till, *Kopt. Chrest. f. den. fay. Dialekt* W. C. Till, *Koptische Chrestomathie für den fayumischen Dialekt*, Vienna 1930
Till, *KR* W. C. Till, *Die Koptischen Rechtsurkunden der Papyrussammlung der österreichischen Nationalbibliothek*, Vienna 1958
Till, *Ostraka* W. C. Till, *Die koptischen Ostraka der Papyrussammlung der österreichischen Nationalbibliothek*, Vienna 1960
Tri O. E. Lemm, *Das Triadon*, St Petersburg 1903
Turin Cat. *Regio Museo di Torino ordinato e descritto da A. Fabretti, F. Rossi e R. V. Lanzone: Antichita egizia*, Turin 1882

Urk. IV K. Sethe, *Urkunden der 18. Dynastie*, Leipzig 1905–9

Vogelsang, *Komm. Bauer* F. Vogelsang, *Kommentar zu den Klagen der Bauern*, Leipzig 1913

Volten, *Dem. Traumdeutung* A. Volten, *Demotische Traumdeutung* (= *Analecta Aegyptiaca*, vol. III), Copenhagen 1942

Wångstedt, *Ausgew. dem. Ostraka* S. V. Wångstedt, *Ausgewählte demotische Ostraka*, Uppsala 1954

Wb. A. Erman and H. Grapow, *Wörterbuch der aegyptischen Sprache*, Leipzig 1926–31

Wenamūn A. H. Gardiner, *Late-Egyptian Stories* (*Bibliotheca Aegyptiaca* I), Brussels 1932

WS W. E. Crum and H. I. Bell, *Coptic Texts from Wadi Sarga* (= *Coptica* III), Copenhagen 1922

WZKM *Wiener Zeitschrift für die Kunde des Morgenlandes*, Vienna 1887–

Xenophon, *Anab.* Xenophon, *Anabasis*

Young, *Misc. Works* }
Works } Thomas Young, *Miscellaneous Works*, London 1858

Z }
Zoega } G. Zoega, *Catalogus codicum Copticorum manuscriptorum qui in Museo Borgiano Velitris adservantur*, Rome 1810

ZÄS *Zeitschrift für ägyptische Sprache*, Leipzig

Zauberspr. f. Mutter u. Kind A. Erman, *Zaubersprüche für Mutter und Kind*, Berlin 1901

ZDMG *Zeitschrift der Deutschen Morgenländischen Gesellschaft*, Dresden, Leipzig and Wiesbaden

Ⲁ

ⲁ-, ⲁ⸗ (Crum 1 a), verbal prefix, from (*Wb.* I, 112, 1–3); (Er. 36, 3), *ỉrỉ*, 'make, do'.

[H]STERN, *Kopt. Gr.*, 215, §374 [1880]; cf. Steindorff, *Kopt. Gr.*, 1st ed., 126, §276, Anm. [1894]; [D]REVILLOUT, *Setna*, 96 [1877]. The Egn. verbal form involved is , *ỉr·f* > L.Egn *ỉry·f* (not , *ỉrr·f* or , *ỉỉr·f*) and Dem. *ỉr·f*.

[H]SPIEGELBERG in *Rec. trav.* 31, 156–7 [1909]; GRIFFITH, *Stories*, 97 [1900]; cf. *Wb.* I, 112, 3 [1926]; Till, *Kopt. Gr.* 159, §313 [1955]. NB. A rival theory (EDGERTON in *JAOS* 55, 259ff. [1935]) considers ⲁ⸗ < ϩⲁ⸗ < *wꜣḥ·*; see ϩⲁ⸗, prefix of Perfect.

[BAF]**ⲁ⸗**, prefix of IInd Present = L.Eg. , *ỉỉr·* + Subj. + Inf. See under [F]ⲁⲁ⸗. The use of Qualitative in the IInd Present (and IInd Future) in which Till, *Kopt. Gr.* 154, §303, sees a decisive objection against deriving this ⲁ⸗ from *ỉrỉ*, must be secondary.

ⲁ- (Crum 1 a), prefix of Imperative = L.Egn. , *ỉ-*; Dem. or (Er. 15, 3), *ỉ-*.

[H]CHABAS, *Voyage*, 82 [1866]; [D]BRUGSCH, *Gr. dém.* 150, §296 [1855]; cf. EDGERTON, *Griffith Studies*, 63 [1932].

ⲁ- (Crum 1 a), adverb of indefiniteness, 'about' = (*Wb.* I, 157, 14ff.), 'arm, district'.

SPIEGELBERG, *ZÄS* 51, 123 [1913]; but see DÉVAUD, *Muséon* 36, 85 [1923].

[F]**ⲁⲁ⸗** (not in Crum), prefix of IInd Perfect = L.Egn. , *ỉỉr·* + Subj. + Inf.

GRIFFITH, *Ryl.* III, 235, n. 2 [1909]; cf. Polotsky, *Études de syntaxe copte*, 71 and n. 1 [1944]. NB. In B, A and F the Eg. construction has resulted in the IInd Present ⲁ⸗, cf. Steindorff, *Lehrbuch*, 148, §321; Mallon-Malinine, *Grammaire copte*, 110, §327.

ⲁⲓⲁⲓ (Crum 1 b), 'increase in size' = (*Wb.* I, 162, 13ff.) *ꜥꜣ*, 'become great'; (Er. 53), *ꜥꜣ*, 'become great'.

[H]DE ROUGÉ, *Œuv. div.* III (= *Bibl. ég.* XXIII), 97 [1856]; [D]BRUGSCH, *Gr. dém.* 119, §243 [1855]. Cf. SETHE, *Verbum* I, 232–3 [1899].

ᴬⲁⲓⲉⲩⲧⲉ is originally an Imperative followed by dependent pers. pronoun of 2nd masc. sing.: 'increase thou'. Rösch, *Vorbemerkungen*, 140, § 120 [1909]. See -ⲧⲉ.

For ⲁⲉⲓⲏⲥ, see separate entry below.

ⲁⲃⲱ (Crum 2a), 'drag net (for fish or animals)', probably connected with , later (*Wb.* I, 65, 1), *ỉbtt*, 'bird trap'.

BRUGSCH, *Wb.* 44 [1867]; but see DÉVAUD, *Muséon* 36, 85 [1923].

ⲁⲃⲱⲕ (Crum 2b), 'crow, raven' = , *ʿbḳ* (as proper name, P. Reinach no. 7, 5); (Er. 59, 4), *ȝbḳ* (as appellative, P. Carlsberg no. 14, f, 6), 'raven'.

SPIEGELBERG in Reinach, *Papyrus grecs et démotiques*, 212 [1905] (as proper name); VOLTEN, *Dem. Traumdeutung*, 105 [1942] (as appellative). ⲃⲁⲗ ⲛⲁⲃⲱⲕ (Crum 2b and 31b), 'raven's eye', leguminous plant, κύαμος ἑλληνική acc. to Zoega 629 and *BIFAO* 28, 91 = , *bỉl n* ⲉⲃⲱⲕ, *Vicia faba* L., acc. to Griffith-Thompson, I, 48, and III, 24, no. 247. The expression seems, however, rather a late modification of an earlier , *ḥr(w)-bỉk*, lit. 'falcon's face', chick peas, *Cicer arientinum* L., Arabic , for which see Keimer in *Anc. Egypt* 1929, 47–8.

HESS, *Rosette*, 67 [1902].

ˢⲁⲃⲉⲣⲏϫ (Crum 2b), a stone = (not in *Wb.*), *brgt* (an incorrect transcription of hieratic instead of , Barguet, *La stèle de la famine*, 24, n. 11), 'smaragd, beryl' (Harris, *Lexicographical Studies*, 105), a loanword from Semitic (cf. Hebrew בָּרֶקֶת, Akkadian *barraqtu*), from which also Sanskrit *marakata*, Greek σμάραγδος. The ϫ (instead of ϭ) of the Saʿîdic probably due to Bohairic form.

ᴮⲁⲃⲥⲱⲛ (Crum 2b), 'wild mint' = ? (*Wb.* I, 64, 16. 17), *ỉbsȝ*, a (medical) plant.

ⲁⲃⲏϣ (Crum 3a; 'meaning unknown'), nn. or adj., epithet of certain edibles (e.g. ⲧⲏⲃⲧ ⲛⲁⲃⲏϣ) = ? (Er. 4, 4), *ȝbḫ* (kind of fish, in *ȝbḫ n yʿm*, 'fishes of sea', lit. prob. 'crowd, mixture', from (*Wb.* I, 8, 8ff.), *ȝbḫ*, 'unite, mix, join' (trans. and intrans.), cf. *ȝbḫt* (*Wb.* I, 8, 21), medical 'mixture' and ⲱⲃϣ.

ⲁⲃⲁϭⲏⲓⲛ (Crum 3a), 'glass' = Persian آبگينه, 'glass'.
ROSSI, *Etym. aegypt.* 1 [1808].

ⲁⲓⲃⲉ Mani (Crum 476a, s.v. **ⲟⲩⲁⲓⲃⲉ**, but see Corrections, p. xxiii), 'stamp, stain', cf. (*Wb.* 1, 6, 23), 'branding-mark' and (Er. 3, 1 and 17, 3) *ꜣb*, *iꜣb*, 'to stamp cattle with a branding mark'.
[HD]H. THOMPSON in Allberry, *A Manichaean Psalm-Book*, II, note on 23, 29 [1938].

ⲁⲉⲓⲕ (Crum 3a), 'consecration (of church)', from (*Wb.* 1, 230, 3ff.), *ʿḳ*, 'to enter' (see **ⲱⲕ**), cf. (*Wb.* 1, 232, 10), *ʿḳy*, 'solemn entrance of the king'; (Er. 56, 7), *ʿyḳ*, 'festival, inauguration'.
[H]GRIFFITH, *Pap. Rylands*, III, 340, s.v. *wyn* [1909]; cf. Erman-Grapow, *Wb.* 1, 232, 10 [1926]; [D]GRIFFITH, *Cat. of Dem. Graffiti*, 1, p. 133, no. 7, and p. 138, no. 35 [1937].

ⲁⲕⲏ (Crum 3b and 674a, *s.v.* **ϩⲁⲙ**, adding **ϩⲁⲙⲁⲕⲏ**, Jernstedt, *Hermitage* p. 54), meaning unknown, prob. a (metal?) instrument = ? Late Aeth. (*Wb.* 1, 136, 17), *iḳyt*, an instrument.

ⲁⲕⲱ (Crum 3b), 'thing destroyed, destruction' = (*Wb.* 1, 21, 22), *ꜣḳyt*, 'loss'.
MASPERO, *Rec. trav.* 20, 152 [1898], whose , *ꜣḳt*, is perhaps only reconstructed; ERMAN-GRAPOW, *Wb.* 1, 21, 22 [1926].

[B]**ⲁⲕⲗⲏ** (Crum 3b), a vessel = (P. Berlin 3108, 3), (Petubastis Vienna R 23), *ʿkr*, a metal object (Er. 74, 1).
BRUGSCH, *ZÄS* 14, 68 [1876]; cf. REVILLOUT, *Rev. ég.* 12, 25 [1907].

ⲁⲕⲗⲏ (Crum 3b), 'weasel', see under **ⲕⲗⲏ**.

ⲁⲕⲟⲩⲗⲁⲩϫⲉ (Crum 3b), nn. f., a vessel, receptacle? from? Gk. κόλλαθον, a measure of 25 sextari, on which see Bell in *WS*, p. 22.

ⲁⲕⲧ, ⲁⲕⲏⲧ (Crum 3b), 'cause to solidify, congeal', is prob. Ar. أعقد, 'cause to thicken', etc. (IVth form of عقد, 'tie, attach').
CRUM, *A Coptic Dict.* 3b [1929].

ⲁⲗ (Crum 3b), 'deaf, dumb' = (Er. 68, 3), *ʿlwꜣ*, 'dumb', in proper name *Tꜣ-ḥf-ʿlwꜣ* ('dumb snake'), cf. **ϩⲟϥⲛⲁⲗ** = ἀσπὶς κωφή, Psalm 57, 4.
SPIEGELBERG, *Kopt. Handwb.* 3 [1921]; but see DÉVAUD, *Muséon* 36, 86 [1923].

ⲁⲗ (Crum 3b), 'pebble' = L.Egn. , (*Wb.* I, 208, 11), *ʿr*, 'pebble'; (Er. 68, 1), *ʿl*, 'stone'.

H CHABAS, *Voyage*, 215–16 and 349 [1866]; D GRIFFITH, *Catalogue of Dem. Graffiti*, I, p. 139, no. 44 [1937].

ⲁⲗⲙⲡⲉ, 'hail' = Egn. **ʿr n pt*, lit. 'pebble of the sky'.

ⲁⲗ (Crum 4a; 'meaning unknown'), always with vb. **ⲁϣ-**, 'cry' = (Er. 6, 12), *ꜣrl*, 'wail, lament' or sim.

ⲁⲗⲉ (Crum 4a), 'mount, go up' = , *iʿr*, later , *ʿr* (*Wb.* I, 41, 14ff.); (Er. 67, 5), *ʿl*, 'mount'.

H DE ROUGÉ, *Chrest. ég.* I, 73 [1867]; cf. SETHE, *Verbum*, II, §664 [1899]; HD BRUGSCH, *Wb.* 204 and 212 [1867]; cf. Griffith in *PSBA* 18, 105 [1896].

See also **ⲱⲗ**.

ⲁⲗⲟⲩ (Crum 5a), 'youth, maiden' = (Er. 68, 2), *ʿlw*, 'child'. From Semitic, cf. Hebr. **עויל**, 'sucking child', Syriac ܥܘܠܐ *ʿulâ* (Brockelmann, *Lex.*, 246).

D LEEMANS, *Aegyptische Papyrus in demotisch schrift met grieksche overschrijvingen*, 47, no. 23 [1839]; S DÉVAUD's slip.

See also next word.

ⲁⲗⲱ, ⲁⲗⲟⲩ (Crum 5a), 'pupil of eye', same word as the preceding, lit. 'maiden (of the eye)', cf. also Egn. (*Wb.* III, 53, 21), *ḥwnt imyt irt*, 'maiden in the eye' = 'pupil'. See VERGOTE, *Muséon* 63, 294 [1950], but envisaged already by Crum though with doubt.

ⲁⲗⲱ (Crum 5b), 'snare, trap' = , (*Wb.* I, 252, 3), *wꜣrt*, 'string (to close a net)'.

DÉVAUD's slip.

BS **ⲁⲗⲟⲕ** (Crum 5b), 'corner, angle', lit. 'bend(ing)', from **ⲱⲗⲕ**, 'bend'. Same word as S **ⲁⲗⲟϭ**, B **ⲁⲗⲟϫ**, 'thigh, knee, arm' (see this).

ⲁⲗⲕⲉ (Crum 5b), 'last day of month' = (*Wb.* I, 212, 8), *ʿrḳy*, older , *ʿrḳw* (*ASAE* 51, 445–6); Dem. (Er. 67, 2), *ʿrḳy*, 'last day of month'.

H KABIS, *ZÄS* 12, 125 [1874]; D SPIEGELBERG, *Dem. Chron.* 47, no. 49 [1914].

ⲁⲗⲓⲕⲧ (Crum 5b), a metal (?) object = (Er. 7, 9), *ꜣlykt*, 'ring(?)', probably from Greek ἑλικτός, 'twisted', or ἕλιξ, anything of spiral shape.
[D]CRUM, *A Coptic Dict.* 5b [1929]; [G]ERICHSEN, *Dem. Glossar*, 7, 9 [1954] (following Griffith-Thompson, I, 95 [1904]).

ⲁⲗⲓⲗ (Crum 6a), 'field mouse' = ?Gr.-R. (*Wb.* I, 210, 7), *ꜥrꜥr*, an eatable animal. Prob. ultimately related to ⲉⲙⲓⲙ.

ⲁⲗⲱⲗ (Crum 6a), Qual. ⲉⲗⲁⲗⲧ (Mani Hom.; Ev. Ver.) 'be worried', perhaps = (not in *Wb.*), *ꜣrr*, 'frustration (?)', P. Brit. Mus. 10083, 25.
EDWARDS, *Hieratic Papyri in the Brit. Mus.*, Fourth Series, I, 3 n. 16 [1960].

[S]ⲁⲗⲧⲕⲁⲥ, [B]ⲁⲧⲕⲁⲥ (Crum 6b), 'marrow', lit. 'pain-remover' (ⲱⲗ 're-move' + ⲧⲕⲁⲥ 'pain', cf. ⲁⲗⲥⲛⲟϥ), [B]ⲁⲧⲕⲁⲥ, however, is 'fat of (the) bone' (ⲱⲧ + ⲕⲁⲥ), this being the original expression, while [S]ⲁⲗⲧⲕⲁⲥ is a transformation due to the belief that animal marrow is an efficient remedy against pain. See TILL, *Die Arzneikunde*, no. 90 [1951] and *Festschrift Grapow*, 324–5 and 337 [1955].

[B]ⲁⲗⲓϫⲓ (Crum 6b), 'fuller's earth', طفل = (not in *Wb.*; ex. Brugsch, *Rec. de mon.* I, pl. XVI, l. 18), *ꜣrkt*, 'fuller's mixture' (*ꜣrkt* of natron, oil, myrrh and wine to bleach a fabric).
BRUGSCH, *Wb.* 11 [1867].

[S]ⲁⲗⲟϭ, [B]ⲁⲗⲟϫ (Crum 7a), 'thigh, knee, arm' = Late (*Wb.* I, 211, 18), *ꜥrḳ*, 'joint of leg?'; (Er. 8, 2), *ꜣlg*, in *ꜥwy n ꜣlg*, 'cover of the thigh', Petubastis Vienna M4; from ⲱⲗⲕ, 'to bend' (see this). Same word as [BS]ⲁⲗⲟⲕ, 'corner, angle', lit. 'bend(ing)'.
KRALL, *Mitt. aus der Sammlung Erzh. Rainer*, VI, 59, no. 9 [1897]; cf. [D]STRICKER, *Oudheidkundige Mededelingen*, N.S. 35, 57 [1954] (translating '*schenkelstuck*').

ⲁⲁⲙ (Crum 7a, Add., p. xv), a medical plant = ? (*Wb.* I, 169, 15), *ꜥꜥm* (and various other spellings), a medical plant.
CHASSINAT, *Pap. méd.* 317 [1921].

ⲁⲙⲉ (Crum 7a), 'herdsman' = (*Wb.* I, 167, 19–21), *ꜥꜣm*, 'Asiatic', as early as XIXth Dyn. also 'herdsman' (*ZÄS* 72, 146); (Er. 55, 5), *ꜥꜣm*, 'herdsman'.

[H]BRUGSCH, *Rhind*, 34, no. 35 [1865]; DE ROUGÉ, *Oeuv. div.* VI (= *Bibl. ég.* XXVI), 12 [1865]; [D]SPIEGELBERG, *Rec. trav.* 28, 201 [1906].

ⲁⲙⲟⲩ (Crum 7b), Imperative 'come!' 2nd sing. masc. = (*Wb.* II, 35, 8); *mỉ*, (Er. 30, 1), *ỉm*, 'come!'.

[H]CHABAS, *Pap. mag. Harris*, 221 (glossary) [1860]; [D]BRUGSCH, *Gr. dém.* 39, §83, and 150, §296 [1855].

ⲁⲙⲏ 'come!' 2nd sing. fem. = (*Wb.* II, 35, 14), *mỉ·ṯ*; *ỉmỉ(·t)* (Dem. mag. Pap. 6, 19).

[H]W. MAX MÜLLER, *ZÄS* 31, 44 [1893]; [D]GRIFFITH-THOMPSON, III, 7, no. 58 [1909].

ⲁⲙⲱⲓⲛⲉ, 'come', 2nd pl. = (*Wb.* II, 35, 15–17), *my·n*, lit. 'let us go!'; *ỉmỉ·n*.

[H]W. MAX MÜLLER, *ZÄS* 31, 50 [1893]; cf. ERMAN, *Näg. Gr.*², 170–1, §362 [1933]; [D]BRUGSCH, *Gr. dém.* 150, §296 [1855].

ⲁⲙⲏⲉⲓⲧⲛ, 'come!', 2nd pl. = **ⲁⲙⲏⲉⲓ** + **ⲧⲛ**, **ⲁⲙⲏⲉⲓ** being the Plural *my* (*Wb.* II, 35, 8ff.) and **ⲧⲛ** the dependent pronoun of 2nd pl. (lit. 'come you!'); *ỉmw·tn*.

SETHE, *Verbum*, II, 214, §512 [1899]; cf. ERMAN, *Näg. Gr.*², 167, §354 [1933]; [D]VOLTEN, *Ägypter und Amazonen*, 89 [1962].

[B]**ⲁⲙⲟⲛⲓ** (Crum 8a), 'be strong, possess' = (*Wb.* II, 419, 4ff.), *rmnỉ*, 'carry'.

BRUGSCH, *Wb.*, Suppl. 727 [1881]; cf. SETHE, *ZÄS* 50, 103 [1912].

[B]**ⲁⲙⲓⲛⲁⲕⲟⲩ** (not in Crum; cf. Peyron, p. [6]), 'styrax' = (not in Er.), *ꜣmwnyꜥk*, from Greek ἀμμωνιακόν, 'Ammoniac' (a gum resin used in medicine and as cement; *The Concise Oxford Dictionary*, 3rd ed., 37).

GRIFFITH-THOMPSON, III, 7, no. 63 [1909].

ⲁⲙⲛⲧⲉ (Crum 8b), 'Hades' = (*Wb.* I, 87, 1ff.), *ỉmntt*, 'the west'; (Er. 31, 4), *ỉmntt*.

[H]ROSELLINI, *Monumenti civili*, III, 476–8 [1836]; [D]BRUGSCH, *Rhind*, 33 and pl. 34, no. 11 [1865].

ⲁⲙⲣⲉ (Crum 8b), 'baker' = (*Wb.* I, 187, 2); (Er. 61, 10), *ꜥmr*, an occupation.

[D]GRIFFITH, *Cat. of Demotic Graffiti*, I, 288–9, no. 820 [1937].

ⲁⲙⲣⲏϩⲉ (Crum 9a), 'bitumen, asphalt' = (*Wb.* II, 111, 1 ff.), *mrḥt*, later (*Wb.* II, 111, 13), *mrḥ*, 'asphalt'; (Er. 169, 11), *mrḥ*.
[H]LORET, *Rec. trav.* 16, 158 and 161 [1894]; [D]MÖLLER, *Pap. Rhind*, p. 23*, no. 155 [1913].

[B]**ⲁⲙϣⲓ** (Crum, Add. XV), 'rope' = L.Egn. (*Wb.* II, 130, 3, 4), *mḫꜣ*, 'rope, fetter'. *ᵉ*mḫeꜣ* became fem. in Coptic.

[S]**ⲁⲙϩⲣⲏⲣⲉ**, 'scarab', [O]**ⲙⲟⲩϨⲣⲏⲣ** (*JEA* 28, 30) = (Er. 177, 6), *mḫrr*; (Volten, *Dem. Traumdeutung*, 110), *mḫll*.
WALKER in GRIFFITH-THOMPSON, III, p. 153 [1909].
NB. Crum (704a s.v. **ϩⲣⲏⲣⲉ**) reads **ⲟⲩⲁⲙϩⲣⲏⲣⲉ**, 'flower-eater', but Demotic shows this wrong since the *ḥ* of **ϩⲣⲏⲣⲉ** (Egn. *ḥrrt*) could not have been rendered as *ḫ* in *mḫrr*.

[S]**ⲁⲙⲁϩⲧⲉ**, [B]**ⲁⲙⲁϩⲓ** (Crum 9a), 'prevail, grasp' = *imḥti*, or *imḥtw*; (Er. 5, 4), *ꜣmḥṯ*, or (Er. 172, 2), *mḥṯ*, 'seize', these being Imperative of (*Wb.* II, 119, 5 ff.), *mḥ*, 'seize' (identical with , *Wb.* II, 116, 6 ff., **ⲙⲟⲩϩ**, 'fill'); (Er. 172, 2), *mḥ*, 'seize', with dependent pronoun of 2nd sing., 'thou'.
[H]CHABAS, *Voyage*, 183 [1866] (deriving **ⲁⲙⲁϩⲓ** from *mḥ*); W. MAX MÜLLER, *ZÄS* 26, 95 [1888] (on **ⲁⲙⲁϩⲧⲉ**); Spiegelberg in *Rec. trav.* 28, 205 [1906] (explaining **-ⲧⲉ**); [D]BRUGSCH, *Wb.* 695 [1868]. For Egn. exx. of this Imperative used as Infinitive, see GARDINER, *JEA* 42, 18 [1956].

ⲁⲛ- (Crum 10b), construct form of **ⲟ** + genit. **ⲛ** = () (*Wb.* I, 163, 1), *ꜥꜣ(n)*; (Er. 54, 1), *ꜥꜣ n*, 'great one of'.
[HD]SPIEGELBERG, *ZÄS* 42, 56 [1905]; cf. SPIEGELBERG, *ZÄS* 51, 124 n. 5 [1913].

ⲁⲛⲙⲏⲧ (δεκάδαρχος) = , *ꜥꜣ n mḏ(w)*, 'great one of ten' (exx. *ZÄS* 42, 56 n. 7; *JEA* 34, 121).
ⲁⲛⲧⲁⲓⲟⲩ (πεντηκόνταρχος) = , *ꜥꜣ dỉyw*, 'great one of fifty' (ex. SPIEGELBERG, *OLZ* 27, 187).
ⲁⲛϣⲉ, *centurio* = * , , *ꜥꜣ n št*, 'great one of hundred', *ZÄS* 42, pl. III, l. 7 and p. 56, XI.
ⲁⲛϣⲟ (χιλίαρχος) = * , *ꜥꜣ n ḫꜣ*, 'great one of thousand'.
ⲁⲛϫⲟⲧⲏ (Till, *KR*, no. 207 1) = * , *ꜥꜣ n 25*, 'great one of twenty-five'.

ⲁⲛⲟⲩⲣϣⲉ (Crum 491 a, s.v. **ⲟⲩ(ⲉ)ⲣϣⲉ**), 'watchman, guard' = * , *ꜥꜣ n wršt*, 'great one of the watch'; SPIEGELBERG, *Rec. trav.* 21, 21–2 [1899].

ⲁⲛ- (Crum 10 b), prefix in collective numerals, = (*Wb.* I, 158, 5 ff.), *ꜥn*, 'piece, unit of': ^{B}**ⲁⲛ{ⲁⲛ}ⲑⲃⲁ**, μυριάς = * , *ꜥn ḏbꜥ*, 'ten thousand'.

SPIEGELBERG, *Rec. trav.* 21, 21 [1899]; cf. SPIEGELBERG, *ZÄS* 51, 124 [1913].

ⲁⲛ-, prefix of words with geographical meaning = (*Wb.* I, 157, 14 ff.), *ꜥn*, 'district of'; or (Er. 53, top, B; but belonging to *ꜥwy* (Er. 52,2), 'arm', not to *ꜥwy* (Er. 52, 6), 'house'): ^{B}**ⲁⲛⲉⲙⲣⲱ** (Crum 183 a, s.v. **ⲙⲣⲱ**), 'harbour' = * , *ꜥn mryt*; ^{B}**ⲁⲛⲧⲱⲟⲩ** (Crum 441 b top), 'mountainous country' = * , *ꜥn ḏw*.

SPIEGELBERG, *Rec. trav.* 21, 21 [1899]; cf. SPIEGELBERG, *ZÄS* 51, 123 [1913].

ⲁⲛ (Crum 10 b), postpositive negative particle = L.Egn. (*Wb.* I, 90, 1), *ỉ(w)n(ꜣ)*; (Er. 5, 5), *ꜣn*, or (Er. 32, 7), *ỉn*.

^{H}GARDINER, *ZÄS* 41, 130–5 [1904]; ^{D}HESS, *Stne*, 10 [1888].

ⲁⲛⲁⲓ (Crum 11 a), Qual. **ⲁⲛⲓⲧ** (Mani Hom.), 'be pleasing' contains (*Wb.* I, 190, 1 ff.), *ꜥn*, 'be beautiful'; (Er. 62, 5), *ꜥn*, 'beautiful, is beautiful'.

^{HD}BRUGSCH, *Wb.* 194 [1867].

ⲁⲛⲁⲓ < **ⲁⲛ** + **ⲛⲁⲓ**, lit. 'pleasing to me', as early as I Kh. 5, 14 , *ꜥn·y* (for *ꜥn-n·y*).

ⲣ ⲁⲛⲁ, 'be pleasing' and 'be pleased' [lit. 'make (a) pleasing, pleased (one)] is secondary, the suffix being omitted, but the prep. **ⲛⲁ⸗** retained; so too in ^{B}**ⲣ ⲁⲛⲉ**. In **ⲣ ⲁⲛ⸗** the suffixes are appended correctly. Qual. **ⲁⲛⲓⲧ** (Crum, Add. xv) is also secondary.

^{S}**-ⲁⲛ** and varr. as adj. in **ⲥϯⲁⲛ**, 'perfume' = * , *sṯỉ ꜥn*, 'pleasant smell'.

See also **ⲛⲁⲛⲟⲩ-**.

^{B}**ⲁⲛⲑⲟⲩⲥ** (Crum 11 b), '(species of) lizard' = (*Wb.* III, 122, 9), *ḥntꜣsw*; (Er. 315, 3), *ḥnṯs*, 'lizard'.

^{H}CHABAS, *Oeuv. div.* II (= *Bibl. ég.* x), 178 [1862]; cf. BRUGSCH, *Rec. de mon.* II, 106 [1863]; ^{D}REVILLOUT, *Poème*, 78 [1885].

ⲁⲛⲟⲕ (Crum 11 b), personal pronoun of 1st sing. = (*Wb.* I, 101, 13); (Er. 36, 2), *ỉnk*, 'I'.

[H]CHAMPOLLION, *Gr. ég.* 246–52 [1836]; [D]BRUGSCH, *Scriptura Aeg. dem.* 31, §22 [1848].

ⲁⲛⲓⲕⲁⲙ (Crum 12 a), kind of 'vitriol' = **ⲱⲛⲉ**, 'stone' + **ⲕⲁⲙⲉ**, 'black' = (Er. 563, bottom), *ỉny km*, 'black stone'.

TILL, *Arzneikunde der Kopten*, §159 b [1951]; [D]SHORE's communication. See also **ⲕⲙⲟⲙ**.

ⲁⲛⲟⲙ (Crum 12 a), 'skin' = (*Wb.* I, 96, 14 ff.), *ỉnm*; (Er. 5, 14), *ỉnm*, 'skin'.

[H]DE ROUGÉ, *Oeuv. div.* I (= *Bibl. ég.* XXI), 245–6, note [1848]; [D]SPIEGELBERG, *Mythus*, 62, no. 13 [1917].

[B]**ⲁⲛⲁⲙⲏⲓ** (Crum 157, s.v. **ⲙⲉ** and 524 a, s.v. **ⲱⲛⲉ**), 'real, precious stone' = (LD III, 194, 32), (BRUGSCH, *Rec. de mon.* IV, 97, col. 13), (*ib.* 9, col. 49), *ʿȝt n mȝʿt*, lit. 'precious stone (*ʿȝt*, *Wb*, I, 165, 13 ff.; Er. 55, 2) of truth'.

BRUGSCH, *Rhind*, 34, no. 41 [1865]; cf. BRUGSCH, *Wb.* 580 [1868]; DÉVAUD, *Muséon* 36, 85 [1923].

Origin of **ⲉⲛⲉⲙⲙⲉ** is different, see **ⲱⲛⲉ**.

ⲁⲛⲟⲛ (Crum 11 b, s.v. **ⲁⲛⲟⲕ**), personal pronoun of 1st pl. = L.Egn. (*Wb.* I, 97, 5. 6); (Er. 35, 6), *ỉnn*, 'we'.

[H]LEGRAIN in Erman, *Äg. Gr.*³, 84 n. 1 [1911]; cf. ČERNÝ, *JEA* 27, 106–7 [1941]; [D]BRUGSCH, *Gr. dém.* 93, §208 [1855].

[B]**ⲁⲛⲛⲉ-** [not in Crum; exx. Kasser, *Pap. Bodmer* III, p. xi], verbal prefix of neg. future condition 'if he will not...', 'unless he...' = Late Egn. * , *ỉnn bn ỉw·f (r) sḏm*, 'if he will not hear, unless he hears'; , *r bn ỉw ỉr·k r šm*, 'if thou art not going' > **ⲁ(ⲛⲟⲛ)** + **ⲛ̄ⲛⲉϥⲥⲱⲧⲉⲙ**.

ČERNÝ, *ZÄS* 90, 13–16 [1963].

ⲁⲛⲥⲏⲃⲉ (Crum 12 a), 'school' = (*Wb.* I, 160, 12; IV, 85, 7), *ʿt-⟨n⟩-sbȝ*, 'house of teaching'; (Er. 420, 5), *ʿt-⟨n⟩-sbȝ*.

[H]LAUTH, *Über die altäg. Hochschule von Chennu* (= *Sitzungsberichte der Kgl. bayer. Ak. der Wiss., Philos.-philol. Classe*, 1872, vol. II), 41 [1872]; [D]GRIFFITH, *Stories*, 129 [1900].

ⲁⲛⲥⲙⲙⲉ (Crum 337a, s.v. **ⲥⲙⲙⲉ**), 'ordinance' = (*Wb.* I, 189, 7), *ʿn-smy*, 'make (lit. return) report'; (Er. 61, 12 and 432, bottom), *ʿn-smy*.

[HD]GRIFFITH, *Stories*, p. 89 [1900].

ⲁⲛⲧⲁϣ (Crum 12b), 'sneeze', from Semitic, cf. Hebrew עֲטִישָׁה, Syr. ܥܛܫܐ (*ʿatāšā*), 'sneezing' (Payne-Smith, p. 411).

W. MAX MÜLLER in GESENIUS-BUHL, *Hebr. und aram. Wörterb.*[14], 527 [1905].

NB. Derivation from , *ʿtš*, proposed by DÉVAUD, *Rec. trav.* 39, 158–9 [1921], was retracted by its author himself, *Muséon*, 36, 88 [1923].

ⲁⲛⲁϣ (Crum 12b), 'oath' = (*Wb.* I, 202, 11ff.); (Er. 63, 7), *ʿnḫ*, 'oath'.

[H]DE ROUGÉ, *Chrest.* I, 52 n. 1 [1867]; cf. Devéria, *Journal asiatique*, 6e série, 8, 192 n. 1 [1866]; [HD]BRUGSCH, *Wb.* 199 [1867]; cf. BRUGSCH, *ZÄS* 6, 73–8 [1868].

ⲁⲛⲁϣ (Crum 12b), **ⲁⲛⲏϣ** (Mani Ps.), 'bunch of flowers' = (*Wb.* I, 204, 3–5), *ʿnḫ*, 'bunch of flowers'; (Er. 64, 2), *ʿnḫ*, same meaning.

[HD]H. THOMPSON, in Allberry, *A Manichaean Psalm-book*, II, 185, note on l. 13 [1938].

[B]**ⲁⲛϣⲓⲣⲓ, ⲁⲛϭⲓⲣⲓ** (Crum 12b), species of 'bean', 'phaseolus' = (not in Er.; ex. Ankhsh. 20, 21), *ỉndr*, 'beans'.

GLANVILLE's index.

ⲁⲛⲁϩ (Crum 13a), 'border (of a garment)', lit. 'a thing which surrounds', from (*Wb.* I, 99, 3ff.), *ỉnḥ*, 'surround, enclose'. Cf. (MACADAM, *Kawa* I, pl. 12, l. 13), *grb ỉw·w ỉnḥ 35*', '35 plaited(?) cloth with embroidered edges'.

MACADAM, *Kawa* I, *Text*, 39 n. 45 [1949].

See also next word.

ⲁⲛϩ (Crum 13a), 'yard, court' = (*Wb.* I, 99, 14), *ỉnḥ*, 'framing of a picture'; (Er. 35, 8), *ỉnḥ*, 'yard', from (*Wb.* I, 99, 3ff.), *ỉnḥ*, 'surround, enclose'. Probably same word as the preceding.

[H]ERMAN-GRAPOW, *Wb.* I, 99, 14 [1926]; [D]REVILLOUT, *Chrest. dém.* 425 (to P. Louvre 2410 and 2418 [*ib.* p. 89]) [1880].

ⲁⲡⲁ (Crum 13a), title of reverence, as well as the less Egyptianized and more formal **ⲁⲃⲃⲁ**, through Gk. ἀββᾶς from Syriac ܐܰܒܳܐ, *'abâ*, 'father'.

LACROZE, *Lexicon*, 5 [1775].

The corresponding f. **ⲁⲙⲁ** through Gk. ἀμμά from Syriac ܐܶܡܳܐ, *'emâ*, 'mother'.

CRUM, *Dict.* 13a [1929].

ⲁⲡⲉ (Crum 13b), 'head' = (*Wb.* v, 293, 3), *tpt*, (Er. 59, 5), *ʿpt*, 'head'.

[H]CHABAS, *Pap. mag. Harris*, 207, no. 84 (glossary) [1860]; [D]BRUGSCH, *De natura et indole*, pp. 22 and 30 (reading *apa*) [1850].

Acc. to SPIEGELBERG, *Rec. trav.* 21, 22 [1899], from , *tp(y)t*, feminine of the adjective *tpy* (*Wb.* v, 276, 10 ff.), lit. 'which is on the top'; with this agrees the accent, on which see TILL, *Festschrift Grapow*, 325 [1955].

ⲁⲡⲉⲓ (Crum 14a), a purple dye-plant, madder, *Rubia tinctorum* L. = (*Wb.* I, 68, 14), *ip3*, 'a red dye'.

ERMAN-LANGE, *Papyrus Lansing*, 53 [1925]; cf. LORET, *Kêmi*, 3, 28 ff. [1930].

[B]**ⲁⲡⲟⲩⲥ** (Crum 14b), 'bald (from ring-worm)', see **ⲟⲩⲥ**.

ⲁⲡⲟⲧ (Crum 14b), 'cup' = (*Wb.* I, 69, 17); early XIXth Dyn. (O.DM, nos. 19, 27, 29), *ipd*; (Er. 29, 5), *ipt*, 'chalice'.

[H]BRUGSCH, *Rec. de mon.* I, p. 29 [1862]; cf. Schäfer, *Nastesen*, 16 and 117 n. 2 [1901], cf. GRAPOW, *OLZ* 26, col. 560 [1923]; cf. [D]BRUGSCH, *Gr. dém.* 33, §67 [1855].

ⲁⲣⲏⲃ (Crum 15a), 'pledge' = , *ʿnrb*, in fem. proper name *Ḫnsw-p3y·s-ʿrb* (SCHIAPARELLI, *Relazione*, etc., I, 203) and in masc. proper name , *'Iʿḥ-p3y·f-ʿrbt* (*BIFAO* 52 [1953], 184 and n. 5); (Er. 7, 13), *3lbw*, 'pledge'. From Semitic (cf. Hebrew עֲרֻבָּה, עֵרָבוֹן, Ar. عرّب) like Gk. Old and New Testament ἀρραβών.

[H]MALININE, *Choix de textes juridiques*, 130, 10 [1953]; [D]VOLTEN, *Dem. Traumdeutung*, 105 [1942]; [S]ROSSI, *Etym. aeg.* 16 [1808].

[B]**ⲁⲣⲓⲙ**, [B]**ⲁⲣⲁⲣⲓⲙ** (Crum 15b), 'an edible plant, saltwort' = Hebrew חֲרֵרִים (Pl. m.), 'sun-burnt places'.

DÉVAUD's slip.

ⲁⲣⲏⲩ (Crum 15b), 'perhaps' = (Er. 66, 1), *ꜥrw*, 'perhaps'.

REVILLOUT, *Setna*, 206 [1877].

ⲁⲣⲟⲟⲩⲉ (Crum 16a), 'burr, thistle' = (*Wb.* I, 114, 16), *ỉrwt*; (Er. 6, 7), *ꜣrwy*, 'thistle'.

[H]KUENTZ, *BIFAO* 28, 161 [1929]; [D]SPIEGELBERG, *Dem. Chronik*, 39, no. 5 [1914].

NB. Different from **ⲡⲟⲟⲩⲉ**.

ⲁⲣⲟϣ (Crum 16a), 'become cold' = (Er. 40, 2), *ỉrš*, 'cold'.

SPIEGELBERG, *Kopt. Handwb.* 9 [1921].

ⲁⲣϣⲓⲛ (Crum 16b), 'lentil, *Lens esculenta* Mch.' = L.Egn. (*Wb.* I, 211, 15); (Er. 66, 4), *ꜥršn*, 'lentil'. From Semitic, cf. Hebrew עֲדָשִׁים, pl. of *עֲדָשָׁה, Ar. عدس, 'lentils'.

[H]BRUGSCH, *Wb.* 209 [1867]; [D]SPIEGELBERG, *Dem. Denkmäler*, II, 211 and pl. 73, 30976, ro. 7 [1908]; [S]ROSSI, *Etym. aeg.* 28 [1808].

See also next word.

ⲁⲣϣⲁⲛ (Crum 16b), a skin disease, 'lentigo' = , *ꜥršn*, a disease. Same word as last.

ČERNÝ, *Crum Memorial Volume*, 35–6 [1950].

[B]**ⲁⲣϣⲏⲧ** (Crum 16b), 'press upon' (ἐπικεῖσθαι) = **ⲁⲣϣ** (part. coni. of **ⲱⲣϣ**) + **ϩⲏⲧ**, 'merciless', lit. 'cold of heart' or **ϩⲁⲣϣ-ϩⲏⲧ**, 'heavy (**ϩⲣⲟϣ**) of heart', i.e. 'patient, persistent'.

See also **ϩⲁϣⲏⲧ**, 'falcon'.

ⲁⲣⲏϫ⸗ (Crum 16b), 'limit, end', is subst. belonging to verb **ⲱⲣϫ**, 'confirm, fasten, imprison', i.e. also 'shut in, limit'.

HESS, *Stne*, 149 [1888].

ⲁⲥ (Crum 17a), 'old' = (*Wb.* I, 128, 7–9); (Er. 43, 4), *ỉs*, 'old'.

[HD]BRUGSCH, *Wb.* 120 [1867]; [D]BRUGSCH, *Gr. dém.* 33, §65; 119, §243 [1855].

ⲁⲉⲓⲏⲥ (Crum 2a, s.v. **ⲁⲓⲁⲓ**), 'greatness' = (*Wb.* I, 163, 12), *ꜥꜣt*, 'greatness' + **ⲥ** (cf. **ϣⲓⲏⲥ** besides **ϣⲓⲏ**).

STEINDORFF in Leipoldt, *ZÄS* 40, 136 n. 2 [1902/3].

ⲁⲥⲁⲓ (Crum 17b), 'be light' = (*Wb.* I, 128, 4), *ỉsỉ*; (Er. 11, 3), *ꜣsꜥ*, 'be light'.

[H]VOGELSANG, *Die Klagen des Bauern* (*Inaug. Diss.*), 22 [1904]; [D]REVILLOUT, *Pap. mor. de Leide*, I, 231 n. 4 [1907].
See also ⲟⲥⲉ, 'loss, damage, fine'.

[B]ⲁⲥⲑⲉⲙ (not in Crum; only John 14, 11 acc. to P. Bodmer III), 'if not, (then)', εἰ δὲ μή, elliptically for *ⲁⲥⲧⲉⲙϣⲱⲡⲓ, Egn. **iw·s* (*ḥr*) *tm ḫpr*, '(if) it does not happen'.

ⲁⲥⲡⲉ (Crum 18a), 'language, speech' = , , *isp*(*t*), Karnak, Temple of Khons, Sanctuary, East wall, 1st register, ll. 15 and 16 (Gr.-Rom. period, unpublished), 'language'
DRIOTON, communicated by Fairman.

ⲁⲥⲟⲩ (Crum 18a), 'price, value' = (*Wb.* I, 131, 2 ff.), *isw*, 'compensation, reward'; (Er. 44, 2), *iswy*(*t*), 'compensation, reward, price'.
[H]BRUGSCH, *ZÄS* 2, 34 [1864]; [D]BRUGSCH, *Wb.* 121–2 [1867].

[B]ⲁⲥⲟⲩⲓ (Crum 18b), 'purse, wallet' = (*Wb.* I, 131, 12), *iswy*, 'testicles'; (Er. 11, 5), *ꜣswꜣt*, 'purse'.
[H]ROSSI, *Grammatica copto-geroglifica*, 242 [1878]; cf. DÉVAUD's slip (who compares the meaning of the French slang word '*les bourses*'); [D]SPIEGELBERG, *Kopt. Handwb.* 10 [1921].

[B]ⲁⲥⲫⲟⲩⲓ (Crum 18b), 'first year' of reign = (*Wb.* III, 26, 6 ff.), *ḥꜣt-sp wꜥt*, '(regnal) year 1'; (Er. 288, 2).
BRUGSCH, *Mat. cal.* 73 [1864]; SETHE, *Beiträge zur ältesten Geschichte Ägyptens*, 95 [1905]; cf. BRUGSCH, *ZÄS* 9, 58–9 [1871]; BRUGSCH, *Wb.* Suppl., 783 [1881]; GARDINER, *JNES* 8, 170–1 [1949].

ⲁⲧ- (Crum 18b), privative prefix = (*Wb.* I, 46, 1 ff.), *iwty*, 'which is not'; (Er. 25, 7), *iwt*(*y*), 'without'.
[H]LE PAGE RENOUF, *A Prayer from the Egyptian Ritual*, 20 n. 70 [1862]; cf. CHABAS, *Voyage*, 137 [1866]; [D]HESS, *Gnost. Pap.* I [1892].

ⲁⲧⲉ (not in Crum; Mani Ps.), 'net' = (*Wb.* I, 36, 8), *iꜣdt*, 'net'.
[H]H. THOMPSON in Allberry, *A Manichaean Psalm-book*, II, 217, note on l. 8 [1938]; [D]despite H. Thompson's statement there seems to be no certain ex. of this word in Demotic.

[B]ⲁⲑⲁϩ, [F]ⲁⲧⲉϩ, 'burden, load', see ⲱⲧϩ, 'draw'.

ⲁⲩ, ⲁⲩⲉⲓⲥ (Crum 19b), Imperative 'give, bring hither!' = , *ỉ3w*, Imperative of (*Wb.* I, 5, 10), *3wỉ*, 'stretch out, hand over'; (Er. 57, 1), *ỉ3w*, Imperative of , *ʿw*, 'to be distant, to stretch out'. In [S]**ⲁⲩⲉⲓⲥ**, [B]**ⲁⲩⲓⲥ** the **-ⲥ** is the old dependent pers. pronoun , *sw*, 'it'.

[H]SPIEGELBERG, *Rec. trav.* 26, 37 [1904]; SETHE, *ZÄS* 47, 6 [1910]; [D]GRIFFITH-THOMPSON, III, 18, no. 179 [1909]; GRIFFITH, *Ryl.* III, 326 [1909].

[B]**ⲁⲓⲟⲩ** (Crum 19b) in **ⲉⲣ ⲁⲓⲟⲩ**, 'go, travel' = (Er. 1, 1), *ỉr 3*, 'betake oneself'.

SPIEGELBERG in *OLZ* 32, col. 923 [1929].

[S]**ⲁⲩⲱ** (Crum 19b), conjunction 'and' = L.Egn. , *ỉ·w3ḥ*, , *r-w3ḥ*, Imperative of (*Wb.* I, 253, 1 ff.); (Er. 76, 7), *w3ḥ*, 'to put, place', also written , *ỉw-ʿ3*. [B]**ⲟⲩⲟϩ** is not Imperative, but Infinitive of the verb with imperative meaning.

[H]STERN, *Kopt. Gr.* 385, §592 [1880]; W. MAX MÜLLER, *ZÄS* 26, 94–5 [1888]; [D]GRIFFITH, *Stories*, 136 [1900]; SPIEGELBERG, *Mythus*, 69, no. 37 [1917].

[B]**ⲁⲩⲗⲏⲟⲩ** (Crum 20b), part of monk's dress = Plural of Gk. αὐλαία > ***ⲁⲩⲗⲁ**, like *[S]**ⲉⲡⲣⲁ**, 'vanity', Pl. [B]**(ⲉ)ⲫⲗⲏⲟⲩ**.

CRUM, *A Coptic Dict.*, p. xvi [1939].

ⲁⲩⲁⲛ (Crum 20b), 'colour' = (*Wb.* I, 52, 10 ff.); (Er. 24, 2), *ỉwn*, 'colour'.

[H]CHABAS, *Voyage*, 255 [1866]; [D]BRUGSCH, *Wb.* 34 [1867].

ⲁⲩⲉⲓⲛ (P. Cai 42573), **ⲟⲩ(ⲉ)ⲓⲛ** (Crum 480a), 'water-channel (?)', 'drain channel (of a bathroom)' (see Chassinat, *Un manuscrit magique copte*, 47) = Gr.-R. (*Wb.* I, 53, 2), *ỉwny* (or *ỉwyn*?), some watercourse. Same word in **ⲥⲓⲟⲟⲩⲛ**, 'bath', see this.

ⲁⲟⲩⲉⲓⲛ (Crum 21a), 'ship's cargo, load' = (Er. 24, 1), *ỉwn*, 'ship's hold, cargo, journey'.

SPIEGELBERG, *ZÄS* 51, 73 n. 1 [1913]; cf. SPIEGELBERG, *Chronik*, 104, no. 364 [1914]. But see DÉVAUD, *Muséon*, 36, 88 [1923].

[A]**ⲁⲩϭⲉ** (Crum 21b), 'all (together)' = **ⲁ** + **ⲟⲩ** + **ϭⲉ**, *, *r wʿ ky*, 'to one form, body', cf. , *m ky wʿ*, lit. 'in one single form', '(all) together' (*Wb.* v, 16, 16; *JEA* 3, 103); , *n wᶜ gy* (I Kh. 6, 20).

SETHE in Spiegelberg, *Kopt. Handwb.* 11 n. 9, 212 n. 1 [1921]; cf. SPIEGELBERG, *Demotica*, I, 25 [1925].

Bⲁⲫⲱⲫ (Crum 21 b), 'giant' = (*Wb.* I, 167, 14–15), *ᶜ3pp*; (Er. 59, 7) *ᶜpᶜp*, 'Apophis, enemy of the sun'.

HCHAMPOLLION, *Dict.* 88 [1841]; DGRIFFITH-THOMPSON, III, 6, no. 54 [1909]; but cf. DÉVAUD, *Muséon*, 36, 89 [1923].

Bⲁϫⲓ, see ⲁϭⲓ.

ⲁϣ (Crum 22 a), 'who? what?' = L.Egn. (*Wb.* I, 123, 12 ff.); (Er. 41, 6), *iḫ*, 'what?' < , *(i)ḫt*, 'a thing, something' (cf. Sethe, *ZÄS* 47, 4).

HCHAMPOLLION, *Gr. ég.* 255 [1836]; DBRUGSCH, *Wb.* 111 [1867].

ⲁϣ (Crum 22 a), 'furnace, oven' = (*Wb.* I, 223, 13), (Er. 69, 4) *ᶜḫ*, 'brazier'.

HDBRUGSCH, *Wb.* 214 [1867]; DBRUGSCH, *De natura et indole*, pp. 23, 35 [1850].

ⲁϣⲁⲓ (Crum 22 b), 'become many' = (*Wb.* I, 228, 8 ff.); (Er. 72, 3), *ᶜš3*, 'become many'.

HDE ROUGÉ, *Oeuv. div.* II (= *Bibl. ég.* XXII), 89 [1851]; DÅKERBLAD, *Lettre*, pp. 42–3 and pl. I, no. 12 [1802]; cf. BRUGSCH, *Gr. dém.* 119, §243 [1855].

Aⲁϣⲉⲉⲓⲧⲉ is originally an Imperative followed by dependent pers. pronoun 'thou'. See under -ⲧⲉ.

RÖSCH, *Vorbemerkungen*, 140, §120 [1909].

ⲁϣⲁⲓ (Crum 22 b), 'multitude, amount' = (*Wb.* I, 228, 22–3 = 229, 1–4).

DÉVAUD's slip.

ⲁϣⲏ (Crum 22 b), 'multitude' = (*Wb.* I, 229, 6–8); (Er. 72, 3), *ᶜš3t*, 'multitude'.

HSTEINDORFF, *Kopt. Gr.*, 1st ed., 47, §70 b [1894]; DBOESER, *Pap. Insinger*, 6 [1922].

Bⲁϣⲉⲃⲉⲛ (Crum 23 a), 'enchanter', from Semitic, cf. Hebrew אַשָּׁפִים (Plural) and Aram. אָשְׁפִין, 'conjurers'.

DÉVAUD in Spiegelberg, *Kopt. Handwb.* 300 [1921].

The resemblance between ⲁϣⲉ and ⲁϣⲉⲃⲉⲛ is therefore fortuitous. To maintain a connexion between them it would have to be assumed that ⲁϣⲉⲃⲉⲛ is ⲁϣⲉⲃ(< ⲁϣⲉⲩ) + ⲉⲛ, the latter an obscure element sometimes added to words containing, and especially ending in, ⲃ (cf. FECHT, *Wortakzent und Silbenstruktur*, p. 54 and n. 164).

[B]ⲁϣⲓⲣⲁ (Crum 23a), 'chameleon', perhaps also 'lizard' and connected with , *ʿš3*, 'lizard' (not in *Wb.*, but see BARNS, *Five Ramesseum Papyri*, 31 n. 21.).

KEIMER, *BIFAO* 36, 95 [1936].

NB. One is tempted to derive ⲁϣⲓⲣⲁ from * , *ʿš3 ỉrw*, 'manifold of forms' (ⲁϣ- from ⲁϣⲁⲓ, for *ỉrw* see *Wb.* I, 113, 13–15) referring to chameleon's well-known change of colour.

[A2]ⲁϣⲥⲓⲟⲩ (not in Crum), 'star-reader, astrologer', see ⲱϣ, 'cry, read'.

[B]ⲁϣⲉⲩ (Crum 23a), 'astrologers', is either secondary Plural of *ⲁϣⲉ (so SPIEGELBERG, *Kopt. Handwb.* 12) = (*Wb.* II, 445, bottom), *rḫ-ỉḫt*, 'scholar', lit. 'he who knows things' (*Wb.* II, 443, 27–30), or L.Eg. , *(ỉw)rḫw*, Pl. of , *(ỉw)rḫ*, older (*Wb.* II, 445, 17, 18), *rḫ*, 'he who knows' = 'scholar'.

See also [B]ⲁϣⲉⲃⲉⲛ, 'enchanter' which is perhaps of different origin.

ⲁϥ (Crum 23a), 'flesh' = (*Wb.* I, 51, 14ff.); (Er. 23, 6), *ỉwf*, 'flesh'.

[H]CHAMPOLLION, *Gr. ég.* 76 [1836]; [D]BRUGSCH, *De natura et indole*, 31 [1850].

ⲁϥ (Crum 23b), 'fly' = (*Wb.* I, 182, 14, 15), *ʿff*, later (*Wb.* I, 182, 10), *ʿfy*, 'fly, bee'; (Er. 59, 10), *ʿf*, 'fly'.

[H]CHAMPOLLION, *Gr. ég.* 74 [1836]; [D]BRUGSCH, *Gr. dém.* 24, §41 [1855].

ⲁϥⲛⲉⲃⲓⲱ (Crum 23b), 'bee', lit. 'honey-fly' = , *ʿfy n bỉt* (*Wb.* I, 182, 11; 434, 10); (Er. 59, 10), *ʿf n ỉbỉ*.

[H]ERMAN-GRAPOW, *Wb.* I, 182, 11, and 434, 10 [1926]; [D]BRUGSCH, *Wb.* 183 [1867].

[B]ⲁϥⲙⲃⲓⲟⲩ (Crum 7a, s.v. ⲁⲙⲏ) stands for ⲁϥⲛⲉⲃⲓⲱ, lit. 'fly of honey' = 'bee' (cf. [A]ⲉⲃⲓⲟⲩ, 'honey'). Through confusion it is used for 'wasp' in Sa. 12, 8.

ⲁϥ-ϫⲓⲣ (Crum 23b), 'greedy of shameful gain', cf. [hieroglyphs] (*Wb.* I, 9, 17), *ꜣfꜥ*, 'greedy', and L.Egn. [hieroglyphs] (*Wb.* I, 182, 12), *ꜥfi*, 'greedy(?)'; [Demotic] (Er. 60, 1), *ꜥfꜥ*, 'be greedy'.

HD SPIEGELBERG, *Dem. Chronik*, 39, no. 4 [1914]. **ⲁϥϫⲓⲣ** more probably = **ⲁϥ** (part. coni. of **ⲱϥⲉ**) + **ϫⲓⲣ**, 'who squeezes out a small fish'.

A **ⲁϩⲧⲛ-** (Crum 23b), 'against, in opposition to' = * [hieroglyphs], *r-ẖt n*, lit. 'against (the) body of'; [Demotic], *r-ẖt-n*, with suffixes [Demotic], *r-ẖt*, 'like, to, from' (Er. 374, Spiegelberg, *Dem. Gr.*, §347, 348b).

H TILL, *Achm.-kopt. Gr.* 210, §181a [1928].

B **ⲁϧⲓ, ⲁⲭⲓ** (Crum 25a under **ⲁϩⲣ**) is everywhere (Ge. 41, 2. 18; Is. 19, 7; Si. 40, 6) a mere transcription of ἄχει of LXX which renders the אחו of the original. They all, however, go back to [hieroglyphs] (*Wb.* I, 18, 8), *ꜣḫy*, 'plants, vegetation', or—less likely—to [hieroglyphs] (*Wb.* I, 18, 9), *ꜣḫt*, 'land under vegetation'; [Demotic] (Er. 10, 4), *ꜣḫy*, 'reed-thicket' or sim.

D BRUGSCH, *Gr. dém.* 26, §51 [1855]; cf. Krall, *Mitt. Erzh. Rainer*, VI, 56, and 59, no. 12 [1897].

ⲁϧⲱⲣⲓ (Crum 23b), 'asp' = [hieroglyphs] (*Wb.* I, 22, 6), *ꜣkr*; [Demotic] (GRIFFITH-THOMPSON III, 15, no. 143), *ỉkr*, spirit or god of the earth, already in Pyramid texts in Pl. for the totality of the spirits (Sethe, *Übersetzung und Kommentar zu den altäg. Pyramidentexten*, II, 144), since N.K. considered as snakes [hieroglyphs] (*Wb.* I, 22, 7), *ꜣkryw*. In the Gk. inscription of a stone amulet Brit. Mus. 56001 the deity [hieroglyph] is called AKWPI (WILKINSON-BIRCH, *The Manners and Customs of the Ancient Egyptians*, II, 514, fig. 494; cf. Spiegelberg in *Archiv für Religionswissenschaft*, 21 [1922], 225–7). Egn. *k* > **ϧ** (instead of > **ⲭ**) is perhaps unique but Crum 516a quotes Gk. words in which **ⲭ** is replaced by **ϧ**. In Pl. also in proper name **ⲡⲁⲛⲁⲭⲱⲣⲉ**, lit. 'He of the asps'.

H NAVILLE in *PSBA* 25, 69 [1903].

ⲁϩ- (Crum 24a), verbal particle in past relative clause = construct form of Qualitative of [hieroglyphs], Dem. [Demotic], **ⲟⲩⲱϩ**: **ⲉⲧ-ⲁϩ-ⲥⲱⲧⲙ** 'who is finished as to hearing' = 'who heard'.

SETHE, *ZÄS* 52, 112–16 [1914].

NB. If Sethe's explanation is correct, then the **ⲁϣ-** listed by Crum as a S[A] form of **ⲁϩ-** must be of different origin, since its **ϣ** cannot go back to *ḥ* of *wꜣḥ*!

^F^ⲁϩⲁ, ⲁϩ, ϩⲁ (Crum 24a), conj. 'and', see ^S^ⲁϩⲁⲛ.

ⲁϩⲉ (Crum 24a), 'length of life' = (*Wb.* I, 222, 18ff.), *ꜥḥꜥw*; , *ꜥḥꜥ* (Er. 69, 1), 'length of life'.

^H^DE ROUGÉ, *Oeuv. div.* II (= *Bibl. ég.* XXII), 132 [1851]; ^D^BRUGSCH, *Gr. dém.* 30, §61 [1855].

ⲁϩⲉ, 'use, profit' (SETHE, *ZÄS* 41, 142–3 [1904]; SPIEGELBERG, *Kopt. Handwb.*, 13; *Wb.* I, 15, 10), non-existent, 'Sethe should have read ⲧⲁ-ϩⲉⲛⲕⲟⲟⲩⲉ = τὴν ἑτέρων ὠφελείαν', CRUM, *JEA* 8, 117 [1922].

ⲁϩⲟ (Crum 24b), 'treasure' = (*Wb.* I, 220, 10ff.), *ꜥḥꜥ*, 'heap', or (*Urk.* IV, 762), *ꜥḥꜥ ꜥꜣ*, 'large heap'.

MASPERO, *Mélanges d'arch. ég. et assyr.* 3, 147 n. 4 [1877] (*ꜥḥꜥ*); DÉVAUD's slip (for *ꜥḥꜥ ꜥꜣ*).

Pl. ⲁϩⲱⲱⲣ = , cf. GRIFFITH, *JEA* 12, 196 n. 13 [1926]. For its ⲣ, see SETHE, *ZÄS* 47, 164 [1910]; ČERNÝ, *ASAE* 41, 335–36 [1942].

^B^ⲁⲛⲁϩⲱⲣ (Crum 24b, also S:BMar 47, 13 [Till]), 'storehouse' < ⲏⲓ + ⲛ + ⲁϩⲱⲣ, 'house of treasures'.

^B^ϫⲉⲙⲙⲁϩⲱⲣ, fem. proper name, see under ϭⲓⲛⲉ, 'find'.

See also ϩⲟ, a measure, and ϩⲟⲓ, 'heap of grain'.

ⲁϩⲟⲙ (Crum 24b), 'sigh, groan' = (*Wb.* I, 118, 20f.), *ỉhm*, 'to mourn'; (Er. 8, 6), *ꜣhm*, 'mourning'.

^HD^BRUGSCH, *Wb.* 12 and 105 [1867]; ^D^BRUGSCH, *Gr. dém.* 34, §68 [1855].

ⲁϩⲱⲙ (Crum 25a), 'eagle, vulture' = (*Wb.* I, 225, 15ff.), *ꜥẖm*; (Er. 70, 8), *ꜥẖm*, 'divine image, falcon'.

^H^CHAMPOLLION, *Gr. ég.* 73 [1836]; ^D^BRUGSCH, *Gr. dém.* 197 (add. to p. 23, §41) [1855].

^SA2^ⲁϩⲁⲛ, ^A2^ⲁϩⲛ (Crum, Add. XVI; 685a, s.v. ϩⲛ- at end), 'to' = ^F^ⲁϩⲁ, ⲁϩ, ϩⲁ (Crum 24a), conj. 'and' prob. = Gr.-Roman (*Wb.* II, 495, 14, 15), *r hn r*, lit. 'to approach, touch' = 'as far as' (of time and place); (Er. 276, 4), *r hn (r)*, 'as far as' (of time). Later development > 'as far as and including' > 'including, and'.

^S^ⲁϩⲣ(ⲉ) (Crum 25a), 'marsh herbage, sedge' = (Er. 10, 3), *ꜣẖr*, 'marsh'. ^B^ⲁϧⲓ, however, is a mere transcription of ἄχει of LXX; see under ^B^ⲁϧⲓ.

DÉVAUD, *Muséon*, 36, 89 [1923].

See also ⲥⲁⲙ-ⲁϩⲏⲣ.

[S]ⲁϩⲣⲟ⸗, [B]ⲁϧⲟ⸗ (Crum 25a), 'what? why?' = (*Wb.* I, 123, 15), *ỉḫ r*+Suffix; (Er. 41, 6), *ỉḫ r·w*, 'why?'.

[H]DE ROUGÉ, *Chrest. ég.* II, 96 [1868]; cf. Brugsch, *Wb.* 111 [1867]; [D]KRALL, *Mitt. aus der Sammlung. Erzh. Rainer*, VI, 60, no. 34 [1897]; cf. Brugsch, *Wb.* 111 [1867].

ⲁϩⲏⲧ (in ⲕⲱⲕ ⲁϩⲏⲧ, Crum 101a, 'strip, make naked'), see under ϩⲏⲧ.

[B]ⲁϫⲱ (Crum 25b), 'viper' = (*Wb.* V, 503, 1 ff.), *ḏt*, 'viper'.

SPIEGELBERG, *ZÄS* 55, 89 [1918]; cf. DÉVAUD, *Rec. trav.* 39, 159–61 [1921].

ⲁϫⲛ-, ⲁϫⲛ⸗ (Crum 25b), prep. 'without' (for ⲁⲧ-ϣⲛ-, lit. 'without asking') = (Er. 514, middle), *ỉwṯ šnṯ·*, 'without asking', 'without'.

STEINDORFF, *Kopt. Gr.*, 2nd ed., §391 [1904]; cf. SPIEGELBERG, *Petubastis*, 1*, no. 7, and 59*, no. 405 [1910].

ⲁϭⲃⲉⲥ (Crum 26a), 'moisture', = ⲱϭⲃ + ⲥ, see under ⲱϭⲃ.

ⲁϭⲟⲗ (Crum, Add. XVI to 26a), 'calf', non-existent. In *Actes 5ᵉ Cong. Papyrol.* μόσχος is 'twig' and Dem. αγ́ολ is ϫⲁⲗ, 'twig'.

ⲁϭⲟⲗⲧⲉ (Crum 26a), 'wagon, cart' = L.Egn. (*Wb.* I, 236, 9), *ʿgrt*; (Dem. Ostr. Strassburg D 191), *ʿklṯ3*, 'cart'. From Semitic, cf. Hebrew עֲגָלָה, Aram. עֲגָלְתָא, Syr. ܥܓܠܬܐ, Ar. عَجَلَة, 'cart'.

[H]BRUGSCH, *Wb.* 226 [1867]; LE PAGE RENOUF, *ZÄS* 6, 8 n. 2 (= *Egypt. and philol. Essays*, I, 386 n. 2) [1868]; [D]SPIEGELBERG, *Kopt. Handwb.* 14 [1921].

ⲁϭⲟⲛ (Crum 26b), 'stand' for jar (for meaning see Allberry, *Manich. Psalm-book*, II, 220, 22) = > L.Eg. (*Wb.* I, 236, 5, 6); *ʿgn*, 'stand for vessels'; (not in Er.; O. Murray 1, 11), *ʿkn*, not derived from but ultimately related to, Semitic √*ʿgl*, cf. Hebrew עָגִיל, 'ring'.

[D]H. THOMPSON's Demotic dictionary.

[B]ⲁϭⲛⲓ (Crum 26b), 'blemish, stain' = (Er. 75, 1), *ʿḏn* (fem.), 'scar'.

SPIEGELBERG, *Kopt. Handwb.* 14 [1921]; but cf. Dévaud, *Muséon*, 36, 89 [1923].

See also ⲱϫⲛ.

ⲁϭⲣⲏⲛ (Crum 26b), 'barren female', from Semitic, cf. Hebrew עָקָר and עֲקָרָה, 'barren', Arabic عاقر, fem. عاقرة.

DÉVAUD, *Muséon*, 36, 90 [1923] and in *ZÄS* 61, 109 [1926].

B

ⲃⲁ (Crum 27b), 'branch of date palm' = L.Egn. (*Wb.* I, 446, 9, 10); (Er. 113, 5), *bꜥỉ*, 'rib of palm leaf'.

[H]LORET, *Flore pharaonique*, 2nd ed., 35 [1892]; [D]GRIFFITH-THOMPSON, III, 24, no. 244 [1909].

ⲃⲁⲓ (Crum 28a), 'night raven, screech-owl' = (*Wb.* I, 410, 10), *bꜣ*, a bird (jabiru, *Ephippiorhynchus senegalensis*; cf. *ASAE* 30, 1–20).

ERMAN-GRAPOW, *Wb.* I, 410, 10 [1926].

[O]**ⲃⲁⲓ** (Crum 28a), lord of spirit(s) = (*Wb.* I, 411, 6ff.), *bꜣ*; (Er. 111, 4), *by*, 'soul'. Ultimately identical with the preceding word.

[H]CHAMPOLLION, *Gr. ég.* 179 [1836]; cf. [H]LEFÉBURE, *Hymne au soleil*, 59 [1868]; MÖLLER, *Rhind*, 15*, no. 102 [1913].

ⲃⲏ (Crum 28a), 'grave' = (Er. 109, 8), *bt*, 'grave'.

BRUGSCH, *Gr. dém.* 33, §65 [1855].

ⲃⲱ (Crum 28a), 'tree' (where its fruit specified) = (*Wb.* I, 416, 5ff.), *bꜣt*, 'bush' (especially of *Cyperus papyrus*); (Er. 109, 7), *b*, 'bush'.

[H]CHABAS, *Voyage*, 225 [1866]; [D]BRUGSCH, *Gr. dém.* 25, §44 [1855].

ⲃⲏⲃ (Crum 28b), 'cave, hole' = (*Wb.* I, 419, 1ff.), *bꜣbꜣ*, 'hole'.

DE ROUGÉ, *Oeuv. div.* IV (= *Bibl. ég.* XXIV), 128 [1861].

ⲃⲁⲁⲃⲉ (Crum 28b), 'be insipid'.

ⲃⲁⲁⲃⲉ-ⲣⲱⲙⲉ, 'boaster', cf. , *ꜥbꜥ*, later (*Wb.* I, 177, 17f.), *ꜥbꜥb* (or *bꜥbꜥ*?), 'boast'.

BRUGSCH, *Wb.* 176 [1867]; cf. SPIEGELBERG, *Rec. trav.* 23, 203–4 [1901].

ⲃⲉⲉⲃⲉ, ⲃⲉⲃⲉ (Crum 28b), 'bubble, well up' = L.Eg. (not in *Wb.*), *b(ꜣ)b(ꜣ)y*, 'well up'; (Er. 115, 3), *bbꜣ*, 'well up', onomatopoetic like 'bubble' and Semitic √בעבע, and it is unnecessary to derive **ⲃⲉⲉⲃⲉ** from the latter (as done by Stricker in *Acta Orientalia*, 15, 3) or from נָבַע (as done by Dévaud in *Sphinx*, 12, 121–2).

[H]MASSART in *Mitt. Kairo*, 15, 178 n. 7 [1957]; [D]LEXA, *Pap. Insinger*, II, 33, no. 141 [1926].

ⲃⲟⲩⲃⲟⲩ (Crum 29a), 'shine, glitter' = (*Wb.* I, 178, 4), *ꜥbꜥb*, 'shine' > **bꜥbꜥ*; (Er. 115, 2), *bwbw*, 'glitter'.

[H]DÉVAUD, *Muséon*, 36, 90 [1923]; [D]REVILLOUT, *Rev. ég.* 4, p. 85 n. 10 [1885].

[B]**ⲃⲱⲕ** (Crum 30a), 'servant, slave' = (*Wb.* I, 429, 6ff.), *bꜣk*; (Er. 124, 2), *bk*, 'servant'.

[H]CHABAS, *Pap. mag. Harris*, pl. I, no. 15; p. 173 n. 3 [1860]; [D]REVILLOUT, *Poème*, 207 [1885].

[B]**ⲃⲱⲕⲓ**, 'female servant' = (*Wb.* I, 430, 5ff.), *bꜣkt*; (Er. 124, 2), *bꜣkt*, 'female servant'.

[H]BRUGSCH, *Wb.* 432–3 [1868]; [D]ERICHSEN, *Dem. Glossar*, 124, 2 [1954].

ⲉⲣ ⲃⲱⲕ, 'serve, labour' = (*Wb.* I, 429, 7); (Er. 124, 1), *ỉrỉ bꜣk*, 'serve'.

[H]DÉVAUD's slip; [D]GRIFFITH, *Pap. Ryl.* III, p. 230 n. 4, and p. 346 [1909].

[B]**ⲃⲁⲕⲓ** (Crum 30b), 'city, town' = (*Wb.* I, 430, 14), *bꜣkꜣt*, 'precincts'; (not in Er.), *bkt*, 'city'.

[H]BRUGSCH, *Wb.* 433–4 [1868]; cf. CHABAS, *Voyage*, 224 [1866]; [D]HESS, *Stne*, pp. 53 and 154 [1888]; BRUGSCH in *ZÄS* 26, 39 [1888].

ⲃⲉⲕⲉ (Crum 30b), 'wage' = (Er. 124, 4), *bk*, 'wage'.

SPIEGELBERG, *Rec. trav.* 26, 39 [1904].

ϫⲓ ⲃⲉⲕⲉ, 'receive wage' = (*Wb.* I, 428, 15), 'receive wage(?)'.

ERMAN-GRAPOW, *Wb.* I, 428, 15 [1926].

ⲣⲙⲃⲉⲕⲉ (Crum 31a), 'wage-man, hireling' = , *rmt-bk*, lit. 'man of wage'.

SPIEGELBERG, *Rec. trav.* 26, 39 [1904].

ⲃⲏⲕⲉ (Crum 31a), 'woof'? = , *bkt*, 'woof(?)'; cf. Aeth. (*Wb.* I, 430, 13), *bꜣk*, a (wooden) instrument used in siege.

GLANVILLE, *Cat. of Dem. Pap.* II, 76 n. 243 [1955].

[B]**ⲃⲟⲕⲓ** (Crum 31a) in **ⲙⲃⲟⲕⲓ, ⲉⲣ ⲃⲟⲕⲓ**, 'conceive' = (*Wb.* I, 481, 12. 13), *bkꜣt*; (Er. 125, 3), *bk*, 'pregnant'.

[H]DE ROUGÉ, *Oeuv. div.* VI (= *Bibl. ég.* XXVI), 344 n. 1 [1859]; [D]GRIFFITH, *Pap. Ryl.* III, 346 [1909].

ⲃⲱⲕⲉ, ⲃⲁⲕ- (Crum 31 a), 'tan' = (*Wb.* I, 426, 3 ff.), *b3k*, 'work', also 'work a hide' (P. Mallet I, 3); (Er. 123, 8), *bk*, 'work'.

H A. BAILLET, *Oeuv. div.* I (= *Bibl. ég.* XV), 35 [1867]; D ERICHSEN, *Dem. Glossar*, 123, 8 [1954].

ⲃⲉϫⲉ (Mani), see **ⲃⲏⲧⲥⲏ** under **ⲃⲱⲧⲥ**.

ⲃⲁⲗ (Crum 31 b), 'eye' = L.Egn. , *bnr*, 'balls (of the eyes)' (Horus and Seth 10, 4); (*Wb.* I, 465, 5), *br*, 'the two eyes'; (Er. 120, 1), *bl*, 'eye'.

H BRUGSCH, *Wb.*, Suppl., 435 (only) [1880]; cf. BLACKMAN, *JEA* 19, 200 [1933] (for *bnr*); D BRUGSCH, *Scriptura Aeg. demotica*, 17, § 14 [1848]; DE ROUGÉ, *Oeuv. div.* I (= *Bibl. ég.* XXI), 241 and pl. I (94), nos. 1 and 2 [1848].

ⲃⲁⲗ ⲛⲁⲃⲱⲕ (Crum 31 b), a plant, lit. 'raven's eye', see under **ⲁⲃⲱⲕ**.

ⲃⲱⲗ (Crum 32 a), 'loosen, untie' = (Er. 120, 4), *bl3*, 'loosen'.

SPIEGELBERG, *Dem. Chronik*, 51, no. 76 [1914]; cf. REVILLOUT, *Rev. ég.* 2, pl. 11 (, **ⲃⲱⲗ**, 'disparaître') [1881].

ⲃⲟⲗ (Crum 33 b), 'the outside' = (*Wb.* I, 461, 1 ff.), *bnr* (*bl*), 'the outside'; (Er. 118, 1), *bnr* (*bl*), 'the outside'.

H CHABAS, *Mélanges égypt.* I, 105 [1862]; D BRUGSCH, *Gr. dém.* 133, § 276 [1855].

For **ⲕⲁ ⲃⲟⲗ**, 'cast forth, vomit', see under **ⲕⲱ**.

B **ⲃⲗⲁ** (Crum 37 a), a musical instrument, probably an error for **ⲛⲁⲃⲗⲁ** = Gk. νάβλα, a musical instrument of ten or twelve strings, a word of Semitic origin, cf. Hebrew נֵבֶל or נֶבֶל, a portable harp or lute.

CRUM, *A Coptic Dict.* 37 a [1929].

ⲃⲟⲗⲃⲗ (Crum 37 b), 'dig up, out' = (Er. 120, 9), *blbl*, 'blister, burn'.

GRIFFITH-THOMPSON, III, 26, no. 267 [1909]; cf. Parker, *JEA* 26, 95 [1940].

ⲃⲗⲃⲓⲗⲉ (Crum 37 b), 'a single grain' = Gr.-Roman (*Wb.* I, 466, 3), *brbr*(*t*) (masc.!), spherical top of the Upper Egyptian crown ; = (Er. 120, 8), *blbyl3*, 'grain'.

HD BRUGSCH, *Wb.* 405–6 [1868].

[A]ⲃⲗⲕⲉ (Crum 38a), 'throne' (Crum: 'wrath', but cf. Dévaud) = (*Wb.* I, 482, 8), *bkrt*, 'throne'.
DÉVAUD, *Kêmi*, 2, 5–6 [1929].

ⲃⲗⲗⲉ (Crum 38a), 'blind person' = , *br*, masc. proper name (RANKE, I, 97, 27), and in m. pers. name *P3-brr* (RANKE, I, 104, 25); (Er. 120, 2), *bl*, 'blind'.
[H]GRIFFITH, *Pap. Ryl.* III, 265 n. 8 [1909]; [D]GRIFFITH, *Pap. Ryl.* III, 225 n. 10 and 265 n. 8 [1909].

ⲃⲁⲗⲟⲧ (Crum 38a), ⲙⲁⲗⲗⲱⲧ (Crum 165a), 'skin garment', from Gk. μηλωτή, 'hide, sheep skin', like Aram. מֵילָתָא (fem.); [B]ⲙⲉⲗⲱⲧⲏ (quoted Crum 38b).
DÉVAUD, *Muséon*, 36, 91 [1923]; DÉVAUD's slip.

ⲃⲗϩⲙⲟⲩ (Crum 38b), Blemys = * in fem. proper name (Turin Cat. 1816), *T-Brhmt*, lit. 'The (female) Blemys'; (Er. 120, 10), *Blhm*, 'Blemys'.
[H]ČERNÝ, *BIFAO* 57, 203–5 [1958]; [D]GRIFFITH, *PSBA* 31, 105 and 291 [1909]; cf. GRIFFITH, *Pap. Ryl.* III, 420 [1909].

ⲃⲗϫⲉ (Crum 38b), 'earthenware, pottery' = (*Wb.* I, 488, 11), *bḏ3*, a pot; (Er. 120, 13), *blḏ*, 'sherd'.
[H]BRUGSCH, *Wb.* 1469 [1868]; [D]BRUGSCH, *Gr. dém.* 33, §66 [1855].

ⲃⲟⲙ (Crum 39a), 'owl', is the Arabic بوم, 'owl'.
CRUM, *A Coptic Dict.* 39a [1939]; cf. Stricker in *Oudheidkundige Mededelingen, N.R.* 38, 10 [1957].

ⲃⲁⲁⲙⲡⲉ (Crum 39a), 'goat' = * (cf. *Wb.* I, 414, 13) *b3 ꜥ3 n pt*, 'great he-goat of heaven' (epithet of a god, prob. of Amūn); (Er. 111, 4), *bỉ-ꜥ3-n-pt*, 'he-goat'.
[D]GRIFFITH-THOMPSON, III, p. 25, no. 250 [1909]. For [H]*b3* see Lauth, *Manetho*, 61 [1865].

ⲃⲱⲱⲛ (Crum 39a), 'bad, evil' = (*Wb.* I, 442, 15ff.); (Er. 112, 3), *bỉn*, 'bad'.
fem. ⲃⲟⲟⲛⲉ (Crum. 39b), 'evil, misfortune' = (*Wb.* I, 444, 10), *bỉnt*, 'evil'.

[H]CHAMPOLLION, *Dict.* 101 [1841]; [D]BRUGSCH, *Gr. dém.* 34, §68 [1855].

[SA2]**ⲃⲁⲛ-** in **ⲃⲁⲛ-ⲓⲉⲓⲣⲉ**, 'malicious', lit. 'evil of eye' (see **ⲉⲓⲁ**), **ⲃⲁⲛϣⲁⲓ** (see under **ϣⲁⲓ**) and **ⲃⲁⲛϩⲟ**.

See also **ⲉⲓⲉⲣ-ⲃⲟⲟⲛⲉ** under **ⲉⲓⲁ**, 'eye'.

ⲃⲏⲛⲉ (Crum 40a), 'swallow' = (*Wb.* II, 68, 2ff.), *mnt*; (Er. 117, 3), *bny*, 'swallow'.

[H]CHAMPOLLION, *Gr. ég.* 73 and 85 [1836]; [D]SPIEGELBERG, *Krüge*, 35 n. 63 and 63, no. 69 [1912].

[B]**ⲃⲓⲛⲓ** (Crum 40a), 'crucible' = Late (*Wb.* II, 68, 16), *mnt*, coppersmith's 'melting fire', and , *mnyt*, *H.O.* XLVII, 1, vo. 8.

FECHT, *Wortakzent und Silbenstruktur*, 230 to §428 [1960].

[S]**ⲃⲟⲓⲛⲉ**, [B]**ⲟⲩⲱⲓⲛⲓ** (Crum 40a), 'harp' = or (*Wb.* I, 457, 5ff.), *b(ỉ)nt*; (Er. 112, 4), *bynt*, 'harp'.

[H]ROSELLINI, *Mon. civili*, III, 21–2 [1836]; [D]REVILLOUT, *Rev. ég.* 3, pl. 3 [1885].

ⲃⲁⲛⲕ (Crum 40a), a bird = (*Wb.* I, 464, 4), *bng*, a bird.

JUNKER in SPIEGELBERG, *Kopt. Handwb.* 18 [1921]; but cf. DÉVAUD, *Muséon*, 36, 91 [1923].

ⲃⲛⲛⲉ (Crum 40a), 'date palm-tree' = (*Wb.* I, 462, 1ff.), *bnrt*; (Er. 117, 1), *bnỉt*, 'date palm-tree'.

[H]BRUGSCH, *Rec. de mon.* I, 49 [1862]; [D]BRUGSCH, *Gr. dém.* 25, §44 [1855].

ⲃⲛϣⲟⲟⲩⲉ (Crum 40b), 'dried dates' = (P. Harris 38b, 3; 54a, 9), *bnr šw*, 'dried dates'.

DÉVAUD's slip.

ϣⲛⲃⲛⲛⲉ (Crum 40b), 'palm-fibre' = L. Eg. (*Wb.* I, 462, 2 and IV, 498, 12), *šny bnr(t)*, lit. 'hair of date palm-tree'; (Er. 513, 1), *šn-bnt*, or , *šr-bnt*. For **ϣⲟⲩⲃⲛⲛⲉ**, cf. Gr.-Rom. , *šw bn(t)* (Dümichen, *Rec.* IV, 90) from Dendara. Gk. σεβένιον, σεβέννιον, 'envelope of the palm-tree flower' (Bally).

[H]BRUGSCH *Dict. geogr.* 891 [1879] (*šnỉ bnrt*); BRUGSCH, *Wb.* 226 [1867] (*šw-bnt*); [D]BRUGSCH, *Gr. dém.* 25, §45 [1855].

For **ⲃⲛⲛⲉⲕⲟⲩⲕ** see **ⲕⲟⲩⲕ**.

ⲃⲉⲛⲓⲡⲉ (Crum 41a), 'iron' = (*Wb.* I, 436, 14f.), *bỉꜣ n pt*, 'iron', lit. 'metal of the heaven'; (Er. 117, 7), *bnpy*, 'iron'.

[H]BIRCH in *Archaeologia*, 38, 377 [1860] (with doubt); cf. BRUGSCH, *Wb.* 1722–3 [1868]; [D]REVILLOUT, *Setna*, pp. 26 and 48 [1877].

ⲃⲟⲛⲧⲉ (Crum 41 a), 'gourd, cucumber' = (Sinai 136, S 1), *bdt*, 'bed (of gourds)'; (P. Chester Beatty II, 6, 9), *bndt*; (*Wb.* I, 432, 8), *bꜣdt*; (*Wb.* I, 464, 13), *bnd*; (*Wb.* I, 458, 2), *bnt* (for Old Kingdom occurrences, see YOYOTTE, *BIFAO* 61, 125–6), 'gourds'; (not in Er.; P. Cairo 30982, ro. 19), *bynt*, a plant.

[H]GARDINER, *Hieratic Papyri in the British Museum, Third Series*, I, p. 15 n. 2 and p. 50 n. 5 [1935]; cf. BRUGSCH, *Wb.* 402 [1868]; [D]SPIEGELBERG, *Dem. Denkmäler*, II, 213 [1908].

[S]**ⲃⲁⲛϩⲟ** (Crum 41 b, 'meaning unknown') < **ⲃⲱⲱⲛ** + **ϩⲟ**, 'bad of face, miserable, negligible', like **ⲃⲁⲛ-ⲓⲉⲓⲣⲉ** (see under **ⲉⲓⲁ**, 'eye') and **ⲃⲁⲛ-ϣⲁⲓ**, 'ill-fated' (see under **ϣⲁⲓ**, 'fortune, fate'). Opposite **ⲛⲁϥⲣϩⲟ** (only as proper name).

CRUM, *Catalogue of the Coptic Manuscripts in the British Museum*, 468 n. 5 (with doubt) [1905].

ⲃⲓⲛⲁϫ (Crum 41 b), 'dish' = (*ZÄS* 14, pl. IV, 5), *bnḏ*; (GRIFFITH-THOMPSON, III, 30, no. 290; not in Er.), *pynꜥks*; from Gk. πίναξ.

[D]BRUGSCH, *ZÄS* 14, 68 [1876]; [G]HARKAVY, *ZÄS* 7, 48 [1869].

ⲃⲓⲣ, ⲃⲁⲓⲣⲉ (Crum 41 b), 'basket (of palm-leaf)' = (Er. 112, 5), *byr*, 'basket'; (*Theban Ostraca*, pl. VII, D 111, ro. 3), *bly*, 'basket'.

PARKER, *JEA* 26, 93 [1940]; cf. H. THOMPSON in *Theban Ostraca*, 64 [1913].

ⲃⲁⲁⲣⲉ (Crum 42 a), 'boat, barge' = (*Wb.* I, 465, 8–9), *br*; (Er. 119, 1), *br*, a kind of ship, βᾶρις.

[H]CHABAS, *Mél. égypt.* II, 142 [1864] (ident. with βᾶρις); [D]ERICHSEN, *Dem. Glossar*, 119, 1 [1954].

NB. **ⲃⲁⲣⲓ** (KIRCHER, *Lingua aeg. restituta*, 133) is non-existent and Kircher's insertion, since it is not found in any MS of the *Scala* that Crum collated (Crum's card to Dévaud of 18 July 1924)!

[S]**ⲃⲱⲣⲉ**, [B]**ϥⲟⲣⲓ** (Crum 42 a), a fish, *Mugil cephalus* = (*Wb.* I, 465, 10), *br*, a Nile fish. From Coptic the Egn. Ar. بوري, 'mullet'.

[H]CHABAS, *Oeuv. div.* I (= *Bibl. ég.* IX), 250 [1858]; [AR]ROSSI, *Etym. aeg.* 283 [1808].

ⲃⲣⲃⲣ (Crum 42b), ‘boil over’ = (*Wb.* I, 466, 1), *brbr*, ‘boil’.
BRUGSCH, *Wb.* 404 [1868]; cf. DAUMAS, *BIFAO* 48, 89 n. 3 [1949].

ⲃⲉⲣⲃⲓⲣ (Crum 42b), ‘missile’ = L.Egn. (*Wb.* I, 459, 12), *brbr*, ‘(pointed) loaf of bread’ and (*Wb.* I, 459, 13. 14), *brbr*, ‘point’ of a pyramid or obelisk; (Er. 119, 3) in *ỉr brbr* ‘hunt’ or sim.
HDERICHSEN, *Dem. Glossar*, 119, 3 [1954].

ⲃⲣⲏ(ⲉ)ⲓⲛⲉ, see **ⲉⲃⲣⲓⲉⲓⲛ**.

F**ⲃⲁⲣⲛⲉϩ**, S**ⲃⲣⲁⲛⲉϩ** (Crum 43a), ‘linseed (?)’ = **ⲉⲃⲣⲁ**, ‘seed’ + **ⲛⲉϩ**, ‘oil’, lit. ‘seed of oil’. See **ⲉⲃⲣⲁ** and **ⲛⲉϩ**.

ⲃⲣⲣⲉ (Crum 43a), ‘new, young’ = (Er. 119, 2), *bry*, ‘young’.
ERICHSEN, *Dem. Glossar*, 119, 2 [1954].

ⲃⲉⲣⲥⲓⲙ (Crum 43b), among names of victuals = **ⲃⲉⲣ** + **ⲥⲓⲙ**, lit. ‘seed of plant’; from it Arabic برسيم, ‘clover’, *Trifolium alexandrinum* L., see Keimer in *BIFAO* 28, 85.

B**ⲃⲁⲣⲏⲓⲧ** (Crum 43b), ‘he-goat’ = **ⲃⲁ** + **ⲣⲏⲓⲧ**. **ⲃⲁ** = , *bꜣ*, ‘he-goat’, as in **ⲃⲁ-ⲁⲙⲡⲉ**; **ⲣⲏⲓⲧ** is obscure.

ⲃⲁⲣⲱⲧ (Crum 43b), ‘brass, bronze’ = (*Wb.* I, 437, 21; II, 410, 15), *bỉꜣ(?)rwḏ*, a metal, lit. ‘strong metal’.
GUNN in Gardiner, *JEA* 4, 36 [1917]; SETHE, *ZÄS* 53, 51 n. 2 [1917].
LEPSIUS, *ZÄS* 10, 117 [1872] thought that **ⲃⲁⲣⲱⲧ** was the town of Beirût, and that **ⲃⲁⲣⲱⲧ** was used shortly for **ϩⲟⲙⲛⲧ ⲛⲃⲁⲣⲱⲧ**, ‘copper from Beirût’. The word for ‘copper’ in Ethiopic: **ብረት**, *bĕrĕtĕ* comes from **ⲃⲁⲣⲱⲧ** (LAGARDE, *Übersicht*, p. 78 [1889]). But see also **ϣⲥⲣⲟⲧ** which speaks against Lepsius’ explanation.

ⲃⲣⲉϣⲏⲩ (Crum 44a), ‘coriander seed’ = (*Wb.* IV, 400, 16), *prt šꜣw*, ‘fruit of *šꜣw*’, a plant.
STERN in Ebers, *Papyros Ebers*, II, 44 (glossary) [1875].

ⲃⲁⲣⲱϩ (Crum 44a), **ϥⲁⲣⲱϩ** (Till, *Ostraka* 43, 6), a transport animal, camel? = (not in Er.), *b[ʿr]ḫ*, a pack animal.
PARKER, *JEA* 26, 109 [1940].

ⲃⲁⲣⲱϩ (Crum 44b), ‘fodderer’ or sim. = (Er. 119, 5), *brḫ*, a title.
BOTTI, *Testi demotici*, I, 51 n. 3 [1941].

ⲃⲱⲣϭ (Crum 44b), 'break asunder' (ῥήγνυσθαι) = late (*Wb.* I, 466, 12), *brg*, 'be open (of doors)'. Probably from Semitic √*brḳ*, therefore properly 'be split in two by lightning'.
See also **ⲉⲃⲣⲏϭⲉ**, 'lightning'.

ⲃⲣϭⲟⲟⲩⲧ (Crum 44b), 'chariot' = (*Wb.* II, 113, 4), *mrkbt*, 'war chariot', from Semitic, cf. מֶרְכָּבָה; HINCKS, *Transactions of the Roy. Irish Academy*, 21, part II, p. 141 and pl. I, no. 11 and 12 [1848, read in 1846].

CHABAS, *Voyage*, 129 [1866].

ⲃⲁⲥ (Crum 44b), a utensil of bronze = (*Wb.* I, 423, 4), *bꜣs*, a vase for unguent; (Er. 122, 5), *bs*, an object of metal, probably a vase.

HDERICHSEN, *Dem. Glossar*, 122, 5 [1954].

ⲃⲏⲥⲉ (Crum 44b), 'pail, well-bucket', perhaps = (not in *Wb.*, exx. O. IFAO 1017, vo. 4; O. Louvre E 3263, vo. 3; O. Cairo, prov. no. 182, 3), also (O. Berlin 11260, 6), *bꜣsꜣ*, a wooden object; from Eg. βησίον of Gk. papyri (Preisigke, Kiessling).

ⲃⲁⲥⲃⲥ (not in Crum; preserved in fem. name **ⲧⲃⲁⲥⲃⲥ**, see *ZÄS* 60, 81) = (*Wb.* I, 477, 1), *bsbs*, 'white-headed duck', *Erismatura leucocephala* Scop.? (cf. Edel, *Zu den Inschriften auf der Jahreszeitenreliefs der "Weltkammer" aus dem Sonnenheiligtum des Niuserre*, II, 97).

HEUSER in Ranke, *ZÄS* 60, 81 [1925]; HEUSER, *Die Personennamen der Kopten*, 30 [1929].

ⲃⲉⲥⲛⲏⲧ (Crum 44b), 'smith' = (*Wb.* I, 477, 5–7), *bsnt*, in the title *ḥry bsnt* of the temple of Ptah; (Er. 122, 11), *bsnṯ*, 'smith'.

HDSPIEGELBERG, *Kopt. Etymologien*, 42–3 [1920].

ⲃⲁⲓⲥⲛⲁⲩ (not in Crum), a wine-measure, see under **ϥⲓ**, 'bear, carry'.

ⲃⲁⲥⲛϭ (Crum 14b), 'tin' = **ⲃⲁ** (as in **ⲃⲁⲛⲓⲡⲉ**, **ⲃⲁⲣⲱⲧ**) + Persian سَنْگ 'stone, weight, ore', which is supposed to be origin of *zinc* (this from German *Zink*), cf. MURET-SANDERS, *Encycl. Wörterbuch der engl. u. deutschen Sprache*, s.v. Zink.

ⲃⲏⲧ (Crum 45a), 'palm-leaf' = ? (not in Er.), *byṯt*, 'palm-leaf' (?).

PARKER, *JEA* 26, 94 [1940].

ⲃⲟⲉⲓⲧ (Crum 45a), 'ox' or 'cow' = ? (*Wb.* 1, 398, 13, 14), *wḏw*, 'freely moving cattle'. Cf. *wḏw*, 'stela' > **ⲟⲩⲟⲉⲓⲧ**. Crum thought of βοίδιον, diminutive of βοῦς.

ⲃⲱⲧⲉ (Crum 45b), 'pollute; hate, abominate' = (*Wb.* 1, 580, 8 ff.), *ft*, 'abominate'; (Er. 126, bottom), *bty*, 'hate, abominate'.

^{H}DÉVAUD's slip.

Contaminated with:

ⲃⲟⲧⲉ (Crum 45b), 'hateful thing, abomination' = (*Wb.* 1, 483, bottom), *btꜣ*, 'crime'; (Er. 126, 2), *btw* (masc.) and , *bty* (fem.), 'abomination, crime'.

^{H}DEVÉRIA, *Pap. judiciaire de Turin*, 163 = *JA*, 6e série, 8, 175–6 [1866]; CHABAS, *Voyage*, 373 (glossary) [1866]; DE ROUGÉ, *Chrest.* 1, 77 [1867]; ^{D}BRUGSCH, *Gr. dém.* 34, §68 [1855].

ⲃⲱⲧⲉ (Crum 45b), 'emmer', a cereal (*Triticum sativum dicoccum*) = (*Wb.* 1, 486, 14 ff.), *bdt*; (Er. 126, 1), *bt*, 'emmer'.

^{H}SALVOLINI, *Analyse grammaticale raisonnée de différents textes anciens Égyptiens*, p. 100 and pl. 41, nos. 13–16 [1836]; ^{D}MALININE in *Kêmi*, 11, 9–12 [1950].

ⲃⲉⲧⲃⲉⲧ (Crum 46a), among vegetables, for ***ⲟⲩⲉⲧⲟⲩⲉⲧ** = Graeco-Roman (*Wb.* 1, 270, 6, 7), *wꜣḏwꜣḏ*, 'green plants' in fields or marshes, from **ⲟⲩⲟⲧⲟⲩⲉⲧ**, 'become green'. See this latter under **ⲟⲩⲱⲧ**, 'be raw, fresh, green'.

^{B}**ⲃⲱⲧⲥ** (Crum 46a), **ⲃⲱϭⲥ** (Mani Ps.), 'to fight, war' = (*Wb.* 1, 483, 5), *bgs*; (Er. 125, 7), *bgs*, 'revolt'.

^{H}SPIEGELBERG, *Die demot. Papyri Loeb*, p. 5 (16) [1931]; ^{D}SETHE, *Hieroglyphische Urkunden der griech.-röm. Zeit*, 221, note h [1904].

ⲃⲏⲧⲥⲏ (read **ⲃⲉⲧⲥⲉ**) (Crum 46a), 'female warrior' = ^{A2}(**ⲃⲉⳉⲉ**), 'rebel', Plural **ⲃⲉⳉⲉⲩⲉ**.

POLOTSKY, *Manich. Homilien*, p. xix and index, p. 6* [1934].

ⲃⲁⲑⲱ (Crum 46a), 'kerchief' < **ⲃⲁⲑⲟ** (Till, *KR* 178, 4), for **ϥⲁⲧ-ϩⲟ** from **ϥⲱⲧⲉ**, 'wipe' + **ϩⲟ** 'face', cf. **ⲃⲁⲧϭⲓϫ** (Crum 625a).

^{A2}**ⲃⲏⲩ** (Mani Hom. 12, 29. 30; 75, 28; Ps.; not in Crum), 'outrage' = (*Wb.* 1, 413, 16), *bꜣw*, 'might, force, wrath'; (Er. 109, 10; 114, 6), *bw*, or *bꜣw*, 'punishment'.

^{S}ⲃⲟⲟⲩ, ^{B}ⲃⲱⲟⲩ (Crum 46b, two items incl. Pbow, فاو, and other place names), 'heap (of stones)' (σωρός, P. Bodmer XXI from Jos. 7, 26 and 8, 29) = , var. (*Wb.* I, 418, 9, where the ref. is now Coffin Texts I, 256, c), *bꜣw*, 'heap'.

^{S}ⲃⲏⲏϣ, ^{B}ⲃⲏϣ (Crum 46b), 'unripe fruit' of fig tree = (*Wb.* I, 478, 10), *bšꜣ*. > L. Eg. , *bš*, kind of fruit (besides corn and dates).

ERMAN-GRAPOW, *Äg. Handwb.* 50 [1921]; but cf. GARDINER, *Onom.* II, 223*–5* [1947].

ⲃⲱϣ (Crum 46b), 'be loosen, release, give leave' = (Er. 123, 2), *bš*, 'strip, abandon'.

PLEYTE-BOESER, *Suten-χeft*, 9 [1899].

^{B}ⲃⲟⲓϣⲓ (Crum 47a), a desert animal, cf. bishârî اباشه (*u b'ašeʰ*), Sudanese jackal.

HESS, *Zeitschrift für Assyriologie*, 31, 28 [1918].

ⲃⲁϣⲟⲣ (Crum 47b), 'fox' = Greek βασσάρα, 'fox'.

ROSSI, *Etym. aeg.* 35 [1808].

ⲃⲁϣⲟⲩⲣ (Crum 47b), 'saw', from Semitic, cf. מַשּׂוֹר, منشار.

ROSSI, *Etym. aeg.* 35 [1808].

ⲃⲁϣⲟⲩϣ (Crum 47b), 'rue' = (Er. 123, 3), *bšwš*, 'rue', from Semitic, cf. Syriac ܒܫܫܐ bašāšå, *ruta sylvestris* (Lagarde, *Ges. Abhandlungen*, 173) *peganum harmala* L. acc. to Brockelmann, p. 47; Aram. בַּשָּׁשָׁא (Dalman), bab. Talm. בַּשָּׁשׁ, wild rue (Margolis, 96*).

^{D}GRIFFITH-THOMPSON, III, 27, no. 272 [1909]; ^{S}ROSSI, *Etym. aeg.* 36 [1808].

ⲃⲁϩ, ϥⲁϩ (Crum 47b), 'penis(?)' = (*Wb.* I, 419, 14), 'penis'.

GOODWIN, *ZÄS* 4, 55 [1866].

Cf. also ⲙⲙⲁϩ.

^{B}ⲃⲱⲱϩ, ⲃⲟϩ (Crum 47b), an idol in Alexandria = prob. (*Wb.* I, 472, 14), *bḫ*, Buchis (Βουχις), sacred bull of Hermonthis; (Er. 121, 7), *bḫ*; s.m. For *ḫ* > Boh. ϩ (instead of the regular ϧ) compare *mꜣḫ* > ^{B}ⲙⲟϩ, 'burn'.

ⲃⲟⲩϩⲉ (Crum 48a), 'eyelid(s)' (also 'eyebrows', Till, *Arz.* D 1–5) = (*Wb.* 1, 467, 3–4), *bht*, 'fan'. Passage of meaning 'fan' > 'eyelid' because of similarity of movement.
See also ⲥⲣⲉⲃⲣⲟⲩⲃⲉ and ϭⲁⲗⲟⲩⲙⲃⲓϩ.

[B]ⲃⲉϩⲃⲉϩ (Crum 48a and 509a s.v. ⲟⲩⲁϩⲃⲉϥ), 'howling, barking', for *ⲟⲩⲉϩⲟⲩⲉϩ, same as *wḥwḥ* > ⲟⲩⲁϩⲃⲉϥ, 'bark, growl' of dog, see this latter. The sole authority for ⲃⲉϩⲃⲉϩ is Labib's dictionary and he might have been influenced by the Arabic وَحْوَح, 'barking dog' (cf. Stricker in *Acta Orientalia*, 15, 3).

CRUM, *A Coptic Dict.* 48a [1929].

ⲃⲉϩⲱⲗ (Crum 48a), kind of date-palm, = (= [ⲃ?]ⲉϩⲱⲗ), from Semitic **baḥal*, cf. بلح.

HESS in Dévaud, *Muséon*, 36, 91–2 [1923] (but ⲃⲉⲣϩⲱⲗ the same as ⲃⲉϩⲱⲗ, ⲃⲉⲣ- being due to influence of ⲃⲉⲣ- , ⲃⲣⲉ- ('fruit'), present in ⲃⲣⲉϣⲏⲩ).

ⲃⲱϩⲛ (Crum 48a), 'canopy, awning' = (*Wb.* 1, 467, 10), *bhn*, 'fan' or sim., in , *ḥbs bhn*, 'protect', lit. 'to hold fan over'. L.E. (Lovesongs Beatty 24, 1), however, is a 'blanket' or 'cloak' which is put over a , *mss*, 'shirt'.

SPIEGELBERG, *Kopt. Handwb.* 21 [1921].

ⲃⲁϩⲥⲉ (Crum 48a), 'heifer' = (*Wb.* 1, 469, 11), *bḥst*, fem. of (*Wb.* 1, 469, 4 ff.), *bḥs*, 'calf'; (Er. 121, 3), *bḥst*, 'calf'.

[H]BRUGSCH, *Geographie*, 125 and Pl. XXX, no. 520 [1857]; LORET, *Manuel*, 73, §171 [1889] (from); [D]GRIFFITH, *Pap. Rylands*, III, 346 [1909].

[B]ⲃⲓϫⲓ (Crum 48b), ⲃⲓϭⲉ (Mani Ps. 165, 18), ⲃⲉϭⲧ⸗ Mani Hom. 78, 17) 'be wrecked' (of ship) = (*Wb.* 1, 431, 2 f.), *bꜣgy*, 'become tired, faint'; cf. (*Wb.* 1, 482, 12), *bgꜣw*, 'shipwrecked person'; (Er. 125, 4), *bky*, 'sink, suffer shipwreck'.

[H]SPIEGELBERG, *ZÄS* 44, 100–1 [1907]; [D]BRUGSCH, *Gr. dém.* 27, §54 [1855].

ⲃⲏϭ (Crum 48b), 'falcon' = (*Wb.* 1, 444, 13 ff.), *bỉk*; (Er. 123, 7), *bk*, 'falcon'.

[H]CHAMPOLLION, *Précis*, 2nd ed., 126 [1828]; [D]LEGRAIN, *Livre des transformations*, 30 [1890].

[B]ⲃⲉϭⲏⲛ, ⲃⲉϫⲏⲛ (Crum 48b), 'rush' βούτομος, from Semitic, cf. Hebrew בִּצָּה, Aram. בִּצָּה, Pl. בִּצִּין (Dalman).

DÉVAUD, *Muséon*, 36, 90 and 92 [1923] and DÉVAUD's slip.

ⲃⲱϭⲥ (Mani Ps.), 'to fight, rebel', see ⲃⲱⲧⲥ.

ⲗ

[F]ⲗⲁⲩⲥⲁϯ, see [S]ⲧⲁⲯⲁⲧⲉ.

ⲉ

ⲉ-, ⲉⲣⲟ⸗ (Crum 50a), preposition, 'to', etc., = 𓂋 (*Wb.* II, 386, 6 ff.), *r*; [demotic] (Er. 236, 2–238), *r*, 'to', etc.

[H]CHAMPOLLION, *Gr. ég.* 452, §294 [1836]; [D]BRUGSCH, *Gr. dém.* 101, §229; 173, §§335, 336 [1855].

[SB]ⲉ⸗, ⲉⲣⲉ- (Crum 52a), verbal prefix = [hieroglyphs] (*Wb.* I, 43, 6 ff.), *ỉw*·; [demotic] and [demotic] (Er. 19, 5), *ỉw*·, 'to be':

(*a*) of 3rd Future: [hieroglyphs], *ỉw·f(r)* + Inf.; [demotic], *ỉw·f r* + Inf. (see *JNES* 7, 233 for a detailed table).

[H]CHAMPOLLION, *Gr. ég.* 412–13, §278 [1836]; [D]BRUGSCH, *Gr. dém.* 141, §288 [1855] (sees in the [demotic] of [demotic] the preposition *n*, but identifies [demotic] with ⲉⲓⲉϫⲱ!);

(*b*) of Circumstantial [hieroglyphs] *ỉw·f (ḥr)* + Inf. or [hieroglyphs] *ỉw·f* + Old Perf.; [demotic] + Inf. or Old Perf. (see *JNES* 7, 231 for a detailed table);

[HD]STERN, *Kopt. Gr.* §§400 and 404 [1880]; [D]BRUGSCH, *Gr. dém.* 126–7, §259 [1855],

and other verbal constructions;

SPIEGELBERG, *Rec. trav.* 31, 156 [1909];

(*c*) of nominal sentences;

[HD]BRUGSCH, *Gr. dém.* 126–7, §259 [1855].

[S]ⲉ⸗, ⲉⲣⲉ-, [B]ⲁ⸗, ⲁⲣⲉ- (Crum 52a), verbal prefix of:

(*a*) 2nd Present = [hieroglyphs], *ỉỉr* + Subj. + Inf.; [demotic], *ỉỉr*· (see complete table of forms in *JNES* 7, 230) + Subj. + Inf.;

[H]POLOTSKY, *Études*, 94 f. [1944]; [D]WILLIAMS, *JNES* 7, 224–6 and 230 [1948];

(*b*) 2nd Future, cf. (Mag. P., vo. 33, 3), *n ỉỉr·k nꜣ wnm*, 'will you eat?' (see, however, under **ⲛⲁ-**, 'go', as verbal prefix (*b*));

WILLIAMS, *JNES* 7, 227 [1948];

(*c*) 2nd Present of habit, cf. (Mag. P. 27, 28), *r-ỉr ḫr ỉr·k dỉ·f*, '(it is into something of glass) that you place it';

WILLIAMS, *JNES* 7, 226 [1948];

(*d*) Adjectival verbs: [S]**ⲉⲛⲁⲁⲕ**, [A2]**ⲉⲛⲉⲉⲕ**, 'you are greater (than)', cf. (P. Insinger 30, 1), *ỉỉr nꜣ-ʿn*, 'it is good'.

WILLIAMS, *JNES* 7, 226 [1948].

ⲉⲃⲏ (Crum 52b), 'darkness' = (Er. 3, 5), *ꜣbt*, 'darkening'.

SPIEGELBERG, *Mythus*, 60, no. 5 [1917].

ⲣ ⲉⲃⲏ, 'to darken, be dark' = , *ỉr ꜣbt*, 'be dark'.

GRIFFITH, *Cat. of Dem. Graffiti*, I, 134, no. 13 [1937].

[B]**ⲙⲉⲧⲉⲃⲏ**, ἔκστασις = **ⲙⲉⲧ** + (*Wb.* I, 440, 3), *bỉꜣt*, 'wonder'.

BRUGSCH, *Wb.* 372 [1868]; cf. Dévaud, *Muséon*, 36, 93 [1923].

ⲉⲃⲓⲱ (Crum 52b), 'honey', Pl. **ⲉⲃⲓⲟⲟⲩⲉ** (Till, *KR* 16, 6) = (*Wb.* I, 434, 6 f.), *bỉt*; (Er. 26, 5), *ỉbỉ*, 'honey'.

[H]CHAMPOLLION, *Gr. ég.* pp. 57 and 229 [1836]; [D]BRUGSCH, *Gr. dém.* 33, §66 [1855].

ⲉⲃⲓⲧ, **ⲉⲃⲉⲓⲧ**, 'honey dealer', Pl. **ⲉⲃⲓⲁⲧⲉ** (Till, *KR* 16, 3) = (*Wb.* I, 434, 13–15), *bỉty*, 'bee-keeper'; (Er. 27, 1), *ỉbỉṯ*, [με]λισσουργός.

[H]KRALL, *Verhandlungen des XIII. Internat. Orientalisten-Kongresses, Hamburg September 1902*, p. 347 [publ. Leiden 1904]; [D]GRIFFITH, *ZÄS* 45, 106 n. 6 [1908].

ⲉⲃⲓⲏⲛ (Crum 53a), 'a wretched person, wretched' = (Er. 112, 3), *ꜣbyn*, 'poor, wretched (person)', from , *bỉn* = **ⲃⲱⲱⲛ** (see this), as loan-word in Hebrew **אֶבְיוֹן**.

[H]BRUGSCH, *Wb.* 4 [1867]; [D]BRUGSCH, *Rhind*, 35 and pl. 35, no. 53 [1865].

ⲉⲃⲣⲁ (Crum 53a) and [B]**ϥⲣⲉ** (Crum 624a), 'seed' of cereals = (*Wb.* I, 530, 9 ff.), *ptr*, , *br*, in a late proper name (*Chronique d'Égypte*, no. 82, 408), 'fruit, seed'; (Er. 135, 2), *prt*, 'grain'.

[HD]BRUGSCH, *Wb.* 479 [1868].

ⲉⲃⲣⲁ ⲥⲱϣⲉ (Crum 53b), ‘seed-corn’ = , *prt-sḫt*, lit. ‘seed of (the) field’.

SPIEGELBERG in Reinach, *Papyrus grecs et démotiques*, 180 [1905].

See also **ⲉϥⲣⲁⲥⲟⲩ**.

For **ⲃⲁⲣ-**, **ⲡⲉⲣ-**, see **ⲃⲁⲣⲛⲉϩ**, **ⲡⲉⲣⲛⲟⲩϥⲉ**, and possibly **(ⲡ)ⲉⲣϣⲓϣ**.

ⲉⲃⲣⲓⲉⲓⲛ (Crum 53b), **ⲃⲣⲏⲉⲓⲛⲉ** (Crum, *Varia Coptica*, 119, 6–7), **ⲃⲣⲏⲓ̈ⲛⲉ** (**ⲟⲩϩⲁⲓⲧⲉ ⲛⲃⲣⲏⲓ̈ⲛⲉ**; Till, *Ostraka*, 140, 10) = *phrygionia*, i.e. *vestis* (Pliny, *Hist. nat.* VIII, 48, 79, § 195), ‘Phrygian’, embroidered woollen material from Phrygia and generally from Asia Minor reputed for their fine sheep and wool (Lat. *phrygio* = ‘embroider’) (see Orth in Pauly-Wissowa XII, 607, under ‘Lana’).

ⲉⲃⲣⲏϭⲉ (Crum 53b), ‘lightning’, from Semitic stem *brḳ*, cf. Hebrew בָּרָק, Aram. בַּרְקָא, Ar. بَرْق.

ROSSI, *Etym. aeg.* 192–3 (s.v. **ⲥⲉⲧⲉⲃⲣⲏϫ**) [1808].

See also **ⲃⲱⲣϭ**, ‘break asunder’.

ⲉⲃⲟⲧ (Crum 53b), ‘month’ = (*Wb.* I, 65, 5 ff.), *ỉbd*; (Er. 27, 3), *ỉbt*, ‘month’.

[HD]YOUNG, *Misc. Works*, III, pl. 4, no. 179 = *Encycl. Brit.*, Suppl. IV, pl. 77, no. 179 [1819], cf. Champollion, *Gr.* 97 [1836].

ⲉⲃⲟⲧ ⲛϩⲟⲟⲩ (Crum 54a) = (*Wb.* I, 65, 5), *ỉbd n hrw*, ‘full month’, lit. ‘month of days’.

SPIEGELBERG, *ZÄS* 58, 158 [1923].

ⲉⲕⲓⲃⲉ (Crum 54a), ‘breast, nipple’ = (*Wb.* V, 11, 2 ff.), *ḳ3bt*, ‘breast’.

BRUGSCH, *Wb.*, Suppl. 433, s.v. *bndt* [1880], and 1240 [1882].

ⲉⲗⲕⲱ (Crum 54b), ripe fruit of sycamore (*Ficus sycomorus* L.) which was always notched in order to destroy through an influx of air the insects that bred in it = (*Wb.* II, 343, 8–12), *nḳʿwt*, from (*Wb.* II, 343, 7), *nḳʿ*, ‘incise’; (Er. 8, 1), *3lkw*, same as Coptic (not ‘Maulbeere’).

[H]KEIMER in *Acta Orientalia* 6, 288–304 [1928]; in *Ancient Egypt*, 13, 65–6 [1928]; in *BIFAO* 28, 65 ff. [1929]; [D]SPIEGELBERG, *Mythus*, 197, no. 484 [1917]; cf. Griffith-Thompson, III, 13, no. 114 [1909].

ⲉⲗⲟⲟⲗⲉ (Crum 54b), 'grape, vine' = (*Wb.* I, 32, 12–14), *ỉꜣrrt*; (*Er.* 7, 16), *ꜣlly*, 'grape, vine'.

HCHAMPOLLION, *Gr. ég.* 79 [1836]; DYOUNG, *Misc. Works*, III, 26–7, no. 54 = *Mus. crit.* 6, pp. 176–7, no. 54 [1815] (a letter to de Sacy of 21 Oct. 1814), cf. Saulcy, *Rosette*, 21 [1845]; Brugsch, *Gr. dém.* 42, §92 [1855].

ⲉⲗⲉⲗϣⲟⲟⲩⲉ (Crum 54b), 'dried grapes, raisins' = **ⲉⲗⲟⲟⲗⲉ** + (*Wb.* IV, 429, 10–14), *šw*, 'dry'; (*Er.* 7, 16), *ꜣll šw*.

HERMAN-GRAPOW, *Wb.* IV, 429, 10 ff. [1930]; DGRIFFITH-THOMPSON, III, 3, no. 7 [1909] (without quoting the Coptic expression).

ϧⲱ ⲛⲉⲗⲟⲟⲗⲉ (Crum 55a), 'vine', lit. 'tree of vine' = , *b ꜣlly*.

SPIEGELBERG, *Dem. Chronik*, 111, no. 413 [1914].

ⲉⲗⲉⲗⲕⲏⲙⲉ (Crum 55a), 'bruise', coloured like grapes, lit. 'grape of Egypt', cf. , *ꜣlly n kmt*, 'grape of Egypt'.

GRIFFITH-THOMPSON, I, 195, n. to l. 7 [1904].

ⲉⲗⲁⲗⲧ, Qual. of **ⲁⲗⲱⲗ**, see this.

B**ⲉⲗⲧⲟϥ** (Crum 55b and 453a under **ⲧⲁϥ**), 'spit on' (προσσιελίζειν) = *, *ndf*, 'spit', though only reduplicated (*Wb.* II, 368, 13), *ndfdf*, 'weep' is actually attested. **ⲉⲗⲧⲟϥ** is ultimately related to Hebrew נָטַף. Boh. stressed **ⲧ** requires Egn. and forbids associating **ⲉⲗⲧⲟϥ** with S**ⲧⲁϥ**, B**ⲑⲁϥ**, 'spittle' = (*Wb.* II, 356, 7. 8), *ntf*, a different word since it has as early as M.K., and of Gr.-R. and quoted by Brugsch, *Wb.* 823, it is impossible to say whether they represent *ntf* or *ndf*.

HSPIEGELBERG, *Kopt. Etym.* 18–19 [1920]; SBRUGSCH, *Wb.*, Suppl. 706 [1881].

ⲉⲗⲟⲓϩ (Crum Add. XVI), 'shepherd' = (*Wb.* I, 119, 21); (Er. 166, top), *mr-ỉḥ(w)*, 'overseer of cattle', Gk. transcription -ελαι- in the proper name Πελαίας = *Pꜣ-mr-ỉḥw* (see GRIFFITH, *Ryl.* III, 257 n. 2), Coptic **ⲡⲉⲗⲁⲉⲓ** (Ranke I, 100, 16).

CRUM, *A Coptic Dict.* p. XVI [1939].

B**ⲉⲗϩⲏⲥ** (Crum 770a, s.v. **ϫⲱⲗϩⲥ**), 'breath' = (not in Er.; Berlin med. P. 105 A/7), *lhs*, 'breath'. Only in **ϩⲓ ⲉⲗϩⲏⲥ**. Sa'îdic form was prob. **ⲗϩⲏⲥ** in **ϫ(ⲉ)ⲗϩⲏⲥ**, see under **ϫⲱⲗϩⲥ**.

H. THOMPSON's Dem. dictionary.

[S]ⲉⲙⲉ, [B]ⲁⲙⲏ (Crum 55b), 'hoe' for digging = Greek ἄμη, a 'shovel' or 'mattock'.

ÉTIENNE LE MOYNE in DÉVAUD, *Muséon* 36, 87, no. 16 [1923].

ⲉⲙⲟⲩ (Crum 55b), 'cat' = (*Wb.* II, 42, 4. 5), *myt*, and (*ASAE* 18, 134, 4), *mỉwt*; (Er. 151, 2), *ỉmỉ*, 'cat'.

[H]BRUGSCH, *Wb.*, Suppl. 543–4 [1881], cf. DE ROUGÉ, *Oeuvr. div.* IV (= *Bibl. ég.* XXIV), 141 n. 2 [1861] (comparing masc. *mỉw*); Goodwin in a letter to Renouf (Dawson, *Ch. W. Goodwin*, pp. 75–6) [1862]; [D]BRUGSCH, *Wb.* 70 [1867].

[O]ⲉⲙⲓⲙ (Crum 55b), 'shrew mouse' = (*Wb.* I, 186, 10; Gr.-R. ex. *ZÄS* 88, 74), *ʿmʿmw*; (Er. 61, 9), *ʿmʿm*, 'shrew mouse'. For the meaning of *ʿmʿmw*, see Brunner-Traut in *Nachr. Ak. Wiss. Göttingen, phil.-hist. Kl.*, 1965, 145 ff.

[HD]GRIFFITH-THOMPSON, I, 84, note [1904]; cf. III, 7, no. 62 [1909].

ⲉⲙⲛⲧ (Crum 56a), nn., 'west' = (*Wb.* I, 86, 15 ff.), *ỉmnty*, 'western, west side'; (Er. 31, 3), *ỉmnṯ*, 'west, western'.

[H]CHAMPOLLION, *Gr.* 67, 97 [1836]; [D]BRUGSCH, *Gr. dém.* 57, §§128, 129 [1855]; LEXA, *Dem. Totb.* 36, no. 19 [1910].

With article ⲡⲉⲙⲛⲧ = , *p*(*r*) *ỉmnṯ*, 'the west'.

[S]ⲉⲙⲏⲣⲉ, [B]ⲁⲙⲏⲣⲓ (Crum 56a), 'inundation, high water' = perhaps of (*Wb.* V, 223, 1 ff.), *tꜣ-mrỉ*, a designation of Egypt. The was later taken for fem. definite article and the word was treated as feminine (*Wb.* I, 223, 10) and *ⲧⲉⲙⲏⲣⲉ became ⲧ + ⲉⲙⲏⲣⲉ.

ⲉⲙⲓⲥⲉ (Crum 56a), 'dill, anise' = (*Wb.* I, 88, 9), *ỉmst*; (not in Er.), *ꜣmys*, 'dill'.

[H]LORET, *Rec. trav.* 7, 106–8 [1886]; [D]SPIEGELBERG, *Kopt. Handwb.* 5 [1921].

ⲉⲙⲏϣ (Crum 56a), 'anvil', from ⲙⲓϣⲉ, 'strike'.

ROSSI, *Etym. aeg.* 8 [1808].

[F]ⲉⲙⲉϣⲏⲓ(ⲉ) (Crum 56a), 'except' = L.Eg. , *ỉw bw rḫ·ỉ*, 'while I do not know'. [F]-ⲙⲉϣⲏⲓ is [S]ⲙⲉϣⲁⲓ, 'I do not know' (Ep. 66; from ⲙⲉϣⲉ), as [F]ⲛⲏⲓ, 'to me', is [S]ⲛⲁⲓ.

SPIEGELBERG, *Kopt. Handwb.* 25 [1921].

ⲉⲙⲉϣϭⲉ (Crum 56b), a Nile fish, *Tilapia* (*Chromis*) *nilotica* L. = (*Wb.* I, 88, 10), *ỉmsk*, a Nile fish.

DÉVAUD, *Kêmi*, 2, 6–7 [1929].

ⲉⲛⲉ (Crum 56b), interrogative particle = (*Wb.* I, 89, 14), *ỉn ỉw*; (Er. 32, 5), *ỉn*.

[H]LEPSIUS in *ZÄS* 2, 87 [1864]; cf. DE ROUGÉ, *Chrest.* III, 75, §328 [1875]; [D]BRUGSCH, *Wb.* 81–2 [1867].

ⲉⲛⲉ-, ⲉⲛⲉ⸗ in past relative clauses, see under **ⲛⲉ-**, prefix of past tenses.

ⲉⲛⲉ- (Crum 56b), verbal prefix of unfulfilled condition = (*Wb.* II, 481, 7), *h(ꜣ)n(ꜣ)*, also (), *hn*, or , *hn wn* (see Till, *ZÄS* 69 [1933], 112–13), all probably from *, *hꜣ wn*, 'if' of unfulfilled condition; (Er. 265, 8), *hwn*, or (Er. 88, 2), *wn*, same meaning.

[D]SPIEGELBERG, *Dem. Gr.* 225, §496 [1925].

ⲉⲛⲕ (Crum 56b), a plant = (*Wb.* I, 97, 10), *ỉnnk*; (Er. 6, 1), *ꜣnḳ*, a plant.

[H]LORET, *Flore*, 2nd ed., 67–8, no. 112 [1892]; [D]GRIFFITH-THOMPSON, I, 104 [1904]; III, 9, no. 90 [1909].

ⲉⲛⲓⲙ (Crum 56b), 'draw lots' (thus, not 'lot' as Crum), for ***ⲉⲣ** (from **ⲉⲓⲣⲉ**) + **ⲛⲓⲙ**, lit. 'make "who?"', to determine who will do or receive a certain thing.

DRESCHER in *Bull. de la Soc. d'Arch. Copte*, 16, 285–6 [1962].

ⲉⲛϩ (Crum 56b), 'eyebrow' = (*Wb.* I, 99, 1), *ỉnḥ*; (Er. 35, 9), *ỉnḥ*, 'eyebrows'.

Also [S]**ⲙϫⲛϩ**, [B]**ⲙⲉϫⲉⲛϩ** (Crum 57a) = **ⲙⲟϫϩ** + **ⲉⲛϩ**, 'girdle of (the) eyebrows'.

[H]PLEYTE, *Études ég.* I, 42 (in **ⲙⲉϫⲉⲛϩ**) [1866]; [D]BRUGSCH, *De natura et indole*, 22 (in **ⲙⲉϫⲉⲛϩ**) [1850].

See also **ⲥⲣⲛϩ**.

ⲉⲛⲉϩ (Crum 57a), 'eternity' = (*Wb.* II, 299, 2 ff.), *nḥḥ*; (Er. 224, 1), *nḥḥ*, 'eternity'.

[HD]BRUGSCH and DE ROUGÉ in BRUGSCH, *Gr. dém.* 182, §358 [1855].

ⲉⲛⲱ (Crum 57b), part of fastening of door = (*Wb.* I, 497, 15), *pꜣyt*, part of fastening of door.

DÉVAUD, *Études*, 57–9 [1922].

ⲉⲡⲏⲡ (Crum 57b), name of 11th month = (*Wb.* I, 69, 4), *ỉpỉp*, name of a festival and month.

GARDINER, *ZÄS* 43, 138 [1906]; cf. LEPSIUS, *Chronologie*, 141 [1848].

ⲉⲡⲣⲁ (Crum 57b), used only as plural, 'vanities' = Late and Gr.-R. (*Wb.* I, 531, 6. 7), *prt*, 'evil, impurity', also 'mourning'. Proper plural would be ***ⲉⲡⲣⲏⲩⲉ** (see ^B^**ⲉϥⲫⲗⲏⲟⲩ**, 'vanity, emptiness'), cf. **ⲉⲃⲣⲁ**, 'seed', pl. **ⲉⲃⲣⲏⲩⲉ**.

BRUGSCH, *Wb.* 476 [1868]; difference in meaning of Egn. and Coptic words (Dévaud, *Muséon*, 36, 96) cannot disprove the etymology, the range of meaning of *prt* is by far too wide to exclude 'vain'.

^O^**ⲉⲡϣⲉ** = (not in Crum), a beetle = (*Wb.* I, 181, 18), *ʿpšꜣy*, a beetle, (*Wb.* I, 181, 19), *ʿpšꜣyt*, a kind of grasshopper, and (*Wb.* I, 182, 1), *ʿpšwt*, an animal. Cf. Aram. חִפּוּשִׁית, 'blackbeetle', Arabic خُنْفُس.

^H^GRIFFITH-THOMPSON, I, 173 [1904]; III, 109, no. 16 [1909]; ^S^DÉVAUD's slip (Aram.) and I. E. S. EDWARDS (Arabic).

ⲉⲡⲱϭⲙ (Crum 286b, s.v. **ⲡⲱϭⲙ**), also **ⲉⲡⲱϭⲛ**, from Greek ἐποίκιον, 'hamlet'.

BARNS in *JEA* 45, 83–4 [1959].

ⲉⲣ- (Crum 57b, adding **ⲡⲉⲣϩⲱⲧⲃ**, 'murderer', Deut. 4. 42 acc. to P. Bodmer XVIII), archaic relative prefix with past tenses, where the relative is subject of the clause = L.Egn. *ỉỉr*; , *ỉỉr*, participles of *ỉrỉ* (*Wb.* I, 108, 5 ff.).

SETHE, *Nachrichten der K. Ges. d. Wiss. zu Göttingen, phil.-hist. Kl.* 1919, 149 ff. [1919].

^B^**ⲉⲣⲃⲓⲛ** (Crum 58a), 'papyrus', from Semitic, cf. Syr. ܐܪܦܐ or ܐܪܦ (LAGARDE, *Mitt.* 2, 65; Brockelmann, p. 25).

ROSSI, *Etym. aeg.* 51 [1808].

ⲉⲣⲱⲧⲉ (Crum 58b), 'milk' = (*Wb.* I, 117, 1 ff.), *ỉrṯt*; (Er. 40, 3), *ỉrt*(*t*), 'milk'.

^H^CHAMPOLLION, *Gr. ég.* pp. 60 and 79 [1836]; ^D^BRUGSCH, *Gr. dém.* 33, §66 [1855].

ⲉⲣⲏⲩ (Crum 59a), 'fellow, companion' = Plural *iryw* of (*Wb.* I, 105, 6), *iry*, 'belonging to, fellow'; (Er. 38, 3), *iry*, 'fellow'.

[HD]BRUGSCH, *Wb.* 94 [1867].

ⲉⲣϣⲁⲛ- (Crum 59a), conditional verbal prefix 'if' = (Er. 37, 7; 361, 3; 489, 1), *ir-ḫn*, 'if'. **-ϣⲁⲛ** < (*Wb.* III, 469, 19 ff.), *sḫn*, 'happen'; **-ⲉⲣϣⲁⲛ-** lit. 'if it happens that'.

[H]BRUGSCH, *Wb.* 1294 [1868]; cf. Brugsch, *Gr. hier.* 66 [1872]; [D]GROFF, *Les deux versions*, 47 [1888].

[B]**ⲉⲣϣⲓϣ** (Crum 59b), 'chick-pea' حمّص, perhaps from ***ⲡⲉⲣϣⲓϣ** (**ⲡ-** being taken for def. article), lit. 'seed of pea'. **ⲡⲉⲣ-** from **ⲉϥⲣⲁ**, 'seed', **ϣⲓϣ** from Latin *cicer* (for the late pronunciation of *cicer* compare French (*pois*) *chiche*.)

[B]**ⲉⲣϣⲓϣⲓ** (Crum 59b), 'have power, have authority' = (*Wb.* IV, 260, 5 ff.), *iri sḫr*, lit. 'make plans' = 'to provide, to take care of'; (Er. 452, 1), *ir sḫy*, 'have power'.

[HD]GRIFFITH, *Stories*, 184, note to l. 6 [1900].

ⲉⲥⲏⲧ (Crum 60a), 'ground, bottom' = (*Wb.* III, 423, 7 ff.), *sꜣṯw*; (Er. 11, 11), *ꜣsṯ*, 'ground'.

[H]PIEHL, *Rec. trav.* 2, 32, §20 [1880]; [D]SPIEGELBERG, *Petubastis*, 1*, no. 5 [1910]; LEXA, *Dem. Totb.* 35, no. 8 [1910].

ⲉⲥⲟⲟⲩ (Crum 61a), 'sheep' = Plural of (*Wb.* III, 462, 7 ff.), *sr*; (Er. 441, 3), usually and sim., *sr*, 'ram', also , *isw*, as sign of zodiac.

[H]CHABAS, *Oeuv. div.* I (= *Bibl. ég.* IX), 84 n. 1 [1856]; [D]W. MAX MÜLLER, *OLZ* 5, col. 135 [1902] (sign of zodiac); SOTTAS, *Pap. de Lille*, I, 44 and pl. 7, no. 20, l. 6 [1921] (as appellativum).

ⲙⲁⲛⲉⲥⲟⲟⲩ (Crum 61a), 'shepherd', see **ⲙⲁⲛⲉ-** under **ⲙⲟⲟⲛⲉ**.

ⲉⲧ- (Crum 61a), relative prefix = (*Wb.* II, 351, lower), *nty*; (Er. 231, 3), *nty*, 'he who, which'.

[H]CHAMPOLLION, *Gr. ég.* 304 ff., §234 [1836]; [D]BRUGSCH, *Scriptura Aeg. dem.* 37, §28 [1848] (but puts the form ⲉ with ⲉⲧ!); *Gr. dém.* 110 ff., §§236–8 [1855].

ⲉⲧⲉ- = , , *nty iw*.

[H]BRUGSCH, *Gr. hier.* 10 [1872]; cf. Erman, *Neuäg. Gr.*, 2nd ed. 484, §846 [1933]; [D]SPIEGELBERG in *OLZ* 32, col. 641 [1929].

[B]**ⲉⲁⲧ** (Crum 61 a), 'end, farthest part, opposite side' = ? (*Wb.* I, 239, 6), *ʿḏ* > , *ʿd*, 'land farthest from the river on border of desert'; (Er. 74, 4), *ʿt*, 'side, region, dry land, shore'.

[HD]SPIEGELBERG, *Kopt. Etym.* 48–50 [1920].

ⲉⲧⲃⲉ-, ⲉⲧⲃⲏⲏⲧ⸗ (Crum 61 a), 'because of, concerning' = (*Wb.* V, 559, 15 ff.), *r-ḏbꜣ*, 'to replace, instead of'; (Er. 620, 1), *r·tbꜣ*, 'because of'. With *t* in st. pron. already in Egn. and Dem., see Dévaud, *Muséon*, 36, 97 [1923].

[H]BRUGSCH, *ZÄS* 3, 90 [1865]; [D]BRUGSCH, *Pap. Rhind*, 43 and pl. 40, no. 271 [1865].

[A]**ⲉⲧⲛⲓϩ** (Crum 61 b), 'ashes' = *, *ỉwtn n ḫt*, 'dust of the fire' (Spiegelberg) or *, *ỉwtn n ḫt*, 'dust of wood' (Dévaud). For **ⲉⲧ-**, see **ⲉⲓⲧⲛ**.

SPIEGELBERG, *ZÄS* 53, 132 [1917]; DÉVAUD in Spiegelberg, *Kopt. Handwb.* 301 [1921].

ⲉⲧⲡⲉ (Kasser, *P. Bodmer XXI*, p. 24), nn. m., 'prison?'—non-existent. Understand **ⲙⲡⲉⲩⲉⲧⲡⲉ**, 'above them', and cf. Crum 260 a, upper (s.v. **ⲡⲉ**).

ⲉⲧⲣⲉ (not in Crum; Mani Ps. 220, 18), 'waste, refuse' = יֶתֶר, 'remainder'.

SÄVE-SÖDERBERGH, *Studies in the Coptic Manich. Psalm-book*, 117 n. 1 [1949].

[B]**ⲉⲧⲏϣⲓ** (Crum 61 b), 'rust (blight), mildew' = **edrēšet* < **edšēret*, fem. of (*Wb.* V, 488, 1 ff.), *dšr*, 'red' (> **ⲧⲣⲟϣ**). See also the next entry.

SETHE, *ZDMG* 77, N.F. II, 1923, 195 [1925].

[B]**ⲉⲧⲏϣⲓ** (Crum 61 b), 'crane' = *, *dšrt* (fem. from *dšr*, 'red', **edrēšet* < **edšēret*, like the prec. entry), where, however, the bird is flamingo, *Phoenicopterus roseus* (Gardiner, *Eg. gr.*, 470, G 27).

SETHE in Spiegelberg, *Kopt. Handwb.* 31 [1921]; cf. Dévaud, *Muséon*, 36, 97 [1923].

[A2]**ⲉⲧⲁϩ**, 'burden, load', see **ⲱⲧϩ**, 'draw'.

ⲉⲟⲟⲩ (Crum 62 a), 'honour, glory' = (*Wb.* I, 28, 1 ff.), *ỉꜣw*, 'praise'.

CHAMPOLLION, *Gr. ég.* pp. 60 and 65 [1836].

ⲉⲩⲱ (Crum 62b), 'pledge, surety' = (*Wb.* I, 49, 17), *iwꜣyt*, 'representative, substitute' or sim.; (Er. 22, 10), *iwit*, 'guarantee'.
[H]GARDINER, *JEA* 37, 111 [1951]; [D]REVILLOUT, *Chrest. dém.* 429 [1880]; cf. BRUGSCH, *Wb.* 516 [1881].

[O]**ⲉⲟⲩⲱⲧ⸗** (Crum 62b), 'hail!' = + Suffix (*Wb.* I, 28, 6; add Amenemope 13, 13), *iꜣwt·*; + Suffix (Er. 2, 7), *ꜣwy*, 'praised is...'.
[HD]BRUGSCH, *ZÄS* 22, 18 [1884]; cf. GRIFFITH, *ZÄS* 38, 86–7 [1900]; Möller, *Pap. Rhind*, 86, no. 108 [1913].

[B]**ⲉⲩⲛⲓ** (Crum 62b), 'nether millstone, mill' = εὐνή, 'bed', or = , *bnwt*, , *bnyt* (*Wb.* I, 458, 13), 'millstone' (**ebnīyet* > **ewnīyet* > *ewnī*).
VON LEMM, *Kleine koptische Studien*, 34 n. 4 [1900] (εὐνή); DÉVAUD, *Muséon*, 36, 97–8, no. 98 [1923] (*bnyt*).

[B](ⲉ)ⲫⲗⲏⲟⲩ (Crum 63a), 'vanity, emptiness' is Boh. pl. form (for ***ⲉⲫⲗⲏⲟⲩⲓ**) of [S]**ⲉⲡⲣⲁ** (see this), pl. ***ⲉⲡⲣⲏⲩⲉ**. For Sa. **ⲣ** = Boh. **ⲗ**, cf. [S]**ϩⲉⲣϣⲓⲣⲉ**, [B]**ϧⲉⲗϣⲏⲣⲓ**.

[B]**ⲉⲫⲱⲧ, ⲁⲫⲱⲧ** (Crum 63a), a kind of 'crocodile (?)', a ghost-word created by a glossary maker from νεφωτ explained by κροκόδειλοι in Epiphanius, *De vita prophetarum*, 8, after deducting ν- as plural definite article. Νεφωτ is, in fact, a god Νεφώτης, Egn. , *Nfr-ḥtp*, lit. 'beautiful as to peace'.
SPIEGELBERG, *ZÄS* 62, 35–7 [1927].

[B]**ⲉϣⲟ, ϣⲟ** (Crum 63a), 'bran' = (not in *Wb.*; ex. Griffith, *Liverpool Annals of Arch.* 9, Pl. 39, l. 175), *wšꜣw*, 'bran'.

[S]**ⲉϣⲱ** (Crum 550a, s.v. **ϣⲱ**), a skin disease, the same word as [B]**ⲉϣⲟ**, cf. Greek πίτυρον, a skin eruption, lit. 'husks of corn, bran'.
TILL, *Die Arzneikunde der Kopten*, p. 33, Q 25 [1951].

ⲉϣⲱ (Crum 63a), 'sow' = (*Wb.* IV, 405, 11), *šꜣt*, (*Wb.* IV, 405, 10), *šꜣi*; (Er. 44, 6), *iš*, 'sow'.
[H]CHAMPOLLION, *Gr. ég.* pp. 61 and 72 [1836]; [D]ERICHSEN, *Dem. Glossar*, 44, 6 [1954]
[S]**ϣⲉ**, [A]**ϣⲁ-.**, Pl. [SB]**ⲉϣⲁⲩ**, [F]**ⲉϣⲉⲩ** = (*Wb.* IV, 405, 7–9), *šꜣi*, 'pig' (male).
RAHLFS, *Die Berliner Handschrift des sahidischen Psalters*, 59, note [1901], cf. DÉVAUD, *Muséon*, 36, 99 [1923].

[SF]ⲉϣϫⲉ, [B]ⲓⲥϫⲉ (Crum 63b), 'if' = ⲉⲓⲥ + ϫⲉ < *, *íw·s (r) ḏd*, '(if) it is that (lit. 'to say')'.

SETHE, *Dem. Urkunden*, 22 [1920]; SETHE, *ZÄS* 57, 139 [1922].

[A](ⲉⲓ)ϩⲡⲉ, [A2]ⲉϣⲡⲉ is a contraction of ⲉϩⲱⲡⲉ (see under ϣⲱⲡⲉ), [A](ⲉⲓ)ϩϫⲉ < *ⲉϩⲱⲡⲉ + ϫⲉ; [SF]ⲉϣϫⲉⲡⲉ < ⲉϣϫⲉ + (ⲉϣⲱ)ⲡⲉ.

ⲉϥⲣⲁⲥⲟⲩ (Crum 64a), a plant, ?*abrotonum*, *artemisia* = ⲉϥⲣⲁ (for ⲉⲃⲣⲁ, 'seed' [see this]) + ⲥⲟⲩ [or ⲁⲥⲟⲩ?] which is obscure, perhaps (*Wb.* I, 127, 21. 22), *isw*, 'reed'.

ⲉϩⲉ (Crum 64a), 'ox & cow' = (*Wb.* I, 120, 5), *iḥt*, 'cow'; (Er. 41, 2), *iḥ*, 'head of cattle'.

[H]CHAMPOLLION, *Précis*, 2nd ed., 126 [1828] (but he derives it wrongly from masc. *iḥ* (*Wb.* I, 119, 15), 'head of cattle', cf. DÉVAUD, *Muséon*, 36, 99 [1923]; SCHWARTZE in Bunsen, *Geschichte*, I, 565 [1845] correctly from fem. *iḥt*; [D]BRUGSCH, *Sammlung dem. Urkunden*, 21 and pl. IV, H 321 [1850].

[S]ⲉϫⲱ, [B]ⲉϭⲟⲩ (Crum 65a), 'tongs, pincers' = [] and , *ṯꜣyt*, 'pincers', from verb (*Wb.* V, 346–7), *ṯꜣi*, 'seize' (Copt. [S]ϫⲓ, [B]ϭⲓ).

CLÈRE, *Revue d'ég.* 11, 157–8 [1957]; cf. DÉVAUD, *Études*, 43–4 [1922].

[S]ⲉϭⲱϣ, [B]ⲉⲑⲱϣ (Crum 65b), 'an Ethiopian, a Nubian' = (Er. 45, 8), *ikš*, 'a Nubian'; from (*Wb.* V, 109, 1), *kꜣš*, 'Nubia'.

[H]TATTAM, *Lexicon*, 108 [1835]; cf. Champollion, *Dict.* 409 [1842]; [D]BRUGSCH, *De natura et indole*, 38 [1850].

Ⲏ

ⲏⲓ (Crum 66a), 'house' = (*Wb.* I, 160, 1–13), *ʿt*, 'room, house', later (masc., *Wb.* I, 159, 15); (Er. 51, 9), *ʿt*, 'room', (Er. 52, 6), *ʿwy*, 'house'.

[H]CHABAS, *Pap. mag. Harris*, 250 [1860]; cf. GARDINER, *Onomastica* II, 206*–7* [1947]; [D]MASPERO, *ZÄS* 20, 125 [1882].

ⲁ- in ⲁⲛⲁϩⲱⲣ, 'storehouse' (see under ⲁϩⲟ) and in ⲁⲛⲥⲏⲃⲉ, 'school'.

ⲏⲓ (Crum 66b), 'pair, couple' = (*Wb.* I, 158, 9–10), *ʿ*, 'pair'; (Er. 52, 2 = 52, 3), *ʿwy*, 'arms, pair'.

^{H}MASPERO, *ZÄS* 20, 126 [1882]; ^{D}BRUGSCH acc. to Spiegelberg in *ZÄS* 37, 27 [1899].

^{O}**ⲏⲓ** (Crum 66b), interjection, = or (*Wb.* I, 25, no exx. given, but see Gardiner, *Gr.*^{3}, §87 n. 4); (Er. 15, 1), *ỉ*, interjection.

^{H}MÖLLER, *Pap. Rhind*, I*, no. I [1913]; ^{D}GRIFFITH, *Pap. Rylands*, III, 325 [1909].

ⲏⲛ (Crum 66b), 'ape' = (*Wb.* I, 41, 6), *ỉʿny*; (Er. 56, 12), *ʿʿn(y)*, 'baboon'.

^{H}CHAMPOLLION, *Gr. ég.* pp. 60, 72, 83 [1836]; ^{D}KRALL, *Mitt. aus der Sammlung Erzh. Rainer*, VI, 60, no. 42 [1897].

^{S}**ⲏⲛⲉ** (Apocr. St John Codex II, 11, 33) m. (var. ^{A2}**ϭⲁⲛⲓ**), 'ape' = (*Wb.* I, 41, 9), *ỉʿnt*, 'female baboon'; became masc. in Coptic.

^{B}**ⲏⲣ** (not in Crum; John 11, 11; 15, 14. 15; 19, 12 acc. to P. Bodmer III), 'friend' (φίλος) = (*Wb.* I, 105, 5), *ỉry*, 'fellow'; singular of **ⲉⲣⲏⲩ**. Cf. Spiegelberg's reconstruction of the Coptic singular as ***ⲏⲣⲉ**: **ⲏⲣⲓ** (*Kopt. Etym.* 24).

KASSER, *Pap. Bodmer III*, p. XI [1958].

^{O}**ⲣⲉ́ⲓ ⲉ̀ⲛⲥⲓ́ⲙⲉ** in **ⲧⲁⲣⲉ́ⲓ ⲉ̀ⲛⲥⲓ́ⲙⲉ** = *, *tȝy·ỉ ỉry n st-ḥmt*, 'my female companion'.

GRIFFITH in *ZÄS* 38, 91 [1900].

ⲏⲣⲡ (Crum 66b), 'wine' = (*Wb.* I, 115, 5–7); (Er. 39, 6), *ỉrp*, 'wine'.

^{H}CHAMPOLLION, *Gr. ég.* pp. 60 and 79 [1836]; ^{D}BRUGSCH, *De natura et indole*, 23 [1850].

^{O}**ⲏⲟⲩ** (Crum 67b), 'limbs (?)' = Plural of (*Wb.* I, 160, 14 ff.); (Er. 51, 10), *ʿt*, 'limb'.

^{H}ERMAN, *ZÄS* 21, 100 and 104 [1883]; ^{D}GRIFFITH, *Stories*, 129, note [1900].

ⲏϭⲉ (Crum 67b), 'leek' = (*Wb.* I, 34, 1), *ỉȝḳt*, 'leek'.

LORET, *Flore pharaonique*, 2nd ed., 138 (index) [1892].

ⲑ

^{B}**ⲑⲟⲩⲙⲉ** (Crum 68b), zodiacal sign *Virgo* = (*Wb.* v, 368, 8), *ṯmꜣt*, name of a decan constellation, Greek τωμ.

BRUGSCH, *Wb.* 1326 [1882].

^{B}**ⲑⲙⲓⲥ** (Crum 68b), 'dust' is Gk. ἀτμίς, 'steam, vapour'.

CRUM, *A Coptic Dict.* 68b [1929].

^{B}**ⲑⲏⲛ** (Crum 69a), 'sulphur' = Greek θεῖον.

ROSSI, *Etym. aeg.* 65 [1808].

^{B}**ⲑⲣⲁⲛ** (Crum 69a), 'tin' = (Er. 648, 6), *trn*, 'tin'. Acc. to Sethe in Spiegelberg, *Kopt. Handwb.* 151, with article **ⲡⲓ-ⲑⲣⲁⲛ** from βρεττανία, Brittany being the chief source of tin in antiquity.

BRUGSCH, *Die Aegyptologie*, 398 [1891]; cf. GRIFFITH-THOMPSON, III, 94, no. 1024 [1909].

^{B}**ⲑⲉⲣϣ**, ^{B}**ⲑⲏⲣϣ** (Crum 69a), 'linseed' = (*Wb.* v, 491, 6), *dšr*, '(red-coloured?) grains'.

BRUGSCH, *Wb.*, Suppl. 1375 [1882]; cf. Chassinat, *Pap. méd.* 114 [1921].

See also **ⲧⲱⲣϣ**, 'be red'.

^{B}**ⲑⲟⲩⲣⲁϫⲓ** (Crum 69a), part of monastic costume, is Gk. θωράκιον, lit. 'breast-plate'.

CRUM, *A Coptic Dict.* 69a [1929].

^{B}**ⲑⲟⲩⲥ** (Crum 69b), 'point' of beard, see under **ⲧⲱⲃⲥ**, 'prick, goad, incite'.

^{B}**ⲑⲟⲩⲉⲗⲟ** (Crum 69b), 'overflow, submerge' is causative of **ⲟⲩⲱⲗⲉ**, 'float, hover' (see under **ⲟⲩⲱⲱⲗⲉ**, 'be well off').

CRUM, *A Coptic Dict.* 69b [1929].

^{B}(***ⲑⲓϥⲓ**), **ⲑⲁϥ⸗** (Crum 69b), 'take out, away' (cf. ^{B}**ⲙⲓⲥⲓ**, **ⲙⲁⲥ**) = or (*Wb.* v, 297, 11 ff.), *tfy*, 'remove (by force)'; (Er. 628, 9), *tfy*, 'take away, remove'.

^{B}***ⲑⲓϥⲓ** is the same word as ^{A2}**ⲧⲁϥⲉ** (Qual.), 'scare up'; see this latter.

[B]ⲑⲟϥⲧⲉϥ (Crum 69b), 'let fall drop by drop' = (*Wb*. v, 573, 13–15), *dfḏf*, 'fall drop by drop', > *ṯfṯf*, cf. (*Wb*. v, 300, 9), in name of a deity, , *ṯfṯf-nwn*, 'he who lets fall Nun (i.e. rain-water) drop by drop'. Cf. Aram. טפטף.

[H]SPIEGELBERG, *Kopt. Handwb.* 159 [1921] (comparing Gr.-Rom. , *ṯfṯf*, which is not in *Wb*., but cf. exx. in Brugsch, *Wb*. 1583–4); [S]ROSSI, *Etym. aeg.* 67–8 [1808].

ⲈⲒ, Ⲓ

ⲉⲓ (Crum 70a), 'come' = (*Wb*. I, 37, 1 ff.); (Er. 18, 2), *ỉy*, 'come'.

[H]CHAMPOLLION, *Gr. ég.* 382 [1836]; [D]BRUGSCH, *Gr. dém.* 39, §83 [1855]. For ⲛⲏⲩ used as its Qualitative, see ⲛⲏⲩ.

ⲉⲓⲁ, ⲉⲓⲉⲣ-, ⲉⲓⲁⲧ⸗ (Crum 73b), 'eye' = (*Wb*. I, 106, 6 ff.); (Er. 38, 2), *ỉrt*, 'eye'.

[H]SETHE in SPIEGELBERG, *Rec. trav.* 17, 93 [1895]; cf. SETHE, *Verbum*, II, p. 6, note [1899]; [D]HESS, *Stne*, 186 [1888].

ⲉⲓⲁ must be a secondary form based on ⲉⲓⲁⲧ⸗, the absolute form is attested only in Mani ⲃⲁⲛ-ⲓⲉⲓⲣⲉ, 'malicious', lit. 'evil of eye' (ALLBERRY, *Kephalaia*, 229, 24a, *Psalm-Book*, II, Index, p. 9*; cf. LACAU in Sainte Fare Garnot, *Mél. Maspero*, I, 4, 161 [1961]. The best pronominal form, with *r* > ⲓ still shown is ⲓⲁϊⲧϥ in ⲙⲁϩ-ⲓⲁϊⲧϥ 'onlooker', lit. 'one who fills his eye (with something)' (Allberry, *A Manichaean Psalm-Book*, II, 10, 10).

[S]ⲙⲟⲩϩ ⲛ-, ⲙⲉϩ-ⲉⲓⲁⲧ⸗ ⲙⲙⲟ⸗, [A]ⲙⲁϩ ϊⲉⲧ⸗ ⲙⲙⲁ⸗ (also A_2, Mani H 85, 20), lit. 'fill eye with', i.e. 'look intently' = + Suff. + , *mḥ ỉrt m*, 'fill eye with' (*LRL* 14, 7, 8; 28, 6; 44, 15; 54, 8); (Petub. 9, 10), *mḥ ỉrt* (also *mḥ n ỉrt*, ib. 16, 1) (Er. 178, middle), same meaning.

SPIEGELBERG in *OLZ* 7, col. 197 [1904]; cf. Spiegelberg, *Petubastis*, 8*, no. 35 [1910]. NB. This expression has nothing to do with [S]ⲙⲟⲩϩ, [A]ⲙⲟⲩϩ (Crum 210b), 'look', whose ancestor requires *ḫ* or *ẖ* (not *ḥ*).

ⲛⲁⲓⲁⲧ⸗ (Crum 74a), 'blessed' art, is etc. for *ⲛⲁⲁ + ⲉⲓⲁⲧ⸗, lit. 'great is thy, his eye', see ⲛⲁⲁ-.

SPIEGELBERG, *Kopt. Etym.* 28 [1920].

ⲧⲟⲩⲛⲉⲓⲁⲧ⸗ (Crum 73 b), 'instruct, inform', lit. 'cause (the) eye (of somebody) to open' = * , *dỉt wn ỉrt·*; (Er. 89, middle), *ty wn ỉrt·*, 'inform'.

[H]SETHE, *Verbum*, I, 22, §37; II, 106, §247, and p. 461 [1899]; cf. SETHE, *ZÄS* 47, 146 [1910]; [D]GRIFFITH-THOMPSON, III, 20, no. 197 [1909].

ⲱⲟⲩ ⲛⲓⲁⲧ-, 'blessing', see under **ⲱⲟⲩ**.

ⲉⲓⲉⲣ ⲃⲟⲟⲛⲉ (Crum 39 b), 'evil eye' = (*Wb.* I, 107, 5; 443, 11); (REVILLLOUT, *Chrest.* 214, from Dem. pap. Louvre 2428), *ỉrt-bỉnt*, 'evil eye', as component in personal names.

SPIEGELBERG, *Rec. trav.* 17, 93–4 [1895].

ⲉⲓⲉ (Crum 74 a), particle, 'then', etc. = L.Egn. (*Wb.* I, 25, 8), *ỉ3*, interjection; (not in Er.), *ỉwy*, 'indeed'.

[H]GOODWIN, *ZÄS* 9, 127 [1871]; cf. ERMAN, *Näg. Gr.* § 140 f (with doubt) [1880]; [D]SPIEGELBERG, *Krüge*, 59, no. 12 [1912].

ⲉⲓⲱ (Crum 75 a), 'wash' = (*Wb.* I, 39, 2 ff.); (Er. 48, 6), *ỉʿ*, 'wash'.

[H]CHAMPOLLION, *Gr. ég.* 37C [1836]; [H]BRUGSCH, *De natura et indole*, 25 [1850].

ⲉⲓⲱ (Crum 75 b), 'ass' = (*Wb.* I, 165, 6–8. 12); (Er. 54, 3), *ʿ3*, 'ass'.

[H]CHAMPOLLION, *Gr. ég.* 83 [1836]; [D]BRUGSCH, *Gr. dém.* 23, §40 [1855].

ⲉⲓⲁ ⲛⲧⲟⲟⲩ (Crum 76 a), 'desert, wild ass' = * , *ʿ3 n ḏww*, 'ass of the desert'.

SPIEGELBERG, *Dem. Chronik*, Glossary, 41, no. 13 [1914].

ⲉⲓⲃ (Crum 76 a), 'hoof, claw, nail' = (*Wb.* I, 7, 21), *3b*, 'finger-nail'; (Er. 49, 9), *ỉb*, 'finger-nail, claw'.

[H]SPIEGELBERG, *Kopt. Handwb.* 23 [1921]; cf. Brugsch, *Wb.* 168 [1867]; *Dict. géo.* 113 [1879] (but he confuses *3b*, 'finger-nail', with *ʿb*, 'horn'); [D]BRUGSCH, *Gr. dém.* 29, §56 [1855].

ⲉⲓⲃⲉ (Crum 76 a), 'to thirst' = (*Wb.* I, 61, 8 f.), *ỉbỉ*, 'to thirst'; (Er. 3, 9), *3bỉ*, 'to thirst'.

[H]CHAMPOLLION, *Gr. ég.* pp. 60, 375 [1836]; [D]BRUGSCH, *Gr. dém.* 44, §94 [1855].

ⲉⲓⲁⲃⲉ (Crum 76b), 'matter from sores, pus' from (*Wb.* I, 29, 19), *ỉꜣb*, adj. and verb of bad meaning (of smell of the corpses, etc.); (Er. 48, 7), *ỉꜥb*, 'ill, tired', as fem. noun 'illness'.

[H]ERMAN-GRAPOW, *Wb.* I, 29, 19 [1926]; [D]REVILLOUT, *Pap. mor.* II, 24 [1908]; cf. Sethe, *Nominalsatz*, p. 40 [1916].

ⲉⲓⲉⲃⲧ (Crum 76b), nn., 'the east' = (*Wb.* I, 30, 16), *ỉꜣbty*; (Er. 17, 5), *ỉꜣbṭ*, 'eastern, east'.

[H]CHAMPOLLION, *Gr.* 67, 97 [1836]; [D]BRUGSCH, *Gr. dém.* 57, §§128–9 [1855]. With article **ⲡⲉⲓⲉⲃⲧ** = , *p(r) ỉꜣbṭ*, 'the east'.

ⲉⲓⲁⲗ (Crum 76b), 'mirror' = (Er. 50, 5), *ỉl*, 'mirror'.

BRUGSCH, *De natura et indole*, 25 [1850].

ⲉⲓⲟⲩⲗ (Crum 77a), 'hart, hind' = (*Wb.* I, 38, 16), *ỉyr*; (Er. 1, 7), *ỉywr*, 'hart', from Semitic *'yl*, cf. אַיָּל, 'hart', إِيَّل.

[H]BURCHARDT, *Die altkanaan. Fremdworte*, II, 1, no. 12 [1910]; [D]BRUGSCH, *De natura et indole*, 22 [1850]; [S]ROSSI, *Etym. aeg.* 45 [1808].

ⲓⲉⲗⲗⲉ (Crum 77a), 'brightness, light' = (Er. 50, 6), *yꜥl*, 'brightness'.

SPIEGELBERG, *Mythus*, 97, no. 142 [1917].

ⲉⲓⲉⲗⲉⲗ (Crum 77a), 'shine, glitter' = Gr.-R. (not in *Wb.*, ex. *Temple of Esna*, 48a), *ỉrr*, 'shed light', from Semitic, cf. הָלַל.

[H]SAUNERON, *Quatre campagnes à Esna*, 46 [1959]; cf. Sauneron in *Mélanges Mariette*, 233 [1961]; [S]ROSSI, *Etym. aeg.* 71 [1808].

ⲉⲓⲟⲙ (1) (Crum 77a), 'sea' = L.Egn. (*Wb.* I, 78, 11); (Er. 50, 1), *ym*, 'sea', from Semitic, cf. יָם.

[H]CHAMPOLLION, *Gr. ég.* 98 [1836]; [D]DE SAULCY, *Rosette*, 21 [1845] (Demotic group reproduced incorrectly); BRUGSCH, *Scriptura Aeg. dem.* 19, §20 [1848]; [S]ROSSI, *Etym. aeg.* 75 [1808].

(2) (Crum 77b), 'wine vat (hardly: press)' already in Demotic: O. Campbell 13, 4; Cairo Cat. 30691 A 33 (= SPIEGELBERG, *Dem. Denkm.* I, 81 and n. 4) , *ym*, a (metal) vessel.

H. THOMPSON's Demotic dictionary.

ⲉⲓⲙⲉ (Crum 77b), 'know, understand' = (*Wb.* I, 184, 16–20), *ꜥm*; (Er. 60, 6), *ꜥm*, 'know'.

[H]DE ROUGÉ, according to a letter by de Horrack to Dévéria of 14 Jan. 1863, publ. in DE HORRACK, *Oeuv. div.* p. XVIII (= *Bibl. ég.* XVII); CHABAS, *Mél. égypt.* I, 208 [1864]; [D]ERICHSEN, *Dem. Glossar*, 60 [1954].

For **ⲛⲁϣⲧⲉⲓⲙⲉ**, **ⲛⲁϣⲧⲙⲙⲉ** (Crum 78b), 'presumptuous', see under **ⲛϣⲟⲧ**.

ⲉⲓⲛⲉ (Crum 78b), 'bring, bear' = (*Wb.* I, 90, 2 ff.), *ỉnỉ*; (Er. 33, 7), *ỉn*, 'bring'.

[H]CHAMPOLLION, *Gr. ég.* 383 [1836]; [D]BRUGSCH, *Sammlung demotischer Urkunden*, 26 and Pl. 5, l. 28 [1850].

ⲉⲓⲛⲉ (Crum 80b), 'resemble, be like' = (Er. 50, 3), *yn*, 'be like'.

GRIFFITH-THOMPSON, III, 16, no. 162 [1909].

ⲉⲓⲛⲉ (Crum 81a), 'thumb, great toe' = (*Wb.* I, 188, 1–7), *ʿnt*, 'nail, claw, thumb'; (Er. 63, 2), *ʿnt*, 'nail, claw'.

[H]MASPERO, *Pap. Louvre*, 23 n. 1 [1875]; [D]ERICHSEN, *Dem. Glossar*, 63, 2 [1954] (identifies the Demotic word with its prototype *ʿnt* without quoting the Coptic form).

See the next word.

ⲉⲓⲛⲉ (Crum 81a), 'carpenter's axe, adze' = (*Wb.* I, 187, 17), *ʿnt*, 'carpenter's axe'.

BRUGSCH, *Wb.* 1407 [1882]; cf. DÉVAUD, *Rec. trav.* 39, 165–6 [1921].

Etymologically identical with the preceding word. Another tool called after a part of body is **ⲧⲱⲣⲉ** (see this).

ⲉⲓⲟⲡⲉ (Crum 81a), 'craft, art, occupation' = (*Wb.* I, 303, 8 ff.), *wpwt*, 'message, task'; (Er. 86, 1), *wpt*, 'work'.

[H]GOODWIN, *ZÄS* 6, 21 [1868]; [D]HESS, *ZÄS* 28, 6–7 [1890].

ⲉⲓⲉⲡ ⲟⲩⲟⲉⲓⲉ (Crum 81b), 'tillage, tilled land'; (cf. *wp n wyʿ*, Er. 86, 1 and 79, 2), *wpt wyʿ*, 'tillage'.

[O]**ⲉⲓⲡⲛ** (not in Crum), postpositive 'this' = (*Wb.* I, 507, 10 f.), *ỉpn*, originally plural of , *pn*, 'this'. In **ⲛⲉⲧ ⲉⲓ̈ⲡⲛ** (*JEA* 28, 25, 8), = prob. , *nṯr pn*, 'this god'; **ⲙⲧⲁ ⲉⲉⲓ̈ⲡⲛ**, ib. 25, 10 = , *m tꜣ pn*, 'in this world', and **ⲙ[illegible]ⲁⲩ ⲉⲓ̈ⲡⲛ** (ib. 25, 12; 26, 37–8, 44, 49) = , *m hrw pn*; (Spiegelberg, *Dem. Gr.* 17, § 12), *m hrw ỉpn*, 'on this day'.

CRUM in *JEA* 28, 28, 8 [1942].

ⲉⲓⲟⲟⲣ (Crum 82 a), 'canal' = (*Wb.* I, 146, 10 ff.), later (P. Sallier I, 7) and (Wenamūn 2, 23), *ỉtrw*, 'river'; (Er. 50, 4), *yr*, 'river, canal'.

ᴴCHABAS, *Oeuv. div.* III (= *Bibl. ég.* XI), 245 [1868]; cf. BRUGSCH, *Geographie des alten Ägyptens*, 8 and Pl. I, no. 16 [1857] (from); ᴰYOUNG, *Misc. Works*, III, 28–9, no. 62 = *Mus. crit.* 6, pp. 178–9, no. 62 [1815] (letter to de Sacy of 21 Oct. 1814); DE SAULCY, *Rosette*, 21 [1845].

ϫⲓⲟⲟⲣ (Crum 82 a and 751 b), 'ferry over, cross river, cross (sea or land)' = (*Wb.* V, 512, 11), *ḏꜣỉ ỉtrw*, 'cross river'; (Er. 665, lower), *tꜣỉ y(ꜥ)r*, 'cross the river'.

ᴴDE ROUGÉ, *Oeuv. div.* II (= *Bibl. ég.* XXII), 198 [1851]; ᴰBRUGSCH, *Thesaurus*, 1029 [1891]; BRUGSCH, *Sieben Jahre der Hungersnot*, 71–2 [1891].

ⲉⲓⲉⲣⲟ (Crum 82 b), 'river', lit. 'great canal' = (*Wb.* I, 146, 17 and 162, 11), *ỉtrw ꜥꜣ*, 'Nile' (especially the main branch), lit. 'the great river'; (Er. 50, 4), *y(ꜥ)r ꜥꜣ*, 'Nile'.

ᴴLEPSIUS, *ZÄS* 3, 41 [1865]; ᴰGRIFFITH-THOMPSON, III, 16, no. 156 [1909].

ⲉⲓⲣⲉ (Crum 83 a), 'make, do' = (*Wb.* I, 108, 5 ff.), *ỉrỉ*; (Er. 36, 3), *ỉr(ỉ)*, 'make, do'.

ᴴCHAMPOLLION, *Gr. ég.* 64 [1836]; ᴰÅKERBLAD in YOUNG, *Misc. Works*, III, 37 [1815]; BRUGSCH, *Scriptura Aeg. dem.* 56, §44, 4 [1848].

Fem. Qual. **ⲟⲉⲓⲧ**, see this latter.

ᴬ²**ⲓⲉⲓⲣⲉ**, 'eye', in Mani **ⲃⲁⲛ-ⲓⲉⲓⲣⲉ**, 'malicious', see **ⲉⲓⲁ**.

ⲉⲓⲥ (Crum 85 a), interjection 'behold, lo' = (*Wb.* I, 130, 12), *ỉs*; , *ꜥs* (?), or , *ỉs* (Er. 70, 9), 'behold'.

ᴴCHAMPOLLION, *Gr. ég.* 500 [1836]; ᴰSPIEGELBERG, *ZÄS* 37, 41–3 [1899]. According to SETHE, *Bürgschaftsurkunden*, 22 and 358 [1920] **ⲉⲓⲥ**, and are nothing else but L.Eg. , *ỉw·s* 'it is (that)'.

ⲉⲓⲥⲧⲉ (Crum 85 b) = L.Eg. , *ỉstw* < , *ỉs·ṯ(w)*, 'behold, thou'. RÖSCH, *Vorbemerkungen*, 175–6 [1909].

ᴮ**ⲓⲱⲥ** (Crum 86 a), 'hasten' = (*Wb.* I, 20, 1), *ỉꜣs*; (Er. 50, 7), *ys*, 'hasten'.

ᴴCHABAS, *Oeuv. div.* II (= *Bibl. ég.* X), 54 [1859]; ᴰREVILLOUT, *Pap. mor.* I, 69 and 70 n. 6 [1905].

ⲉⲓⲱⲧ (Crum 86b), 'father' = (*Wb.* I, 141, 10), *ỉt*, usually written (*ỉtf*); (Er. 46, 4), *yt* (written *ytf*), 'father'.

[H]CHAMPOLLION, *Gr. ég.* 65 and 104 [1836]; [D]ÅKERBLAD in YOUNG, *Misc. Works*, III, 37 [1815]; DE SAULCY, *Rosette*, 20 [1845].

ⲉⲓⲱⲧ (Crum 87a), 'barley' = (*Wb.* I, 142, 10 ff.), *ỉt*; (Er. 46, 1), *ỉt*, 'barley'.

[H]BRUGSCH, *Wb.* 1527 [1868] and Suppl. 167 [1880]; [D]SPIEGELBERG, *Die demot. Urkunden des Zenon-Archivs*, 31 [1929]; cf. MALININE in *Kêmi*, 11, 12 ff. [1950].

ⲉⲓⲱⲧⲉ (Crum 87b), 'dew' = (*Wb.* I, 36, 1), *ỉꜣdt*; (Er. 49, 6), *yꜥḏꜣt*, 'dew'.

[H]BIRCH in *Archaeologia*, 38, 387 [1860] (with doubt); DE ROUGÉ, *Oeuv. div.* IV (= *Bibl. ég.* XXIV), 133 [1861]; [D]BRUGSCH, *De natura et indole*, 25 [1850].

ⲉⲓⲧⲛ (Crum 87b), 'ground, earth, dust' = (*Wb.* I, 58, 6–10), *ỉwtn*, 'ground'; (Er. 47, 4), *ỉwtn*, 'ground'.

[H]CHABAS, *Oeuv. div.* I (= *Bibl. ég.* IX), 297 n. 2 [1858]; [D]BRUGSCH, *Wb.* 31 [1867]; 549 [1868].

ⲉⲡⲓⲧⲛ (Crum 88a and Add. p. XVII), = **ⲉ-ⲡ-ⲓⲧⲛ**, lit. 'to the ground, downwards', substantivized (hence **ⲟⲩⲉⲡⲓⲧⲛ**, **ⲛⲉⲡⲓⲧⲛ**) with the meaning 'space leading downward, hole'. See parallel development of **ⲉ-ⲧⲡⲉ**, 'to the sky, upward', under **ⲧⲡⲉ**.
See also [A]**ⲉⲧⲛⲓⳉ**.

ⲉⲓⲁⲁⲩ (Crum 88a), 'linen' = (*Wb.* I, 166, 6), *ꜥꜣt*, kind of linen; (Er. 55, 3), *ꜥꜣyw*, 'linen'.

[HD]REVILLOUT, *Poème*, 71 [1885]; cf. DÉVAUD in *ZÄS* 49, 113 [1911].

[B]**ⲓϣ** (Crum 88a), 'urine' = (*Wb.* I, 358, 1), *wsšt*, 'urine'.

ASMUS, *Über Fragmente im mittelägyptischen Dialekt*, 52 [1904].

ⲉⲓⲟⲩⲉ, ⲉⲓⲟⲟⲩⲉ (Crum 88a), pl., 'waters(?)' = *ỉywt*, *ỉywꜣt* in, *st-ỉywt*, or, *st-ỉywꜣt*, 'bath' (GRIFFITH-THOMPSON, III, 71, no. 702). Identical with or related to, the old (*Wb.* I, 49, 1, 2), *ỉwy*, 'inundate, pour out'? Different from (**ⲓ**)**ⲟⲟⲩⲛ** in **ⲥⲓⲟⲟⲩⲛ**, see this.

ⲉⲓϣⲉ (Crum 88b), 'hang, suspend' = (*Wb.* I, 224, 2 ff.), *ꜥḫi*, 'lift up'; (Er. 70, 1), *ꜥḫi*, 'hang up'.

[H]CHAMPOLLION, *Gr. ég.* 368 [1836]; [D]BRUGSCH, *Wb.* 213 [1867].

ⲉⲓϣⲟⲩⲉⲓ (Crum 89a), 'roast, dry (by heating)' is Ar. إشْوِ, Imperative of شَوَى, 'roast'.

CRUM, *A Coptic Dict.* 89a [1930].

[B]**ⲓϧ** (Crum 89a), [A2]**ⲓϩ** (Mani Ps.), 'demon' = (*Wb.* I, 16, 10), *ꜣḫ*, 'spirit, demon'; (Er. 42, 3), *ỉḫy*, 'spirit'.

[H]LAUTH, *Manetho*, 161 [1865]; cf. BRUGSCH, *Wb.* 31 and 113 [1867]; [D]BRUGSCH, *Gr. dém.* 36, §73 [1855].

ⲉⲓⲱϩⲉ (Crum 89b), 'field' = (*Wb.* I, 12, 17), *ꜣḥt*; (Er. 9, 1), *ꜣḥ*, 'field'.

[H]BUNSEN, *Ägyptens Stelle in der Weltgeschichte*, I, 565 [1845]; [D]YOUNG, *Misc. Works*, III, 26–7, no. 53 = *Mus. crit.* 6, p. 176–7, no. 58 [1815] (letter to de Sacy of 21 Oct. 1814).

ⲉⲓⲉϩ-ⲉⲗⲟⲟⲗⲉ (Crum 89b), 'vineyard' = , *ꜣḥ n ỉrr*; (in Plural), *ꜣḥw ꜣrly*, lit. 'field of grapes'.

[H]SPIEGELBERG, *Der demot. Text der Priesterdekrete*, 107, no. 40 [1922]; [D]BRUGSCH, *Scriptura Aeg. dem.* 15, §9 [1848].

See also ⲥ(ⲉ)ⲧⲉⲓⲱϩⲉ under ⲥⲱⲧ.

ⲉⲓϭⲣⲓ (Crum 90b, 'meaning unknown') is very prob. Ar. إجْرِ, Imperative of جَرَى, 'hasten'.

Ⲕ

-ⲕ, suffix of 2nd person sing. masc. = (*Wb.* V, 83, 2–3), *·k*; (Er. 555, 1), *·k*.

[H]CHAMPOLLION, *Précis*, 1st ed., Tableau général, no. 13, and p. (2), 13 [1824]; [D]BRUGSCH, *Scriptura Aeg. dem.* 32–3 [1848].

ⲕ-, prefix of Ist Present 2nd person sing. masc. = L.Eg. (*Wb.* V, 246, upper), (Er. 609, 5), *tw·k*, and , *ỉr·k*.

[HD]ERMAN, *Näg. Gr.* 135–6, §209 [1880].

ⲕⲉ (Crum 90b), ‘another’ = (*Wb.* v, 110, 7), *kỉỉ*; (Er. 557, 6), *kỉ*, ‘another’.

[H]CHAMPOLLION, *Gr. ég.* 314 [1836]; [D]DE SAULCY, *Rosette*, 34 [1845].

ⲛⲕⲉⲥⲟⲡ, ‘another time’, cf. (*Wb.* v, 110, 9, and III, 436, 3), *kỉỉ sp*, ‘another time’.

ⲡⲕⲉ- (Crum 91b), ‘also, even’ = L.Eg. *, *pꜣ kỉỉ* (attested in fem. , *ḥnᶜ ḳtỉ Kš*, ‘and also Kush’, P. Chester Beatty v, 5, 12); (Er. 559, middle), *pꜣ kỉ*, ‘also’.

[H]GARDINER, *Hieratic Papyri in the Brit. Mus., Third Series*, I, 47 n. 3 [1935].

ⲕⲟⲟⲩⲉ (Crum 91b) [plural of **ⲕⲉ**] = , L.Eg. (*Wb.* v, 110, lower), *kỉwỉ*; (Er. 558, top), *kyw*, ‘others’.

[H]BRUGSCH, *Wb.* 1488–9 [1868]; [D]BRUGSCH, *Gr. dém.* 118, §241, 7°A [1855].

ⲕⲉⲧ (Crum 92a), ‘another’ = , L.Eg. (*Wb.* v, 110, lower), *ḳtỉ*, fem. of ; (Er. 559, lower), *ḳtỉt*.

[H]CHABAS, *Voyage*, 234 [1866]; [D]BRUGSCH, *Scriptura Aeg. dem.* 39, VI [1848].

Plural [S]**ⲕⲉⲕⲟⲟⲩⲉ** (Crum 91b), = Singular **ⲕⲉ** + Plural **ⲕⲟⲟⲩⲉ**.

[B]**ⲕⲏ** (Crum 92a), nn. f., ‘river-bank?’—The word cannot have anything to do with , *kỉỉ*, **ⲕⲉ**, ‘other’ (Crum, s.v.; Calice in *OLZ* 35, 254) since Boh. **ⲕ** in accented syllable must derive from , *ḳ* (and not , *k*). Perhaps a misspelling of [B]**ⲕⲟⲓ** = [S]**ⲕⲟⲓⲉ**, ‘field’.

[O]**ⲕⲟ** (Crum 92a), ‘bull’(?) = (*Wb.* v, 94, 7 ff.); (Er. 555, 12), *kꜣ*, ‘bull’.

[H]MÖLLER in PREISENDANZ, *Papyri graeca magicae*, I, 75 n. 16 [1928]; cf. Spiegelberg, *Mythus*, 276, no. 848 [1917].

ⲕⲟⲓⲉ (Crum 92b), ‘field’ = (*Wb.* v, 6, 4 ff.), *ḳꜣyt*; (Er. 532, 1), *ḳy*, ‘high ground’.

[H]GOODWIN, *ZÄS* 5, 58 [1867]; [D]SPIEGELBERG, *Mythus*, 270–1, no. 804 [1917].

[S]**ⲕⲟⲩⲓ** (Crum 92b), ‘small person’ or ‘thing’ = (Er. 575, 2), *gwy*, or , *ky*, ‘small’.

SETHE in Spiegelberg, *Dem. Chron.* 136, no. 565 [1914].

[B]**ⲕⲟⲩϫⲓ** though synonymous must be a different word.

ⲕⲱ (Crum 94b), 'place, permit, abandon' = (*Wb.* III, 227, 3 ff.), *ḫ3ʿ*, 'throw, place, abandon'; (Er. 345, 7), *ḫ3*(ʿ).

ᴴBIRCH in *Archaeologia*, 35, 123 n. c and pl. IV, no. 26 [1853]; ᴰBRUGSCH in HESS, *ZÄS* 28, 4 [1890], cf. BRUGSCH, *Thesaurus*, V, p. x, n. xx and p. 1014 [1891].

NB. *ḫ* > *k* as early as by XXth Dyn., cf. , 'do not abandon me', GRAPOW, *Sitzber. Preuss. Ak. Wiss., Phil.-hist. Kl.* XXVIII, 330 n. 1 [1938]; for later exx. see *Revue d'ég.* 14 (1962), 50.

ⲕⲁ ⲃⲟⲗ (Crum 37a), 'vomit', is either **ⲕⲱ** () + **ⲃⲟⲗ**, 'outside' (SPIEGELBERG, *Kopt. Handwb.* 35 [1921]), or , *ḳ3ʿ*, 'spit out, vomit' + **ⲃⲟⲗ** (ERMAN-GRAPOW, *Wb.* V, 7, 5 [1931]).

ⲕⲱⲃ (Crum 98b), 'to double' = (*Wb.* V, 8, 7–8 and 9, 1), *ḳ3b*, 'to double', cf. (Er. 533, 10), *ḳb*, 'the double'.

ᴴDE ROUGÉ, *Oeuv. div.* III (= *Bibl. ég.* XXIII), 206 [1857]; ᴰSPIEGELBERG, *Mythus*, 271, no. 805 [1917].

ᴮ**ⲕⲱⲃ** (Crum 99a), 'leaven', lit. 'doubling' = **ⲕⲱⲃ**, 'to double'.

ᴮ**ⲕⲁⲃⲁⲓ** (Crum 99a), 'cages, baskets (?) of wickerwork' = (Er. 534, 3), *ḳb3t*, 'mat'.

ERICHSEN, *Dem. Glossar*, 534, 3 [1954].

ᴮ**ⲕⲏⲃⲓ** (Crum 99b), 'jar, pitcher' = (*Wb.* V, 25, 2–6), *ḳby*(*t*), 'jar, jug'; (Er. 534, 2), *ḳbt*, a vessel.

ᴴBRUGSCH, *Wb.* 1444 [1868], cf. MACADAM, *The Temples of Kawa*, I, 63 n. 120 [1949]; ᴰERICHSEN, *Dem. Glossar*, 534, 2 [1954].

ⲕⲱⲱⲃⲉ, ⲕⲱⲱϥⲉ (Crum 99b), 'compel, seize by force' = (*Wb.* V, 121, 2 ff.), *kfʿ*, 'make booty'; (Er. 534, 4), *ḳby*, 'compel'.

ᴴCHAMPOLLION, *Dict.* 408 [1841]; ᴰGRIFFITH-THOMPSON, III, 89, no. 950 [1909].

ⲕⲃⲁ (Crum 99b), 'vengeance', belongs to **ⲕⲃⲟ** (Crum 100a), 'become cool', see the next entry.

ˢ**ⲕⲃⲟ**, ᴮ**ϫⲃⲟⲃ** (Crum 100a), 'be, become cool' = (*Wb.* V, 22, 5 ff.), *ḳb*, *ḳbb*; (Er. 533, 11), *ḳb*, 'become cool'.

ᴴDE ROUGÉ, *Oeuv. div.* III (= *Bibl. ég.* XXIII), 206 [1857]; ᴰBRUGSCH, *Wb.* 1442 [1868].

ⲕⲃⲁ (Crum 99b), 'vengeance' = (Er. 534, 1), *ḳb* (*ḳb3*), 'vengeance, take vengeance'.

KRALL, *Mit. aus der Sammlung Erzh. Rainer*, VI, 76, no. 321 [1897].

[B]ⲕⲃⲱⲟⲩ (Crum 100a) = *ḳbwy* (*ASAE* 25, 233 n. 2; = *ḳbb*, *Wb.* v, 24, 13), 'northern wind'; (not in Er., ex. Ankhsh. 20, 14), *ḳbbw*, 'cold winds'.

[H]STERN, *Kopt. Gr.* 58, § 122 [1880]; cf. SPIEGELBERG, *Kopt. Etym.* 11 [1920]; [D]GLANVILLE's index.

ⲕⲱⲃϩ (Crum 100a), 'sinew, cord' = (*Wb.* v, 26, 1–2 and 3), *ḳbht*, 'tendon'; (Er. 535, 4), *ḳbḥ*, 'sinew'.

[H]BOTTI-PEET, *Il Giornale della necropoli*, 36 n. 3 [1928]; cf. GARDINER, *Onom.* II, 255* [1947]; KLASENS, *A Magical Statue Base*, 110 [1952]; [D]GRIFFITH-THOMPSON, III, 89, no. 951 [1909].

[A2]ⲕⲃϩⲱ⸗ (not in Crum; Natura rerum [Till]), refl., 'cool (oneself)', 'calm down' = (*Wb.* v, 26, 6 ff.), *ḳbḥ*, 'become, make cool'; (Er. 534, 8), *ḳbḥ*, same meaning.

ⲕⲁⲕ (Crum 100b, 'part of bird'), evidently 'feathers' since it is in plural and corresponds to ريش. Identical with or related to ⲕⲟⲩⲕ ('a bird?'), see next entry.

ⲕⲟⲩⲕ (Crum 100b) is, since listed between ⲙⲉϩⲉ and ⲧⲉⲛϩ 'feather', rather a part of a bird than 'a bird', despite the existence of (*Wb.* v, 71, 11), *ḳḳ*, a bird. This ⲕⲟⲩⲕ is perhaps the same word as the preceding ⲕⲁⲕ.

ⲕⲟⲩⲕ (Crum 100b), nuts of 'dûm-palm (*Hyphaene thebaica* Mart.)' = (*Wb.* v, 21, 14–15), *ḳ(w)ḳ(w)*; (Er. 569, 1), *kk*, 'dûm-palm nuts'.

ⲃⲛⲛⲉ ⲕⲟⲩⲕ (Crum 100b), 'dûm-palm', lit. 'date-palm of (i.e. bearing) *kūk*' = (Er. 569, 1), *bny kwk*.

[HD]SPIEGELBERG, *Mythus*, 280, no. 872 [1917].

ⲕⲱⲕ (Crum 100b), 'peel, strip off' = (*Wb.* v, 71, 12), *ḳḳ*, 'peel'.

PEET in *JEA* 11, 46 n. 2 [1925].

ⲕⲱⲕ ⲁϩⲏⲩ (Crum 101a), 'strip, make naked', for *ⲕⲱⲕϩⲏⲩ, see ϩⲏⲩ.

ⲕⲟⲩⲕⲉ (Crum 101a), 'rind, skin' = (Er. 551, 1), *ḳḳt*, 'rind'; cf. (*Wb.* v, 71, 13), *ḳḳty*, 'rind?'.

[H]ERMAN-GRAPOW, *Wb.* v, 71, 13 [1931]; [D]HESS, *Gnost. Pap.* 15 [1892].

ⲕⲱⲕ (Crum Add. xvii–xviii), rubric in magical texts = ^{O}ϫⲱⲱϫ (Crum 101 b, s.v. ⲕⲁⲕⲉ), demon of darkness = (*Wb.* v, 144, 13), *kkw*, one of the eight primaeval gods, personification of darkness.

GRIFFITH-THOMPSON, I, 45 [1904].

ⲕⲁⲕⲉ (Crum 101 b), 'darkness' = (*Wb.* v, 142, bottom, and 143, 1 ff.), *kkw*; (Er. 568, 11), *kky*, 'darkness'.

^{H}CHAMPOLLION, *Gr. ég.* 62, 79 [1836]; ^{D}BRUGSCH, *Scriptura Aeg. dem.* 29, II [1848].

^{O}ϫⲱⲱϫ, see above under ⲕⲱⲕ, demon of darkness.

^{A2}**ⲕⲟⲩⲕⲟⲩ** (not in Crum; Mani Ps. 165, 2), vb. = 'coo' of doves, and prob. of other birds; found also as first part in ⲕⲁⲕⲟⲩ-ⲡⲁⲧ, 'hoopoe' and ^{B}ϫⲁⲕⲕⲁ-ⲙⲁⲩ, 'small night owl'. Cf. also various European words cited by D. W. Thompson, *Glossary of Greek Birds* (Oxford, 1936), s.v. κικκάβη and κοῦκκος, and Arabic قوقى, 'to cluck (of hen)'. All onomatopoetic.

ⲕⲟⲩⲕⲗⲉ (Crum 101 b), 'hood, cowl' of monks, like Gk. κουκούλλιον from Latin *cucullа*, itself perhaps of Gaulish origin (Pauly-Wissowa IV, col. 1739) though the Coptic word and Anglo-Saxon *cugle* (borrowed between 450 and 650) perhaps directly from Gaulish. Cf. GASELEE, *Journal of Theological Studies*, 34, 331 [1933].

ⲕⲁⲕⲟⲩⲡⲁⲧ (Crum 102 a), 'hoopoe' = (Er. 551, 3), *k̰k̰pt*, 'hoopoe'; for the first part., cf. (*Wb.* v, 71, 11), *k̰k̰*, a bird.

^{H}GARDINER in DAVIES, *The Tomb of Menkheperrasonb*, 25 and 26 [1933]; cf. GARDINER, *Onomastica*, I, 9 [1947]; ^{D}BRUGSCH, *Scriptura Aeg. dem.* 17, § 15 [1848].

The second part -ⲡⲁⲧ is onomatopoetic like דוּכִיפַת, Greek ἔποψ, Latin *upupa* and Arabic هُدْهُد; ⲕⲁⲕⲟⲩ- is perhaps a more general word for 'bird', cf. ϫⲁⲕⲕⲁ-ⲙⲁⲩ under ⲕⲟⲩⲕⲟⲩ above.

^{O}**ⲕⲉⲗ** (Crum 102 a), [illegible], unidentified animal = (Er. 545, 8), *k̰l*, an animal, and possibly (Ankhsh. 15, 11; 23, 15), *kl*, an animal.

VOLTEN, *Dem. Traumdeutung*, 116 [1942].

^{S}**ⲕⲗⲉ**, ^{B}**ⲕⲗⲏ** (Crum 102 a), vessel for liquids; from Semitic, cf. Hebrew כְּלִי.

CALICE in *OLZ* 35, col. 254 [1932].

[S]ⲕⲗⲏ (Crum 102a), 'cat' = (Er. 545, 8, confused with *ḳl*, ⲕⲉⲗ), *ḳlỉt*, 'cat'.

CRUM, *A Coptic Dict.* 102a [1930].

ⲙⲁϫⲉ ⲕⲗⲏ = , *msḏ n ḳlỉt*, lit. 'cat's ears', a plant (Dem. Mag. Pap., vo. 7, 1).

CHASSINAT, *Pap. méd.* 245 [1921].

[B]ⲁⲕⲗⲏ, [SB]ⲕⲁⲗⲏ (Crum 102a and 3b under ⲁⲕⲗⲏ), 'weasel' = (Er. 573, 14), *gꜥlꜣt*, 'weasel', from Greek γαλέη, γαλῆ, 'weasel' and akin animals.

[D]CHASSINAT, *Pap. méd.* 244 [1921]; [G]PEYRON, *Lex.* 3 [1835].

ⲕⲗⲟ (Crum 102b), vegetable (?) poison used for arrows = (Er. 565, 7), *ḳrꜥꜣ*, 'poison'.

[D]GRIFFITH-THOMPSON, III, 87, no. 919 [1909].

ⲕⲉⲗⲉⲃⲓⲛ (Crum 102b), 'axe, pickaxe' = Dem. κολεβειν (*Actes 5e Cong. Papyrol.* 1938, 79), translated ἀξίνη; from Semitic, cf. Aramaic כַּלְבָּא (Dalman, p. 188b) as also Greek πέλεκυς.

[S]ROSSI, *Etym. aeg.* 84 [1808].

[B]ⲕⲉⲗⲕⲁ (Crum 102b), [S]ⲕⲗⲕⲁ (Ex. 45, 19, acc. to P. Bodmer XVI; cf. *CdÉ* 37, 418), 'lump, pustule,' cf. ? (*Wb.* v, 109, 9), *kꜣkꜣwt* (Plural of *kꜣkꜣt*?), 'blister'. Prob. also contained in ⲕⲉⲗⲕⲟⲩⲗⲉ (Crum 103a), same meaning as ⲕⲉⲗⲕⲁ.

VON DEINES and WESTENDORF, *Wörterbuch der medizinschen Texte*, 898 n. 1 [1962].

[B]ⲕⲁⲗⲟⲩⲕⲓ (Crum 103a), 'young camel' or 'ox'; perhaps only 'young animal' = ?Gk. κουλουκής, a word for dog (Sophocles, 685).

ⲕⲁⲗⲕⲓⲗ and sim. (Crum 103a), ϭⲁⲗⲓⲗ (Crum 810b), 'wheel', a loan-word from Semitic, cf. Hebrew גַּלְגַּל and גְּלִיל.

ROSSI, *Etym. aeg.* 310 [1808].

ⲕⲗⲁⲕⲗⲉⲕ (Crum 103a), 'astragalus (the plant or its gum)', see ⲗⲟⲕⲗⲉⲕ under ⲗⲱⲕ, 'be soft, fresh'.

ⲕⲗⲁⲗ (Crum 103a), 'chain' esp. on neck = (Er. 547, 1), *ḳll*, 'chain'; as loan word in Gk. κλάλιον, κλανίον.

GRIFFITH, *Ryl.* III, 399 [1909].

ⲕⲗⲉⲗ (Crum 103b, s.v. ⲕⲗⲁⲗ), 'pill' (e.g. ⲕⲗⲉⲗ ⲛϩⲁⲥⲙ, 'pill of natron', ⲕⲗⲉⲗ ⲛϩⲙⲟⲩ, 'pill of salt') = Aramaic גְּלָל, 'pill' (Dalman, p. 75).
DÉVAUD's slip.

ⲕⲗⲗⲉ (Crum 103b), 'bolt, joint' = [hieroglyphs] (*Wb.* v, 12, 2 ff.), *ḳ3rt*; [demotic] (Er. 545, 9), *ḳl3t*, 'bolt'.
HBRUGSCH, *ZÄS* 1, 42 [1863]; DREVILLOUT, *Rev. ég.* 1, fasc. 4, pl. 3 and 4 [1880].

ⲕⲉⲗⲉⲛⲕⲉϩ (Crum 104a), 'elbow' = ⲕⲗⲗⲉ, 'joint' + [hieroglyphs] (*Wb.* v, 19, 6 ff.), *ḳʿḥ*, 'upper arm, shoulder'.
ERMAN, *Äg. Glossar*, 133 [1904].

ⲕⲉⲗⲱⲗ (Crum 104a), 'pitcher, jar' = ?[hieroglyphs] (*Wb.* v, 135, 8), *krr*, a vessel, Dem. κρωρι (*Actes 5e Cong. Papyrol.* 1938, 79, translated κεράτιον); [demotic] (not in Er., ex. Ankhsh. 23, 23), *krl*, 'pitcher'; from Semitic, cf. Arabic قُلَّة, 'earthernware pot' and Aramaic קְלָל (Dalman, p. 362). Semitic ق and ק show that the Egn. word must have originally begun with *ḳ*.
HSCHÄFER, *Eine äthiopische Königinschrift*, 116 [1901]; DGLANVILLE's index; SROSSI, *Etym. aeg.* 246 [1808].

ⲕⲗⲟⲟⲗⲉ (Crum 104a), 'cloud' = [hieroglyphs] or [hieroglyphs] (*Wb.* v, 58, 6 ff.), *ḳrr*, *ḳr*, 'cloud'; [demotic] (Er. 546, 7), *ḳll*, 'cloud'.
HGARDINER, *Onomastica*, 1, 5* [1947]; DSPIEGELBERG, *Mythus*, 273, no. 824 [1917].

ⲕⲉⲗⲗⲟϫ (Crum 104b), (1) puppy, whelp; (2) buffalo. Earlier only as proper name, [hieroglyphs] (Ranke 1, 336, 15–16), *ḳrḏ*; [demotic] (Er. 545, 10), *ḳlwḏ*; Κολλούθης, ⲕⲉⲗⲗⲟⲩϫ and sim. Cf. Spiegelberg, *Äg. und griech. Eigennamen*, 18*, no. 121a, and p. 40. fem. ⲕⲟⲩⲗⲱϫⲉ (only as name) = [hieroglyphs], *ḳrrwḏt* (quoted by Spiegelberg, loc. cit.).
CRUM in *Byzantinische Zeitschrift* 30, 323–5 [1929/30].

ⲕⲗⲟⲙ (Crum 104b), 'crown, wreath' = [demotic] (Er. 546, 3), *ḳlm*, 'wreath'.
BRUGSCH, *De natura et indole*, 38 [1850].
See also ϫⲗⲟⲙⲗⲉⲙ, 'to crown'.

ⲕⲗⲙⲉ (Crum 105a), 'pad, poultice' = [demotic] (Er. 546, 4), *ḳlmỉt*, 'poultice'.
CHASSINAT, *Pap. méd.* 125–6 [1921].

Bⲕⲱⲗⲡ (Crum 105b), 'steal, rob', from Greek κλέπτω, 'steal'.

ROSSI, *Etym. aeg.* 91 [1808].

NB. If ⲕⲱⲗⲡ came from , *ḫnp* (Stern in *Pap. Ebers.* II, 60 [1875]) one would expect it to begin with ϫ, as Sⲕⲱ, Bϫⲱ from *ḫ3ꜥ*.

ⲕⲗⲯ (Crum 105b), 'blow' = (Er. 546, 2), *ḳlps*, 'beat', from Greek κόλαφος, 'a buffet, blow'.

DSPIEGELBERG, *Krüge*, 75, no. 221 [1912]; GROSSI, *Etym. aeg.* 337 [1808].

Bⲕⲁⲗⲧ- (Crum 106a), 'be hairless' < *ⲕⲁⲗⲡ- from Sϭⲱⲗⲡ, Bϭⲱⲣⲡ, 'uncover, open, reveal'. Bⲕⲁⲗⲧϫⲱϥ = Sϭⲁⲗⲡϫⲱϥ.

ⲕⲱⲗϩ (Crum 106b), 'knock, strike' = (Er. 547, 2), *ḳlh*, 'knock, strike'.

HESS, *Gnost. Pap.* 15 [1892].

ⲕⲁⲗⲁϩⲏ (Crum 107a), 'womb' = (*Wb.* v. 62, 12 f.), *ḳrḥt*, '(earthenware) vessel, container, recipient' > (*Wb.* v, 63, 10), *ḳrḥt*, 'ancestral matrice', also personified as goddess (*Wb.* v, 63, 5), *ḳrḥt*; Graeco-Roman , *ḳrḥt*, , *ḳrḥt* (temple of Esna), or (*Wb.* v, 183, 11), *grḥt*, or (P. Carlsberg I), *khr3t*, 'womb'.

SAUNERON, *Quatre campagnes à Esna*, 46 [1959]; cf. Sauneron in *Mélanges Maspero*, I, fasc. 4, 113–20 [1961]; cf. LANGE in LANGE-NEUGEBAUER, *Papyrus Carlsberg No. I*, 82 [1940] (implies the identification by translating *khr3t*, 'Mutterleib').

ⲕⲱⲗϫ (Crum 107b), 'bend' = (Er. 567, 10), *kḏ*, 'bend'.

SPIEGELBERG, *Mythus*, 279, no. 865 [1917].

ⲕⲁⲙ (Crum 108a), 'reed, rush', probably *Juncus maritimus* Lam. = (*Wb.* v, 37, 14), *ḳm3*, 'reed', and (*Wb.* v, 170, 5), *gmy*, a plant; (Er. 537, 3), *ḳm*, 'reed'. Borrowed into Hebrew as גֹּמֶא.

HDBRUGSCH, *Wb.* 1452 [1868]; cf. Keimer in *OLZ* 30, col. 153 [1927]; CAMINOS, *LEM*, 167 [1954].

ⲕⲓⲙ (Crum 108a), 'move, be moved' = (*Wb.* v, 33, 8 ff.), *ḳm3*, 'throw, move'; (Er. 537, 2), *ḳm*, 'move'.

HSPIEGELBERG in *Rec. trav.* 26, 165 [1904]; DHESS, *Gnost. Pap.* 15 [1892].

For Oⲕⲙⲡⲧⲟ̑, see separate entry below.

ⲕⲙⲕⲙ (Crum 109a), 'strike, beat a musical instrument' = (Er. 564, 2), *kmkm*, 'strike'.

ROSSI, *Grammatica egizia*, 37 [1901].

'drum' = (stela Cairo J. 49566 from Edfu, XVIIth Dyn.), , (*Wb.* v, 40, 5), *ḳmḳm*, kind of drum; (Er. 538, 3), *ḳmḳm*, kind of drum.

[H]SPIEGELBERG, *Anc. Egypt* 1, 110 n. 5 [1914]; [D]REVILLOUT, *Rev. ég.* 14, 11 n. 11 [1914].

ⲕⲙⲟⲙ (Crum 109b), 'become black' = (*Wb.* v, 124, 6–8); (Er. 563, 2), *km(m)*, 'become black'.

[H]BRUGSCH, *Wb.* 1450 [1868]; [D]SPIEGELBERG, *Mythus*, 278, no. 855 [1917].

ⲕⲁⲙⲉ (Crum 109b), 'black' = (*Wb.* v, 123, 1 ff.); (Er. 563, 2), *km*, 'black'.

[H]CHAMPOLLION, *Gr. ég.* 319, 320–1 [1836]; [D]BRUGSCH, *Gr. dém.* 120, §243 [1855].

-ⲕⲁⲙ in **ⲁⲛⲓⲕⲁⲙ** (see this), a kind of vitriol, lit. 'black stone'.

ⲕⲙⲏⲙⲉ (Crum 110b), 'darkness' = (Er. 563, bottom), *kmmt*, also , *kmỉmỉt*, 'darkness'.

CRUM, *A Coptic Dict.* 110b [1930].

ⲕⲏⲙⲉ (Crum 110a), 'black' land = Egypt, (*Wb.* v, 126, 7 ff.), *kmt*; (Er. 564, 1), *kmy*, 'Egypt'.

[H]CHAMPOLLION, *Gr.* 152 [1836]; [D]ÅKERBLAD, *Lettre*, 32–3 and Pl. 1, no. 10 [1802].

ⲣⲙⲛⲕⲏⲙⲉ (Crum 110a and 295b), 'Egyptian' = (*Wb.* II, 423, 9; v, 127, 13, 14), *rmṯ n kmt*, lit. 'man of Egypt'; (Er. 247, middle; 564, middle), *rmt (n) kmy*.

[H]CHABAS, *Voyage*, 350 [1866]; [D]BRUGSCH, *Scriptura Aeg. dem.* 3 [1848].

ⲙⲛⲧⲣⲙⲛⲕⲏⲙⲉ (Crum 110a), 'Egyptian nationality, speech' = L.Eg. (*Wb.* v, 127, 17), *mdt rmṯ n kmt*, lit. 'speech of man of Egypt'; , *mt rmt n Kmy*.

[H]ERMAN-GRAPOW, *Wb.* v, 127, 17 [1931]; [D]BRUGSCH, *De natura et indole*, 7 [1850].

ⲕⲟⲙⲙⲉ (Crum 110b), 'gum' = (*Wb.* v, 39, 3 ff.), *ḳmyt*, 'resin, gum'; (Er. 537b), *ḳmỉ*, 'gum'.

^H DE ROUGÉ, *Oeuv. div.* IV (= *Bibl. ég.* XXIV), 140–1 [1861]; ^D BRUGSCH, *Gr. dém.* 26, §51 [1855].

ⲕⲏⲙⲉ ⲛϣⲟⲛⲧⲉ (Crum 110b) = (*Wb.* V, 39, 4 and IV, 521, 3), *ḳmyt nt šndt* 'resin of acacia'.

ERMAN-GRAPOW, *Wb.* IV, 521, 3 [1930].

^O **ⲕⲙⲡⲧⲟ̄**, ^O **ⲕⲟⲙⲧⲱ** (Crum 109a, s.v. **ⲕⲓⲙ**), 'creator of earth' = * (*Wb.* V, 34, 3), *ḳmꜣ-tꜣ*; (Griffith-Thompson, III, 122, no. 239); *ḳm-tꜣ*, 'creator of earth' (*sic*, rather than **ⲕⲙⲧⲟ**, 'earthquake').

MÖLLER in Preisendanz, *Papyri graecae magicae*, I, 61 n. 8 [1928].

^B **ⲕⲏⲛ** (Crum 111a), 'cease, finish' = (*Wb.* V, 49, 1 ff.), *ḳn*, 'finish'; (Er. 538, 5), *ḳn*, 'cease'. **ⲕⲏⲛ**, originally a Qual. (from Inf. ***ⲕⲱⲛ**), does double duty for Inf. and Qual. (Steindorff, *Lehrbuch*, §230).

^H BRUGSCH, *Wb.* 1463–4 [1868]; ^D BRUGSCH, *Gr. dém.* 37, §78 [1855].

ⲕⲟⲩⲛ⸗ (Crum 111b), 'bosom' = (*Wb.* V, 50, 13 ff.), *ḳnỉ*, 'embrace, bosom'; (Er. 538, 7), *ḳn*, 'lap'.

^H CHAMPOLLION, *Dict.* 453 [1841]; ^D GRIFFITH, *Stories*, 167 [1900].

^B **ⲕⲛⲓⲕⲓϫⲓ** (Crum 111b), vessel or measure for liquids, prob. corrupted from ***ⲕⲛⲓϫⲓ**, i.e. κνίδιον, sc. κεράμιον, 'Cnidian (vessel)'.

ⲕⲛⲛⲉ (Crum 111b), 'be fat' = (*Wb.* V, 40, 8 ff.), *ḳn*, 'become fat, (be) fat'.

STERN in *Pap. Ebers*, II, 34 [1875]; cf. BRUGSCH, *Wb.* 1460 [1868].

See also **ⲕⲓⲱⲟⲩ**.

ⲕⲱⲛⲥ (Crum 112a), 'pierce, slay' = (Er. 541, 4), *ḳns*, 'slay', from Semitic, cf. Aram. כְּנַס, Syr. ܟܢܣ. See also next entry.

^D SPIEGELBERG, *Mythus*, 272, no. 815 [1917]; ^S DÉVAUD, *Kêmi*, 2, 7 [1929].

ⲕⲛⲟⲥ (Crum 112b), 'stink, be putrid', cf. , *ḳnst* (fem.), 'stinking', perhaps IInd Infinitive of the preceding word.

^D BRUGSCH, *ZÄS* 26, 33 [1888].

ⲕⲛⲧⲉ (Crum 112b), 'fig' = (*Wb.* V, 117, 6), *kwnt*, name of a sacred tree; (Er. 543, 1), *ḳnṯ*, 'fig'.

^H DÜMICHEN, *Bauurkunde der Tempelanlagen von Dendera*, 35 [1865]; cf. BRUGSCH, *Wb.* 1490 [1868]; ^D BRUGSCH, *Gr. dém.* 26, §51 [1855].

ⲕⲛⲁⲁⲩ (Crum 112b), 'sheaf' = (*Wb.* v, 52, 5), *ḳnỉw* (pl.), 'sheafs'.

ERMAN-GRAPOW, *Äg. Hdwb.* 190 [1921]; SPIEGELBERG, *Kopt. Handwb.* 42 [1921].

[B]**ⲕⲉⲛⲉⲫⲓⲧⲉⲛ** (Crum 113a), kind of loaf or cake, = (*Wb.* v, 32, 16), *ḳfn*, kind of bread; (Er. 536, 8), *ḳfn*, or (Er. 541, 2), *ḳnf*, kind of bread, + (*Wb.* I, 146, 6), *ỉtnw*, 'ashes'(?).

BRUGSCH, *Dict. géo.*, Suppl. 1204 [1880] + VERGOTE, *Muséon*, 63, 293 [1950]; but cf. SPIEGELBERG in *ZÄS* 53, 132–3 [1917].

[B]**ⲕⲉⲛⲉϥⲓⲧⲏⲥ** (Crum 113a), 'baker', Greek formation from **ⲕⲉⲛⲉϥⲓⲧⲉⲛ**.

SPIEGELBERG, *ZÄS* 53, 133 [1917].

[B]**ⲕⲁⲛⲟⲩϥⲓ** (Crum 113a), a fish, *barbus bynni* = (Er. 362, 7), *ḫnfy*.

BRUGSCH, *Wb.* 1097 [1868].

ⲕⲛϩⲉ (Crum 113a), 'porch, shrine' = (*Wb.* v, 133, 13), fem., *ḳnḥ*, a designation of palace; (P. mag. Salt 18, 6; not in *Wb.*), *ḳnḥ*, 'shrine'; (Er. 541, 3), *ḳnḥ*, 'shrine', lit. 'dark (place), from (not in *Wb.*; exx. *ZÄS* 86, 113–14), *ḳnḥ*, 'grow, make dark'.

[D]BRUGSCH, *Wb.* 1462 [1868].

ⲕⲟⲩⲛϫⲟⲩ (Crum 113a adding **ⲕⲛϫⲟⲩ** *Klio* 13, 174), a vessel = (Er. 543, 3), *ḳnḏw*, 'container, large plate'. Same as the older (O. DM 347, 1), *ḳḏ*?

SPIEGELBERG, *Kopt. Handwb.* 42 [1921].

ⲕⲁⲡ (Crum 113a), 'string (of a harp), shread, strand', cf. ? (*Wb.* v, 118, 13. 14), *ḳp*, material for bandages.

DE MEULENAERE in *Chronique d'Égypte*, vol. 41, no. 82, 408 [1966].

ⲕⲱⲡ (Crum 113b), 'hide, be hidden' = (*Wb.* v, 104, 14 ff.), *ḳ3p*; (Er. 535, 7), *ḳp*, 'to hide'.

[H]CHABAS, *Voyage*, 157 and 225 [1866]; [D]LEXA, *Beiträge*, no. 508 [1916].

ⲕⲁⲡⲁⲓ (Crum 114a), [B]**ⲕⲁⲫⲁⲓ** (Crum 130a), '(Egyptian) partridge' ('sandgrouse' acc. to Calice, *OLZ* 35, col. 254) = (*Wb.* v, 105, 2), *ḳ3pw*, name of a bird.

BRUGSCH, *Wb.*, Suppl. 1275 [1882]; cf. LORET, *ZÄS* 30, 26 [1892]; cf. VERGOTE, *Muséon*, 63, 292 [1950].

ⲕⲏⲡⲉ (Crum 114a), 'vaulted place, cellar, canopy' = (*Wb.* v, 104, 6), *kꜣpw*, 'roof', or (*Wb.* v, 104, 7), *kꜣpt*, 'roof (of the sky)'; (Er. 536, 2), *ḳp*, 'vault, roof'.

HDSPIEGELBERG, *Kopt. Handwb.* 42 [1921]; cf. VERGOTE, *Muséon*, 63, 291 [1950].

Different from **ⲕⲩⲡⲏ** which is Greek κύπη (γύπη).

ⲕⲟⲩⲡⲣ (Crum 114a), a plant, *Lawsonia inermis* = (Er. 536, 4), *ḳpr*, 'henna', from Semitic (cf. כֹּפֶר) like Greek κύπρος. As pers. name (Ranke I, 333, 29), *ḳwpr* (masc.), fem. in Coptic **ⲕⲟⲩⲡⲉⲣ** = , Young, *Hieroglyphics*, I, Pl. 5; , ib. Pl. 6.

HEUSER, *Die kopt. Eigennamen äg. Ursprungs*, 35; 72 n. 2 [1929].

DBRUGSCH, *Gr. dém.* 26, §44 [1855].

B**ⲕⲁⲡϣⲱ** (Crum 114b), 'sandy land', from the expression S(**ⲟⲩⲥⲱϣⲉ ⲉⲥ**)**ⲕⲏ ⲉⲡϣⲱ**, '(a field) lying on sand'.

SPIEGELBERG, *Kopt. Etymologien*, 32 [1920].

ⲕⲟⲩⲣ (Crum 115a), 'pivot, hinge' of door = (Er. 576, 1), *gwri*, 'pivot'. Prob. from Semitic, cf. קוּר. قار, 'cut a round hole'.

CRUM, *A Coptic Dict.* 115a [1930].

ⲕⲱⲣ, ϭⲱⲣ (Crum 115a), (1) quantity of money, less than carat; (2) **ⲕⲱⲣ**, a wine measure, from Aramaic כּוֹר (Dalman 185b) which is translated into Greek as κόρος; it contained 10 Attic medimni. The subform **ⲕⲟⲩⲣⲓ** was probably influenced by Ionian κοῦρος for κόρος, 'boy'.

KRALL, *Kopt. Texte*, I (= *Corpus pap. Raineri*, II), p. 41 [1895].

ⲕⲣⲟ (Crum 115a), 'shore, further side, limit' = (Er. 543, 4), *ḳr*, 'shore'.

REVILLOUT, *Setna*, 193 [1877].

ⲕⲁⲓⲣⲉ (Crum 115a), 'gullet, belly' from Semitic, cf. Hebrew גָּרוֹן, Arab. جِران.

DÉVAUD's slip.

S**ⲕⲟⲣϩ**, B**ⲕⲟⲣⲕⲥ** (Crum 115b), also B**ⲕⲉⲣⲁϩ** (K 124) '(iron) hoe' and an instrument of torture = Greek κόραξ, lit. 'raven', also an instrument of torture (Lucian, *Necyomantia*, 11).

J. J. HESS in DÉVAUD, *Rec. trav.* 39, 157 n. 4 [1921].

ⲕⲱⲱⲣⲉ (Crum 115b), 'cut down (trees, crops)', from Semitic, cf. Hebrew קָרַע, 'tear to pieces'.

STRICKER in *Acta Orientalia* 15, 4 [1937].

ⲕⲱⲣⲙ (Crum 116a), 'smoke' = (Er. 544, 3), *ḳrm*, 'smoke'.

SPIEGELBERG, *Mythus*, 273, no. 820 [1917].

See also **ⲕⲣⲙⲧⲥ**, 'smoke, mist'.

ⲕⲣⲙⲣⲙ (Crum 116a), 'murmur, be vexed' = (Er. 544, 5), *ḳrmrm*, 'murmur'.

GRIFFITH-THOMPSON, III, 89, no. 960 [1909].

ⲕⲣⲟⲙⲣⲙ (Crum 116b), 'be dark', reduplication of **ⲕⲱⲣⲙ**, 'smoke'; **ⲕⲣⲙⲧⲥ** 'smoke, mist', see separate entry below.

^{S}**ⲕⲣⲙⲉⲥ**, ^{B}**ⲕⲉⲣⲙⲓ** (Crum 117a), 'ash, soot, dust', cf. (*Wb.* v, 60, 12), *ḳrmt*, 'ashes' (of burnt tents); (Er. 565, 9), *krb*, or (Volten, *Ägypter und Amazonen*, 114), *krm*, fem. 'ashes'.

^{H}BURCHARDT, *Die altkanaan. Fremdworte*, II, 47, no. 919 [1910]; ^{D}LEXA, *Papyrus Insinger*, II, 121, no. 526 [1926].

ⲕⲣⲙⲧⲥ (Crum 116b, s.v. **ⲕⲣⲟⲙⲣⲙ**), 'smoke, mist' = (Er. 544, 6), *ḳrmṯs*, 'darkness'.

REVILLOUT, *Rev. ég.* 4, 87 n. 4 [1885].

See also **ⲕⲱⲣⲙ**, 'smoke'.

ⲕⲣⲟⲩⲣ (Crum 117a), 'frog' = (*Wb.* v, 61, 5); (Er. 544, 7), *ḳrr*, 'frog'.

^{H}BRUGSCH, *Wb.*, Suppl. 1235 (in the name *Tꜣ-kr*) [1882]; STEINDORFF, *ZÄS* 30, 63 (in the proper name *Pꜣ-ḳrr*) [1892]; SPIEGELBERG, *Rec. trav.* 15, 67 (appellative) [1893]; ^{D}KRALL, *Mitteil. Erzherzog Rainer*, VI, 55 (in *Pꜣ-ḳrr*) [1897]; SPIEGELBERG, *Mythus*, 273, no. 823 (appellative) [1917].

ⲕⲁⲣⲟⲩⲥ (Crum 117b), 'yellowish' of hair = or (not in Er.), *ḳr(w)s*, 'yellowish', a loan-word from Greek κιρρός, 'orange-tawny'.

^{DG}SPIEGELBERG in *Rec. trav.* 35, 88 n. 3 [1913].

ⲕⲉⲣⲏⲧ (Crum 117b), 'dung, dirt', see **ϭⲉⲣⲏⲧ**.

ⲕⲱⲣϣ (Crum 117b), 'request, persuade, cajole' = (Er. 545, 2), *ḳrš*, 'cajole'.

REVILLOUT, *Pap. mor.* II, 72 n. 3 (ad 35, 1) [1908] (= *Journal as.* XI, 310 [1908]).

ⲕⲱⲣϥ (Crum 118a), 'bring to naught, cancel, destroy' and (ϭⲱⲣϥ) (Crum 829b), 'nip off' and B(ϫⲱⲣⲉⲃ) (Crum 785a), 'cut open (?)' = (*Wb.* v, 135, 6), *krp*, 'remove, efface' (an inscription); (Er. 565, 13), *krf*, 'refuse' or sim. Perhaps from Semitic, cf. جَرَفَ, 'remove, rake'.

HERMAN-GRAPOW, *Wb.* v, 135, 6 [1931]; DGRIFFITH, *Ryl.* III, 399 [1909]; SSTRICKER in *Acta Orientalia* 15, 5 [1937].

ⲕⲣⲟϥ (Crum 118b), 'guile, ambush', cf. (*Wb.* v, 60, 7), *ḳrf*, 'bend'; (Er. 544, 1), *ḳrf*, 'guile'.

HERMAN-GRAPOW, *Wb.* v, 60, 7 [1931]; DBRUGSCH, *Gr. dém.* 35, § 70 [1855].

ⲕⲉⲣϩⲉ (Crum 119a), 'bald person', from Semitic, cf. Hebrew and Aram. קֵרֵחַ, Syriac ܩܪܚܐ, 'bald' (Lagarde, *Übersicht*, 69).

ROSSI, *Etym. aeg.* 87 [1808].

ⲕⲱⲣϫ (Crum 119a), 'cut down, break off', = (not in Er.), [*kr*]*ḏ*, 'cut off', from Semitic, cf. Hebrew קָרַץ.

DSPIEGELBERG in *Aegyptus* 11, 74 [1931]; SSPIEGELBERG, *Kopt. Handwb.* 44 [1921].

ⲕⲣⲟⲩϫ (Crum 119b), a baked or fried cake, from Semitic, cf. Aram. גְּרִיץ גְּרִיצְתָּא (fem.), Pl. גְּרִיצָן (Dalman), Ar. قُرْص 'round and flat bread' (Belot).

DÉVAUD's slip.

ⲕⲁⲥ, ⲕⲉⲉⲥ (Crum 119b), 'bone' = (*Wb.* v, 68, 2 ff.), *ḳs* (for *ḳrs*, see Lacau in *Syria*, 31, 299); (Er. 548, 3), *ḳs*, 'bone'.

HCHABAS, *Pap. mag. Harris*, 249, no. 869 [1860]; DBRUGSCH, *Gr. dém.* 74, § 161 [1855].

ⲕⲁⲥ (Crum 120a), 'carat', a coin, lit. 'bone', a translation of Greek κεράτιον, $\frac{1}{24}$ of *solidus* (diminutive of κέρας, 'horn'); from the latter Ar. قِيرَاط and from this our 'carat'.

ⲕⲟⲉⲓⲥ (Crum 120a), vessel for liquids, κόϊς (Preisigke III, 360) = Late Aeth. (*Wb.* v, 108, 17), *kꜣs*, a vessel (of metal); (Er. 560, 6), *kys*, a vessel.

ⲕⲱⲱⲥ (Crum 120a), 'dress, prepare corpse for burial, bury' = (*Wb.* v, 63, 11 ff.), *ḳrs*; (Er. 548, 4), *ḳs*, 'bury'.

HCHAMPOLLION, *Gr. ég.* 372 and 374 [1836]; DBRUGSCH, *Scriptura Aeg. dem.* 19, § 21 [1848].

ⲕⲁⲓⲥⲉ (Crum 121a), 'preparation for burial, embalming' = (*Wb.* v, 64, 8), *ḳrst*, 'burial'; (Er. 549, 1), *ḳst*, 'burial, embalming'.

HERMAN, *ZÄS* 21, 95 [1883]; DBRUGSCH, *Rhind*, 47 and Pl. 43, no. 383 [1865].

ⲕⲁⲥⲉ (Crum 121a), 'shoemaker' = (*Wb.* v, 203, 1 ff.), *gs*, 'shoemaker' > ?L.Egn. (O. Michaelides 6, 2), *ḳs*; (Er. 549, middle), *ḳs*, 'shoemaker'.

HDDE MEULENAERE in *ZÄS* 80, 80 [1955].

ⲕⲁⲥⲕⲉⲥ (Crum 121a), 'whisper' = (Er. 550, 5), *ḳsḳs*, 'whisper'. From Semitic, cf. Arabic كَشْكَش, 'to rustle'.

DREVILLOUT, *Rev. ég.* 2, fasc. 2–3, pl. 23 [1881]; SROSSI, *Etym. aeg.* 244 [1808]; cf. STRICKER in *Acta Orientalia* 15, 3 [1937].

ⲕⲟⲥⲕⲥ ⲉⲃⲟⲗ (Crum 121b), refl. 'bend, entwine' = L.Egn. (*LES* 43, 8), *ksks*, 'bend down'; (not in *Wb.*; exx.: O. IFAO 1263, vo. 5; O. Berlin 12343, 6), *ksks*, fem., a basket (with legs), and (not in *Wb.*; exx.: O. DM 146, 7; P. BM 10052, 3, 20; 4, 4), *ksksty*, fem., a basket, lit. '(an object) in wicker-work'.

ϭⲟⲩⲣ (Crum 121b), 'finger-ring' = (*Wb.* v, 206, 15–17), *gsr*; (Er. 568, 3), *kswr*, 'finger-ring'. From Semitic, cf. Hebrew קֶשֶׁר, 'bond', Aram. קִשְׁרָתָא, 'girdle'.

HBRUGSCH, *Wb.*, Suppl. 1305 [1882]; DBRUGSCH, *ZDMG* 6, 250 [1852]; SALBRIGHT, *The Vocalization of the Egyptian Syllabic Orthography*, 55 [1934].

ⲕⲱⲧ (Crum 122a), 'build, form' = (*Wb.* v, 72, 8 ff.), *ḳd*, 'turn pottery, build, form'; (Er. 551, 4), *ḳt* (*ḳd*), 'build'.

HCHAMPOLLION, *Gr. ég.* 381 [1836]; DBRUGSCH, *Wb.* 1478 [1868].

ⲉⲕⲱⲧ (Crum 122b), 'builder, mason, potter' = (*Wb.* I, 138, 20, and v, 74, 1 ff.), (*ỉ*)*ḳdw*, 'potter, mason, creator'; (Er. 551, 5), *ḳt* (*ḳd*), 'builder'.

H DÉVAUD, *Rec. trav.* 39, 163–5 [1921] and *Études*, 5–7 [1922]; D SPIEGELBERG, *Chronik*, 83, no. 257 [1914].

ⲥⲉ-ⲕⲱⲧ (Crum 123a), 'potter's place, workshop' = *, *st* (*ỉ*)*ḳdw*, 'potter's place', in Plural (in an inscription at Philae).

JUNKER, *WZKM* 31, 60 and 69 n. 44 [1924]; cf. Crum in Crum and Bell, *Wadi Sarga*, p. 144 n. 4 [1922] and Dévaud, *Études*, 9 [1922].

ⲕⲓⲧⲉ (Crum 123b), 'double drachma' = ½ stater = (*Wb.* v, 79, 15), *ḳdt*, weight of 9·1 gr.; , (Er. 552, 1), *ḳt*, weight of 9·1 gr.

H BIRCH in *Archaeologia* 35, 126 n. i [1853]; D BRUGSCH, *ZÄS* 29, 72 [1891]; BRUGSCH, *Thesaurus*, 1058 [1891].

ϭⲓⲥⲕⲓⲧⲉ (Crum 124a), 'half a kite = 1 drachma' = , ½ *ḳtt*, 'half a kite'.

GRIFFITH-THOMPSON, I, 151 [1904]; III, 90, no. 972 [1909].

ⲕⲓⲧⲉ (Crum 124a), 'sleep' = (*Wb.* v, 79, 7–8), *ḳdt*, 'sleep'; or (Er. 552, 3), *ḳtt* (*ḳdt*), 'sleep'.

H ERMAN, *ZÄS* 33, 58 [1895]; D GRIFFITH, *Stories*, 88 [1900].

ⲕⲱⲧⲉ (Crum 124a), 'go round, turn (trans.), turn self' = (*Wb.* v, 78, 1 ff.), *ḳdỉ*, 'go round'; (Er. 552, 4), *ḳty* (*ḳdy*), 'go round, surround'.

H GOODWIN in a letter to Renouf (Dawson, *Ch. W. Goodwin*, p. 78) [1862]; cf. CHABAS, *Voyage*, 270 [1866]; D REVILLOUT, *Chrest. dém.* 419 [1880].

ⲕⲱⲧⲉ (Crum 126a), nn. 'turning round, circuit, surroundings' = L.Egn. (*Wb.* v, 78, 9, 10), *ḳd*, 'circuit'; (Er. 553, middle), *ḳtỉt*, 'surroundings'.

H BRUGSCH, *Wb.* 1480 [1868]; D HESS, *Stne*, 181 [1888].

ⲕⲧⲟ (Crum 127b), 'turn, make to turn' (causative of ⲕⲱⲧⲉ, from *ⲧⲕⲧⲟ) = *, *dỉt ḳd*; (Er. 553, upper), *tỉ ḳt*, 'cause to go round'.

H ERMAN, *ZÄS* 22, 30 [1884]; D GRIFFITH-THOMPSON, III, 90, no. 973 [1909].

ⲕⲧⲟⲕ, ⲕⲧⲟⲟ[ⲕ] in ⲁⲧⲕⲧⲟⲕ, ⲛⲕⲧⲟⲟ[ⲕ], 'untimely', ἄωρος (P. Bodmer VI; not in Crum), this latter for *ⲛϭⲧⲟϭ, since the MS. does not use ϭ,

= (GRIFFITH-THOMPSON, III, 88, no. 938), *n gtg*, or . (P. Cairo 31213, 24), *n gtgt* (Er. 594, 8 and 595, 2), 'quickly', from *gtg*, an incomplete reduplication of *gtgt*, 'be quick, hurry' = (*Wb.* v, 146, 1 f.), *ktkt*, 'tremble, move'.

κωτϥ (Crum 129b), 'gather' corn, fruit, wood, etc., = (*Wb.* v, 81, 12), *ḳdf*, 'gather' fruit, sayings; perhaps from Semitic, cf. Hebrew קָטַף.

HSETHE in GARDINER, *Admonitions*, 97 [1909]; cf. DÉVAUD, *Kêmi*, 2, 7–9 [1929]; ČERNÝ, *Crum Memorial Volume*, 36–7 [1950]; SROSSI, *Etym. aeg.* 95 [1808].

κιωογ (qualitative) (Crum 129b), 'be fat, soft', from **κηνε**, 'become fat' and equivalent of B**κενιωογτ** which comes from B**κενι**. See **κηνε**.

DÉVAUD, *Kêmi*, 2, 9 [1929]; cf. POLOTSKY, *ZÄS* 65, 130 [1930].

κιωογ (Crum 129b, s.v. **κιωογ**, 'be fat', *in fine*), 'cyperus, κυπείρων, a sweet-smelling marsh plant' (Lidell-Scott) = ?Pl. of (*Wb.* v, 157, bottom), *gỉw*, a sweet-smelling plant; (Er. 531, 6), *ḳỉ*, a plant of which mats are made.

HBRUGSCH, *Wb.* 1507 [1868]; DMÖLLER, *Pap. Rhind*, 57*, no. 390 [1913]. NB. The word is a *hapax* and Crum doubts its existence, but his emendation of P 44, 82 into **βω ηκιωογ** ('soft shrub') is not satisfactory: **κιωογ** becoming thus Qual. could not join the preceding noun by means of **η-**.

κοογ (Crum 130a), 'length of time', often with **ηοϭ**: **ηοϭ ηκοογ**, 'great length of time', identical with, or related to, (*Wb.* v, 4, 1 ff.), *ḳ3w*, 'height, length', not attested in the meaning 'length of time', but the Adj. (*Wb.* v, 1, 2 ff.), *ḳ3*, 'high, long' is often used in the meaning 'long' of a lifetime (*Wb.* v, 2, 23), so also , *ḳy* in Dem. (Er. 531, bottom). Cf. also place-name **τκωογ**, later **τκοογ** = , *Ḏw-ḳ3w*.

B**καϕαι** (Crum 130a), 'Egyptian partridge', see S**καπαι**.

καϣ (Crum 130a), 'rush', especially *Saccharum aegypt.* Wild, = (*Wb.* v, 156, 8 ff.), *g3š*, 'rush'; (Er. 593, 7), *gš*, 'rush'.

HPLEYTE, *Ét. ég.* 146 [1866]; cf. Brugsch, *Wb.* 1520 [1868]; DSPIEGELBERG, *Mythus*, 274, no. 834 [1917].

ⲕⲱⲱϣⲉ (Crum 130b), 'break' = (Er. 545, 3), *ḳrš*, 'break'.
SPIEGELBERG in LEXA, *Dem. Totenbuch*, 51, no. 258 [1910].

ⲕⲁϣⲁⲃⲉⲗ (Crum 131a), 'earring' = (not in Er.), *kšbr*, 'earring'. From Old Persian **gauša-bâra* > New Persian گوشوار, 'earring', lit. 'what is worn in ear' (Bartholomä, *Altiranisches Wörterbuch*, 486).
[D]WÅNGSTEDT, *Ausgew. dem. Ostraka*, 165 and Index, p. 215 [1954]; [PER]JERNSTEDT in Crum, *A Coptic Dict.* XVIII b [1939].

ⲕⲟⲩϣⲧ (Crum 131a), a (odorous) plant = (Er. 533, 7), *kwšṭ*, probably Greek κόστος, a spice root (Griffith-Thompson, III, 88, no. 945).
CHASSINAT, *Pap. méd.* 192 [1921].

ⲕⲁϥ (Crum 131a), 'trunk' of tree, = (*Wb.* V, 120, 9), *kfꜣ*, part of plant.
STERN in Ebers, *Pap. Ebers*, II, 19 [1875].

ⲕⲁϩ (Crum 131a), 'earth, soil' = (*Wb.* V, 12, 9 f.), *ḳꜣḥ*, 'earth'; (Er. 547, 3), *kḥ*, 'earth'.
[H]ERMAN, *Äg. Glossar*, 133 [1904]; [D]GRIFFITH-THOMPSON, III, 89, no. 965 [1909].
ⲕⲁϩ (Crum 131b), 'district, province' is of different origin, see next entry.

ⲕⲁϩ (Crum 131b), in certain place-names 'district, province' = (*Wb.* V, 20, 9), *ḳꜥḥt*, 'district'; (Er. 547, 7), *kḥ*, 'district'.
[HD]SPIEGELBERG, *Rec. trav.* 26, 162 [1904].
ⲧⲕⲁϩ ϣⲙⲓⲛ = (*Wb.* V, 20, 11), *tꜣ ḳꜥḥt Ḫnty-Mn*; (*ZÄS* 51, Pl. III, 4), *tꜣ kḥ Ḫn-Mn*.
[HD]SPIEGELBERG, *ZÄS* 51, 70 [1913]; cf. Spiegelberg, *Rec. trav.* 26, 162 [1904].

ⲕⲉϩ (Crum 131b), 'arm (?)' = (*Wb.* V, 19, 6 ff.), *ḳꜥḥ*, 'upper arm, shoulder'; (Er. 548, 1), *kḥ*, 'arm'.
[H]CHAMPOLLION, *Gr. ég.* 73 and 93 [1836]; [D]SPIEGELBERG, *Mythus*, 273, no. 327–8 [1917].
For **ⲕⲉⲗⲉⲛ-ⲕⲉϩ**, see **ⲕⲗⲗⲉ**.

ⲕⲟⲉⲓϩ (Crum 132a), 'sheath'. For **ⲕⲟⲉⲓϩ ⲛϫⲱⲱⲙⲉ**, see under **ⲕⲓϩⲉ** and **ⲕⲁϩⲓ**. **ⲕⲁⲓϩ**, 'inner corner' of eye, prob. = **ⲕⲟⲟϩ**, 'angle, corner'.

ⲕⲟⲟϩ (Crum 132a), 'angle, corner' = (*Wb.* v, 19, 16 ff.), *ḳʿḥ*, 'corner, angle, side'; (Er. 547, 6), *ḳḥ*, 'corner side, angle'.

ᴴCHABAS, *Oeuv. div.* I (= *Bibl. ég.* IX), 89 [1856]; ᴰBRUGSCH, *Wb.* 1440 [1868].

ⲕⲁⲓϩ (Crum 132a, s.v. **ⲕⲟⲉⲓϩ**), 'inner corner' of eye is probably this word, cf. (*Wb.* v, 20, 4), *ḳʿḥw n irty*, 'corners of eyes'.

(**ⲕⲱϩ**), **ⲕⲉϩ-**, **ⲕⲁϩ⸗** (Crum 133a), 'make level, smooth, tame' = (*Wb.* v, 66, 8–10), *ḳḥ*, 'to tame'.

BRUGSCH, *Wb.* 1472 [1868].

For **ⲕⲁϩⲕϩ**, 'hew out', see separate entry below; for ᴮ**ⲕⲉϩⲑⲱⲣⲓ**, see under **ⲧⲱⲣⲉ**, 'hand'.

ᴮ**ⲕⲁϩⲓ** (Crum Add. XVIII) in **ⲟⲩⲕⲁϩⲓ ⲛϫⲱⲙ** Ps. 39, 7; Hebr. 10, 7 = κεφαλὶς βιβλίου, perhaps the same as ˢ**ⲕⲓϩⲉ**, see this. ˢ**ⲟⲩⲕⲟⲉⲓϩ ⲛϫⲱⲱⲙⲉ** of ShP. 130, 4; 157, must be the same expression, but through confusion uses the word **ⲕⲟⲉⲓϩ** ,'cover, case' (lit. 'sheath') containing a book.

ⲕⲓϩⲉ (Crum 130b, s.v. **ⲕⲏϣⲉ**, and Add. XVIII) has hardly anything to do with **ⲕⲏϣⲉ**. **ⲧⲕⲓϩⲉ ⲛⲭⲁⲣⲧⲏⲥ** suggests that **ⲕⲓϩⲉ** = (*sic l.*, *Wb.* v, 21, 7), *ḳʿḥt*, also , 'sheet, page' of papyrus (Posener in *Mélanges Maspero*, I, 333–4). Related to, or even identical with, **ⲕⲁϩⲓ** (**ⲛϫⲱⲙ**), see previous entry.

BRUGSCH, *Wb.* 1440 [1868] (for **ⲕⲁϩⲓ**).

NB. There was evidently a considerable confusion among the words **ⲕⲁϩ**, **ⲕⲉϩ**, **ⲕⲟⲉⲓϩ**, **ⲕⲟⲟϩ**, **ⲕⲓϩⲉ** and **ⲕⲟⲓϩⲓ**.

ⲕⲟⲓϩⲓ (Crum 133b), possibly corrupted from **ⲙⲟⲓϩⲓ**; see **ⲙⲟⲓϩⲓ**.

ⲕⲟⲓⲁϩⲕ (Crum 133b), name of 4th month = (*Wb.* III, 131 top, and v, 86 bottom; 93, 1–3), name of a festival and of a month, lit. 'spirit upon spirit'.

LEPSIUS, *Chronologie*, 137–8 [1848]; cf. ERMAN, *ZÄS* 39, 129 [1901].

ⲕⲁϩⲕϩ (Crum 133a), 'hew out, smooth' = (not in *Wb.*), *kḥkḥ*, 'cut, smoothe' (stone).

DÉVAUD, *Kêmi* 2, 9–10 [1929]; cf. ČERNÝ, *Crum Mem. Vol.*, 38 [1950].

ⲕⲱϩⲧ (Crum 133b), 'fire', cf. (*Wb.* v, 12, 8), *ḳꜣhd*, 'smoke (meat)'.

DE MEULNAERE in *Chronique d'Égypte*, vol. 41, no. 82, 408 [1966].

κεϩτε (Crum 134a), 'loin, hip' = Dual of (*Wb.* v, 19, 15), *kꜥḥt*, 'shoulder of an ox'; (Er. 547, 5), *kḥṯ*, 'shoulder piece'.

HERMAN-GRAPOW, *Wb.* v, 19, 15 [1931]; DGRIFFITH, *Cat. Dem. Graffiti*, I, 184, no. 352 [1937].

καϫι (Crum 134b), 'pitcher, bucket' = (*Wb.* v, 148, 20), *kḏ*, a vessel, from Semitic, cf. Aram. כֻּזָא, 'small jug' (Dalman), כּוּזָא (Buxtorf), Syr. ܟܽܘܙܳܐ (Brockelmann, 154), 'pot'.

HSCHÄFER, *Nastesen*, 116 and 117 n. 2 [1901]; SDÉVAUD's slip.

B**κουϫι** (Crum 92b, s.v. **κουι**), 'small person or thing' = , *kṯ*, a proper name (Ranke, I, 350, 1), lit. 'small one', from Semitic, cf. Aram. גוץ, fem. גוּצָא (Margolis, 97*, and Dalman, 70), 'small'.

HSPIEGELBERG, *ZÄS* 51, 67 n. 1 [1913]; SDÉVAUD's slip.

See also **κουι**.

λ

λα (Crum 134b), 'envy, slander' = (Er. 260, 10), *lꜥ*, 'punishment' or sim., 'slander'.

ERICHSEN, *Dem. Gloss.* 260, 10 [1954].

λα- (Crum 135a) + noun, forming adjectives, 'possessing, endued with' = ? , *ny* > , *n* (*Wb.* II, 196, 3), 'belonging to'.

SETHE, *Verbum*, I, 134, §229 and 135, §231 [1899].

λο (Crum 135a), 'cease, stop' = (*Wb.* II, 406, 2 ff.), *rwi*, 'go away'.

DE ROUGÉ, *Oeuv. div.* III (= *Bibl. ég.* XXIII), 272–3 [1858]; cf. LACAU in *Rec. trav.* 25, 148 [1903].

αλοκ (Imperative) = L.Egn. (in) + Suffix **-κ**; (I Kh. 5, 6), *r-lk·k*, 'cease!'.

SPIEGELBERG, *ZÄS* 53, 127 [1917]; EDGERTON, *ZÄS* 70, 123–4 [1934].

λαβοι (Crum 136b), 'lioness, she-bear' = ? (*Wb.* II, 403, 9) > L.Egn. (Plural), *rwꜣbw* > *rby*, 'lion'; (Er. 262, 1), *lby*, 'bear, lion'. From Semitic, cf. Hebrew לָבִיא, fem. לְבִיָּא, Ar. لَبَاة, لَبَاءَة, لَبُوَة, Akkadian *lābu*.

[H]CHAMPOLLION, *Gr. ég.* 83 [1836]; cf. SPIEGELBERG, *Rec. trav.* 17, 96 [1895]; GARDINER, *Hierat. Papyri in the Brit. Mus., Third Series*, I, 3 n. 4 [1935]; [D]BRUGSCH, *Gr. dém.* 23, §40 [1855]; [S]HINCKS in *Transactions of the Roy. Irish Academy*, 21, 144 [1848, read in 1846].

ⲗⲓⲃⲉ (Crum 136b), 'be mad; madness' = (Er. 261, 10), *lby*, 'be mad; madness'. From Semitic?; see **ⲗⲱⲃⲗⲉⲃ** below.

BRUGSCH, *Numerorum apud veteros Aegyptios demoticorum doctrina*, 5 [1849].

ⲗⲟⲩⲃⲟⲓⲉ (Crum 137b), kind of Nile ship, evidently the same as λουφ(ο)ιων (Plural); the latter is clearly the classical λοφεῖον, 'a crest-case, any case'.

[B]**ⲗⲱⲃⲗⲉⲃ** (Crum 137b), 'feel violent love', reduplication of **ⲗⲓⲃⲉ**. From Semitic; cf. Arabic لَبْلَبَ, 'be tender towards her young (of a mother)'.

ROSSI, *Etym. aeg.* 104 [1808]; cf. Stricker in *Acta Orientalia* 15, 4 [1937].

ⲗⲱⲃϣ (Crum 137b), 'be hot, glow' = (*Wb.* II, 224, 10–12), *nwḫ*, 'be burnt, become warm'.

DÉVAUD's slip.

ⲗⲱⲃϣ (Crum 138a), 'set crown upon, adorn' = (Er. 262, 3), *lbš*, 'to arm, clothe', a loan-word from Semitic, cf. Hebrew לָבַשׁ, 'to clothe', לְבוּשׁ, 'clothing', Akkad. *lubūšu*, Arabic لَبِسَ, 'make stockade, bulwark of reeds', لَبُوس, 'coat of mail', Syr. ܠܒܺܝܫܳܐ, 'loricatus' (Brockelmann, p. 172).

GRIFFITH, *Ryl.* III, 365 [1909].

ⲗⲱⲃϣ, 'crown, coping, battlement' of roof = (*Wb.* II, 414, 6), Pl., *rbšy*, '(leather) coat of mail'; (Er. 262, 3), *lbšt* (always in Plural) 'armour, coat of mail', from Semitic, see above under the verb **ⲗⲱⲃϣ**.

See also **ϩⲁⲗⲃϣⲉ**.

ⲗⲟⲕ (Crum 138a), 'bowl, cup', as measure for oil, = (Er. 264, 2), *lḳ*, a measure for liquids. From Semitic, cf. לֹג, liquid measure.

[D]BRUGSCH, *De natura et indole*, 38 [1850]; [S]ROSSI, *Etym. aeg.* 103 [1808].

ⲗⲱⲕ (Crum 138b), 'be soft, fresh', from Semitic √*rkk*, cf. Hebrew רַךְ, 'be tender, weak', Aram. רְכַךְ, Arabic رَقَّ, Syriac ܪܰܟ, 'be made soft' (Brockelmann, p. 354).

DÉVAUD, *Muséon*, 36, 87 [1923].

ⲗⲟⲕⲗⲕ (Crum 138b), 'become soft, soften', cf. (*Wb.* II, 458, 8) *rkrk[y]t* in (Edel, *Zeitschr. des Deutschen Palästina-Vereins*, 69, Pl. 7, l. 6), lit. 'came stepping softly'. From Semitic, cf. Arabic رَكْرَكَ, 'be weak'.

[S]STRICKER in *Acta Orientalia* 15, 4 [1937].

Cf. also **ⲣⲁⲕⲣⲉⲕ** (Crum 293a), 'soften' (iron).

ⲗⲟⲕⲗⲉⲕ (Crum 139a), **ⲕⲗⲁⲕⲗⲉⲕ** (Crum 103a), 'astragalus (plant or its gum)', *Orobus niger* = (*Wb.* II, 458, 7), *rkrk*, a medical plant.

ⲗⲁⲕⲗⲁⲕ (Crum 139a), kind of sweet paste or jelly (made of astragalus gum).

ⲗⲁⲕⲙ (Crum 139a), 'piece, fragment', from Semitic, cf. Ar. لَقَّمَ, 'break (bread)', لُقْمَة, Pl. لُقَيْم, 'piece of bread'.

ROSSI, *Etym. aeg.* 100 [1808].

ⲗⲁⲕⲛⲧ (Crum 139b, adding **ⲗⲁⲕⲛ**, Till, *Ostraka*, 141, 2), 'jug, bowl, plate' from oblique cases of Greek λαγυνύς, Gen. -ίδος, fem. (Sophocles), diminutive of λάγυνος (later λάγηνος), fem. 'flask, flagon'. This latter is also found in Coptic as **ⲗⲁⲕⲱⲛ** (exx. TILL, *Ostraca*, 285, 7 and note) and is probably the Dem. (Er. 265, 2), *lgns* or , *lgn*, 'jug'. The Greek word is a loan-word from Semitic (cf. Aram. לְגֵינְתָא, 'jug', Dalman, 203), Latin *lagōna*, *lagūna*, *lagoena*, etc. are from Greek (Ernout-Meillet).

[D]WÅNGSTEDT, *Ausgew. dem. Ostraka*, 165 and 205 [1954] (equates *lgn* directly with **ⲗⲁⲕⲛⲧ**); [G]TILL, *Ostraka*, Index, p. 94 (**ⲗⲁⲕⲛ**), 108 (**ⲗⲁⲕⲱⲛ**) [1960] (identifying the two Coptic words).

ⲗⲱⲕⲥ (Crum 139b), 'bite, pierce, stab' = (not in Er.; P. Louvre 3229, II, 29 = Maspero, *Mémoire sur quelques papyrus du Louvre*), *lks*, 'bite, sting'.

H. THOMPSON's Demotic dictionary.

ⲗⲓⲕⲧ (Crum 140a), 'veil, covering', prob. derived from **ⲗⲱϭⲉ** (Crum 152b), 'hide'.

DÉVAUD's slip.

ⲗⲁⲕϩ (Crum 140b), 'corner, extremity, top', perhaps from , *rḳ* (= **ⲣⲓⲕⲉ**), 'incline, bend, turn'. Despite Crum prob. the same as [S]-**ⲗⲁⲕ**, [B]-**ⲗⲁⲕϩ** in [S]**ⲡⲓⲗⲁⲕ**, [B]**ⲡⲓⲗⲁⲕϩ**, Gr.-R. , *p(ꜣ)-ỉw-rḳ* (*Wb.* I, 47, 9), Philae, lit. 'the island of (the) corner, extremity'.

^Bⲗⲟⲩⲕⲟϫⲓ (Crum 140 b) = ^Sϩⲟⲗⲟⲕⲟⲧⲧⲓⲛⲟⲥ = Gk. ὁλοκόττινος, a name for the gold coin *solidus* of the Late Roman Empire (first occurrence of the word in the Diocletian's tariff of 301 A.D.). ὁλ. is a hybrid Graeco-Latin formation from ὅλος, 'entire', and *coctus*, 'cooked, purified', therefore = 'entirely of pure gold'; cf. SCHROTTER, *Wörterbuch der Munzkunde* [1913], 274.

KRALL, *Mitt. aus der Papyrussammlung Erz. Rainer*, 2, 47 and n. 2 [1887].

ⲗⲏⲗ (Crum 140 b), 'necklace' = (Er. 262, 9), *ll*, 'necklace, bracelet' or sim.

GRIFFITH, *Ryl.* III, 269 n. 5, and 366 [1909].

ⲗⲁⲗⲉ, ⲗⲟⲟⲗⲉ (Crum 141 a), 'smear, paint, overlay' = (Er. 263, 3, wrongly under *llwl*; further exx. in Caminos, *LEM*, 452), *lꜥlꜥ*, 'overlay, apply.'

SPIEGELBERG, *Kopt. Handwb.* 50 [1921].

Perhaps compare the epithet of Isis (Er. 261, 1), *tꜣ lꜥlyt*, 'the gilded'(?), unless *lꜥlyt* = ⲗⲉⲗⲟⲩ (see the latter).

GRIFFITH, *Cat. Dem. Graffiti*, I, 90 and 164, no. 205 [1937].

NB. Identity of ⲗⲁⲗⲉ with L.Egn. (*Wb.* I, 209, 15–18), *ꜥrꜥr*, 'carry out', suggested by Spiegelberg in *Rec. trav.* 23, 204 [1901] is very doubtful.

^Bⲗⲉⲗⲉ (Crum 141 a), 'wander about' = (Er. 261, 6), *lwlw*, or (Er. 243, 6), *rwrw*, 'wander about' or sim.

LEXA, *Papyrus Insinger*, II, 72, no. 269 [1926].

ⲗⲉⲗⲟⲩ (Crum 141 b), 'youth, maiden' = (*Wb.* II, 215, 20), and (*Wb.* II, 272, 4), *nn*, 'child'; (Er. 262, 8), *ll*, 'boy, girl', also written , *rrwy* (Pl.) (Volten, *Ägypter und Amazonen*, 105); perhaps also the epithet of Isis *tꜣ lꜥlyt* (Er. 261, 1), unless this latter comes from ⲗⲁⲗⲉ.

^HSETHE in Spiegelberg, *Kopt. Handwb.* 50 [1921]; ^DERICHSEN, *Dem. Glossar*, 262, 8 [1954].

ⲗⲟⲩⲗⲁⲓ (Crum 141 b), 'shout' = (Er. 263, 3), *llwl*, in the expression , *š-llwl*, 'jubilation' (Dem. = Coptic ⲱϣ, ⲉϣ-, ϣ-, i.e. , *ꜥš*, 'call').

BRUGSCH, *Gr. dém.* 38, §80 [1855].

ᴬⲗⲓⲗⲱⲓ = (Vienna Petubastis, N 11), *lylʿy*.

STRICKER, *Oudheidkundige Mededelingen, N.R.* 35, 58 n. 56 [1954].

For ⲱϣ ⲗⲟⲩⲗⲁⲓ, ⲉϣⲗⲟⲩⲗⲁⲓ, ϣⲗⲟⲩⲗⲁⲓ (Crum 141b), see under ϣⲗⲟⲩⲗⲁⲓ. Cf. also ⲁϣ-ⲁⲗ under ⲁⲗ.

ⲗⲗⲏⲃ (Crum 142a), 'jesting, buffoonery', from Semitic, cf. Aram. לְעֵיב, Hebrew לָעַב, Arab. لعب, 'to jest'.

DÉVAUD, *Études*, 47–8 [1922].

ⲗⲟⲟⲙⲉ (Crum 142b), nn., 'bait'. ⲙⲟⲟⲗϥ seems a different word, *q.v.*

ⲗⲱⲱⲙⲉ (Crum 142b), 'wither, fade', from Semitic?, cf. Ar. رمّ, 'be decayed'.

STRICKER in *Acta Orientalia* 15, 3 n. 1 [1937].

ⲗⲱⲙⲥ (Crum 143a), 'be foul, foulness, a kind of sour wine' = (not in Er.), *lms*, 'sour wine(?)'.

PARKER, *JEA* 26, 111 [1940].

ⲗⲉⲙⲏⲏϣⲉ (Crum 143b), 'warrior, champion' = (*Wb.* II, 94, 5; 155, 16), *ỉmy-r mšʿ*, 'chief of the army', later also written (*Wb.* II, 388, 11), *r-mšʿ*; (Er. 165, 5, and 181, 2), *mr-mšʿ*, as military and priestly title.

ᴴᴰGRIFFITH, *PSBA* 21, 270–2 [1899].

ⲗⲁⲙϫⲁⲡⲧ (Crum 143b), 'tar, pitch' = (Er. 262, 7), *lndp*, 'pitch'. The second part *dp*, -ϫⲁⲡⲧ is a loan-word from Semitic, cf. זֶפֶת, Arab. زفت; which itself is prob. borrowed from Egn. (*Wb.* IV, 118, 11), *sft*, name of one of seven (sacred) oils (Coptic ⲥⲓϥⲉ).

ᴰBRUGSCH, *ZÄS* 26, 62 [1888]; ˢROSSI, *Etym. aeg.* 99 [1808].

ⲗⲁⲓⲛ (Crum 143b), 'steel' = (Er. 260, and 5), *lʾyn*, *lyn*, 'steel'.

REVILLOUT, *Rev. ég.* 14, 21 n. 11 [1914].

ⲗⲁⲉⲓⲛⲉ, 'steel-smith' = , *ly{l}ny*, and sim. in late proper names, *Kêmi*, 16, 36–7; (Er. 260, 5), *lyn*, 'steel-smith'.

ᴴDE MEULENAERE in *Chronique d'Égypte* 41, no. 82, 408 [1966]; ᴰSPIEGELBERG in PREISIGKE–SPIEGELBERG, *Äg. und griech. Inschriften und Graffiti aus...Gebel Silsile*, 16, no. 268 [1915].

ⲗⲉⲟⲛ (Crum 143b), 'earring, bracelet' = (not in Er.; P. Berlin 3108, 4), *lἰn*, 'earring', from Greek ψέ(λ)λιον, 'armlet, anklet', or ποδοψέλλιον, 'anklet'.

^{D}BRUGSCH, *ZÄS* 14, 68 [1876]; ^{G}CRUM, *A Coptic Dict.* 143b [1930].

^{B}**ⲗⲉⲛϫⲓ** (Crum 144a), 'coat of mail, cuirass' = Greek λέντιον from Latin *linteum*, 'cloth, napkin'. As S. form a **ⲗⲏⲛⲧⲥⲉ** is attested with **ⲧⲥ** for **ϫ** (as in **ⲧⲥⲟⲩⲧⲥⲟⲩ** for **ϫⲟⲩϫⲟⲩ**).

CRUM, *A Coptic Dict.* 144a [1930] (with doubt).

^{B}**ⲗⲁⲡⲥⲓ** (Crum 144a), 'bite, seize' = (?) (*Wb.* II, 334, 11–14), *nsb*, 'swallow' or sim., 'lick, lick off'.

ERMAN-GRAPOW, *Äg. Hdwb.* 87 [1921]; SPIEGELBERG, *Kopt. Handwb.* 52 [1921].

^{S}**ⲗⲉⲯⲉ**, ^{B}**ⲗⲁⲡⲥⲓ** (Crum 144b), 'fragment, small portion', lit. 'a bit', substantivized inf. of the preceding ^{B}**ⲗⲁⲡⲥⲓ**, 'bite', where also etymology.

ⲗⲁⲥ (Crum 144b), 'tongue' = (*Wb.* II, 320, 8 ff.); (Er. 263, 8), *ls*, 'tongue'.

^{H}DE ROUGÉ in his course in 1864 (acc. to Lauth, *Manetho*, 119 [1865]); CHABAS, *Voyage*, 388 [1866]; ^{D}BRUGSCH, *Gr. dém.* 28, §56 [1855].

^{S}**ⲗⲱⲱⲥ**, ^{B}**ⲗⲁⲥ⸗** (Crum 145a), 'be bruised, crushed; bruise, crush' = (*Wb.* II, 336, 12 and 13), *nss*, 'to damage', ultimately akin to Aram. כְּסַס, 'crush' (Dalman, 386).

^{H}ERMAN-GRAPOW, *Wb.* II, 336, 12 and 13 [1928]; ^{S}DÉVAUD, *Muséon* 36, 87 [1923].

^{S}**ⲗⲁⲧⲡ**, ^{B}**ⲗⲁⲡⲧ** (Crum 145b), 'turnip', from Semitic, cf. Arabic لِفْت, Aram. לְפַת 'spice', Pl. 'white turnip', and לִפְתָּא, also Syriac ܠܶܦܬܳܐ. The Boh. form, therefore, is more correct; cf. ^{S}(**ⲗⲁⲙ**)**-ϫⲁⲧⲡ**, ^{B}(**ⲗⲁⲙ**)**-ϫⲁⲡⲧ** from زِفْت.

DÉVAUD's slip; STRICKER in *Acta Orientalia* 15, 17 [1937].

^{SF}**ⲗⲁⲁⲩ**, ^{SAA_2}**ⲗⲁ(ⲁ)ⲩⲉ**, ^{F}**ⲗⲁⲩⲓ**, ^{F}**ⲗⲁⲩⲉⲓ** (Crum 146a), 'anyone, -thing, something', in neg. sentences 'any', perhaps < **ⲗⲁ-ⲟⲩⲁ**, lit. 'belonging to one', 'single'.

ⲗⲁϣⲓⲉ (Crum 148a), Pl., 'hypocrites', cf. ? (Er. 263, 6), *lḫi*, also , *lš*, 'fool, blasphemer'.

ⲗⲁϣⲁⲛⲉ (Crum 148a), village magistrate or official, = (*Wb.* IV, 496, 13 ff.), *mr šn*, a title; (Er. 166, middle, and 512, 3), *mr šn*, chief priest, λεσῶνις or λασᾶνι (*LD* VI, 93, no. 349).

GRIFFITH, *PSBA* 21, 272 [1899]; cf. GRIFFITH, *Stories*, 99 [1900]; cf. however, Stricker, *Acta Orientalia* 16, 92–3 [1938].

[B]**ⲗⲉⲓϥⲓ** (Crum 148b), fish *Cyprinus niloticus*, [S]**ⲗⲁⲃⲏⲥ** = (not in Er.), *lbs*, is from Greek ἀλάβης, ἀλλάβης, λεβίας.

GRIFFITH-THOMPSON, I, 68 n. on l. 9 [1904]; cf. CHASSINAT, *Pap. méd.* 236–7 [1921].

(**ⲗⲱⲱϥⲉ**), Qual. **ⲗⲟⲟϥⲉ** (Crum 148b), 'be prone to fall, decadent', cf. ? (Er. 246, 2), *rfꜥy*, 'folly (?), vaccillation (?)'.

H. THOMPSON, *A Family Archive*, Index, p. (110), no. 180 [1934].

ⲗⲟϥⲗϥ (Crum 148b), 'mortify, become rotten, perish', cf. (*Wb.* II, 252, 10), *nfnf*, = (not in *Wb.*, quoted by Champollion), *rfrf*, 'creeping creature, worm', probably from Semitic, cf. Arab. لَقْلَقَ, 'totter'.

[H]CHAMPOLLION, *Gr. ég.* 87 (*rfrf*) [1836]; GOODWIN, *ZÄS* 5, 85 (adding *nfnf*) [1867]; [S]DÉVAUD's slip.

[O]**ⲗϭⲏ** (*JEA* 28, 25), 'plebeians' = (*Wb.* II, 447, 9 ff.), *rḫyt*, 'plebeians'.

GARDINER in CRUM, *JEA* 28, 28 [1942]; cf. GARDINER, *Onomastica*, I, 98*, no. 232 [1947].

ⲗⲉϩ (Crum 149a), 'care, anxiety' = ? (*Wb.* II, 281, 1), 'loss, diminution', identical (?) with (*Wb.* I, 12, 4 f.), *ꜣhw*, 'pain, anxiety, sadness'; (Er. 263, 4), *lh*, 'care, anxiety'.

[H]DÉVAUD's slip; [D]HESS, *Stne*, 13 and 165 [1888].

ⲗϩⲱⲃ (Crum 149b), 'steam, vapour' = (*Wb.* II, 440, 3), *rhb*, 'glow of the fire'; (Er. 263, 5), *lhb*, 'smoke'; from Semitic, cf. לַהַב and לֶהָבָה, لهب, اَلْهُوب, 'ardour' (LAGARDE, *Übersicht*, 67).

[HS]ERMAN-GRAPOW, *Wb.* II, 440, 3 [1928]; [DS]BRUGSCH, *Gr. dém.* 27, §53 [1855].

[S]ⲗⲱϩⲙ, [B]Qual. ⲗⲁϧⲉⲙ (Crum 149b), 'be boiling, boil' = [demotic] (Er. 263, 7), *lḫm*, 'boil'.
BRUGSCH, *Gr. dém.* 121, §244 [1855].

ⲗϩⲏⲙ (Crum 150a), 'roar' esp. of lions, probably from Semitic, cf. Aram. נְהַם, Arab. نَهَمَ, 'roar (of lions)', these latter akin to Egn. 𓈖𓉔𓅓𓀁 (*Wb.* II, 285, 7 ff.), *nhm*, 'jubilate', and 𓈖𓉔𓅓𓉔𓅓𓀁 (*Wb.* II, 286, 3), *nhmhm*, 'roar (of lions)'.
DÉVAUD's slip.

ⲗⲱϫ (Crum 150a): (1) 'be sticky, stick', from Semitic, cf. Arabic لَزَّ, 'stick'.
DÉVAUD, *Études*, 49 n. 5 [1922].
(2) 'crush', from Semitic, cf. Hebrew רָצַץ, Aram. רְצַץ ('smash, crush'), Syr. ܪܥ (Brockelmann, 359).
See also ⲗⲟϫⲗⲉϫ, 'languish, be sickly'.
DÉVAUD's slip; STRICKER in *Acta Orientalia* 15, 2 [1937].

ⲗⲱϫⲕ, ⲗⲱϫϭ (Crum 150b), 'be sticky, adhesive', perhaps from Semitic, cf. لَزِجَ, 'to stick to'.

ⲗⲟϫⲗϫ (Crum 150b), 'languish, be sickly' = [demotic] (P. Kasan, l. 9), *ldld*, 'be ill'. Probably the same as ⲗⲟϫⲗϫ, 'rub, crush, oppress' (Crum 150b, s.v. ⲗⲱϫ, 'be sticky'). Reduplication of ⲗⲱϫ (2), 'crush'.
H. THOMPSON's Demotic dictionary.

ⲗⲱϫϩ (Crum 151a), 'be crushed, crush', from Semitic, cf. לָחַץ, 'oppress', and רָצַח 'kill'.
DÉVAUD, *Muséon* 36, 87 [1923], and DÉVAUD's slip; cf. STRICKER in *Acta Orientalia* 15, 4 [1937].

ⲗⲱϫϩ (Crum 151a, not distinguished from preceding), 'lick' = [demotic] (Er. 264, 5), *lkḥ*, 'lick', from Semitic, cf. Hebrew לָחַךְ, Syr. ܠܚܟ, *lkḥ*, 'lick' (Brockelmann, 176).
[D]BRUGSCH, *Wb.* 885 [1868]; [S]DÉVAUD's slip.

ⲗⲟϭ (Crum 151a), 'impudent, persistent person', from Semitic, cf. لَاجَّ, 'quarrel obstinately'.
ROSSI, *Etym. aeg.* 101 [1808].

[S]ⲗⲁϭⲉ, [B]ⲗⲱϫⲓ (Crum 151b), 'cease, recover from sickness' = (Er. 264, 6), *lg*, and (Er. 264, 4), *lk*, 'cease'.

BRUGSCH, *Wb.* 874 [1868].

See also ⲧⲁⲗϭⲟ.

ⲗⲱϭⲉ (Crum 152b), 'lie hid, hide' = late (*Wb.* II, 459, 9), *rgy*, 'to bandage (?)'; (Er. 264, 7), *lg*, 'hide'.

[H]ERMAN-GRAPOW, *Wb.* II, 459, 9 [1928]; [D]HESS, *Stne*, 166 [1888].

Cf. also ⲗⲓⲕⲧ, 'veil, covering'.

Ⲙ

ⲙⲁ (Crum 153a), 'place' = (Er. 149, 1), *mꜣꜥ*, 'place'.

BRUGSCH, *Lettre à M. le Vicomte Em. de Rougé*, p. 34 and pl. II, no. 14 [1850].

NB. The much favoured identification with (*Wb.* I, 450, 8 ff.), *bw*, 'place', first proposed by Brugsch, *Wb.* 366, should be definitely abandoned: the Fayyûmic form ⲙⲉ requires ʿAyin at the end (**maꜥ* or sim.), not *w* (**baw*), see TILL in *BIFAO* 30, 363–4 [1930].

[SF]ⲙⲁ-, ⲙⲁ⸗, [S]ⲙⲉ⸗ (Crum 155b), vbal pref. 'if'; attested are ⲙⲁⲕ-, ⲙⲁⲗ (2nd sing. f.), ⲙⲁⲩ-, ⲙⲁ + noun. *ⲙⲁϥⲥⲱⲧⲙ < ⲙⲁ + ⲁϥⲥⲱⲧⲙ or ⲙ + ⲁϥⲥⲱⲧⲙ < *, *mỉ ỉry·f sḏm*, 'if he (has) heard'. For *mỉ* = 'according as, if', see Gardiner, *Eg. Gr.*, 2nd ed., §170; Erman, *Äg. Gr.*, 4th ed., §541.

CRUM in *ZÄS* 65, 125 [1930].

ⲙⲁ- (Crum 155b), imperative of ϯ 'give' and of causatives formed with ⲧ- = (*Wb.* I, 76, 14), *ỉmỉ*, 'give!'; (Er. 150, bottom), *my*, 'give!'.

[H]CHABAS, *Pap. mag. Harris*, 206 [1860]; [D]BRUGSCH, *Gr. dém.* 146, §291 [1855].

See also ⲙⲁⲣⲉ- optat. prefix.

[B]ⲙⲁⲓⲏ (Crum 156a), 'size, age, kind'.

[B]ϭⲓ ⲙⲁⲓⲏ, 'grow in size, increase' = (Ankhsh. 6, 9), *ṯꜣy-ꜣmyt*, 'adult age'.

STRICKER in *Oudheidkundige Mededelingen, N.R.*, 39, 61 [1958].

ⲙⲉ (Crum 156a), 'to love' = (*Wb.* II, 98, 12), *mrỉ*, 'to love'; (Er. 167, 1), *mr*, 'to love'.

[H]CHAMPOLLION, *Précis*, 1st ed. 142–5, and Tableau gén., no. 348 ff. and pp. (37)–(38) [1824]; [D]YOUNG, *Misc. Works*, III, 26–7, no. 42 (= *Mus. crit.* 6, 176–7, no. 42), letter to de Sacy of 21 October 1814 [May 1815]; cf. BRUGSCH, *Gr. dém.* 38, §79 [1855].

ⲙⲁⲓ̈- (part. coni.) (Crum 156b), 'loving' = (*Wb.* III, 101, 11); (Er. 167, bottom), *mr*, 'loving'.

ⲙⲉⲣⲓⲧ (Crum 156b), 'beloved' = (*Wb.* II, 103, 11 ff.), *mrwty* > *mrỉty*; (Er. 169, 4), *mr(ỉ)ṯ*, 'beloved'.

[H]SETHE, *Verbum*, II, 286, §658 [1899]; [D]SPIEGELBERG, *Mythus*, 144, no. 327 [1917].

ⲙⲉ (Crum 156b), 'truth, justice' = (*Wb.* II, 18, 12 ff.), *mꜣꜥt*; (Er. 149, middle), *mꜣꜥt*, 'truth'.

[H]CHAMPOLLION, *Dict.* 296 [1841]; [D]BRUGSCH, *Gr. dém.* 185, §369 [1855].

(ⲙ)ⲙⲉ (Crum 157a), (adj.) 'truthful, real, genuine' = (*Wb.* II, 19, 9–11), *n mꜣꜥt*, 'of truth'; (Griffith-Thompson, III, 40, no. 413), *n mt*, same meaning.

ERMAN, *Näg. Gr.*, 2nd ed., 95, §211 [1933].

For the initial ⲁ of the word (in ⲛ-ⲁⲙⲉ, 'in truth', and ⲁⲛ-ⲁⲙⲏⲓ, 'precious stone', lit. 'precious stone of truth') see Vergote in *BIFAO* 61, 72 [1962].

ⲙⲏⲧ (Crum 158a), 'true, real' in magic, = (*Wb.* II, 173, top), *mtr*, 'accurate'; , *mtỉ* (Er. 149 bottom; 192, 5; Griffith-Thompson, III, 41, no. 418), 'true', belongs to *mtr*, ⲙⲁⲧⲉ, 'correctness' (see this latter) and not to ⲙⲉ.

[HD]BRUGSCH in *ZÄS* 22, 24 [1884]; cf. SPIEGELBERG, *Mythus*, 155, no. 374 [1917].

ⲙⲏ (Crum 158a), 'urine' = (*Wb.* II, 53, 7), *mwyt*, 'dampness, urine'; (Er. 147, 8), *mꜣt*, 'urine'.

[H]CHABAS, *Mél. égypt.* I, 76 [1862]; [D]BRUGSCH, *Gr. dém.* 27, §54 [1855].

ⲙⲓⲟ⸗ (Crum 158b), 'hail! thanks!'. Allberry, *A Manichaean Psalm-book*, II, 210 n. 14, compares Mani ϫⲣⲟ ⲙⲛϩⲓⲥⲉ, 'strength and praise!' and ϫⲣⲟ ⲙⲛⲓⲁⲕ, ϫⲣⲟ ⲙⲛⲓⲟ (2nd sg. f.), 'strength and thy . . . '. It seems therefore that ⲙⲓⲟ⸗ is only a contraction of an earlier ⲙⲛⲓⲟ⸗ and that ⲓⲟ⸗ is a subst. with suffix. The only somewhat satisfactory candidate seems to be  (*Wb.* I, 25, 11), *ỉ3wy*, 'old age'.

ⲙⲟ (Crum 159a), imperative 'take!' =  (*Wb.* II, 36, 1), *mỉ* (?), 'take!'.

SETHE, *Verbum*, II, 214, §513, and 227, §541 (with doubt) [1899]; ERMAN, *Aeg. Gr.*, 3rd ed. 199, §384 [1911].

ⲙⲟⲩ (Crum 159a), 'die' =  (*Wb.* II, 165, 8 ff.), *m(w)t*, 'die';  (Er. 157, 7), *mwt*, 'die'.

HGOODWIN, *Sur les papyrus hiératiques*, 17 (= *Rev. arch.* N.S. 1, vol. 2, 235) [1860]; CHABAS, *Pap. mag. Harris*, Pl. I, no. 27, and p. 223, no. 373 [1860]; DBRUGSCH, *Gr. dém.* 34, §68 [1855].

ⲙⲟⲩⲉ (Crum 160a), 'light, brightness' =  (*Wb.* II, 28, 1), *m3wt*, 'sunrays'; 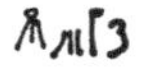 (not in Er.), *mwy*, 'light'.

HCHAMPOLLION, *Gr. ég.* 79 [1836]; DBRUGSCH, *Scriptura Aeg. dem.*, 22, §29 [1848].

ⲙⲟⲩⲉ (Crum 160b), 'island' =  (*Wb.* II, 27, 8), *m3wt*, 'new land' that has recently emerged from the Nile, probably an abbreviation of *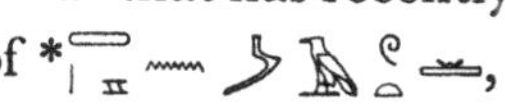, *ỉw n m3wt*, 'new island' (lit. 'island of newness'); 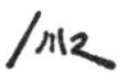 (Er. 148, 2), *m3y*, 'island'.

HBRUGSCH, *Wb.* 563 [1868], cf. GARDINER, *Onomastica*, I, 12*, no. 60 [1947]; DBRUGSCH, *ZÄS* 13, 13 [1875].

Fⲙⲟⲩⲓ (Crum 160b), 'new' =  (*Wb.* II, 27, 3–5), 'new' (lit. 'of newness', replacing the old adjective , *Wb.* II, 26, 5 ff., *m3*, 'new');  (Er. 148, 1), *(n)m3y*, 'new, newness'.

DHBRUGSCH, *Wb.* 564 [1868]; cf. DSPIEGELBERG, *Petubastis*, 22*, no. 140 [1910].

ⲙⲟⲩⲓ (Crum 160b), 'lion' =  (*Wb.* II, 11, 14), *m3ỉ*, 'lion';  (Er. 148, 3), *m3ỉ*, 'lion'.

HCHAMPOLLION, *Gr. ég.* 73 [1836]; DBRUGSCH, *Gr. dém.* 23, § 40 [1855].

ⲙⲟⲩⲓⲏ, ⲙⲓⲏ, 'lioness' =  (*Wb.* II, 12, 6), *m3(ỉ)t*, 'lioness' as a designation for goddesses; 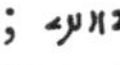 (Er. 148, 3), *m3ỉt*, 'lioness'.

HERMAN-GRAPOW, *Äg. Hdwb.* 59 [1921]; DSPIEGELBERG, *Mythus*, 137, no. 293 [1917].

ⲙⲟⲩⲓ (Crum Add. p. xix); metal utensil, lit. 'lion' (see prec. entry), probably bronze (later iron) lion serving as bolt in a certain type of Egn. locks, on which see *ASAE* 58, 86 ff. (with bibliography, p. 86 n. 1). For locks in form of a lion from modern Iran, see Brugsch, *ZÄS* 1, 43–4.

ⲙⲁⲁⲃ (Crum 161 a), 'thirty' = (*Wb.* II, 46, 15), *mꜥbꜣ*, 'thirty'.

DE ROUGÉ, *Chrest.* II, 110 n. 2 [1868].

^{S}**ⲙⲃⲟⲛ, ⲛⲃⲁⲛ** in **ⲣ̄ⲛⲃⲁⲛ** (Mani Ps. 15, 31; 18, 26), ^{O}-**ⲃⲁⲛ** (i.e. *nban*, Hor. 122) (Crum 161 a, 'be wrath', subst. 'wrath' = (Spiegelberg, *Petubastis*, 18*, no. 112; Volten, *Dem. Traumdeutung*, 105), *ỉnbꜣn*, 'evil', the latter connected with *bỉn*, 'bad' (**ⲃⲱⲱⲛ**)?

ⲙⲓⲕⲉ (Crum 161 b), intr. 'rest', refl. 'rest oneself' = (*Wb.* II, 160, 15), *mkỉ*, 'protect (limbs)'; (Er. 183, 4), *mky*, 'protect, pamper' (limbs). Cf. also the reduplicated form (*Wb.* II, 159, 1), *mḳmḳ*, 'rest, sleep'.

H. S. SMITH, *JEA* 44, 122 [1958].

See also **ⲙⲟⲕⲙⲉⲕ** below.

ⲙⲟⲕⲓ (Crum 161 b), 'jar, vessel, quiver', container generally = (not in *Wb.*; ex. P. BM 10795, frg. C, II, 13), *mk*, a vessel.

^{B}**ⲙⲟⲩⲕⲓ** (Crum 161 b), 'ladder' = (*Wb.* II, 33, 6), *mꜣḳt*; (Er. 183, 3), *mky*, 'ladder'.

^{H}A. BAILLET, *Oeuv. div.* I (= *Bibl. ég.* XV), 31 [1867]; ^{D}SPIEGELBERG, *Petubastis*, 25*, no. 168 [1910].

ⲙⲟⲕⲙⲉⲕ (Crum 162 a), 'think, ponder' = (Er. 183, 6), *mkmk*, or , *mḳmḳ*, 'think', probably < (*Wb.* II, 159, 1), *mḳmḳ*, 'rest, sleep'. Reduplication of **ⲙⲓⲕⲉ**.

^{D}GRIFFITH, *Pap. Rylands*, III, 357 [1909].

ⲙⲁⲕⲣⲟ (Crum 162 b), 'trough, mortar' = ? (*Wb.* II, 159, 4), *mḳr*, a vessel, late (Ritual of the Festival of the Valley, 2, 12), *mkr*.

ⲙⲁⲕϩ (Crum 162 b), 'neck' of man or beast = (*Wb.* II, 163, 6), *mkḥꜣ*; (Er. 183, 2), *mkḥ*, 'neck'.

^{H}BRUGSCH, *Wb.* 620 [1868]; ^{D}SPIEGELBERG in SPIEGELBERG–RICCI, *Pap. Reinach*, 213 n. 6 and Pl. XVI, l. 8 [1905].

ⲙⲟⲩⲕϩ (Crum 163a), 'afflict, oppress', see **ⲙⲕⲁϩ**.

ⲙⲕⲁϩ (Crum 163a), 'be painful, be grieved' = (Er. 183, 1), *mkḥ*, 'be grieved'.

GRIFFITH, *Stories*, 190 [1900].

[B]**ⲙⲓⲟⲗⲱⲛ** (Crum 165a), 'bitumen' = (*Wb.* II, 82, 9–14), *mnnn*, 'asphalt'.

LORET in *Rec. trav.* 16, 161 [1894].

ⲙⲁⲗⲗⲱⲧ (Crum 165a), see under **ⲃⲁⲗⲟⲧ**, 'skin garment'.

ⲙⲉⲗⲱⲧ (Crum 165a), 'ceiling, canopy', from Semitic, cf. Hebrew מֶלֶט (Jer. 43, 9, 'mortar'), translated by προθύραι, 'porch' by LXX; Syr. ܡܠܛܐ. Arab. ملط, properly 'make something smooth', then 'cover' wall with lime or cement, مِلاط, 'cement covering', Gk. μάλθα or μάλθη, mixture of wax and pitch for caulking ships and laying over writing tablets. Perhaps same word as (Er. 153, 2), *mylt*, a textile.

[S]ROSSI, *Etym. aeg.* 113 [1808]; cf. Spiegelberg, *Kopt. Handwb.* 58 [1921]; Lacau in *BIFAO* 58, 158–9 [1959].

ⲙⲟⲗⲟϫ (Crum 165a), planet 'Mars' = (Er. 170, 7), *mlẖ*, 'Mars', from Μολοχ, Greek transcription of the name of the Ammonite god מֹלֶךְ.

BRUGSCH, *Wb.* 683 [1868]; cf. BRUGSCH, *Gr. dém.* 30, §60 [1855]; cf. BRUGSCH, *Mémoire sur les observations planétaires*, 45 n. 4 [1856].

ⲙⲟⲟⲗϥ (Crum 142b, under **ⲗⲟⲟⲙⲉ**), nn., m., 'bait', seems different from **ⲗⲟⲟⲙⲉ**, being attested as verb 'attract, seduce' in phrase *ẖr mlf·s ḥ*ʿ[*·f?*], 'she seduced his [heart]', P. Fay, D7.

H. THOMPSON's Demotic dictionary.

[B]**ⲙⲗⲁϫ** (Crum 165b), 'fight, quarrel' = (Er. 170, 8), *mlẖ*, 'fight', prob. from Semitic, cf. Hebrew לָחַם, 'to fight'.

BRUGSCH, *Wb.* 683 [1868].

ⲙⲟⲩⲗϩ (Crum 165b), 'make salt', from Semitic, cf. Hebrew מֶלַח, Aram. מִלְחָא, Arab. مِلْح, 'salt'. So also

ⲙⲗϩ (Crum 166a), 'salt'.

SETHE, *Verbum*, I, 193, §318 [1899]; cf. VON LEMM, *Kleine Kopt. Studien*, 243 [1904].

ⲙⲟⲩⲗϩ (Crum 166a), 'wax' = (*Wb.* II, 83, 4), *mnḥ*, 'wax'; (Er. 162, 13), *mnḥ*, 'wax'; cf. , *mlḥỉ*, 'pickling, waxing'.

HGOODWIN, *ZÄS* 5, 86 [1867]; DGRIFFITH-THOMPSON, III, 37, no. 370 [1909] (for *mnḥ*); GRIFFITH, *Cat. Dem. Graffiti*, I, 153, no. 142 [1937] (for *mlḥỉ*).

Sⲙⲟⲩⲗϩ, Bⲙⲟⲗϩ (Crum 166a), 'be hooked into, attached to, involve, enmesh' = (*Wb.* II, 87, 8), *mnḫ*, 'to thread (beads), to hang up'.

SPIEGELBERG, *Kopt. Etym.* 25–6 [1920]; cf. LORET in LALLEMAND, *BIFAO* 22, 98 n. [1923].

Bⲙⲟⲩⲗⲁϫ (Crum 166b), Sⲙⲟⲩⲗⲁϩϫ (Crum 339b, l. 10 down), 'owl' (for meaning see *OLZ* 35, 254) = (Er. 5, 3), *ỉmwlḏ*, 'owl'. ⲙ- or ⲙⲟⲩ- is probably the constr. form of the lost word for the bird which the sign 𓅓, *m*, represents (*Wb.* II, 1, 1); the abs. form prob. in Bⲭⲁⲕⲕⲁ-ⲙⲁⲩ.

HSETHE in *Nachr. Ges. Wiss. Gött.* 1916/17 [1916] = *Der Ursprung des Alphabets*, 153 [1926]; DBRUGSCH, *Gr. dém.* 23, §41 [1855].

ⲙⲟⲩⲙⲉ (Crum 198b, s.v. ⲙⲟⲟⲩ), 'spring, fountain' = (*Wb.* II, 59, 3), *mmwy*, 'spring', older 𓅓𓅓 *mmt* (above a list of nomes in one of the small rooms at the back of the temple of Ramesses III at Medînet Habu); (not in Er.), *mm*, 'fountain'.

HDÉVAUD's slip; DGRIFFITH, *Ryl.* III, 353 [1909].

Akhmîmic equivalent ⲙⲟⲩⲛⲙⲉ is a reinterpretation: 'true water', lit. 'water of truth'.

Sⲙⲙⲛ-, Bⲙⲙⲟⲛ (Crum 166b), 'not to be' = L.Eg. (*Wb.* II, 59, 5), *mn*, 'there is not', L.Eg. writing of the old , *nn wn*, 'there is not'); (Er. 158, 2), *mn*, 'there is not'.

HBRUGSCH, *Wb.* II, 641 [1868]; cf. BRUGSCH, *ZÄS* 14, 121 ff. [1876]; ERMAN, *Näg. Gr.* 233, §351 [1880]; DBRUGSCH, *Rhind*, p. 40 and Pl. 37, no. 168 [1865].

ⲙⲛⲧⲉ⸗ (Crum 167 b) = L.Eg. (*Wb.* II, 59, 7–9), *mn mdỉ·*, 'there is not with', 'has not'; (Er. 158, middle), *mn mtw*.

HERMAN, *Näg. Gr.* 84, §116 n. 2 [1880].

ⲙⲙⲟⲛ (Crum 169a), 'verily, for' = , *mn*, 'verily'. Etymologically the same word as Bⲙⲙⲟⲛ, 'is not', but the reason for passage of meaning is obscure (cf. *ZÄS* 44, 134).

ERICHSEN, *Eine neue demotische Erzählung*, 17 [1956].

ⲙⲁⲛ (Crum 169 b), 'a certain person, or thing' =  (*Wb.* II, 64, 13 f.), *mn*, 'so and so';  (Er. 158, 3), *mn*, 'someone'. Often replaced by **ⲛⲓⲙ**, 'so and so', see the latter.

H CHABAS, *Mél. ég.* I, 111 [1862]; D BRUGSCH, *Gr. dém.* 117, §241, 6° [1855].

S **ⲙⲛ-**, B **ⲛⲉⲙ-** (Crum 169 b), preposition 'with' = L.Eg.  (*Wb.* I, 115, 17–20), *ỉrm*;  (Er. 39, 9), *ỉrm*, 'with', written  (*Wb.* II, 263, 6), *nm*, in Graeco-Roman period.

H GOODWIN, *ZÄS* 5, 87–8 [1867]; D YOUNG, *Misc. Works*, III, 24–5, no. 26 (= *Mus. Crit.* 6, 174–5, no. 26) [1815], letter to de Sacy of 21 October 1814); HESS, *Stne*, 163 [1888]. , *ỉrm*, originates in  *r-mn*, 'together with' < 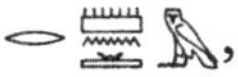, *r-mn-m*, lit. 'to remain in', see GARDINER, *Eg. Gr.*, 2nd ed. 136, §180, Obs. [1950].

A **ⲙⲛ-** (Crum 170 b), negative imperative (vetitive) =  (*Wb.* II, 3, 3 ff.), *m*;  (Er. 116, 1), *bn*.

H STEINDORFF, *Die Apokalypse des Elias*, 43 n. 4 [1899]; D GRIFFITH-THOMPSON, I, 130 [1904]; III, 25, no. 256 (2) [1909].

ⲙⲁⲉⲓⲛ (Crum 170 b), 'sign, mark' =  (*Wb.* II, 69, 9 ff.), *mnw*, 'monument',  (*Wb.* II, 71, 3 f.), *mnw*, '(monumental) statue'; 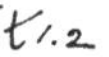 (Er. 158, 4), *mn*, 'divine statue', in proper name *ꜣḫ-mnw* (Ranke, I, 2, 25).

H DE ROUGÉ, *Oeuv. div.* I (= *Bibl. ég.* XXI), 181 and 233 [1847]; D ERICHSEN, *Dem. Glossar*, 158, 4 [1954].

ⲙⲟⲩⲛ (Crum 171 b), 'remain, continue' =  (*Wb.* II, 60, 6 ff.), *mn*, 'remain';  (Er. 159, 2), *mn*, 'remain'.

H CHAMPOLLION, *Gr. ég.* 65 [1836]; D BRUGSCH, *Rhind*, 38, no. 126, and Pl. 37, no. 125 [1865].

ⲙⲙⲏⲛⲉ (Crum 172 a), 'daily, every day' = (*Wb.* II, 65, 9), *m mnt*; 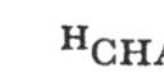 (Er. 160, 4), (*n*)-*mn*, 'daily'.

H CHABAS, *Voyage*, 384 [1866]; LAUTH, *ZÄS* 4, 63 [1866]; D BRUGSCH, *Wb.* 638 [1868].

ⲙⲓⲛⲉ (Crum 172 a), 'sort, quality, manner' = 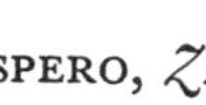 (*Wb.* II, 65, 6–8), *mnt*;  (Er. 161, 3), *mnt*, 'manner'.

H GARDINER, *PSBA* 38, 181–3 [1916]; D MASPERO, *ZÄS* 15, 139, no. 79 [1877].

ⲛⲧⲉⲓⲙⲓⲛⲉ (Crum 173a), 'of this sort' = (*Wb.* II, 65, 8), *m tꜣy mnt*, 'in this manner'.

ⲙⲟⲛⲏ, Pl. [B]**ⲙⲟⲛⲱⲟⲩⲓ** (Crum 177b) is not Egn. word (Vycichl, *ZÄS* 85, 73), but Gk. μονή, 'stopping place, station, on the road', from μένω, 'stay'. Resemblance to Egn. , *mn*, 'stay' (**ⲙⲟⲩⲛ**) is fortuitous. See also **ⲧⲙⲟⲟⲛⲉ** in Geographical Names.

[S]**ⲙⲟⲟⲛⲉ**, [B]**ⲁⲙⲟⲛⲓ** (Crum 173a), 'to pasture, feed' = (*Wb.* II, 75, 11), *mnỉ*, 'to pasture, guard'; (Er. 160, middle), *ỉmn*, 'pasture'.

[D]GRIFFITH, *Pap. Rylands*, III, 328 [1909].

ⲣⲉϥⲙⲟⲟⲛⲉ (Crum 173b), 'one who pastures' = , *rmt-ỉw.f-mn*, lit. 'man who pastures', 'shepherd'.

MATTHA, *Dem. Ostraca*, 171, note on 225, 2 [1945].

ⲙⲁⲛ-, **ⲙⲁⲛⲉ-** (Crum 173b), 'herdsman, pastor' = (*Wb.* II, 74, bottom), *mnỉw*; (Er. 160, 1), *mn*, 'herdsman'.

[H]CHAMPOLLION, *Dict.* 455 [1841]; [D]SPIEGELBERG in *ZÄS* 46, 114 [1909] (identified the Demotic group without mentioning **ⲙⲁⲛ(ⲉ)-**).

ⲙⲁⲛ-ⲉⲥⲟⲟⲩ (Crum 61a, s.v. **ⲉⲥⲟⲟⲩ**), 'shepherd' = , *mnỉw srw*, lit. 'pastor of sheep'.

ČERNÝ, *Miscellanea Gregoriana*, 58 [1941].

ⲙⲁⲛ-ϩⲏⲩ (Crum 173b, and Addenda, p. xix a), 'herdsman' = , *mỉnw-ʿwt*; , *mỉnw ỉꜣwt*, 'pastor of (small) cattle'.

ČERNÝ, *Miscellanea Gregoriana*, 59 [1941].

ⲙⲁⲛⲉ-ϩⲧⲟ (Crum 723a, s.v. **ϩⲧⲟ**), 'groom', lit. 'pastor of horses' = , *mnỉww* (Plural)-*ḥtr*.

ČERNÝ, *Miscellanea Gregoriana*, 60–1 [1941]; ČERNÝ, *Crum Memorial Volume*, 39 [1950].

ⲙⲁⲛ-ϭⲁⲙⲟⲩⲗ (Crum 173b), 'camelherd' = (Er. 160, 1; 581, 1), *mnỉw-gmwl*, 'camelherd'.

ČERNÝ in *Miscellanea Gregoriana*, 58 [1941].

[S]**ⲙⲟⲟⲛⲉ**, [B]**ⲁⲙⲟⲛⲓ** (Crum 173b), 'be made fast, come to land, into port' = (*Wb.* II, 73, 13 f.), *mnỉ* (*mỉnỉ*), 'to land'; (Er. 160, 2), *mn*, 'to land'.

[H]CHAMPOLLION, *Gr. ég.* 372 [1836]; [D]BRUGSCH, *Rhind*, 38 and Pl. 37, no. 126 [1865].

ⲙⲟⲟⲛⲉ (Crum 174a), ‘nurse’ = (*Wb.* II, 78, 1 ff.), *mnʿt*, ‘nurse’.
CHAMPOLLION, *Gr. ég.* 77 [1836].

(ⲉ)ⲙⲛⲁⲓ (Crum 174a), ‘here, hence, hither’ = (*Wb.* II, 44, 1; attested since Middle Kingdom, see CAMINOS, *LEM* 273), *mỉnꜣ*, ‘hither’; (Er. 113, 12), *r-bw-nꜣỉ*, ‘hither’.
[H]ERMAN, *Näg. Gr.* 69, §95, 2 [1880]; [D]REVILLOUT, *Setna, Avantpropos*, p. 33 n. 1 (*ad* Setna 5, 2), and pp. 111, 121, 144 where the comparison is not yet made [1877–80].

ⲙⲛⲏ (Crum 174b), ‘there, thither’ has the same etymology as the preceding **ⲙⲛⲁⲓ**; hierogl. and Demotic writings do not show the difference in vowels, as also in **ⲧⲁⲓ**, ‘here’, and **ⲧⲏ**, ‘there’, both = , *dỉ*.

ⲙⲟⲩⲛⲕ (Crum 174b), ‘make, form’ = (*Wb.* II, 84, 13), *mnḫ*, ‘work with chisel’; (Er. 164, 5), *mnky*, ‘form’.
[H]CHAMPOLLION, *Gr. ég.* 372 [1836]; [D]SPIEGELBERG, *Mythus*, 143, no. 321 [1917].

ⲙⲟⲩⲛⲕ (Crum 175a), ‘cease, make to cease’, etc. = (*Wb.* II, 89, 16), *mnḳ*, ‘bring to end, finish’; (Er. 164, 5), *mnḳ*, ‘finish, accomplish’.
[H]BRUGSCH, *Wb.* 665 [1868]; [D]BRUGSCH, *Rhind*, 38 and Pl. 37, no. 129 [1865].

[B]**ⲙⲟⲛⲙⲉⲛ** (Crum 176a), ‘shake, be shaken’ = (*Wb.* II, 80, bottom), *mnmn*, ‘move (oneself)’; (Er. 162, 11), ‘move, tremble’.
[H]BRUGSCH, *Wb.* 649 [1868]; [D]BOESER, *Pap. Insinger*, 14 (= *Oudh. Med.*, *N.R.* III, 1) [1922].

[B]**ⲙⲟⲛⲙⲉⲛ** (Crum 176a), ‘twisted’ = (*Wb.* II, 47, 9), *mnn*, ‘twisted rope’, and cf. (*Wb.* II, 47, 7), *mnn*, ‘be wound round’; , *mnn*, ‘torsion, twisting’, LEFEBVRE, *Petosiris*, I, 73 n. 5, and III, Pl. 13.
BRUGSCH, *Wb.* 605 [1868].

ⲙⲛⲧ- (Crum 176a), prefix forming abstracts = construct form of (*Wb.* II, 181, 7 f.; forming abstracts only in Graeco-Rom. period, II, 182, 3. 4), *mdt*, ‘speech, matter’; (Er. 184, 7), *mt*, ‘speech, matter’.
[H]W. MAX MÜLLER, *Rec. trav.* 9, 21 ff. [1887], cf. HESS, *Stne*, 12–13 [1887]; [D]BRUGSCH, *De natura et indole*, 4 ff. [1850].

ⲙⲛⲟⲧ (Crum 176b), 'breast' = (*Wb.* II, 92, 11 ff.), *mnḏ*, 'breast'; (not in Er.; P. Berlin [Thoth] 4/1), *mnṯ*, 'breasts'.

[H]CHAMPOLLION, *Gr. ég.* pp. 62, 73 [1836]; [D]H. THOMPSON's Dem. dictionary.

ⲙⲛⲟⲩⲧ (Crum 176b), 'porter, door keeper' = (not in *Wb.*), *mnty*, 'porter'; (Er. 165, 3), *mnṯ*, 'porter'.

[H]PEET, *Tomb Robberies*, 173 n. 1 [1930]; [D]REVILLOUT, *Setna*, 68, cf. 2 (autogr.) [1878].

ⲙⲛⲧⲣⲉ (Crum 177a), 'witness, testimony' = (*Wb.* II, 172, 5), *mtrw*; (Er. 192, 1), *mtr*, 'witness'. From **emtor*, 'be present', see ⲙⲧⲟ, 'presence'.

[H]BRUGSCH, *ZÄS* I, 32 [1863]; cf. BRUGSCH, *Rec. de mon.* II, 73, note * [1863]; [D]BRUGSCH, *Gr. dém.* 37, §78 [1855].

[B]**ⲙⲉⲛϧⲏ** (Crum 177b), nn. with **ⲥⲁ-** forming prep., 'after', see under **ⲥⲁⲙⲉⲛϧⲏ**.

ⲙⲁⲛϭⲁⲗⲉ (Crum 177b), 'pick, hoe', might have been as to its meaning influenced by Gk. μάκελλα (or μακέλη), but must come, as its form shows, from Semitic, cf. Hebrew מַגָּל, 'sickle' (from **mingal*), Arabic مِنْجَل, 'sickle', Syriac ܡܓܠܐ 'sickle', Brockelmann, p. 199 (the Arab. word is held for a loan-word from Syriac by Fränkel, *Aram. Fremdwörter im Arabischen*, 133). From Semitic comes evidently also μάκελλα, 'pick-axe with one point' though Greeks felt the word to come from μία, 'one', and κέλλω, 'to drive on', and formed δίκελλα, 'two-pronged hoe' (δίς, 'twice' and κέλλω).

[S]KABIS, *ZÄS* 13, 105 [1875].

[S]**ⲙⲡⲁⲓ**, [B]**ⲙⲃⲁⲓ** (Crum 177b), 'spindle' = (*Wb.* II, 243, 5–7), *nbꜣ*, 'pole (for carrying)'; (not in Er.), *mbꜥ*, 'spindle(?)'.

[D]BRUGSCH, *ZÄS* 14, 65 [1876].

ⲙⲡⲉ- (Crum 178a), prefix of negative 1st Perfect = M.Eg. (*Wb.* I, 495, 2), *n pꜣ-* 'has never done' > L.Eg. (*Wb.* I, 453, 3), *b(w)p(w)-*, (Er. 116, 3), *bn-pw*.

[H]BRUGSCH, *Gr. hiérogl.* 70 [1872]; cf. ERMAN, *Näg. Gr.* 228, §345 [1880] (L.Eg.); ERMAN, *ZÄS* 20, 7 [1882] (M.Eg.); GARDINER, *ZÄS* 45, 73 ff. [1908]; [D]GRIFFITH, *Stories*, 71 [1900].

[S]ⲙⲡⲟ, [B]ⲉⲃⲟ (Crum 178a), 'dumb person' = (*Wb.* I, 96, 2; further exx. *Revue d'ég.* 17, 192–3), *ỉnbꜣ*, 'be dumb'; (Er. 3, 10), *ꜣbw*, 'be dumb'.

[H]SETHE in Spiegelberg, *Kopt. Handwb.* 23 [1921]; [D]ERICHSEN, *Dem. Glossar*, 3, 10 [1954].

ⲙⲡⲱⲣ (Crum 178b), 'do not! by no means!' is not a direct descendant of (*Wb.* II, 3, 3), *m ỉr*, 'do not do!' but a secondary absolute state to the construct state ⲙⲡⲣ-.

RAHLFS in *ZÄS* 43, 151–2 [1906].

ⲙⲡⲣ- (Crum 178b), prefix of negative imperative = (*Wb.* II, 3, 4 and I, 112, 7), *m ỉr* + infinitive; (Er. 37, top), *m·ỉr*, 'do not . . . !'

[H]LE PAGE RENOUF, *Lifework*, I, 305–16 (= *On Some Negative Particles*) [1862]; GOODWIN, *Mél. ég.* 1, 89 [1862]; [D]HESS, *Stne*, 73 [1888]; cf. BRUGSCH, *Gr. dém.* 151, §297 [1855].

ⲙⲡⲁⲧⲉ- (Crum 179a), prefix of negative Perfect of what *has not yet happened* = (*bw ỉr·t·*) + Subject + Infinitive (ERMAN, *Näg. Gr.*, 2nd ed. §445); (Er. 114, 3), *bw-ỉr·tw*.

[HD]ERMAN, *ZÄS* 50, 106–7 [1912]; cf. BRUGSCH, *Wb.* 369 [1868].

ⲙ(ⲡ)ϣⲁ (Crum 179a), 'be worthy, worth' = (*Wb.* IV, 404, 17) *m šꜣw*, 'in the worth (of)'; (Er. 493, 1), *n pꜣ šꜣ*, written as if it meant 'of the value'.

[H]SETHE, *ZÄS* 47, 143–5 [1910]; cf. GARDINER, *JEA* 42, 14 [1956]; [D]REVILLOUT, *Poème*, 51 [1885]; cf. [HD]SPIEGELBERG, *Rec. trav.* 16, 69 [1894].

See also ϣⲁⲩ, 'use, value'.

[AA2]ⲙⲡϣⲁ (Crum 180a), 'much, very', prob. < *ⲙϣⲁ (see under ⲙⲁϣⲟ) with ⲡ inserted under influence of ⲙⲡϣⲁ, 'be worthy, worth'; this ⲡ has nothing to do with def. article in , *pꜣ m-šs*, 'much, very' (Griffith, *Stories*, 85; Möller, *Rhind*, 56*, no. 387).

ⲙⲏⲣ (Crum 180a), 'shore' of river, especially 'opposite shore' = (*Wb.* II, 109, 5), *mrw*, 'desert'; (Er. 168, 1), 'across the river', 'the other side'.

[H]SPIEGELBERG, *Kopt. Handwb.* 63 [1921]; [D]GRIFFITH-THOMPSON, I, 72 [1904].

ⲉⲙⲏⲣ, 'to the other side' = , *r mr.*

GRIFFITH-THOMPSON, I, 72 [1904] and III, [37], no. 377 [1909].

ϩⲓⲙⲏⲣ, 'on the other side' = , *ḥr mrw.*

SPIEGELBERG, *Kopt. Handwb.* 63 [1921]; cf. CAMINOS, *LEM* 129 [1954] (*Wb.* lists under *mryt*, 'port', II, 109, 12 ff.!).

NB. Demotic , *r mrt*, and , *ḥr mrt*, 'to ship-board' and 'on board' do not contain **ⲙⲏⲣ** but the feminine word for 'ship', *mrt* (Er. 168, 3)!

ⲙⲟⲩⲣ (Crum 180a), 'bind, gird, tie' = (*Wb.* II, 105, 1 ff.), *mr*; (Er. 166, 2), *mr*, 'bind'.

HCHAMPOLLION, *Gr. ég.* 385 [1936]; DBRUGSCH, *Gr. dém.* 36, §76 [1855].

ⲙⲏⲣ (Crum 182a), 'bundle' = (*Wb.* II, 105, 9 f.), *mrw*, 'bundle'.

DÉVAUD's slip.

ⲙⲁⲓⲣⲉ and **ⲙⲏⲣⲉ** (Crum 182a) = (*Wb.* II, 105, 16), 'bundle of cloths'.

ERMAN-GRAPOW, *Wörterbuch der äg. Sprache*, II, 105, 16 [1928].

ⲙⲁⲣⲉ- (Crum 182b), prefix of optative = , *imi iry*, lit. 'cause that . . . makes'; , *my iri·* (Spiegelberg, *Dem. Gr.* §186).

HERMAN, *ZÄS* 22, 32–3 [1884]; DBRUGSCH, *Gr. dém.* 146, §291 [1855]. See also **ⲙⲁ-**.

ⲙⲉⲣⲉ-, **ⲙⲉ⸗** (Crum 182b), prefix of negative aorist = , *bw ir·*; (Er. 114, 2), *bw·ir.*

HDE ROUGÉ, *Chrest.* III, 128, §395 [1875] (as to **ⲙ-**); DHESS, *Stne*, 66 [1888].

ⲙⲉⲉⲣⲉ (Crum 182b), 'midday' = (*Wb.* II, 174, 6), *mtrt*; (Er. 192, 2), *mtr*, 'midday'.

HBRUGSCH, *ZÄS* I, 35 [1863]; DBRUGSCH, *Gr. dém.* 30, §61 [1855].

ⲙⲣⲱ (Crum 183a), 'harbour, landing stage' = (*Wb.* II, 109, 12 ff.), *mryt*, 'river shore', 'landing place'; (Er. 168, 2), *mr(t)*, 'harbour'.

HCHABAS, *Oeuv. div.* II (=*Bibl. ég.* X), 97 [1860]; DGRIFFITH, *Pap. Rylands*, III, 225 n. 15 [1909].

B**ⲙⲉⲣⲁⲛ** (Crum 183a), 'trough, tank' = ? (not in *Wb.*; only P. BM 10795, frg. C, II, 11), *mrynt*, a vessel; if so, **ⲙⲉⲣⲁⲛ** < ***ⲙⲉⲣⲁⲛⲧ**.

[B]**ⲙⲁⲩⲣⲉⲥ** or **ⲙⲁⲣⲓⲥ** (Crum 183a), nn. f., 'jug, jar' = Greek μάρις (masc.), 'measure for liquids of 6 cotylae', acc. to Polyaenus 4, 3, 32 of 10 Attic khoes. Cf. also μαῦρα, Preisigke, II, 55.

DÉVAUD's slip.

ⲙⲣⲓⲥ (Crum 183a), 'new wine, must' = (*Wb.* II, 112, 15), *mrsw*, kind of wine.

DÉVAUD, *Rec. trav.* 39, 168–70 [1921].

ⲙⲟⲣⲧ (Crum 183b), 'beard' = (*Wb.* II, 113, 6), *mrt*, 'chin'; (Er. 169, 14), *mrt*, 'beard', probably a loan-word from Hamitic, cf. Berber *t-amart*.

[H]CHAMPOLLION, *Notice sur le pap. hiératique et les peintures du cercueil de Petaménoph*, [1827] (= CHAMPOLLION in CAILLIAUD, *Voyage à Méroé*, IV, 39 n. 4 [1827]); [D]GRIFFITH-THOMPSON, III, 38, no. 387 [1909]; cf. BRUGSCH, *Wb.* 683 [1868] (with doubts); [HAM]ADELUNG, *Mithridates*, III, 77 [1812]; cf. STERN, *ZÄS* 21, 26 n. 2 [1883].

[A2]**ⲙⲣⲁⲩⲧ** (not in Crum; Mani Ps. 200, 13), [S]**ⲙⲣⲟⲟⲩⲧ** (only in place-name **ⲧⲉⲙⲣⲟⲟⲩⲧ**, **ⲧⲉⲙⲣⲁⲩⲧ**, cf. Ep. 433 n. 13), f., 'crop-land?' = (Griffith, *Ryl.* III, 354, and Er. 169, 9), *mrwṭ*, 'yielding corn' (σιτοφόρος).

ⲙⲣⲟϣ (Crum 183b), 'be red' or 'yellow' = (*Wb.* II, 113, 1), *mrš*, 'bright red'; (Er. 170, 9), *mlš*, same meaning.

[H]DÜMICHEN, *Geogr. Inschriften altäg. Denkmäler*, Text, 69 [1866]; [D]VOLTEN, *Dem. Traumdeutung*, 110 [1942].

ⲙⲣⲱϣⲉ (Crum 184a), 'vessel of clay', perhaps identical with **ⲙⲣⲱϩⲉ** (Crum 184a, 'vessel prob. of metal') = (*Wb.* II, 112, 11), *mrẖt*, kind of vessel; (Er. 169, 12), *mrẖ*, a metal tool.

[H]CRUM, *A Coptic Dict.* 184a (s.v. **ⲙⲣⲱϩⲉ**) [1930]; [D]CRUM, *The Monastery of Epiphanius*, II, 293, no. 549 n. 2 [1926].

[B]**ⲙⲣⲟϧⲧ** (Crum 184a), 'fuller's clay' (not 'pipe-clay' as Crum), if a genuine word—Rossi, *Etym. aeg.* 112, is the only authority for it—and is Gk. μόροχθος which acc. to Dioscorides, *De mat. med.* 5, 134, came from Egypt (ἐν Αἰγύπτῳ γεννᾶται, ed. Wellmann), it would be a noun formed by prefix *m-* to (*Wb.* II, 448, 8), *rẖt*, [B]**ⲣⲱϧⲓ**, 'wash'. Since the final *t* is preserved in ⲙⲣⲟϩⲧ this latter would have to have come into Coptic through a Semitic language. In Sem. 'wash' is רָחַץ, with *ṣ*, Arabic رحض.

ⲙⲉⲣⲉϩ (Crum 184a), 'spear, javelin' = (*Wb.* II, 112, 4), *mrḥ*, 'spear', loan-word from Semitic, cf. רֹמַח, رُمْح, 'spear'.

BRUGSCH, *Wb.* 608 [1868].

ⲙⲣⲱϩⲉ (Crum 184a), a vessel, see ⲙⲣⲱϣⲉ.

ⲙⲁⲣϫⲱϫⲉ (Crum 184a), a garment = ⲙⲁⲣ- (part. coni. of ⲙⲟⲩⲣ, 'bind, tie') + ϫⲱϫ 'head', 'that which ties the head'.

CRUM, *A Coptic Dict.* 184a [1930].

ⲙⲓⲥⲉ (Crum 184b), 'bear, bring forth' = (*Wb.* II, 137, 4 ff.), *msỉ*; (*Er.* 177, 10), *ms*, 'bear, bring forth'.

HCHAMPOLLION, in YOUNG, *Misc. Works*, III, 245 [1822]; CHAMPOLLION, *Précis*, 1st ed., pp. 69–70 and pl. V, nos. 3 and 4; pp. 135–7; Tableau gén. pp. (30) and (37), and pl. 14 and 17, nos. 258a and 346 [1824]; DBRUGSCH, *Scriptura Aeg. dem.* p. 23, §14; p. 21, §28 [1848].

ϩⲟⲟⲩⲙⲙⲓⲥⲉ, ϩⲟⲩⲙⲓⲥⲉ (Crum 185a), 'birthday' = Gr.-Roman ; (Er. 178 [upper]), *h(rw) ms(yt)*, 'birthday'.

HDCHAMPOLLION, in Young, *l.c.* 245 [1822]; cf. DBRUGSCH, *Wb.* 906 [1868].

Oⲙⲉⲥⲓⲉ (Crum 185b), 'whom ... bore' = Relative form of , *msỉ*; .

HDERMAN, *ZÄS* 21, 103 [1883].

ⲙⲁⲥ (Crum 185b), 'young', mostly of animal or bird = (*Wb.* II, 139, 1 ff.), *ms*, 'child'; (Er. 179, 1), *ms*, 'young' (of animals).

HMALLON, *Sphinx*, 9, 125 [1906]; DGRIFFITH, *Pap. Rylands*, III, 356 [1909].

ⲙⲁⲥⲉ (Crum 186a), 'young animal', especially 'calf, bull' = (*Wb.* II, 140, 8), *ms*, 'calf'; (Er. 179, 2), *ms*, 'calf'.

HCHAMPOLLION, *Gr. ég.* 321 [1836]; DSPIEGELBERG, *Mythus*, 149, no. 351 [1917].

ⲙⲏⲥⲉ (Crum 186a), 'usury, interest' = (*Wb.* II, 142, 2), *ms*, 'grain received as interest'; (Er. 178, lower), *mst*, 'interest'.

HERMAN-GRAPOW, *Wörterbuch der äg. Sprache*, II, 142, 2 [1928]; DREVILLOUT, *Nouv. chrest. dém.* 152 [1878].

ϯ ⲉⲙⲏⲥⲉ (Crum 186a), 'give at interest' = , *rdit r msy*, 'give at an interest' (of birds, hence the determinative).

CAMINOS, *LEM* 238 [1954].

ⲙⲉⲥⲓⲱϯ (Crum 186a), see under **ⲟⲟⲧⲉ**.

ⲙⲉⲥ ϩⲛⲏⲓ (Crum 186b), 'one born in the house' = *, *ms m-ẖnw ʿt*, 'born in (the) house', cf. (*Wb.* II, 139, 6), *msw n pr.f*, 'his household', lit. 'children of his house'.

ERMAN-GRAPOW, *Wörterbuch der äg. Sprache*, II, 139, 6 [1928].

ⲙⲉⲥⲟⲣⲏ (Crum 186b), name of the 12th month = (*Wb.* II, 141, 13), 'birth of Rēʿ', name of a festival.

GARDINER, *ZÄS* 43, 136 ff. [1906]; cf. LEPSIUS, *Chronologie*, 142 [1848]; BRUGSCH, *Die Ägyptologie*, 361 [1891].

^{B}**ⲥⲉⲙⲓⲥⲓ** (Crum 186b), lit. 'birth-place, seat', so 'childbirth, parturition' = *, *st-mst*, 'place of birth'.

SPIEGELBERG, *Zeitschrift für Assyriologie*, 14, 269 [1899]; cf. SPIEGELBERG, *Ägyptol. Randglossen*, 20 [1904].

ⲙⲉⲥⲓⲟ (Crum 186b), 'bring to birth, act midwife' < ***ⲧⲙⲉⲥⲓⲟ** < *dit msy.*, 'cause to be born', causative of **ⲙⲓⲥⲉ**.

STEINDORFF, *Kopt. Gr.*, 1st ed. 110, §242 [1894].

ⲙⲉⲥⲓⲱ (Crum 186b), 'midwife, nurse' = (Er. 178, 1), *ms-ʿꜣ(t)*, 'midwife', in the fem. proper name *Tꜣ-ms-ʿꜣt*, lit. 'The midwife'.

SPIEGELBERG, *Ägyptische und griechische Eigennamen*, 14* [1901].

(**ⲙⲥⲱⲃⲉ**), **ⲉⲙⲥⲱⲃⲉ** (Crum 186b), 'large needle' = prob. L.Eg. , *mssbt*; a metal tool (unpubl. hierat. Ostr. Gardiner 146, l. 4).

ⲙⲟⲥⲛⲉ (Crum 186b), a vessel or dry measure = (*Wb.* II, 145, 1), *msn*, name of the sign representing a reed basket for transport of dates (Brugsch, *Wb.* II, 703).

CRUM, *Coptic Ostraca*, 59, no. 216 n. 1 [1902].

ⲙⲟⲥⲧⲉ (Crum 187a), 'hate' = (*Wb.* II, 154, 1 ff.), *msḏi*; (Er. 180, 2), *mst*, 'hate'.

^{H}CHAMPOLLION, *Gr. ég.* 384 [1836]; ^{D}BRUGSCH, *Wb.* 714 [1868].

ⲙⲉⲥⲧⲉ, f. **ⲙⲉⲥⲧⲏ**, 'hated person', cf. (*Wb.* II, 154, 10. 11), *msḏyt* (fem.), 'that which is hated'.

ⲙⲉⲥⲑⲏⲧ, ⲙⲉⲥⲧⲛ̄ϩⲏⲧ (Crum 187b), 'breast' = L.Eg. (*Wb.* II, 151, 5), *mstỉ* (same as , *Wb.* II, 152, 14, *msdt*), 'basket' + , *ḥ3ty*, 'heart', ϩⲏⲧ, lit. therefore 'basket of (the) heart'.

ⲙⲥⲁϩ (Crum 187b), 'crocodile' = (*Wb.* II, 136, 10); (Er. 179, 6), *msḥ*, 'crocodile'.

[H]CHAMPOLLION, *Précis*, 2nd ed., 125 [1828]; [D]BRUGSCH, *Gr. dém.* 23, §40 [1855].

ⲙⲉⲥϩⲱⲗ (Crum 187b), 'file', is Arabic مِسْحَل.

ROSSI, *Etym. aeg.* 112 [1808].

ⲙⲏⲧ (Crum 187b), numeral 'ten' = ∩ (*Wb.* II, 184, 1), *mḏw*, 'ten'.

[HD]YOUNG, *Misc. Works*, III, Pl. 4, no. 197 = *Encycl. Brit.*, Suppl. IV, Pl. 77, no. 197 [1819].

ⲣⲉⲙⲏⲧ, pl. ⲣⲉⲙⲁⲧⲉ, 'tenth part' = , *r mḏw*, m., 'tenth part, tithe' (Fairman in Pendlebury, *The City of Akhenaten*, III, 168).

SETHE, *ZÄS* 47, 1 n. 2 [1910].

[A2]ⲙⲏⲧ (*Manich. Psalm-book*, 87, 27; 147, 53), masc. = ⲙⲧⲟ masc. (Crum 193a, there confused with fem. ⲙⲧⲱ, see THOMPSON in ALLBERRY, *Manich. Psalm-book*, 87 n.), 'deep water, depth of sea' = (*Wb.* II, 174, 8), *mtr*, 'flood' > ; (Er. 192, 3), *mtr*, 'flood'.

[H]BRUGSCH, *ZÄS* 1, 22–4 [1863]; [D]REVILLOUT, *Setna*, 51 and 53 [1877]; [HD]SPIEGELBERG, *Dem. Chronik*, 59, no. 121 [1914].

ⲙⲓⲧ (Crum 188a), 'parsley' or 'celery' = (*Wb.* II, 33, 11–15), *m3tt*, 'celery', 'parsley' (for the meaning, see v. Deines and Grapow, *Wörterbuch der äg. Drogennamen*, 216–17).

LORET in *Rec. trav.* 16, 6–11 [1894].

ⲙⲟⲉⲓⲧ (Crum 188a), 'road, path' = (*Wb.* II, 176, 1 ff.), *mṯn*, 'road' > L.Eg. (*Wb.* II, 41, 13), *myt* (fem.); (Er. 153, 11), *myt* (masc.), 'road'.

[H]CHABAS, *Oeuv. div.* II (= *Bibl. ég.* X), 295 [1863]; [D]BRUGSCH, *Rhind*, 44, no. 290 [1865].

ϫⲓ ⲙⲟⲉⲓⲧ, 'take road' before, 'lead, guide' = Late (*Wb.* V, 347, 20), *ṯ3y mṯn*, 'show the way'; (Er. 666, upper), *ṯ3y mỉt*, 'show the way'.

[D]MÖLLER, *Rhind*, 22*, no. 137 [1913].

ⲙⲟⲩⲧ (Crum 189a), 'sinew, nerve' = (*Wb.* II, 167, 9), *mt*, 'vein'; or (Er. 184, 3), *mwt*, 'vein, muscle'.

ᴴEBERS, *Pap. Ebers*, I, 32 n. ** [1875]; ᴰERICHSEN, *Dem. Glossar*, 184, 3 [1954].

ⲙⲁⲧⲉ (Crum 189a), 'reach, obtain, enjoy' = (*Wb.* II, 173, 1 ff.), *mtr*, 'correct, accurate' or sim. (Adj.); (Er. 190, 2), *mtr* (*mti*), 'fit, be content, agree'.

ᴴBRUGSCH, *ZÄS* I, 26 [1863]; ᴰBRUGSCH, *Gr. dém.* 37, §78 [1855]; cf. BRUGSCH, *Wb.* 725–6 [1868].

ⲙⲁⲧⲉ (Crum 189b), 'attainment, success' = , *mꜣꜥt*, 'success'.

SPIEGELBERG, *Mythus*, 138, no. 296, 2 [1917].

See also the following word.

ⲙⲁⲧⲉ in ⲉⲙⲁⲧⲉ (Crum 190a) > ⲙⲙⲁⲧⲉ 'greatly, very' = ? (*Wb.* II, 174, 1), *r mtr*, 'correctly, accurately' (lit. 'according to correctness'). But cf. DÉVAUD, *Muséon* 36, 95 [1923] who suggests *ⲙ + ⲁⲧⲟ, lit. 'in multitude'.

See also ⲙⲏⲧ under ⲙⲉ, 'truth'.

ⲙⲁⲧⲟⲓ (Crum 190b), 'soldier' = and (*Wb.* II, 186, 4), *mdy*; (Er. 185, 2), *mty*, 'Persian', 'Persia', lit. 'Mede', through Aramaic *Māday*.

NB. *Wb. l.c.* confuses *mdy* with the African people *mḏꜣy*!

ᴴGRIFFITH, *Pap. Rylands*, III, 319 [1909]; cf. SETHE, *Nachr. aus der K. Ak. Wiss. zu Göttingen, Phil.-hist. Kl.* 1916, 124 ff. [1916]; ᴰBRUGSCH, *Gr. dém.* 38, §81; 41, §90 [1855].

ⲙⲏⲧⲉ (Crum 190b), 'middle' = perhaps in () (*Wb.* II, 168, 3–6), *m mtt (nt) ib*, 'gladly', lit. 'from (the) middle of (the) heart'; (Er. 191, 1), 'centre'.

ᴴERMAN-GRAPOW, *Wörterbuch der äg. Sprache*, II, 168, 3–6 [1928]; cf. GOODWIN, *ZÄS* 2, 39 [1864]; ᴰBRUGSCH, *Gr. dém.* 72, §158 [1855].

ⲛⲧⲙⲏⲧⲉ (Crum 191a), 'in midst' = L.Eg. , ⟨*m*⟩*tꜣ mt n*, '(in) the middle of'.

WENTE, *Late Ramesside Letters*, 25 n. b [1967].

ⲙⲟⲩⲧⲉ (Crum 191b), 'speak, call' = (*Wb.* II, 179, 2 ff.), *mdw*, 'speak'; (Er. 184, 7), *mt* (*md*), 'speak'.

ᴴᴰBRUGSCH, *De natura et indole*, 3 ff. [1850]; cf. W. MAX MÜLLER, *Rec. trav.* 9, 23 [1887].

ⲙⲧⲟ (Crum 193a), 'face, presence' = (*Wb.* II, 171, 9), *mtr*, 'be present', and L.Eg. (*Wb.* II, 172, 1–4), *mtr*, 'presence'; (Er. 191, 3), *mtr*, 'be present, presence'.

ⲙⲡⲙⲧⲟ, 'before' = , *n pꜣ mt*, lit. 'in the presence (of)' = 'before'; ⲙⲡⲉϥⲙⲧⲟ ⲉⲃⲟⲗ, 'before him' = , *n pꜣy·f mt r-bl*, 'in his presence' = 'before him'.

[H]SETHE, *ZÄS* 38, 145 [1900]; [D]BRUGSCH, *Gr. dém.* 174, §339 [1855].

ⲙⲧⲟ (Crum 193a, not distinguished from following word), masc. 'depth of sea', see [A2]ⲙⲏⲧ.

ⲙⲧⲱ (Crum 193a, where not distinguished from the preceding word), fem. 'depth' = (*Wb.* II, 184, 8 ff.), *mḏwt*; (Er. 191, 2), *mtỉ*, 'depth'.

[H]ERMAN, *Äg. Glossar*, 58 [1904]; [D]SPIEGELBERG, *Mythus*, 155, no. 373 [1917].

ⲙⲧⲟⲛ (Crum 193b), 'be at rest' = (*Wb.* II, 182, 8), *mdn*, 'be quiet'; (Er. 189, 10), *mtn*, 'repose'.

[H]BIRCH, *Harris*, 18 n. 17 [1876]; [D]ERICHSEN, *Dem. Glossar*, 189 [1954]. See also the following word.

ⲙⲟⲩⲧⲛ (Crum 195b), 'rest, set at rest' = L.Eg. , *mdn*, transitive infinitive of ⲙⲧⲟⲛ, see the latter.

GUNN, *JEA* 41, 92 [1955].

ⲙⲧⲱⲧⲉ (Crum 196a), meaning unknown, if a vessel then = L.Eg. (*Wb.* II, 183, 18), *mdd*, vessel for measuring wine, also and (Hayes, *Ostraka and Name Stones*, 35–6). For = -ⲧⲱⲧⲉ, see ⲙϣⲧⲱⲧⲉ.

[B]**ⲙⲧⲁⲩ** (Crum 196a), 'wizardry, magic' = (*Wb.* II, 180, 4 ff.), *mdw*, 'words, speech', especially in ϫⲉ ⲙⲧⲁⲩ, 'say magic' = or (*Wb.* II, 180, 8–9), *ḏd mdw*; (Er. 691, middle), *ḏd md(t)*, 'saying words' as heading of magical spells to be recited.

SPIEGELBERG, *ZÄS* 59, 160 [1924]; ZYHLARZ, *WZKM* 32, 173 [1925].

ⲙⲁⲧⲟⲩ (Crum 196a), 'poison' = (*Wb.* II, 169, 5–8), *mtwt*; (Er. 189, 5), *mtwt*, 'poison'.

[H]BRUGSCH, *ZÄS* 1, 22 [1863]; GOODWIN in a letter to Renouf (Dawson, *Ch. W. Goodwin*, p. 88) [1863]; [D]REVILLOUT, *Pap. mor.* I, 251 n. 4 [1907].

[A2]ⲙⲁⲧⲉϭⲧⲉ (not in Crum; exx. *Mani. Hom.*), 'army' = (Er. 193, 6), *mtgṯ*, fem. 'army', masc. 'army camp', from Semitic, cf. Akkadian *madaktu*, 'army camp'.

[D]POLOTSKY, *Manich. Homilien*, p. xix and Index, p. 9* [1934]; cf. ČERNÝ, *BIFAO* 57, 205 [1958].

ⲙⲙⲁⲩ (Crum 196b under ⲙⲁⲩ), 'there, therein' = , L.Eg. (*Wb.* I, 72, 4), *ỉm*; (Er. 201, 4), *n·ỉmw*, 'there'.

[H]BRUGSCH, *Gr. hiérogl.* 10 [1872]; [D]GRIFFITH, *Stories*, 112 [1900].

ⲙⲁⲁⲩ (Crum 197a), 'mother' = (*Wb.* II, 54, 1 ff.), *mwt*; (Er. 155, 2), *mwt*, 'mother'.

[H]CHAMPOLLION, *Précis*, 1st ed., 71 and Tabl. gén., pl. 14, no. 250 (cf. 258b) [1824]; [D]BRUGSCH, *Scriptura Aeg. dem.* 11 [1848].

ⲙⲟⲟⲩ (Crum 197b), 'water' = (*Wb.* II, 50, 7 ff.), *m(ỉ)w*, or *mwy* acc. to Lacau in *Syria*, 31, 291; (Er. 154, 14), *mw*, 'water'.

[H]CHAMPOLLION, *Gr. ég.* 98 [1836]; [D]BRUGSCH, *Gr. dém.* 27, §54 [1855].

ⲙⲟⲩⲙⲉ (Crum 198b), 'spring, fountain', see under ⲙⲟⲩⲙⲉ.

ⲙⲁⲩⲁⲁ⸗ (Crum 198b), 'alone, single' = ⲙ + ⲟⲩⲁⲁ⸗, see ⲟⲩⲱⲧ.

ⲙⲉⲉⲩⲉ (Crum 199a), 'think' = (*Wb.* II, 34, 17 f.), *mỉṯ*; (Er. 156, 3), *mwy*, 'think'.

[H]BRUGSCH, *Wb.* 582 [1868]; [D]BRUGSCH, *Wb.* 636 [1868].

[O]ⲙⲁⲟⲩⲥⲉ (Crum 201a), an internal organ = (*Wb.* II, 44, 11), *mỉst*, 'liver' (see Gardiner, *Onomastica*, II, 245*, no. 598); (Er. 157, 4), *mws*, 'liver'.

[H]GRIFFITH-THOMPSON, I, 141, n. on l. 31 [1904]; [D]GRIFFITH, *ZÄS* 38, 92 [1900].

ⲙⲟⲩⲟⲩⲧ (Crum 201a), 'kill', transitive Infinitive of ⲙⲟⲩ, 'die' (see the latter) formed on its Qual. ⲙⲟⲟⲩⲧ. Not attested in pre-Coptic.

ⲙⲁϣⲉ (Crum 201a), 'balance' = (*Wb.* II, 130, 8), *mḫỉt*; (Er. 176, 1), *mḫyt*, 'balance'.

[H]CHAMPOLLION, *Précis*, 2nd ed., 126 [1828]; [D]BRUGSCH, *Gr. dém.* 26, §50 [1855].

S**ⲙⲁϣⲟ**, B**ⲙⲁϣⲱ**, F**ⲙⲁϣⲁ** (Crum 201 b) in **ⲉⲙⲁϣⲟ**, etc. 'greatly, very'. **ⲙⲁϣⲟ** = ?? (*Wb.* IV, 542, 4), *mỉ-šs* > (*Wb.* IV, 542, 5 ff.), *m šs*, 'in (good) state, in order'; (Er. 521, upper), *m šs*, 'very'.

HDGRIFFITH, *Stories*, 85 [1900]; cf. Spiegelberg, *Dem. Gr.* 175–6, §394 [1925].

Phonetic details quite obscure! Dévaud, *Muséon*, 36, 95 [1923] thinks of ***ⲙ** + **ⲁϣⲟ**, 'in multitude' (**ⲁϣⲟ** from **ⲁϣⲁⲓ**). See also AA2**ⲙⲡϣⲁ**, 'much, greatly'.

ⲙⲉϣⲉ, **ⲙⲉϣⲁ**⸗ (Crum 201 b) = L.Eg. , *bw rḫ*, '... does not know'; (Er. 114, 1), *bw rḫ*.

HERMAN, *ZÄS* 32, 128–30 [1894]; DGRIFFITH-THOMPSON, III, 24, no. 241 [1909].

ⲙⲏⲏϣⲉ (Crum 202 a), 'multitude, crowd, troop' = (*Wb.* II, 155, 2 ff.), *mšꜥ*, 'army, troops'; (Er. 181, 2), *mšꜥ*, 'people, multitude, army'.

HDGRIFFITH, *PSBA* 21, 271 [1899].

ⲙⲓϣⲉ (Crum 202 b), 'fight' = (*Wb.* II, 131, 1), *mḫꜣ*, 'measure (one's strength with)'; (Er. 176, 3), *mḫy*, 'strike, fight'.

SETHE in Spiegelberg, *Kopt. Handwb.* 68 n. 13 [1921]; DBRUGSCH, *Scriptura Aeg. dém.* 20, §23 [1848].

ⲙⲟⲟϣⲉ (Crum 203 b), 'walk, go' = L.Eg. (*Wb.* II, 156, 5), *mšꜥ* (*mšꜥỉ*?), 'march'; (Er. 181, 1), *mšꜥ*, 'go'.

HCHABAS, *Pap. mag. Harris*, Pl. I, no. 28 [1860]; DBRUGSCH, *Gr. dém.* 39, §83 [1855].

NB. A**ⲙⲁ(ⲁ)ϩⲉ** and A2**ⲙⲁϩⲉ** show that the middle consonant was not *š*, but , *ḫ*; see Rösch, *Vorbemerkungen*, pp. 31–2 [1909]. There are also Dem. writings with *ḫ*.

S**ⲙⲉϣⲡⲉⲗⲧ** (Crum 206 a), meaning unknown, cf. ? (Er. 182, 2), *mšprtyt*, 'lamp' or 'vessel', probably a loan-word from Semitic.

ⲙϣⲓⲣ (Crum 206 a), name of 6th month = (*Wb.* II, 131, 14), *mḫỉr*, abbreviated from (*Wb.* I, 493, top; II, 131, 13; cf. *ASAE* 43, 174 and 179), *pꜣ n pꜣ mḫỉr*, 'that (*i.e.* festival) of the *mḫỉr*', name of a festival. For the object *mḫỉr* see the following word.

ERMAN, *ZÄS* 39, 129–30 [1901]; cf. BRUGSCH, *Die Ägyptologie*, 360 [1891].

ⲙϣⲓⲣ (Crum 206a), 'pot, box for incense, censer' = (not in *Wb.*), *mḫir*, a basket. ⲙϣⲓⲣ and *mḫir* seem to be characteristic objects used at the eponymous festival of the sixth month; it is not certain if they were named after the festival, or vice versa.

ČERNÝ, *BIFAO* 57, 206–8 [1958].

ⲙⲁϣ(ⲉ)ⲣⲧ (Crum 206a), 'cable' of palm fibre = (not in Er.; ex. Spiegelberg, *Petubastis*, 25*, no. 167), *mšḫti*, 'cable' (used as fetters) in *mšḫti n Gtiwtin*, 'cable of Gatiton' (for this latter, see ϭⲁϭⲓⲧⲱⲛ). Crum compares the Arabic مشاط, one of ship's cables (Almkvist, *Le Monde Oriental*, 19 [1925], 103) which according to Almkvist is a Plural of مُشْط, 'comb', and cannot have anything to do with the Coptic word.

ⲙⲟⲩϣⲧ (Crum 206b), 'examine, search out, visit' = (Er. 182, 4), *mšt*, 'examine, inspect'. Basic meaning prob. 'pass through'. See also ⲙⲏϣⲧⲉ and ⲙϣⲧⲱⲧⲉ.

GRIFFITH, *Pap. Rylands*, III, 357 [1909].

ⲙⲏϣⲧⲉ (Crum 207a), 'ford, ferry (?)' = (*Wb.* II, 158, 14), *mšdt*; (Er. 182, 6), *mšty*, 'ford'. Derivative of ⲙⲟⲩϣⲧ.

[H]CRUM, *A Coptic Dict.* 207a [1930].

ⲙϣⲧⲱⲧⲉ (Crum 207b), 'comb' = (Hierat. Ostr. Nat. Library, Vienna, Aeg. 1, l. 10; not in *Wb.*), *mšdd*, 'comb', probably from Semitic, cf. Arabic مُشْط, 'comb'.

[S]ROSSI, *Etym. aeg.* 109 [1808].

ⲙϣⲓϣ (Crum 207b), 'vengeance' = (Er. 182, 1), *mšyḫ*, 'vengeance (?)'.

[D]SPIEGELBERG, *Mythus*, 149, no. 359 [1917].

[O]**ⲙⲟⲩϧⲣⲏⲣ**, 'scarab', see under [S]ⲁⲙϩⲣⲏⲣⲉ.

ⲙⲁϩ-, always ⲙⲙⲁϩ- (Crum 208a), 'before' = (*Wb.* I, 420, 1 ff.), *m-bꜣḥ*, 'in presence of, before'; (Er. 110, 2), *m-bꜣḥ*, 'before'. *b* > *m* since N.K., cf. Sauneron, *Crum Memorial Vol.* 155–7 [1950]; Posener in *Revue d'ég.* 5, 252–4 [1946].

[H]GOODWIN, *ZÄS* 4, 55 [1866]; [D]HESS, *Stne*, 8 [1888].

Cf. also ⲃⲁϩ, ϥⲁϩ.

ⲙⲁϩ (Crum 208 a), 'nest, brood (of young)' = (*Wb.* II, 121, 10); (incomplete facsimile in Er. 173, 5, see P. Carlsberg I, 4, 25), *mḥ*, 'nest'.

HBRUGSCH, *Wb.* 692 [1868].

ⲙⲁϩⲟⲩⲁⲗ (Crum 208 a), 'nest, dovecote' = (*Wb.* II, 128, 2), *mḥwn*; (Er. 175, 1), *mḥwl*, 'dovecote'. From ⲙⲁϩ, 'nest' +ⲟⲩⲁⲗ, L.Eg. (not in *Wb.*; ex. *H.O.* XXXVIII, 1, vo. 3), *wr*, 'young bird (which can neither walk nor fly), fledgling'.

HDSPIEGELBERG, *Dem. Texte auf Krügen*, 31 n. 45 [1912].

ⲙⲟⲉⲓϩ (Crum 208 a), measure for fodder = (*Wb.* II, 31, 2. 3), *m3ḥ*, 'wreath' as measure; (Er. 153, 5), *myḥ*, a measure for fodder, *mḥ*, 'wreath' (SPIEGELBERG, *Mythus*, 145, no. 338 listed in Er. 173, 4), origin of Greek μώϊον.

DMATTHA, *Dem. Ostraca*, 189, n. on no. 261, 3 [1945] where a vessel (also ⲙⲁⲉϩⲓ Ep. 549) perhaps = (*Wb.* II, 126, 11–14), *mḥt*, 'bowl'.

Bⲙⲟⲓϩⲓ (Crum 133 b, s.v. ⲕⲟⲓϩⲓ) 'arm', perhaps = (*Wb.* II, 120, 1), *mḥ*, 'arm'.

ⲙⲟⲩϩ (Crum 208 a), 'fill' = (*Wb.* II, 116, 6 ff.); (Er. 171, 6), *mḥ*, 'fill'.

HCHAMPOLLION, *Gr. ég.* 323, 365, 521 [1836]; DBRUGSCH, *Gr. dém.* 121, §244 [1855].

For ⲙⲉϩ ⲉⲓⲁⲧ-, see ⲉⲓⲁ.

ⲙⲉϩ ⲣⲱ⸗ (Crum 209 a), 'fill mouth, eat' = (*Wb.* II, 116, 17), *mḥ r*, as subst. ⲙⲉϩⲣⲟ = as masc. proper name.

ⲙⲉϩ- (Crum 210 a), prefix to ordinal numerals = (*Wb.* II, 117, 19 ff.), *mḥ*, 'filling, completing'; (Er. 172, 1), *mḥ*: *mḥ 2*, 'completing 2' = 'second'.

HYOUNG, *Misc. Works*, III, Pl. 4, nos. 189 and 191 = *Encycl. Brit.*, Suppl. IV, Pl. LXXVII [1819]; cf. CHAMPOLLION, *Gr. ég.* 239 [1836]; DBRUGSCH, *Scriptura Aeg. dem.* 48–9, §33 [1848].

ⲙⲟⲩϩ (Crum 210 a), 'burn, glow' = (*Wb.* II, 31, 8), *m3ẖ*; (Er. 177, 4), *mẖ*, 'burn'.

HBRUGSCH, *Wb.* 588–9 [1868]; DBRUGSCH, *Gr. dém.* 121, §244 [1855].

ⲙⲁϩⲉ (Crum 210b), 'ell, cubit' = (*Wb.* II, 120, 2); (Er. 173, 1), *mḥ*, 'cubit'.

[H]CHAMPOLLION, *Gr. ég.* 224 and 228 [1836]; [D]REVILLOUT, *Nouvelle chrest. dém.* 114 and 118 [1878].

ⲙⲁϩⲉ (Crum 211a), 'flax' = (*Wb.* II, 121, 4), *mḥy*; (Er. 173, 3), *mḥỉ*, 'flax'.

[H]CHAMPOLLION, *Gr. ég.* 77 [1836]; [D]REVILLOUT, *Rev. ég.* I, 60 n. 5 and Pl. I (fasc. 2) [1880].

ⲙⲏϩⲉ (Crum 211a), 'feather' = (*Wb.* II, 123, 6), *mḥt*; (Er. 174, 3), *mḥy*, 'feather'.

[H]CHAMPOLLION, *Gr. ég.* 68 [1836]; [D]SPIEGELBERG, *Mythus*, 146, no. 342 [1917].

ⲙⲟⲉⲓϩⲉ (Crum 211b), 'wonder' = (Er. 153, 3), *myh*, 'wonder'.

SPIEGELBERG, *Petubastis*, 22*, no. 142 [1910].

[A2]**ⲙϩⲏ** fem. (not in Crum, see Allberry, *Manich. Psalm-book*, II, Index, p. 17*), 'breath' = (*Wb.* II, 125, 6–8), *mḥyt*; (Er. 175, 4), *mḥtt*, 'north wind'.

POLOTSKY, *JEA* 25, 113 [1939]; cf. SPIEGELBERG, *ZÄS* 65, 131 [1930].

[A]**ⲙⲉϩⲏⲗ** (211b), 'bald place' on head = (Er. 171, 4), *mhl*, translated ἀναφάλαντος, 'bald in front'.

STERN, *ZÄS* 24, 125 n. 3 [1886].

ⲙⲉϩⲙⲟⲩϩⲉ (Crum 211b), 'purslane' = (*Wb.* II, 131, 15), *mḥmḥwt*, a kind of flowers.

MASPERO, *Journal As.* 8e série, I, 41 n. 1 [Jan. 1883].

[A2]**ⲙⲁϩⲛϭⲛⲟⲩⲧ** (Crum 823b, s.v. **ϭⲛⲟⲩⲧ**) = (Er. 174, 1), *mḥ-n-knwṯ*, a plant-name.

ⲙⲁϩⲧ (Crum 211b), 'bowels, intestines' = (*Wb.* II, 135, 4 ff.), *mẖtw*; (Er. 177, 9), *mẖṯ*, 'entrails'.

[H]DÜMICHEN, *ZÄS* 4, 61 [1866]; [D]BRUGSCH, *Gr. dém.* 29, §56 [1855].

ⲙⲉϩⲧⲟ (Crum 212a), 'great intestine' = , *mẖṯỉ ꜥ3*, 'great intestine' (BRUGSCH, *Wb.* 614).

ⲙϩⲓⲧ (Crum 212a), 'north' = (*Wb.* II, 125, 10 ff.), *mḥty*; (Er. 175, 3), *mḥt*, 'north'.

[H]CHAMPOLLION, *Gr. ég.* 97 [1836]; [D]BRUGSCH, *Gr. dém.* 57, §§128, 129 [1855].

Plural only in place-name **ⲡⲙϩⲁⲧⲉ** = *, *nꜣ-mḥtyw*, lit. 'The Northerners'.

ČERNÝ in *Festschrift Grapow*, 31 [1955].

ⲙϩⲁⲁⲩ (Crum 212b), 'tomb, cavern' = (Er. 174, 6), *mhw*, 'tomb'.

BRUGSCH, *Rhind* 38–9 and Pl. XXXVII, no. 144 [1865]; cf. MÖLLER, *Pap. Rhind*, p. 24*, no. 157, and p. 22* n. 2 [1913].

[O]**ⲙϩⲁⲟⲩⲉ** (not in Crum†), 'family' = (*Wb.* II, 114, 7), *mhwt*; (Er. 171, 2), *mhwt*, 'family'.

[O]**ⲥⲛⲛⲙϩⲁⲟⲩⲉ** = (*Wb.* II, 114, 12), *sn n mhwt*, 'relative', lit. 'brother of (the) family'.

ČERNÝ in *Festschrift Grapow*, 30–1 [1955].

ⲙⲁⲁϫⲉ (Crum 212b), 'ear' = (*Wb.* II, 154, 13), *msḏr*; (Er. 180, 4), *msḏr* > *msḏ*ᶜ, 'ear'.

[H]CHAMPOLLION, *Gr. ég.* 92 [1836]; [D]DE ROUGÉ, *Oeuv. div.* I (= *Bibl. ég.* XXI), 243 and Pl. I [94], no. 3 [1848]; cf. BRUGSCH, *Gr. dém.* 28, §56 [1855].

On *msḏ*ᶜ postulated by the Coptic forms, see POLOTSKY, *ZÄS* 67, 76 [1931]; ČERNÝ, *Crum Memorial Volume*, 39 [1950].

ⲙⲁⲁϫⲉ (Crum 213a), a measure of grain, fruit, etc. Greek μάτιον = (*Wb.* II, 186, 15), *mḏꜣ*, a measure for dates; (Er. 194, 3), *mḏꜣt*, a measure.

[H]LANGE, *Das Weisheitsbuch des Amenemope*, 78 [1925]; cf. GARDINER, *JEA* 26, 157–8 [1940]; [D]CRUM, *Coptic Ostraca*, 25, no. 165 [1902].

ⲙⲁϫⲉ (Crum 213a), 'chisel, axe, pick' = (*Wb.* II, 188, 5), *mḏꜣt*; (Er. 194, 4), *mḏy*, 'chisel'.

[H]BRUGSCH, *Wb.*, Suppl. 657 [1881]; cf. GRIFFITH, *PSBA* 21, 270 [1899]; [D]GARDINER, *Onomastica*, I, 72* [1947].

ⲙⲁϫⲁⲕⲓⲛ (Crum 213b), meaning unknown, named with embroiderers = (Er. 195, 6; adding *ZÄS* 66, 39–40), *mḏkn*, a title.

† Listed 212b, s.v. ⲙϩⲁⲁⲩ, 'tomb'.

ⲙⲉϫⲏⲗ (Crum 213b, adding Ex. 9, 8 from P. Bodmer xvi), 'soot' = *md͗l*, with the superscribed gloss μετηλ (Spiegelberg, *Demotica*, ii, 45 and Pl. 10).

ⲙϫⲱⲗ (Crum 213b), 'onion' = (Er. 195, 4), *md̲l*, 'onion', from Semitic, cf. Hebrew בְּצָלִים (Plural only, from Sing. *בָּצָל), Arab. بَصَل, Akkadian *bisru* (or *bišru*), 'onion'.

ⲉⲙϫⲱⲗ ϩⲉⲩⲧ (or **ϩⲟⲟⲩⲧ**), 'wild onion' = , *md̲wl hwṯ*, 'wild (lit. 'male') onion'.

[D]HESS, *Gnost. Pap.* 8 [1892]; [S]ROSSI, *Etym. aeg.* 129 [1808].

ⲙⲉϫⲡⲱⲛⲉ (Crum 213b), 'ulcer, eruption' = (*Wb.* ii, 157, 6), *mšpnt*, a disease.

LORET in a University course in 1909 according to Dévaud's slip.

[S]**ⲙⲟϫϩ**, [A]**ⲙⲁϫϩ**, [B]**ⲙⲟϫϧ** (Crum 213b), 'girdle' of soldier or monk = (Er. 195, 5), *md̲ḥ*, 'girdle', probably a loan-word from Semitic, cf. Hebrew, מֵזַח, Akkadian *mēzeḫu*.

[D]GRIFFITH-THOMPSON, iii, 42, no. 427 [1909]; [S]ROSSI, *Etym. aeg.* 125 [1808].

NB. Against identification of this word with (*Wb.* ii, 189, 11), *md̲ḥ*, 'fillet' (= , *mdḥ*, *Wb.* ii, 190, 1), see GUNN, *JEA* 25, 218–19 [1939].

See also [S]**ⲙϫⲛϩ**, [B]**ⲙⲉϫⲉⲛϩ**, 'eyebrow', under **ⲉⲛϩ**.

ⲙϫⲁϩⲧ (Crum 214a), 'mortar' = (*Wb.* ii, 193, 2; also *JEA* 31, 38), *md̲ḥt*, 'mortar'.

DÉVAUD, *Rec. trav.* 39, 171–2 [1921].

ⲙⲟⲩϫϭ (Crum 214a, adding [S]**ⲙⲟⲩϣϭ** Apocr. St John ii, 28, 18), 'be mixed, mix', cf. (not in Er., exx. Ankhsh. 4, 18; 5, 15), *mṯk*, 'mixed drink', and in the name of Psammetichus, *P͗-s-(n)-mṯk*, lit. 'the man (= vendor) of mixed drink' where *mṯk* is sometimes determined with , see Griffith, *Ryl.* iii, 201 n. 3; from Semitic, cf. Hebrew מָסַךְ, 'mix', מֶסֶךְ, 'mixture', i.e. wine mixed with spices, New Hebrew מָזַג, Aram. מְזַג, Arab. مَزَجَ, Syr. ܡܙܓ, 'mix' (Brockelmann, 182).

[D]GRIFFITH, *Ryl.* iii, 201 n. 3 [1909]; cf. Glanville's index; [S]ROSSI, *Etym. aeg.* 125 [1808]; cf. SETHE, *ZÄS* 30, 55–6 [1892].

ⲙⲉϭⲧⲱⲗ (Crum 214b), 'tower' = L.Eg. (*Wb.* II, 164, 2. 3), *mktr*; (Er. 183, 9), *mkṯr*, 'fortification tower', from Semitic, cf. Hebrew מִגְדָּל.

HA. BAILLET, *Oeuv. div.* I (= *Bibl. ég.* XV), 37 [1867]; cf. BRUGSCH, *Wb.* 621 [1868]; DGRIFFITH, *Pap. Rylands*, III, 357 [1909].

Ⲛ

ⲛ- (Crum 215a, Ia), particle of genitive = ; *nì* > , *n* (*Wb.* II, 196, 3), adjective 'belonging to' from the preposition *n*, 'to'; Dem. (Er. 196, 2), *n*.

HCHAMPOLLION, *Précis*, 1st ed., p. 76 and Tableau gén. p. (4) and nos. 33 and 34 [1824]; DÅKERBLAD in Young, *Misc. Works*, III, 37 [1815]; cf. BRUGSCH, *Scriptura Aeg. dem.* 29, II [1848].

ⲛ-, ⲙⲙⲟ⸗ (Crum 215a, Ib), partitive preposition 'of' = , *m*, with suffix , L.E. also , *ìm-* (*Wb.* II, 1, 16); Dem. , *n*, with suffix and sim., (*n*)-*ìm-* (Er. 198, lower). See below, preposition **ⲛ-** < , *m*.

ⲛ-, ⲙⲙⲟ⸗ (Crum 215b, II), preposition introducing the object after durative tenses (see Plumley, §187; Till, §259; first recognised by Jernstedt, *Comptes rendus de l'Académie des sciences de l'URSS* 1927, 70 ff.) = Dem. , *n*, with suffix , (*n*)-*ìm·* (not yet in L.Eg.). Deriving from partitive use of the preposition *m* (see last entry).

DSPIEGELBERG, *Rec. trav.* 26, 34–5 [1904].

ⲛ-, ⲙⲙⲟ⸗ (Crum 215b, bottom; also 215b, middle, IIb, c), preposition 'with', etc. = , *m*, with suffix , L.E. also , *ìm·* (*Wb.* II, 1, 2 ff.), preposition 'in', etc.; Dem. , *n*, with suffix , (*n*)-*ìm·*, and sim. (Er. 198, lower), 'in', etc.

HCHAMPOLLION, *Précis*, 1st ed., p. 76, 2nd para., and Tableau gén., p. (2), nos. 35 and 36 [1824]; DBRUGSCH, *Gr. dém.* 169–70, §325; 159, §314, 6° and 7° [1855].

ⲛ-, ⲛⲁ⸗ (Crum 216a), preposition of dative, 'to' = (*Wb.* II, 193, 3 ff.), *n*, preposition 'to'; Dem. (Er. 196, 3), *n*, preposition of dative 'to'.

[H]CHAMPOLLION, *Précis*, 1st ed., Tableau gén., p. (3) and nos. 18–20 [1824]; [D]BRUGSCH, *Scriptura Aeg. dem.* 29, III [1848].

ⲛ- (Crum 10b, under **ⲁⲛ**), negative particle = (*Wb.* II, 195, 6 ff.), *n*, in L.E. written (*Wb.* I, 456, 7 ff.), (*b*)*n*; Dem. (Er. 115, 6), (*b*)*n*, negative particle.

[H]CHAMPOLLION, *Gr. ég.* 443, §286, 1° and 2° [1836]; SETHE, *Nominalsatz*, 15, §13 [1910]; cf. Sethe in *ZDMG* 79, 299 n. 2 [1925]; [D]GRIFFITH, *Stories*, 85 n. [1900]; cf. MÖLLER, *Pap. Rhind*, 230*, no. 200 [1913].

ⲛ- (Crum 258b, under **ⲡ-**), plural of definite article = , *nꜣ n*, > , *nꜣ* (*Wb.* II, 199, 2, IIb); Dem. (Er. 202, 5), *nꜣ*, plural of definite article.

[H]CHAMPOLLION, *Gr. ég.* 179–80 [1836]; cf. CHAMPOLLION, *Précis*, 75 [upper] and Tableau gén., p. 1, no. 3 [1824]; [D]ÅKERBLAD, *Lettre*, 38 and Pl. I, no. 11 [1802]; cf. BRUGSCH, *Scriptura Aeg. dem.* 25 [1848].

[B]**ⲛⲉⲛ-** and [F]**ⲛⲉⲛ-** go back to the construction , *nꜣ n*; ROSSI, *Grammatica copto-geroglifica*, 31 [1877]; cf. ERMAN, *Näg. Gr.* p. 20, §22 [1880].

-ⲛ, suffix of 1st pers. pl. = (*Wb.* II, 194, bottom), ·*n*; Dem. (Er. 201, 2), ·*n*, suffix of 1st pers. pl.

[H]CHAMPOLLION, *Gr. ég.* 261 [1836]; [D]BRUGSCH, *Scriptura Aeg. dem.* 32–3 [1848].

ⲛⲁ (Crum 216b), 'have pity, mercy' = (*Wb.* II, 266, 4), *nꜥ*, 'merciful, have mercy'; Dem. (Er. 208, 2), *nꜥ*, 'merciful, be merciful'.

[H]BRUGSCH, *Wb.* 739 [1868]; [D]REVILLOUT, *Pap. mor. de Leide*, I, p. 122 n. 3 [1906].

ⲛⲁⲏⲧ (Crum 217b) < **ⲛⲁϩⲏⲧ**, 'pitiful of heart, compassionate', from * , *nꜥ ḥꜣty*, 'merciful of heart', without **ϩ** already in Demotic , *nꜥṯ* (after masc.! Ankhsh. 10, 15).

ⲛⲁ, [AA2]**ⲛⲛⲁ** (Crum 217b), 'go' = (*Wb.* II, 206, 7), *nꜥy*, 'travel in a boat', L.E. , *nꜥy*, 'proceed, go'; Dem. (Er. 207, 8), 'go'. See also **ⲛⲟⲩ**, 'go'.

[H]CHAMPOLLION, *Gr. ég.* 383 [1836]; cf. SETHE in *ZÄS* 47, 145 n. 1 [1910]; [D]GRIFFITH, *Stories*, 92 [1900].

[AA2]ⲛⲛⲁ appears in Dem. as , *ỉn(y)nꜥ(k)* (SPIEGELBERG, *Petubastis*, 30*, no. 189).

DÉVAUD's slip.

As verbal prefix of

(*a*) Ist Future ϯⲛⲁⲥⲱⲧⲙ = L.Eg. *, *twꜣ m nꜥy r sḏm*, 'I am in going to hear', Dem. 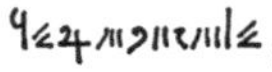, *twy nꜣỉ ḥys* 'I shall praise', ⲛⲁ being written unetymologically *nꜣỉ*, instead of *nꜥy*, cf. SPIEGELBERG, *Dem. Gr.* § 139.

[H]GARDINER, *ZÄS* 43, 97–8 [1906]; cf. also , *st (m) nꜥy r mšꜥ*, 'they are going to travel' (Pap. Strassburg 24 v, vo. 2 [XXIst Dyn.] = *ZÄS* 53, 19); [D]GRIFFITH and THOMPSON, III, 43, no. 431, (1) [1909].

(*b*) IInd Future ⲉⲓ ⲛⲁⲥⲱⲧⲙ = L.E.*, *ỉw·ỉ m nꜥy r sḏm*, 'I am in going to hear', see perhaps  *ỉw·w ⟨m⟩ nꜥy r ḳbḥ* 'they are going to cool down', Wenamūn 2, 66 (XXIst Dyn.); Dem. *ỉ·ỉr Pꜣ-Rꜥ*  (*nꜣỉ*) *ḫꜥ n-ỉm·f* 'the sun will rise', Dem. mag. Pap. 29, 2–3.

[D]SPIEGELBERG, *Dem. Gr.* 77, § 162 [1925].

NB. The rival theory, however, maintains that ⲉ⸗ of IInd Future derives from verb *ỉry*, see under ⲉ⸗, ⲉⲣⲉ-, verbal prefix of second tenses (*b*).

(*c*) Imperfect of Future ⲛⲉⲓⲛⲁⲥⲱⲧⲙ = L.E.  , *wn·ỉ m nꜥy r sḏm*, 'I was in going to hear'; cf.  , *wn·f ⟨m⟩ nꜥy ⟨r⟩ smy*, 'he was going to report' (Pap. Strassburg 24, v, 5 [XXIst Dyn.] = *ZÄS* 53, 18).

For Qual. ⲛⲏⲩ, see this latter below.

ⲛⲁ- (Crum 259 a under ⲡⲁ-), pl. possessive prefix 'those of' = , *nꜣ n* > , *nꜣ* (*Wb.* II, 199, 5, 6), 'this (neutr.) of', 'those of';  (Er. 203, 2), *nꜣỉ*, 'those of'.

[H]DE ROUGÉ, *Chrest.* II, p. 32 [1868]; cf. Spiegelberg, *ZÄS* 54, 109–10 [1918]; [D]BRUGSCH, *Gr. dém.* 83, §§ 185, 186 (knows only Dem. examples of sg. m. and f.) [1855].

ⲛⲁⲁ (Crum 218 b), 'be great' =  (cf. *Wb.* II, 200, 1), *nꜣ-ꜥꜣ*, 'great is...' in proper names like , *nꜣ-ꜥꜣ-tꜣy·s-nḫt*, 'great is her might';  (Er. 54, top; 202, 6), *nꜣ-ꜥꜣ*, 'great is...'.

[H]ERMAN, *ZÄS* 44, 109–10 [1907]; [D]REVILLOUT, *Poème*, 80 [1885].

ⲛⲁⲓⲁⲧ⸗, 'blessed', see under ⲉⲓⲁ, 'eye'.

ⲛⲁⲓ (Crum 259a under ⲛⲁⲓ), pl. demonstrative pronoun, 'these' =  (*Wb.* II, 199, 1. 2), *nꜣ*, 'this' > L.E. 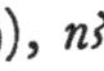 (*Wb.* II, 199, 9), *nꜣỉ*, 'these';  (Er. 203, 3), *nꜣỉ*, 'these'.

[H]CHAMPOLLION, *Gr. ég.* 182 [1836]; [D]BRUGSCH, *Gr. dém.* 79, §172 [1855].

ⲛⲁⲉⲓⲱ (Crum 218b), 'peg, stake' = 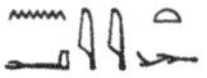 (*Wb.* II, 207, 17), *nꜥyt*, 'stake on the prow of a ship to tie it to shore';  (Er. 208, 3; 206, 2; 207, 1), *nꜥyt*, 'stake'.

[H]BRUGSCH, *Wb.*, Suppl. 660 [1881]; [D]SPIEGELBERG, *Petubastis*, 30*, no. 190 [1910].

ⲛⲉ- (Crum 219a), prefix of past tenses =  (*Wb.* I, 308–9), *wn*, 'be';  (Er. 88, 2), *wnw*, 'be' to form Imperfect.

[H]STERN, *Kopt. Gr.* 214, §373 [1880]; [D]REVILLOUT, *Chrest. dém.* 420; 143 n. 1 [1880].

ⲉⲛⲉ-, verbal prefix in relative clauses with past meaning = (*a*) after defined antecedent ⲉⲛⲉ- = L.E. , *ỉwn* + subj.; , *r-wnnꜣw*, i.e. (past) Relative form of , 'to be'.

[HD]SPIEGELBERG, *Dem. Gr.* 248–9, §549; 252, §555 [1925].

(*b*) after undefined antecedent ⲉⲛⲉ⸗ = ⲉ + ⲛⲉ⸗ = L.E.  + subj., *ỉw wn*.

-ⲛⲉ (Crum 260b, under -ⲛⲏ), enclitic as plural copula = L.E.  (*Wb.* II, 199, 10), *nꜣỉ*;  (Er. 203, bottom), *nꜣw*, pl. demonstrative subject in non-verbal sentence.

[H]ERMAN, *Näg. Gr.* 57–8, §78 [1880], and *Spr. Westcar*, 50 n. 2 [1889]; cf. Maspero, *ZÄS* 15, 111–13 [1877]; [D]BRUGSCH, *Gr. dém.* 125, §257 [1855].

ⲛⲉⲓ (Crum 219a), 'time' = 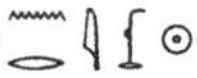 (*Wb.* II, 279, 11, 12), *nrỉ*, 'specified time, term'; perhaps Dem. 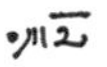 (Er. 205, 5), *nꜣy*, 'time'.

[H]ERMAN-LANGE, *Pap. Lansing*, 40 [1925].

ⲛⲏ (Crum 260b, under ⲛⲏ), pl. demonstrative pronoun 'that' =  (*Wb.* II, 199, 1), *nꜣ* > L.E.  (*Wb.* II, 199, 9), *nꜣỉ*, 'those'.

NB. The form **nꜣw*, postulated by STEINDORFF, *Kopt. Gr.*[2], §96, Anm. [1904], and by ERMAN, *Äg. Gr.*[3], §168, Anm., is not attested in L.E.

ⲛⲟⲩ (Crum 219a), 'go' = (*Wb.* II, 206, 7), *nʿỉ*, 'travel in a boat'; (Er. 207, 8), *nʿ*, 'go'.

[H]SETHE, *Verbum*, II, 268, §615 [1899]; [D]GRIFFITH, *Stories*, 92 [1900]; cf. Griffith–Thompson, III, 44, no. 433 [1909].

See also under **ⲛⲁ**, 'go' of which **ⲛⲟⲩ** is a masc. (infinitive) substitute acc. to SETHE, *ZÄS* 47, 145 n. 1 [1910]. Neither in Egn. nor in Dem. are **ⲛⲁ** and **ⲛⲟⲩ** distinguishable, see PARKER, *JEA* 26, 90.

For **ⲛⲏⲩ** (Crum 219b), see this latter.

ⲛⲟⲩ⸗ (Crum 260b, under **ⲡⲱ⸗**), pl. absolute possessive pronoun, 'mine' (lit. 'those of mine') = + suff. (*Wb.* II, 199, 7), *nꜣy*; (Er. 205, 1), *nꜣỉ·*, 'mine'.

[H]CHAMPOLLION, *Gr. ég.* 265 [1836]; [D]BRUGSCH, *Scriptura Aeg. dem.* 33, §25 [1848].

ⲛⲏⲃ (Crum 221a), 'lord' = (*Wb.* II, 227, 5 ff.), *nb*, 'lord'; (Er. 212, 3), *nb*, 'lord'.

[H]CHAMPOLLION, *Précis*, 1st ed., Tableau gén., p. (43) and pl. 20, no. 415 ff. [1824]; [D]BRUGSCH, *Gr. dém.* 38, §81 [1885], cf. Åkerblad in Young, *Misc. Works*, III, 38 [1815].

ⲛⲟⲩⲃ (Crum 221b), 'gold' = (*Wb.* II, 237, 6), *nb*, 'gold'; (Er. 214, 1), *nb*, 'gold'.

[H]CHAMPOLLION, *Gr. ég.* 89 [1836]; [D]YOUNG, *Mus. crit.* 6, 169–70, no. 74 = *Misc. Works*, III, 28–9, no. 74 [1815, letter to de Sacy of 21 Oct. 1814].

ϩⲁⲙⲛⲟⲩⲃ, 'goldsmith', see under **ϩⲁⲙ**, 'craftsman'.

ⲛⲏⲏⲃⲉ (Crum 222a), 'float, swim' = (*Wb.* II, 236, 10), *nbỉ*, 'swim'; (Er. 215, 2), *nby*, 'swim'.

[H]CHAMPOLLION, *Gr. ég.* 376, 427 [1836]; [D]VOLTEN, *Dem. Traumdeutung*, 111 [1942].

ⲛⲟⲃⲉ (Crum 222a), 'sin' = Gr.-R. (not in *Wb.*; only Rochemonteix, *Edfou*, I, 543; quoted by Möller), *nb*; (Er. 214, 6), *nby*, , *nbỉt*, 'damage, sin'.

[H]MÖLLER, *Pap. Rhind*, 30*, no. 194 [1913] (who, however, does not consider its identity with **ⲛⲟⲃⲉ**); [D]REVILLOUT, *Poème*, 14 [1885].

ⲛⲟⲩⲃⲥ (Crum 222b), a tree = (*Wb.* II, 245, 10), *nbs*, Christ's thorn tree, *Zizyphus spina Christi*; (Er. 215, 7), *nbs*, a tree.

[H]BRUGSCH, *ZÄS* 22, 20 [1884]; [D]GRIFFITH-THOMPSON, III, 46, no. 458 [1909].

ⲛⲟⲩⲃⲧ (Crum 222b), 'weave' = (*Wb.* III, 246, 4), *nbd*, 'to plait'; (not in Er.; Apisritual XI, 19; XII, 6), *nbt*, 'wrap'.

[H]BIRCH in *Archaeologia*, 38, 386 [1860]; cf. BRUGSCH, *Wb.* 752 [1868]; [D]H. THOMPSON's Demotic dictionary.

ⲛⲏⲃⲧⲉ, 'plait, tress' = L.E. (*Wb.* II, 246, 9), *nbd*, also often (Ostracon Dêr el-Medîna Cat. no. 304, 4) and sim., *nbdt*, 'wicker-work'; (Er. 215, 8), *nbt*, 'wicker-work'.

[HD]JUNKER, *Pap. Lonsdorfer I*, 15 n. 9 [1921]; cf. Champollion, *Gr. ég.* 382 [1836].

ⲛⲟⲉⲓⲕ (Crum 222b), 'adulterer' = (*Wb.* II, 345, 11), *nkw*, 'fornicator'; (Pap. Insinger 7, 24; cf. Er. 229, 8), *nk*, and (Ankhsh. 13, 12; 19, 1), *nyk*, 'fornicator'.

[H]ERMAN-GRAPOW, *Wb.* II, 345, 11 [1928]; [D]REVILLOUT, *Pap. mor.* I, 45 n. 2 [1906].

[S]**ⲛⲁⲁⲕⲉ**, [A]**ⲛⲉⲕϩⲉ**, [B]**ⲛⲁⲕϩⲓ** (Crum 223a), 'pains of travail' = **nahḳet*' from (*Wb.* II, 288, 1), movement of a woman which reveals whether she is pregnant or not.

DÉVAUD's slip (as parallel he quotes [S]**ⲛⲁϫϩⲉ**, **ⲛⲁⲁϫⲉ**, [B]**ⲛⲁϫϩⲓ** = *nḏḥt*, 'tooth'); cf. SAUNERON in *BIFAO* 64, 8–10 [1966].

ⲛⲕⲁ (Crum 223a), 'thing' = (*Wb.* II, 347, 10 ff.), *nkt*, 'a little of..., thing'; (Er. 229, 9), *nkt*, 'thing'.

[H]CHABAS, *Mél. ég.* II, 202 [1864]; [D]REVILLOUT, *Poème*, 253 [1885].

ⲛⲕⲁ ⲛⲓⲙ (Crum 223b), 'everything' = (*Wb.* II, 347, 15. 16), *nkt nb*, 'all things, something'; (Er. 230, middle; e.g. P. Berlin 3078, 6), *nkt nb*, 'everything'.

ⲛⲟⲕⲛⲉⲕ (Crum 223b), 'have affection, inclination to', reduplication of (*Wb.* II, 345, 3 f.), *nk*, 'have sexual intercourse'; (Er. 229, 8), *nk*, or (Er. 229, 5), *nḳ*, same meaning.

ⲛⲟⲩⲕⲉⲣ (Crum 224a), 'prick, incise' = Dem. (Er. 229, 6), *nḳr*, 'scrape, chisel off', loan-word from Semitic נָקַר, 'bore, pick, dig'.

ᴰGRIFFITH, *Pap. Ryl.* III, 363 [1909]; ˢSPIEGELBERG, *Kopt. Handwb.* 76 [1921].

ⲛⲕⲟⲧⲕ, ⲛⲕⲟⲧⲉ (Crum 224a), 'sleep' = L.E. (*Wb.* II, 345, 1; see corr. in vol. of examples), *nḳdd*, 'sleep'; (Er. 229, 7), (*ỉ*)*nḳty*, 'sleep'.

ᴴSPIEGELBERG in GRIFFITH, *Pap. Kahun*, Text, 99 [1898]; cf. CHABAS, *Mél. ég.* I, Appendice, 43 n. 3 [1863]; ᴰGRIFFITH, *Stories*, 114 and 154 [1900]; cf. HESS, *Stne*, 16 [1888].

ⲕⲧⲟⲕ, 'untimely', see **ⲕⲧⲟⲕ**.

ⲛⲓⲙ (Crum 225a), 'who?' = (*Wb.* II, 263, 7–9), *nm*, L.E. , *nm*, 'who?'; (Er. 218, 2), *nm*, 'who?'.

ᴴGOODWIN in Chabas, *Mél. ég.* I, 86 [1862]; ᴰBRUGSCH, *Wb.* 743 [1868].

ⲛⲓⲙ (Crum 225a), 'certain person, so and so' replaces ᴮ**ⲙⲁⲛ** (see the latter): ᴼ**ⲛⲓⲙ ⲉⲙⲉⲥⲓⲉ ⲛⲓⲙ** (Preisendanz, *Papyri graecae magicae*, I, 72, 120), 'so and so whom so and so has borne' = , *mn r·ms mn* of Dem. Mag. Pap., passim, older , *mn ms·n mnt* (*Wb.* II, 65, 1).

ᴰERMAN, *ZÄS* 21, 103 [1883].

ⲛⲓⲙ (Crum 225b), 'every' = (*Wb.* II, 234, 3 ff.), *nb*, 'every'; (Er. 213, 3), *nb*, 'every'.

ᴴGELL in YOUNG, *Misc. Works*, III, 420 [1827]; CHAMPOLLION, *Précis*, 2nd ed., Tableau gén., p. (46) and pl. 20, no. 423, 426–8 [1828]; ᴰBRUGSCH, *Scriptura Aeg. dem.* 40, § 30, II (1848).

ᴼ**ⲛⲉⲙⲉ** (Crum 226a), 'flame' as goddess (?) = (*Wb.* II, 244, 11), *nbỉt*, 'fire, glow'; (Er. 214, 5), *nbt*, 'flame', and (Er. 218, 7), *mmỉt*, 'flame' as goddess.

ᴴᴰGRIFFITH in *ZÄS* 46, 124 [1909]; cf. ᴰSpiegelberg, *Petubastis*, Glossary, 32*, no. 202 [1910].

ⲛⲟⲙⲧⲉ (Crum 226a), 'strength, power' = (Er. 220, 2), *nmṭ*(*t*), 'strength, power'; cf. (*Wb.* II, 271, 2 ff.), *nmtt*, 'step', despite the difference in meaning.

ᴴERICHSEN, *Dem. Glossar*, 220, 2 [1954]; ᴰBRUGSCH, *Gr. dém.* 36, § 76 [1855].

ⲛⲟⲉⲓⲛ (Crum 226b), 'shake, tremble' = (*Wb.* II, 203, 7), *nyny*, 'shake' (of legs); (Petubastis, Pap. Krall, H 18), or (Ankhsh. 22, 5), *nyn*, 'tremble'.

[H]GLANVILLE's index; [D]STRICKER, *Oudheidkundige Mededelingen, N.R.* 35; 53 n. 29 [1954].

ⲛⲟⲩⲛ (Crum 226b), 'abyss (of hell)' = (*Wb.* II, 214, 18 ff.), *nwn(w)*, 'primeval ocean'; and (Er. 211, 2), *nwn*, 'primeval ocean'.

[H]CHAMPOLLION, *Gr. ég.* 98 [1836]; [D]BRUGSCH, *Gr. dém.* 27, §54 [1855].

ⲛⲁⲛⲟⲩ- (Crum 227a), 'be good, fair' = , *n-ꜥn*, 'be good', in fem. proper name , *n-ꜥn-n(ꜣy)s ḥryw*, 'may her masters be good' (Ranke, I, 182, 15; II, 366, *ad* I, 182, 15); (Er. 62, 4), *nꜣ-ꜥn·*, 'be good'.

[H]RANKE, *Die äg. Personennamen*, II, 366 [1953]; [D]BRUGSCH, *Wb.* 194–5 [1867]. Contains , *ꜥn*, 'be pleasing', **ⲁⲛⲁⲓ**, STEINDORFF, *Kopt. Gr.* 2nd ed., 130, §269, Anm. [1904].

NB. The fem. proper name in which Erman (*ZÄS* 44, 109–10) thought to recognize **ⲛⲁⲛⲟⲩ≈ⲥ**, is to be read and interpreted *nꜥ-n·s-Wbꜣstt*, '(goddess) Ubaste be merciful to her'; see Ranke, I, 182, 17.

ⲛⲏⲛⲓ (Crum 227b), 'honeycomb' = (Er. 220, 8), *nnyt*, 'honeycomb'. Perhaps through assimilation from (*Wb.* II, 66, 6 ff.), *mnỉ*, later , or (but m. like **ⲛⲏⲛⲓ**), kind of jug. Egyptian bee keepers used pots as honeycombs (Klebs, *Die Reliefs und Malereien des mittleren Reiches*, 83–4; Davies, *Rekhmire* Pl. 49; Säve-Söderbergh, *Four Tombs*, Pl. 9).

[D]BRUGSCH, *Gr. dém.* 33, §66 [1855].

ⲛⲟⲩⲛⲉ (Crum 227b), 'root' = (*Wb.* II, 77, 2), *mnyt*, 'root'; (Er. 220, 6), *nnt*, 'root'.

[H]DÉVAUD's slip; [D]GRIFFITH-THOMPSON, III, 47, no. 466 [1909].

ⲛⲛⲉ- (Crum 228a), prefix of neg. 3rd Future = , *nn ỉw·f(r sḏm)* > L.E. , *bn ỉw·f (r sḏm)* > late , *bn·f (sḏm)* (*Wb.* I, 456, 12), 'he shall not (hear)'; (Er. 115, 7), *bn-ỉw·*, 'he shall not (hear)' (for a table of forms, see *JNES* 7, 235).

[H]SETHE, *Verbum*, II, 465, corr. to §568c [1899]; [D]GRIFFITH-THOMPSON, III, 25, no. 256 [1909]; GRIFFITH, *Ryl.* III, 345 [1909].

[O]ⲛⲉⲛⲉⲃⲉ (Crum 228a), 'styrax(?)' = (*Wb.* II, 276, 9), *nnyb*, 'styrax'.

GRIFFITH-THOMPSON, I, 85 n. [1904].

ⲛⲁⲡⲣⲉ (Crum 228a), 'grain, seed' = (*Wb.* II, 249, 4, 5), *npri*, 'grain'.

CHAMPOLLION, *Gr. ég.* 77 [1836].

For ⲛⲁⲡⲛⲉ (in Pistis Sophia), compare (*Wb.* II, 248, 13) and (*Wb.* II, 249, 2), *npnn*, 'grain', both probably sub-forms of *npri*.

DÉVAUD's slip.

ⲛⲁⲣⲟ, ⲛⲁⲣⲉ-, ⲛⲁⲣⲟ⸗ (P. Bodmer VI; not in Crum), 'observe, watch, see'. The pron. form is from ⲛⲁⲩ ('see') + ⲉⲣⲟ⸗, absolute and construct infinitives are secondary, formed on the pronominal; analogous to ϫⲉ + ⲉⲣⲟ⸗ > ϫⲉⲣⲟ⸗, 'mean'.

KASSER in *ZÄS* 92, 114 [1966].

ⲛⲟⲩⲣⲉ (Crum 228b), f., 'vulture' = (*Wb.* II, 277, 1), *nrt*, 'vulture'; (Er. 221, 1), *nr*, 'vulture'.

[H]CHAMPOLLION, *Gr. ég.* 73 [1836]; [D]BRUGSCH, *Gr. dém.* 24, §41; 73, §159 [1855].

Masc. 'male vulture' = , *nwr*, 'male vulture'.

SPIEGELBERG, *Mythus*, 173, no. 422 [1917].

[A2]ⲛⲟⲩⲣⲥ, ⲛⲁⲣⲥ⸗, Qual. ⲛⲁⲣⲥ (not in Crum; Mani Ps.), 'destroy' = ?lit. 'burn', (*Wb.* II, 335, 4–11), *nsr*, 'burn' intrans., in Graeco-Roman period also transitive.

ⲛⲏⲥⲉ (Crum 229a), 'bench, seat(?)' = , (*Wb.* II, 321, 6), *nst*, 'throne, seat'; (Er. 228, 1), *nsꜣt*, 'seat, bench' or sim.

[HD]SPIEGELBERG, *OLZ* 14, col. 258 [1911].

(ⲛⲉⲥⲃⲟ, or better ⲛⲉⲥⲃⲉ), ⲛⲉⲥⲃⲱⲱ⸗ (Crum 229a), 'be wise', adjectival verb ⲛⲉ + ⲥⲃⲟ ('teaching', here with passive meaning 'being taught').

CRUM, *A Coptic Dict.* 229a [1930]; cf. Steindorff, *Lehrbuch*, 136–7, §297 [1951].

ⲛⲁⲧ (Crum 229a), 'loom, web' = (*Wb.* II, 376, 18), *nḏ*, 'thread'; (P. Lille, no. 32, 15; not in Er.), *nt*, 'loom'.

[H]BRUGSCH, *Wb.* 829 [1868]; [D]SOTTAS, *Pap. dém. de Lille*, I, 84 and pl. 18 [1921].

ⲛⲟⲩⲧ (Crum 229a), 'grind, pound' = (*Wb.* II, 369, 11 ff.), *nḏ*, 'grind'; (Er. 231, 1), *nt*, 'grind'.

[H]CHABAS, *Oeuv. div.* II (= *Bibl. ég.* x), 178 [1862]; [D]BRUGSCH, *Wb.* 827–8 [1868].

ⲛⲟⲉⲓⲧ (Crum 229b), 'meal, flour' = (*Wb.* II, 370, 16), *nḏ(w)*, 'flour; (Er. 231, 1), *nyt*, 'flour'.

[H]BRUGSCH, *Wb.* 828 [1868]; [D]GRIFFITH–THOMPSON, III, 45, no. 444 [1909].

[SA2]**ⲛⲟⲩⲧ** (Crum 229b, under **ⲛⲟⲩⲧ**, 'grind', and Add. XIX), f., 'gathering of waters, pool', only in **ⲛⲟⲩⲧ ⲙⲙⲟⲟⲩ** = (Couyat-Montet, *Hammâmât*, no. 1, 6), *nwt nt mw*, 'pools of water', *nwt* being different from (*Wb.* II, 221, 14 f.), *nw(y)t*, 'water, flood'. For final **-ⲧ** cf. **ⲙⲟⲩⲧ**, 'sinew.

DÉVAUD's slip (despite Spiegelberg, *Kopt. Etym.* 56).

ⲛⲧⲉ- (Crum 229b), prefix of Conjunctive = L.E. + suffix or nom. subj. (*Wb.* II, 165, 2 ff.), *mtw·*, prefix of Conjunctive; (Er. 185, 8), *mtw·*, prefix of Conjunctive.

[H]ERMAN, *Näg. Gr.* 139, §216 [1880]; [D]BRUGSCH, *Scriptura Aeg. dem.* 54, §41 [1848].

NB. The ultimate origin of L.E. , *mtw·k sḏm*, from (*ḥnʿ*) *ntk sḏm*, 'and you (shall) hear', was established by GARDINER, *JEA* 14, 86 ff. [1928]; see also Černý, *JEA* 35, 25–30 [1949].

ⲛⲧⲉ, ⲛⲧⲁ⸗ (Crum 230a), particle of genitive = (*Wb.* II, 176, 14 ff.), *mdy·*, 'with'; (Er. 188, 1), *mtw·*, 'with'.

[H]ERMAN, *Näg. Gr.* 84, §110 n. 2 [1880]; [D]BRUGSCH, *Scriptura Aeg. dem.* 36 [1848].

ⲛⲟⲩⲧⲉ (Crum 230b), 'god' = (*Wb.* II, 358, 1 ff.), *nṯr*, 'god'; (Er. 232, 6), *ntr*, 'god'.

[H]YOUNG, *Misc. Works*, III, Pl. 1, no. 1 = *Encycl. Brit.*, Suppl. IV, Pl. 74, no. 1 [1818]; [D]YOUNG, *Misc. Works*, III, pp. 24–5, no. 29 = *Mus. crit.* 6, 174–5, no. 29 [1815].

[O]**ⲛⲉⲧ-** in **ⲛⲉⲧ ⲉϊⲡⲛ**, 'this god', see under **ⲉϊⲡⲛ**. Also in [O]**ⲛⲉⲧⲟ**, 'great god'.

CRUM in *JEA* 28, 28, 4 [1942].

ⲛⲧⲱⲣⲉ (Crum 230b; for further examples, see *JEA* 25, 110), 'goddess' = (*Wb.* II, 362, 4), *nṯrt*, 'goddess'; (Er. 233, bottom), *ntrt*, 'goddess'.

ⲛⲧⲟ (Crum 11 b, under **ⲁⲛⲟⲕ**), personal pronoun of 2nd pers. sing. fem., 'thou' = (*Wb.* II, 357, 7), *nṯt*, 'thou (fem.)'; (Er. 187, top), *mtwt*.

[H]CHAMPOLLION, *Gr. ég.* 253 [1836]; [D]BRUGSCH, *Scriptura Aeg. dem.* 31, §22 [1848].

ⲛⲧⲟⲕ (Crum 11 b, under **ⲁⲛⲟⲕ**), pers. pronoun of 2nd pers. sing. masc., 'thou, you' = (*Wb.* II, 357, 2), *ntk*, 'you'; (Er. 187, top; 147, 4), (*m*)*ntk*, 'you'.

[H]CHAMPOLLION, *Gr. ég.* 252 [1836]; [D]BRUGSCH, *Scriptura Aeg. dem.* 31, §22 [1848].

ⲛⲟⲩⲧⲙ (Crum 231 b), 'become sweet', [B]**ⲛⲟⲩⲧⲉⲙ**, 'sweet' = (*Wb.* II, 378, 9 ff.), *nḏm*, 'become, be sweet'; (Er. 232, 5), *ntm*, 'be pleasant, sweet'.

[H]DE ROUGÉ, *Oeuv. div.* III (= *Bibl. ég.* XXIII), 68 [1855]; [D]BRUGSCH, *Rhind*, 40, no. 178, and Pl. 38, no. 178 [1865].

ⲛⲧⲉⲣⲉ- (Crum 232 a), prefix in temporal clauses: **ⲛⲧⲉⲣⲉϥⲥⲱⲧⲙ** < *, *m-ḏr ỉry.f sḏm*, 'after he had heard', **ⲛⲧⲉ-** = (*Wb.* V, 593, 15), *m-ḏr*; Dem. , *mtw-*, , *n-t*(*t*), etc. (Er. 645, bottom).

[H]DE ROUGÉ, *Chrest.* III, 61, §311 [1875]; [D]BRUGSCH, *Rhind*, 40, and pl. 38, no. 175–6 [1865].

NB. That **ⲛⲧⲉ-** only, not **ⲛⲧⲉⲣⲉ-**, corresponds to , *m-ḏr*, has not always been realized; first clearly formulated by SPIEGELBERG, *Dem. Gr.* 233, §513 [1925]; cf. Sethe, *ZÄS* 62, 6, 3 [1927].

ⲛⲧⲟⲥ (Crum 11 b, under **ⲁⲛⲟⲕ**), pers. pronoun of 3rd pers. sing. fem., 'she' = (*Wb.* II, 356, 14), *nts*, pers. pronoun of 3rd pers. sing. fem.; (Er. 187, middle), *mtws*.

[H]CHAMPOLLION, *Gr. ég.* 254 [1836]; [D]BRUGSCH, *Gr. dém.* 94, §213 [1855].

ⲛⲧⲱⲧⲛ (Crum 11 b, under **ⲁⲛⲟⲕ**), pers. pronoun of 2nd pers. pl., 'you' = (*Wb.* II, 357, 8), *nṯtn*, pers. pronoun of 2nd pers. pl.; (Er. 187), *mtwtn*.

[H]CHAMPOLLION, *Gr. ég.* 255–6 [1836]; [D]BRUGSCH, *Scriptura Aeg. dem.* 31, §22 [1848].

ⲛⲧⲟⲟⲩ (Crum 11 b, under ⲁⲛⲟⲕ), pers. pronoun of 3rd pers. pl. = (*Wb.* II, 355, 15), *nt·w*, pers. pronoun of 3rd pers. pl., 'they'; (Er. 187), *mtww*.

[H]STERN, *Kopt. Gr.* 120, §254 [1880]; [D]BRUGSCH, *Scriptura Aeg. dem.* 31, §22 [1848].

ⲛⲧⲟⲟⲩⲛ (Crum 232 a), 'then' = (*Wb.* V, 432, 11–13), *m dwn*, 'then, further'; (Er. 615, 1), *ntwn*, 'indeed'.

[H]CHABAS, *Mél. ég.* 3e sér., I, 32 and 185 [1870]; [D]LANGE in LANGE-NEUGEBAUER, *Papyrus Carlsberg No. I*, 32 [1940].

See also ⲧⲱⲟⲩⲛ, 'arise'.

ⲛⲟⲩⲧϥ (Crum 232 a), 'loosen, dissolve' = (*Wb.* II, 356, 9), *ntf*, 'loosen'; (Er. 232, 4), *ntf*, 'loosen'.

[HD]SPIEGELBERG, *ZÄS* 53, 131 [1917].

ⲛⲧⲟϥ (Crum 11 b, under ⲁⲛⲟⲕ), pers. pronoun of 3rd pers. sing. masc., 'he' = (*Wb.* II, 356, 3), *ntf*; (Er. 187), *mtwf*, 'he'.

[H]CHAMPOLLION, *Précis*, 1st ed., 76 and Tableau gén., no. 17 on p. (2)–(3) and Pl. I [1824]; [D]BRUGSCH, *Scriptura Aeg. dem.* 31, §22 [1848].

ⲛⲧⲟϥ (Crum 232 b), same pronoun used as particle, 'rather, but, again' = L.E. (*Wb.* II, 356, 3, this shade of meaning not recorded).

[H]SETHE, *Nominalsatz*, p. 1, §6 [1916], but his L.Eg. ex. is non-existent. P. Anast. 4, 5, 1, should be translated 'if I were it' (i.e. 'my heart, thought'); [D]STRICKER, in *Oudheidkundige Mededelingen, N.R.* 35, 73 n. 22 [1954].

ⲛⲁⲩ (Crum 233 b), 'look, behold' = (*Wb.* II, 218, 3 ff.), *nw* (from an older , *nwꜣ* (*Wb.* II, 221, 20), see Gardiner, *JEA* 31, 113), 'look'; (Er. 209, 3), *nw*, 'see'.

[H]DE ROUGÉ, *Oeuv. div.* III (= *Bibl. ég.* XXIII), 66 [1855]; [D]MASPERO, *ZÄS* 15, 138 n. 9 [1877].

With preposition , *r* > ⲉ-, *nw* is attested since XXIst Dyn. in weakened meaning 'see' (*Wb.* II, 218, 9).

Imperative ⲁⲛⲁⲩ = Dem. , *ỉ·nw*, *r·nw* (Er. 209, lower).

KRALL, *Mitt. aus der Sammlung Erz. Rainer*, VI, 67, no. 153 [1897].

ⲛⲁⲩ (Crum 234b), 'hour, time' = (*Wb.* II, 219, 1 ff.), *nw*, 'time'; (Er. 210, 1), *nw*, 'time, hour'.

Hᴄʜᴀʙᴀs, *Mél. ég.* II, 205 [1864]; Dʙʀᴜɢsᴄʜ, *Gr. dém.* 30, §61 [1855].

(ⲛ)ⲧⲛⲁⲩ, ⲧⲛⲛⲁⲩ (Crum 235b), 'when?' = (*Wb.* V, 373, 1), *tnỉ*, 'where?' + , *nw*, 'time'; spelt , *n-dnw*, Schäfer, *Nastesen*, 101 n. 11.

sᴇᴛʜᴇ in Spiegelberg, *Kopt. Handwb.* 148 [1921].

ⲛⲏⲩ (Crum 219b), 'be coming, about to come', acting as Qual. of **ⲉⲓ**, 'to come', and generally derived from **ⲛⲁ** and **ⲛⲟⲩ**, 'to go', and consequently from (*Wb.* II, 206, 7), *nꜥy*, 'to travel in a boat', is in reality L.E. (Wenamūn 2, 63), for old , *m ỉwt*, 'in coming'; Dem. (Er. 21, 1), *(ỉ)n·ỉw*.

HDɢʀɪғғɪᴛʜ, *Stories*, 153–4 [1900]; cf. also Spiegelberg, *Kopt. Etym.* 50 ff. [1920] and ɢᴀʀᴅɪɴᴇʀ, *LES* p. 73a [1932] (for *m ỉwt*).

B**ⲛⲁⲩⲓ** (Crum 235b), 'spear' = (*Wb.* II, 202, 15), *nỉwy*, 'spear'; (Er. 210, 2), *nw*, 'spear'.

Hᴅᴇ ʀᴏᴜɢé in his course of lectures in 1863, acc. to de Horrack's letter to Chabas (de Horrack, *Oeuv. div.* p. xviii); printed in *Rev. ég.* 5, 162 n. 3 = de Rougé, *Oeuv. div.* V (= *Bibl. ég.* XXV), 345 n. 2 [1888]; Dsᴘɪᴇɢᴇʟʙᴇʀɢ, *Sitzber. Bayr. Ak.* 1925, 4. Abh. 23–4 [1925].

B**ⲛⲱⲟⲩϯ** (Crum 235b), 'swaddling-bands' = (*Wb.* II, 225, 12), *nwdt*, 'swaddling-bands' of a child.

ʟᴇ ᴘᴀɢᴇ ʀᴇɴᴏᴜғ, *Egypt. and Philol. Essays*, I, 458 (= *ZÄS* 10, 96) [1872].

ⲛⲟⲉⲓϣ (Crum 236a), 'spleen' = (*Wb.* II, 276, 17), *nnšm* > , *nš* (Abydos, temple of Sethos I = Jéquier, *L'architecture et la décoration dans l'Ég. anc.* II, Pl. 19), 'spleen'; (Er. 207, 5), *nyš*, 'spleen'.

Hʙʀᴜɢsᴄʜ, *Wb.* 784 [1868]; Dʙʀᴜɢsᴄʜ, *Gr. dém.* 29, §56 [1855].

ⲛⲁϣⲉ-, ⲛⲁϣⲱ⸗ (Crum 236a), 'be many, much' = (Er. 72, 3), *nꜣ-ꜥšꜣ*, 'be many'.

ʀᴇᴠɪʟʟᴏᴜᴛ, *Pap. mor.* I, 46 n. 6, and p. 118 n. 1 [1906].

ⲛⲟⲟϣⲉ (Crum 236a), Qual. (of *ⲛⲟⲩⲟⲩϣⲉ as **ⲃⲟⲟⲣⲉ** is of **ⲃⲱⲱⲣⲉ**, etc.), 'be strong' (of bad smell) = (*Urk.* IV, 1963, 4), *nꜥḥ* > L.Eg. (*Wb.* II, 209, 12 f.), *nꜥš*, 'strong'; (Er. 208, 4), *nꜥš*, 'strong' or sim.

ⲛⲟⲩϣⲡ (Crum 236a), 'blow, agitate' = (*Wb.* II, 339, 1), *nšp*, 'breathe'.

SPIEGELBERG, *Kopt. Etymologien*, 11 [1920].

ⲛⲟϣⲣ (Crum 237a), 'vulture, falcon' = (Er. 229, 4), *nšr*, 'vulture, falcon', from Semitic (Ar. نَسْر, Hebr. נֶשֶׁר, Akkadian *našru*).

[D]BRUGSCH, *Gr. dém.* 24, §41 [1855]; [S]ROSSI, *Etym. aeg.* 138 [1808].

[S]**ⲛⲟⲩϣⲧ**, [A]**ⲛⲟⲩⳉⲧ** (Crum 237a), 'make hard, oppress, do violence', 1st Inf. of **ⲛϣⲟⲧ**, 'become hard', etc. See the latter for etymology.

ⲛϣⲓⲧ (Crum 237a), 'lock of hair' = (not in Er.), *nšyt*, 'lock of hair'; cf. (*Wb.* II, 337, 6), *nšt* (fem.), 'hairdresser'.

H. S. SMITH, *JEA* 44, 122 [1958].

ⲛϣⲟⲧ (Crum 237a), 'become hard, strong' = (*Wb.* II, 314, 6 ff.), *nḫt*, 'be strong'; (Er. 226, 5), *nḫt*, 'become strong'. **ⲛϣⲟⲧ** is 2nd Inf. of **ⲛⲟⲩϣⲧ**.

[H]CHAMPOLLION, *Gr. ég.* 380 [1836]; [D]DE ROUGÉ, *Oeuv. div.* I (= *Bibl. ég.* XXI), 248–50 and Pl. 2 [95], nos. 25, 26, 29, 30, 31 [1848].

ⲛⲁϣⲧⲉⲓⲙⲉ, ⲛⲁϣⲧⲙⲙⲉ (Crum 78b), 'presumptuous, impudent, obdurate' = , *nḫt ỉmy(t)*, 'hard of character'. The orig. form is **-ⲙⲙⲉ** which corresponds to (Er. 5, 1), *ỉmyt*, 'soul, character' or sim. (not to the homonymous *ỉmyt*, 'fist', so Spiegelberg); **-ⲉⲓⲙⲉ**, is a re-interpretation influenced by the verb **ⲉⲓⲙⲉ** which is, however, related.

SPIEGELBERG in *Rec. trav.* 31, 159–60 [1909].

ⲛⲁϣⲧϩⲣⲁ⸗ (Crum 237b), 'hard of face, impudent' = (*Wb.* II, 315, 2), *nḫt-ḥr*, 'impudent'.

DÉVAUD, *Kêmi*, I, 29 [1928].

ⲛⲁϣⲧⲉ (Crum 238a), 'strength' = (*Wb.* II, 317, 15–22), *nḫtt*, 'stiffness in limbs, strength, victory'; (Er. 226, 5), *nḫṯt*, 'strength, victory'.

[H]W. MAX MÜLLER, *Der Bündnisvertrag Ramses' II, und des Chetiterkönigs*, 13 n. 4 [1902]; [D]REVILLOUT, *Pap. mor.* I, 174 n. 2 [1906].

ⲛⲉⲉϥ (Crum 238b), 'sailor' = (*Wb.* II, 251, 1 ff.), *nfw*, 'sailor'; (Er. 216, 7), *nf*, 'sailor'.

[H]BRUGSCH, *Wb.* 754–6 [1868]; [D]BRUGSCH, *Sammlung dem. Urk.* p. 36 and Pl. 10, col. IV, 13 [1850]; BRUGSCH, *De natura*, 31 [1850].

ⲛⲓϥⲉ (Crum 238b), 'blow, breathe (of wind)' = (*Wb.* II, 250, 11), *nfy*, 'breathe'; (Er. 216, 6), *nyf*, 'blow, breathe'.

[H]CHAMPOLLION, *Gr. ég.* 374 [1836]; [D]BRUGSCH, *De natura*, 31 [1850].

ⲛⲓϥⲉ, 'mist' (Crum 239a) = (*Wb.* II, 251, 8), *nfy*, 'darkness (?), mist (?)'.

ERMAN-GRAPOW, *Wörterbuch der äg. Sprache*, II, 251, 8 [1928].

ⲛⲉϥⲣ- (Crum 239b), 'is good, profitable' = , *nꜣ-nfr*, 'good is' in late personal names like , *nꜣ-nfr-sḫmt*, 'Sakhme is good' (Ranke, I, 169, 24 ff.); (Er. 217, bottom), *nꜣ-nfr*, 'good is'.

[HD]SPIEGELBERG, *Rec. trav.* 37, 22 [1915], but cf. WILLIAMS, *JEA* 38, 63 [1952].

ⲛⲟⲩϥⲉ (Crum 240a), 'good' (Adjective) = (*Wb.* II, 253, 1 ff.), *nfr*, 'good, be good'; (Er. 216, 8), *nfr*, 'good'.

[H]CHAMPOLLION, *Gr. ég.* 65 and 319 [1836]; [D]DE ROUGÉ, *Oeuv. div.* I (= *Bibl. ég.* XXI), pp. 250–2 and Pl. 2 (95), no. 37 [1848].

[A2]**ⲛⲁϥⲣϣⲁⲓ** (Mani Ps.), lit. 'good of fate', 'blessed(ness)'. See also under **ϣⲁⲓ**, 'fortune'.

ALLBERRY, *A Manichean Psalm-book*, II, 4 n. on l. 16 [1938].

ⲛⲟϥⲣⲉ (Crum 239b), 'good, profit' (Subst.) = (*Wb.* II, 259, 3–8), *nfrt*, 'good (thing)'; (Er. 217), *nfrt*, 'good (thing)'.

[H]LORET, *Manuel de la langue ég.* 73, §171 [1889]; [D]HESS, *Stne*, 12 [1888].

ⲛⲟⲩϥⲧ (Crum 240a), 'swell, be distended' = (*Wb.* II, 263, 3), *nft*, 'displace'.

BREASTED, *The Edwin Smith Surgical Pap.* 348, 596 [1930].

ⲛⲉϩ (Crum 240b), 'oil' = (*Wb.* II, 302, 17–20), *nḥḥ*, '(sesame) oil'; (Er. 224, 2), *nḥḥ*, 'oil'.

[H]BRUGSCH, *Wb.* 797 [1868]; [D]BRUGSCH, *Gr. dém.* 63, §133; 185 n. 1 [1855].

ⲛⲉϩ ⲙⲉ or **ⲙⲙⲉ**, 'true, genuine oil', i.e. olive oil = , *nḥḥ n mꜣꜥt*, lit. 'oil of truth'.

CHASSINAT, *Le manuscrit mag. copte*, 100 [1955].

ⲛⲉϩ ⲛⲥⲓⲙ, 'radish oil', ῥαφάνιον of Dioscorides I, 45 = , *nḥḥ n sym*, lit. 'oil of herbs'.

MASPERO in *Rec. trav.* I, 39 n. 63 [1870].

ⲥⲁ ⲛⲛⲉϩ (Crum 241 a), 'oil-dealer' = , *s-n-nḥḥ*, 'oil-dealer', lit. 'man of oil'.

GRIFFITH-THOMPSON, III, 153 (Add. to 47, no. 468) [1909].

ⲛⲟⲩϩ (Crum 241 a), 'rope, cord' = (*Wb.* II, 223, 6 ff.), 'rope, cord'; (Er. 211, 5), *nwḥ*, 'cord'.

[H]CHAMPOLLION, *Gr. ég.* 77 [1836]; [D]REVILLOUT, *Revue ég.* 4, 80 n. 2 [1885].

[B]ϣⲉ ⲛⲛⲟϩ, a land measure, see under ϣⲉ, 'wood'.

ϣⲱϣ ⲛⲟⲩϩ, 'twist rope', see under ϣⲱϣ, 'twist'.

ⲛⲟⲩϩⲉ (Crum 241 b), 'shake' = (*Wb.* II, 282, 5), *nh*, 'shake' in , *nhnh*, *ⲛⲟϩⲛϩ, 'shake', see this latter.

LORET, *Rec. trav.* 16, 143 [1894].

NB. Distinction is to be made between ⲛⲟⲩϩⲉ, ⲛⲉϩ-, ⲛⲁϩ⸗, ⲛⲏϩ† and ⲛⲟⲩⲟⲩϩ, ⲛⲁⲩϩ-, ⲛⲁⲩϩ⸗, ⲛⲁⲩϩ†; see TILL, *ZÄS* 73, 136 f. [1937]; ALLBERRY, *JEA* 25, 172 [1939].

ⲛⲟⲩϩⲉ (Crum 242 b), 'sycamore (*Ficus sycomorus*)' = (*Wb.* II, 282, 6 ff.), 'sycamore'; (Er. 221, 7), *nhy*, 'sycamore'.

[H]CHAMPOLLION, *Précis*, 2nd ed., 125–6 [1828]; [D]BRUGSCH, *Gr. dém.* 25, §48 [1855].

ⲛⲟⲩϩⲃ (Crum 243 a), 'make ready by yoking beasts' = (*Wb.* II, 293, 3 ff.), *nḥb*, 'harness horses'; (not in Er.), *nḥb*, 'harness'; cf. (Er 222, 8), *nḥb*, 'yoke-tax'.

[H]BRUGSCH, *Wb.* 794 [1868]; [D]VOLTEN, *Ägypter und Amazonen*, 102 [1962].

ⲛⲁϩⲃ (Crum 243 a), 'yoke' = (*Wb.* II, 293, 1, 2), *nḥb*, 'yoke'.

CHABAS, *Voyage*, 85 [1866]; DÜMICHEN, *ZÄS* 4, 84 n. [1866].

ⲛⲁϩⲃ(ⲉ) (Crum 243 a), 'shoulders, back' = (*Wb.* II, 292, 9 ff.), *nḥbt*, 'neck'; (Er. 223, 1), *nḥbt*, 'shoulders'.

[H]CHAMPOLLION, *Gr. ég.* 62 [1836]; [D]SPIEGELBERG, *Petubastis*, p. 32*, no. 206 [1910].

ⲛⲟⲩϩⲃ (Crum 243 b), 'copulate' = (*Wb.* II, 284, 3, 4), *nhp*, 'copulate'. For *p* > ⲃ at the end of a word, compare (*Wb.* II, 294, 9 ff.), *nḥp*, 'potter's wheel' written also , *nḥb* (XIXth Dyn.).

DÉVAUD's slip.

ⲛⲉϩⲃⲏⲗ (Crum 243b), 'wine-skin' is Hebrew נֵבֶל, νέβελ of Septuagint, 'skin-bottle'.

STERN, *Kopt. Gr.* 52, §101 [1880].

ⲛⲟⲩϩⲙ (Crum 243b), 'be saved, save' = (*Wb.* II, 295, 12 ff.), *nḥm*, 'take away, rob'; (Er. 223, 2), *nḥm*, 'rob, save'.

[H]CHAMPOLLION, *Gr. ég.* 380, 389 [1836]; [D]DE SAULCY, *Rosette*, 106 n., 178–9 [1845].

(**ⲛⲟϩⲛϩ**), **ⲛⲉϩⲛⲟⲩϩ⸗** (Crum 244b), 'shake' = (*Wb.* II, 282, 5), *nhnh*, and (*Wb.* II, 286, 6), *nhnh*, 'shake'; perhaps a loan-word from Semitic, cf. New Hebrew נִעְנֵעַ, Eth. *něhnûh*, 'shake'.

[H]LORET, *Rec. trav.* 16, 143 [1894]; [S]LAGARDE in DILLMANN, *Lexicon*, 634 (for Eth.), and DÉVAUD's slip (for New-Hebr.).

ⲛⲉϩⲡⲉ (Crum 245a), 'mourn' = (*Wb.* II, 284, 17), *nhp*, 'mourn'; (Er. 221, 10), *nhp*, 'mourn'.

[H]CHABAS, *Pap. mag. Harris*, 72 [1860]; [D]BRUGSCH, *Gr. dém.* p. 34, §68 [1855].

ⲛϩⲟⲩⲣ (Crum 245a), 'tremble, cause to tremble', 'fear (Subst.)' = (*Wb.* II, 286, 12), *nhr*, a designation of god Seth, lit. 'terror'; (Er. 222, 2), *nhr*, 'terror'.

[HD]SPIEGELBERG, *Petubastis*, p. 32*, no. 205 [1910].

ⲛⲉϩⲥⲉ (Crum 245b), 'awake, arise' = (*Wb.* II, 287, 3), *nhsỉ*, 'awake'; (Er. 222, 3), *nhs*, 'awake'.

[H]DE ROUGÉ, *Oeuv. div.* III (= *Bibl. ég.* XXIII), 274 [1856]; [D]BRUGSCH, *Gr. dém.* p. 40, §88 [1855].

ⲛⲁϩⲧⲉ (Crum 246a), 'trust, believe' = (*Wb.* II, 303, 14 and 15), *nḥty*, 'trust' (*Wb.* differently!); (Er. 225, 1), *nḥṱ*, 'believe, trust'.

[H]CHABAS, *Pap. mag. Harris*, 132 [1860]; [D]SPIEGELBERG, *Petubastis*, p. 32*, no. 208 [1910]; cf. Spiegelberg, *Sitzber. Bayr. Ak.* 1925, Abh. 4, pp. 24 ff.

ⲛⲟⲩϫ (Crum 246b), 'lying, false' = , *nꜥwḏ* (e.g. in , *mdt nꜥwḏ*, lit. 'false speech', ⲙⲛⲧⲛⲟⲩϫ), 'lie', probably a derivative from (Er. 74, 10), *ꜥḏ*, 'injustice, lie'.

DÉVAUD, *ZÄS* 61, 110–11 [1926].

Sⲛⲟⲩϫⲕ, Bⲛⲟⲩϫϧ (Crum 249a), 'sprinkle, asperge, scatter' = (Er. 235, 9), *ndḫ*, 'asperge, scatter', a loan-word from Semitic; cf. Arabic نضخ, 'asperge', Hebrew נָזָה, same meaning.

DBRUGSCH, *Script. Aeg. dem.* 19, §21 [1848]; SROSSI, *Etym. aegypt.* 139 [1808].

ⲛⲁϫϩⲉ (Crum 249b), 'tooth' = (*Wb.* II, 384, 2), *ndḥt*, 'tooth'; (not in Er.; Apisritual XI, 12 etc.), *ndḥy*, 'tooth'.

HBIRCH in *Archaeologia* 35, 134 n. c, and Pl. IV, no. 94 [1853]; DH. THOMPSON's Demotic dictionary.

Sⲛⲟϭ, Bⲛⲓϣϯ (Crum 250a), 'great, large'. Since Boh. form clearly comes from , , *nḫt* (see ⲛϣⲟⲧ), it is tempting to interpret ⲛⲟϭ as < *ⲛⲟⲧϣ, a metathesis of *ⲛⲟϣⲧ, i.e. *nḫt*. However, *ⲛⲟⲧϣ should > ⲛⲟϫ also in Sa. (though thus attested only in Boh. and F.).

GRIFFITH, *Ryl.* III, 363 [1909]; cf. Spiegelberg, *Mythus*, 175, no. 436 [1917].

(ⲛⲉϭⲉ-), ⲛⲉϭⲱ(ⲱ)⸗ (Crum 252a), 'be ugly, unseemly, disgraceful', nom. verb ⲛⲉ + ϭⲁ ('be ugly, ugliness').

STEINDORFF, *Lehrbuch*, 137, §297 [1951]; cf. STERN, *Kopt. Gr.* 147, §308 [1880].

ⲛⲏϭⲉ, Bⲛⲉϫⲓ (Crum 252a), 'belly, womb' = (not in *Wb.*), *ngy*, 'belly', Ostr. Turin 9572, 2 (Ramesside; follows , *mḫtw*, 'intestines').

ⲛϭⲓ, BFⲛϫⲉ (Crum 252a), particle introducing nominal subject in proleptic verbal clause, 'namely' = * (), *m kỉ* (*n*) (*Wb.* V, 15, 5), 'in the form (of), namely'; (Er. 230, 1; 583, 2), *ng*, 'namely'.

HGARDINER, *JEA* 5, 190 n. 4 [1918]; DW. MAX MÜLLER, *Rec. trav.* 13, 151 [1890].

ⲛⲟⲩϭⲥ (Crum 252b), 'be, make wroth' = (*Wb.* II, 336, 15), *nsḳ*, 'bite(?)' and L.Eg. (*Wb.* II, 336, 16), *nsḳ*, 'cut, prick, irritate' or sim. *Nsḳ* > ⲛⲟⲩϭⲥ as *psg* > ⲡⲱϭⲥ.

O

-ⲟ (Crum 253a), 'great' = (*Wb.* I, 161, 5 ff.), *ꜥꜣ*, 'great'; (Er. 54, 1), 'great'.

[H]STERN, *Kopt. Gr.* pp. 91–2 (§194) [1880]; [D]HESS, *Stne*, 148 [1888].

ⲡⲓⲟ ⲡⲓⲟ (Crum 253b), 'the great one, the great one' as epithet of Thoth = *, *pꜣ ꜥꜣ pꜣ ꜥꜣ*, 'the great one, the great one' (cf. , *ꜥꜣ ꜥꜣ*, *Wb.* I, 163, 5, 'great, great', and the proper name (Ranke, II, 261, 18), *ỉꜥḥ pꜣ ꜥꜣ ꜥꜣ*, 'Moon, the great, great'.

ERMAN, *ZÄS* 21, 94 [1883].

ⲁ- in **ⲁⲡⲁϩⲧⲉ** (Crum 253b) = (*Wb.* I, 539, 19), *ꜥꜣ pḥty*, 'great of strength' as epithet of gods; (Er. 138, bottom), *ꜥꜣ pḥṱ*, 'great of strength' as epithet of god Miysis.

[H]ERMAN, *ZÄS* 21, 95 [1883]; [D]SPIEGELBERG, *Mythus*, 133, no. 277 [1917].

ⲟⲃⲛ (Crum 254a), 'alum' = (*Wb.* I, 63, 8), *ỉbnw*, a mineral, alum?; (Er. 4, 1), *ꜣbn*, 'alum'.

[H]LORET, *Rec. trav.* 15, 199–200 [1893]; [DH]W. MAX MÜLLER, *Asien und Europa*, 188–9 n. [1893].

ⲟⲃϩⲉ (Crum 254a), 'tooth' = (*Wb.* I, 64, 2–4), *ỉbḥ*, 'tooth' (with change of gender); (Er. 4, 2), *ꜣbḥ*, 'tooth'.

[H]CHAMPOLLION, *Gr. ég.* pp. 60, 73, 92 [1836]; [D]BRUGSCH, *De natura*, 22 [1850].

ⲟⲉⲓⲕ (Crum 254a), 'bread, loaf' = (*Wb.* I, 232, 16 ff.), *ꜥḳw*, 'income, food, bread'; (Er. 73, 1), *ꜥḳ*, 'bread, income'.

[H]CHABAS, *Pap. mag. Harris*, p. 204 (glossary) and Pl. I, no. 68 [1860]; [D]SPIEGELBERG, *Dem. Chron.* 48, no. 55 [1914].

[B]**ⲥⲁ ⲛⲱⲓⲕ** (Crum 254b), 'bread seller' = , *s n ꜥḳ*, lit. 'man of bread'.

SPIEGELBERG, *l.c.*

ⲟⲉⲓⲕ (Crum 254b), 'reed', can hardly be separated from the Dem. word for 'reed' appearing in writings like (Er. 12, 4), *ꜣk*, (Er. 12, 2), *ꜣkyr*, , *ꜥkr* (Er. 73, 8, where other spellings without *r*, but possibly different words, are quoted).

ⲟⲕⲉ (Crum 254b), 'sesame' = (Er. 12, 1), *ꜣkỉ*, or , *ꜣky*, 'sesame', probably the older (*Wb.* I, 139, 9; further exx. Caminos, *Chronicle*, 149–50), *ỉk*, a grain, also used for making bread.

[H]GOODWIN in *ZÄS* 12, 64 [1874]; [D]BRUGSCH, *Gr. dém.* 25, §44; 26, §51 [1855].

See also [B]**ⲟⲩⲟⲕⲓ**, 'dregs of sesame'.

ⲟⲉⲓⲗⲉ (*sic*, Crum 254b), 'ram', from Semitic (cf. אַיִל, Akkadian *ajalu*). See also **ⲉⲓⲟⲩⲗ**.

ROSSI, *Etym. aegypt.* 249 [1808].

ⲟⲙⲉ (Crum 254b), 'clay, mud' = (*Wb.* I, 185, 17), *ꜥmꜥt*, and (*Wb.* I, 186, 12), *ꜥmꜥ⟨{m}⟩t*, 'mud'; see also Gardiner, *Onom.* I, 10*–11*, for the word; (Er. 60, 4), *ꜥm*, 'clay'.

[H]BRUGSCH, *Wb.* 231 [1867]; [D]SPIEGELBERG, *Kopt. Handwb.* 88 [1921].

[S]**ⲟⲉⲓⲙⲉ**, [B]**(ϩ)ⲱⲓⲙⲓ** (Crum 255a and 676a), 'hook', from (*Wb.* III, 31, 12 f.), *ḥꜣm*, 'to fish'; (Er. 305, 2), *ḥm*, 'to fish, to catch birds'.

[HD]SPIEGELBERG, *Petubastis*, 41*, no. 267 [1910].

ⲟⲛ (Crum 255b), 'again' = (*Wb.* I, 189, 8–16), *ꜥn*, 'again'; (Er. 61, 13), *ꜥn*, 'again'.

[H]CHABAS, *Mél. ég.* II, 217 [1864]; [D]REVILLOUT, *Poème*, pp. 7 and 28 [1885].

ⲟⲉⲓⲡⲉ (Crum 256a), a measure of grain, etc., one sixth of the artaba (**ⲣⲧⲟⲃ**) = (*Wb.* I, 67, 6), *ỉpt*, measure of 40 hin; (Er. 29, 1), *ỉpyt*, a measure. A unique XIth Dyn. writing shows that **ⲟⲉⲓⲡⲉ** goes back to **aypat* < **apyat* (James, *Ḥekanakhte*, 65). Hebrew אֵיפָה is from **aypat*.

[H]BRUGSCH, *Wb.* 49 [1867]; [D]BRUGSCH, *Thes.* 1052 [1891], acknowledged by Hess, *Stne*, 17 [1888].

ⲟⲣⲃⲉ (Crum 256b), 'wafer, thin cake', from Aramaic עֲרוֹב (Ex. 29, 2; Lev. 8, 26). The existence of the word in Aramaic is, however, doubtful. It may be a mistake for עֲרוֹךְ.

DÉVAUD's slip.

ⲟⲥⲉ (Crum 256b), m. 'loss, damage, fine' = , mostly, however, (not in *Wb.*; many hieratic exx. on unpubl. Ramesside weights from Deir el-Medînah), *ỉsy*, nn. m., 'shortage, unfavourable difference, loss' in weight, lit. 'lightness'; (Er. 10, 8), *ꜣsy*, 'loss, fine'. From **ⲁⲥⲁⲓ**, 'be light'.

[D]BRUGSCH, *Wb.* 16 [1867].

[B]**ⲟⲥⲓ** (Crum 257a), 'tamarisk' = (*Wb.* I, 130, I f.), *ỉsr*, 'tamarisk'; (Er. 11, 6), *ꜣsr*, 'tamarisk'. Ultimately related to Semitic word for 'tamarisk': Hebrew אֶשֶׁל, Arabic أَثْل, Akkadian *ašlu*.

[H]CHAMPOLLION, *Gr. ég.* 88 [1836]; [D]SPIEGELBERG, *Hauswaldt*, p. I n. 5 (translates 'tamarisk' but does not mention the Coptic word) [1913].

ⲟⲉⲓⲧ (Crum 257a), Qual. = *, *ỉr·tỉ* (3rd pers. sing. fem. of Old Perfective of , *ỉry*, 'do, make', **ⲉⲓⲣⲉ**, lit. 'has been made' = 'is'; , *ỉrṯ*, , *ỉryṯ* and sim. (Er. 36, lower), same meaning. **ỉŏrtey* > **ⲟⲉⲓⲧ**, like **ḥkŏrtey* > **ϩⲕⲟⲉⲓⲧ**, 'is hungry'.

SPIEGELBERG in *ZÄS* 62, 44–5 [1926].

ⲟⲟⲧⲉ (Crum 257a), 'womb' = (*Wb.* I, 142, 21), *ỉdt*, 'vulva' (for the reading, see Gardiner, *Onom.* II, 259*–61*); (Er. 13, 5), *ꜣt(ỉ)t*, 'vulva'.

[H]BRUGSCH, *Wb.* 135 [1867]; [D]BRUGSCH, *ZDMG* 9, 496, and Pl. I, no. 13 [1855]; *Gr. dém.* 41, §90 [1855].

Same word in **ⲟⲩⲁⲙ-ⲉϯ** (Crum 479a, s.v. **ⲟⲩⲱⲙ**), 'gangrene, cancer', lit. 'eater (from **ⲟⲩⲱⲙ**) of **ⲉϯ**' < ***ⲟⲩⲁⲙ-ⲟϯ** (cf. , *wnmt m ỉdt*, in P. Ebers 95, 6–7 and 'cancer uteri' (lit. 'eater of uterus') acc. to Ebbell, *ZÄS* 63, 73 [1928], but in [B]**ⲙⲉⲥⲓⲱϯ** (Crum 186a), 'womb', **ⲓⲱϯ** should be a word for 'child' (lit. 'bearer of child', **ⲙⲉⲥ-** from **ⲙⲓⲥⲉ**), perhaps , *ỉd* (*Wb.* I, 151, 8f.).

ⲟⲟⲩϣ (Crum 257a), 'gruel' of bread or lentils = (*Wb.* I, 58, 2, 3), *ỉwšš*, 'pastry, gruel'; (Er. 2, 11), *ꜣwš*, 'gruel (?)'.

[H]STERN, *Pap. Ebers*, II (glossary), p. 13 [1875]; [D]PARKER, *JEA* 26, 100 [1940].

ⲟⲉⲓϣ (Crum 257b), 'cry' (subst.) = (*Wb.* I, 227, 14), *ʿš(w)* (see Gunn, *JEA* 12, 135), 'cry' (subst.); (Er. 71, 5) *ʿš*, 'cry', from **ⲱϣ**.

[H]GRIFFITH, *Ryl.* III, 340, s.v. *wyn* [1909].

For **ⲧⲁϣⲉ ⲟⲉⲓϣ**, 'proclaim, preach', see under **ⲧⲁϣⲟ**.

ⲟⲓϩ (Crum 257b, 'meaning unknown'), nn. m. = ? (*Wb.* I, 119, 15 f.), *ỉḥw*, 'cattle', Plural of **ⲉϩⲉ**. See also **ⲉⲗ-ⲟⲓϩ**.

ⲟⲟϩ (Crum 257b, adding SO**ⲱϩ** 536b), 'moon' = (*Wb.* I, 42, 7), *ỉʿḥ*, 'moon'; (Er. 19, 4), *ỉʿḥ*, 'moon'.

H CHAMPOLLION, *Gr. ég.* pp. 60, 75 [1836]; D BRUGSCH, *Wb.* 108 [1867].

ⲟϩⲉ (Crum 258a), 'yard' of house = (*Wb.* I, 118, 5–7), *ỉhw*, 'camp, cattle yard'; (Er. 40, 8), *ỉhy*, 'stall'.

H HINCKS in *Transactions of the Roy. Irish Ac.* XXI, part II, 48 and Pl. I, no. 30 [1848, read in 1846]; D BRUGSCH, *Wb.* 105 [1867].

B**ⲟϫⲓ** (Crum 258b), 'iniquity' = (*Wb.* I, 240, 14), *ʿḏꜣ*, 'injustice' and sim.; (Er. 74, 10), *ʿḏ*, 'injustice, lie'.

H CHABAS, *Oeuv. div.* II (= *Bibl. ég.* X), 37 [1859]; D BRUGSCH, *Sammlung dem. Urk.* 26 and Pl. 5, l. 29 [1850].

Ⲡ

ⲡ- (Crum 258b), masc. definite article = (*Wb.* I, 492, middle), *pꜣ*, def. article; (Er. 127, 2), *pꜣ*, def. article.

H CHAMPOLLION, *Précis*, 1st ed., p. 74 and Tableau gén., no. I on p. (I) and pl. I [1824]; D SAULCY, *Rosette*, 26 [1845].

ⲡⲁ-, with suffixes **ⲡⲉ-** (Crum 258b), masc. possessive article 'my...' = + suffix (*Wb.* I, 493, 1), *pꜣy*, possessive article; (Er. 128, 3), *pꜣy*, possessive article.

H CHAMPOLLION, *Gr. ég.* 264–5 [1836]; ÅKERBLAD in Young, *Works*, III, 37 [1815].

ⲡⲁ- (Crum 259a), masc. possessive prefix, 'the (man) of' = , (*Wb.* I, 492, 7), *pꜣ n*, masc. possessive prefix; (Er. 128, 1), *pa* (*pꜣ n*), masc. possessive prefix.

H DE ROUGÉ, *Chrest. égypt.* II, 31–2 [1868]; D BRUGSCH, *Script. Aeg. dem.* p. 38, §28, II [1848].

ⲡⲁⲓ (Crum 259a), masc. demonstrative pronoun 'this', before substantive **ⲡⲉⲓ-** =  (*Wb.* I, 493, 3, 4), *pꜣi*, 'this';  (Er. 128, 2), *pꜣi*, 'this'.

[H]CHAMPOLLION, *Gr. ég.* 182 [1836]; [D]BRUGSCH, *Gr. dém.* 78, § 171 [1855]; for construct form BRUGSCH, *Script. Aeg. dem.* 27, § 19 [1848].

ⲡⲉ (Crum 259a), 'heaven, sky' =  (*Wb.* I, 490, 10 f.; 492, 1), *pt*, 'sky'; 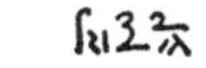 (Er. 127, 1), *p(t)*, 'sky'.

[H]CHAMPOLLION, *Dict.* 1–2 [1841]; [D]BRUGSCH, *Gr. dém.* 32, §63 [1855].

-ⲡⲉ (Crum 260a; 260b under **ⲡⲏ**), enclitic joining subject and predicate in nominal clause =  (*Wb.* I, 493, 5), *pꜣi*;  (Er. 128, 2), *-pꜣi*.

[H]ERMAN, *Neuäg. Gr.* 57–8, § 78 [1880]; [D]BRUGSCH, *Gr. dém.* 125–6, § 257 [1855].

ⲡⲉⲓ (Crum 260a), 'kiss' = 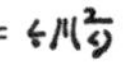 (Petubastis 16, 22; not in Er.), *pʿy*, 'to kiss'.

KLASENS, *Bibl. Or.* 13, 222 [1956].

[O]ⲡⲏ (not in Crum), 'patricians' =  (*Wb.* I, 503, 2 ff.), *pʿt*, 'patricians'.

GARDINER in CRUM, *JEA* 28, 28 [1942].

ⲡⲏ (Crum 260b), demonstr. pronoun 'that (one)' perhaps =  (*Wb.* I, 493, 6), *pꜣw*, a subform of the demonstr. pronoun , *pꜣi*.

STEINDORFF, *Kopt. Gr.*[2], p. 46, § 96 n. [1904].

ⲡⲏⲓ (Crum 260b), 'a leap' =  (*Wb.* I, 494, 8–11), *pꜣ*, of any swift movement; 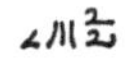 (Er. 130, 2), *pꜣy*, 'to run, hasten'.

[B]**ϭⲓ-ⲫⲉⲓ**, 'take a leap' = 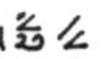 (Er. 130, 2), *ṯꜣy pꜣy pꜣy*, lit. 'take (a) leap leap'.

[H]ERICHSEN, *Dem. Glossar*, 130, 2 [1954]; [D]BRUGSCH, *Gr. dém.* 130, § 269 [1855].

ⲡⲏⲓ, 'flea' (lit. 'a leaper') = (*Wb.* I, 502, 2), *py*, 'flea'.

STERN, *Pap. Ebers*, II, *Glossar*, p. 31 [1875].

ⲡⲟⲓ (Crum 260b), 'bench' =  (*Wb.* I, 489, 4–7), *p*, 'base, throne'; 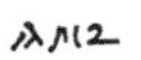 (Er. 130, 6), *py*, 'seat'.

[H]BRUGSCH, *Wb.*, Suppl. 466 [1881]; [D]ERICHSEN, *Dem. Glossar*, 130, 6 [1954].

ⲡⲱ⸗ + suffix (Crum 260 b), masc. possessive article used absolutely, 'mine' = + suffix (*Wb.* I, 493, 2), *pꜣy*, 'mine'; (Er. 129, 1), *pꜣy*, same use.

[H]ERMAN, *Spr. Westcar*, 50, §97 n. 1 [1889]; [D]GRIFFITH-THOMPSON, III, 29, no. 283 [1909].

ⲡⲁⲕⲉ (Crum 261 a), 'become light, thin' = (*Wb.* I, 499, 6–7), *pꜣk*, 'thin', 'become thin', Caminos, *Chronicle*, 93–4; (Er. 141, 2), *pk*, in *pk-ḥꜣt*, 'faint of heart'.

[H]ERMAN-GRAPOW, *Wörterbuch der äg. Sprache*, I, 499, 6–7 [1926]; [D]KRALL, *Mitt. aus der Sammlung... Erzh. Rainer*, VI, 63, no. 100 [1897].

ⲡⲁⲕⲉⲛϩⲏⲧ, [A]**ⲡⲁⲕϩⲏⲧ**, 'small, poor of heart'; (Petubastis, P. Krall, L, 20), *pḳy n ḥꜣt*, or (P. Insinger 22, 22), *pk-ḥꜣt*, 'faint of heart, discouraged'; cf. the earlier (*Wb.* I, 499, 7), *pꜣḳ ib*, 'be longing for'.

[D]KRALL, *l.c.*

ⲡⲱⲗϩ (Crum 261 a), 'wound', from Semitic, cf. فَلَحَ, 'split'.

ROSSI, *Etym. aeg.* 238 [1808]; cf. Stricker in *Acta Orientalia* 15, 4 [1937].

ⲡⲱⲗϭ (Crum 261 b), 'be agreed, deliver, decide' = (*Wb.* I, 511, 2), *png*, 'detach?'; (Er. 137, 3), *plk*, 'to detach, free, liberate, reconcile' etc. Ultimately connected with Sem. √*plg*, cf. Ar. فلج, Hebrew, פָּלַג, Syr. ܦܠܓ, 'divide'.

[H]BURCHARDT, *Altkanaan Fremdworte*, II, 22, no. 406 [1910]; [D]SOTTAS, *Pap. dém. de Lille*, I, 69 [1921]; [S]BURCHARDT, *l.c.*

[S]**ⲡⲉⲗϫⲉ** prob. under influence of **ⲃⲗϫⲉ**, 'earthenware, sherd'.

ⲡⲗϭⲉ (Crum 262 b), nn., 'split, torn cloth, rag', from **ⲡⲱⲗϭ**, 'detach'.

[S]**ⲡⲟⲙⲡⲉⲙ** (Crum 263 a), [B]**ⲫⲟⲛⲡⲉⲛ** (Crum 514 a), 'to swell, overflow', redupl. of **ⲡⲱⲛ**, 'be poured, flow'; **ponpen* > **pompen* > *pompem*.

ⲡⲓⲛ (Crum 263 a), 'mouse' = (*Wb.* I, 508, 6), *pnw*, 'mouse'; (Er. 131, 10), *pn*, 'mouse'.

[H]CHAMPOLLION, *Gr. ég.* pp. 84, 107 [1836]; [D]BRUGSCH, *Gr. dém.* 23, §40 [1855].

ⲡⲱⲛ (Crum 263a), 'be poured, flow' = (*Wb.* I, 501, 2), *pnn*, 'spray' powder; (not in Er.), *pn*, 'be poured out'.

[H]ERMAN-GRAPOW, *Wörterbuch der äg. Sprache*, I, 510, 2 [1926]; [D]KLASENS in *Bibl. Or.* 13, 222 [1956].

ⲡⲁⲱⲛⲉ (Crum 263b), name of 10th month = (*Ann. du Service*, 43, 175), *P(ꜣ)-n-ỉnt*, 'that (sc. festival) of the Valley', name of a Theban festival.

ČERNÝ, *Archiv für Orientforschung* 5, 114 [1929].

ⲡⲱⲱⲛⲉ (Crum 263b), 'turn' = (*Wb.* I, 508, 11 ff.), *pnꜥ*, 'turn'; (Er. 131, 12), *pnꜥ*, 'turn'.

[H]CHABAS, *Voyage*, 37 [1866]; [D]REVILLOUT, *Rev. ég.* I, 172 and pl. 9, 3rd line from bottom [1880].

ⲡⲱⲛⲕ, ⲡⲱⲛϭ (Crum 265b), 'draw, bail, empty out' water = (*Wb.* I, 510, 12 f.), *pnḳ*, 'draw water'; (Er. 132, 3), *pnk*, 'draw water'.

[H]CHABAS, *Pap. mag. Harris*, 229 [1860]; [D]SPIEGELBERG, *Petubastis*, 21*, no. 130 [1910].

[S]**ⲡⲛⲛⲏ**, [B]**ⲃⲉⲛⲛⲏ** (Crum 266a), 'doorpost, threshold, step' = (*Wb.* I, 509, 14), *pnꜥyt*, 'threshold' (*Wb.* differently), later (*Wb.* I, 460, 15), *bnnt*, 'threshold'; (Er. 131, 11), *pnt*, 'threshold'.

[H]DÉVAUD, *Études*, 59–60 [1922] (for *pnꜥyt*); ERMAN-GRAPOW, *Wb.* I, 460, 15 [1926] (for *bnnt*); [D]ERICHSEN, *Dem. Glossar*, 131, 11 [1954].

ⲡⲁⲟⲡⲉ (Crum 266b), name of 2nd month = (*Wb.* I, 68, 6; 492, bottom), *p(ꜣ)-n-ỉpt*, 'that (sc. festival) of Opet (i.e. Luxor)', a Theban festival. For **-ⲟⲡⲉ**, see Geogr. Index under **ⲡⲁⲡⲉ**.

ERMAN in *ZÄS* 39, 128–9 [1901].

ⲡⲁⲡⲟⲓ (Crum 266b), 'bird, chicken(?)' = **ⲡⲁ** (possessive article) + **ⲡⲟⲓ**; **ⲡⲟⲓ** = singular of (*Wb.* I, 494, 15), *pꜣyw* (Plural), 'birds' (lit. 'flying ones'); (Er. 131, 5), *ppy*, 'young bird'.

[H]BRUGSCH, *Wb.* 456 [1868] (**ⲡ-ⲁⲡⲟⲓ**); [D]BRUGSCH, *Gr. dém.* 23, §41 [1855].

ⲡⲱⲱⲡⲉ (Crum 266b), 'make bricks' = (*Wb.* I, 502, 6, 7), *pỉp*, 'knead (clay), make bricks'; (Er. 131, 6), *ppy*, 'make bricks'.

[H]BRUGSCH, *Wb.*, Suppl. 471 [1881]; [D]GRIFFITH, *Ryl.* III, 349 [1909].

ⲡⲁⲡⲉⲓⲧ, 'brick-maker', <**ⲡⲁⲡ-ⲉⲓⲧⲛ**, lit. 'clay-kneader'; final **ⲛ** discarded perhaps under influence of **ⲉⲃⲓⲧ**, **ⲉⲃⲉⲓⲧ**, 'honey dealer' and other nouns denoting occupation.

For **ⲡⲁⲡⲥⲟⲧ**, see **ⲥⲟⲧ**.

-ⲡⲱⲣ, ⲡⲉⲣ- (Crum 267a), 'house' = (*Wb.* I, 511, 7 ff.), *pr*, house; see **ⲡⲉⲣⲓⲡⲉⲣⲟⲓ, ϫⲉⲛⲉⲡⲱⲣ**.

ⲡⲁⲣⲁ (Crum 267a and Add. xx, Kahle, *Bal.* II, 720), nn. m. and f., 'receipt' = Arabic براءة.

CRUM, *A Coptic Dict.* p. xx [1939].

ⲡⲏⲣⲉ (Crum 267a), 'quail' = (*Wb.* I, 504, 14), *pꜥrt*; (not in Er.; O. F. Ll. Griffith 4, 7. 8; O. Murray I, 3), *pꜥr*, a bird; related to Arab. فرّة.

[H]LORET, *ZÄS* 30, 25–6 [1892]; [D]H. THOMPSON's Demotic dictionary.

ⲡⲉⲓⲣⲉ (Crum 267a), 'come forth' = (*Wb.* I, 518, bottom), *prỉ*, 'come forth'; (Er. 134, 7), *pr(y)*, 'come forth'.

[HD]BRUGSCH, *Nouvelles recherches sur la division de l'année*, 4–7 [1856].

ⲡⲱⲱⲣⲉ (Crum 268a), 'dream' = (*Wb.* I, 564, I ff.), *ptr*, 'see'; (Er. 136, 2), *prỉ*, 'dream'.

[H]BRUGSCH, *Wb.* 484 [1868]; [D]GRIFFITH, *Stories*, 184–5 [1900].

NB. For the loss of *t*, cf. the writings (Totb. ed. Lepsius 55, 2; 58, I; 99, 25; 149, 24; 163, 12); Gr.-Rom. (*Wb.* I, 564, top) (*Edfou* VII, 249, 5); (*ibid.* VII, 235, 8), the latter two for *prw* (*Wb.* I, 526, 14), 'surplus'. Also conversely *ptrt* (*Wb.* I, 565, 6) for *prỉ*, 'battle-field'. The meaning 'to see (a dream)' is attested for *ptr* since XXth Dyn. (P. Dêr el-Medîna 6, vo. 3).

ⲡⲣⲱ (Crum 268a), 'winter' = (*Wb.* I, 530, 7), *prt*, the second season of Egyptian year, lit. 'the coming forth' (of vegetation); (Er. 135, I), *prt*, same meaning.

[HD]BRUGSCH, *Nouvelles recherches sur la division de l'année*, 7–10; 14, and Pl. I, nos. 14, 15 [1856].

ⲡⲟⲣⲕ (Crum 268a), outer mantle of clerics, monks, *pallium* = (Er. 136, 8), *prk*, 'cloak'.

H. THOMPSON, *A Family Archive*, Index, p. (100), no. 117 [1934].

See also **ϩⲁⲡⲟⲣⲕ**, 'saddle, saddle-cloth'.

πωρκ (Crum 268b), 'pluck, root out' = (Er. 136, 7), *prk*, 'root out', from Semitic, cf. פָּרַק, 'tear apart, away'.

[D]GRIFFITH-THOMPSON, III, 31, no. 311 [1909]; [S]S. GROLL's information.

παρμοῦτε (Crum 269a), name of 8th month = , *p(ꜣ)-n-Rnnwtt*, 'that (sc. festival) of harvest goddess Ernūte'.

ČERNÝ, *Annales du Service* 43, 175 [1943]; cf. Brugsch, *Dict. géogr.* 1313–14 [1880].

παρμϩοτπ (Crum 269a); name of 7th month = (*Wb.* I, 493, top), *p(ꜣ)-n-ʾImnḥtp*, 'that (festival) of (deified king) Amenḥotpe'.

ERMAN, *ZÄS* 39, 129–30 [1901].

περνοῦϥε (Crum 269a), a plant = (not in Er.; ex. Dem. mag. Pap. 10, 13), *pr-nfr*, a plant. From this Arabic بِرْنُوف, *conyza odorata* (Kazimirski), lit. 'good seed', see **εϐρα** and **νοῦϥε**.

[Ar]CHASSINAT, *Pap. méd.* 206 [1921].

περιπερο (Crum 269b); **πρεπρρο**, Mani Hom. 24, 8, 'royal palace' = , *pryt-Prʿꜣ*, 'courts of Pharaoh'; (Er. 132, 4), *pr-Prʿꜣ*, 'king's palace'.

[H]H. THOMPSON, *A Coptic Palimpsest*, p. 384 (ad P. 349) [1911]; actual examples supplied by Gardiner, *Eg. Gr.* p. 481 [1927]; [D]SPIEGELBERG, *Mythus*, 130, no. 266 [1917].

πηρϣ (Crum 269b), 'red-coloured substance' = (*Wb.* I, 532, 13), *prš*, 'red ochre' (see Iversen, *Det Kongel. Danske Videnskabernes Selskab, Hist.-filol. Meddelelser*, 34, 31 [1955]; (Er. 136, 6), *prš*, 'red ochre'.

[H]ERMAN-GRAPOW, *Wörterbuch der äg. Sprache*, I, 532, 13 [1926]; [D]HESS, *Stne*, 156 (glossary), cf. p. 3 [1888].

πωρϣ (Crum 269b), 'spread, stretch' = (*Wb.* I, 532, 7–11), *prḫ*, Gr.-R. , *prš*, 'open up (of bloom), stretch out'; (Er. 136, 4), *prḫ*, 'stretch out'. From Semitic, cf. פָּרַח, 'sprout, flower, bear fruit'.

[H]ERMAN-GRAPOW, *Wörterbuch der äg. Sprache*, I, 532, 7 [1926]; [D]BRUGSCH, *De natura*, 30 [1850]; [S]STRICKER in *Acta Orientalia* 15, 4 [1937].

NB. (*Wb.* I, 533, 1) is probably the same word, 'stretch out (for thrashing)'.

ⲡⲱⲣϫ (Crum 271 b), 'divide' = [hieroglyphs] (*Edfou* II, 221, 37), *prṯ*, or [hieroglyphs] (*Edfou* VI, 163, 10), *prḏ*, 'separate'; [demotic] (Er. 137, 1), *prḏ*, 'separate', from Semitic, cf. פְּרַץ, 'separate'.

ᴴJ.-CL. GOYON (letter of 15. iv. 1969); ᴰBRUGSCH, *De natura*, 30 [1850]; ˢSPIEGELBERG in *ZÄS* 46, 115 n. 1 [1909].

ⲡⲓⲥⲉ (Crum 273 a), 'boil, bake, melt' = [hieroglyphs] (*Wb.* I, 551, 5), *fsỉ* > *psỉ*, 'cook'; [demotic] (Er. 139, 7), *psỉ*, 'cook'.

ᴴCHAMPOLLION, *Gr. ég.* 378 [1836]; cf. *Dict.* 428 [1841]; ᴰBRUGSCH, *Gr. dém.* 27, §53 [1855].

ⲯ(ⲉ)ⲣⲙⲟⲟⲩ (Crum 273 b), some blistery itch < **ⲯ(ⲉ)ⲣ-** (constr. state of Gk. ψώρα, 'itch') + **ⲙⲟⲟⲩ**, 'water'. Also **ⲯⲱⲣⲁ ⲙⲙⲟⲟⲩ**.

CRUM, *A Coptic Dict.* 273 b [1932].

ⲯⲓⲥ (Crum 273 b), 'nine' = [hieroglyphs] (*Wb.* I, 558, 10), *psḏ*, 'nine'.

BRUGSCH, *ZÄS* 2, 78 [1864].

ⲡⲥⲧⲁⲓⲟⲩ (Crum 273 b), 'ninety' = [hieroglyphs] alliterating with [hieroglyphs], *psḏt*, 'ennead (of gods)' in Pap. Leiden 350, 4, 1. See Gardiner in *ZÄS* 42, 42 [1903]; Sethe in *ZÄS* 47, 27–8 [1910].

ⲡⲁⲧ (Crum 273 b), 'knee' = [hieroglyphs] (*Wb.* I, 500, 9 f.), *pꜣd*, 'knee'; [demotic] (Er. 142, 1), *pt*, 'knee, foot'.

ᴴCHAMPOLLION, *Gr. ég.* 83, 95 [1836]; ᴰBRUGSCH, *Scriptura Aegypt. dem.* 17, §14 [1848].

ᴮ**ⲣⲁⲧ-ϥⲁⲧ** (Crum 273 b), 'hare', lit. 'one whose foot is covered with a growth (of hair)'; **ⲣⲁⲧ-** from **ⲣⲱⲧ**.

RAHLFS *ap.* Polotsky in *JEA* 25, 111 [1939].

ⲡⲱⲧ (Crum 274 a), 'run, flee, go' = [hieroglyphs] (*Wb.* I, 500, 13 f.), *pd*, 'knee, run'; [demotic] (Er. 141, 8), *pt*, 'run, flee'.

ᴴCHABAS, *Oeuv. div.* I (= *Bibl. ég.* IX), 150 n. [1857]; ᴰBRUGSCH, *Gr. dém.* 39, §83 [1855].

ⲡⲁⲓⲧⲏ (Crum 276 a) and **ⲙⲡⲁⲓⲧⲏ**, 'eggplant' (بَدِنْجان, *bedengân*) are a transcription of Arabic بَيْضاء, 'white'.

CRUM, *A Coptic Dict.* 276 a [1932]; cf. Chassinat, *Le manuscrit magique copte*, 51–2 [1955].

ⲡⲓⲧⲉ (Crum 276a), 'bow (arcus)' = (*Wb.* I, 569, 8 f.), *pḏt*, 'bow'; (Er. 142, 2), *ptyt*, 'bow'.

[H]CHAMPOLLION, *Précis*, 2nd ed. 125–6 [1828]; [D]SPIEGELBERG, *Mythus*, 133, no. 282 [1917].

ⲡⲁⲧⲁⲗⲁⲥ (Crum 276a, 'meaning unknown') = Gk σπαταλᾶς, 'living lewdly', Part. of σπαταλάω.

DRESCHER's communication.

ⲡⲟⲧⲡⲧ (Crum 276a), 'fall away, make fall, drop' = (*Wb.* I, 563, 9 f.), *ptpt*, 'tread on something'.

BRUGSCH, *Wb.* 523 [1868].

ⲡⲱⲧⲥ (Crum 276a), 'divide, split, crack' = (*Wb.* I, 566, 16 f.), *pds*, 'crush, destroy'.

ⲡⲁⲧⲥⲉ (Crum 276b), 'thing divided, split off, plank' = (*Wb.* I, 567, 2. 3), *pdst*, 'small ball, pill'; (not in Er.; ex. *Mitt. Inst. Or.* 2, 368, l. 1), *pts*, 'pill'.

ⲡⲱⲧϩ (Crum 276b), 'carve, engrave' = Gr.-R. (*Wb.* I, 565, 11), *ptḥ*, 'to form'; (Er. 142, 4), *ptḥ*, 'carve'. From Semitic, cf. פִּתַּח, 'engrave'.

[H]BRUGSCH, *Wb.* 528 [1868]; [D]GRIFFITH-THOMPSON, III, 33, no. 326 [1909]; [S]ROSSI, *Etym. aegypt.* 242 [1808].

ⲡⲧⲁϩ (Crum 277a, s.v. ⲡⲱⲧϩ), god Ptah = (*Wb.* I, 565, 9), *ptḥ*; (Er. 142, 3), *ptḥ*.

[H]CHAMPOLLION, *Précis*, 1st ed. 97–8 and 'Tableau général', no. 48; 141 [1824]; [D]BRUGSCH, *Scriptura Aeg. dem.* 11 [1848].

ⲡⲁϣ (Crum 277a), 'trap, snare' = (*Wb.* I, 543, 15–16), *pḫꜣ*, 'bird trap'; (Er. 139, 1), *pḫ*, 'trap, snare'.

[H]MASPERO, *Journal asiatique*, 8e série, I, 31 n. 1 [1883]; [D]GRIFFITH, *Ryl.* III, 350 [1909].

ⲡⲟⲉⲓϣ (Crum 277a), 'rung, step' of ladder = lit. 'divider' from ⲡⲱϣ, 'divide', see next entry.

ⲡⲱϣ (Crum 277a), 'divide' = (*Wb.* I, 553, 6 ff.), *pss̆* > , *ps̆*, 'divide'; (Er. 140, 2), *ps̆*, 'divide'.

[H]BRUGSCH, *Wb.* 511–12 [1868]; [D]BRUGSCH, *Scriptura Aegypt. dem.* 35 [1848].

παϣε (Crum 378a), 'division, half' = (*Wb.* I, 554, 4 f.), *psšt* > , *pšt*, 'share, half'; (Er. 140, 2), *pšt*, 'half'.

HBRUGSCH, *Wb.* 512 [1868]; DBRUGSCH, *Scriptura Aegypt. dem.* 24 and passim [1848].

παϣε (Crum 278b), a disease producing pustules, swelling = (not in *Wb.*), *pš*, a disease.

EDWARDS, *Oracular Amuletic Decrees*, 11, n. 30 [1960].

πωϣν (Crum 278b), 'do service, serve' as priest = (Er. 140, 3), *pšn*, 'penetrate, call into office'. The earlier (*Wb.* I, 560, 3 f.), *pšn*, means still only 'split'.

SPIEGELBERG, *Petubastis*, p. 21*, no. 134 [1910].

παϣοης (Crum 279a), name of 9th month = (*Wb.* III, 300, bottom), *p(ꜣ)-n-ḫnsw*, 'that (festival) of Khons', a Theban festival.

ČERNÝ, *Annales du Service* 43, 175 [1943]; cf. Lauth, *Manetho*, 56 [1865]; cf. Lepsius, *Chronologie*, 141 [1848].

πωϣς (Crum 279b), 'be amazed, beside oneself' = (*Wb.* I, 550, 16–18), *psḫ*, 'confuse, be disarranged' and sim.

DÉVAUD, *Études*, 12–14 [1922].

πωϩ (Crum 280a), 'break, burst, tear' = (*Wb.* I, 542, 12 f.), *pḫꜣ*, 'split'; (not in Er.), *pḫ*, 'tear up' (a document).

HCHABAS, *Voyage*, 299 [1866]; DPARKER, *JEA* 26, 108 [1940].

πωϩ (Crum 281a), 'reach' = (*Wb.* I, 533, 12 ff.), *pḥ*, 'reach'; (Er. 137, 7), *pḥ*, 'reach'.

HBRUGSCH, *Geographie des alten Ägyptens* 189 and Pl. XXXVII, no. 844 [1857]; HDBRUGSCH, *Rhind*, 37, no. 108 and Pl. XXXVI, no. 107 [1865].

(B**ϕωϧερ**), Qual. **ϕαϧερ** (Crum 282b), 'charm, bewitch' = (*Wb.* I, 544, 14), *pḫr*, 'turn round, charm'; (Er. 139, 4), *pḫr*, 'to charm'.

HSPIEGELBERG, *Kopt. Handwb.* 97 and n. 17 [1921]; cf. GRIFFITH, *Stories*, 92 [1900]; DSPIEGELBERG, *Dem. Chron.* 55, no. 94 [1914].

παϩρε (Crum 282b), 'drug, medicament' = (*Wb.* I, 549, 1 ff.), *pḫrt*, 'medicament'; (Er. 139, 5), *pḫrt*, 'medicament'.

HSTEINDORFF, *ZÄS* 27, 108 [1889]; DHESS, *Gnost. Pap.* 9 [1892].

ⲡⲱϩⲥ (Crum 283a), 'to bite' = (*Wb.* I, 550, 1–10), *psḫ*, 'bite'; (Er. 137, 6), *phs*, also (Ankhsh. 14, 14), *pḥs*, 'to bite'.

[H]RÖSCH, *Vorbemerkungen*, 104 [1909]; [D]SPIEGELBERG, *Kopt. Etym.* 14–15 [1920].

ⲡⲱϩⲧ (Crum 283a), 'bend self, fall' = (*Wb.* I, 544, 7–11), *pḫd*, 'hang down, be thrown down'; (Er. 139, 6), *pḫṭ*, 'throw down'.

[H]LE PAGE RENOUF, *Egyptol. and Philol. Essays*, II, 63 [1867]; [HD]BRUGSCH, *Wb.* 505 [1868].

ⲡⲁϩⲧⲉ (Crum 284b), 'strength, valiance' = (*Wb.* I, 539, 5 ff.), *pḥty*, 'strength'; (Er. 138, 2), *pḥṭ*, 'strength'.

[H]ERMAN, *ZÄS* 21, 95 [1883]; [D]HESS, *Gnost. Pap.* 6 [1892].

ⲡⲁϩⲟⲩ (Crum 284b), 'hinder part, back' = (*Wb.* I, 535, 14 f.), *pḥwy*, 'hinder part, end'; (Er. 138, 1), *pḥw*, 'hinder part, end'.

[H]CHAMPOLLION, *Dict.* 115 [1841]; [D]BRUGSCH, *Gr. dém.* 175, §340 [1855].

ⲡⲟϫ Qual. (Crum 285a), 'amorous (?)' = (Er. 142, 7), *pḏ*, 'to love'.

GRIFFITH–THOMPSON III, 33, no. 330 [1909].

ⲡⲉϫⲉ- (Crum 285a), 'say' = (*pꜣ ỉdd·*) + Subject, 'that which...said'; (Er. 691, middle), *pꜣ ỉdd·*.

[H]ERMAN, *Näg. Gr.* pp. 105, 256, 265 [1880]; [D]REICH, *JEA* 10, 285–8 [1924].

ⲡⲱϫϭ (Crum 285b), 'beat flat, broad' = (Er. 142, 8), *pḏḫ* 'spread out'. For ḫ > ϭ, cf. *nḏḫ* > ⲛⲟⲩϫⲕ.

[A]**ⲡⲟⲩⲟⲩϫⲉ** (Crum 285b, s.v. ⲡⲱϭⲉ), 'break', from Semitic, cf. Hebrew פָּצַע, 'bruise'.

STRICKER in *Acta Orientalia* 15, 4 [1937].

[A]**ⲡⲁⲓϭⲉ** (Crum 285b), 'mouth', originally perhaps slang subst. 'split, fissure', from ⲡⲱϭⲉ, 'break, burst', see this latter.

TILL, *Festschr. Grapow*, 328 [1955].

ⲡⲟϭⲉ (Crum 285b), ⲡⲁϭⲉ Mani Hom. 11, 7; 71, 27 (?), prob. 'battle-field' = (*Wb.* I, 562, 14), *pgꜣ*, 'battlefield'.

SPIEGELBERG in Crum, *A Coptic Dictionary*, 285b [1932].

ⲡⲱϭⲉ (Crum 285b), ‘break, burst’ = (*Wb.* I, 562, 1–7), *pgꜣ*, ‘spread, open’; (Er. 141, 3), *pk*, ‘separate’; also (Ankhsh. 10, 13), *pgy*, ‘open’ (heart).

[H]BAILLET, *Oeuv. div.* I (= *Bibl. ég.* XV), 40 [1867]; [D]ERICHSEN, *Dem. Glossar*, 141, 3 [1954].

ⲡⲟϭⲉ (Crum 286a), ‘broken piece, fragment, piece of wood’ = (*Wb.* I, 563, 6), *pgꜣ*, ‘pieces of wood’; (Er. 141, 3), *pk*, ‘fragment’.

[H]HINCKS, *Transactions of the Roy. Irish Ac.* 21, Part II, p. 151 and Pl. I, no. 45 [1848, read in 1846]; [D]BRUGSCH, *Wb.* 516–17 [1868].

[A]**ⲡⲟⲩⲟⲩϫⲉ** is a different word, see this.

-ⲡⲱⲕⲉ in **ⲟⲩⲡⲱⲕⲉ**, see the latter, Geogr. Names.

[S]**ⲡⲟϭⲗⲉ** (Crum 286b, ‘meaning unknown’), [A2]**ⲡⲁϭⲗⲉ** (Mani Ps.), ‘cluster’ of vegetables or fruit (thus Allberry), through metathesis from ***ⲡⲟⲗϭⲉ**, this synonymous with **ⲡⲟⲗϭⲥ** (Crum 262b), ‘clod, lump’, from **ⲡⲱⲗϭ**, ‘deliver, free’.

ⲡⲱϭⲙ (Crum 286b, ‘meaning unknown’); read **ⲉⲡⲱϭⲙ**, see this latter.

***ⲡⲟϭⲡϭ** is the correct form of **ϩⲡⲟϭⲡϭ**, **ϩⲡⲟϫⲡϫ**, [A2]**ϩⲡⲁϭⲡϭ** (Crum 743a under **ϩϫⲟⲡϫⲡ**), ‘break into small pieces’, reduplication of **ⲡⲱϭⲉ**, ‘break’. For **ϫ** replacing **ϭ**, cf. **ϫⲣⲟⲟⲙⲡⲉ**, **ϫⲁϩϫⲉϩ**, **ϩⲱⲣϫ** quoted by Crum 745a.

ⲡⲱϭⲥ (Crum 286b), ‘sweat, drip’, and *pgs* < *psg* (*Wb.* I, 555, 4 f.), ‘spit’, see below.

ⲡⲁϭⲥⲉ, ‘spittle’ = (*Wb.* I, 555, 15), *pgs* (fem.), ‘spittle’ by metathesis from (*Wb.* I, 555, 4–14), *psg*, ‘spit’; (Er. 141, 6), *pkst*, ‘spittle’.

[H]LANGE, *Das Weisheitsbuch des Amenemope*, 116 [1925]; cf. Brugsch, *Geographie des alten Ägyptens*, 298 [1857]; [D]REVILLOUT, *Rev. ég.* 4, p. 76, n. 4 [1885].

P

ⲣⲁ (Crum 287a), 'state, condition' = (*Wb.* II, 394, 11 f.), *rꜣ-ʿ*, prefix: 'state of . . . '; (Er. 242, 6), *rʿ*, prefix: 'state of . . . '.

[H]ERMAN, *Näg. Gr.* 189, §285 [1880]; [D]SPIEGELBERG, *Dem. Gr.* 27, §33 [1925].

In **ϣⲁⲛⲣⲁ**, 'to the extent, as far as, until', **ⲣⲁ** = (*Wb.* II, 394, 1–8), *rꜣ-ʿ*, 'end of . . . '; (Er. 239, 8; 242, 5), *r-ʿ*, 'as far as'.

-ⲣⲉ (Crum 287b), interrog. enclitic = ? (Er. 246, 3), *rm*, interrog. particle.

[O]**ⲣⲉ́ⲓ** in **ⲣⲉ́ⲓ ⲉ̀ⲛⲥⲓ́ⲙⲉ**, 'female companion', see under **ⲏⲣ**, 'friend'.

ⲣⲏ (Crum 287b), 'sun' = (*Wb.* II, 401, 5 f.), *rʿ*, 'sun'; (Er. 242, 2), *rʿ*, 'sun'.

[H]CHAMPOLLION, *Précis*, 1st ed., Tableau gén., p. (5) and Pl. 3, no. 47; p. 28 and Pl. 14, no. 237a [1824]; [D]ÅKERBLAD in Young, *Misc. Works*, III, 37 [1815].

ⲣⲓ (Crum 287b), 'cell, room' possibly related to (or contracted from?) , , (*Wb.* II, 407, 13–14), *rryt* (*Wb.*: *rwyt*?), '(office) room'; (Er. 241, 3), *ryt*, 'room'.

[H]GARDINER, *The Chester Beatty Papyri, No. I*, 36 n. 1 [1931]; [D]BRUGSCH, *Gr. dém.* 32, §63 [1855].

ⲣⲟ (Crum 288a), (1) 'mouth', = (*Wb.* II, 389, 1 f.), *rꜣ*, 'mouth'; (Er. 239, 12), *rꜣ*, 'mouth'.

[H]CHAMPOLLION, *Gr. ég.* 92 [1836]; [D]BRUGSCH, *Gr. dém.* 28, §56 [1855].

(2) 'gate' (Crum 289a) = (*Wb.* II, 390, 10 f.), *rꜣ*, 'opening, door'; (Er. 240, 1), *rꜣ*, 'door, entrance'.

[H]CHAMPOLLION, *Gr. ég.* 80 [1836]; [D]BRUGSCH, *Gr. dém.* 32, §63 [1855].

ⲣⲁ- (Crum 289b), 'part, fraction' = (*Wb.* II, 392, 2 f.), *rꜣ*, 'part' (lit. 'mouth'); (Er. 240, 2), *rꜣ*, 'part'.

[H]CHAMPOLLION, *Gr. ég.* 243–4 [1836]; [D]BRUGSCH, *Scriptura Aeg. dem.* 46 [1848].

ⲕⲱ ⲛⲣⲱ⸗, ⲕⲁ ⲣⲱ⸗ (Crum 288b), 'leave mouth, be silent' = *ḫꜣʿ rꜣ*, 'be silent'.

KRALL, *Mitt. Erzh. Rainer*, VI, 71, no. 227 [1897].

ᴮϫⲉⲕ ⲣⲱ⸗ (Crum 289a), 'fill mouth, satisfy' = , *ḏk rꜣ*, 'complement'.

GRIFFITH-THOMPSON, III, 99, no. 1092 [1909].

ⲉⲣⲛ, ⲉⲣⲟ ⲛ (Crum 289b), prep., 'to mouth of, to, upon' = (*Wb.* II, 391, 11. 12), *r rꜣ* . . . , 'at the door (of a building)', also weakened 'at the entrance (of a gate), at (the gate)'; (Er. 239, 12; Spiegelberg, *Dem. Gr.* §331), *r-rꜣ*, 'to, at'.

ᴴJUNKER, *Gram. der Denderatexte*, 174, §240b [1906]; ᴰGRIFFITH-THOMPSON, III, 51, no. 486 (1) [1909].

ˢϩⲁⲣⲛ-, ᴮϧⲁⲣⲉⲛ-, ˢϩⲁⲣⲱ⸗, ᴮϧⲁⲣⲱ⸗ (Crum 289b), 'under mouth of, beneath, before', (mostly = Gk dative) = , *ẖr-rꜣ·*, 'under mouth of'.

SPIEGELBERG, *Dem. Gr.* 150, §332d [1925].

ϩⲓⲣⲛ-, ϩⲓⲣⲟ ⲛ- (Crum 290a), 'at mouth of, at door of, at, upon' = Gr. (*Wb.* II, 391, 13), 'at the entrance of . . .'; (Spiegelberg, *Dem. Gr.* §332), *ḥr-rꜣ*, 'upon, at'.

ᴴJUNKER, *Gram. der Denderatexte*, 174, §240c [1906].

ⲣⲟ (Crum 290a), 'goose' = (*Wb.* II, 393, 1–3), *rꜣ*, 'goose'; (Er. 241, 1), *rꜣ*, 'goose' (reading uncertain; might also be *ꞽpt*, 'fowl, goose').

ᴴERMAN, *ZÄS* 35, 108–9 [1897]; ᴰERICHSEN, *Dem. Glossar*, 241, 1 [1954].

ⲣⲱ (Crum 290a), enclitic particle, emphatic or explicative, 'same, again, also', etc., probably = Gr. *rw* (*Wb.* I, 104, lower) for N.K. , *ꞽr(y)w*, plural of adjective , *ꞽry* (*Wb.* I, 103, 18), 'belonging to'.

DAUMAS, *BIFAO* 48, 102 [1949].

NB. Erman-Grapow, *Wb.* II, 395, 7 [1928] and Erman, *Neuäg. Gr.*, 2nd ed. 341, §683 [1933] equate **ⲣⲱ** with L.Eg. () (*Wb.* II, 395, 7–11), *(m)-rꜣ-ʿ*, 'also'.

ⲡⲓⲕⲉ (Crum 291b), 'incline' (cf. Gardiner in *Festschrift Grapow*, p. 3) = (*Wb.* II, 456, 9 f.), *rḳ*, 'deviate from the level', etc.; (Er. 256, 3), *rḳ*, 'deviate'.

[H]BAILLET, *Oeuv. div.* I (=*Bibl. ég.* XV), 30 [1867]; DEVÉRIA, *Le papyrus judiciaire de Turin*, 188–9 [1868] = *Journal As.* 1867, 467–8 [1867]; [D]SPIEGELBERG, *Mythus*, 196, no. 483 [1917].

ⲣⲁⲕⲣⲉⲕ, [Sf]**ⲗⲉⲕⲗⲱⲕ⸗** (Crum 293a), prob. 'soften' (tr. and intr.) = **ⲗⲟⲕⲗⲉⲕ**, see this under **ⲗⲱⲕ**, 'be soft'.

ⲣⲉⲕⲣⲓⲕⲉ (Crum 293a, Add., p. xx), 'bending, nodding of head in sleep', reduplication of **ⲣⲓⲕⲉ**, 'incline', see this.

ⲣⲱⲕϩ (Crum 293a), 'burn' = (*Wb.* II, 458, 9–14), *rkḥ*, 'burn'; (Er. 256, 4), *rḳh*, 'burn'.

[H]CHAMPOLLION, *Gr. ég.* 99, 378 [1836]; [D]BRUGSCH, *Scriptura Aeg. dem.* 19, §22 [1848].

ⲣⲁⲙⲉ (Crum 294a), fish *tilapia* = (*Wb.* II, 416, 12–17), *rm*, 'fish'; (Er. 246, 4), *rm*, 'fish'.

[H]CHAMPOLLION, *Gr. ég.* 74 [1836]; [D]BRUGSCH, *Gr. dém.* 24, §42 [1855].

ⲣⲓⲙⲉ (Crum 294a), 'weep' = (*Wb.* II, 416, bottom), *rmy*, 'weep'; (Er. 246, 5), *rmy*, 'weep'.

[H]CHAMPOLLION, *Gr. ég.* 373, 389 [1836]; [D]BRUGSCH, *Gr. dém.* 34, §68; 128, §262 [1855].

ⲣⲙⲉⲓⲏ (Crum 294b), 'tear' = (*Wb.* II, 417, 14–15), *rmyt*, 'tear'.

BRUGSCH, *Wb.* 857–8 [1868].

ⲣⲱⲙⲉ (Crum 294b), 'man, human being' = (*Wb.* II, 421, 9 ff.), *rmṯ* 'man'; (Er. 247, 5), *rmt*, 'man'.

[H]CHABAS, *Voyage*, 350 [1866]; [D]ÅKERBLAD in Young, *Misc. Works*, III, 37 [1815].

ⲣⲙⲛⲣⲁⲧⲟⲩ (Crum 295b from Ex. 12, 37), **ⲣⲙⲣⲁⲧⲟⲩ**, 'on foot, pedestrians' = (Er. 247, bottom), *rm rt·w*, 'pedestrians, infantry'.

KRALL, *Mitt. Erzh. Rainer*, VI, 68, no. 176 [1897].

ⲣⲙⲛⲕⲏⲙⲉ (Crum 295b), 'Egyptian', see **ⲕⲏⲙⲉ**, under **ⲕⲙⲟⲙ**.

ⲣⲉϥ- (Crum 295b), prefix forming agent of verbs = (*Wb.* II, 422, 7), *rmṯ ỉw·f* . . ., 'one who . . . ' (lit. 'man he being . . . '); , *rmt ỉw·f*, 'one who . . . '.

ERMAN, *Näg. Gr.* 16, §14 [1880]; [D]BRUGSCH, *Scriptura Aeg. dem.* 66 [1848].

NB. Though Coptic and Dem. (Spiegelberg, *Dem. Gr.* §27) alike use indiscriminately **ⲣⲉϥ-** and *rmt ỉw·f*, P. Bodmer VI according to the syntactic need still differentiates **ⲣⲙⲉϥ-**, **ⲣⲙⲉⲥ-** (fem.), **ⲣⲙⲉⲩ-** (pl.) and **ⲣⲙⲉⲧ-** (after definite article), and uses **ⲡⲣⲱⲙⲉ ⲉϥ-** and **ⲟⲩⲣⲱⲙⲉ ⲉϥ-** instead of **ⲣⲱⲙⲉ ⲛⲣⲉϥ-**.

KASSER, *Papyrus Bodmer*, VI, p. xxiv [1960].

ⲣⲙⲙⲁⲟ (Crum 296a), 'great man, rich man' = (*Wb.* I, 162, 12; II, 424, 7), *rmṯ ꜥꜣw*, 'important (old, rich?) people'; (Er. 247, 5), *rmt ꜥꜣ*, 'great man, rich man'.

HSTERN, *Kopt. Gr.* p. 92 [1880]; cf. Schäfer, *Nastesen*, pp. 101, 103 [1901]; DKRALL, *Mitt. Erzh. Rainer*, VI, 68, no. 176 [1897].

ⲣⲟⲙⲡⲉ (Crum 296b), 'year' = (*Wb.* II, 429, bottom), *rnpt*, 'year'; (Er. 250, 3), *rnpt*, 'year'.

HYOUNG, *Misc. Works*, III, Pl. 4, no. 180 = *Encyclopaedia Britannica*, Suppl. IV, Pl. 77, no. 180 [1819]; DÅKERBLAD in Young, *Misc. Works*, III, 38 [1815].

ⲧⲣⲟⲙⲡⲉ, ⲛⲧⲣⲟⲙⲡⲉ (Crum 296b), 'this year' = L.Eg. (*Wb.* II, 430, 12), *m tꜣ rnpt*, 'in this year'.

ⲧⲛⲣⲟⲙⲡⲉ, ⲧⲉⲣⲣⲟⲙⲡⲉ (Crum 297a), 'each year, annually' = (*Wb.* V, 378, 1–4), *tnw rnpt*, 'each year, annually'; (Er. 635, 1), *tn rnpt*, same meaning.

HGOODWIN in Chabas, *Mél. égypt.* I, 85 [1862]; DBRUGSCH, *Wb.* 1551 [1868].

ⲣⲁⲙⲥ (not in Crum; Allberry, *Manichaean Psalm-Book*, Part II, 163, 4; 178, 11), 'ship(?)' = (Er. 247, 4), *rms*, kind of ship, from the Greek ῥώμσιν (acc. sg.), ῥώψ.

H. THOMPSON in Allberry, *A Manichaean Psalm Book*, Part II, p. 163 [1938].

ⲣⲙϩⲉ (Crum 297a), 'free person' = (*Wb.* II, 268, 4–6), *nmḥw*, 'poor man'; (Er. 219, 6), *nmḥ*, 'free'.

HDSPIEGELBERG, *ZÄS* 53, 116 [1917]; cf. Lacau, *Rec. Champollion*, 722–3 [1922].

ⲙⲛⲧⲣⲙϩⲉ (Crum 297a), 'freedom' = , *mdt rmt-nmḥ*, 'freedom' (**ⲣⲙ-** being interpreted through 'Volksetymologie' as *rmt*, 'man').

GLANVILLE, *Cat. of Demotic Papyri*, II, 66 [1955].

ⲣⲁⲛ (Crum 297b), 'name' = (*Wb.* I, 425, 1 ff.), *rn*, 'name'; (Er. 249, 1), *rn*, 'name'.

HCHAMPOLLION, *Précis*, 2nd ed., 126 [1828]; DBRUGSCH, *Sammlung dem. Urk.* Pl. VI, l. 24 [1850].

ⲣⲡⲉ (Crum 298b), 'temple' = (*Wb.* II, 397, 6), *rꜣ-pr*, 'temple'; (Er. 245, 2), *rpy*, 'temple'. Preceded by definite article **ⲡ-** in Egyptian Arabic بربة (ÅKERBLAD, *Lettre*, 39).

HBRUGSCH, *Nouvelles recherches*, p. 3 [1856]; DYOUNG, *Misc. Works*, III, pp. 24–5, no. 16 = *Mus. crit.* 6, pp. 174–5, no. 16 [1815]; cf. Åkerblad, *Lettre*, 38–9 and Pl. I, no. 11 [1802].

(**ⲣⲡⲱ**), **ⲉⲣⲡⲱ** (Crum 298b), nn., meaning uncertain, related to vine leaves = (*Wb.* II, 435, 2 f.), *rnpwt* > , *rnpyt*, 'fresh plants'; (Er. 244, 5), *rpy*, 'fresh plants, greens'.

B**ⲣⲓⲡⲓⲑⲓ** (MS. **ⲣⲓⲧⲓⲑⲓ**, Crum 306a), zodiacal sign *Aquarius* = (*Wb.* I, 571, 1–5), *ḥry-pḏt*, lit. 'Commander of bowmen', which of course should be *Sagittarius*. **-ⲡⲓⲑⲓ** (instead of **-ⲫⲓⲑⲓ**) through a Greek transcription (*ῥιπιθι), similarly **ⲣⲓⲡⲓϯ** K 217 'fan' from Gk. ῥιπίδιον.

ČERNÝ in *Festschrift Grapow*, 31–2 [1955].

ⲣⲓⲣ (Crum 299a), 'swine, pig' = (*Wb.* II, 438, 7), *rrỉ*, 'pig'; (Er. 251, 3), *ryr*, as proper name.

HGELL in Young, *Misc. Works*, III, 460 [1828]; Champollion, *Gr. ég.* 72 [1836].

ⲣⲏⲣ in proper name **ⲫⲣⲣⲏⲣ** (i.e. **ⲡ** + **ϩⲣ** + **ⲣⲏⲣ**) = **pꜣ-ḥr-rrỉ*, lit. 'The pig-face', cf. fem. proper name , *Ḥr-rrꜣ*, Lichtheim, *Dem. Ostraca*, 71, no. 158 n. 2 [1957].

ⲣⲁⲁⲣ(ⲉ), **ⲣⲁⲓⲣⲉ** (Crum 299a), f., 'sucking pig' = (*Wb.* II, 438, 8 ff.), *rrt*, 'swine'; (Er. 251, 3), *ryr(ꜣ)t*, 'swine', the hippopotamus constellation.

DCRUM, *A Coptic Dict.* 299a [1932].

ⲣⲣⲟ (Crum 299a), 'king, queen' = (*Wb.* I, 516, 2 ff.), *pr-ꜥꜣ*, 'palace, king', lit. 'great house'; (Er. 133, 5), *pr-ꜥꜣ*, 'king'.

HDE ROUGÉ, *Oeuv. div.* III (= *Bibl. ég.* XXIII), 92–8 [1856]; DÅKERBLAD, *Lettre*, 47–9 and Pl. I, no. 15 [1802]; cf. YOUNG, *Encycl. Brit.*, Suppl. IV, Pl. 76, no. 137 [1819]; Hess, *Stne*, pp. 9, 82 and 155 [1888].

ⲣⲣⲱ, 'queen' = (Volten, *Ägypter und Amazonen*, 97), *pr-ꜥꜣt*, 'queen'.

ⲣⲉⲣⲙⲏ (Crum 299b), m., quantity, measure of land, ½ arura = (*Wb.* II, 420, 16; 421, 1, 2), *rmnyt*, 'domain' (see Gardiner, *The Wilbour Papyrus*, III, 110–11) which seems to have an identical form with (*Wb.* II, 419, 3), '½ arura', being but an abbreviated spelling. ***rem-nēyet* > **renmēyet* > **rermēyet* > **ⲣⲉⲣⲙⲏ**.

KUENTZ, *Bulletin de la Société d'archéologie copte*, 5, 245–9 [1939].

ⲣⲏⲥ (Crum 299b), 'south' = (*Wb.* II, 452–3), *rsy*, 'southern, south'; (Er. 254, 2), *rs*, 'south, southern'.

[H]CHAMPOLLION, *Gr. ég.* 97 [1836]; [D]BRUGSCH, *Scriptura Aeg. dem.* 43 [1848].

ⲙⲁⲣⲏⲥ (Crum 300b), 'Southern Country, Upper Egypt' = , *mꜣꜥ-rs*, 'southern place (= part)' of a locality, perhaps also 'Upper Egypt'.

SPIEGELBERG, *Die dem. Pap. Loeb*, p. 5 (19) [1931].

ⲣⲟⲉⲓⲥ (Crum 300b), 'be awake, watch' = (*Wb.* II, 449, 8 f.), *r(ỉ)s*, 'to awake, watch'; (Er. 253, 5), *rsy*, 'watch'.

[H]BIRCH in *Archaeologia* 35, p. 120 and Pl. 4, no. 16 [1853]; [D]BRUGSCH, *Wb.* 871 [1868].

ⲣⲥⲱ (Crum 302a), 'fold' for cattle and sheep = , , Plural (not in *Wb.*, but see Yoyotte in *Mitt. Kairo* 16, 417), *rsyt*, 'the watch'; (Er. 254, 1), *rst*, 'fold, dwelling, watch'.

[H]SPIEGELBERG, *Kopt. Handwb.* 103 [1921]; [D]GRIFFITH, *Ryl.* III, 226 n. 9; 367 [1909].

ⲣⲁⲥⲧⲉ (Crum 302a), 'morrow' = (Er. 255, 7), *rsṯ*, 'morrow', originally , *r(ỉ)s tw*, 'wake up, thou' (Imperative of , *r(ỉ)s*, **ⲣⲟⲉⲓⲥ**, 'wake' and dependent pers. pronoun < *ṯw*, 'thou'), the beginning of the morning prayer to the rising sun (*Wb.* II, 449, 12); compare **ⲁⲙⲁϩⲧⲉ** and others under **-ⲧⲉ**.

[D]GRIFFITH, *Stories*, p. 170 (n. to II Kh. 3, 24) [1900].

ⲣⲁⲥⲟⲩ (Crum 302b), 'dream' = (*Wb.* II, 452, 1–3), *rswt*, 'dream'; (Er. 255, 3), *rswt*, 'dream'.

[H]BRUGSCH, *Wb.* 871 [1868]; [D]BRUGSCH, *Gr. dém.* 40, §88 [1855].

ⲣⲁⲧ⸗ (Crum 302b), 'foot' = (*Wb.* II, 461, 1 ff.), *rd*, 'foot'; (Er. 258, 1), *rt*, 'foot'. Not from the Dual **radwey* which would have given ***ⲣⲁⲧⲟⲩ** like **paḥwey* > **ⲡⲁϩⲟⲩ**.

ᴴCHAMPOLLION, *Précis*, 2nd ed., 125–6 [1828]; ᴰBRUGSCH, *Gr. dém.* 29, §56 [1855].

ⲕⲁ ⲣⲁⲧ (Crum 303a), 'lay, set foot' = , *ḫꜣ* *rt*, 'depart'.

KRALL, *Mitt. Erzh. Rainer*, VI, 71, no. 227 [1897].

ⲟⲩⲉϩ ⲣⲁⲧ ϩⲓϫⲱ⸗ (Crum 303a), 'set foot upon', cf. , *wꜣḥ rdwy ḥr*, same meaning.

CAMINOS, *Chronicle*, 84 [1958].

ⲉⲣⲁⲧ⸗ (Crum 303a), 'to foot of, to', cf. (*Wb.* II, 461, 17–19), *r rdwy*, 'to the feet of'; (Er. 258, 1), *r rt*, 'to'.

ϩⲁⲣⲁⲧ⸗ (Crum 303b), 'under foot of, beneath', cf. (*Wb.* II, 462, 3–7; III, 388, 5), *ẖr rdwy*, 'under the feet of, at the feet of'; (Er. 258, 1), *ẖr rt*, 'beneath'.

ϩⲓⲣⲁⲧ⸗ (Crum 303b), 'toward', cf. (*Wb.* II, 462, 1–2), *ḥr rdwy*, 'on the feet'; (Er. 258, 1), *ḥr rt*, 'before (?)'.

ⲣⲏⲧ (Crum 303b), a title? = (*Wb.* II, 413, 12 f.), *rwḏw*, 'administrator, controller'; (Er. 256–7), *rt*, 'administrator'.

ᴰGRIFFITH, *Dem. Graffiti Dodekaschoinos*, I, 295, no. 845 [1937] (with doubt).

ⲣⲱⲧ (Crum 303b), 'grow, be covered with a growth' = (*Wb.* II, 462, 20 f.), *rd*, 'grow'; (Er. 257, 1), *rt*, 'grow'.

ᴴCHAMPOLLION, *Gr. ég.* 363 [1836]; ᴰBRUGSCH, *Gr. dém.* 25, §47 [1855].

ᴮ**ⲣⲁⲧ-ⲫⲁⲧ**, see under **ⲡⲁⲧ**.

ⲣⲱⲧ (Crum 304a), 'a growth' = (*Wb.* II, 463, 8–10), *rd*, 'plant, growth'; (Er. 257, 1), *rt*, 'growth'.

ᴴᴰBRUGSCH, *Wb.* 878 [1868].

-ⲣⲱⲧ, -ⲣⲟⲧ (not in Crum), adj. 'hard, strong' = (*Wb.* II, 410, 13 f.), *rwḏ*, adj., 'strong' (the verb being **ⲟⲩⲣⲟⲧ**). See **ⲃⲁⲣⲱⲧ, ⲥⲓⲙⲣⲱⲧ** and **ϣⲥⲣⲟⲧ**.

ⲣⲁⲓⲧⲉ (Crum 304b), 'kindred, kinship', cf. [demotic] (Er. 242, 1), *ryṯt*, a fem. subst.

GRIFFITH-THOMPSON, III, 52, no. 499 [1909].

ⲣⲏⲧⲉ (Crum 304b), 'manner, fashion, likeness' = [demotic] (Er. 258, 2), *rtṯ*, 'manner'.

GRIFFITH, *Stories*, 133–4 [1900].

Originally ?'feet' (from **ⲣⲁⲧ**); GRIFFITH, *Dem. Graffiti Dodekaschoinos*, I, 164, no. 202 [1937].

ⲣⲧⲱ (Crum 305b), 'span', perhaps (ⲧ)**ⲣⲧ-ⲱ**, *[hieroglyphs], *ḏrt-ꜥꜣt*, 'great hand' = [hieroglyphs], a subdivision of the cubit (for which see Griffith in *PSBA* 14, 404).

BONDI, *ZÄS* 32, 132–3 [1894].

ⲣⲧⲟⲃ (Crum 305b), measure of grain, etc. = [demotic] (Er. 259, 3), *rtb*, measure of grain, ἀρτάβη, إِرْدَب, Syr. ܐܪܕܒܐ, etc., all from Aramaic אַרְדַּב, this perhaps from Persian.

DThat Dem. [demotic] = ἀρτάβη was known to BRUGSCH, *Thes.*, 1051 [1891], but he transcribed the Demotic group incorrectly; the correct interpretation of [demotic] alone as [hieroglyphs] and as an abbreviation for ἀρτάβη was suggested by MALININE, *Kêmi* 11, 19 ff. [1950]. SSETHE, *Nachrichten von der K. Gess. Wiss. zu Göttingen, Phil.-hist. Kl.* 1916, 112 ff. [1916]; cf. Rossi, *Etym. aeg.* 53 [1808].

B**ⲣⲓⲧⲓⲑⲓ** (Crum 306a), corrupted from **ⲣⲓⲡⲓⲑⲓ**, see this latter.

ⲣⲁⲩⲏ (Crum 306a), 'quarter' of town, 'neighbourhood' = [hieroglyphs] (*Wb.* II, 396, 6–11), *rꜣ-wꜣt*, 'neighbourhood'.

SETHE, *Einsetzung des Veziers*, 36 [1909].

ⲣⲁⲟⲩⲱ (Crum 306a), 'happen, fall, be subject, be caught' from **ⲣ-ⲁⲟⲩⲱ**, = *[hieroglyphs], *ỉrt ỉw* (*Wb.* I, 48, 5 f.) or *[hieroglyphs], *ỉrt ỉwyt* (*Wb.* I, 48, 11), 'suffer (lit. 'do') evil'; [demotic] (Er. 22, 9), *ỉr ỉw(ỉ)t*, 'suffer harm'.

HDERICHSEN, *Dem. Lesestücke*, I, 2, 1 [1937]; cf. Erichsen, *Dem. Glossar*, 22, 9 [1954].

ⲣⲟⲟⲩⲉ (Crum 306b), 'stubble' = [hieroglyphs] (*Wb.* II, 408, 2), *rwyt*, 'straw, stubble'.

BRUGSCH, *Wb.* Suppl. 722 [1881]; cf. Lange, *Das Weisheitsbuch des Amenemope*, 41 [1925]; Gunn in *ZÄS* 62, 84 n. 2 [1927].

ⲣⲟⲟⲩⲛⲉ (Crum 306b), 'virgin' = , *rwnt*, 'young girl', and or (*Wb.* II, 409, 1), *rwnt*, 'young cow', also related is (*Wb.* II, 435, 18), *ỉnnt*, 'young girl, virgin'; (Er. 249, 2), *rnt*, 'virgin'.

HCLÈRE in *Archiv Orientální* 20, 635–9 [1952]; cf. Erman-Grapow, *Wb.* II, 409, 1 [1928]; DBRUGSCH, *Wb.* 862 [1868].

ⲣⲟⲟⲩϣ (Crum 306b), 'have care for, be intent on' = (not in *Wb.*), *rwš*, 'have care for'; (Er. 243, 8), *rwš*, 'have care for'.

HBIRCH in *Revue arch., Nouv. sér.* IVe année, 7e vol. 129 [1863]; cf. Černý, *Crum Mem. Vol.* 40 [1950]; DBRUGSCH, *Wb.* 852 [1868].

-ⲣⲁϣ (Crum 308a) only in **ⲣⲙ-ⲣⲁϣ**, 'mild, gentle person' = *, *rmṯ-rḫ*; (Er. 247, 5), *rmt rḫ*, 'scholar' (lit. 'man who knows').

W. MAX MÜLLER in *Rec. trav.* 9, 22 n. 1 [1887].

ⲣⲱϣ (Crum 308a), 'to measure' = Infinitive of the verb (*Wb.* II, 442, 7 ff.), *rḫ*, 'recognize, learn, investigate' (only its Old Perfective means 'to know'); (Er. 252, bottom), *rḫ*, 'establish, measure'.

DMATTHA, *Dem. Ostraca*, 23 [1945].

ⲣⲁϣⲉ (Crum 308b), 'rejoice' = (*Wb.* II, 454, 1–12), *ršw*, 'rejoice'; (Er. 256, 2), *ršy*, 'rejoice'.

HCHAMPOLLION, *Gr. ég.* 205 [1836]; DBRUGSCH, *Gr. dém.* 38, §80 [1855].

ⲣⲁϣⲉ (Crum 309a), 'gladness, joy' = (*Wb.* II, 454, 14 ff.), *ršwt*, 'joy', Infinitive of the verb *ršw* (see above).

ⲣⲱϣⲉ (Crum 309a), 'to suffice, to content' = *, *rḫt*.

Subst. **ⲣⲱϣⲉ** (in **ⲣ ⲡⲣⲱϣⲉ**, 'be, do enough', Crum 310a), '(right, sufficient) amount' = (*Wb.* II, 448, 12 f.), *rḫt* (masc.), 'list, amount'.

SETHE in Spiegelberg, *Kopt. Handwb.* 106 [1921]; cf. Gunn, *JEA* 12, 132 [1926].

ⲣϣⲱⲛ (Crum 310a), 'cloak, covering' = (Er. 35, 11), *ỉnšn*(?), some kind of cloth, see Hughes, *JNES* 16, 57 [1957]. Spellings beginning with (= *ỉr-ỉn*) show perhaps that the Dem. word reads in reality *ỉršn* and suggest that it originates in *, *ỉry-šny*, 'companion of (the) hair'; cf. Lüddeckens, *Acta Orientalia* 25, 245–6 [1961].

ERICHSEN, *Auswahl frühdem. Texte*, II, 39 [1950]; cf. H. THOMPSON *ap.* Mattha, *Dem. Ostraca*, 163–4, note on no. 208, 2 [1945].

[S]**ⲣⲁϣⲣⲉϣ**, [A2]**ⲣⲉϣⲣⲉϣ** (Mani) (Crum 310a; correct Crum's 2nd ex. into **ϩⲟⲩⲣⲉϣⲣⲉϣ**, cf. Allberry, *A Manichaean Psalm-book*, II, 8, note on l. 9), 'rejoice' = (*Wb.* II, 456, 1), *ršrš*, 'rejoice'; reduplication of **ⲣⲁϣⲉ**, Mani **ⲣⲉϣⲉ** < , *rš*.

ϩⲟⲩⲣⲉϣⲣⲉϣ (Mani Ps. 8, 19; 91, 8), 'rejoice' = **ϩⲟⲩ-** (St. constr. of **ϩⲓⲟⲩⲉ**) + **ⲣⲉϣⲣⲉϣ**.

ⲣⲟⲩϩⲉ (Crum 310b), 'evening' = (*Wb.* II, 409, 4–6), *rwhꜣ*, 'evening'; (Er. 251, 7), *rhy*, 'evening'.

[H]HINCKS in *Trans. of the Roy. Irish Ac.* 21, Part II, 149–50 and Pl. I, no. 36 and 39 [1848, read in 1846]; [D]BRUGSCH, *Gr. dém.* 30, §61 [1855].

ⲣⲱϩⲉ (Crum 310b), 'wash' = (*Wb.* II, 448, 8), *rḫt*, 'wash (clothes)'; (not in Er.; ex. P. Loeb 21, 54), *rḫt*, 'wash'.

[H]CHAMPOLLION, *Gr ég.* 365, 407 [1836].

ⲣⲁϩⲧ (Crum 311a), 'cleaner, fuller' = (*Wb.* II, 448, 9–11), *rḫty*, 'washerman'; (Er. 253, 2), *rḫṭ*, 'washerman'.

[H]MASPERO, *Études ég.* I, 91 n. 1 [1879]; [D]BRUGSCH, *Sammlung dem. Urk.*, 36 and Pl. X, col. 4, l. 5 [1850].

(**ⲣⲁϩⲣⲉϩ**), **ⲣⲉϩⲣⲱϩ⸗** (Crum 311a), 'warm up?' = Gr.-R. (*Wb.* II, 442, 8), *rḥrḥ*, 'warm up (of heart)', reduplication of the older (*Wb.* II, 442, 1), *rḥwy*, 'be burnt'; (Er. 252, 3), *rḥrḥ*, 'to glow'.

ⲣⲁϩⲧⲉ (Crum 312a), 'cauldron' = (*Wb.* II, 441, 5–7), *rhdt*, 'metal cauldron'; (not in Er.; P. Cairo 31206, 12), *rht*, 'cauldron'.

[H]STERN, *Pap. Ebers*, II, Gloss. 36 [1875]; [D]SPIEGELBERG, *Dem. Denkmäler*, II, 300 [1908].

ⲣⲁϩⲧⲟⲩ (Crum 312b), a monkish garment, leather apron (?) = (not in Er.), *rḥṯw*, a garment.

PARKER, *JEA* 26, 105 [1940].

ⲣⲁϭⲣⲉϭ (Crum 312b, 'hiss'(?), adding **ⲣⲉϭⲣⲉϭ** from Mani Ps. 8, 18; Hom. 20, 16), 'glitter, sparkle' = ? (not in Er.), *rḳrḳ*.

SPIEGELBERG, *Die dem. Pap. Loeb*, 57, (5) [1931].

ⲥ

ⲥ, suffix of 3rd person sing. fem. = (*Wb.* IV, 1, 4); (Er. 399, 1), *·s*.

HCHAMPOLLION, *Précis*, 1st ed., 82 and Tableau gén. no. 16 on p. (2) and Pl. 1 [1824]; DBRUGSCH, *Scriptura Aeg. dem.* 32–3 [1848].

-ⲥ in S**ⲁⲩⲉⲓⲥ**, B**ⲁⲩⲓⲥ** is the old dependent pers. pronoun , *sw*, 'it': 'give it!' See **ⲁⲩ**, **ⲁⲩⲉⲓⲥ**, 'give, bring hither!' So also in **ⲁϥϫⲟⲟⲥ** and its Imperative **ⲁϫⲓⲥ** ('say it!') from **ϫⲱ**.

ⲥ-, prefix of 1st Present, 3rd person sing. fem. = L.E. for *s*(*t*), Erman, *Näg. Gr.* 2nd ed., §419 < M.E. , , *sy* (*Wb.* IV, 28, 5–7); (Er. 399, 2), *s*.

SETHE in *ZÄS* 49, 25 [1911]; cf. Till, *WZKM* 33, 126–7 [1926].

ⲥⲁ (Crum 313a), 'side, part' = (*Wb.* IV, 8, 14 f.), *sꜣ*, 'the back'; Dem. only in (Er. 404, 2), *m-sꜣ*, 'behind, after'. **ⲥⲁ** is unstressed form of **ⲥⲟⲓ**, 'back' (Spiegelberg, *Kopt. Handwb.*, 108).

ⲛⲥⲁ- (Crum 314a), 'behind, after' = (*Wb.* IV, 10, 4 f.), *m-sꜣ*, 'behind, after', lit. 'at the back of'; (Er. 404, 2), *m-sꜣ*, 'behind, after'.

HCHAMPOLLION, *Gr. ég.* 494 ff. [1836]; DBRUGSCH, *Gr. dém.* 176–7, §342 [1855].

ⲙⲛⲛⲥⲁ- (Crum 314b), 'after' of time = (Er. 405, middle), *bn m-sꜣ*, 'after' of time.

HESS, *Stne*, 159 [1888] with doubts; cf. GRIFFITH-THOMPSON, III, 70, no. 698 [1909].

ⲥⲁ (Crum 316a), 'man' = (*Wb.* III, 404, 6 f.), *s*, 'man'; (Er. 400, 1), *s*, 'person'.

ⲥⲁ ⲛ-, 'man of . . . ' = , *s n-*, 'man of . . . '.

HDE ROUGÉ, *Chrest. ég.* II, 5 and 77–8 [1868]; DREVILLOUT, *Rev. ég.* 2, pl. 40 [1881].

See also **ⲥⲁ ⲛⲛⲉϩ** under **ⲛⲉϩ**, and B**ⲥⲁ ⲛⲱⲓⲕ** under **ⲟⲉⲓⲕ**.

ⲥⲉ-, prefix of 1st Present 3rd person plural L.E. (*Wb.* IV, 325, 1), *st*, 'they'; (Er. 471), *st*, 'they'.

HERMAN, *Näg. Gr.* 40, §47 [1880]; DGRIFFITH-THOMPSON, III, 71, no. 703a [1909].

-ⲥⲉ, dependent pronoun of 3rd person plur. as object of a verb, 'them', same origin.

LAUTH, *Manetho*, 225 [1865].

ⲥⲉ (Crum 316a), 'yea' = (Er. 470, 7), *st*, lit. 'they (are so)'.

GRIFFITH-THOMPSON, I, 122 [1904].

ⲥⲉ-, ⲥⲓ- (Crum 316b), 'seat, place' = (*Wb.* IV, 1, bottom), *st*, 'seat'; (Er. 400, 2), *s(t)*, 'place, seat'.

[HD]HESS, *Rosette*, 41 [1902].

In **ⲥⲉⲕⲱⲧ** (see under **ⲕⲱⲧ**), **ⲥⲉⲙⲓⲥⲓ** (see **ⲙⲓⲥⲉ**), **ⲥⲉⲥⲃⲟϩ** (see **ⲥⲃⲱϩ**), **ⲥⲓⲟⲟⲩⲛ** (see this latter).

ⲥⲉⲓ (Crum 316b), 'be filled, satisfied, enjoy' = (*Wb.* IV, 14, bottom), *sꜣy*, 'become sated'; (Er. 407, 5), *sy*, 'become sated'.

[H]BRUGSCH, *Wb.* 1156 [1868]; [D]BRUGSCH, *ZÄS* 16, 48 and Pl. III, l. 21 [1878].

-ⲥⲓ-, 'son' = (*Wb.* III, 408, 1 ff.), *sꜣ*, 'son'; (Er. 402, 5), *sꜣ*, 'son'.

[H]CHAMPOLLION, *Précis*, 1st ed., 68 and Pl. V, no. 2 [1824]; Hess, *Stne*, 173 [1888].

E.g. in **ⲱⲣ-ⲥⲓ-ⲏⲥⲉ**, a proper name of person = , *Ḥr-sꜣ-ꜣst*, 'Horus, son of Isis'; Champollion, *Précis*, 128 [1824].

ⲥⲟⲓ (Crum 317b), 'back' of man or beast = (*Wb.* IV, 8, 14–16), *sꜣ*, 'back'; in (Er. 404, 2), *m-sꜣ*, 'behind', lit. 'at the back of'.

[H]BRUGSCH, *ZÄS* 2, 17 [1864] after Lauth; [D]HESS, *Gnost. Pap.* 12 [1892].

For unstressed form, see **ⲥⲁ**, 'side, part'.

ⲥⲟⲓ (Crum 317b), 'beam' of wood = (*Wb.* III, 419, 14–17), *sꜣw* > , *sꜣy*, 'beam' of wood; (Er. 407, 4), *sy*, 'beam' of wood.

[H]BRUGSCH, *Wb.* 1156 [1868]; [D]REVILLOUT, *Chrest. dém.* 500 (correcting p. 376, col. 2) [1880].

ⲟⲩⲉϩⲥⲟⲓ (Crum 318a), nn. f., 'addition of beams, roof' = , *wꜣḥ sy*, 'lay, place a beam', as verb: P. BM 10524, 2, 3; as noun, 'roof', P. Turin Suppl. 6089, 20 (Botti, *L'Archivio demotico da Deir el-Medinah*, no. 17, Pl. XXII, 20); cf. Mustafa el-Amir in *BIFAO* 68, 113.

H. THOMPSON's Demotic dictionary.

ⲥⲱ (not in Crum; gloss in Dem. Mag. Pap. 2/8), 'amulet' = or (*Wb.* III, 414, 9 f.), *s3*, 'protection, amulet'; or (Er. 403, 1), *s3(w)*, 'protection, amulet'.

GRIFFITH-THOMPSON, I, 27 [1904].

ⲥⲱ (Crum 318a), 'soaked reed, mat of reeds' = ? (*Wb.* IV, 58, 7 f.), *swt*, kind of reed.

SPIEGELBERG, *ZÄS* 64, 93–4 [1929].

ⲥⲱ (Crum 318a), 'drink' = (*Wb.* III, 428, 5 f.), *swr* (*zwr*) > *swi*, 'drink'; (Er. 415, 4), *swr*, 'drink'.

HCHAMPOLLION, *Gr. ég.* 376 [1836]; DBRUGSCH, *Gr. dém.* 33, §66; 129, §265 [1855].

ⲥⲃ (Crum 318b) in A**ⲥⲃ-ⲛ-ⲥⲉⲧⲉ**, 'burnt offerings' = , (*Wb.* III, 430, 19), 'burnt offerings', lit. 'gone in flame', from (*Wb.* III, 429, 10 f.), *sby* (*zby*), 'go, disappear, perish' and , (*Wb.* IV, 376, 12 f.), *sdt*, 'fire, flame'.

C. SCHMIDT, *Der erste Clemensbrief in altkopt. Übersetzung*, 11 [1908].

See Schäfer, *Klio* 6, 2, 291 n. 4.

See also **ϣⲟⲩⲥⲟⲟⲩϣⲉ**.

O**ⲥⲏⲃ** (*JEA* 28, 27), 'enemy' = (*Wb.* IV, 87, 14 f.), *sbi*, 'rebel'; (Er. 420, 3), *sb3*, 'enemy'.

GARDINER and GUNN in Crum, *JEA* 28, 27 [1942].

ⲥⲓⲃ (Crum 318b), 'tick', insect = (*Wb.* III, 440, 17–18), *sp*, kind of worm causing irritation; cf. also (*Wb.* III, 432, 15), *sbt*, 'vermin'; = (Er. 419, 4), *sb*, 'vermin'.

HGRIFFITH-THOMPSON, I, 105, note on 15, 3 [1904] (*sp*); BRUGSCH, *Wb.*, Suppl. 1027 [1882] (*sbt*); DGRIFFITH-THOMPSON, III, 72, no. 718 [1909].

ⲥⲁⲃⲉ (Crum 319a), 'wise person', cf. (*Wb.* IV, 85, 1–5), *sb3w*, 'teacher'.

ERMAN-GRAPOW, *Wörterbuch der äg. Sprache* IV, 85, 1–4 [1930]; cf. Lepsius, *Chronologie*, 49 n. 1 [1848].

ⲥⲉⲃ (Crum 319b), 'knowing, cunning person', cf. the preceding.

ⲥⲃⲟⲩⲓ (Crum 319b), 'disciple, apprentice', cf. 𝄑 ⋆ 𝄑 (*Wb.* IV, 84, 16–18), *sbȝ*, 'ward, apprentice'.

ERMAN-GRAPOW, *Wörterbuch der äg. Sprache* IV, 84, 16–18 [1930].

ⲥⲃⲱ (Crum 319b), 'doctrine, teaching' = 𝄑 𝄑⋆ 𝄑𝄑 ⌣ (*Wb.* IV, 85, 10 f.), *sbȝyt*, 'teaching, punishment'; ⲇⲍⲇ⳥ (Er. 421, 1), *sbȝt*, 'teaching'.

HCHABAS, *Oeuv. div.* II (= *Bibl. ég.* x), 80 [1860]; cf. Goodwin, *Sur les papyrus hiératiques*, 18 [1860], cf. Lepsius, *Chronologie*, 49 n. 1 [1848]; DREVILLOUT, *Poème*, pp. 20, 52 [1885].

ⲥⲏⲃⲉ (Crum 320b), 'reed' = 𝄑 𝄑 ⌐ 𝄖 (*Wb.* IV, 82, 3–5), *sbt*, 'reed'; ⳥ⲙⲇ⳥ (Er. 421, 6), *sbyt*, 'reed, flute'.

HROSELLINI, *Mon. stor.* III, 28–9 [1836]; CHAMPOLLION, *Gr. ég.* 61, 75 [1836]; cf. Pleyte, *Et. ég.* II, 146 [1866]; DSPIEGELBERG, *Mythus*, 245, no. 661 [1917].

ⲥⲱⲃⲉ (Crum 320b), 'laugh' = — 𝄑 ⇌ ⌀ (*Wb.* III, 434, 6–10), *sbṯ* (*zbṯ*), 'laugh'; ⳥ⲙⲇ⳥ (Er. 421, 5), *sby*, 'laugh'.

HDBRUGSCH, *Wb.* 1188 [1868].

ⲥⲱⲃⲉ (Crum 321b), 'edge, fringe' of garment, see ⲥⲱⲡⲉ.

ⲥⲃⲉ (Crum 321b) 'door' = 𝄑 𝄑⋆ 𝄖 𝄗 (*Wb.* IV, 83, 9 f.), *sbȝ*, 'gate, door'; ⳥⳥ (Er. 419, 3), *sb(ȝ)*, 'door'.

HCHAMPOLLION, *Gr. ég.* 80 [1836]; DBRUGSCH, *Pamonth*, 3, 9 [1850].

ⲥⲃⲃⲉ (Crum 321b), 'circumcise' = 𝄑 𝄑 ⌢ (*Wb.* IV, 81, 15), *sby*, 'circumcise'.

CAPART, *Une rue de tombeaux*, I, 51 [1907].

ⲥⲃⲟⲕ (Crum 322a), 'become small' = ⌐ⳤ⳥ (Er. 422, 7), *sbk*, 'small, become small'.

BRUGSCH, *Scriptura Aeg. dem.* 57 [1848] (though misinterpreting the determinative).

ⲥⲃⲗⲧⲉ, ⲥⲗⲃⲧⲉ (Crum 322b), intr. 'roll over, about' = ?— 𝄑 ∿ (*Wb.* III, 433, 7 ff.) *sbn*, Late 𝄑 𝄗, *snb*, 'slip, fall'; Imperative ⲥⲃⲗ + ⲧⲉ, 'thou'. See also -ⲧⲉ.

SPIEGELBERG, *Kopt. Etymologien*, 35–6 [1920].

[B]**ⲥⲉⲃⲉⲛ** (Crum 322b), 'bandage, selvage' = (*Wb.* IV, 89, 12–13), *sbn*, 'bandage'; (Er. 421, 8), *sbn*, 'bandage', and ? (Er. 438, 7), *snb*, 'bandage'.

[H]MASPERO, *Mémoire sur quelques papyrus du Louvre*, 21 n. 3 [1875]; [D]BRUGSCH, *Wb.* 1189 [1868].

ⲥⲓⲃⲧ (Crum 322b), 'hill' = (Er. 423, 3), *sbt*, 'hill'.

HESS, *Stne*, 175 [1888].

ⲥⲟⲃⲧ (Crum 323a), 'wall, fence' = (*Wb.* IV, 95, 10 ff.), *sbty*, 'wall, fortification'; (Er. 423, 4), *sbt*, 'wall'.

[H]CHAMPOLLION, *Gr. ég.* 76, 198 [1836]; [D]BRUGSCH, *Scriptura Aegypt. dem.* 16, §11 [1848].

ⲥⲟⲃⲧⲉ (Crum 323a), 'become ready, prepare' = (*Wb.* IV, 112, 10 ff.), *spdd*, 'make ready, prepare'; (Er. 424, 1), *sbt*, 'equip'.

[H]DE ROUGÉ, *Oeuv. div.* III (= *Bibl. ég.* XXIII), 168 [1856]; [D]BRUGSCH, *Gr. dém.* 37, §78 [1855].

ⲥⲃϣⲉ (Crum 324a), 'shield' = (*Wb.* IV, 92, 1), *sbẖt*, 'gate, palace' and (*Wb.* IV, 92, 10), *sbẖt*, a breast amulet, from (*Wb.* IV, 91, 10 f.), *sbẖ*, 'enclose, protect (as shield)'; (Er. 422, 6), *sbšy*, 'shield'.

[H]GRAPOW in *OLZ* 26, col. 560 [1923]; [D]KRALL, *Mitt. aus der Sammlung Erzh. Rainer*, VI, 56 and 72, no. 249 [1897].

ⲥⲱⲃϩ (Crum 324b), 'leprosy' = (not in *Wb.*), *sbḥ*, 'leprosy'; (Er. 422, 3), *sbḥ*, 'leprosy'.

[H]ČERNÝ in *Festschrift Grapow*, 32–3 [1955]; [D]GRIFFITH, *PSBA* 31, 104 n. 19 [1909].

ⲥⲃⲱϩ (not in Crum; ex. Mani Hom. 36, 28), 'implore' = (*Wb.* IV, 90, 14), *sbḥ*, 'cry aloud'; (Er. 422, 4), *sbḥ*, 'implore'.

[H]POLOTSKY, *Manich. Homilien*, p. xix, and Index, p. 11* [1934].

ⲥⲉⲥⲃⲟϩ (Crum 358b), 'place of atonement' = *, *st-sbḥ*, 'place of atonement'; (Er. 422, 4), *st-sbḥ*, 'place of atonement'.

GRIFFITH–THOMPSON, III, 71, no. 702 [1909]; cf. Spiegelberg, *Rec. trav.* 28, 208 [1906].

ⲥⲟⲕ (Crum 325a), 'sack, sackcloth, bag' = *, *sꜣḳ* (cf. the determinative of , (*Wb.* IV, 25, 6 f.), *sꜣḳ*, 'join together, collect'), (*Urk.* IV, 1332, 3), *s(ꜣ)ḳ*, 'sack', and the Gr.-R. (*Wb.* IV, 26, 14–16), *sꜣḳ*, 'mat'; (Er. 411, 9), *sʿḳ*, 'sack?, mat?'.

[H]ERMAN–GRAPOW, *Wörterbuch der äg. Sprache* IV, 25, 6 [1930]; [D]VOLTEN, *Dem. Traumdeutung*, 114 [1942].

NB. Hebrew שַׂק is a loan-word from Egyptian and so too is Greek σάκκος, σάκος, this perhaps through a Semitic intermediary.

ⲥⲱⲕ (Crum 325a), 'flow (as water), draw, gather' = (*Wb.* IV, 25, 7 f.), *sꜣḳ*, 'draw together, gather'; (Er. 466, 2), *sḳ*, 'gather'.

[H]BRUGSCH, *Wb.*, Suppl. 1030–1 [1882]; [D]BRUGSCH, *Gr. dém.* 36, §76 [1855].

ⲥⲉⲕ ϩⲣⲟⲟⲩ (Crum 326a), 'snort', cf. (Er. 466, 2), *sḳ n ḫrw*, 'snort'.

ⲥⲁϫⲟ (Crum 384a, s.v. **ⲥϩⲁⲓ**, adding [F]**ⲡⲗⲉⲙⲥⲁϫⲏ** CMSS, 31, cf. προμ σαχα *PGM* II, 111, 'esteemed man') = ***ⲥⲁⲕ-ϩⲟ**, 'esteemed, dignified person', lit. 'gatherer of face' = (Er. 466, 2), *sḳ-ḥr*, 'esteemed' or sim. See also **ⲥⲕⲉⲛϩⲟ**.

ⲥϫⲁⲧ (Crum 387a), 'marriage gift' (from bridegroom) = ***ⲥⲕ-ϩⲁⲧ**, lit. 'gathering, saving money'. The young man had to collect or save to get married.—**ⲣⲙⲛⲥϫⲁⲧ**, 'collector of money'.

PLUMLEY, *An Introductory Coptic Grammar*, 3, §3 [1948].

ⲥⲱⲕ ϩⲏⲧ (Crum 716a) 'draw heart, persuade' = (*H.O.* XXXVIII, 1, vo. 1–2), *sꜣḳ ḥꜣty*, 'persuade', cf. too the earlier (*Wb.* IV, 26, 1–2), *sꜣḳ-ib*, 'self-possessed'.

ⲥⲓⲕⲉ (Crum 328a), 'grind, pound' = (*Wb.* IV, 314, 14), *sk*, 'grind'; (Er. 466, 6), *sk*, 'grind'.

[H]STERN, *Pap. Ebers*, II, Glossary, 38 [1875]; [D]GRIFFITH–THOMPSON, I, 36 [1904].

ⲥⲕ- (not in Crum), in place-names, see **ϣϭⲉ-**.

ⲥⲕⲁⲓ (Crum 328b), 'to plough' = (*Wb.* IV, 315, bottom), *skꜣ*, 'to cultivate (plough and sow)'; (Er. 467, 4), *skꜣ*, 'to plough'.

ᴴCHAMPOLLION, *Précis*, 2nd ed., 125–6 [1828]; ᴰREVILLOUT, *Nouv. chrest. dém.* 154 [1878].

ⲥⲕⲓⲙ (Crum 328b), 'discoloured, grey hair' = (*Wb.* IV, 318, 1) *skm*, 'greying of hair'.

STERN, *Pap. Ebers*, II, 33 (s.v. *km*) [1875].

ᴮ**ⲥⲕⲉⲛ, ⲥⲕⲉⲛⲧ** (Crum 329a), 'side of' in compound prepositions **ⲉⲥⲕⲉⲛ** = (*Wb.* V, 194, 11 ff.), *r-gs* + **ⲛ** 'of'; **ϩⲓⲥⲕⲉⲛ** = (*Wb.* V, 193, 6. 7), *ḥr-gs* + **ⲛ**, 'of', 'at the side of' = 'beside'.

PIEHL, *PSBA* 15, 478–9 [1893].

ⲥⲕⲉⲛϩⲟ is of different origin, see next entry.

ⲥⲕⲉⲛϩⲟ (Crum 329a, under **ⲥⲕⲉⲛ**), 'good appearance' in **ϭⲓ ⲥⲕⲉⲛϩⲟ**, 'to make (lit. "to take") a fair show' (translating εὐπροσωπεῖν) = *sḳ-n-ḥr* (Er. 466, 2), *sḳ-ḥr*, 'honour, esteem'. See also **ⲥⲁϫⲟ** under **ⲥⲱⲕ**, 'flow, draw, gather'.

SPIEGELBERG, *Rec. trav.* 34, 157–8 [1912].

ⲥⲕⲁⲛ (Crum 329a), nn., in **ⲟⲉⲓⲕ ⲛⲥⲕⲁⲛ**, 'stale bread', lit. 'bread of cooling-room', (*Wb.* V, 305, 12), *sḳbbwy* > , *sḳbw*, 'cooling-room' for food and beverages.

ⲥⲕⲟⲣⲕⲣ (Crum 329a), 'roll' (trans. and intr.) = (O. IFAO 2208, 3), *sḳrḳr*, 'roll' (in bed, of a feverish patient), cf. late , *sgrgr* (not in *Wb.*), 'trembling twigs' and (*Wb.* V, 66, 5), *ḳrḳr*, 'roll' (of the waters of inundation).

POSENER's comm. (for *sḳrḳr*) [1963]; cf. SETHE, *Amun und die acht Urgötter*, 97 n. 6 [1929] (for *sgrgr*); ERMAN-GRAPOW, *Wörterbuch der äg. Sprache* V, 66, 5 [1931] (for *ḳrḳr*).

ⲥⲟⲕⲥⲉⲕ (Crum 330a), 'pull, gather' = (not in Er.; ex. Ankhsh. 17, 24), *sksk*, 'gather, scavenge', reduplication of **ⲥⲱⲕ**, 'flow, draw, gather'.

GLANVILLE's index.

ᴮ**ⲥⲉⲕⲉϩ** (Crum 330a), 'clear out' a house = ? (*Wb.* IV, 304, 1), *sḳ3ḥ*, 'clear out'; cf. (*Wb.* IV, 304, 2), *sḳ3ḥ*, 'to plaster, whitewash'.

ⲥⲟⲗ (Crum 330a), 'wick' = (Er. 444, 3), *sl*, or (Er. 491, 7), *šʿl*, 'wick', from Semitic, cf. Arabic شَعَل, 'kindle'.

BRUGSCH, *Gr. dém.* 39, §84 [1855]; ˢSTRICKER in *Acta Orientalia* 15, 5 [1937].

ⲥⲱⲗ (Crum 330a), 'dissipate, pervert', see **ⲥⲱⲣ**, 'scatter'.

ⲥⲗⲏ (Crum 330a), 'coffin' = (not in Er.), *slꜣt*, 'coffin'.

SPIEGELBERG, *ZÄS* 56, 8 [1920].

ⲥⲁⲗⲟ (Crum 330b), 'basket', from Semitic, cf. Aram. סַלָּא, Arabic سَلَّة, Syr. ܣܰܠܳܐ.

CRUM, *A Coptic Dict.* 330b [1932].

ⲥⲱⲗⲡ (Crum 330b), 'break, cut off', from Semitic, cf. Arabic سَلَبَ.

DÉVAUD in Crum, *A Coptic Dict.* 331a [1932].

ⲥⲉⲗⲉⲡⲓⲛ (Crum 331b), 'spleen', under influence of **ⲥⲉⲗⲉⲡⲓⲛ**, 'little finger, toe', from ***ⲥⲡⲗⲏⲗⲓⲛ**, the latter from Gk. σπληνίον, diminutive of σπλήν, 'spleen'. See also **ⲥⲡⲗⲏⲗⲓⲛ**, 'poultice'.

ⲥⲉⲗⲉⲡⲓⲛ (Crum 331b), 'little finger, toe' = (Er. 406, 3), *sꜣlʿpyn*, 'little finger'.

LEEMANS, *Aeg. Pap. in demot. Schrift*, 48 [1839].

ˢ(**ⲥⲟⲗⲥⲗ**), ᴮ**ⲥⲟⲗⲥⲉⲗ** (Crum 331b), 'adorn' = (Er. 444, 6), *slsl*, 'adorn, adornment'. Reduplication of (Er. 444, 2), *sl*, 'arrange, distribute' (***ⲥⲱⲗ**).

SPIEGELBERG, *Petubastis*, 54*, no. 372 [1910].

ⲥⲟⲗⲥⲗ (Crum 332a), 'comfort, encourage' = (*Wb.* IV, 201, 13), *srsr*, 'comfort'; from Semitic?, cf. سَلَّى, 'to comfort', سَلْوَى, subst. 'comfort'.

ᴴSCHÄFER, *Die äthiopische Königsinschrift*, 102 [1901]; ˢDÉVAUD's slip.

ⲥⲁⲗⲁϣⲉⲓⲉ (Crum 333a). The parallel descriptions of Antichrist demand a word for 'tall (man)', therefore **ⲥ.** is probably a corruption of **ϭⲁⲗⲁϣⲓⲣⲉ**, 'giant' and existence of **ⲥⲁ**, 'man', and **ⲗⲁϣⲓⲏ** (Crum 135a, s.v. **ⲗⲁ-**) might have helped the corruption. The Akhm. version substitutes for **ϭⲁⲗⲁϣⲓⲣⲉ** the more familiar **ϩⲣϣⲓⲣⲉ**.

ⲥⲱⲗϭ (Crum 333b), 'smear, wipe, obliterate' = (Er. 444, 7), *slk*, 'anoint'.

GRIFFITH-THOMPSON, III, 76, no. 769 [1909].

ⲥⲗⲟϭⲗϭ (Crum 333b), 'make smooth' = (Er. 443, 9), *srkrk*, 'whet, sharpen'.

BRUGSCH, *Gr. dém.* 29, §58 [1855].

ⲥⲓⲙ (Crum 334a), 'grass, fodder, herbs' = (*Wb.* IV, 119, 11 f.), *smw*, 'herbs'; (Er. 430, 2), *sm*, 'herbs'.

^{H}CHAMPOLLION, *Gr.* 89 [1836]; ^{D}BRUGSCH, *Scriptura Aeg. dem.* 18, §17 [1848].

ⲛⲉϩ ⲛⲥⲓⲙ (Crum 334a), 'radish oil' = (Er. 430, 2), *nḥ n sym*, lit. 'oil of herbs'.

MASPERO, *Rec. trav.* I, 39, note 63 [1870].

ⲥⲁⲙ-, see under **ⲥⲁⲙⲁϩⲏⲣ**.

ⲥⲓⲙ-ⲉⲛϩ < ?**ⲥⲓⲙ** + **ⲛⲉϩ** ('oil'); **ⲥⲓⲙ-ⲣⲱⲧ**, see **-ⲣⲱⲧ**, **-ⲣⲟⲧ**, 'hard, strong'.

ⲥⲱⲙ (Crum 334b), 'subdue, press, pound' = (*Wb.* III, 446, 3 ff.), *smꜣ*, 'unite'.

CHASSINAT, *Pap. méd.* 111 [1921].

ⲥⲙⲏ (Crum 334b), 'voice, sound' = L.E. (*Wb.* IV, 121, 2, from Černý, *LRL* 67, 13) or (Černý–Gardiner, *H.O.*, Pl. LXXIX, 6), fem., 'reputation'; cf. **ⲣⲉⲙⲥⲙⲏ** (Crum 335a), 'famed person', lit. 'man of fame', and **ⲉⲣ ⲥⲙⲏ**, 'be famed', lit. 'make fame'.

ⲥⲙⲟⲩ (Crum 335a), 'bless' = (*Wb.* IV, 125, 17–18), *smꜣʿ*, 'pray to god'; (Er. 430, 3), *sm*, 'bless, greet'.

^{H}ABEL, *Kopt. Untersuchungen*, 420 [1876]; ^{D}BRUGSCH, *Gr. dém.* 42, §92 [1855]; cf. Spiegelberg, *ZÄS* 42, 59, xxiv [1905].

Qual. ^{B}**ⲥⲙⲁⲣⲱⲟⲩⲧ** (Crum 335b) is not for ***ⲥⲙⲁϧⲣⲱⲟⲩⲧ** (from *Wb.* IV, 125, 10 f.), *smꜣʿ-ḫrw*, 'to make (somebody's) voice just' = 'to let (him) win in the court' as thought by Brugsch, *Wb.* 578 [1868], but a secondary Qual. from ***ⲥⲙⲁⲣⲟ** which goes back to **ⲥⲙⲟⲩ** + **ⲉⲣⲟ⸗** like **ⲛⲁⲣⲟ** to **ⲛⲁⲩ** + **ⲉⲣⲟ⸗**.

ⲥⲙⲙⲉ (Crum 336b), 'to appeal' = (*Wb.* IV, 127, 7 f.), *smỉ*, 'to report'; (Er. 432, 2), *smy*, 'to sue in court'.

[H]DEVÉRIA, *Journal as.* 6e série, 8, 185 [1866] = *Pap. judiciaire de Turin*, 113 [1868]; [D]REVILLOUT, *Setna*, 66, n. 1 [1877–80].

For ⲁⲛⲥⲙⲙⲉ, 'ordinance', see this latter.

ⲥⲙⲓⲛⲉ (Crum 337a), 'establish, construct, set right' = (*Wb.* IV, 131, bottom), *smn*, 'to make endure, fix', etc.; (Er. 433, 7), *smn*, 'to fix'.

[H]CHAMPOLLION, *Gr.* 108 [1836]; *Dict.*, 386–7 [1841]; [D]DE ROUGÉ, *Oeuv. div.* I (= *Bibl. ég.* XXI), 258 and Pl. 3 (95), no. 69 [1848]; BRUGSCH, *Scriptura Aeg. dem.* 55, §42, III [1848].

ⲥⲙⲟⲩⲛⲉ (Crum 339a), 'Nile goose (*Chenalopex aegyptiaca*) = (*Wb.* IV, 136, 2–4), *smn*, kind of goose; (Er. 433, 6), *smn*, kind of goose.

[H]LEPSIUS, *Lettre à Rosellini*, 52 and Pl. B, no. 55 f [1837]; [D]GRIFFITH–THOMPSON, III, 74, no. 748 [1909].

Arabic سُمَانَى does not go back to the Coptic but is a derivative from √שמן, 'is fat' (de Lagarde, *Übersicht*, 191).

[B]**ⲥⲁⲙⲉⲛϩⲏ** (Crum 177b, adding 640a s.v. ϩⲉ), 'after' = ⲥⲁ-ⲙⲉⲛ-ϩⲏ, 'behind together with back' (ϩⲏ < , *Wb.* III, 10, 1 ff.). Prep. *ḥr* fell out before ⲥⲁ; ⲙⲉⲛ < ⲛⲉⲙ.

STERN, *Kopt. Gr.* 375, §562 [1880].

ⲥⲓⲙⲥⲓⲙ (Crum 340b), 'sesame', a loanword from South Semitic (cf. Arabic, سِمْسِم, Akkadian *šamaššammu*), while Mycenaean Greek (Linear B) *sa-sa-ma* and Greek σήσαμον come from West Semitic, cf. *ššmn* in Ugaritic. From West Semitic probably also [B]ⲥⲓⲥⲁⲙⲏⲛ of K197 and ⲥⲁⲥⲓⲙⲏⲛ of P44, 66. [Information on Semitic and Mycenaean forms is due to K. A. Kitchen.] The native Egn. word for sesame is ⲟⲕⲉ.

ⲥⲁⲙⲓⲧ (Crum 340b), 'fine flour', from Greek σεμίδαλις (fem.), 'the finest wheaten flour'.

PEYRON, *Lex.* 203 [1835].

Arabic سميذ, 'very white flour' (Bellot) goes back to Coptic word.

ⲥⲙⲟⲧ (Crum 340b), 'form, character, likeness, pattern' = (Er. 434, 4), *smt*, 'kind, likeness'.

BRUGSCH, *Gr. dém.* 38, §79 [1855].

ⲥⲙⲁⲩ (Crum 342a), 'temples (tempora), eyelids' = Dual of (*Wb.* IV, 122, 1–5), *smꜣ*, part of head covered with hair; ? (not in Er.; P. Berlin 6750, 3, 7), *smwỉ(t)*, part of body.

[H]PLEYTE, *Études ég.* I, 64 [1866]; [D]H. THOMPSON's Demotic dictionary.

ⲥⲙⲁϩ (Crum 342a), 'bunch' of fruit, flowers, cf. (*Wb.* IV, 140, 8. 9), *smḥ*, 'twig', 'bunch' of grapes; (not in Er.; exx. Spiegelberg, *Kopt. Handwb.* 118, and *JEA* 26, 96, A. 36), *smḥ*, 'bunch (of grapes)'.

[H]JUNKER in Spiegelberg, *Kopt. Handwb.* 118 [1921]; [D]SPIEGELBERG, l.c.

ⲥⲁⲙⲁϩⲏⲣ (Crum 342a), 'fennel' or 'spinach' = **ⲥⲁⲙ** (construct form of **ⲥⲓⲙ**, 'plant') + **ⲁϩⲏⲣ**, 'marsh' (see under **ⲁϩⲣ**). Greek transcriptions in place-names Σαμαχήρ, -ρε, Σαμαήρ (P. Lond. 4, 597) and probably σεμουερ = λυχνὶς ἀγρία of Dioscorides. σαμ- as constr. form of **ⲥⲓⲙ** also in σαμψοῦχος of Hesychius (= *sm-Sbk*, 'plant of [god] Sobek') and σαμψώς of Dioscorides (= *sm-Šw*, 'plant of [god] Show').

ⲥⲁⲉⲓⲛ (Crum 342b), 'physician' = (*Wb.* III, 427, 7 f.), *swnw*, 'physician'; (Er. 415, 3), *swnw*, 'physician'.

[H]STERN, *Pap. Ebers*, II, Glossary, 39 [1875]; [D]REVILLOUT, *Poème*, 173, n. 1 [1885], cf. GRIFFITH–THOMPSON, III, 72, no. 721 [1909].

ⲥⲟⲛ (Crum 342b), 'brother' = (*Wb.* IV, 150, 8 f.), *sn*, 'brother'; (Er. 435, 5), *sn*, 'brother'.

[H]CHAMPOLLION, *Précis*, 1st ed., 72; Tableau général, p. (31) and Pl. 14, no. 260 [1824]; [D]DE ROUGÉ, *Oeuv. div.* I (= *Bibl. ég.* XXI), 254–5 and Pl. 3, no. 57 [1848].

ⲥⲱⲛⲉ (Crum 343a), 'sister' = (*Wb.* IV, 151, 5 f.), *snt*, 'sister'; (Er. 436, 1), *snt*, 'sister'.

[H]CHAMPOLLION, *Gr.* 66, 104 [1836]; [D]BRUGSCH, *Gr. dém.* 76, §167 [1855].

ⲥⲱⲱⲛ (Crum 343a), 'meaning unknown' = Gk. ζῷον, 'living being, animal'. Also **ⲥⲱⲟⲛ** in M. 578, 110[2] where it is said of God **ⲡⲉⲛⲧⲁϥⲧⲁⲙⲓⲟ ⲥⲱⲟⲛ ⲛⲓⲙ**. For **ⲥ** replacing Gk. ζ, see Crum 65a.

Communicated by R. G. COQUIN, Cairo [1970].

ⲥⲏⲛⲉ, ⲥⲉⲛⲏ (Crum 343b), 'granary, bin' also 'hut' (κλισία) = (*Wb.* IV, 156, 7), *snyt*, 'cabin' or sim.; (Er. 437, 5), *snꜣ*, only in the title *ḥm-snꜣ*, 'box-maker' or sim.

[H]ERMAN-GRAPOW, *Wb.* IV, 156, 7 [1930]; [D]SPIEGELBERG, *Kopt. Handwb.* 118 [1921]; cf. SPIEGELBERG, *Die demot. Papyri der Musées royaux du Cinquantenaire*, 8 [1909].

ⲥⲓⲛⲉ (Crum 343b), 'ploughshare' = [GR] (*Wb.* III, 458, 3), *sn*, 'ploughshare'.

DÜMICHEN, *ZÄS* 4, 84 [1866].

ⲥⲓⲛⲉ (Crum 343b), 'pass by, through' = (*Wb.* III, 454, 14 f.), *sny*, 'pass by'; (Er. 437, 7), *sny*, 'pass by'.

[H]CHAMPOLLION, *Gr.* 383 [1836]; [D]BRUGSCH, *Gr. dém.* 39, §83 [1855].

ⲥⲟⲟⲛⲉ (Crum 344 b), 'robber', originally perhaps 'vagrant', a derivative of **ⲥⲓⲛⲉ**, 'pass by', see last entry.

ⲥⲱⲛⲕ (Crum 344b), 'suck' = (*Wb.* IV, 174, 7 f.), *snḳ*, 'suck'; (Er. 439, 3), *snḳi*, 'suck'.

[H]BAILLET, *ZÄS* 5, 68 n. 2 = *Oeuv. div.* I (= *Bibl. ég.* XV), 30 [1867]; [D]VOLTEN, *Dem. Traumdeutung*, 114 [1942].

ⲥⲛⲁⲉⲓⲛ (Crum 345a), 'skip, stroll, wander' = L.Eg. , *snny* < **snyny*, 'pass, move'; (Er. 438, 2), *snyn*, 'go to and fro'.

[H]GARDINER, *Rec. trav.* 36, 201 [1914] (= *Notes on the Story of Sinuhe*, 160 [1916]); cf. Gardiner, *Anc. Eg. Onomastica*, I, 28*–9* [1947]; [D]HESS, *Stne*, 175 [1888]; cf. *ZÄS* 1875, 140.

NB. *Wb.* III, 454, bottom, takes to be the L.Eg. spelling of , *sny*, 'pass by'.

ⲥⲛⲏⲓⲛⲓ (Crum 345a), 'irrigation machine' = (Er. 438, 4), *snꜣynt*, 'water, source'.

SPIEGELBERG, *Mythus*, 248, no. 681 [1917].

ⲥⲁⲛⲛⲉϩ (Crum 345a), 'grasshopper' = (*Wb.* III, 461, 6–8), *snḥm*, 'locust'. The Coptic form is due to 'Volksetymologie' (**ⲥⲁⲛⲛⲉϩ** = 'oil dealer').

CHABAS, *Oeuv. div.* II (= *Bibl. ég.* X), 94 [1860].

ⲥⲁⲛⲓⲥ (Crum 345a), 'doubt', is related to **ⲥⲛⲁⲩ**, 'two' (so is Lat. *dubium* to *duo*, Walde, *Lat. etym. Wörterbuch*, 3rd ed., 1938).

STERN, *Kopt. Gr.* 51, §99 [1880]; cf. Sethe in *ZÄS* 47, 13 [1916].

ⲥⲛⲥⲛ (Crum 345a), 'resound' = (*Wb.* IV, 171, 15–16), *snsn*, 'to praise, worship', completed reduplication of (*Wb.* IV, 171, 5–10), *snsy*, 'to praise'; (not in Er.; P. Berlin [Thoth] 2, 3), *snsn*, 'worship, revere'.

[D]H. THOMPSON's Demotic dictionary.

ⲥⲱⲛⲧ (Crum 345a), 'create' = (*Wb.* IV, 177, 10 f.), *snṯ*, 'found, create'; (Er. 439, 5), *snṱ*, 'found, create'.

[H]CHAMPOLLION, *Gr.* 386 [1836]; cf. BRUGSCH, *Wb.* 1255–6 [1868]; [D]BRUGSCH, *Gr. dém.* 37, §78; 38, §79 [1855].

ⲥⲛⲧⲉ (Crum 345b), 'foundation' = (*Wb.* IV, 179, 9–14), *snṯt*, 'foundation'; (Er. 439, bottom), *snṱ*, 'creation'.

[H]CHABAS, *Oeuv. div.* III (= *Bibl. ég.* XI), 39 [1865]; cf. Champollion, *Gr.* 386 [1836]; [D]SPIEGELBERG, *Rec. trav.* 33, 177 [1911].

ⲥⲱⲛⲧ (Crum 346a), 'custom = (not in *Wb.*; Canopus 27), *snṯ*, 'custom'; (Rosetta 11), (Canopus 53), (Er. 439, bottom), *snṱ*, 'habit, custom'.

[HD]BRUGSCH, *Wb.* 1256 [1868].

ⲥⲛⲁⲧ (Crum 346b), 'fear' = (*Wb.* IV, 182, 2 f.), *snḏ*, 'fear'; (Er. 440, 1), *snt*, 'fear'.

[H]DE ROUGÉ, *Oeuv. div.* III (= *Bibl. ég.* XXIII), 261–2 [1856]; [D]REVILLOUT, *Revue ég.* 4, 84 n. 3 [1885].

ⲥⲟⲛⲧⲉ (Crum 346b), 'resin' = (*Wb.* IV, 180, 18 f.), *snṯr*, 'incense'; (Er. 440, 2), *sntr*, 'incense'.

[H]HINCKS in *Transactions of Roy. Irish Ac.* 21, Part II, 157 and Pl. I, nos. 79–81 [1848, read in 1846], cf. Schwartze in Bunsen, *Geschichte*, I, 583 [1845]; [D]BRUGSCH, *Rhind*, 41 and Pl. 39, no. 223 [1865].

ⲥⲛⲁⲩ (Crum 346b), 'two' = (*Wb.* IV, 148, 6), *snw*, 'two', fem. **ⲥⲛⲧⲉ** = , *snty*.

BIRCH, *Rev. arch.* n.s. 12, 60 [1865]; cf. Sethe in *ZÄS* 47, 22–5 [1910].

ⲥⲛⲟⲟⲩⲥ(ⲉ) (Crum 347 a), in **ⲙⲛⲧⲥⲛⲟⲟⲩⲥ**, ‘twelve’, etc., cf. (*Wb.* IV, 149, 14. 15), *ḥr snwsy*, ‘again, anew’, therefore **ⲥⲛⲟⲟⲩⲥ** = either **ⲥⲛⲁⲩ** + **ⲥ** (ending of fem. nouns), or ‘its two’, i.e. of the new set from 10 to 20, etc.?

SETHE in *ZÄS* 47, 13–14 [1910].

ⲙⲡⲉⲥⲛⲁⲩ (Crum 347 a), ‘both together’, cf. (*Wb.* III, 405, 7), *m pꜣ s 2*, ‘both’, lit. ‘as the two men’; , *n pꜣ s 2*, ‘both’.

HD SPIEGELBERG in *Rec. trav.* 34, 157 [1912].

ⲥⲁⲁⲛϣ (Crum 347 b), ‘make live’ = (*Wb.* IV, 46, 4 f.), *sꜥnḫ*, ‘make live’; (Er. 410, 10), *sꜥnḫ*, ‘feed’.

H BRUGSCH, *Rosettana*, 32 [1851]; cf. Brugsch, *Wb.* 198 [1867]; D HESS, *Gnost. Pap.* 12 [1892].

ⲥⲛⲟϥ (Crum 348 a), ‘blood’ = (*Wb.* III, 459, 2–14), *snf*, ‘blood’; (Er. 438, 9), *snf*, ‘blood’.

H CHAMPOLLION, *Gr.* 99 [1836]; D BRUGSCH, *Scriptura Aegypt. dem.* 17, §14 [1848].

ⲥⲛⲟⲩϥ (Crum 348 b), ‘last year’ = (*Wb.* IV, 162, 12. 13), (Drioton, *Médamoud 1925*, 127), *snf*, ‘last year’; (not in Er.; Harpist 82), *snfỉ*, ‘last year’.

H BRUGSCH, *Wb.* 1209 [1868]; D BRUGSCH, *ZÄS* 26, 38–9 [1888].

ⲥⲱⲛϩ (Crum 348 b), ‘to bind, fetter’ = (*Wb.* IV, 168, 12–24), *snḥ*, ‘bind, fetter’; (Er. 439, 1), *snḥ*, ‘to bind, fetter’.

H CHAMPOLLION, *Gr.* 365, 380, 381 [1836]; D BRUGSCH, *Gr. dém.* 36, §76 [1855].

ⲥⲛⲁⲩϩ (Crum 349 a), ‘bond, fetter’ = (Er. 439, 1), *snḥw*, always in Plural, ‘bonds, fetters’.

SPIEGELBERG, *Mythus*, 248, no. 683 [1917].

B**ⲥⲓⲛⲁϩⲃⲓ** (Crum 349 a), ingredient in boiling cauldron, and S**ⲥⲓⲛⲁⲡⲉ** and varr., prob. = Gk. σίναπι, later form of νᾶπυ, ‘mustard’. Dem. (Er. 438, 6; Griffith–Thompson, I, 158 n.; III, 75, no. 755) is prob. to be read *sn(n)w*, as done by *Wb.* IV, 157, 6, for earlier exx. of the word, and not *snwpt*. In P. Louvre 3229, III, 27, a gloss . . .]ροχλου is written above this word, undoubtedly the Greek name of the plant. E. Lobel points out that there is ἀνδράχλη, -λος (also -νη, -νος) and that [ἄνδ]ροχλος may be still another form of the name. If so, *snnw* was purslane, *Portulaca oleracea* (see Pauly–Wissowa, I, s.v. Ἀνδράχλη) which was also called **ⲙⲉϩⲙⲟⲩϩⲉ**.

ⲥⲡ- (Crum 349a), 'year' in dating events, documents = (*Wb.* III, 26, 6 f.; 437, middle), *ḥꜣt-sp*, 'regnal year', lit. 'year of . . . occurrence'; (Er. 288, 2), *ḥꜣt-sp*, 'regnal year'.

[HD]BRUGSCH, *Matériaux pour servir à la reconstruction du calendrier égyptien*, 73 [1864]; cf. Sethe, *Untersuchungen*, III, 91 ff. [1905]; Gardiner, *JNES* 8, 165 ff. [1949].

ⲥⲟⲡ (Crum 349b), 'occasion, time (*vices*), turn' = (*Wb.* III, 435, 1 ff.), *sp* (*zp*), 'time, occurrence'; (Er. 425, 1), *sp*, 'time, occurrence'.

[H]CHAMPOLLION, *Gr.*, 506 ff. [1836]; [D]SAULCY, *Rosette*, 27 [1845].

ⲛⲥⲟⲡ (Crum 349b), 'at the time' = (*Wb.* III, 438, 8), *m sp*, 'together, at one time'.

ϩⲁϩ ⲛⲥⲟⲡ (Crum 350b, 742a, s.v. **ϩⲁϩ**), 'multitude of times, often' = (*Wb.* III, 153, 8), *ḥḥ n sp*, 'multitude of times, infinitely often'.

GOODWIN in a letter to Le Page Renouf (Dawson, *Charles Wycliffe Goodwin*, p. 72) [1862]; [D]BRUGSCH, *Gr. dém.*, 184, § 367 [1855].

ⲧⲙⲡⲥⲟⲡ (Crum 350b), 'at the moment in question' (thus, not as Crum, see Polotsky, *JEA* 25, 111) from ***ⲉⲧⲙⲡⲥⲟⲡ** = *, *nty m pꜣ sp*, lit. 'who was at the time'.

GARDINER in *JEA* 26, 158–9 [1940].

ⲥⲱⲡ (Peyron 210 from Kircher 257; Spiegelberg, *Kopt. Handwb.* 121), 'rebel', non-existent, see CRUM in *JEA* 8, 119 [1922].

ⲥⲱⲡ (Crum 351a), 'dip, soak' = (not in *Wb.*), *sp*, 'dip, soak'; (Er. 426, 1), *sp*, 'dye'.

[H]LORET, *Rec. trav.* 16, 136 n. 1 [1894]; [D]HESS, *Gnost. Pap.* p. 12 [1892].

ⲥⲱⲡ (Crum 351a), 'eyelid', see below under **ⲥⲱⲡⲉ**.

ⲥⲉⲉⲡⲉ (Crum 351a), 'remain over, be remainder' = (*Wb.* III, 439, 7–15), *spy* (*zpy*), 'remain over'; (Er. 426, 4), *spy*, 'remain over'.

[H]DE ROUGÉ, *Chrest.* II, 87–8 [1868]; BRUGSCH, *Wb.* 1197 [1868]; [D]SPIEGELBERG, *Mythus*, 246, no. 667 [1917].

ⲥⲉⲉⲡⲉ (Crum 351 b), 'remainder' = (*Wb.* III, 440, 8–15), *spyt*, 'remainder'; cf. (Er. 426, bottom), *sp* (masc.), 'remainder'.

ᴴCHABAS, Voyage, 143–5 [1866]; ᴰBRUGSCH, *Gr. dém.* 68, § 146; 115, § 241, 2° [1855].

ˢ**ⲥⲱⲡⲉ, ⲥⲱⲃⲉ,** ᴮ**ⲥⲱⲡⲓ** (Crum 321 b s.v. **ⲥⲱⲃⲉ**), f. 'edge, fringe' of garment = (*Wb.* IV, 99, 13 ff.), 'lip', also 'edge' (of wound, pot, well) (*Wb.* IV, 100, 9–13); (not in Er.; Petubastis ed. Krall, L 28), *spy*, and (O. Brussels E 354, 28), *sby*, 'edge' of garment; cf. Hebrew שָׂפָה, 'lip, edge', and English 'lip' of a cup. In Egn. **sōpet·* the final *t* is not feminine ending, see Lacau, *Syria* 31, 292–4; in Coptic f. because **ⲥⲱⲡⲉ** ended in **-ⲉ**, so perhaps already in L.E.; Lefebvre, *Tableau des parties du corps*, 19, § 20.

ᴰKLASENS in *Bibl. Or.* 13, 223 [1956]; ˢROSSI, *Etym. aeg.*, 213 [1808].

ⲥⲱⲡ(ⲉ) m. (Crum 351 a), 'eyelid', properly 'edge (of eyelid)', is the same word; (Apis Ritual XVII, b, 8), *spy*, 'eyelid'.

ᴰSPIEGELBERG, *ZÄS* 56, 31 [1920].

See also **ⲥⲡⲟⲧⲟⲩ**.

ᴬ**ⲥⲡⲉⲓ** (Crum 351 b), Plural, 'chosen, elect' < ***ⲥⲧⲡⲉⲓ**, ˢ***ⲥⲧⲡⲏ**, feminine collective from **ⲥⲱⲧⲡ**, 'choose' (see this latter).

LACAU in *Rec. trav.* 31, 80 [1909].

ⲥⲡⲗⲏⲗⲓⲛ (Crum 351 b), 'poultice' = (not in Er.), *splllyn*, 'compress, poultice', after assimilation of the first ν to the preceding λ from Greek σπληνίον, 'pad' or 'compress of linen' laid on a wound, lit. 'small spleen', diminutive of σπλήν, 'spleen'. The Demotic word is therefore determined by as part of a body. See also **ⲥⲉⲗⲉⲡⲓⲛ**, 'milt, spleen'.

GRIFFITH–THOMPSON, I, 182 note [1904]; III, 74, no. 745, and 104, no. 51 [1909].

ⲥⲡⲓⲣ (Crum 351 b), 'rib' = Plural (< **spīrew*) from (*Wb.* IV, 101, 10 ff.), *spr*, 'rib'; (Er. 427, 3), *spyr*, 'rib, side'.

ᴴCHAMPOLLION, *Gr.* 61, 73 [1836]; ᴰGRIFFITH–THOMPSON, III, 74, no. 744 [1909].

ⲥⲟⲡⲥ (Crum 352 a), 'pray, entreat, comfort', abbreviated from **ⲥⲟⲡⲥⲡ**, see next entry.

SETHE, *Verbum*, I, 206, § 338 [1899].

ⲥⲟⲡⲥⲡ (Crum 352b), ‘pray, entreat, comfort’, reduplication of (*Wb.* IV, 103, 13 ff.), *spr*, ‘approach someone with request or complaint’, after disappearance of the final *r* [**sōpĕ*]); = (Er. 428, 1), *spsp*, ‘pray, entreat, comfort’.

HDE ROUGÉ, *Oeuv. div.* VI (=*Bibl. ég.* XXVI), 82 n. 1 [1865]; DBRUGSCH, *Gr. dém.* 38, §80; 128, §264 [1855].

ⲥⲡⲟⲧⲟⲩ (Crum 353a), m. ‘lips’ (dual) = Dual (**spŏtwey*) of (*Wb.* IV, 99, 13 ff.), *spt*, ‘lip’; (Er. 428, 2), *spt*, ‘lips’. The Dual of Egn. word is m. (P. Smith 9, 12 *sptwy wbꜣ*, ‘lips opening).

HCHAMPOLLION, *Gr.* 61, 73, 92 [1836]; DBRUGSCH, *Gr. dém.* 38, §56 [1855].

See also **ⲥⲱⲡⲉ**, ‘edge’ of garment, and **ⲥⲱⲡ(ⲉ)**, ‘eyelid’.

ⲥⲓⲣ (Crum 353a), ‘first milk (colostrum), butter’ = (Er. 442, 3), *syr*, ‘butter’.

HESS, *Gnost. Pap.* 12 [1892].

ⲥⲓⲣ (Crum 353a), ‘leaven’, almost certainly the same word; a loan-word from Semitic √*sꜣr*, cf. Hebrew שְׂאֹר, Aram. סְיאוֹרָא, ‘leaven’.

SDÉVAUD, *Études*, 50–1 [1922].

Note. Somehow connected may be Old Slav. *syrъ*, ‘cheese’ (Dévaud’s slip). If the latter is identical with Greek τῡρός, ‘cheese’, and Avestan *tūri-*, ‘sour milk’, the original Indo-European form would have been **tūros*.

ⲥⲓⲣ (Crum 353b), ‘hair, line, stripe’ = (*Wb.* IV, 191, 3. 4), *sr*, ‘hair’ of an animal; cf. also the Graeco-Roman (*Wb.* IV, 191, 5), *srt*, ‘hair (of cattle)’, unless this latter belongs to **ⲥⲟⲣⲧ**, ‘wool’.

For **ⲥⲣ-**, ***ⲥⲉⲣ-**, see **ⲥⲣⲛϩ**, ‘eyebrow’, and **ⲥⲣⲉⲃⲣⲟⲩⲃⲉ**, ‘eyelashes?’ (not ‘handfuls’).

ⲥⲱⲣ (Crum 353b), ‘scatter, spread’, etc. = (*Wb.* IV, 189, 15 f.), *sr*, ‘foretell, announce, divulge’, consequently > (Graeco-Roman; *Wb.* IV, 191, 15), *sr*, ‘spread’ and sim.; (Er. 441, 4), *sr*, ‘announce’; (Er. 442, 1), *sr*, ‘give order, distribute’; (Er. 442, 2), *sr*, ‘let loose’. The development of the meaning therefore is: ‘foretell’→ ‘announce’→‘divulge (news, order)’→‘spread, scatter, distribute’, and

ⲥⲱⲗ (Crum 330a), 'dissipate, pervert' is probably identical with **ⲥⲱⲣ**.

[H]DE ROUGÉ, *Oeuv. div.* III (= *Bibl. ég.* XXIII), 161–2 [1856]; cf. Gardiner, *JEA* 21, 222 (*e*), and n. 1 [1935]; [D]BRUGSCH, *Rhind*, 42 and Pl. 39, no. 237 [1865].

ⲥⲁⲣ(ⲁ)-, see **ⲥⲁⲣⲁⲕⲱⲧⲉ**, **ⲥⲁⲣⲁⲧⲏⲩ** (under **ⲧⲏⲩ**) and **ⲥⲁⲣϭⲁⲧⲥⲉ**.

ⲥⲟⲩⲣⲉ (Crum 354a), 'thorn, spike, dart' = (*Wb.* IV, 190, 24 f.), *srt*, 'thorn, spike'; (Er. 442, 5), *swrt*, 'thorn, spike'.

[H]STERN, *Pap. Ebers*, II, Glossary, 41 [1875]; [D]BRUGSCH, *Gr. dém.* 26, §50 [1855].

[O]**ⲥⲣⲟ** (Crum 354b, adding *JEA* 28, 24), 'ram' = (*Wb.* III, 462, 7 f.), *sr*, 'ram'; (Er. 441, 3), *sr*, 'ram'.

[HD]GRIFFITH, *ZÄS* 46, 129 [1909].

ⲥⲣⲉⲃⲣⲟⲩⲃⲉ (Crum 354b), 'handfuls', حفن. Read prob. جفن, 'eyelid' for the latter and emend **ⲥ.** into **ⲥⲉⲣ-ⲃⲟⲩϩⲉ**, 'eyelashes'. Cf. **ⲥⲓⲣ**, 'hair', and **ⲥⲣⲏϩ**, 'eyebrow'.

ⲥⲁⲣⲁⲕⲱⲧⲉ (Crum 354b), 'wanderer, vagrant' < **ⲥⲁⲣ-ⲕⲱⲧⲉ**, from **ⲥⲱⲣ**, 'spread' and **ⲕⲱⲧⲉ**, 'go round', therefore lit. 'he who spreads going round', cf. *gyrovagus*, κυκλευτής.

BSCIAI in *ZÄS* 25, 70 [1887].

ⲥⲟⲣⲙ (Crum 355a), 'lees, dregs' of wine, oil, etc., cf. (*Wb.* III, 463, 7–11), *srmt*, a beverage. Perhaps ultimately related to Semitic √*šmr*, cf. Hebrew *שֶׁמֶר (always in Plural).

[H]ERMAN-GRAPOW, *Wb.* III, 463, 7 [1929]; [S]ROSSI, *Etym. aeg.* 204 [1808]; cf. Stricker in *Acta Orientalia* 15, 5 [1937].

ⲥⲱⲣⲙ (Crum 355a), 'go astray, err, get lost' = (Er. 443, 2), *srm*, 'go astray'.

GRIFFITH, *Dem. Graffiti from Dodekaschoinos*, 177, no. 307 [1937].

ⲥⲣⲏϩ (Crum 356a), 'eyebrow' = **ⲥⲓⲣ** + **ⲉⲛϩ**, 'hair line, stripe of eyebrow'. Cf. **ⲙϫⲛϩ**, lit. 'girdle of eyebrow', under **ⲉⲛϩ**.

[O]**ⲥⲁⲣⲡⲟⲧ**, [B]**ⲥⲁⲣⲫⲁⲧ** (Crum 356b), 'lotus' = L.E. (*Wb.* IV, 195, 2. 3), *srpt*, 'lotus leaf' and (*Wb.* IV, 195, 4), *srpt*, 'fan' (from its form) < M.E. (*Wb*, IV, 18, 5–7), *sȝpt*, 'lotus leaf'; (Er. 442, 8), *srpt*, 'lotus leaf', from Semitic, cf. סַרְפַּד, a plant, but שַׂרְפָּה (*sic*), 'fan', quoted by Burchardt, II, p. 80, is non-existent.

[H]GRIFFITH–THOMPSON, I, 22 [1904]; [D]KRALL, *Verhandlungen des XIII. Internat. Orientalisten-Kongresses Hamburg, September 1902*, 346 [publ. Leiden, 1904]; [S]BRUGSCH, *Wb.* 1265 [1868].

(**ⲥⲟⲣⲥⲣ**), Qual. **ⲥⲉⲣⲥⲱⲣ** (Crum 356b), 'spread abroad, display', reduplication of **ⲥⲱⲣ**, 'scatter, spread'. Cf. the place name Πσαρσωρτωϩ, lit. 'The spreading of chaff', quoted by Crum 453b, s.v. **ⲧⲱϩ**, 'chaff'.

ⲥⲣⲓⲧ (Crum 356b), 'glean' = (*Wb.* IV, 204, 17), *srd* > L.E. , 'glean'.

BRUGSCH, *Wb.* 1270 [1868].

ⲥⲟⲣⲧ (Crum 356b), 'wool' of sheep, goat, etc. = (*Wb.* IV, 49, 2), *sʿrt*, 'wool' > ?Graeco-Roman (*Wb.* IV, 191, 5), *srt*, 'hair (of cattle)'; (Er. 411, 2), *sʿrt*, 'wool'. From Semitic, cf. Hebrew שַׂעֲרָה, Ar. شَعْر or شَعَر, 'hair'.

[H]CHABAS, *Mél. ég.* 3rd Series, II, 69 n. 1 [1873]; [D]THOMPSON, *Mag. Texts*, in *Brit. Ac. Proc.* 17, 249 (note on VIII, 2) [1931]; [S]W. MAX MÜLLER in Gesenius–Buhl, *Hebr. und Aram. Handwörterbuch*, 14th ed., 721 [1905].

(**ⲥⲱⲣϣ**), Qual. **ⲥⲟⲣϣ** (Crum 356b), vb., in **ⲟⲩⲣⲱ, ⲁⲣϣⲓⲛ ⲉϥⲥⲟⲣϣ**, 'split(?) beans, peas' (refs. now Kahle, *Bal.* II, 747) = ?L.Eg. (*Wb.* IV, 199, 15), *srḫ*.

ⲥⲣϥⲉ (Crum 357a), 'be at leisure, unoccupied' = (*Wb.* IV, 197, 5–8), *srf*, 'rest, bring to rest'; (Er. 443, 1), *srf*, 'be at leisure, rest'.

[H]SETHE, *Verbum*, I, 123, §215, 3 [1899], cf. Maspero in *Journ. as.*, 7ème série, 15, 128 n. 3 [1880]; [D]REVILLOUT, *Pap. mor.* II, 61 n. 2 [1908].

ⲥⲣⲟϥⲣⲉϥ (Crum 357b), 'fall, wither' = (not in Er.; II Kh. 3, 9), *srf{s}rf* (confused writing), 'shrink, wither'. Reduplication of **ⲥⲣϥⲉ**.

GRIFFITH, *Stories*, I, 166 n. [1900].

ⲥⲁⲣϭⲁⲧⲥⲉ (Crum 358a), 'flatus ventris' = **ⲥⲁⲣ-ϭⲁⲧⲥⲉ**, lit. 'scatterer of print(s)'; **ⲥⲁⲣ-** from **ⲥⲱⲣ**, 'scatter', **ϭⲁⲧⲥⲉ** < **ⲧⲁϭⲥⲉ**, '(foot)-print'. [B]**ϫⲟⲕⲥⲓ** with omission of **ⲥⲁⲣ-**.

Sⲥⲁⲣⲁϭⲱⲟⲩϣ, Bϧⲁⲣⲁϭⲱⲟⲩⲧⲥ, Fϭⲁⲛϭⲱϣ (Crum 358a, adding ϭⲁⲗⲁⲛϭⲱϣ 812a), 'hare', from Persian خَرگوش (not خرخوش as La Croze).

LA CROZE, *Lexicon*, 144 [1775]; cf. Rossi, *Etym. aeg.* 286 [1808].

ⲥⲱⲥ (Crum 358a), 'overthrow' = ? (*Wb.* IV, 25, 1) *sꜣsꜣ*, 'attack (an enemy or a town)'.

GARDINER in *Rec. trav.* 36, 198 [1914] = GARDINER, *Notes on Sinuhe*, 157 [1916].

For Bⲥⲟⲥⲓ, see under **ⲥⲁⲥⲉ**.

ⲥⲁⲁⲥⲉ (Crum 358b), 'tow', noun derived from this verb. Connected? with Ar. ساس (de Sacy, *Abdellatif*, 151); cf. W. B. BISHAI, *JNES* 23, 44 [1964].

S**ⲥⲁⲥⲉ** (Crum 358b), 'pull', B**ⲥⲟⲥⲓ** (Crum 358a, s.v. **ⲥⲱⲥ**), 'lift up' (ἐπαίρειν Acts 27, 40) = (not in *Wb.*; XIIth Dyn. inscr. in *Sudan Notes and Records* 15, Pl. XV–XVI), (*Urk.* IV, 8, 9), *sꜣsꜣ*, 'tow (a boat)'; (Er. 411, 8), *sʿsʿ*, 'lift up, set up'.

DSPIEGELBERG, *Petubastis*, 51*, no. 346 [1910].

ⲥⲉⲥⲃⲟϩ (Crum 358b), 'place of atonement', see under **ⲥⲃⲱϩ**.

ⲥⲁⲧ (Crum 358b), 'tail' = (*Wb.* IV, 363, 6 f.), *sd*, 'tail'; (Er. 472, 6), *st*, 'tail'.

HLEPSIUS, *Chronologie*, 110 n. 1 [1848]; DBRUGSCH, *Wb.* 1349 [1868].

-ⲥⲎⲦ (not in Crum), god Sētekh (Seth), in **ϣⲉⲛⲉⲥⲏⲧ** = () , (*Nꜣ-*)*šny-n-Stḫ*, lit. '(the) trees of Seth', a town in Upper Egypt, Greek Χηνοβοσκία (see Gardiner, *Onom.* II, 31*–2*).

DARESSY, *Rec. trav.* 17, 119 [1895].

Also Oⲥⲏⲧ, god Sētekh = (*Wb.* IV, 345, 3), *stš* (*stḫ*); (Er. 472, 10), *sṭ*, Sētekh.

ERMAN in *ZÄS* 21, 109 n. 1 [1883].

ⲥⲏⲧ Qual. (Crum 359a), 'spun' = (*Wb.* IV, 355, 4. 5), *sṯꜣ*, 'spin'; (Er. 474, 1), *stꜣ*, 'spin'.

HCHAMPOLLION, *Dict.* 363 [1841].

ⲥⲓⲧ (Crum 359a), 'basilisk' =  (*Wb.* III, 410, 16. 17), *sꜣ-tꜣ*, name of a serpent, lit. 'son of (the) earth'; 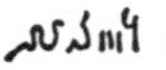 (Er. 472, 9), *syṯ*, 'serpent'.

ᴴBRUGSCH, *Wb.*, Suppl. 1147 [1882], but cf. Chassinat, *Le manuscrit magique copte*, 43 n. 1 [1955]; ᴰBRUGSCH, *Scriptura Aeg. dem.* 18, §16 [1848].

ⲥⲟⲧ (Crum 359a), 'dung, excrement' =  (not in *Wb.*), *sḏꜣw*, 'excrements' in 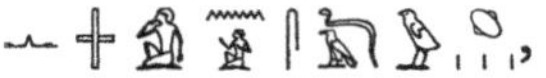, *n wnm·n·ỉ sḏꜣw*, 'I did not eat excrements', P. Berlin 10482, ro., 19 (M.K.) [Dévaud's slip] >  and sim. (*Wb.* IV, 355, 13), *stꜣ*, 'dung'; 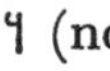 (not in Er., Harpist 81), *st*, 'dung'.

ᴴBRUGSCH, *Wb.* 1334 [1868]; ᴰSPIEGELBERG, *Kopt. Handwb.* 125 [1921].

ⲡⲁⲡⲥⲟⲧ, 'dung-kneader' (from **ⲡⲱⲱⲡⲉ**, 'knead') to make cakes or bricks of dung for fuel.

ⲥⲟⲉⲓⲧ (Crum 359a), 'fame, report' =  (Er. 409, 14), *syt*, 'glory, praise'.

SPIEGELBERG, *Kopt. Handwb.* 126 [1921].

ⲥⲱⲧ (Crum 360a), measure of land =  (*Wb.* IV, 356, 1 f.), *sṯꜣt*, measure of surface of 100 square cubits;  (Er. 472, 12), *stꜣ*, measure of land, arura.

ᴴDÜMICHEN, *Geogr. Inschr.* Text, p. 8 [1866].

ⲥⲧ- in **ⲥⲧⲉⲓⲱϩⲉ** f. =  (*Wb.* IV, 356, 5. 6), *sṯꜣt-ꜣḥt*, lit. '*sōt* of field', same measure as above; , *stꜣ-ꜣḥ*, same meaning.

ᴴGARDINER, *PSBA* 38, 184 [1916]; cf. Brugsch, *Sieben Jahre der Hungersnot*, 135 [1891]; ᴰREVILLOUT, *PSBA* 14, 64 [1891].

ⲥⲁⲧⲉ (Crum 360a), 'fire' =  (*Wb.* IV, 375, 12 f.), *sḏt*, 'fire, flame'; 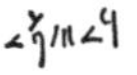 (Er. 475, 7), *styt*, 'fire, flame'.

ᴴCHABAS, *Oeuv. div.* I (= *Bibl. ég.* IX), 216 n. 3 [1858]; ᴰBRUGSCH, *Gr. dém.* 27, §53 [1855].

ⲥⲓⲧⲉ (Crum 360b), 'throw, sow' = 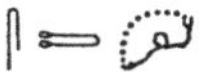 (*Wb.* IV, 346, 13 f.), *sṯy*, 'sow, spread', which when *ṯ* > *t* coalesced with , *sty*, 'throw, put' (*Wb.* IV, 328, 3–5), 'throw out' (*Wb.* IV, 328, 6–8), 'pour out (a liquid)' (*Wb.* IV, 328, 9 ff.); 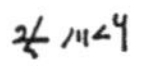 (Er. 475, 4), *sty*, 'throw, shoot' and 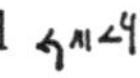 (Er. 475, 5), *sty*, 'spit, drive out, ejaculate (seed)'.

ᴴᴰBRUGSCH, *Wb.* 1336–7 [1868].

ⲥⲟⲧⲉ (Crum 361 b), 'arrow, dart' = (Caminos, *Literary Fragments*, Pl. 2, col. 2, 7), *stw*, Graeco-Roman (*Wb.* IV, 328, 1), *sty*, 'arrow'; (Er. 475, 6), *s(ʿ)tyt*, 'arrow'.

[H]CHAMPOLLION, *Gr.* 76 [1836]; [D]REVILLOUT, *Rev. ég.* 14, 7 n. 2 [1914].

ⲥⲓⲧⲉ (Crum 362 a), 'beam' of light? = singular (**sītet*) of (*Wb.* IV, 331, 2 f.), *stwt* (**satwet*), 'sunrays', later ; (Er. 476, 3), *stw*, 'sunrays' (Plural).

[H]STERN, *ZÄS* 22, 71 [1884]; [D]SPIEGELBERG, *Kopt. Handwb.* 126 [1921].

ⲥⲱⲧⲉ (Crum 362 a), 'redeem, rescue' = (*Wb.* IV, 351, 7 ff.), *sṯꜣ*, 'draw', etc.; (Er. 473, 1), *stꜣ* (*stꜣṯ*), 'draw back, turn (back), rescue' etc.

[H]SPIEGELBERG, *Kopt. Handwb.* 126, and n. 6 [1921]; [D]GRIFFITH–THOMPSON, III, 78, no. 801 [1909].

ⲥⲧⲟⲓ (Crum 362 b), 'smell' = (*Wb.* IV, 349, 5 f.), *sṯy*, 'smell'; (Er. 475, 2), *sty*, 'smell'.

[H]CHAMPOLLION, *Gr.* 61 [1836]; [D]BRUGSCH, *Wb.* 1338 [1868].

ⲥⲁⲧⲃⲉ (Crum 363 a), 'chew, ruminate' = (*Wb.* IV, 368, 12 f.), *sdb*, 'chew, drink'.

SPIEGELBERG, *Kopt. Handwb.* 127 [1921].

ⲥⲟⲧⲃⲉϥ (Crum 363 b), 'tool, weapon' = or (Er. 477, middle), *stbḫf*, 'weapon', evidently ***ⲥⲟⲧⲃⲉϩ** + **ϥ**, possibly Singular of **ⲥⲧⲉⲃⲁⲉⲓϩ** (see this).

ERICHSEN, *Dem. Glossar*, 477 [1954].

ⲥⲧⲉⲃⲁⲉⲓϩ (Crum 363 b), only as Pl., 'tool, utensil' = (*Wb.* IV, 369, 9 f.), Pl., 'equipment'; (Er. 476, 5), *stbḫ*, 'tool, weapon', also (Vienna Petubastis, Bresciani, p. 172), *stbḫf* which gave origin to **ⲥⲟⲧⲃⲉϥ** (see this).

[HD]GRIFFITH, *Ryl.* III, 390 and 258 n. 4 [1909].

ⲥⲱⲧⲙ (Crum 363 b), 'hear' = (*Wb.* IV, 384, 4 f.), *sḏm*, 'hear'; (Er. 478, 4), *stm* (*sdm*), 'hear'.

[H]CHAMPOLLION, *Gr.* 379; 387–8 [1836]; [D]BRUGSCH, *Gr. dém.* 196, §401 [1855].

ⲥⲧⲏⲙ (Crum 364b), 'stibium, antimony, kohl' = (*Wb.* II, 153, 8 f.), *msdmt*, a black mineral, and (*Wb.* IV, 370, 9) > L.E. (Lovesongs Beatty 24, 1), *sdm*, 'eye-paint'; (Er. 180, 3), *mstm*, or (Er. 478, 3), *stm*, 'eye-paint'.

HCHAMPOLLION, *Gr.* 90 [1836]; DBRUGSCH, *Gr. dém.* 26, §52 [1855].

ⲥⲧⲏⲙⲟⲩ (Crum 365a, 'meaning unknown'), in a list of vegetables, cf. ? (Er. 479, 1), *stm*, kind of fruit or sim.

ⲥⲱⲧⲡ (Crum 365a), 'choose' = (*Wb.* IV, 337, 5 f.), *stp*, 'choose'; (Er. 477, 1), *stp*, 'choose'.

HCHAMPOLLION, *Précis*, 1st ed., Tableau gén. p. (41) and pl. 19, no. 396 ff. [1824]; cf. Champollion, *Gr.* 356–7 [1836]; DCHAMPOLLION, *Gr.* 357 [1836].

Metathesis ⲥⲱⲡⲧ is found in Dem. , *sbt*, P. Insinger 9, 3 (Klasens in *Bibl. Or.* 13, 223 [1956]).

ⲥⲁⲧⲉⲉⲣⲉ (Crum 366a), 'stater' coin and weight, from Greek στατήρ through Aram. סתתריא. The Dem. form is (Er. 482, 2), *sttr*.

DBRUGSCH in *ZÄS* 29, 66 [1891]; SROSSI, *Etym. aeg.* 180 [1808]; cf. Sethe, *Nachr. von der K. Gess. Wiss. zu Göttingen, Phil. hist. Kl.* 1916, 115 n. 4.

ⲥⲧⲱⲧ (Crum 366b), 'tremble' = (*Wb.* IV, 366, bottom), *sdꜣdꜣ*, 'tremble'.

SALVOLINI, *Obél. Paris*, 28 and Pl. 1 (7), right col., gr. 8 [1837].

ⲥⲱⲧϥ (Crum 366b), 'purify, cause to drip, pour' = (*Wb.* IV, 342, 5), *stf*, 'to drip off' a liquid in medical treatment; (Er. 478, 2), *stf*, 'pour out, purify'.

HDE ROUGÉ, *Oeuv. div.* IV (= *Bibl. ég.* XXIV), 106 n. 1 [1860]; DBRUGSCH, *De natura*, 31 [1850].

ⲥⲁⲧϥⲉ (Crum 367a) f., 'canal' from ⲥⲱⲧϥ = (Er. 483, 3), *sdf* f., and , *stf*, 'ditch (for cleaning the fields of water), drain'.

MATTHA, *Dem. Ostraca*, 199, note on 275, 4 [1945].

ⲥⲧⲁϫⲟⲩⲗ (Crum 367a), 'spider', for *ⲥⲁⲧϫⲟⲩⲗ, lit. 'thread-spinner', ⲥⲁⲧ-, Part. coni. of *ⲥⲱⲧ (see ⲥⲏⲧ Qual.), 'to spin', and ϫⲟⲩⲗ, 'thread', a Semitic loan-word, cf. Hebrew *קוּר in קוּרֵי עַכָּבִישׁ, 'spider-threads'.

SPIEGELBERG, *Kopt. Handwb.* 128 [1921] (for **ⲥⲧⲁ-**); DÉVAUD's slip (for **-ϫⲟⲩⲗ**).

ⲥⲏⲩ, ⲥⲟⲩ- (Crum 367b), 'time, season' = (*Wb.* IV, 57, 8 f.), *sw*, 'time'; (Er. 461, 7), *sw* (*ssw*), 'term, time'.

[H]SETHE, *Verbum*, III, 75 [1902]; [D]BRUGSCH, *Gr. dém.* 182, §360 [1855].

ⲥⲟⲩ- (Crum 368a), 'day' (with a date or festival) = (*Wb.* IV, 58, 2), *sw*, 'day' of a month; (Er. 462, 1), *ssw* (*sw*), 'day' of a month.

[H]CHAMPOLLION, *Gr.* 225 [1836]; cf. CHABAS, *Mél. ég.* I, 85 [1862]; BRUGSCH, *Rec. de mon.* 40, n. *) [1862]; [D]BRUGSCH, *Wb.* 1304 [1868].

ⲥⲓⲟⲩ (Crum 368a), 'star' = (*Wb.* IV, 82, 7 f.), *sbꜣ*, 'star'; (Er. 413, 1), *sw*, 'star'. For the passage *b* > *w* as early as XXIInd Dyn., see Caminos, *Chronicle*, 81.

[H]CHAMPOLLION, *Gr.* 76 [1836]; [D]BRUGSCH, *Scriptura Aeg. dem.* 22, §30 [1848].

ⲥⲟⲩⲕⲏ (Crum 368b), planet Mercury, see under **ⲥⲟⲩⲕⲏ**.

ⲥⲟⲟⲩ (Crum 368b), 'six' = (*Wb.* IV, 40, 7), *sis*, 'six'; alliterates with , *sw*, in P. Leiden I, 350, ro. 1, 2.

BIRCH, in *Revue arch.* 5, 512 [1849].

ⲥⲉ, 'sixty' = alliterating with , *s*(*ꜣwy*), in P. Leiden I, 350, ro. 3, 6.

PLEYTE, *ZÄS* 5, 13 [1867].

[O]**ⲥⲏⲟⲩⲉ** (Crum 368b), 'bandage(s)(?)' = (Er. 412, 6), *siw*, 'bandage(s)' or sim.

GRIFFITH, *ZÄS* 46, 128 [1909].

ⲥⲟⲩⲟ (Crum 369a), 'corn, wheat' = (*Wb.* III, 426, 12 ff.), *swt* (*zwt*), 'wheat'; (Er. 412, 5), *sw*, 'wheat'.

[H]CHAMPOLLION, *Précis*, 2nd ed., 126 [1828]; [D]REVILLOUT, *Nouvelle chrest. dém.* 122, 123 [1878]; cf. Malinine, *Kêmi* 11, 5 ff. [1950].

[B]**ⲥⲱⲟⲩⲃⲉⲛ** (Crum 369a), 'grass' = , *sbn*, late form of (*Wb.* IV, 160, 8), *snb*, a plant.

MASPERO, *Mém. sur quelques papyrus*, 29 n. 5 [1875].

For metathesis compare (Er. 438, 7), *snb*, and (Er. 421, 8), *sbn*, 'bandage', **ⲥⲉⲃⲉⲛ**.

ⲥⲟⲩⲕⲏ (Crum 368b, s.v. **ⲥⲓⲟⲩ**), planet Mercury = (*Wb.* IV, 95, 8), *sbg*, Mercury(?); (Er. 418, 1), *swgꜣ*, 'Mercury'; , *Sbkỉ*, or , *Sbk* (Stobart tablets; Brugsch, *Mémoire sur des observations planétaires* [1856], 20). The word has, therefore, nothing to do with **ⲥⲓⲟⲩ**, 'star', but is derived from the name of Egyptian god Suchos (*Sbk*).

HD GRIFFITH, *ZÄS* 38, 77 [1900]; D SPIEGELBERG, *Dem. Denkmäler* III, 106 n. 1 [1932].

ⲥⲟⲩⲉⲛ (Crum 369b), 'value, price' = (*Wb.* IV, 68, 3 f.), *swnt*, 'trade, price'; (Er. 414, 1), *swn*, 'value'.

H CHABAS, *Voyage*, 259–60 [1866]; D BRUGSCH, *Scriptura Aeg. dem.* 18, §19 [1848].

ⲥⲓⲟⲟⲩⲛ (Crum 369b) f., 'bath' = (Er. 401, 1), *s(t)-ỉn*, 'bath; bath tax'. Evidently from **ⲥⲉ-** (or **ⲥⲓ-**), 'seat, place' + **ⲁⲩⲉⲓⲛ** (or **ⲟⲩⲉⲓⲛ**), 'water-channel', see **ⲁⲩⲉⲓⲛ**; the presence of *n* in the Coptic and Demotic words forbids the identification with (Griffith–Thompson, III, 71, no. 702), *st-ỉyw*, 'bath', which probably contains **ⲉⲓⲟⲩⲉ**, 'waters?', see this latter.

BRUGSCH, *Gr. dém.* 32, §63 [1855].

ⲥⲟⲟⲩⲛ (Crum 369b), 'know' = , *swn* (not in *Wb.*; P. BM 10383, 3, 1 [Ramesside], 'recognize', late (*Wb.* IV, 69, 1), *swn*, 'know'; (Er. 413, 6), *swn*, 'recognize, know'.

H PEET, *The Great Tomb-Robberies*, 127 n. 11 [1930]; ERMAN–GRAPOW, *Wb.* IV, 69, 1 [1930]; D BRUGSCH, *Gr. dém.* 39, §82 [1855].

B **ⲥⲟⲩⲏⲛ** (Crum 370b), 'well known, famous person' = , *swn* (Rosetta decree, 31), *swn*, 'known'.

YOUNG, *Misc. Works*, III, Pl. 3, no. 52 (cf. p. 177, no. 159) = *Encycl. Britannica*, Suppl. IV, pl. LXXVI, no. 159 [1819].

ⲥⲓⲟⲩⲣ (Crum 371a), 'eunuch' = ? (*Wb.* IV, 188, 3 ff.), *sr*, 'noble person, magistrate'; (Er. 441, 2), *srỉ*, 'noble person, officer'.

H BRUGSCH, *Wb.* 1261 [1868]; D ERICHSEN, *Dem. Glossar*, 441 [1954].

ⲥⲟⲩⲥⲟⲩ (Crum 371a), meaning doubtful, 'guide, lead (?)', cf. ? (Er. 417, 6), *swsw*, a verb.

ⲥⲟⲩⲥⲟⲩ (Crum 371a), nn., 'point, atom, moment'. Since in Luke 4, 5 [B]**ⲥⲟⲩⲥⲟⲩ** renders Gk. στιγμὴ χρόνου ([S]**ⲥⲧⲓⲅⲙⲏ ⲛⲟⲩⲟⲉⲓϣ**), **ⲥⲟⲩⲥⲟⲩ** probably < **ⲥⲉ** (cstr. state of **ⲥⲁϣ**, 'stroke') + **ⲥⲏⲩ**, 'time', lit. 'prick of time', cf. **ⲥⲉ ⲙⲙⲉϩⲧⲱⲡ**, 'prick of needle'.

DÉVAUD's slip.

ⲥⲟⲟⲩⲧⲛ (Crum 371a), 'straighten, stretch' = (*Wb.* IV, 368, 4; M.K. ex. *JEA* 20, 218), *sdwn*, 'fall to pieces' of a ship; 'stretch out' > Gr.-Rom. (*Wb.* IV, 368, 5), *stwn*, 'stretch'; (Er. 418, 7), *swtn*, 'straighten'.

[H]STEINDORFF, *Kopt. Gr.* 1st ed., 105, §233 [1894]; [D]HESS, *Gnost. Pap.* 12 (with doubt) [1892]; cf. Griffith–Thompson, III, 73, no. 733 [1909].

ⲥⲱⲟⲩϩ (Crum 372b), 'gather, collect' = (*Wb.* IV, 211, 13 f.), *sḥw*, 'gather'; (Er. 416, 4), *swḥ*, 'gather'. Metathesis **sóḥᵉw* > **sówᵉḥ* (Till, *ZÄS* 73, 133).

[H]SCHWARTZE in Bunsen, *Geschichte*, I, 586 (reading *sah*) [1845]; [D]BRUGSCH, *Wb.* 1277 [1868].

ⲥⲟⲟⲩϩⲉ (Crum 374a), 'egg' = (*Wb.* IV, 73, 1 ff.), *swḥt*, 'egg'; (Er. 417, 1), *swḥt*, 'egg'.

[H]CHAMPOLLION, *Précis*, 2nd ed. 126 [1828]; [D]BRUGSCH, *Gr. dém.* 42, §90 [1855].

[B]**ⲥⲫⲣⲁⲛϣ** (Crum 374a), 'soothsayer' = , *sẖ pr-ʿnḫ*, 'scribe of the House of life' (for *pr-ʿnḫ*, see *Wb.* I, 515, 6; Gardiner in *JEA* 24, 157 f.); (Er. 460, bottom), *sẖ n pr-ʿnḫ*, 'scribe of the House of life'.

[H]GUNN, *JEA* 4, 252 [1917]; [D]SPIEGELBERG, *Der demot. Text der Priesterdekrete*, 125, no. 119 [1922].

[B]**ⲥⲁϫⲟⲗ** (Crum 374b), 'muzzle' = ?Late Eth. (*Wb.* IV, 319, 1), *skr*, a (metal) vessel.

[O]**ⲥⲁϫⲙⲓ** (not in Crum) = (*Wb.* IV, 250, 7), *sḫmt*, goddess Sakhmet; (Er. 455, 2), *sḫmt*.

ⲥⲟⲉⲓϣ (Crum 374b), 'pair' of animals = (Er. 409, 9), *syḫ*, 'pair'.

SPIEGELBERG in Spiegelberg–Ricci, *Pap. Th. Reinach*, 194, and Pl. 12, l. 9 [1905].

ⲥⲱϣ (Crum 374b), 'strike' = [hieroglyphs] (*Wb.* III, 466, 13 f.), *sḫ* (*zḫ*), 'strike'; [demotic] (Er. 451, 1), *sḫy*, 'strike'.

ⲥⲁϣ, Pl. **ⲥⲏϣⲉ** (Crum 374b), m. and f., 'stroke, blow, sore' = [hieroglyphs] (*Wb.* III, 467, 14 f.), *sḫt* (*zḫt*), 'stroke'; [demotic], *sḫ* (m.) and [demotic] *sḫy* (f.) (Er. 451, bottom), 'stroke'.

[H]CHABAS, *Voyage*, 129 [1866]; [D]HESS, *Rosette*, 93 [1902]; cf. Brugsch, *Wb.* 1286 [1868].

[S]**ⲥⲱϣ**, [B]**ϣⲱϣ** (Crum 375a), 'despise' = [demotic] (Er. 462, 5), *sš*, 'despise'; also [demotic], *ššy*. From **ⲥⲱϣϥ**, 'despise', through confusion with **ⲥⲱϣ**, 'strike'.

BRUGSCH, *Gr. dém.* 35, §70 [1855].

ⲥⲓϣⲉ (Crum 376b), 'be like gall, bitter' = [demotic] (Er. 453, 2), 'bitter'.

SPIEGELBERG, *Kopt. Handwb.* 130 [1921]; cf. Krall, *Mitt. aus der Sammlung Erz. Rainer* IV, 142 [1888].

From **ⲥⲓϣⲉ**, 'bitterness', [hieroglyphs] (*Wb.* IV, 228, 9. 10), *sḫ*, 'gall'; [demotic] (Er. 453, 2), *sḫy*, 'gall'.

[H]BRUGSCH, *Wb.* 87 (s.v. *ȧn*) [1867], 1287 [1868]; [D]BRUGSCH, *Gr. dém.* 29, §56 [1855].

ⲥⲱϣⲉ (Crum 377a), 'field, meadow, country' opp. town = [hieroglyphs] (*Wb.* IV, 229, 8 f.), *sḫt*, 'field'; [demotic] (Er. 450, 4), *sḫt*, 'field'.

[H]LE PAGE RENOUF, *Egyptol. and Philol. Essays*, I, 350 [1865], but in *ZÄS* 4, 60 [1866] he says that Brugsch had suggested the reading, *sḫt* 'long ago'; DE ROUGÉ, *Oeuv. div.* VI (= *Bibl. ég.* XXVI), 69 n. 1 [1866]. [D]REVILLOUT in *Revue ég.* 6, 10, no. 9 [1888] (translates correctly the Dem. word but does not quote **ⲥⲱϣⲉ**, cf. Griffith, *Stories*, 177); Griffith-Thompson, III, 76, no. 779 [1909].

ⲥⲱϣⲙ (Crum 377a), 'to fatigue, annoy', 'faintness, exhaustion' = [hieroglyphs] (*Wb.* IV, 546, 1), *šsm*, 'inflamed, irritated', or sim. (of eyes); [demotic] (Er. 464, 1), *ssm*, 'excitement, anger' or sim., as verb 'become furious' or sim.

[H]BRUGSCH, *Wb.*, Suppl. 1204 [1882]; [D]GRIFFITH, *Stories*, 206 [1900].

ⲥⲱϣⲧ (Crum 377b), 'impede, hinder' = [demotic] (Er. 458, 1), *sḫt*, [demotic] (Er. 465, 6), *sšt*, 'keep away, hinder'.

BRUGSCH, *Wb.* 1316 [1868].

Sϣⲟϣⲧ, Bⲥⲱϣⲧ, ϣⲱϣⲧ (Crum 608b and 378a), 'hindrance, impediment', so 'key', belongs here.

ⲥⲁϣϥ (Crum 378a), 'seven' = (*Wb.* IV, 115, 15), *sfḫw*, 'seven'.
CHAMPOLLION, *Gr.* 210–11 [1836].
ϣϥⲉ, 'seventy' = , 'seventy', alliterates with , *sfḫ*, 'loosen', in P. Leiden I 350, ro. 1, 3.
GOODWIN in *ZÄS* 2, 39 [1864]; cf. Pleyte in *ZÄS* 5, 13 [1867].

S**ⲥⲱϣϥ**, Bϣⲱϣϥ, Aϩⲱⲥϥ (Crum 376a, s.v. ⲥⲱϣ), 'despise' = (*Wb.* III, 335, 6 f.), *ḫsf*, 'repel'; (Er. 369, 6), *ḫsf*, also (Er. 363, 6), *sšf*, 'repel, despise'. Confused with ⲥⲱϣ, 'strike'.
HSETHE, *Verbum*, I, 123, §215, 3 [1899]; III, 75 [1902]; DBRUGSCH, *Gr. dém.* 35, §70 [1855] (for *sšf*); GRIFFITH, *Stories*, 192 [1900] (for *ḫsf*).

ⲥⲁϥ (Crum 378b), 'yesterday' = (*Wb.* IV, 113, 2 f.), *sf*, 'yesterday'; (Er. 429, 1), *sf*, 'yesterday'.
HCHAMPOLLION, *Gr.* 97 [1836]; DBRUGSCH, *Wb.* 1208 [1868].

ⲥⲱⲱϥ (Crum 378b), 'defile, pollute' = (*Wb.* IV, 37, 3), *sṯf*, 'offend' (a goddess); (Er. 429, 2), *sf*, 'pollute, be impure'.
HERMAN–GRAPOW, *Wb.* IV, 37 [1930], cf. Brugsch, *Wb.* 1165 [1868]; HDREVILLOUT, *Poème satyrique*, 156 [1885].

ⲥⲏϥⲉ (Crum 379a), f. and m. (once), 'sword, knife' = (*Wb.* III, 442, 7–10), *sft*, m. 'knife', f. 'sword'; (Er. 429, 3), *sfy*, 'sword, knife'. New Hebrew סיף and Greek ξίφος are loan-words from Egyptian.
HBIRCH in *Archaeologia* 35, 62 n.a (ad *Urk.* IV, 666, 6) [1853]; DBRUGSCH, *Gr. dém.* 40, §86 [1855].

ⲥⲓϥⲉ (Crum 379a), 'tar' = (*Wb.* IV, 118, 11), *sfṯ*, name of one of the seven oils > (*Wb.* IV, 114, 15–19), *sfy*, 'resin' of coniferous trees; (Er. 429, 4), *sfy*, 'resin'.
HBIRCH in *Transactions of the Royal Soc. of Lit.*, N.S. II, 46 [1847]; DBRUGSCH, *Rhind*, 41, and Pl. 38, no. 219 [1865].

A**ⲥϩⲉ** (not in Crum), twice in ϩⲛ ⲟⲩⲥϩⲉ (Mic. 2, 3; Mal. 3, 1), ἐξαίφνης LXX, 'on a sudden'. Both editors (Till, *Coptica*, IV, 107; Malinine, *Crum Mem. Vol.* 394) emend into ⲥϩⲛⲉ. In Canopus decree l. 24 (= Sethe,

Urk. II, 142) ἐξαίφνης translates , *m sẖꜣẖ*, where *sẖꜣẖ* is the old verb (*Wb.* IV, 235, 12. 13), 'carry away quickly, speed up'. For further exx. of *m sẖꜣẖ*, cf. ***Wb.*** IV, 235, 14. This *sẖꜣẖ* seems to guarantee that **ϩⲛⲟⲩⲥϩⲉ** is a genuine expression (lit. 'in a speeding-up') and not a mere mistake for **ϩⲛⲟⲩⲥϩⲛⲉ**; see also this latter under **ϣⲥⲛⲉ**.

DÉVAUD's slip.

ⲥⲁϩ (Crum 379b), 'awl, borer' = , (not in *Wb.*, exx. in Spiegelberg, *Kopt. Handwb.* 133 n. 5), *s(ꜣ)ḥ*, 'borer'.

BIRCH, *ZÄS* 7, 133 [1869].

ⲥⲱϩ (Crum 379b), 'deaf person', from (*Wb.* III, 473, 16 f.), *sẖỉ*, 'be deaf'.

CHABAS, *Voyage*, 268 [1866]; LEPSIUS, *ZÄS* 4, 103 [1866].

ⲥⲓϩⲉ (Crum 379b), 'be removed, displaced, move, remove self, withdraw' = Late Egn. (*Wb.* IV, 207, 1 f.), *shꜣ*, 'turn something back, deceive'; (Er. 444, 9), *shy*, 'turn back, flee'.

HD SPIEGELBERG, *Rec. trav.* 36, 173 [1914]; cf. Fecht in *Orientalia*, N.S. 24, 292 [1955].

ⲥⲟⲟϩⲉ (Crum 380a), 'remove'; prob. of same etymology as the next entry (thus Spiegelberg, *Kopt. Handwb.* 133 [1921]); differently Fecht in *Orientalia*, N.S. 24, 242 [1955].

ⲥⲟⲟϩⲉ (Crum 380b), (1) 'set up, upright'; (2) 'reprove, correct, dispute with' = (*Wb.* IV, 53, 2 ff.), *sꜥḥꜥ*, 'to cause to stand, erect, accuse'; (Er. 411, 6), *sꜥḥꜥ*, 'reprove'.

H SPIEGELBERG, *Studien und Materialien*, 128–9 [1892]; D REVILLOUT, *Pap. mor.* I, 73 n. 3 [1905].

ⲥⲱϩⲉ (Crum 381a), 'weave' = (*Wb.* IV, 263, 6f.), *sẖt*, 'plait, weave'; (Er. 457, 5), *sẖt*, 'weave'.

H CHAMPOLLION, *Dict.* 389; 399 [1841]; D ERICHSEN, *Glossar*, 457, 5 [1954]. See also **ϣϯⲧ**, 'weaver', and **ϣⲧⲁϯ**, 'edge' of garment.

ⲥϩⲁⲓ (Crum 381b), 'write, paint' = (*Wb.* III, 475, 6 ff.), *sš* (*zš*), better *sẖ* (*zẖ*), 'write, paint; (Er. 458, 3), *sẖ*, 'write'.

H CHAMPOLLION, *Précis*, 1st ed., Tableau gén., p. (35) and Pl. 16, no.

312 ff. [1824]; [D]BRUGSCH, *Scriptura Aeg. dem.* 15, §8 [1848]; cf. [HD]YOUNG, *Misc. Works*, III, Pl. 2, no. 103 = *Encycl. Brit.*, Suppl. IV, Pl. 75 [1819]. But [B]ⲥϧⲓ (Crum 383b), 'written copy, diploma' is perhaps Late Egn. (*Wb.* IV, 234, 18), *sh͟ꜣ(w)*, 'notes, document, memorandum', from (*Wb.* IV, 232, 12 f.), *sh͟ꜣ*, 'remember'.

ⲥⲁϩ (Crum 383b), 'writer, teacher, master' = (*Wb.* III, 479, 14 f.), *sh͟* (*zh͟*), 'scribe'; (Er. 460, 1), *sh͟*, 'scribe'.

[H]CHAMPOLLION, *Gr.* 104 [1836]; [D]BRUGSCH, *Scriptura Aeg. dem.* 35 [1848].

ⲥⲁϫⲟ (Crum 384a), not 'great scribe', but = *ⲥⲁⲕ-ϩⲟ, see under ⲥⲱⲕ, 'flow, draw, gather'.

(ⲥ)ϩⲃⲏⲏⲧⲉ (Crum 384b), 'foam' of waves, mouth = (Er. 273, 8), *hbtt*, 'foam'.

BRUGSCH, *Gr. dém.* 33, §66 [1855].

[S]ⲥⲱϩⲙ (Crum 384b), [B]ⲥⲱϩⲉⲙ, Qual. ⲥⲁϩⲉⲙ, 'cause to fall, overwhelm, press down' = (*Wb.* IV, 215, 9 f.), *sḥm*, 'to pound, crush', ultimately related to Arabic زحم, 'press'.

BRUGSCH, *Wb.* 1290–1 [1868]; cf. KUENTZ, *Bull. Soc. Ling.* 34, 199 [1933].

[A2]ⲥⲁϩⲙⲉⲗⲱ (not in Crum; exx. in Mani Ps.), not 'pitfall' as Allberry, *A Manichaean Psalm-book*, 210, n. on l. 24), but 'he who (or 'that which') presses down (the) trap (ⲉⲗⲱ)', 'trap-setter'.

ⲥⲁϩⲙⲉⲥ (Crum 384b), 'pestle', from ⲥⲱϩⲙ + ⲥ; cf. (not in *Wb.*, but see O. Cairo 25362, 3, etc.), *sḥmy*, 'pestle'; and (not in Er.), *sḥm*, 'pestle'.

[H]SPIEGELBERG, *Kopt. Handwb.* 134 [1921] (compares *sḥm*, 'to pound'); [D]PARKER, *JEA* 26, 100 [1940].

[S]ⲥⲱϩⲙ (Crum 384b), [B]ⲥⲱϧⲉⲙ, Qual. ⲥⲁϧⲉⲙ, 'pluck, draw' = (Er. 461, 2), *sh͟m*, 'destroy, tear' or sim. < (*Wb.* IV, 269, 12), *sh͟m*, 'to comb (flax)'.

[H]SPIEGELBERG, *Kopt. Handwb.* 134 [1921]; [D]SPIEGELBERG, *Mythus*, 253, no. 706 [1917].

ⲥϩⲓⲙⲉ (Crum 385a, adding Pl. [S]ⲥϩⲓⲟⲙⲉ Böhlig-Labib 154, 33), 'woman' = (*Wb.* III, 407, 9 f.), *st-ḥmt*, 'woman', lit. 'woman-woman' (the addition of *ḥmt*, *Wb.* III, 76, 16 f., became necessary when, after the disappearance of the fem. ending *t*, the word *st* (*zt*) (*Wb.* III, 406, 13 f.), 'woman', became in M.K. homonymous with , *s* (*z*) (*Wb.* III, 404, 6 f.), 'man'; (Er. 306, 3), *s-ḥmt*, 'woman'.

[H]CHAMPOLLION, *Gr.* 77 [1836]; [D]GRIFFITH, *Stories*, 87 [1900]; cf. Brugsch, *Gr. dém.* 54, §122 [1855].

[B]**ⲛⲟⲩϯ ⲛⲥϩⲓⲙⲓ**, 'goddess', lit. 'god, woman', cf. (*Wb.* III, 77, 2), *ntrw ḥmwt*, 'goddesses', lit. 'gods, women', and (*Wb.* II, 362, 14; early exx. *Revue d'ég.* 11, 53 n. 5), *ntrwt ḥmwt*, 'goddesses', lit. 'goddesses, women'; , *ntrw sḥmwt*, 'gods, women'.

[HD]GRIFFITH–THOMPSON, I, 56 [1904].

[B]**ⲥⲛⲏⲩ ⲛⲥϩⲓⲙⲓ**, 'sisters', lit. 'brothers-women', cf. , *snw·f ḥmt*, 'his brothers, women', Macadam, *The Temple of Kawa*, I, 50 n. 59, and Pl. 16, l. 24.

[O]**ⲣⲉ́ⲓ ⲉ̀ⲛⲥⲓ́ⲙⲉ**, 'female companion', see under [B]**ⲏⲣ**.

ϣⲉⲉⲣⲉ ⲛⲥϩⲓⲙⲉ, 'daughter' = (*Wb.* IV, 527, 2), *šrît st-ḥmt*, 'girl', lit. 'girl-woman'.

See also **ϩⲓⲙⲉ**.

ⲥⲁϩⲙⲉⲗⲱ, see under **ⲥⲱϩⲙ**, 'cause to fall, press down'.

ⲥⲁϩⲛⲉ (Crum 385b), 'provide, supply' = (*Wb.* IV, 216, 8), *sḥn*, 'to commission, equip'; (Er. 446, 2), *sḥn*, 'to commission'.

[H]BRUGSCH, *Wb.* 1278–9 [1868]; [D]HESS, *Stne*, 106 [1888].

ⲣⲥⲁϩⲛⲉ, 'make agreement', = (*Wb.* IV, 217, 12. 13), *îrt sḥn*, 'give order, carry out an order'; cf. , *sḥn*, 'agreement', Parker, *JEA* 26, 90 [1940].

ⲟⲩⲉϩ ⲥⲁϩⲛⲉ, 'lay a command, bid' = (*Wb.* IV, 217, 15), 'give (lit. 'lay') an order'; (Er. 447, middle), *wꜣḥ-sḥn*, 'to order'.

[H]SETHE, *ZÄS* 47, 148 [1910]; [D]HESS, *Stne*, 106 [1888].

ⲥⲱϩⲛⲉ(?), **ⲥⲁϩⲛ-** (Crum 386a), 'bring near'(?) = Gr.-R. (not in *Wb.*; *Edfou*, II, 16, 2, parallel to , *îny*, 'bring'), *sẖn*, 'bring near'.

ⲥⲱϩⲡ (Crum 386a), 'suck in, drink, swallow' = (*Wb.* IV, 269, 7–9), *sẖp*, 'swallow, suck in', and (*Wb.* IV, 268, 13 f.), *sẖb*, 'suck in'.

DÉVAUD in *Rec. trav.* 39, 174–5 [1921], and *Études*, 14–16 [1922].

ⲥⲱϩⲣ (Crum 386a), 'sweep' = (*Wb.* IV, 219, 9 ff.), *sḥry*, 'remove'; (Er. 448, 3), *sḥr*, 'sweep'.

H DE ROUGÉ, *Oeuv. div.* III (= *Bibl. ég.* XXIII), 68–9 [1855]; D REVILLOUT, *Setna*, 140 [1877–80].

B **ⲥⲁϩⲥ** (Crum 386b), 'rub down, pound', incomplete reduplication instead of **ⲥⲁϩⲥϩ**, see the next entry.

S (**ⲥⲁϩⲥϩ**), B **ⲥⲁϩⲥⲉϩ** (Crum 386b), 'roll down, rub down, plane' = (not in *Wb.*, but see Brugsch, *Wb.* 1281, and , *Edfou*, V, 26, 14–15; , *Edfou*, II, 131, 8), *sḥsḥ*, 'rub down'; (Er. 449, 2), *syḥsyḥ*, 'thrashing' or sim.

H BRUGSCH, *Wb.* 1281 [1868]; D LEXA, *Pap. Insinger*, II, 101, no. 400 [1926].

ⲥⲉϩⲧ (Crum 386b), 'leprosy' = (*Wb.* IV, 227, 3–5), *sḥḏw*, a disease; (Er. 449, 3), *sḥt*, 'leprosy'.

H GRAPOW, *OLZ* 26, col. 560 [1923]; D SPIEGELBERG, *Demot. Denkmäler*, II, 23, 294 [1908].

ⲥϫⲁⲧ (Crum 387a), 'marriage gift' (from bridegroom), see under **ⲥⲱⲕ**, 'flow, draw, gather'.

ⲥⲁϩⲧⲉ (Crum 387a), 'kindle fire, burn' = (*Wb.* IV, 224, 16 f.), *sḥḏ*, 'cause to be lit, illuminate'; (Er. 450, 1), *sḥḏ* (*sḥṯ*), 'illuminate'.

H SPIEGELBERG, *Correspondances*, 45–6 [1895]; D BRUGSCH, *Scriptura Aeg. dem.* 19, §22 [1848].

ⲥⲁϩⲧⲉ, 'fire' = (*Wb.* IV, 226, 9), *sḥḏwt*, 'light'; (Er. 450, 1), *sḥt*(*y*), 'light, flame'.

D GRIFFITH-THOMPSON, III, 76, no. 773 [1909].

ⲥⲁϩⲟⲩ (Crum 387a), 'to curse' = (*Wb.* IV, 213, 4–6), *sḥwr*, 'to curse'; (Er. 445, 6), *sḥwr*, 'to curse'.

H BRUGSCH, *Wb.* 1280 [1868]; D BRUGSCH, *De natura*, 38 [1850]; *Dem. Urk.* p. 27 and Pl. VI, l. 25 [1850].

ⲥⲏϭ (Crum 388a), 'foal' of ass, horse = (*Wb.* IV, 315, 12), *sk*, foal of ass'; (Er. 467, 5), *skl*, 'foal of ass'.

H MASPERO, *Du genre épistolaire*, 14 [1872]; D GRIFFITH, *Ryl.* III, 271 n. 3; 389 [1909].

ⲥⲟϭ (Crum 388a), 'fool' = Late Egn. (*Wb.* IV, 76, 8), *swg3*, '(be) foolish'; (Er. 417, 8), *swg*, 'foolish, stupid' or sim.

[H]BRUGSCH, *Wb.* 1328 [1868]; [D]BRUGSCH, *Gr. dém.* 34, §68 [1855].

ⲥⲱϭ (Crum 388a), 'become rigid, paralysed', see the following.

ⲥⲓϭⲉ (Crum 388b), same meaning as prec. = (*Wb.* IV, 320, 5–6), *sg3*, 'become rigid from surprise'; (Er. 468, 6), *sg*, 'become rigid' or sim.

[H]ERMAN-GRAPOW, *Wb.* IV, 320, 5 [1930]; [D]SETHE, *ZÄS* 53, 45 [1917]; SPIEGELBERG, *Mythus*, 255, no. 723 [1917].

ⲥⲟϭⲛ (Crum 388b), 'ointment' = (*Wb.* IV, 322, 17 f.), *sgnn*, 'ointment, oil'; (Er. 469, 7), *sgn*, 'ointment'.

[H]BRUGSCH, *Rec. de mon.* II, 119 [1863]; [D]BRUGSCH, *Scriptura Aeg. dem.* 19, §21 [1848].

ⲥϭⲏⲣ (Crum 388b and **ϣϭⲏⲣ** 619a), 'sail' on river or sea = (Er. 470, 2), *sgr*, 'sail'.

BRUGSCH, *Wb.* 1321 [1868].

ⲥϭⲣⲁϩⲧ (Crum 389b), 'rest, pause, be quiet' = 3rd pers. sg. f. of the Old Perfective (**segrăḥtey*) of (*Wb.* IV, 324, 7 f.), *sgrḥ*, 'bring to rest'; (Er. 470, 5), *sgrḥ*, 'bring to rest, be at rest'.

[H]CHAMPOLLION, *Gr.* 382 [1836]; [D]BRUGSCH, *Lettre à M. le Vicomte de Rougé*, 37 [1850].

ⲧ

ⲧ-, ⲧⲉ- (Crum 390a), definite article fem. sing. = (*Wb.* V, 211, 11), *t3*; (Er. 597, 3), *t3*.

[H]CHAMPOLLION, *Précis*, 1st ed., Tableau général, no. 2 on p. (1) and Pl. 1 [1824]; [D]BRUGSCH, *Gr. dém.* 72–3, §§158–9 [1855]; cf. BRUGSCH, *Lettre à M. le Vicomte de Rougé*, 67 [1850].

ⲧⲁ⸗, ⲧⲉ⸗ (Crum 258b, s.v. **ⲡⲁ-**), sing. fem. of possessive pronoun = + suffix (*Wb.* V, 212, 2), *t3y·*, 'mine' (orig. 'this of mine'); (Er. 602, 1), *t3y·*, same meaning.

[H]CHAMPOLLION, *Gr.* 266 [1836]; [D]BRUGSCH, *Scriptura Aeg. dem.* 33, §25 [1848].

ⲧⲁ- (Crum 259a, s.v. **ⲡⲁ-**), fem. possessive article, 'she of...' = (*Wb.* v, 212, 1), *tꜣ nt*; (Er. 598, 1), *tꜣ*, 'she of..., daughter of...'.

[H]CHAMPOLLION, *Gr.* 188–9 [1836]; [D]BRUGSCH, *Scriptura Aeg. dem.* 38 [1848].

[SB]**ⲧⲁⲓ**, [O]**ⲧⲉï** (Crum 390a), 'here' = (*Wb.* v, 420, 5), *dy*, here'; (Er. 604, 1), *tꜣy*, 'here'.

[H]SPIEGELBERG, *Rec. trav.* 21, 46 [1899]; [D]HESS, *Stne*, 59 note, 132, 182 [1888].

ⲧⲉï ⲙⲡⲟⲟⲩ, 'here to-day' = (Dem. Mag. Pap. 1, 13 and often), *tꜣy n pꜣ hrw*, same meaning.

GRIFFITH in *ZÄS* 38, 92 [1900]; cf. Spiegelberg, *Dem. Gr.* 177, §398 [1925].

ⲧⲁï (Crum 259a, s.v. **ⲡⲁⲓ**), fem. sing. of demonstrative pronoun 'this' used absolutely = (*Wb.* v, 211, 5), *tꜣ*, > (*Wb.* v, 212, 4), *tꜣy*, 'this'; (Er. 601, 1), *tꜣy* ,'this'.

[H]CHAMPOLLION, *Gr.* 182 [1836]; [D]SPIEGELBERG, *Der dem. Text der Priesterdekrete*, 198, §380 [1922].

ⲧⲉⲓ-, construct form of preceding = (*Wb.* v, 211, 6), *tꜣ*, > (*Wb.* v, 212, 3), *tꜣy*; (Er. 601, 1), *tꜣy*, same.

[H]CHAMPOLLION, *Gr.* 182 [1836]; [D]BRUGSCH, *Gr. dém.* 79, §172 [1855].

ⲧⲁⲉⲓⲟ (Crum 390b), 'honour, pay respect to, adorn' = + suff., *dỉt ꜥꜣ·*, lit. 'cause to become great'; (Er. 53, bottom), *tỉ ꜥꜣ·*, 'honour'.

[H]STERN, *Kopt. Gr.* 192, §362, 2b [1880]; [D]GRIFFITH–THOMPSON, III, 4, no. 23 [1909].

-ⲧⲉ (Crum 391b), enclitic fem. = (*Wb.* v, 212, 5), *tꜣy*; (Er. 601, middle), *tꜣy*, same use.

[H]MASPERO in *ZÄS* 15, 111–13 [1877]; cf. ERMAN, *Näg. Gr.* 57–8, §78 [1880]; [D]BRUGSCH, *Gr. dém.* 125, §257 [1855].

-ⲧⲉ = , *ṯw*, > , *tw* (*Wb.* v, 358, 7. 8), 'thou', 2nd pers. sing. of dependent personal pronoun after Imperative for emphasis.

SPIEGELBERG in *Rec. trav.* 28, 205 [1906]; cf. Till in *WZKM* 33, 125–6 [1926].

See **ⲁⲙⲁϩⲧⲉ**, A**ⲁⲓⲉⲩⲧⲉ** (under **ⲁⲓⲁⲓ**), A**ⲁⲣⲏϩⲧⲉ** (under **ϩⲁⲣⲉϩ**), A**ⲁϣⲉⲓⲧⲉ** (under **ⲁϣⲁⲓ**), **ⲣⲁⲥⲧⲉ**, **ⲥⲃ̀ⲗⲧⲉ**, A**ⲟⲩϫⲉⲓⲧⲉ** (under **ⲟⲩϫⲁⲓ**); also **ⲉⲓⲥⲧⲉ** (under **ⲉⲓⲥ**). For Demotic verbs coalescing with , *tỉ*, 'thou', see Spiegelberg, *Petubastis*, 30*, no. 191 (*nw*, 'see') and 37*, no. 231 (*rỉs*, 'wake').

ⲧⲉ-, prefix of 2nd pers. fem. sing. of 1st Present = ; (Er. 609, middle), *twt*.

HD MASPERO, *Des formes de la conjugaison*, 14, 43, 59 [1871].

ⲧⲏ (Crum 391 b), 'time, season' = (*Wb.* v, 313, 12 ff.), *tr*, 'time'; (Er. 600, 3), *tꜣ*, 'time'.

H STERN, *Kopt. Gr.* 28, §32 [1880]; D BRUGSCH, *Wb.* 1524 [1868].

O**ⲧⲏ** (Crum 392 a), 'underworld' = (*Wb.* v, 415, 3 f.), *dꜣt*, 'underworld'; (Er. 613, 6), *t(w)ꜣt*, 'underworld'. Cf. also the late writing, (*mt(r)-dꜣ(t)*) for **ⲙⲛⲧⲏ**, 'fifteen' (*ZÄS* 9, 139).

H ERMAN, in *ZÄS* 21, 94 and Pl. III, l. 7 [1883]; D HESS, *Stne*, 182 [1888].

B**ⲧⲏ** (Crum 392 a), 'there' = (*Wb.* v, 420, 6), *dy*, 'there'; (Er. 604, 1), *tꜣy* or , *tꜣ*, 'there'.

H SETHE in *ZÄS* 50, 100 [1912]; D SETHE, *Dem. Urk.* 430, §66 [1920].

ⲧⲏ (Crum 260 b, s.v. **ⲡⲏ**), demonstr. pronoun 'that' = (*Wb.* v, 211, 5), *tꜣ* > , *tꜣy*, (*Wb.* v, 212, 3 f.), 'this, that'.

STEINDORFF, *Kopt. Gr.* 2nd ed. 46, §96, Anm. [1904].

ϯ-, prefix of 1st pers. sing. of 1st Present = (*Wb.* v, 246, top), *twỉ*; (Er. 609, middle), *twy*, same.

HD MASPERO, *Des formes de la conjugaison*, 14, 43, 59 [1871].

ϯ (Crum 392 a), 'give' = (*Wb.* II, 464, 1 ff.), *rdy*, 'give'; (Er. 604, 7), *ty*, 'give'.

H CHAMPOLLION, *Dict.* 88–90, 359–61 [1841]; D BRUGSCH, *Gr. dém.*, 129, §265 [1855].

ϯ ⲉⲃⲟⲗ (Crum 394b), 'give forth, away, sell' = L.Eg., *dít r-bnr*, 'sell', lit. 'give out(side)'; (P. Hauswaldt, Pl. 14, 10a, 3), *ty r-bl*, 'sell'.

[H]PEET, *Tomb Robberies*, 68 [1930]; [D]SPIEGELBERG, *Die dem. Papyri Hauswaldt*, 7* n. 9 [1913]; cf. MALININE, *Choix de textes juridiques*, 82 n. 13 [1953].

ϯ ⲙⲛ- (Crum 393b), 'fight with' = (Er. 606, 1), *ty írm*, 'fight with'.

GRIFFITH, *Stories*, 193 [1900].

ⲡⲉⲧⲉ- + name of a deity, in masc. proper names = , *pꜣ dy*..., 'he whom...has given' (*Wb.* II, 464, 7); (Er. 605, bottom), *pꜣ ty*....

[H]SETHE in *ZÄS* 30, 51 and n. 1 [1892].

ⲧⲉⲧⲉ- + name of a deity, in fem. proper names = (*Wb.* II, 464, 7), *tꜣ dy*....; or , *tꜣ ty*..., 'she whom...has given'.

SPIEGELBERG, *Aeg. u. griech. Eigennamen*, 80–1 [1901].

ⲧⲁⲓ- (Crum 395b), part. coni., 'giver', still independent in proper names , *Pꜣ-[n]-pꜣ-ty*, 'He of the Giver (i.e. God), παπτάις, and , *Pꜣ-[n]-ty*, 'He of Giver', Πατῆς, Παταί, Πατῖς.

MATTHA, *Dem. Ostraca*, 92, note on 38, 1 [1946].

ϭⲓⲛϯ (Crum 396a), 'giving, selling' = (Er. 605, bottom), *gy-n-ty* 'giving'.

THOMPSON, *Theban Ostraca (Demotic)*, 42 and Pl. V, D 135, l. 1 [1913].

ⲧⲟ (Crum 396a), 'land, earth' = (*Wb.* V, 212, 6 ff.), *tꜣ*, 'earth, ground'; (Er. 598, 2), *tꜣ*, 'land, earth, world'.

[H]CHAMPOLLION, *Précis*, 1st ed. Tableau général, p. (43) and Pl. 20, no. 417 [1824]; [D]BRUGSCH, *De natura*, 32 [1850].

[O]**(ⲡ)ⲧⲟ ⲧⲏⲣϥ**, [B]**ⲡⲓⲑⲟ ⲧⲏⲣϥ**, οἰκουμένη = (*Wb.* V, 216, top), *tꜣ r ḏr·f*, 'the whole earth'.

[O]**ⲧⲁ-** in **ⲧⲁ ⲉⲉⲓ̈ⲡⲛ**, 'this world', see under **ⲉⲓ̈ⲡⲛ**.

For [O]**ⲕⲙⲡⲧⲟ̀**, see this.

ⲧⲟⲉ (Crum 396a), 'part, share' = (*Wb.* V, 465, 9 f.), *dnyt*, 'part, share'; (Er. 638, 5), *tnyt* (*dnyt*), 'part, share, piece'.

[H]SETHE, *Von Zahlen und Zahlworten*, 89 [1916]; cf. SALVOLINI, *Analyse gramaticale raisonnée*, 42, and Pl. F, no. 175 [1836]; [D]BRUGSCH, *Scriptura Aeg. dem.* 8 and 47 [1848].

ⲧⲟⲉ (Crum 396b), 'spot' = (*Wb.* v, 238, 9), *tyt*, 'something used by painter besides colours, clay, gold and sim.' and (*Wb.* v, 239, 1 f.), 'sign, mark, figure'.

Spiegelberg, *Kopt. Etymologien*, 29–30 [1920].

ⲧⲱ⸗ (Crum 260b, s.v. **ⲡⲱ⸗**), fem. of possessive pronoun used absolutely = + suffix (*Wb.* v, 212, 2), *tꜣy·*, 'mine'; (Er. 603, bottom) *tꜣy·k*, 'thine'.

[H]Erman, *Spr. Westcar*, 50, §97 n. 1 [1889]; [D]Not identified.

ⲧⲁⲓⲃⲉ, ⲧⲏⲏⲃⲉ (Crum 397a), 'chest, coffin, pouch' = (Er. 622, 7), *tbyt* or *tybt*, 'coffin, shrine, chest'. Both Coptic and Demotic seem to be fusion of two separate words still carefully distinguished in L.Egn.:

1. (*Wb.* v, 561, 8–12), *ḏbꜣt*, fem., 'shrine, coffin', also (O. DM. 233, 4, 10; O. Cairo 25521, 10; O. IFAO 128, 6; O. Černý 20, 4 and vo. 1; > Graeco-Roman (*Wb.* v, 261, 6), *tbt*, perhaps > **ⲧⲏⲏⲃⲉ** (because of its broken vowel, cf. **ⲧⲱⲱⲃⲉ**, 'repay').

2. (*Wb.* v, 434, 10), *dbt*, fem., 'chest, box', also on the lid of a box which contained garments from Tutʿankhamūn's tomb, Cairo J.E. 61500B; identical with (*Wb.* v, 261, 11), *tbỉ*, also written P. Turin Cat. 2104, vo. II, 7 ('*t.* for garments') and very often , *tbt*, O. Berlin 12343, vo. 2; O. Gardiner 119, 2; O. IFAO AG 33, vo. 5 ('*t.* for garments'), and Gr.-R. (*Wb.* v, 261, 6), rendered in Hebrew as תֵּבָה, 'chest, box', LXX θῖβις, > perhaps **ⲧⲁϊⲃⲉ**.

[H]de Rougé, *Oeuv. div.* II (= *Bibl. ég.* XXII), 139 (read in 1849) [1851]; [D]Brugsch, *Gr. dém.* 33, §65 [1855]; [S]Rossi, *Etym. aeg.* 65 [1808]. According to Steindorff (in Crum, Add., p. xxii) there are two different words: **ⲧⲁⲓⲃⲉ, -ⲃⲓ** < *ḏbꜣt*, and **ⲧⲏ(ⲏ)ⲃⲉ, ⲑⲏⲃⲓ** < *tbt*.

ⲧⲉⲃⲓ (Crum 397a), 'obol' coin = (Er. 552, 1, reading *ḳt*) *tbʿ*, 'obol', properly 'seal' because of the figures stamped on the coin.

Pierce in *JEA* 51, 158–9 [1965]; Lüddeckens in *OLZ* 60, col. 143 [1965].

ᴮτεβι (Crum 397a), ‘strip, bandage’ of linen = (plural) ‘mummy bandages’, *Zauberspr. f. Mutter u. Kind*, 8, 8; (*Wb.* v, 560, 10. 11), *ḏbꜣ*, ‘kind of garment for gods’.

DÉVAUD’s slip.

τηηβε (Crum 397b), ‘finger’ = (*Wb.* v, 562, 12 f.), *ḏbꜥ*, ‘finger’; (Er. 623, 1), *tbꜥ* (*ḏbꜥ*), ‘finger’.

ᴴCHAMPOLLION, *Gr.* 93 [1836]; ᴰBRUGSCH, *Rhind*, 44 and Pl. 40, no. 295 [1865].

As measure ‘finger’s breadth, digit’, = , *ḏbꜥ*, ‘finger’ as a part of cubit, *Wb.* v, 565, 11 and for **ογτηηβε μμοογ** cf. ( ), *ḏbꜥ n mrḥt* (*bỉt*) ‘finger, a little of fat (honey)’, *Wb.* v, 565, 12.

CRUM, *Cat. of the Coptic MSS in the Brit. Mus.* 258b, n. 2 [1905].

τωβε (Crum 397b), name of 5th month = , *tꜣ ꜥ(ꜣ)bt*, lit. ‘The offering’, this being the old word (*Wb.* I, 167, 10), *ꜥꜣbt*, ‘offering’.

ČERNÝ in *ASAE* 43, 173–18 [1943].

τωωβε (Crum 398a), ‘brick’ = (*Wb.* v, 553, 7 f.), *ḏbt*, ‘brick’; (Er. 617, 6), *tb*, ‘brick’. From **τωωβ** is Arabic طوب (so already ROSSI, *Etym. Aeg.* 227 [1808]).

ᴴCHAMPOLLION, *Gr.* 100 [1836]; ᴰGRIFFITH, *Rylands*, III, 403 [1909]; GRIFFITH–THOMPSON, III, 93, no. 1003 [1909]; SPIEGELBERG, *Die dem. Papyrus der Musées royaux du Cinquantenaire*, 19 [1909].

See also **τερποσε**.

τωωβε (Crum 398a), ‘to seal’ = (*Wb.* v, 566, 12 f.), *ḏbꜥ*, ‘to seal’; (Er. 623, 2), *tbꜥ* (*ḏbꜥ*), ‘to seal’.

ᴴBRUGSCH, *Wb.* 1678 [1868]; ᴰGRIFFITH, *Stories*, 162, note [1900].

τββε (Crum 398b), subst. ‘seal’ = (*Wb.* v, 566, 5 f.), *ḏbꜥt*, ‘seal’; (Er. 623, 2), *tbꜥ* (*ḏbꜥ*), subst. ‘seal’.

ᴴBRUGSCH, *Wb.* 1678 [1868]; LEFÉBURE, *Traduction comparée des hymnes au soleil*, 41 [1868].

τωωβε (Crum 398b), ‘repay, requite’ = (*Wb.* v, 555, 5 f.), *ḏbꜣ*, ‘replace, compensate, repay’; (Er. 618, 10), *tbꜣ* (*ḏbꜣ*), ‘compensate, repay, punish’.

[H]DE ROUGÉ, *Oeuv. div.* II (=*Bibl. ég.* XXII, 139 (read in 1849) [1851]; [D]BRUGSCH, *Wb.* 1624 [1868]; GRIFFITH–THOMPSON, III, 93, 1002 [1909].

ⲡⲉⲧⲃⲉ (**ⲡⲉ**+**ⲧⲃⲉ**) (Crum 399a), 'Requiter', name of a god= (Er. 619, middle), *pꜣ tbꜣ* (*dbꜣ*), 'Requiter', also as a deity.

GRIFFITH, *PSBA* 22, 162 [1900]; cf. SPIEGELBERG, *Mythus*, 296–7 [1917].

ⲧⲃⲁ (Crum 399a), 'ten thousand'= (*Wb.* V, 565, 13 f.), *ḏbꜥ*, 'ten thousand'; (Er. 623, 3), *tbꜥ* (*dbꜥ*), 'ten thousand'.

CHAMPOLLION, *Gr.* 236 [1836].

[O]**ⲧⲃⲁⲓ-** (Crum 399b), in **ⲧⲃⲁⲓⲧⲱⲟⲩ**, title of Anubis= (*Wb.* V, 543, 7 f.), *tpy ḏw(·f)*, 'he upon (his) mountain'; (Er. 627, middle from Dem. Mag. Pap. 6, 24); also Brugsch, *Thes.* 1001), *tp-tw·f*, same.

[H]ERMAN in *ZÄS* 21, 95 [1883]; [D]GRIFFITH–THOMPSON, III, 93, no. 1011 [1909]; cf. Möller in Preisendanz, *Papyri graecae magicae*, I, 67 n. 6 [1928]. NB. [B]**ⲑⲃⲁⲓ** is not this word, but=[B]**ⲑⲟⲩⲁⲓ**, [S]**ⲧⲟⲩⲁ**, 'door-post, lintel'.

ⲧⲃⲃⲟ (Crum 399b), 'make pure, purify'=*, *dỉt wꜥb·*, 'cause to be pure'; , *dỉt wꜥb·*, same meaning.

[H]BRUGSCH, *Wb.* 171 [1867]; more explicit STEINDORFF, *Kopt. Gr.* 1st ed. 108, §236 [1894]; [D]ERICHSEN, *Auswahl frühdem. Texte*, 2 (Glossary), 111b [1950].

(**ⲧⲃⲕⲟ**), **ⲧⲃⲕⲉ-** (Crum 400b adding **ⲧⲟⲩⲕⲉ-**, **ⲧⲟⲩⲕⲟ≈**, **ⲧⲟⲩⲕⲱ≈** from P. Bodmer XXI, p. 25), 'send'=**ϯ**, 'cause'+**ⲃⲱⲕ**, 'go'.

CRUM, *A Coptic Dict.* 400b [1934].

[S]**ⲧⲃⲏⲗ**, [B]**ⲑⲃⲏⲗ** (Crum 400b), 'fold (?)' for sheep, prob. same as **ⲧⲃⲏⲣ**, 'blow with foot', see this latter.

ⲧⲃⲛⲏ (Crum 400b), 'beast', domestic animal=, *tp n ꜥwt* > , *tp n ỉꜣwt* (*Wb.* V, 267, 4), lit. 'head (=choicest) of animals', 'cattle', Late Aeth. (*Wb.* V, 438, 17), *dbnt*, 'cattle', (Er. 17, 1), *tp n ỉꜣw(w)*, 'cattle'.

[HD]NIMS, *JEA* 22, 51–4 [1936]; cf. Gardiner, *JEA* 38, 30–1 [1952]; for Aeth. ex. cf. Maspero, *Ét. de myth. et arch.* III (=*Bibl. ég.* VII), 253 n. O [1876].

ⲧⲁⲃⲓⲣ (Crum 400 b), 'sanctuary' = (*Wb.* v, 439, 4), *dbr*, also (*Edfou* IV, 328, 8), 'god's shrine', a loan-word from Hebrew דְּבִיר, 'innermost chamber of the temple'.

BRUGSCH, *Wb.* 1634 [1868]; cf. GARDINER, *Onom.* I, 66*–7* [1947]; ^{S}ROSSI, *Etym. Aeg.* 216 [1808].

ⲧⲃⲏⲣ (Crum 401 a), 'blow with foot', prob. the same word as ^{S}ⲧⲃⲏⲗ, ^{B}ⲑⲃⲏⲣ (Crum 400 b), 'fold(?)' for sheep, contained in Gr.-Roman (not in *Wb.*; ex. *Edfou*, III, 136, 5), *mtbr*, 'battlefield' or sim., lit. 'place of thumping of feet'; (Er. 189, 7), *mṯbl*, 'net, cage'. Probably from Semitic, cf. Ar. مُوبَالَة (Belot), *m-* being the Semitic prefix forming words of places.

^{H}SAUNERON's oral communication [Febr. 1963]; cf. SAUNERON, *Revue d'ég.* 15, 54 [1963]; ^{S}DÉVAUD's slip.

ϯⲃⲥ (Crum 401 a), 'heel' = (*Wb.* v, 262, 9), *tbs*, 'heel'; (Er. 625, 2), *tbs*, 'heel'.

^{H}CHAMPOLLION in Caillaud, *Voyage à Meroé*, IV, p. 40 n. 9 [1827]; ^{D}REVILLOUT, *Revue ég.* I, 172 and Pl. 9, last line [1880].

ⲧⲱⲃⲥ (Crum 401 a), 'prick, goad, incite' = Gr.-Roman (*Wb.* v, 262, 10), *tbs*, 'to prick (of thorn)' < , *dbs*, 'to prick (of thorn)'.

ERMAN-GRAPOW, *Wb.* v, 262, 10 [1931]; cf. GARDINER, *Chester Beatty Pap.* II, 17 n. 2 [1935].

^{A2}**ⲧⲟⲩⲟⲥ** (not in Crum; Mani Ps.), 'point' of spear, for *ⲧⲃⲟⲥ, 'point, prick', from preceding verb.

^{B}**ⲑⲟⲩⲥ** (Crum 69 b), 'point' of beard, same as the preceding ⲧⲟⲩⲟⲥ.

ⲧⲃⲧ (Crum 401 b), 'fish' = (*Wb.* v, 261, 5 = *Edfou*, VIII, 242, 6), plural, *tbt*, 'fish'; (Er. 625, 3), *tbṯ*, 'fish'; * , *nꜣ tbṯ·w*, 'fishes' (name of decan).

^{H}BRUGSCH, *Geographie*, 166 and Pl. XXXIV, no. 697 [1857]; ^{D}SPIEGELBERG in W. Max Müller, *OLZ* 5, col. 136 [1902] (decan); GRIFFITH–THOMPSON, III, 93, no. 1006 [1909] (appellative).

ⲧⲟⲟⲃⲉϥ (Crum 402 a), 'foliage', connected with (*Wb.* v, 562, 2. 3), *ḏbꜣw*, 'foliage'.

SPIEGELBERG, *Rec. trav.* 26, 37 [1904].

ⲧⲱⲃϩ (Crum 402a), 'pray, entreat, console' = (*Wb.* v, 439, 6 ff.), *dbḥ*, 'require, entreat'; (Er. 624, 5), *tbḥ*, 'pray, entreat'.
[H]CHAMPOLLION, *Gr.* 378 [1836]; [D]HESS, *Gnost. Pap.* 16 [1892].

ⲧⲟⲕ (Crum 403a), 'knife, razor' = (Er. 659, 3), *tk*, 'knife, razor'.
GRIFFITH–THOMPSON, III, 95, no. 1044 [1909].

ⲧⲱⲕ (Crum 403a), 'be strong, thick, strengthen', Qual. **ⲧⲏⲕ**? = Gr.-R. (*Wb.* v, 325, 15), *tḫ*, 'fat'.
DÉVAUD in *Kêmi* 2, 11–12 [1929].

ⲧⲱⲕ (Crum 403b), 'throw, cast' = (Er. 659, 7), *tkꜣ*, 'throw'.
SPIEGELBERG in *ZÄS* 45, 97 n. 7 and Pl. III (right) [1908].

ⲧⲱⲕ (Crum 404a), 'kindle' (fire), 'bake' = (*Wb.* v, 332, 14 f.), *tkꜣ*, 'burn (trans.), warm up (trans.)'; (Er. 659, 4), *tk*, 'burn (trans.), kindle'.
[H]BRUGSCH, *Wb.* 1569 [1868]; [D]SPIEGELBERG, *Mythus*, 303, no. 958 [1917].
ϯⲕ (Crum 404b), 'spark' = (*Wb.* v, 331, 5 f.), *tkꜣ*, 'flame, torch, candle'; (Er. 659, 4), *tyk*, 'spark'.
[H]CHAMPOLLION, *Gr.* 99 [1836]; [D]GRIFFITH–THOMPSON, III, 92, no. 992 [1909].
ⲛⲛⲧⲱⲕ (Crum 404b), 'oven' of bath, from **ⲡⲛⲛⲧⲱⲕ** = *, *pr n tkꜣ*, lit. 'house of baking'.
VON LEMM in *ZÄS* 25, 115 n. 1 [1887]; cf. Steindorff in *ZÄS* 27, 108 [1889].

ⲧⲁⲕⲟ (Crum 405a), 'destroy' = *, *dit ꜣḳ·*, 'cause to perish' (*ꜣḳ*, *Wb.* I, 21, 11 f.); (P. Ins. 9, 10; 10, 10 etc.), *dit ꜣḳ·* (*ꜣḳ*, Er. 11, 12).
[H]CHABAS, *Oeuv. div.* II (= *Bibl. ég.* X), 96 [1860]; [D]REVILLOUT, *Pap. mor.* I, 64 n. 5; 246 n. 6 [1907].

ⲧⲱⲕⲙ (Crum 406a), 'pluck, draw, drag' = (*Wb.* v, 500, 6. 7), *dgm*, 'become exhausted, worried' (cf. **ⲧⲱⲕⲙ ⲛϩⲏⲧ**, 'be troubled at heart'); (Er. 659, 1), *tḳm*, 'draw out, pluck'.
DRIOTON in *Revue de l'Ég. anc.* 2, 182 [1929]; [D]KRALL, *Mitt. aus der Sammlung Erzh. Rainer*, VI, 77, no. 346 [1897].

ⲧⲕⲟⲩⲣ (Crum 406b), ‘speed’ is non-existent, the true reading being **ⲧⲣⲟⲩⲣ**, see this.

KAHLE *ap.* Černý in *Festschrift Grapow*, 34 [1955].

ⲧⲱⲕⲥ (Crum 406b), ‘pierce, bite, goad’ = Gr.-Roman [hieroglyphs] (*Wb.* v, 331, 2, 3), *ṯks*, ‘pierce’. Late Egn. [hieroglyphs], *tks* (XXIst Dyn. Pap. Cairo), ‘to pain’; XIXth Dyn. [hieroglyphs] (*Wb.* v, 335, 18), *tks*, ‘torture’ and M.K. [hieroglyphs] (*Wb.* v, 335, 17), *tks*, ‘penetrate’; [demotic] (Er. 660, 4), *tks*, ‘pierce’.

[H]BRUGSCH, *Wb.*, Suppl. 1343 [1882]; [D]HESS, *Gnost. Pap.* 16 [1892].

ⲧⲟϭⲥ (Crum 407a), ‘a thing firmly fixed, seat’ = [demotic] (Er. 660, 5), *tks*, ‘throne, chair’. The resemblance with Greek θᾶκος, θῶκος, ‘chair’ (Dévaud’s slip) is purely accidental.

GRIFFITH, *Dem. Graffiti Dodekaschoinos*, I, 190, no. 392 [1937] (with doubt); ERICHSEN, *Dem. Glossar*, 660, 5 [1954].

See also **ⲧⲕⲁⲥ** ‘pain’.

ⲧⲕⲁⲥ (Crum 407a), ‘pain’, from **ⲧⲱⲕⲥ**, ‘pierce’, see the latter, especially XIXth Dyn. *tks*, ‘to torture’, ‘to pain’.

ϯ ⲧⲕⲁⲥ (Crum 407b), ‘give pain’, when meaning ‘have pain’ probably through assimilation from ***ϫⲓ ⲧⲕⲁⲥ**.

[B]**ⲧⲁⲕⲧⲟ** (Crum 407b), ‘put, go around’, from **ϯ** ‘cause’ + **ⲕⲱⲧⲉ** ‘go round’. For Sa‘îdic, see **ⲕⲧⲟ**.

STEINDORFF, *Kopt. Gr.* 1st ed. 109, §238 [1894].

ⲧⲁⲗ (Crum 408a), ‘heap, hillock’? = [hieroglyphs] (*Wb.* v, 384, 6), *tnr*, ‘a place where vegetables grow’, a loan-word from Semitic, cf. Arabic تَلّ, Hebrew תֵּל, ‘mound’.

[H]ERMAN-GRAPOW, *Wb.* v, 384, 6 [1931]; [S]ROSSI, *Etym. Aeg.* 62 [1808].

[F]**ⲧⲁⲗⲁⲧⲏⲗ**, ‘heap, hillock’, from Semitic, cf. New Hebrew תַּלְתַּל*, plural תַּלְתַּלִּים (Gesenius s.v. תל), ‘hill’.

DÉVAUD’s slip.

ⲧⲁⲗⲟ (Crum 408a), ‘lift, offer up, set on’ = *[hieroglyphs], *dit ‘r*, lit. ‘cause to ascend’ (*i‘r*, *Wb.* I, 41, 15 f.); [demotic], *ty-‘l‘yṱ* (= Qual. **ⲧⲁⲗⲏⲟⲩⲧ**), ‘mounted (on horseback)’.

[H]ERMAN, *ZÄS* 22, 36 [1884]; cf. SETHE, *De aleph prosthetico*, 36 [1892]; [D]GRIFFITH–THOMPSON, III, 12, no. 109a [1909].

Bⲧⲓⲗⲓ (Crum 409b), 'fenugreek', *Trigonella foenum graecum* L. = (not in Er.; P. BM 10516, 3 unpublished), *tlꜣ* < Gk. τῆλις.
KEIMER in *BIFAO* 28, 84 and n. [1929].

ⲧⲱⲗⲕ (Crum 410a), 'pluck out' = (Er. 649, 7), *ṯlg*, 'loosen'.
MÖLLER, *Rhind*, 60*, no. 427 [1913].

ⲧⲉⲗⲏⲗ (Crum 410a), 'rejoice' = (Er. 590, 3, reads *gll*), *tll*, 'rejoice', from Semitic תִּלֵּל*, (הִלֵּל)?
DREVILLOUT in *Rev. ég.* 14, 14 n. 6 [1912]; SSETHE, *Verbum*, I, 10, §11 [1899] and Spiegelberg, *Kopt. Handwb.* 144 [1921].
NB. The reading *tll* initiated by Revillout and adopted by Spiegelberg, *Mythus*, p. 30, is acc. to Shore at least as justifiable as *gll*, Spiegelberg, *op. cit.* p. 34, and 84, nos. 886 and 887, followed by Erichsen.

Sⲧⲱⲗⲙ, Bⲑⲱⲗⲉⲃ (Crum 410b), 'be defiled, besmirched, defile', connected with Gr.-R. (*Wb.* v, 312, 9), *tnm*, 'dirt (which is washed off)'.
HBRUGSCH, *Wb.* 1646 [1868].

ⲧⲗⲟⲙ, ⲧⲏⲟⲙ (Crum 411a), 'furrow' = (*Wb.* v, 312, 8), *tnm*, 'furrow' probably < (*Wb.* v, 381, 8), *ṯnm*, 'cauldron, hole' or sim., from Semitic, cf. Hebrew תֶּלֶם, 'furrow'; Arabic تَلَم.
HLANGE, *Amenemope*, 49 [1925]; SLACROZE, *Lexicon*, 23 [1775]; cf. Rossi, *Etym. Aeg.* 66 [1808].

ⲧⲗⲧⲗ (Crum 411a), 'drip, let drop'.
ⲧⲗϯⲗⲉ (Crum 411b), 'a drop' = (Er. 649, 8), *tltlt*, 'a drop'.
BRUGSCH, *Gr. dém.* 33, §66 [1855].

ⲧⲁⲗϭⲟ (Crum 411b), 'make to cease, heal' (causative of ⲗⲁϭⲉ) = (Er. 264, 6), *ty* (ꜥ)*lg*, 'cause to stop' (from , *lg*, 'to cease').
SETHE, *Verbum*, 93, §212 [1899]; DGRIFFITH-THOMPSON, III, 54, no. 528 [1909].

Fⲧⲁⲉⲓⲙ (Crum 412a), 'to help' = (Er. 607, 10), *tym*, 'protect'.
SPIEGELBERG in *Sitzber. bayer. Ak.* 1925, Abh. 4, 15 [1925]; cf. Sottas, *Revue de l'Ég. anc.* I, 231 [1927].

ⲧⲙ- (Crum 412a), negation of infinitive, etc. = (*Wb.* v, 302, 5 f.), *tm*, negation of certain verbal forms; (Er. 629, 3), *tm*, same.
[H]CHAMPOLLION, *Gr.* 446 (§289, 4°) [1836]; [D]BRUGSCH, *Gr. dém.* 149, §§294–5; 152, §299; 186, §375 [1855].

ⲧⲟⲙ (Crum 412b), masc., 'mat' of reeds = (*Wb.* v, 307, 2–9), *tmꜣ*, 'mat'; (Er. 631, 3), *tm*, 'mat'.
[H]ERMAN-GRAPOW, *Wb.* v, 307, 2 [1931]; [D]GRIFFITH, *Stories*, 148 note [1900].
NB. This masc. word is to be distinguished from fem. ⲧⲙⲏ; see this latter.

ⲧⲱⲙ (Crum 412b), 'to shut' = (*Wb.* v, 308, 5 f.), *tmm*, 'to shut'; (Er. 631, 4), *tm*, 'to shut'.
[H]BIRCH in *Archaeologia* 35, 132 n. k (ad *Urk.* IV, 752, 14) [1853]; [D]ERICHSEN, *Dem. Glossar*, 631, 4 [1954].

ⲧⲱⲙ (Crum 413a), 'be sharp, sharpen' = (*Wb.* v, 448, 7 f.), *dm*, 'sharpen, make pointed'; (Er. 632, 1), *tm*, 'sharpen'.
[H]BRUGSCH, *Wb.* 1636 [1868]; [D]SPIEGELBERG, *Petubastis*, p. 66*, no. 465 [1910].

ⲧⲁⲙⲟ (Crum 413b), 'tell, inform' (causative of ⲉⲓⲙⲉ) = L.Eg. (*Wb.* I, 184, 22), *dỉt ꜥm·*, 'announce', lit. 'cause to know'.
BRUGSCH, *Wb.* 188 [1867].

ϯⲙⲉ (Crum 414a), 'village' = (*Wb.* v, 455, 6 ff.), *dmy*, 'locality'; (Er. 632, 6), *tmy (dmy)*, 'town, village'.
[H]DE ROUGÉ, *Oeuv. div.* IV (= *Bibl. ég.* XXIV), 141 n. 2 [1861]; [D]KRALL, *Mitt. Erzh. Rainer*, VI, 54 and 77, no. 334 [1897].

ⲧⲱⲱⲙⲉ (Crum 414b), 'join' (trans. and intr.) = (*Wb.* v, 453, 6 f.), *dmy*, 'touch, join'; (Er. 631, 2), *tm*, 'join, clothe'.
[H]DE ROUGÉ, *Oeuv. div.* IV (= *Bibl. ég.* XXIV), 125 and 141 n. 2 [1861]; [D]SPIEGELBERG in *Rec. trav.* 35, 161 [1913].
Qual. ⲧⲟ(ⲟ)ⲙⲉ, 'be fitting, appropriate', cf. , impersonal, with , *n* (*Wb.* v, 455, 1), 'it is fitting for'.
SETHE, *Untersuchungen*, v, 81 [1909].

ⲧⲱⲱⲙⲉ (Crum 415a), fem., 'purse, wallet' = (*Wb.* v, 307, 15–17), *tmꜣ*, masc., 'sack' for grain.

BRUGSCH, *Wb.*, Suppl. 1328 [1882] (though comparing *tmꜣyt*).

[A]ⲧⲱⲙⲉⲥ, 'purse, wallet' = (Er. 633, 1), *tms*, 'hatch' of the boat, belongs more probably to ⲧⲱⲙⲥ, 'bury' (or ⲧⲱⲙ, 'to shut'?).

ERICHSEN, *Dem. Lesestücke*, I, 2, 87 [1937].

ⲧⲙⲁ(ⲉ)ⲓⲟ (Crum 415b), 'justify, praise' = *, *dỉt mꜣꜥ·*, 'cause to become just'; (Er. 149, lower), *ty mꜣꜥ*, 'justify'.

[H]STEINDORFF, *Kopt. Gr.* 1st ed. 112, §244 [1894]; [D]SETHE, *Demot. Urkunden*, 277 and 358 [1920].

ⲧⲙⲏ (Crum 415b), 'mat' of reeds = (*Wb.* v, 307, 10. 11), *tmꜣyt*, 'mat'; (Er. 631, 3), *tmỉt*, 'mat'. Acc. to Vycichl, *ZÄS* 85, 72 ⲧⲙⲏ is a collective of ⲧⲟⲙ, 'mat'.

[H]ERMAN-GRAPOW, *Wb.* v, 307, 10 [1931]; cf. Maspero, *Ét. ég.* I, 90 note [1880] (deriving ⲧⲙⲏ inaccurately from *tmꜣ*); [D]HESS, *Gnost. Pap.* 16 [1892].

ⲧⲉⲙⲑⲁⲙ (Crum 416a), 'mule' = , *tmṯm*, in , *nꜣ ꜥꜣw n ṯmṯm* (O. Turin, Cat. 2167, 1), 'the donkeys of *ṯmṯm*', where *ṯmṯm* is a receptacle for grain, (*Wb.* v, 371, 2), *ṯmṯm*.

ⲧⲙⲙⲟ (Crum 416a), 'feed, nourish' (causative of ⲟⲩⲱⲙ) = , *dỉt wnm·* (de Rougé, *I.H.*, Pl. 158, 16; also P. Orb. 1, 9; O. DM 412, 3; 428, 2; *LRL* 8, 3, etc.), lit. 'cause to eat'; , *ty wnm*, 'cause to eat'.

[H]SETHE, *De aleph prosthetico*, 33 [1892]; cf. Stern, *Kopt. Gr.* 157, §328 [1880]; [D]GRIFFITH–THOMPSON, III, 19, no. 194 [1909].

ⲧⲱⲙⲥ (Crum 416a), 'bury' = Late Egn. (*Wb.* v, 369, 6), *ṯms*, 'bury'; (Er. 633, 1), *tms*, 'bury'.

[H]GARDINER, *Egn. Hieratic Texts*, I, 27 n. 22 [1911]; [D]BRUGSCH, *Gr. dém.* 33, §65 [1855].

ⲧⲱⲙⲧ (Crum 416b), 'meet, befall' = (*Wb.* v, 457, 4 f.), *dmḏ*, 'join together'; (Er. 634, 1), *tmt*, 'join together', possibly fused with (Er. 631, 2), *tm*, which is > ⲧⲱⲱⲙⲉ.

[H]PLEYTE in *ZÄS* 3, 53 [1865]; [D]Not identified.

ⲧⲱⲙⲧ (Crum 416b), 'be amazed, stupefied' = 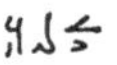 (Er. 634, 3), *tmṯ*, 'deceive, confuse, be embarrassed'.

BRUGSCH in *ZÄS* 26, 32 [1888].

[O]ⲧⲙⲉⲧ (*JEA* 28, 26, 47), [A2]ⲧⲙⲉⲧ (Mani Keph. 128, 3; 135, 3; 162, 29; Ps. 154, 15–16 and 203, 17), mostly in connection with [O]ⲉⲛⲉϩ, [A2]ⲁⲛⲏϩⲉ, 'eternity' =  (*Wb.* v, 460, 5 f.), *dmḏ*, 'totality;  (Er. 634, 2), *dmḏ*, 'total'.

VOLTEN in *Studia Orientalia Ioanni Pedersen...oblata*, 364–5 [1953].

ⲧⲙⲧⲙ (Crum 417a), 'be heavy, oppressed, strike upon, resound' =   (*Wb.* v, 309, 7. 8), *tmtm*, 'crush' (a medicament) > Late 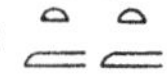 (*Wb.* v, 309, 10), *tmtm*, 'annul'.

ⲧⲙϩⲟ (Crum 417a), 'set on fire, kindle' (causative of ⲙⲟⲩϩ) = *, *dit mꜣḫ·*, 'cause to burn'; 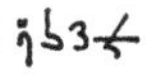 (Er. 177, 4), *ty mḫ*, 'cause to burn'.

[H]STEINDORFF, *Kopt. Gr.* 1st ed. 107, §234 [1894]; [D]GRIFFITH–THOMPSON, III, 38, no. 391 [1909].

-ⲧⲛ, suffix 2nd pers. pl. =  (*Wb.* v, 371, 14, 15), *·tn*, < 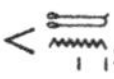, *·ṯn*, 'your';  (Er. 634, 4), *·tn*.

[H]CHAMPOLLION, *Gr. ég.* 261 [1836]; [D]BRUGSCH, *Scriptura Aeg. dem.* 32–3 [1848].

ⲧⲛ-, prefix of 1st per. pl. of 1st Present = L.Eg.  (*Wb.* v, 246, middle), *tw·n*, 'we' as subject in sentences with adverbial predicate; , 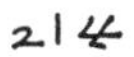 and sim. (Er. 609, bottom), *tw·n*.

[HD]MASPERO, *Des formes de la conjugaison*, 14, 43, 60 [1871].

ⲧⲱⲛ (Crum 417b), 'where?' =  (*Wb.* v, 373, 1 ff.), *ṯny*, 'where, wherefrom, whereto?';  (Er. 634, 5), *tn*, 'where(from)?'.

[H]GOODWIN in Chabas, *Mél. égyptol.* I, 81–2 [1862]; [D]REVILLOUT, *Pap. mor.* II, 50 n. 4 [1908].

ⲧⲏⲛⲉ (Crum 418b), 'dam, dyke' =  (*Wb.* v, 465, 1), fem., *dnyt*, 'dam' > L.Eg.  (*Wb.* v, 465, 4), masc., *dny*, Gr.-R. 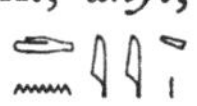 (*Wb.* v, 465, 3), masc., *dny*, 'dam as limit of fields';  (Er. 637, 3), masc., *tn*, 'dam'.

[H]VOGELSANG, *Komm. Bauer*, 174 [1913]; [D]LEXA, *Mél. Maspero*, I, 404 [1938].

S-ⲧⲏⲛⲟⲩ, B-ⲑⲏⲛⲟⲩ, A-ⲧⲏⲛⲉ, suffix of 2nd pers. pl. = , *ṯnw*, (Saite Period; *Wb.* v, 371, 16, 17), *tnw*, suffix of 2nd pers. pl., also as abs. pronoun (*Wb.* v, 371, 6), (Er. 640, 3), *tnw*, suffix of 2nd pers. pl.
HSTERN, *Kopt. Gr.* 47, §89 [1880]; DGRIFFITH, *Rylands*, III, 405 [1909].

ⲧⲏⲛⲟ (Crum 419a), 'pound, tread down' = *, *dỉt nꜥꜥ*, 'to cause to become fine, smooth' (for *nꜥꜥ*, see *Wb.* II, 208, 2 f.; for the meaning 'smooth', cf. Gardiner, *Hierat. Papyri in the Brit. Mus., Third Series*, Text, 41 n. 5; 49 n. 1); (Er. 208, 1), *ty-nꜥ*, 'grind finely, pound'.
DGRIFFITH–THOMPSON, III, 4, no. 432 [1909].

ⲧⲏⲛⲟⲟⲩ (Crum 419b), 'send' = (e.g. Wenamūn 2, 39), *dỉt ỉn·w*, 'cause that they should bring'; (Er. 33, bottom), *ty ỉn·w*, same.
SETHE in Spiegelberg, *Kopt. Handwb.* 148 [1921].

ⲧⲟⲛⲧⲛ (Crum 420a), 'be like, liken' = ?reduplication of *, *ṯny*, from which (causative?) (*Wb.* IV, 359, 9), *sṯny*, 'bear comparison with'.
DÉVAUD's slip (Dévaud draws attention to Arabic ثَنَّ, 'compare'; ثِنّ, 'similar, equal'); 'estimate, speculate' = reduplication of (*Wb.* v, 374, 1 f.), *ṯny*, 'lift up, distinguish'.

ⲧⲛϩ (Crum 421a), 'wing' of birds, angels, etc. = (*Wb.* v, 577, 6), *ḏnḥ*, 'wing'; (Er. 640, 9), *tnḥ*, 'wing'.
HCHAMPOLLION, *Précis*, 2nd ed. 125–6 [1828]; DBRUGSCH, *Gr. dém.* 41, §90 [1855].

(ⲧⲱⲛϩ), ⲧⲟⲛϩ⸗ (Crum 421a), Qual. ⲧⲁⲛϩ (Mani Ps.) 'entangle, be in converse with' = (*Wb.* v, 578, 8, 9), *ḏnḥ*, 'seize (birds) by wings, seize'.
SPIEGELBERG in *Rec. trav.* 26, 36 [1904].

ⲧⲁⲛϩⲟ (Crum 421a), 'make, keep alive' (causative of ⲱⲛϩ) = , *dỉt ꜥnḫ·*, 'cause to live'; (Er. 63, middle), *ty ꜥnḫ·*, 'keep alive'.
HDBRUGSCH, *Wb.* 198 [1867].

ⲧⲛⲁϩⲥⲟ, ⲧⲛⲁϩⲥⲉ- (not in Crum; ex. Mani Hom. 32, 5) 'arouse', causative of ⲛⲉϩⲥⲉ = *, *dỉt nhs·*, 'cause to awake'.
ALLBERRY, *A Manichean Psalm-Book*, Part II, Index, p. 27* [1938].

ⲧⲁⲛϩⲟⲩⲧ (Crum 421 b), 'trust, believe', connected with **ⲛⲁϩⲧⲉ**, see the latter.

ⲧⲁⲡ (Crum 422 a), 'horn' = (*Wb.* v, 434, 3), *db*, 'horn'; (Er. 625, 5), *tp*, 'horn'.

[H]BRUGSCH, *Wb.* 1628 [1868]; [D]BRUGSCH, *De natura*, 32 [1850].

ⲧⲟⲡ (Crum 422 a), 'edge, end, border of garment' = (Er. 625, 6), *tp*, 'edge of garment'.

STRICKER in *Oudheidkundige Mededelingen*, N.S. 29, 76 n. 1 [1948].

ⲧⲱⲡ (Crum 422 b), 'stitch, stop, caulk' = (not in *Wb.*), *tp*, 'to stitch', also spelt ; (not in Er.), *tp*, 'to stitch'.

[H]ČERNÝ in *Festschrift Grapow*, 33 [1955]; [D]PARKER in *JEA* 26, 93 [1940].

ⲙⲉϩⲧⲱⲡ, ⲙⲁϩⲛⲧⲱⲡ (Kasser, *Pap. Bodmer*, XIX, p. 37) and ϩⲁⲙⲛⲧⲱⲡ 'needle' = (Er. 174, 2), *mḥ-n-tp*, 'needle', but probably through metathesis and simplification from *ϩⲟⲙⲛⲧ + ⲛ + ⲧⲱⲡ, 'copper for (lit. 'of') sawing' as suggested by ϩⲁⲙⲛⲧⲱⲡ < ϩⲁⲙⲛ⟨ⲧ⟩ⲧⲱⲡ.

GRIFFITH–THOMPSON, III, 39, no. 394 [1909].

ⲧⲱ(ⲱ)ⲡ (Crum 422 b), 'be accustomed, accustom' = (Er. 626, 1), *tp*, 'accustom'.

ERICHSEN, *Dem. Glossar*, 626, 1 [1954].

Probably identical with ⲧⲱⲡⲉ, 'to taste'; see this.

ϯⲡⲉ (Crum 423 a), 'loins' = (*Wb.* v, 445, 13 f.), *dpt*, a double part of body, 'loins'.

DÉVAUD, *Étymologies coptes*, 18–20 [1922]; cf. LEFÉBURE, *Oeuv. div.* III (= *Bibl. ég.* XXVI), 205 = *Sphinx* 2, 81) [1898] (with doubts).

ⲧⲱⲡⲉ (Crum 423 a), 'to taste' = (*Wb.* v, 443, 7 f.), *dp*, 'to taste'; (Er. 625, 4), *tp*, 'to taste'.

[H]CHABAS, *Voyage*, 131–2 [1866]; [D]GRIFFITH–THOMPSON, III, 93, no. 1007 [1909].

ϯⲡⲉ, subst. 'taste' = (*Wb.* v, 444, 16 f.), *dpt*, subst. 'taste'; < (Er. 628, 3), *tpyt*, subst. 'taste'.

[H]BRUGSCH, *Wb.* 1634 [1868]; [D]SPIEGELBERG, *Mythus*, 298, no. 921 [1917].

ⲧⲡⲉ (Brugsch, *Wb.*, Suppl. 827–8; Spiegelberg, *Kopt. Handwb.* 148, and *Kopt. Etym.* 23), 'head'—non-existent. The word is **ⲧ-ⲡⲉ**, 'the sky'. **ⲉ-ⲧⲡⲉ**, lit. 'to the sky, upwards' became substantivized (hence **ⲡⲉⲧⲡⲉ**, **ⲉⲡⲉⲩⲉⲧⲡⲉ**) with the meaning 'the above, top'. See parallel development of **ⲉⲡⲓⲧⲛ** under **ⲉⲓⲧⲛ**.

CRUM, *A Coptic Dict.* 260a, top [1932].

ⲧⲁⲡ(ⲉ)ⲛ (Crum 423a), 'cumin' =  (*Wb.* v, 296, 9, 10), *tpnn*, 'cumin'.

EBERS in *Papyros Ebers*, I, 18 [1875]; STERN in *Papyros Ebers*, Gloss. 49 [1875].

ⲧⲁⲡⲣⲟ (Crum 423b), fem., 'mouth' =  (*Wb.* v, 287, 4 f.), *tp-rỉ* and 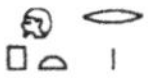 (*Wb.* v, 287, 13 f.), *tpt-rỉ*, 'utterance'.

BIRCH, *ZÄS* 2, 93 n. 7 [1864]; BRUGSCH, *Matér. cal.* 49–50 [1864].

[S]**ⲧⲁⲯⲁⲧⲉ**, **ⲧⲁⲡⲥⲟⲧⲉ**, [F]**ⲧⲁⲩⲥⲁϯ**, **ⲗⲁⲟⲩⲥⲁϯ** (exx. *JEA* 46, 111–12), farmer's name of the month Epēp (25 June to 24 July jul.) = probably **ⲧⲁⲡ-ⲥⲁⲧⲉ**, 'horn of Sirius', the name of Sirius  (*Wb.* IV, 111, 9 f.), *Spdt*, was later pronounced *sŏte* or *săte* (cf. Gk. Σῶθις; Sethe in *ZÄS* 50, 80). The heliacal rising of Sirius fell within this month (on 19 July) and coincided with the beginning of the Nile inundation which brought food to the country. Sirius was early identified with goddess Isis and Graeco-Roman terracottas represent her carrying as attributes ears of corn and a horn of plenty (Weber, *Äg.-greich. Terrakotten*, Pl. 3).

ⲧⲏⲣ⸗ (Crum 424a), 'all, whole, every' =  + suffix (*Wb.* v, 589, 6 f.), *r-ḏr·*, 'all, whole', lit. 'to the frontier of';  (Er. 641, 3), *tr·(dr·)*, 'whole'.

[H]BIRCH in *Transactions of the Royal Society of Literature of the United Kingdom*, New Series 4, p. 227 n. 27 [1853, read on 14 Nov. 1850] (acc. to Brugsch, *ZDMG* 9, 207 [1855]); [D]YOUNG, *Misc. Works*, III, 26–7, no. 49 = *Mus. crit.* 6, pp. 176–7, no. 49 [1815] (letter to de Sacy of 21 Oct. 1814); BRUGSCH, *Gr. dém.* 124, §253 [1855].

ⲧⲁⲣⲉ-; **ⲧⲁⲣⲉϥ-** (Crum 424b), prefix of 'Finalis' = *  (*dỉ·ỉ ỉry·f*) + Infinitive, lit. 'I cause him to...'.

POLOTSKY, *Études de syntaxe copte*, 11 ff. [1944].

ⲧⲱⲣⲉ (Crum 424b), 'willow' = (*Wb.* v, 385, 13 f.) *ṯrt*, 'willow', *Salix safsaf* Forsk.; (Er. 647, 2), *trt*, 'willow'.

[H]BRUGSCH, *Rec. de mon.* I, 49 [1862]; [D]BRUGSCH, *Gr. dém.* 25, §44 [1855].

ⲧⲱⲣⲉ (Crum 425a), (1) 'hand' = (*Wb.* v, 580, 3 f.), *ḏrt*, > , 'hand'; (Er. 643, 1), *trt* (*drt*), 'hand'.

[H]SETHE, *ZÄS* 50, 91 [1912].

See also ϩⲙⲛⲧⲱⲣⲉ.

(2) 'spade, pick' = (Er. 647, 3), *trt*, 'hoe' or sim.; from ⲧⲱⲣⲉ the modern Eg. Arabic طورية, *ṭūrīyya* (Peyron, *Lex.* 249).

[B]ⲕⲉϩⲑⲱⲣ(ⲓ) (Crum, Add. xviii b & 425a, under ⲣ ⲧⲱⲣⲉ), ἀνακρούεσθαι, 'strike up' (in music = (*Wb.* v, 18, 8 f.), *kꜥḥ ḏrt*, 'stretch out a bent hand (i.e. arm) over offerings', lit. 'bend the hand'.

WESTENDORFF, *Kopt. Handwb.* 73 [1965].

ⲣ ⲧⲱⲣⲉ (Crum 425a), 'use hand, clap hands, stamp (with feet)' = (Er. 642, 1), *ỉr tr*, 'dance'.

SPIEGELBERG, *Mythus*, 301, no. 938 [1917].

ϣ(ⲉ)ⲡ ⲧⲱⲣⲉ (Crum 425a), 'grasp hand, undertake, be surety for' = (Er. 500 and 643), *šp trt*, 'to warrant, go bail for'.

SETHE in *ZÄS* 50, 91 and n. 2 [1912]; cf. SETHE, *Dem. Urk.* 38 [1920].

ϣ(ⲉ)ⲡ ⲧⲱⲣⲉ (Crum 427a), 'grasp hand' in greeting = + suffix (*Wb.* IV, 532, 5, 6), *šsp ḏrt*, 'grasp hand' in friendly way, also to help.

ERMAN–GRAPOW, *Wb.* IV, 532, 5 [1930].

ⲧⲟⲟⲧ⸗

[H]CHAMPOLLION, *Gr.* 93 [1836]; [D]BRUGSCH, *Gr. dém.*, 29, §56; 103, §232 [1855].

[S]ⲉⲓⲣⲉ ⲛⲁⲧⲟⲟⲧ⸗ : [B]ⲉⲣ ⲁⲩⲧⲟⲧ⸗ (Crum 426a), 'endeavour', lit. 'make one who stretches, applies (part. coni. of , *ꜣw*, cf. Sethe in *Rec. trav.* 24, 189 [1902]) (the) hand' = (Er. 57, 2), *ỉr ꜥw-trt*, 'endeavour, make an effort'; also 'stretch out hand', as sign of warning (Erichsen, *Dem. Lesest.*, Gl. 12).

[HD]SPIEGELBERG in *Rec. trav.* 23, 202–3 [1901].

[S]ϩⲁⲧⲛ-, [B]ϧⲁⲧⲉⲛ- (Crum 428b), 'under the hand of', so 'beside' = (Er. 381, top), *ẖr ṯrt n*, 'under (the) hand of'.

GRIFFITH, *Ryl.* III, 380 [1909].

ⲧⲣⲉ (Crum 429b), 'kite' = (*Wb.* v, 596, 2 f.), *ḏrt*, a bird of prey; (Er. 647, 1), *trt*, bird of prey, according to Loret (*ZÄS* 30, 29) *Milvus ater.*

HDBRUGSCH, *Wb.* 1559–60 [1868].

ⲧⲣⲟ (Crum 430a), 'cause to do' (causative of **ⲉⲓⲣⲉ**) = , *dỉt ỉry·*, 'cause...to do'; (P. Ryl. IX, 10, 16), *dỉt ỉr·*, same meaning.

HERMAN in *ZÄS* 22, 33 [1884]; DERICHSEN, *Auswahl frühdem. Texte*, 2 (Glossar), 111b [1950].

ⲧⲣⲉ-, prefix of causative infinitive = *, *dỉt ỉry·*; , *ty ỉr·*.

HDE ROUGÉ, *Chrest. égypt.* III, 96, §354 [1875]; cf. SALVOLINI, *Traduction et analyse grammaticale*, 191 [1836]; DBRUGSCH, *Gr. dém.* 192, §393 [1855].

ⲧⲣⲃⲏⲓⲛ (Crum 430a), 'papyrus plant' from Semitic, cf. Syriac ܐܪܒܢܐ.

ROSSI, *Etym. aeg.* 51 [1808].

ⲧⲁⲣⲕⲟ (Crum 430a), 'make to swear, adjure, entreat' (causative of **ⲱⲣⲕ**) = *, *dỉt ʿrḳ·*, 'cause to swear'.

STEINDORFF, *Kopt. Gr.* 1st ed. 110, §241 [1894].

ⲧⲣⲓⲙ (Crum 430b), 'trefoil, clover' = (Er. 14, 1), *ꜣtrm*, 'clover', from Gk. θέρμος, 'lupine (*Lupinus albus*)', for which see Keimer in *BIFAO* 28, 83.

Also **ⲑⲁⲣⲙⲟⲩⲥ** = (Er. 648, 5), *trmws*, Egn. Arabic تُرْمُس, cf. Hess, *Gnost. Pap.* 16 [1892].

SPIEGELBERG in *Rec. trav.* 26, 36 [1904]; CRUM in Thompson, *A Family Archive*, Index p. (90), no. 44; cf. 19 n. 67 [1934].

A2**ⲧⲣⲙⲓⲟ** (not in Crum; Mani Ps.), 'make to weep' (causative of **ⲣⲓⲙⲉ**) = , *dỉt rmy·*, 'cause to weep'; (Lexa, *Dem. Totenbuch*, 46, no. 160), *tỉ-rmy*, same meaning.

ALLBERRY, *A Manichean Psalm-Book*, Part II, Index, p. 27* [1938].

ⲧⲱⲣⲡ (Crum 430b), 'seize, rob', from Semitic, cf. Hebrew טָרַף, 'rend, pluck'.

ROSSI, *Etym. aeg.* 226 [1808].

ⲧⲱⲣⲡ (Crum 431a), 'sew, stitch' = (Er. 648, 3), *ṯrp*, 'bind, sew', from Semitic, cf. Hebrew תָּפַר, 'sew (together)'.

[D]SPIEGELBERG, *Dem. Texte auf Krügen*, 43 n. 115; 77, no. 254 [1912]; [S]ROSSI, *Etym. aeg.* 70 [1808].

ⲧⲉⲣⲡⲟⲥⲉ (Crum 431 b), 'baked brick' from *ⲧⲉⲃ-ⲡⲟⲥⲉ (von Lemm, *Kopt. Misz.* CXXI 518; Jernstedt, *ZÄS* 64 [1929], 124–5) ⲧⲱⲃⲉ + ⲡⲟⲥⲉ (Qualit. of ⲡⲓⲥⲉ) = , *tb psy*, 'baked brick'.

SPIEGELBERG, *Die dem. Papyrus der Musées royaux du Cinquantenaire*, 19 [1909].

ⲧⲣⲓⲣ (Crum 431 b), fem., 'oven' = (*Wb.* v, 318, 18), *trr*, fem., 'oven' of baker; (Er. 648, 8), *ṯrry*, 'oven'.

[H]BRUGSCH, *Wb.* 1579 (cf. p. 621, s.v. *mgꜣ*) [1868]; [D]SPIEGELBERG, *Dem. Chronik*, 88, no. 294 [1914].

ⲧⲣⲟⲩⲣ (correct reading instead of ⲧⲕⲟⲩⲣ of Crum 406 b), 'speed' = (*Wb.* v, 319, 2), *trr*, 'to run a race'.

ČERNÝ in *Festschrift Grapow*, 34 [1955].

ⲧⲣⲣⲉ (Crum 431 b), 'become afraid' = ? (*Wb.* v, 318, 1 ff.), *trỉ*, 'treat respectfully, honour'; ? (Er. 647, 7), *tryꜣ*, nn., 'fear, tremble?'.

[H]SPIEGELBERG in *Rec. trav.* 37, 20 [1915].

ⲧⲱⲣⲧ (Crum 431 b), 'staircase' = (*Wb.* v, 226, 2, 3), *tꜣ-rd*, 'ramp, staircase', lit. 'earth of (the) foot'; (Er. 649, 3), *trt*, 'staircase, terrace'.

[H]SPIEGELBERG, *Kopt. Handwb.* 151 [1921]; [D]REVILLOUT, *Setna*, 140 [1880].

ⲧⲱⲣⲧⲣ (Crum 432 a), 'ladder, step, stair' is ⲧⲱⲣⲧ interpreted as a half-reduplication and for that reason ultimately completed into ⲧⲱⲣⲧⲣ.

GARDINER, *Onom.* II, 211*, no. 434 [1947].

ⲧⲣⲟⲩⲁⲛ (Crum 432 a), 'cheese?' = prob. Gk. τυρίον, 'small cheese' (Liddel–Scott, Sophocles, Preisigke), diminutive of τυρός, 'cheese'.

CRUM, *The Monastery of Epiphanius at Thebes*, II, 217, no. 256 n. 3 [1926].

ⲧⲱⲣϣ (Crum 432 a), 'be red, red' = (*Wb.* v, 488, 1 f.), *dšr*, 'be red, red'; (Er. 658, 6), *tšr*, 'be red, red'; also , *trš*.

[H]CHAMPOLLION, *Gr.* 375 [1836]; [D]Not identified.

ⲧⲣⲟϣ, ‘become red’, same etymology as preceding.

***ⲧⲣⲱϣ**, ‘flamingo’, to be inferred from Egn. Arabic بشروش < ***ⲡⲉ-ⲧⲣⲱϣ** = (*Wb.* v, 487, 9), *dšr*, ‘flamingo’.

KUENTZ in *Bull. Soc. Ling.*, 36, 162 [1935].

ⲧⲣⲟϣⲣ(ⲉ)ϣ (Crum 432b), ‘become red’, reduplication of **ⲧⲣⲟϣ**, but بشروش, ‘flamingo’ not from this, but from ***ⲡⲉ** + **ⲧⲣⲱϣ**, see above. See also ᴮ**ⲑⲉⲣϣ**, ‘linseed’.

ⲧⲁⲣϣⲟ (Crum 432b, ‘increase, multiply’), ‘make heavy, weigh heavily’, is a subform of **ⲧϩⲣϣⲟ**, ‘make heavy’; see this latter. Omission of (initial) **ϩ** in Boh. is frequent (so also in **ⲁⲣϣⲏⲧ**) and there seems to be some confusion with **ⲁⲣⲟϣ**, ‘become cold’, which is ᴮ**ϩⲣⲟϣ**.

ⲧⲱⲣϩ (Crum 432b), ‘be keen, alert, sober, upright’, noun: **ⲧⲱϩⲣ** = (not in *Wb.*, but see Borchardt, *Sahurēʿ*, I, 125, frg. 1), *dhr*, ‘be upright’.

ᶠ**ⲧⲓⲥ** (Crum 433a), ‘give, pay, send(?)’ = **ϯ** + **ⲥ**, lit. ‘give it’ < *, *dỉt sw*. The Inf. *rdỉt* takes as pron. object the dependent pronoun in Demotic and stands then in absolute form (not in pronominal as in **ⲧⲁⲁⲥ⸗ϥ**), see Sethe, *Dem. Urk.* 28.

ⲧⲟ(ⲉ)ⲓⲥ (Crum 433a), ‘piece, rag’ of cloth, linen = (Er. 608, 5), *tys* (*dys*), ‘piece of cloth’.

BRUGSCH, *Wb.* 1597 [1868]; cf. BRUGSCH, *Gr. dém.* 39, §84 [1855].

ⲧⲱⲥ (Crum 433b), ‘become, be hard, stiff, dry; to fix’ = (*Wb.* v, 243, 2, 3), *tys*, ‘plant firmly’.

GUNN in Gardiner, *JEA* 24, 125 n. 3 [1938].

ⲧⲁⲥⲟ(?) (Crum 433b), ‘make light’ (causative of **ⲁⲥⲁⲓ**) = *, *dỉt*, **ϯ**, ‘to cause’ + , *ỉs*, **ⲁⲥⲁⲓ**, ‘to be light’.

CRUM, *A Coptic Dict.* 433b [1934].

ⲧⲥ(ⲉ)ⲓⲟ (Crum 434a), ‘make satisfied, sate’ (causative of **ⲥⲉⲓ**) = , *dỉt*, ‘to cause’ + (), *sỉy*, ‘to become sated’ (ex. Davies, *El Amarna*, v, Pl. XXIX, 10); , *tỉ sy*, ‘cause to be sated’ (exx. Spiegelberg, *Petubastis*, 51*, no. 347).

STEINDORFF, *Kopt. Gr.* 1st ed. 111, §243 [1894].

ⲧⲥⲟ (Crum 434a), 'give to drink, slake' (causative of **ⲥⲱ**) = , *dìt swr·*, 'cause to drink' (ex. de Rougé, *I.H.* 158, 16); (Er. 416, top), *ty swr* 'give to drink'.

STEINDORFF, *Kopt. Gr.* 1st ed., 108, §236 [1894].

ⲧⲥⲁⲃⲟ (Crum 434b), 'make wise, teach, show' (causative of **ⲥⲁⲃⲉ**) = *, *dìt sbꜣ·*, 'cause to learn' (the meaning 'learn' of *sbꜣ* being late; cf. *Wb.* IV, 84, 15); , *ty sbꜣ·*, 'teach' (e.g. Harpist, 2; II Kh. 6, 13; see Er. 420, lower).

[H]STEINDORFF, *Kopt. Gr.* 1st ed. 111, §244 [1894]; cf. ERMAN in *ZÄS* 22, 30 [1884]; [D]SOTTAS, *Revue ég.* N. série, 1, 130 [1919]; cf. BRUGSCH, *Die Ägyptologie*, 100 [1891].

ⲥⲃⲟ (Crum 435a), 'learn' = ?★ (*Wb.* IV, 84, 15), *sbꜣ*, 'learn' [late and insufficiently attested].

ERMAN–GRAPOW, *Wb.* IV, 84, 15 [1930]; cf. LEPSIUS, *Chronologie*, 49 n. 1 [1848].

ⲧⲥⲃⲕⲟ (Crum 435b), 'make small, diminish' (causative of **ⲥⲃⲟⲕ**) = *, *ty sbḳ·*, 'cause to become small'.

STEINDORFF, *Kopt. Gr.* 1st ed. 109, §240 [1894].

ⲧⲥⲁⲛⲟ (Crum 435b), 'adorn, set in order, provide' = *, *dìt sꜥn·*, 'cause to become beautiful', *sꜥn* (*Wb.* IV, 46, 1–3) itself being an *s*-causative of , *ꜥn*, 'to become beautiful'.

STEINDORFF, *Kopt. Gr.* 1st ed. 111, §244 [1894].

ⲧⲥ(ⲉ)ⲛⲕⲟ (Crum 435b), 'to give suck' (causative of **ⲥⲱⲛⲕ**) = *, *dìt snḳ·*, 'cause to suck'.

STEINDORFF, *Kopt. Gr.* 1st ed. 109, §240 [1894].

(ⲧ)ⲥⲧⲟ (Crum 436a), 'bring, pay back, repeat' (causative of **ⲥⲱⲧ(ⲉ)**) = *, *, *dìt stꜣ*, 'cause to return'.

ERMAN in *ZÄS* 22, 30 [1884].

ⲧⲥⲟⲩⲧⲥⲟⲩ (Crum 437b), 'twitter' = **ϫⲟⲩϫⲟⲩ**, see this. For **ⲧⲥ : ϫ**, cf. e.g. **ⲟⲗⲟⲕⲟⲧⲥⲓ** = **ⲗⲟⲩⲕⲟϫⲓ**.

[O]**ⲧⲁⲧ** (Griffith–Thompson, III, [132], nos. 478, 479) = (*Wb.* V, 626, 11), *ḏd*, the *djed*-pillar; (Er. 617, 4), *twtw*, holy pillar of Osiris.

^{H}GRIFFITH in *ZÄS* 46, 124–5 [1909]; ^{D}MÖLLER, *Pap. Rhind*, 65*, no. 458 [1913].

ⲧⲟⲉⲓⲧ (Crum 437b), 'mourn' = (Er. 608, 12), *tyṯ*, 'shout, mourn'.
BRUGSCH, *Wb.* 1603 [1868].

ⲧⲱⲧ (Crum 437b), 'be joined, persuaded, agreeable; agree to; content heart', etc. = , *twt*, in (*Wb.* v, 258, 23), *twt ỉb*, 'heart is agreeable (with)'; (Er. 617, 2), *twtw*, 'rejoice'.
^{H}DÉVAUD, *Études*, 20–2 [1922]; ^{D}ERICHSEN, *Dem. Glossar*, 617, 2 [1954].

ϯϯ (Crum 439a), vb. 'tread(?)' as fuller = (*Wb.* v, 244, 3 f.), *tyty*, 'tread upon'.
DÉVAUD in Crum, *A Coptic Dict.* 439a [1934].

(ⲧⲧⲟ), (ⲧ)ⲧⲉ-, (ⲧ)ⲧⲟ⸗ (Crum 439b), 'make give, require' (causative of ϯ) = , *dỉt dỉ·*, 'cause to give' (e.g. Eskhons 6, 17); (Er. 605, lower), *ty tw·*, 'make give'.
SETHE, *Nachr. Gess. Wiss. Göttingen*, 1919, 139f. [1919]; cf. SPIEGELBERG, *Kopt. Etym.* 15–16 [1920].

ⲧⲉⲧⲛ-, prefix of 2nd person plural of 1st Present = (*Wb.* v, 246, middle), *tw·tn*, dependent pers. pronoun of 2nd person plural; (Er. 609, lower), *tw·tn*.
^{HD}MASPERO, *Des formes de la conjugaison*, 14, 43, 59 [1871].

^{B}ⲧⲁⲧϩⲟ (Crum 439b), 'impede, restrain' (causative of ⲱⲧϩ) = *, *dỉt ỉtḥ·*, 'cause to drag'.

ⲧⲏⲩ (Crum 439b), 'wind' = (*Wb.* v, 350, 12 f.), *ṯꜣw* > , *t(ꜣ)w* (already *CT* III, 208d; 209c), 'air, breath, wind'; (Er. 669, 9), *ṯꜣw*, 'breath, wind'.
^{H}PIERRET, *Voc. hiér.* 738 [1875]; cf. W. MAX MÜLLER, *ZÄS* 24, 86–7 [1886]; ^{D}REVILLOUT, *Poème*, 69 [1885].
ⲁⲛϣ-ⲧⲏⲩ, ⲁⲛ(ⲁ)ϩ-ⲧⲏⲩ (Crum 440a), 'take breath' = ⲱⲛϩ, 'live' (prob. in Part. coni.) + ⲧⲏⲩ, 'wind, breath', lit. 'living as to breath', cf. (*Wb.* v, 351, 18), *ꜥnḫ m ṯꜣw*, 'live on breath'.
GRIFFITH–THOMPSON, I, 20, n. on l. 3 [1904].

ⲥⲁⲣⲁⲑⲏⲟⲩ (Crum 440a), 'whirlwind' < ***ⲥⲁⲣⲑⲏⲟⲩ**, lit. 'scatterer of wind', from **ⲥⲱⲣ**, 'scatter, spread' + **ⲑⲏⲟⲩ**.

ϫⲓⲛⲧⲏⲩ (Crum 440b), 'blight' from parching wind = (*Wb.* v, 534, 1), *ḏʿ n ṯꜣw*, 'windy storm', lit. 'storm of wind'. **ϫⲓ-** from [A]**ϫⲟ**, 'tempest', see this latter.

SPIEGELBERG, *Kopt. Etym.* 55 [1922].

ϯⲟⲩ (Crum 440b), 'five', fem. **ϯⲉ** = (*Wb.* v, 420, 9 f.), *dyw*, 'five'; fem. , *dyt*.

SETHE in *ZÄS* 62, 60 [1927]; cf. Sidney Smith and Gadd in *JEA* 11, 236 [1925].

ⲧⲟⲟⲩ (Crum 440b), 'mountain' = (*Wb.* v, 541, 7 ff.), *ḏw*, 'mountain'; (Er. 611, 3), *tw*, 'mountain, desert'.

[H]CHAMPOLLION, *Gr.* 100 [1836]; [D]BRUGSCH, *Gr. dém.* 26, §52 [1855]. For plural **ⲧⲟⲩ(ⲉ)ⲓⲏ**, cf. ? , *ḏwwt kmwt*, 'black mountains'? ERMAN-GRAPOW, *Wb.* v, 545, 2 [1931].

ⲧⲟⲟⲩ (Crum 441b), 'buy' = * , *dỉt dỉ·w*, 'cause that they should give'.

SETHE, *Nachr. Gess. Wiss. Göttingen* 1919, 142–4 [1919]; SPIEGELBERG, *Kopt. Etym.* 15–16 [1920].

ⲧⲁ(ⲟ)ⲩⲟ (Crum 441b), 'send; produce; proclaim, account' = * , *dỉt ỉw·* 'cause to go'; (Er. 20, bottom), *ty ỉw·w*, 'send; proclaim, account'.

[HD]HESS, *Stne*, 143 [1888].

ⲧⲟⲟⲩⲉ (Crum 443b), 'shoe', pair of shoes = (*Wb.* v, 247, 5 f.), *twt* (*twy*), pl., 'sandals'; (Er. 611, 4), *tw*, masc., 'sandal'.

[H]SCHWARTZE in Bunsen, *Geschichte*, I, 589 [1845]; [D]SPIEGELBERG in *Rec. trav.* 30, 155 [1908].

ⲧⲟⲩⲟ (Crum 443b), 'show, teach' = * , *dỉt wbꜣ·*, 'cause to open', for *wbꜣ*, 'open = make accessible (an information)', cf. *Wb.* I, 291, 7.

SPIEGELBERG, *Kopt. Handwb.* 155 [1921].

ⲧⲟⲩ(ⲉ)ⲓⲟ (Crum 444a), 'remove, wean' (causative of **ⲟⲩⲉ**) = *, *dỉt wꜣy·*, 'cause to become distant'; (Er. 78, middle), *ty wy·*, 'allow to be removed'.

ᴴSTEINDORFF, *Kopt. Gr.* 1st ed. 111, §243 [1894]; ᴰBRUGSCH, *Wb.* 245 [1867].

ⲧⲟⲩⲱ⸗ (Crum 444b), 'bosom'. The meaning 'bosom' is perhaps secondary, and the word is identical with Gr.-R. (*Wb.* v, 250, 13), *twꜣt*, 'leg', lit. 'support (of the body)'.

ⲉⲧⲟⲩⲛ-, ⲉⲧⲟⲩⲱ⸗, 'besides, at, with' = (Er. 612, 1), *r twn·*, 'next to, at';

ˢ**ϩⲁⲧⲟⲩⲱ⸗**, ᴮ**ϧⲁⲑⲟⲩⲱ⸗**, 'beside, at with' = , *ḫr tw·w*, 'beside'.

ϩⲓⲧⲟⲩⲛ-, ϩⲓⲧⲟⲩⲱ⸗, 'beside, next' = , *ḥr-twn-*, , *ḥr-tw·f*, 'near, at, beside'.

GRIFFITH, *PSBA* 18, 105 [1896]; cf. Griffith, *Stories*, 132 [1900] (deriving the word ultimately from **ⲧⲟⲟⲩⲉ**, 'sandals').

(**ⲧⲟⲩⲕⲟ**), **ⲧⲟⲩⲕⲉ-, ⲧⲟⲩⲕⲟ⸗, ⲧⲟⲩⲕⲱ⸗** (P. Bodmer XXI, p. 25), 'send', (ἐξ)-αποστέλλειν, see (**ⲧⲃ̄ⲕⲟ**), **ⲧⲃ̄ⲕⲉ-**, 'send'.

ⲧⲱⲟⲩⲛ (Crum 445a), 'arise; raise, carry' = (*Wb.* v, 431, 1 ff.), *dwn*, 'stretch out', etc.; (Er. 614, 3), *twn*, 'arise'.

ᴴCHAMPOLLION, *Gr.* 383 [1836]; ᴰBRUGSCH, *Wb.* 1619 [1868].

(**ⲧⲟⲩⲛⲟ**), **ⲧⲟⲩⲛ** (Crum 446b), 'make to open' (causative of **ⲟⲩⲱⲛ**), only in **ⲧⲟⲩⲛⲉⲓⲁⲧ** (see under **ⲉⲓⲁ**) and in **ⲧⲟⲩⲛⲟⲥ** (see the next entry).

ⲧⲟⲩⲛⲟⲥ (Crum 446b), 'wake, raise, set up' = *, *dỉt wn·s*, 'cause that it opens', where **-ⲥ** < , *·s*, refers to the feminine , *ỉrt*, 'eye', which is to be supplied. Compare **ⲧⲟⲩⲛⲉⲓⲁⲧ⸗** under **ⲉⲓⲁ**, 'eye'.

SETHE, *ZÄS* 47, 145–6 [1910]. For an alternative etymology (**ϯ**+**ⲧⲱⲟⲩⲛ** with **-ⲥ** originally a reflexive object *sw*), see STRICKER, *Oudheidkundige Mededelingen*, N.S. 29, 81 n. 3 [1948].

ⲧⲟⲩⲟⲥ (not in Crum; Mani Ps.), 'point of spear', see under **ⲧⲱⲃ̄ⲥ**, 'prick, goad, incite'.

ⲧⲟⲩⲱⲧ (Crum 447a), 'idol, pillar' = (*Wb.* v, 255, 8 f.), *twt*, 'statue, image'; (Er. 616, 1), *twtw*, 'statue' and sim.

HCHAMPOLLION, *Gr.* 76 [1836]; DBRUGSCH, *Scriptura Aeg. dem.* 22, §30 [1848].

ⲧⲟⲟⲩⲧⲉ (Crum 447b), 'gather, collect' = (*Wb.* v, 259, 5 f.), *twt*, 'gather, be gathered'; (Er. 616, 2), *twtw*, 'collect, gather, be gathered'.

HBRUGSCH, *Wb.* 1531 [1868]; DDE ROUGÉ, *Mém. sur l'inscription du tombeau d'Ahmès*, 177 n. 1 (read in 1849) [1851] (= *Oeuv. div.* II [= *Bibl. ég.* XXII], 183 n. 1).

ⲧⲏⲩⲧⲛ, suffix of 2nd person plural = (*Wb.* v, 247, 2, 3), *twtn*, dep. pers. pronoun of 2nd person plural (as object after *sḏm·f* and Imperative); (Er. 609, lower), *twtn*.

HERMAN, *Äg. gr.* 3rd ed. 83, §149 [1911] (with doubt); cf. Steindorff, *Lehrbuch*, 44, §82, Anm. [1951] (also with doubt); DLEXA, *Dem. Totb.* 22 (ad II, 30) [1910].

Bⲧⲟⲩϩⲟ (Crum 448b), 'add' (causative of ⲟⲩⲱϩ) = , *dỉt wꜣḥ·*, 'cause to stay' (ex. Gardiner, *LEM*, 81, 12).

STEINDORFF, *Kopt. Gr.* 1st ed. 108, §236 [1894].

ⲧⲟⲩϫⲟ (Crum 448b), 'make whole, save', causative of ⲟⲩϫⲁⲓ = * , *dỉt wḏꜣ·*, 'cause to become safe'; (Er. 108, 2), *ty wḏꜣ·*, 'to save, to free'.

HSTEINDORFF, *Kopt. Gr.* 1st ed. 108, §236 [1894]; DBRUGSCH, *Wb.* 313 [1867].

ⲧⲱϣ (Crum 449b), 'be boundary, be fixed, be moderate', etc. = (*Wb.* v, 236, 15 f.), *tꜣš*, 'limit, divide'; (Er. 656, 5), *tš*, 'determine hand over'.

HSPIEGELBERG, *Kopt. Handwb.* 159 [1921]; DREVILLOUT, *Chrest. dém.* 52 [1880]; HESS, *Rosette*, 97 [1902].

ⲧⲟϣ (Crum 451b), 'border, limit; nome' = (*Wb.* v, 234, 15), *tꜣš*, 'frontier', later also 'district, nome'; (Er. 656, 6), *tš*, 'province, nome'.

HCHAMPOLLION, *Gr.* 98 [1836]; DBRUGSCH, *Gr. dém.* 56, §126 [1855].

NB. Also in ϫⲕⲱⲟⲩ, ⲧϣⲕⲱⲟⲩ, see Geogr. Names.

ⲧⲉϣⲉ (Crum 452b), 'borderer, neighbour, that which adjoins' = (not in Er., ex. Ankhsh. 9, 13), *tšꜣ*, 'neighbour'.

GLANVILLE's index.

ⲧⲁϣⲟ (Crum 452b), 'increase', causative of ⲁϣⲁⲓ = *, *dỉt ꜥšꜣ·*, 'cause to become numerous'; , *ty ꜥšꜣ* (e.g. Harpist 2, 11), 'increase'.

STEINDORFF, *Kopt. Gr.* 1st ed. 108, §236 [1894]; cf. CHABAS, *Mél. ég.* II, 6 [1864].

ⲧⲁϣⲉ-, 'cause to cry, call' = *, *dỉt ꜥš·*, 'cause to cry'; chiefly in ⲧⲁϣⲉ ⲟⲉⲓϣ (Crum 257b, s.v. ⲟⲉⲓϣ), 'proclaim, preach'; lit. 'cause (a) herald to call'; , *ty ꜥš pꜣ ꜥyš*, 'cause the herald to call'; ⲧⲁϣⲉ- confused with ⲧⲁϣⲟ, 'increase'.

STRICKER in *ZÄS* 91, 133–5 [1964].

^{F}(ⲧϣⲁ), ⲧϣⲉ- (Crum 453a), 'send', causative of ϣⲉ = ?, *dỉt šm·*, 'cause to go'.

CRUM, *A Coptic Dict.* 453a [1934].

ⲧϣⲙⲟ (Crum 453a), 'make small', causative of ϣⲙⲁ = *, *dỉt šmꜥ·*, 'cause to become small, thin'.

DÉVAUD's slip.

ⲧϣⲟⲩⲓⲟ (Crum 453a), 'make dry, parch', causative of ϣⲟⲟⲩⲉ = (*Wb.* IV, 429, 7); (P. mag. Harris 11, 8), *dỉt šw·*, 'cause to become dry'; (Er. 494, lower), *ty šw·*, 'let become dry'.

^{H}STEINDORFF, *Kopt. Gr.* 1st ed. 110, §242 [1894]; ^{D}GRIFFITH–THOMPSON, III, 81, no. 834 [1909].

ⲧⲁϥ (Crum 453a), 'spittle' = (*Wb.* V, 297, 9), *tf*, 'spittle'.

BRUGSCH, *Wb.* 1543–4 [1868].

^{B}ⲉⲗ ⲧⲟϥ, 'spit on', see under ⲉⲗⲧⲟϥ.

^{A2}ⲧⲁϥⲉ (Crum 453a, 'meaning unknown') is Qual. of Inf. *ϯϥⲓ, 'to scare up, to start (a wild animal) = L.Eg. (*Wb.* V, 297, 11 f., especially 298, 7), 'to scare up'. ^{A2}ⲧⲁϥⲉ is the same word as ^{B}(ⲑⲓϥⲓ), ⲑⲁϥ⸗, 'remove (by force)', see this latter above.

ⲧⲱϩ (Crum 453b), 'chaff', viz. chopped straw known as *tibn* in modern Egypt, Greek ἄχυρον (Caminos, *LEM*, 190) = (*Wb.* v, 481, 1 f.), *ḏḥꜣ*, 'straw, chaff'; (Er. 651, 5), *tḥ*, 'straw'.

[H]CHAMPOLLION, *Gr.* 89 [1836]; [D]SPIEGELBERG, *Rechnungen aus der Zeit Setis I*, 42 n. 2 [1896].

ⲁⲙⲧⲱϩ (= ⲟⲙⲉ + ⲧⲱϩ), 'clay mixed with chaff' = (Amenemope 24, 13), *ꜥmꜥ-ḏḥꜣ*, 'clay-chaff'.

CAMINOS, *LEM* 190 [1954].

ⲧⲱϩ, [B]ⲑⲟϩ (Crum 453b), 'be disturbed, stir' = (*Wb.* v, 233, 9, 10), *tꜣḥ*, 'dip in water, submerge' (attested in MK: *CT* III, 98 n.); (not in Er.), *tyḥ*, 'rinse' (ex. Botti, *Testi demotici*, Pl. III, vo. 5).

[H]DÉVAUD, *Études* 22–4 [1922]; [D]REVILLOUT, *Setna*, 110 [1880]; REVILLOUT, *Rev. ég.* 1, Pl. 16 [1880].

ⲧⲱϩ, [A]ⲧⲱϩ, [B]ⲑⲱϧ (Crum 453b), 'be mixed, mix' = (Er. 654, 3), *tẖ*, 'mix'; in older Egn. so far only the reduplicated , *tẖtẖ* > ⲧⲁϩⲧϩ is attested, see ⲧⲁϩⲧϩ.

GRIFFITH–THOMPSON, III, 95, no. 1038 [1909].

ⲧⲁϩⲟ (Crum 455a), 'make to stand', etc. (causative of ⲱϩⲉ) = (*Wb.* I, 219, 15–17), *dit ꜥḥꜥ*, 'cause to stand'; (Er. 68, lower), *ty ꜥḥꜥ*, 'place'.

[H]BRUGSCH, *Wb.* 927 [1868]; [D]BRUGSCH, *Gr. dém.* 103, 104 [1855].

ϯϩⲉ (Crum 456b), 'become drunken' = (*Wb.* v, 323, 13 f.), *tẖy*, 'become drunken'; (Er. 654, 5), *tẖy*, 'become drunken'.

[H]BRUGSCH, *Wb.* 1565 [1868]; [D]BRUGSCH, *Rhind*, 44 and Pl. 40, no. 287 [1865].

ⲧϩⲓⲟ (Crum 457a), 'make fall', causative of ϩⲉ = , *dit hꜣy*, 'cause to descend, fall' (e.g. *LD* III, 165, 16. 17).

BRUGSCH, *Wb.* 911 [1868].

ⲧϩⲟ (Crum 457a), 'become bad' (not 'make bad'!) = (*Wb.* v, 482, 14 f.), *ḏḥr*, '(become) bitter'; (Er. 653, 1), *tḥr*, or , *tḥ* (Inf.) 'become bad, ill, sad, suffer'.

[H]SETHE, *Verbum* I, 137, §237, 1; 144, §242; 147, §249, 2; 251, §404, 2b; II, 466, corr. to §624, 3 [1899]; III, 79 [1902]; [D]GRIFFITH, *Stories*, 85 [1900].

ⲧⲱϩⲃ (Crum 457b), 'moisten, soak' = (*Wb.* v, 326, 1 f.), *ṯhb*, 'dip in a liquid, moisten'; (Er. 653, 4), *ṯhb*, 'moisten, dip in liquid, anoint'.

[H]SPIEGELBERG, *Kopt. Handwb.* 160 [1921]; [D]GRIFFITH, *Dem. Graffiti Dodekaschoinos*, I, 190, no. 389 [1937].

ⲑⲃⲃⲓⲟ (Crum 457b), 'humiliate' (causative of **ϩⲓⲃⲉ**, **ϩⲃⲃⲉ**, see the former) = *, *dỉt hb·*, 'cause to become humble'; , *dỉt ḥb·*, same meaning.

[H]STEINDORFF, *Kopt. Gr.* 1st ed. 110, §242 [1894]; [D]GRIFFITH, *Stories*, 191 n. [1900].

ⲑⲗⲟ (Crum 458a), 'make to fly, drive away, scatter' (causative of **ϩⲱⲗ**) = *, *dỉt ḥry·*; *, *ty ḥl·*, 'cause to fly'.

STEINDORFF, *Kopt. Gr.* 1st ed. 107, §235 [1894].

ⲧⲱϩⲙ (Crum 458b), 'knock (on door), summon, invite' = (*Wb.* v, 321, 6 f.), *thm*, 'be pierced', etc., 'knock (on the door)' (*Wb.* v, 322, 3); (Er. 650, 2), *thm*, 'invite'.

[H]DÉVÉRIA in *Journal as.* 1865, 466 [1865] = *Pap. jud.* 187 [1868] = *Mém. et fragm.* II, 243; [D]HESS, *Gnost. Pap.* 16 [1892].

ϯϩⲙⲉ (Crum 459a), a receptacle for water, grain, meal, etc. = (not in *Wb.*; O. Cairo J. 72454, vo. 2, XIXth Dyn., unpubl.), *thm* (masc.), a large vessel, as receptacle for wicks; (Er. 650, 3), *thm*, a measure.

[D]MATTHA in Mond–Myers, *The Bucheum*, II, 56 and I, Pl. LXVII, no. 97 [1934].

ⲑⲙⲟ (Crum 459b), 'to warm' (causative of **ϩⲙⲟⲙ**) = *, *dỉt šmm·*; (Er. 381, middle), *ty ḫmm·*, 'cause to become warm'.

[H]STEINDORFF, *Kopt. Gr.* 1st ed. 109, §239 [1894]; [D]SPIEGELBERG, *Mythus*, 209, no. 532 [1917].

ⲑⲙⲕⲟ (Crum 459 b), 'ill use, afflict, humiliate' (causative of **ⲙⲟⲩⲕϩ**, **ⲙⲕⲁϩ**) = with metathesis *, *ty mkḥ*, 'cause to become sad'.

[H]STEINDORFF, *Kopt. Gr.* 110, §240 [1894]; [D]SPIEGELBERG, *Kopt. Handwb.* 161 [1921].

ⲑⲙⲥⲟ (Crum 460 a), 'make to sit, seat', causative of **ϩⲙⲟⲟⲥ** = (*Wb.* III, 98, 22), *rdì ḥms·*, 'let sit down'; (Er. 308, bottom), *ty ḥms·*, 'let sit down'.

[H]BRUGSCH, *Wb.* 960 [1868]; [D]HESS, *Stne*, 2–3 [1888].

ⲧⲁϩⲛⲟ (Crum 460 a), 'hinder' = *, *dìt rhn·*, 'cause to flee' (*rhn*, *Wb.* II, 440, 14); (Er. 277, 2), *ty hn·*, 'hinder'.

[H]DÉVAUD's slip; [D]BRUGSCH, *Wb.* 902–3 [1868], and Suppl. 759 [1881].

ⲧⲉϩⲛⲉ (Crum 460 b), 'forehead' = (*Wb.* v, 478, 6 f.), *dhnt*, 'forehead; (Er. 651, 1), *thn*, 'point, forehead'.

[H]CHAMPOLLION, *Gr.* 73 [1836]; [D]GRIFFITH, *Ryl.* III, 203 n. 19; 424 [1909] (in a place-name).

ⲧϩⲛⲟ, [A]**ⲧϩ̄ⲛⲟ** (Crum 460 b), 'make to approach' (causative of **ϩⲱⲛ**) = *, *dìt ẖn·*, 'cause to approach'.

STEINDORFF, *Kopt. Gr.* 1st ed. 107, §235 [1894].

ⲧϩⲡⲟ (Crum 461 a), 'cause to reach, bring back, accompany' (causative of **ⲡⲱϩ**) = *, *dìt pḥ·*, 'cause to reach'; *dy pḥ·*, same meaning.

[H]ERMAN, *ZÄS* 22, 30 [1884]; [D]SPIEGELBERG, *Mythus*, 131, no. 272 [1917].

ⲧϩⲣϣⲟ (Crum 461 a), 'make heavy, terrify' (causative of **ϩⲣⲟϣ**) = *, *ty ḥrš·*, 'cause to become heavy'. See also **ⲧⲁⲣϣⲟ**, 'increase, multiply .

[D]BRUGSCH, *Die Ägyptologie*, 100 [1891].

ⲧⲱϩⲥ (Crum 461 b), 'anoint' = (*Wb.* v, 323, 5–6), *tḥs*, 'crush' and , *tḥs*, 'smear, spread'; (Er. 653, 2), *tḥs*, 'anoint'.

[H]MASSART in *Mitt. Kairo* 15, 178 n. 11 [1957]; [D]BRUGSCH, *Scriptura Aeg. dem.* 19, §21 [1848].

ⲧⲁϩⲧ (Crum 462 a), 'lead' = (*Wb.* v, 606, 4 f.), *ḏḥty*, 'lead'; (Er. 651, 3), *tḥth*, 'lead'.

Demotic agrees with Coptic sub-form ⲧⲁϩⲧϩ, an erroneously completed reduplication.

[H]CHAMPOLLION, *Gr.* 89 [1836]; [D]REVILLOUT, *Pap. mor.* I, 242 n. 9 [1907].

ⲧⲁϩⲧϩ (Crum 462 a), 'confuse' (reduplication of ⲧⲱϩ, 'mix') = (*Wb.* v, 328, 8 f.), *tḫtḫ*, 'put in disorder'; or (Er. 655, 6), *tḫtḫ*, also , *thth*, 'confuse'.

[H]BRUGSCH, *Nouvelles recherches*, 10 n. 4, and Pl. I, no. 15 [1856]; [D]BRUGSCH, *Wb.* 1568 [1868]; cf. SAULCY, *Analyse grammaticale*, 103 [1845].

ⲑⲟⲩⲣⲉ (P. Bodmer VI; not in Crum), in ⲛⲁⲛⲉ...ⲑⲟⲩⲣⲉ..., 'good is... bad (thing is)...' = , *tḥrt*, fem. adj. (e.g. P. Ryl. IX, 12, 10), 'bad' from (Er. 653, 1), *tḥ(r)*, 'be afflicted, be bad', ⲧϩⲟ (see this latter).

ⲑⲟⲟⲩⲧ (Crum 462 a), name of first month = name of the god Thoth , *ḏḥwty* (*Wb.* v, 606, 1); in Late Egn. also name of a festival and of the first month , *ḏḥwty* (*Wb.* v, 606, 2 and *ASAE* 43, 174).

ERMAN, *ZÄS* 39, 128–9 [1901]; cf. LEPSIUS, *Chronologie*, 135–6 [1848]; BRUGSCH, *Die Ägyptologie*, 359 [1891].

ⲧⲁϫⲟ (Crum 462 b), 'judge, condemn' (causative of ⲱϫ) = (*Wb.* I, 241, 6), *dỉt ʿḏꜣ·*, 'accuse (before court)', lit. 'cause to become guilty'; (Er. 75, top), *ty ʿḏ·*, 'accuse'.

[H]C. SCHMIDT, *Der erste Clemensbrief in altkopt. Übersetzung*, 11 [1908]; [D]SPIEGELBERG in Sethe, *Dem. Urk.* 357 [1920].

ⲧϫⲁ(ⲉ)ⲓⲟ (Crum 462 b), 'make to rise (?), appear' > 'triumph', almost certainly causative of ϣⲁ; if so then = * , *dỉt ḫʿy·*, 'cause to appear' (**d-ḫeʿyŏ*; for *dḫ* = ϫ, cf. ϫⲡⲟ < *d-ḫeprŏ*); (BM 57371, 33, unpublished) *dỉt·f ḫʿ*, 'he caused to be resplendent'.

[H]CRUM, *A Coptic Dict.* 462 b [1934]; [D]SHORE's information.

ⲧⲁϫⲣⲟ (Crum 462 b), 'make strong, firm, fast', causative of ϫⲣⲟ = (Er. 683, lower), *ty ḏr*, 'fasten, strengthen'.

SETHE, *Verbum*, II, 93, §212 [1899]; [D]HESS, *Stne*, 185 [1888].

ⲧⲁϭ (Crum 464a), 'lump, piece, cake' = (Er. 659, 5), *tk*, 'lump'.
GRIFFITH–THOMPSON, I, 33 [1904]; cf. III, 92, no. 991 [1909].

Sϯϭⲉ: Bϫⲓϫⲓ (Crum 464a), 'gourd' or 'vegetables' generally = , *dḳr* > , *dg(ꜣ)* (*Wb.* v, 495, 8 f.), Graeco-Roman (*Wb.* v, 497, 3), *dg*, 'vegetables', 'fruit'; (Er. 662, 1), *tgy*, 'fruit'.
HDÉVAUD, *Études*, 24–6 [1922]; DSPIEGELBERG, *Der demot. Text der Priesterdekrete*, 206, no. 410 [1922].

ⲧⲱ(ⲱ)ϭⲉ (Crum 464a), 'be fixed, joined, plant' = (*Wb.* v, 496, 4), *dḳr*, 'be fixed' > L. Egn. (*Wb.* v, 499, 7 f.), *dgꜣ*, 'plant stones, plant'; (Er. 661, 5), *tg*, 'plant'.
HBRUGSCH, *Wb.* 1662 [1868]; DHESS, *Rosette*, 98 [1902].

ⲧϭⲁ(ⲉ)ⲓⲟ (Crum 465b), 'make ugly', hence 'disgrace, condemn', causative of ϭⲁ(ⲉ)ⲓⲉ, see this latter.
ϭⲁ(ⲉ)ⲓⲉ (Crum 466a), 'ugly one, ugliness, disgrace', see below under ϭⲁ(ⲉ)ⲓⲉ.

Bⲧϭⲟ (Crum 466a), 'plant', see Sϫⲟ, B(ⲧ)ϭⲟ, 'sow, plant'.

Sⲧⲏϭⲙⲉⲥ, Bϫⲓⲥⲙⲓⲥ (Crum 466a), 'castor-oil plant' *Ricinus communis* L. (Palma Christi), see Keimer, *Kêmi* 2, 100 ff.; Dawson, *Aegyptus* 10, 57 ff. (= ⲧⲏϭⲙⲉ + ⲥ) = (*Wb.* v, 500, 9 f.), *dgm*, a tree or bush (ricinus?); (Er. 662, 2), *tgm*, '(ricinus) plant, fruit, oil'.
HDLORET in *Revue de médecine* 22, 694–5 [1902] (for ϫⲓⲥⲙⲓⲥ); cf. HSPIEGELBERG, *Die dem. Urkunden des Zenon-Archivs*, 3 n. 5; 8–9 n. 4 [1929].

ⲧⲱϭⲛ (Crum 466a), 'push, repel' = = (*Wb.* v, 333, 10 f.), *tkn*, 'approach', 'repel, remove' (for this latter meaning, see Dévaud, *Études*, 27–8); (Er. 659, 11), *tkn*, 'be near, approach', also (not in Er.; ex. Ankhsh. 16, 8), 'repress, push back'.
HDÉVAUD, *Études*, 26–8 [1922]; cf. MASPERO, *Les mémoires de Sinouhit*, 178 (with doubts) [1908]; DREVILLOUT, *Revue ég.* 1, fasc. 4, pl. 3 and 4 [1880].
Note. *Tkn* > L.Egn. *tgn*, cf. for *dgn·f*, Edinburgh stone 912.

ⲧⲱϭ(ⲉ)ⲣ, ⲧⲱⲣϭ (Crum 466b), 'become fixed, joined' = Graeco-Roman (*Wb.* v, 330, 15–17; *Mélanges Mariette*, 237), 'become joined with...(?)' < ? (*Wb.* v, 478, 3), *drg*.

ⲧⲁϭⲥⲉ (Crum 466b), 'foot-sole, foot-print' (from [*Wb.* v, 501, 1 f.], *dgs*, 'tread') = (Er. 661, 2), *tkst*, 'step'.

[H]SPIEGELBERG, *Kopt. Handwb.* 155 [1921]; cf. CHABAS, *Voyage*, 116–17 [1866] and BRUGSCH, *Wb.* 1662 [1868]; [D]SPIEGELBERG, *Petubastis*, 67*, no. 478 [1910].

(**ⲧⲟϭⲧϭ**), Qual. **ⲧⲉϭⲧⲱϭ** (Crum 467b), 'press firmly' = (*Wb.* v, 501, 11 f.), *dgdg*, 'trample' < ? (*Wb.* v, 336, 13), *tktk*, 'attack' or sim.

ČERNÝ, *Crum Mem. Volume*, 40 [1950].

ⲞⲨ

ⲟⲩ (Crum 467b), interrog. pronoun 'what? who?' = (*Wb.* I, 273, 3), *wꜥ*, 'one, someone'.

SETHE, *ZÄS* 47, 4 [1910].

-ⲟⲩ, suffix of 3rd person plural = L.Eg. (*Wb.* I, 243, 12–14), *·w*, suffix 3rd person plural; (Er. 75, 3, sub. 1), *·w*, same.

[H]Not identified; [D]BRUGSCH, *Scriptura Aeg. dem.* 36 (table of suffixes) [1848].

ⲟⲩⲁ (Crum 468b), 'blasphemy' = (*Wb.* I, 279, 14), *wꜥꜣ*, 'speak evil'; (Er. 82, 3), *wꜥy*, 'to revolt', 'blasphemy'.

[H]BRUGSCH, *Wb.* 240 [1867]; [D]BRUGSCH, *Gr. dém.* 34, §68 [1855].

ϫⲓ-ⲟⲩⲁ, ϫⲉ-ⲟⲩⲁ = , *ḏd-wꜥ* (Lexa, *Totb.* 2, 27), 'say a blasphemy'.

ⲟⲩⲁ (Crum 469a), 'one, someone' = (*Wb.* I, 273, 3 f.), *wꜥ*, 'one'; (Er. 81, 1), *wꜥ*, 'one'.

[H]DE ROUGÉ, *Oeuv. div.* III (= *Bibl. ég.* XXIII), 172 f. [1856]; cf. *Oeuv. div.* II (= *Bibl. ég.* XXII), 133 (read in 1849) [1851], and *Oeuv. div.* III (= *Bibl. ég.* XXIII), 65 [1855]; [D]BRUGSCH, *De natura*, 26 [1850].

ⲟⲩⲁ ⲟⲩⲁ (Crum 469a), 'one by one, one after another' = (*Wb.* I, 276, 6), *wꜥ wꜥ*, 'each one'.

ⲟⲩ- (Crum 470a), indefinite article = L.Eg. (*Wb.* I, 276, 8–9), *wꜥ*, indefinite article, < , *wꜥ n*, 'one of...'; (Er. 81, 1), *wꜥ*, indefinite article.

[H]DE ROUGÉ, *Oeuv. div.* III (= *Bibl. ég.* XXIII), 175 [1856], according to Brugsch, *Gr. dém.* 76, § 168 [1855]; [D]BRUGSCH, *Gr. dém.* 76, § 168 [1855]. See also ⲗⲁⲁⲩ.

ⲟⲩⲁ- (Crum 470a), verbal prefix indicating future = ? (*Wb.* I, 246, 5–9), *wꜣ*, 'to be about to...'.

ERMAN–GRAPOW, *Wb.* I, 246, 5 [1926].

ⲟⲩⲁⲁ⸗ (Crum 470a), 'alone, self', see **ⲟⲩⲱⲧ**.

ⲟⲩⲉ (Crum 470b), 'be distant, far-reaching' = (*Wb.* I, 245, 3 f.), *wꜣy*, 'be distant'; (Er. 78, 2), *wy*, 'be distant'.

[H]BRUGSCH, *Wb.*, Suppl. 378–9 [1880]; [D]BRUGSCH, *De natura*, 26 [1850].

ⲟⲩⲟ(ⲉ)ⲓ (Crum 472a), masc., 'rush, course', swift movement = (*Wb.* I, 246, bottom), *wꜣt*, 'way, side'; fem., sometimes treated as masc. (*Wb.* I, 246, 17).

BRUGSCH, *Wb.* 320–1 [1868].

ϯ ⲟⲩⲟⲉⲓ, 'go about seeking, seek, go forward' = , *dỉt wꜣt*, 'direct one's way to', lit. 'give way' (P. Lansing 8, 4), besides , *dỉt tꜣ wꜣt* (P. Harris 7, 3).

SPIEGELBERG, *Kopt. Etymologien*, 12–13 [1920]; cf. BLACKMAN, *JEA* 16, 70 n. 6 [1930].

ⲟⲩⲟ(ⲉ)ⲓ (Crum 472b), interjection 'woe!' = (*Wb.* I, 272, 11; N.K. ex. *H.O.*, Pl. 80), *wy*, 'woe!'; (Er. 78, 3), *wy*, 'woe!'.

[H]ERMAN–GRAPOW, *Wb.* I, 272, 11 [1926]; [D]HESS, *Stne*, 151 [1888].

ⲟⲩⲟⲉⲓⲉ (Crum 473a), 'husbandman, cultivator' of fields or vines = , *ꜥwꜣw*, 'reaper?' (not in Wb., but see Gardiner, *JEA* 27, 21 n. 5), from (*Wb.* I, 171, 19 f.), *ꜥwꜣy*, 'to harvest'; (Er. 79, 2), *wyꜥ*, 'farmer'.

[H]SETHE in Spiegelberg, *Kopt. Handwb.* 165 [1921]; [D]REVILLOUT, *Nouvelle chrestomathie dém.* 154, 155 [1878].

ⲟⲩⲱ (Crum 473b), 'cease, stay, finish' = (*Wb.* I, 255, top), *wꜣḥ*, 'to last'; (Er. 76, 8), *wꜣḥ*, 'finish, cease'.

HSPIEGELBERG, *Kopt. Handwb.* 165 [1921]; DGRIFFITH–THOMPSON, III, 21, no. 213 [1909].

ⲟⲩⲱ (Crum 474b and 751b s.v. **ϫⲓ**), 'news, report' = (Er. 77, 2), *wꜣḥ*, 'message, matter, news'.

GRIFFITH, *ZÄS* 38, 87 and 89 [1900].

ⲣ ⲟⲩⲱ (Crum 474b), 'make reply' or merely 'speak' = , *ỉr wꜣḥ*, 'answer' (vb. and nn.).

GRIFFITH–THOMPSON, III, 21, no. 214 [1909].

ϫⲓ ⲟⲩⲱ (Crum 475a), 'bring news, announce' = (Er. 77, 2), *ḏd wꜣḥ*, unetymologically , *tꜣy-wꜣḥ*, 'answer, give an oracle'.

HESS, *Stne* 152 [1888]; SPIEGELBERG, *Die dem. Pap. Loeb.* p. 33 (14) [1931].

ϫⲓ ⲡⲟⲩⲱ (Crum 475a), 'bring news, announce' = , *ḏd pꜣ wꜣḥ*, same meaning.

GRIFFITH–THOMPSON, III, 21, no. 214 [1909].

ⲟⲩⲃⲉ- (Crum 476a), preposition 'opposite, towards, against' = Roman , (not in *Wb.*), *wbꜣ*, 'opposite'; (Er. 84, 13), *wbꜣ*, 'against, for'.

HSAUNERON, *BIFAO* 55, 21–2 [1955]; DBRUGSCH, *Scriptura Aegypt. dem.* 58, VI [1848].

ⲟⲩⲃⲁϣ (Crum 476b), 'become white' = (*Wb.* I, 295, 12 f.), *wbḫ*, 'be bright, emit light'; (Er. 85, 6), *wbḫ*, 'be bright, illuminate'.

HGOODWIN in *ZÄS* 9, 104 [1871]; DBRUGSCH, *De natura*, 35 [1850].

B**ⲟⲩⲟⲕⲓ** (Crum 477a), 'dregs of sesame' in oil-press, undoubtedly related to **ⲟⲕⲉ**, 'sesame' (see this), perhaps identical if the initial **ⲟⲩ-** (hardly indefinite article) is a mistake. Or rather read ⟨**ⲙ**⟩**ⲟⲩ-ⲟⲕⲓ**, 'water (from **ⲙⲟⲟⲩ**) of sesame'?

KUENTZ, *Bull. Soc. Ling.* 36, 162 [1935].

ⲟⲩⲱⲱⲗⲉ (Crum 477a), (1) 'be well off, flourish' = (*Wb.* I, 286, 8 f.), *wꜥr*, 'to flee'; (Er. 93, 2, and 84, 4), *wr*, *wꜥly*, 'have abundance', and (Er. 96, 3, and 84, 3), *wl*, *wꜥl*, 'flee, float'.

HMÖLLER, *Rhind*, 14*, no. 89, and n. 1 [1913]; DREVILLOUT, *Revue ég.* 4, p. 75 n. 8 [1885].

(2) **ⲟⲩⲱⲗⲉ, ⲟⲩⲁⲗⲉ-** (refl.), **ⲟⲩⲁⲗⲉ†** (Mani Ps.), 'float, hover', same as **ⲟⲩⲱⲱⲗⲉ**, 'be well off'.

H. THOMPSON in Allberry, *A Manichaean Psalm-Book*, II, 193, n. on l. 30 [1938].

See also causative B**ⲑⲟⲩⲉⲗⲟ**, 'overflow, submerge'.

ⲟⲩⲗⲁⲓ (Crum 477a), 'curly-haired' = (Er. 96, 3), *wl*, 'hanging over (of hair)', therefore derived from **ⲟⲩⲱⲱⲗⲉ**, but Peyron (*Lex.* 142a) thinks of Greek 'οὐλή capillus'. Such a word does not seem to exist, but there is οὖλος 'woolly', and in Odyssey is found οὖλαι κόμαι, 'crisp, close-curling hair'.

BRUGSCH, *Rhind*, 32, note *) [1865].

ⲟⲩⲗⲗⲉ (Crum 477a), 'melody, music', cf. L.Eg. (*Wb.* I, 252, 1), *wnr*, and (*Wb.* I, 252, 13), *wr*, 'flute (made of reed)?', perhaps also Graeco-Roman (*Wb.* I, 252, 11), *w(ꜣ)r*, 'dance, sing', and (*Wb.* I, 252, 10), *w(ꜣ)r*, a priestly title at Ombos ('singer?'); = (Er. 96, 4), *wl*, 'sing; melody', (Er. 76, 6), *wꜣlylꜥw*, 'singer', and in the title *dd*(?)*wl*, 'singer(?) of melody'. Probably all from Semitic, cf. **ⲟⲩⲉⲗⲟⲩⲉⲗⲉ**.

HSPIEGELBERG, *Kopt. Handwb.* 166 [1921]; DGRIFFITH, *Dem. Graffiti Dodekaschoinos*, I, 142, no. 74; 306, no. 879 [1937]; cf. SPIEGELBERG, *Mythus*, 107, no. 177 [1917].

ⲟⲩⲱⲗⲡ (Crum 477b, 'meaning uncertain'), 'become, make blunt' = (Er. 93, 6), *wrp*, 'become blunt'.

ⲟⲩⲗⲡⲉ, therefore, 'insensitive place' (on skin).

ⲟⲩⲱⲗⲥ (Crum 477b), 'lean, be bent, confounded; bend, humiliate' = (Er. 96, 8), *wls*, 'overturn, turn to flight'. Perhaps also connected with (*Wb.* I, 335, 9), *wrs*, 'headrest'.

HERICHSEN, *Dem. Glossar*, 96, 8 [1954]; DGRIFFITH, *Ryl.* III, 342 [1909].

ⲟⲩⲉⲗⲟⲩⲉⲗⲉ (Crum 478a), 'yelp, howl', reduplication of **ⲟⲩⲗⲗⲉ**, see the latter. From Semitic, cf. Arabic وَلْوَلَ, though not necessarily connected, since Latin too has *ululare*. Correct **ⲟⲩⲉⲗⲟⲩⲉⲗⲉ** into **ⲟⲩⲉⲗⲟⲩⲉⲗ** with Sethe, *Verbum*, II, §635.

[S]DÉVAUD's slip; cf. Crum, *A Coptic Dict.* 478a [1934].

ⲟⲩⲱⲙ (Crum 478a), 'eat, bite' = (*Wb.* I, 320, 1 ff.), *wnm*, 'eat'; (Er. 91, 2), *wnm*, 'eat'.

[H]DE ROUGÉ, *Oeuv. div.* II (= *Bibl. ég.* XXII), 175 (read in 1849) [1851]; [D]REVILLOUT, *Setna*, 157 [1877]; cf. MASPERO, *ZÄS* 16, 80 n. 26, and Pl. 5, nos. 87–95 [1878].

ⲟⲩⲁⲙ-ⲉϯ (Crum 479a), 'gangrene, cancer', see under **ⲟⲟⲧⲉ**.

ⲟⲩⲙⲟⲧ (Crum 479b), 'become thick' = (*Wb.* I, 306, 9–11), *wmt*, 'become thick'.

BRUGSCH, *Wb.* 253 [1867].

ⲟⲩⲟⲙⲧⲉ (Crum 480a), 'tower' = (*Wb.* I, 307, 6. 7), *wmtt*, 'surrounding wall'; (Er. 87, 8), *wmṯ*, 'tower'.

[H]BRUGSCH, *ZÄS* I, 24 [1863]; [D]GRIFFITH, *Ryl.* III, 341 [1909].

[B]**ⲟⲩⲱⲙⲧ** (Crum 480a), 'swell, become swollen', same origin as **ⲟⲩⲙⲟⲧ**.

ⲟⲩⲁⲛ (Crum 480a), 'dyke' = (*Wb.* I, 315, 2), *wnt*, 'fortress', (*Wb.* I, 315, 1), *wnt*, 'sanctuary' or sim.; (Er. 89, 5), *wn*, 'wall, dyke (χῶμα)'.

[H]BAILLET, *Oeuvres diverses*, I (= *Bibl. ég.* XV), 303 [1887]; [D]BRUGSCH, *Gr. dém.* 32, §63 [1855].

ⲟⲩⲉⲓⲛ (Crum 480a), 'water-channel (?)', see **ⲁⲩⲉⲓⲛ**.

ⲟⲩⲟⲉⲓⲛ (Crum 480a), 'light' = (*Wb.* I, 315, 4), *wny*, 'light' (attested since XXIInd Dyn., cf. Yoyotte, *BIFAO* 54, 104 n. 2); (Er. 79, 6), *wyn*, 'light'.

[H]CHAMPOLLION, *Gr.* 377 [1836]; [D]BRUGSCH, *Scriptura Aeg. dem.* 22, §29 [1848].

ⲟⲩⲟⲛ (Crum 481a), 'to be' = (*Wb.* I, 308, 1 f.), *wn*, 'to be'; (Er. 88, 1), *wn*, 'it is'.

[H]CHAMPOLLION, *Dict.* 125 [1841]; [D]BRUGSCH, *Gr. dém.* 97, §219; 127, §260, 2° [1855].

ⲟⲩⲛⲧⲉ-, 'to have' = L.Eg. (*Wb.* I, 309, 5; II, 177, 7), *wn mdỉ* + suff., 'to have', lit. 'it is with'; (Er. 88, middle), *wn mtw·*, 'to have'.

[H]ERMAN, *Näg. Gr.* 84, § 110 n. 2 [1880].

ⲟⲩⲟⲛ (Crum 482 a), 'some one, some thing, some' = , *wn*, 'he who is, being', partic. of *wn* (*Wb.* I, 308, 1 ff.). Actual ex. is (P. BM 10052, 3, 19), *bḥy wn sp n·tn*, 'nothing remained for you'; (Er. 87, 10), *wn*, 'some one'.

[H]FECHT, *Wortakzent und Silbenstruktur*, 54–5 [1960]; [D]SPIEGELBERG, *Petubastis*, 13*, no. 82 [1910].

ⲟⲩⲱⲛ (Crum 482 b) 'to open' = (*Wb.* I, 311, 2 f.), *wn*, 'to open'; (Er. 89, 1), *wn*, 'to open'.

[H]CHAMPOLLION, *Gr.* 373, 381 [1836]; [D]BRUGSCH, *Wb.* 254 [1867].

ⲟⲩⲱⲛ (Crum 483 a), 'part' = (*Wb.* I, 273, 9), *wʿ*, 'one', in , *wʿ 10 m*, 'one tenth of', lit. 'one ten in'; (Er. 89, 6), *wn*, 'part, sum'.

[H]SETHE, *ZÄS* 47, 6–7 [1910]; [D]SPIEGELBERG, *Rec. trav.* 35, 161 [1913].

ⲟⲩⲉⲓⲛⲉ (Crum 483 b), 'pass by' = (*Wb.* I, 313, 10 f.), *wny*, 'hurry, pass by'; (Er. 80, 1), *wyn*, 'pass by'.

[H]BRUGSCH, *Wb.* 257–8 [1867]; [D]GRIFFITH, *Stories*, 178 [1900].

ⲟⲩⲛⲁⲙ (Crum 483 b), 'right hand' = L.Eg. (*Wb.* I, 322, 1 f.), *wnmy*, 'right (hand)'; (Er. 91, 4), *wnm*, 'right, right-hand side'.

[H]CHABAS, *Oeuv. div.* II (= *Bibl. ég.* X), 226 f. [1865]; cf. CHABAS, *Oeuv. div.* III (= *Bibl. ég.* XI), 15 f. [1865]; cf. LEPSIUS, *ZÄS* 3, 12–13 [1865]; [D]BRUGSCH, *Wb.* 261 (with doubts) [1867]; GRIFFITH–THOMPSON, III, 20, no. 200 [1909].

ⲟⲩⲉⲉⲓⲉⲛⲓⲛ (Crum 484 a), 'Ionian, Greek' = (Er. 80, 2), *wynn*, 'Greek', *Wayanīn*, through double metathesis (*way* < *yaw* and *yan* < *nay*) from Aramaic plural * *Yawnayīn*, the latter from Ἰᾱϝων (> Ἴων), 'Ionian'.

[D]ÅKERBLAD, *Lettre*, 49–50 and Pl. I, no. 16 [1802]; cf. SETHE, *Nachr. K. Gess. Wiss. zu Göttingen, Phil.-hist. Kl.* 1916, 131–3 [1916].

ⲟⲩ(ⲉ)ⲛⲧ (Crum 484 a), 'deep, hollow place, hold (of ship)' = (*Wb.* I, 326, 1), *wnḏwt*, 'hold (of ship)'; (Er. 92, 4), *wnṭ*, 'hold (of ship)'.

[H]DÉVAUD's slip; cf. ERMAN–GRAPOW, *Wb.* I, 326, 1 [1926]; [D]SPIEGELBERG, *Petubastis*, 15*, no. 89 [1910].

ⲟⲩⲛⲟⲩ (Crum 484b), 'hour' = (*Wb.* I, 316, 1 f.), *wnwt*, 'hour'; (Er. 90, 5), *wnwt*, 'hour'.

[H]CHAMPOLLION, *Gr.* 96, 241 [1836]; [D]BRUGSCH, *Wb.* 256 [1867].

ⲛ̄ⲧⲉ(ⲟ)ⲩⲛⲟⲩ (Crum 484b), 'on the instant, forthwith' = L.Eg. (*Wb.* I, 316, 11), *m tꜣ wnwt*, 'in this hour, now'.

ⲧⲉⲛⲟⲩ (Crum 485a), 'now', same origin as **ⲛ̄ⲧⲉ(ⲟ)ⲩⲛⲟⲩ**.

ⲟⲩⲱⲛϣ (Crum 485b), 'wolf' = (*Wb.* I, 324, 16), *wnš*, 'wolf'; (Er. 92, 3), *wnš*, 'wolf'.

[H]CHAMPOLLION, *Gr.* 72 [1836]; [D]BRUGSCH, *Gr. dém.* 23, §40 [1855].

ⲟⲩⲛⲟϥ (Crum 485b), 'rejoice' = (*Wb.* I, 319, 11 f.), *wnf*, 'rejoice'; (Er. 91, 1), *wnf*, 'rejoice'.

[H]BRUGSCH, *Wb.* 259 [1867]; [D]SPIEGELBERG, *Mythus*, 106, no. 170 [1917].

ⲟⲩⲱⲛϩ (Crum 486a), 'reveal, be revealed, appear' = (*Wb.* I, 312, 15), *wn-ḥr*, 'open the face'; (Er. 92, 1), *wnḥ*, 'reveal'.

[H]BRUGSCH, *Rec. de mon.* II, 77 [1863]; [D]BRUGSCH, *De natura*, 26 [1850].

ⲟⲩⲟⲡ (Crum 487b), 'be pure, innocent' = (*Wb.* I, 280, 12 f.), *wꜥb*, 'to purify, be pure'; (Er. 82, 7), *wꜥb*, 'be pure, pure'.

[H]CHAMPOLLION, *Gr.* 376 [1836]; [D]BRUGSCH, *Gr. dém.* 28, §54; 121, §244 [1855] (but he reads the Demotic word *AeW*).

ⲟⲩⲏⲏⲃ (Crum 488a), 'priest' = (*Wb.* I, 282, 13 f.), *wꜥb*, 'priest'; (Er. 83, 1), *wꜥb*, 'priest'.

[H]CHAMPOLLION, *Gr.* 104, 105 [1836]; [D]ÅKERBLAD, *Lettre*, 18 [1802]; cf. ÅKERBLAD in Young, *Works*, III, 37 [1815]; BRUGSCH, *Scriptura Aeg. dem.* 8, §8 [1848].

(ⲟⲩⲏⲣ), ⲟⲩⲏⲣⲉ (Crum 488b), 'great' = (*Wb.* I, 326, bottom), *wr*, 'great, be great'; (Er. 92, 8), *wr*, 'great', fem. (Er. 93, 1), *wrt*. Only in proper names **ⲉⲥⲟⲩⲏⲣⲉ-** = (*Wb.* IV, 8, 13), *ꜣst wrt*, '(goddess), Isis the Great', Greek Ἐσουῆρις, and **ⲡⲟⲩⲉⲣⲧⲉⲓⲟⲩ** = (Ranke, I, 104, 7), *Pꜣ-wr-dỉw*, 'The great one of five', Greek Πόρτις.

STEINDORFF, *ZÄS* 28, 52 [1890]; GRIFFITH, *Ryl.* III, 441, and 283 n. 4 [1909].

ⲟⲩⲏⲣ (Crum 488b), 'how great, how many, how much?' = (*Wb.* I, 331, 4), *wr*, 'how much?'. For demotic exx. see now Parker, *Dem. Math. Pap.*, Problem 37, 19; 38, 14.

[H]STEINDORFF, *Kopt. Gr.* 1st ed., 41, §60 [1894]; cf. Brugsch, *Rosettana*, 29 [1851] and *Dict. géo.* 589 [1879]; [D]PARKER *op. cit.* [1972].

ⲟⲩⲣⲱ (Crum 489a), 'bean' = (*Wb.* I, 56, 14. 15), *ἰwryt*, 'bean'; (Er. 93, 3), *wrꜣ*, 'bean', ἄρακος, *Vigna sinensis* Endl., Arabic لوبيه (Keimer, *BIFAO* 28, 90).

[H]BIRCH, *Harris*, 17 n. 27 [1876]; [D]SETHE, *Bürgschaftsurk.* 46–8 [1920].

ⲟⲩⲣⲓⲥ (Crum 489b), plant κόστος = (Er. 94, 7), *wrs*, a plant.

ⲟⲩⲣⲧ (Crum 490a), 'rose' = (Er. 95, 6), *wrṯ*, 'rose', from Semitic (Aram. וְרָד, Arabic وَرْد), there as well as in Sanskrit (*vr̥dhi-*), Armenian (*vard*), Greek (ῥόδον) and Latin (*rosa*) from Persian *gul* < **u̯r̥da*.

[D]BRUGSCH, *Scriptura Aeg. dem.* 18, §17 [1848]; [S]ROSSI, *Etym. aeg.* 38 [1808].

ⲟⲩⲣⲟⲧ (Crum 490a), 'be glad, eager, ready', = (*Wb.* II, 410, 13 f.), *rwḏ*, 'be firm'; (Er. 243, 9), *rwṯ*, 'be firm, fresh'.

[H]SETHE, *Verbum*, I, 104, §178; 188, §311, 3; 227, §379 [1899]; [D]SPIEGELBERG, *ZÄS* 42, 60 [1905]; cf. SPIEGELBERG, *Dem. Pap. Loeb*, 62, (12) [1931].

See also **-ⲣⲱⲧ**, **-ⲣⲟⲧ** as adj. 'firm, strong'.

ⲟⲩⲉⲣⲏⲧⲉ (Crum 491a), 'foot' = Dual , *wꜥrty* (**weꜥrĕtey*), of (*Wb.* I, 287, 4), *wꜥrt*, 'leg'.

BRUGSCH, *ZDMG* 9, 206 [1855]; cf. BRUGSCH, *Wb.* 244 [1867]; ERMAN, *Pluralbildung*, 40, note **) [1878].

NB. Sing. **ⲟⲩⲏⲣⲉ** (Spiegelberg, *Kopt. Etymologien*, 7) is non-existent. Job 13, 27 should read **ⲧⲁⲟⲩⲏⲣⲉϫⲉ ϫⲉ** = δέ μου τὸν πόδα, CRUM, *JEA* 8, 187 [1922]. The Singular would be ***ⲟⲩⲁⲣⲉ** < *waꜥret*, see Steindorff, *Lehrbuch*, 71, §135.

ⲟⲩ(ⲉ)ⲣϣⲉ (Crum 491a), 'watch, watch tower' = (*Wb.* I, 336, 5), *wršyt*, 'watch', L.Eg. (*Wb.* I, 336, 15) *wršt*, 'watch tower', from (*Wb.* I, 335, 10 f.), *wrš*, 'spend the day, to wake'; (Er. 95, 1), *wrš*, 'to spend day, wake', 'the watch'.

[H]SPIEGELBERG, *Rec. trav.* 21, 21–2 [1899]; [D]HESS, *Gnost. Pap.* 5 [1892].
ⲁⲛⲟⲩⲣϣⲉ, 'watchman, guard' = *, *ꜥꜣ n wršt*, lit. 'great one of the watch'.

SPIEGELBERG, *op. cit.*

[B]**ⲟⲩⲟⲣϣϥ** (Crum 491 b, 'meaning unknown'), 'watch-tower' or sim. < ***ⲟⲩⲱⲣⲉϣ** (from , *wrš*, see under **ⲟⲩ(ⲉ)ⲣϣⲉ**) + **ϥ**.

ⲟⲩⲱⲣϩ (Crum 491 b), 'set free, open, renounce' = (Er. 94, 2), *wrḥ*, 'set free, admit'.

GRIFFITH–THOMPSON, III, 21, no. 208 [1909] (with doubt); SPIEGELBERG, *Kopt. Handwb.* 171 [1921].

ⲟⲩⲣⲉϩ (Crum 492 a), 'free space' = (Er. 94, 3), *wrḥ*, '(building) site, plot'.

BRUGSCH, *Scriptura Aeg. dem.* 16, § 11; 43 [1848].

[S]**ⲟⲩⲱϩⲣ**, [A]**ⲟⲩⲁϩⲣⲉ**, see below under **ⲟⲩⲱϩⲣ**.

ⲟⲩⲥ (Crum 492 a), 'bald person' = (*Wb.* I, 20, 12), *(i)ꜣs*, (*Wb.* I, 33, 8), *iꜣs*, 'bald'.

DÉVAUD, *Études*, 28–31 [1922]; cf. SPIEGELBERG, *ZÄS* 63, 154 [1928].

[B]**ⲁⲡⲟⲩⲥ** (Crum 14 b) probably under influence of **ⲁⲡⲁⲥ**, 'old'.

ⲟⲩⲉⲓⲥⲉ (Crum 492 a), 'to saw' = (*Wb.* I, 358, 10 f.), *wsy*, 'to saw'; (Er. 99, 6), *ws*, 'to saw'.

[H]CHAMPOLLION, *Gr.* 372 [1836] (comparing *wsy* with **ⲃⲁⲥ**); *Dict.* 150 [1841]; [D]SPIEGELBERG, *Mythus*, 110, no. 189 [1917].

ⲟⲩⲟⲥⲣ (Crum 492 a), 'oar' = (*Wb.* I, 364, 1–4), *wsr*, 'oar'; (not in Er.; P. Dodgson, ro. 25), *wsr*, 'oar'.

[H]DE ROUGÉ, *Oeuv. div.* III (= *Bibl. ég.* XXIII), 147 [1856]; cf. SCHWARTZE in Bunsen, *Geschichte*, I, 585 [1845], who reads the Egn. word *ssr* and compares it with [B]**ⲟⲩⲟⲥⲉⲣ**; [D]H. THOMPSON's Demotic dictionary.

ⲟⲩⲟⲥⲧⲛ (Crum 492 b), 'become broad, broaden' = (*Wb.* I, 367, 9 f.), *wsṯn*, 'walk freely'; (Er. 101, 4), *wstn*, 'be free, unhindered'.

[H]DE ROUGÉ, *Oeuv. div.* III (= *Bibl. ég.* XXIII), 66 [1855]; [D]REVILLOUT, *Pap. mor.* I, 67 n. 1, and passim [1906]; cf. REVILLOUT, *Rev. ég.* 2, IV, pl. 61, ll. 4 and 7 [1881].

ⲟⲩⲱⲥϥ (Crum 492 b), 'be idle, brought to naught' = (*Wb.* I, 357, 2 f.), *wsf*, 'be lazy, idle'; (Er. 100, 6), *wsf*, 'be lazy'.

HCHABAS, *Mél. égypt.* I, 88 [1862]; DREVILLOUT, *Pap. mor.* I, 238 n. 4 [1907].

ⲟⲩⲟⲉⲓⲧ (Crum 493 a), 'pillar' = (*Wb.* I, 398, 15 f.), *wḏ*, 'stela'; (Er. 105, 6), *wty* (also *wyt*), 'stela'.

HBRUGSCH, *Wb.* 293 [1867]; DDE SAULCY, *Rosette*, 226 [1845].

ⲟⲩⲱⲧ (Crum 493 a), 'be raw, fresh, green' = (*Wb.* I, 264, 12 f.), *wꜣḏ*, 'be green, flourish'; (Er. 104, 4), *wt* (and *wṯ*), 'be green; green, fresh'.

HCHAMPOLLION, *Gr.* 317 [1836]; DBRUGSCH, *Rhind*, 36 and Pl. [35, no. 82 [1865].

ⲁϥ ⲉϥⲟⲩⲱⲧ, 'raw meat', cf. , *ἰwf w(ꜣ)ḏ*, 'raw meat'.

GARDINER, *Onom.* II, 255*, no. 608 [1947].

ⲟⲩⲟ(ⲟ)ⲧⲉ (Crum 493 b), 'greens, herbs' = (*Wb.* I, 266, 13), *wꜣḏt*, 'vegetables'; (Er. 105, 1, 'papyrus stem'), *wt* (*wṯ*), 'plants'.

HBRUGSCH, *Wb.*, Suppl. 403–4 [1880]; DBRUGSCH, *Gr. dém.* 25, §44 [1855].

ⲟⲩⲟⲧⲟⲩⲉⲧ (Crum 493 b), 'become, be green, palid' = (*Wb.* I, 270, 4. 5), *wꜣḏwꜣḏ*, 'be green'; (Er. 106, 5), *wtwt*, 'become, be green'.

HDBRUGSCH, *Wb.* 360 [1868]; cf. Brugsch, *Geographie*, 103 [1857]: as noun 'greenness, herbs, pallor', cf. (*Wb.* I, 408, 1), *wꜣḏwꜣḏ*, 'greenness'.

CHAMPOLLION, *Gr.* 89 [1836].

See also **ⲃⲉⲧⲃⲉⲧ**.

ⲟⲩⲱⲧ (Crum 494 a), 'single, alone, any, one and same' = (*Wb.* I, 278, 9), *wꜥty*, 'alone'; (Er. 81, 3), *wꜥṯ*, 'single, alone'.

HBRUGSCH, *Wb.* 242 [1867]; DHESS, *Gnost. Pap.* 5 [1892].

ⲟⲩⲁ ⲛⲟⲩⲱⲧ, 'single one, each one', cf. L.Eg. (*Wb.* I, 279, 1), *wꜥ wꜥty*, 'single one'.

ⲟⲩⲁⲁ⸗, ⲟⲩⲁⲁⲧ⸗ (Crum 470 a), 'alone, self' = L.Eg. + suffix, as in (Horus and Seth 4, 1), *ἰw·f wꜥt·f*, 'he being alone', (d'Orb. 5, 1), *wꜥ·ṯ*, 'you (fem.) alone', this for ⟨*n*⟩ *wꜥt*·+suffix, cf.

(Israel Stela, 6), *n wꜥ.f*, 'he alone' or for ⟨*ḥr*⟩ *wꜥt·* + suffix, cf. , *ḥr wꜥt.f*, 'alone' (James, *Ḥeḳanakhte*, 21); (Er. 81, bottom), *wꜥṯ·*, 'alone'.

[H]DE ROUGÉ, *Oeuv. div.* III (= *Bibl. ég.* XXIII), 173 [1856]; [D]REVILLOUT, *Pap. mor.* II, 46–7 n. 5 [1908] = *Journal as.*, 1908, 284–5 n. 5.

ⲙⲁⲩⲁⲁ⸗, ⲙⲁⲩⲁⲧ⸗ (Crum 198b), 'alone, single', from **ⲙ** + **ⲟⲩⲁⲁ⸗**, = L.Eg. + suffix, cf. (P. Millingen 1, 4), *m wꜥ.k*, 'you alone'.

GARDINER, *Late Eg. Stories*, 14a, note *c* to 5, 1 [1932].

(*N*) *wꜥt·* and *m wꜥt·* perhaps contain the pronominal form of the Infinitive of the verb *wꜥy*, 'to be alone' (*Wb.* I, 277, 1), and may literally mean 'of (his) being alone' and 'in (his) being alone'.

ⲟⲩⲱⲧ (Crum 495b), impers. 'it is different'.

ⲟⲩⲉⲧ...ⲟⲩⲉⲧ... (Crum 496a), 'one (thing) is...another is...' = L.Eg. ... (*Wb.* II, 408, 3), *rw(iꜣ)t(y)*, same meaning; .... (Er. 104, 1), *wṯ...wṯ...*, same meaning.

[H]SETHE, *Nachr. Ges. Wiss. zu Göttingen, Phil.-Hist. Kl.* 1925, 142–5 [1925]; cf. SETHE, *ZÄS* 63, 99–101 [1928]; [D]KRALL in Revillout, *Poème*, 245 [1885].

ⲟⲩⲧⲉ-, ⲟⲩⲧⲱ⸗ (Crum 494b), 'between, among' = (*Wb.* I, 58, bottom), *r iwd*, 'between', lit. 'to separate'; (Er. 26, 1), *iwt (iwṯ)*, 'between'.

[H]BRUGSCH, *Rec. de mon.* I, 43 [1862]; [D]BRUGSCH, *Gr. dém.* 167, §322 [1855].

ⲟⲩⲏⲧⲉ (Crum 495a), 'lightning?, calamity' = (Er. 105, 5), *wti*, 'fire, lightning' and (Er. 106, 4), *wty*, 'destruction'.

GRIFFITH, *Dem. Graffiti Dodekaschoinos*, I, 144, no. 83 [1937].

ⲟⲩⲉⲓⲧⲉ (Crum 495a), 'waste away, dry up' = (Er. 106, 1), *wyt*, 'melt, soften, dissolve'.

GRIFFITH, *Stories*, 106 [1900].

ⲟⲩ(ⲱ)ⲱⲧⲉ (Crum 495a), 'send' = (*Wb.* I, 397, 11), *wḏy*, 'send, leave for a journey'; (Er. 103, 5), *wt (wṯ)*, 'send away, dismiss'.

[H]DÉVAUD's slip; [D]GRIFFITH, *Ryl.* III, 344 [1909] (with doubt).

ⲟⲩ(ⲱ)ⲱⲧⲉ (Crum 495b), 'separate' = (*Wb.* I, 404, 3 f.), *wḏꜥ*, 'separate, judge'; (Er. 104, 1), *wṯ*, 'separate, choose'.

ᴴSETHE, *Verbum* I, 89, §145, 3; 187, §310 [1899]; ᴰSPIEGELBERG, *Mythus*, 113, no. 205 [1917].

ⲟⲩⲟⲧ (Qual.) **ⲉ-** (Crum 495b), 'separated, choice' = (Er. 104, 1), *wṯỉ*, 'better (than)'.

SPIEGELBERG, *Mythus*, 112, no. 204 [1917].

For **ⲟⲩⲱⲧ**, 'it is different', see this.

ⲟⲩⲱⲧⲃ, ⲟⲩⲱⲧϥ (Crum 496a), 'change (place), remove, transfer' = (*Wb.* I, 408, 3 f.), *wḏb*, 'turn (round)'; (Er. 106, 6), *wtb*, 'turn, pass over, make slip in writing'.

ᴴSCHWARTZE in Bunsen, *Geschichte*, I, 569 [1845]; cf. SALVOLINI, *Analyse grammaticale raisonnée*, 146, note ** and Pl. 42, no. 47 [1836]; ᴰREVILLOUT, *Chrest. dém.* 23, 150. 153 [1880].

ⲁⲧⲟⲩⲱⲧⲃ (Crum 497b), 'immutable' = (B. of D. 78, 38), *ỉwty wḏb*, 'immovable'.

ⲟⲩⲱⲧⲃ (Crum 496a), 'pass through, traverse, pierce' = (*Wb.* I, 306, 7), *wft*, 'pierce' > Dem. **wtf*, cf. (Er. 106, 7), *wtf*, 'hole'.

ᴴDÉVAUD, *Rec. trav.* 39, 155–6 [1921]; DÉVAUD–JUNKER in Spiegelberg, *Kopt. Handwb.* 173 [1921]; ᴰSPIEGELBERG, *Rec. trav.* 25, 10–11 [1903].

ⲟⲩⲁⲧⲃⲉ, ⲟⲩⲁⲧϥⲉ (Crum 497b), 'pierced place, hole' = , *wtby*, 'pierced place, hole' (of window and door).

PARKER, *JEA* 26, 107 [1940].

ⲟⲩⲱⲧⲛ (Crum 497b), 'pour' = (*Wb.* I, 391, 1 f.), *wdn*, 'make an offering'; (Er. 107, 1), *wtn*, 'libation'.

ᴴCHAMPOLLION, *Gr.* 108 [1836]; ᴰSAULCY, *Analyse grammaticale*, I, 226 [1845].

ⲟⲩⲱⲧⲛ (Crum 498a), 'pierce' = (*Wb.* I, 380, 10. 11), *wtn*, 'pierce'.

CHABAS, *Oeuv. div.* I (= *Bibl. ég.* IX), 289 n. 2 [1858].

ⲟⲩⲟⲧⲟⲩⲉⲧ, 'become green', see under **ⲟⲩⲱⲧ**, 'be raw, fresh, green'.

ⲟⲩⲧⲁϩ (Crum 498a), 'fruit' = Gr.-Roman (*Wb.* I, 410, 4), *wḏḥ*, 'fruit'; (Er. 107, 3), *wtḥ*, 'ripen; fruit'.

[HD]BRUGSCH, *Wb.*, Suppl. 1410 [1882]; cf. Brugsch, *Wb.*, Suppl. 362 [1880].

ⲟⲩⲱⲧϩ, ⲱⲧϩ (Crum 498b), 'pour, melt' = [hieroglyphs] (*Wb.* I, 393, 6 f.), *wdḥ*, 'pour'; [demotic] (Er. 107, 4), *wtḥ*, 'melt', and [demotic] (Er. 14, 4), *ꜣtḥ*, 'pour'.

[H]RÖSCH, *Vorbemerkungen*, 105 [1909]; [D]BRUGSCH, *De natura*, 26 [1850]; cf. PARKER, *JEA* 26, 91 [1940].

NB. **ⲟⲩⲱⲧϩ**, 'draw (water)' is confused with **ⲱⲧϩ**, 'draw' < Egn. *ꜣtḥ*.

ⲟⲩⲟⲧϩ and **ⲟⲩⲟⲧϩⲉ** (Crum 499a), 'pouring thing, cup' = [hieroglyphs] (not in *Wb.*, but cf. O.DM 318, 5; 434, II, 8; P. Leiden 344, 7, 14), *wḏḥ* (for *wdḥ*), a vessel; [demotic] (Er. 107, 5), *wtḥ*, a vessel.

[H]DÉVAUD's slip; [D]BRUGSCH, *Gr. dém.* 33, §66 [1855].

ⲟⲩⲱⲧϩ, ⲱⲧϩ (Crum 532b, s.v. **ⲱⲧϩ**), 'tie, sew, weave' = [hieroglyphs] (not in *Wb.*; exx. O. Gardiner 120, 1; vo. 1), *wꜣḏḥ*.

[B]**ⲟⲩⲫⲁϫⲓ** (Crum 499a), 'liver' = Gk. ἡπάτιον, 'small liver', diminutive of ἧπαρ, 'liver'.

ⲟⲩⲟⲉⲓϣ (Crum 499b), 'time, occasion' = Saite [hieroglyphs] (*Wb.* I, 336, 2), *wrš*, a length of time, from [hieroglyphs] (*Wb.* I, 335, 10), *wrš*, 'spend the day'; [demotic], *wrš*, or [demotic], *wš* (Er. 95, 2), 'time'.

[H]SETHE, *Verbum*, I, 141, §242 [1899]; [D]REVILLOUT in Groff, *Décr. Canope*, 62 (cf. 26) [1888].

ⲟⲩⲱϣ (Crum 500a), 'to desire, love' = [hieroglyphs] (*Wb.* I, 353, 14 f.), *wḫꜣ*, > L.Eg. [hieroglyphs], *w(ꜣ)ḫ*, 'search for, wish'; [demotic] (Er. 98, 8), *wḫ(ꜣ)*, 'search for, wish, request'.

[H]BRUGSCH, *Wb.* 269–70 [1867]; [D]GRIFFITH, *Stories*, 91 [1900].

ⲟⲩⲱϣ (Crum 501b), 'cleft, gap, interval' = [hieroglyphs] (*Wb.* I, 368, 5 f.), *wš(r)*, 'be empty, fall out' > [hieroglyphs] (*Wb.* I, 374, 10 f.), *wšr*, 'dry up, be missing, be bold, etc.'; [demotic] (Er. 101, 5), *wš*, 'hole, gap, space'.

[H]MÖLLER, *Rhind*, 14*, no. 94 [1913]; [D]GRIFFITH, *Stories*, 101 [1900].

ⲛⲟⲩⲉϣⲛ- (Crum 502a), 'with lack, absence of, without' = *[hieroglyphs], *m wš n*, cf. [hieroglyphs] + Infinitive (*Wb.* I, 368, 13, 14), *m wš r*, 'in the lack of, without'; [demotic], [demotic] (Er. 101, lower), *(n) wš (n)*, 'without'.

[H]BRUGSCH, *Wb.* 283 [1867]; [D]BRUGSCH, *Wb.* 289 [1867].

See also **ϣⲟⲩ, ⲥⲟⲩ-**.

ⲟⲩϣⲏ (Crum 502a), 'night' = (*Wb.* I, 352, 11), *wḫt*, 'darkness' (of the night), > L.Eg. , *wḫ(ꜣ)*; (Er. 98, 6), *wḫ*, 'night'.
[H]CHAMPOLLION, *Gr.* 97 [1836]; [D](SETHE *ap.* Spiegelberg in *ZÄS* 65, 54 [1930]).

ⲟⲩⲱ(ⲱ)ϣⲉ (Crum 502b), 'consume' by burning = (*Wb.* I, 370, 6f.), *wšꜥ*, 'chew, eat, consume (by fire)'; (Er. 101, 7), *wš*, 'consume (of fire), burn'.
[H]BRUGSCH, *Wb.* 285 [1867]; [D]GRIFFITH–THOMPSON, III, 22, no. 227 [1909].

ⲟⲩⲱϣⲃ (Crum 502b), 'answer' = (*Wb.* I, 371, 6 f.), *wšb*, 'answer'; (Er. 102, 4), *wšb*, 'answer'.
[H]CHAMPOLLION, *Gr.* 378, 474 [1836]; [D](BRUGSCH in *ZÄS* 26, 7 [1888]).

ⲟⲩⲱϣⲙ (Crum 503a), 'knead' = (*Wb.* I, 373, 9. 10), *wšm*, 'to mix something with liquid'; (not in Er.), *ꜣwšm*, 'knead?'.
[H]STERN in *Pap. Ebers*, Gloss. p. 57 [1875]; [D]PARKER, *JEA* 26, 100 [1940].

ⲟⲩϣⲁⲡ (Crum 503a), 'loan' = (not in Er.), *wšyp*, 'loan'; cf. (P. Lansing 6, 9), *wšby*, 'loan'.
[H]CAMINOS, *LEM*, 395 [1954]; [D]PARKER, *JEA* 26, 99 [1940].

ⲟⲩⲱϣⲥ (Crum 503b), 'become, be broad, at ease' = (*Wb.* I, 364, 11 f.), *wsḫ*, 'be broad, broad'; (Er. 101, 1), *wsḫ*, 'be broad'.
[H]CHAMPOLLION, *Gr.* 439 [1836]; [D]BRUGSCH, *De natura*, 26 [1850].
As noun: 'breadth' = (*Wb.* I, 365, 6 f.), *wsḫ*, 'breadth'; (Er. 101, 3), (Griffith–Thompson, III, 22, no. 224), *wsš*, 'breadth'.
[D]GRIFFITH–THOMPSON, III, 22, no. 224 [1909].

ⲟⲩⲁϣⲥⲉ (Crum 504a), 'breadth' = (*Wb.* I, 365, 13–15), *wsḫt*, 'breadth' (as measure); (Er. 101, 1), *wsḫt*, 'breadth'.
[H]STEINDORFF, *Kopt. Gr.*[2], 53, § 105 [1904]; cf. BRUGSCH, *Wb.* 279 (from *wsḫ*) [1867]; DÉVAUD in *Rec. trav.* 38, 193–4 [1917].

ⲟⲩⲱϣⲧ (Crum 504a), 'worship, greet, kiss' = (*Wb.* I, 375, 7 f.), *wšd*, 'address, greet, worship'; (Er. 102, 6), *wšt*, 'worship, greet'.
[H]ERMAN, *Die Sprache des Pap. Westcar*, 22 [1889]; [D]BRUGSCH, *Wb.* 352 [1868].

ⲟⲩⲁϣⲧⲉ (Crum 504b), 'worship, adoration' = (Er. 102, 6), *wšd(ỉ)t*, 'adoration'.

DSPIEGELBERG, *Rec. trav.* 17, 97 [1895]; cf. Brugsch, *Gr. dém.* 38, §79 [1855] who compared **ⲟⲩⲁϣⲧⲉ** with Infinitive *wšd*.

ⲟⲩⲟϣⲟⲩⲉϣ (Crum 504b), 'strike, thresh' = L.Eg. (*Wb.* I, 370, 16 f.), *wšwš*, 'smash'. Unrelated to **ⲟⲩⲟϭⲟⲩϭ**, 'to chew, crush.'

DE ROUGÉ, *Oeuv. div.* VI (= *Bibl. ég.* XXVI), 399 [lecture delivered in 1859, printed in 1874]; CHABAS, *Voyage*, 135–6 [1866].

ⲟⲩⲱϣϥ (Crum 505a), 'wear down, crush, destroy' = (Er. 102, 5; different from *wš*, 'consume'; read *wšf⟨·f⟩* in II Kh. 7, 4), *wšf*, 'destroy'.

SPIEGELBERG, *Kopt. Handwb.* 175 [1921].

ⲟⲩⲟϥ (Crum 505a), 'lung' = (*Wb.* I, 306, 3), *wfꜣ*, 'lung'; (Er. 87, 6), *w(ỉ)f*, 'lung'.

HBRUGSCH, *Wb.* 252 [1867] and 331 [1868]; DBRUGSCH, *Gr. dém.* 29, §56 [1855].

ⲟⲩⲱϩ (Crum 505b), 'put, set' = (*Wb.* I, 253, 1 ff.), *wꜣḥ*, 'put, lay'; (Er. 76, 7), *wꜣḥ*, 'lay'.

HDE ROUGÉ, *Oeuv. div.* I (= *Bibl. ég.* XXI), 288 n. [1849]; DHESS, *Stne*, 152 [1888].

ⲟⲩⲉϩ ⲥⲁϩⲛⲉ, see under **ⲥⲁϩⲛⲉ**; **ⲟⲩⲉϩ-ϫⲱ** under **ϫⲱ**.

(**ⲟⲩⲱϩ**), **ⲟⲩⲉϩ-** (Crum 508b), 'interpret' = (*Wb.* I, 348, 3 ff.), *wḥꜥ*, 'undo, disentangle, explain, interpret'.

DÉVAUD's slip.—But **ⲟⲩⲉϩ-** in **ⲡⲉϥⲟⲩⲉϩ ⲣⲁⲥⲟⲩ** is perhaps only a mistake for **ⲟⲩⲉϩⲙ-** (from **ⲟⲩⲱϩⲙ**); CRUM, 508b. The verb *wḥꜥ* is otherwise not found in Demotic.

ⲟⲩⲁϩⲉ (Crum 508b), 'oasis = (*Wb.* I, 347, 18), *wḥꜣt*, 'oasis'; (Er. 98, 4), *wḥy*, 'oasis'. Greek Ὄασις is a loan-word from Egn., Arabic واح from Coptic.

HGRIFFITH, *PSBA* 16, 51 [1893]; cf. SETHE, *ZÄS* 56, 45 [1920]; DGRIFFITH–THOMPSON, III, 22, no. 216 [1909].

ⲟⲩⲓϩⲉ (Crum 508b), 'to miss, be unsuccessful' = (*Wb.* I, 339, 1 f.), *why*, 'escape, miss, be unsuccessful'; (Er. 97, 4), *why*, 'miss, make mistake'.

ⲟⲩⲁϩⲓϩⲏⲧ, 'cruel' = *, *why-ḥ3ty*, 'one whose heart is passing by'; (Ankhsh. 21, 21), *whyṯ* (after masc.!), 'merciless, cruel' without *ḥ* of *ḥ3ty*, cf. ⲛⲁⲏⲧ for *nʿ-ḥ3ty*; see ⲛⲁⲏⲧ.

HDČERNÝ, *Crum Memorial Vol.* 41–2 [1950].

ⲟⲩⲟⲟϩⲉ (Crum 509a), 'scorpion', see the next entry.

ⲟⲩⲟⲟϩⲉ (Crum 509a), 'scorpion' = (*Wb.* I, 351, 1), *wḥʿt*, 'scorpion'; (Er. 98, 3), *wḥit*, 'scorpion'.

HSTERN, *ZÄS* 12, 91 [1874]; DREVILLOUT, *Setna*, 28 [1877].

ⲥⲓⲙ ⲛⲟⲩⲟⲟϩⲉ, plant *Erythraea spicata* = (*Wb.* I, 351, 8), *sm wḥʿt*, 'scorpion plant', thorny and therefore used in magic against scorpion sting.

ⲟⲩⲱϩⲉ (Crum 509a), 'fisher' = (*Wb.* I, 350, 1), *wḥʿ*, 'fisher'; (Er. 98, 2), *wḥ(i)*, 'fisher'.

HLAUTH in *Sitzungsberichte bayer. Ak. Wiss., Philos.-philol. Cl.* 1872, II, 57 [1872]; BRUGSCH, *Wb.*, Suppl. 440 [1880] (he reads the Egn. word *beḥā*; the reading *wḥʿ* was established by Maspero, *ZÄS* 22, 87 [1884]); cf. Dévéria, *Mém. et fragments*, I, 132 [1859]; DBRUGSCH, *Lettre à M. le Vicomte de Rougé*, 54 [1850].

ⲟⲩⲁϩⲃⲉϥ (Crum 509a), 'bark, growl' of dog = (*Wb.* I, 351, 10), *wḥwḥ*, 'bark'.

DÉVAUD in Spiegelberg, *Kopt. Handwb.* 305 [1921]; cf. DÉVAUD, *Études*, 31–3 [1922].

ⲟⲩⲱϩⲙ (Crum 509a), 'repeat, answer' = (*Wb.* I, 340, bottom), *whm*, 'repeat'; (Er. 97, 5), *whm*, 'repeat'.

HBRUGSCH, *ZDMG* 9, 193 f. [1855]; DBRUGSCH, *Wb.* 769 [1868] (though he reads the Egn. word *nem*).

ⲛⲟⲩⲱϩⲙ (Crum 510b), 'again' = (*Wb.* I, 343, 4), *m whm*, 'again', lit. 'in repeating'; (Er. 97, lower), *n whm*, 'again'.

ⲟⲩⲁϩⲙⲉ [510b], 'what is added', 'storey' of house, cf. (Er. 97, 5), *wḥm (n) ẖt 2*, 'two-storey' house.

SPIEGELBERG, *Dem. Pap. Strassburg*, 45 n. 1 [1902].

Sⲟⲩⲱϩⲣ, Aⲟⲩⲁϩⲣⲉ (Crum 492a, s.v. ⲟⲩⲱⲣϩ), 'put aside, save, spare?' = ? Late (*Wb.* I, 355, 8. 9), *wẖr*, 'take care of, provide' (*ẖ* required by Akhmîmic ϩ).

ⲟⲩϩⲟⲣ, fem. **ⲟⲩϩⲟ(ⲟ)ⲣⲉ** (Crum 510b), 'dog' = , *whr* (only in proper name *Pꜣ-whr*, Ranke I, 104, 12); fem. , *whrt* (only in proper names, *Wb.* I, 346, 6); (Er. 97, 6), *whr*, 'dog'.

[H]CHAMPOLLION, *Gr.* 72 [1836]; [D]BRUGSCH, *Scriptura Aeg. dem.* 17, §14 [1848].

ⲟⲩⲱ(ⲱ)ϫⲉ (Crum 511a), 'cut' = (*Wb.* I, 404, 3), 'separate (by cutting)'.

SPIEGELBERG, *Kopt. Etym.* 43–5 [1920].

ⲟⲩϫⲁⲓ (Crum 511b), 'be whole, safe, sound' = (*Wb.* I, 399, 14 f.), *wḏꜣ*, 'be intact', etc.; (Er. 108, 2), *wḏꜣ*, 'be intact'.

[H]DE ROUGÉ, *Oeuv. div.* II (= *Bibl. ég.* XXII), 193 f. (read in 1849) [1851]; [D]BRUGSCH, *Rhind*, 36 and Pl. 36, no. 86 [1865]; cf. BRUGSCH, *Wb.* 313 [1867].

[A]**ⲟⲩϫⲉⲓⲧⲉ** is originally an imperative followed by dependent pers. pronoun 'thou'. See under **-ⲧⲉ**.

RÖSCH, *Vorbemerkungen*, 140, §120 [1909].

ⲟⲩⲱϭ (Crum 512b), **ⲟⲩⲉϭ-** (in **ⲟⲩⲉϭⲣⲟ**), 'door(-planks)' = (*Wb.* I, 376, 7. 8), *wg*, 'plank', also part of ship; (Er. 102, 7), *wg*, part of ship.

ⲟⲩⲉϭⲣⲟ (Crum 512b, s.v. **ⲟⲩⲟⲟϭⲉ**), 'door's jawbone, door-post' = **ⲟⲩⲱϭ** + **ⲣⲟ** ('door'); cf. (not in Er.; Pap. Louvre E 7862, 5, see *ZÄS* 91, *Tafel* II), *wgyt pꜣ rꜣ*, 'door-post'.

[H]ERMAN–GRAPOW, *Wb.* I, 376, 7 [1926]; [D]MALININE in *ZÄS* 91, 128 n. *g* [1964].

ⲟⲩⲟ(ⲟ)ϭⲉ (Crum 512b), 'jaw, cheek' = dual (?) of (*Wb.* I, 376, 3–5), *wgyt*, 'lower jaw'; (Er. 103, 1), *wggy*, 'lower jaw'.

[H]STERN in *Pap. Ebers*, Gloss. 56 [1875]; [D]VOLTEN, *Dem. Traumdeutung*, 107 [1942].

ⲙⲁⲣⲟⲩⲟ(ⲟ)ϭⲉ (Crum 512b), 'jaw-bone' = **ⲙⲟⲩⲣ** ('bind') + **ⲟⲩⲟ(ⲟ)ϭⲉ**. For **ⲙⲟⲩⲣ** < , *mr*, of ligament on the jaw, cf. *Wb.* II, 105, 7.
For **ⲟⲩⲉϭⲣⲟ**, see **ⲟⲩⲱϭ**.

ⲟⲩⲱϭⲡ (Crum 513a), 'break' = (*Wb.* I, 377, 5), *wgp*, 'crush something in a liquid, destroy'; (Er. 102, 8), *wgp*, 'destroy'.

[H]ERMAN, *Zur äg. Wortforschung*, III (= *Sitzber. Preuss. Ak., phil.-hist. Kl.* XXXIX), 951 [1912]; [D]GRIFFITH, *Ryl.* III, 302 n. 1; 344 [1909].

ⲟⲩⲟϭⲟⲩⲉϭ (Crum 513b), 'chew, crush', reduplication of (*Wb.* I, 376, 1. 2), *wgy*, 'chew', connected with **ⲟⲩⲟ(ⲟ)ϭⲉ**, 'jaw'.

STERN in *Pap. Ebers*, Gloss. 56 [1875].

Ⲫ

ⲫⲓⲏ (Crum 514a), 'sprout, blossom' = (Er. 136, 1), *pryw*, 'sprout' or sim. from (*Wb.* I, 518 bottom), *pry*, 'to come out'.

[H]SPIEGELBERG, *Kopt. Handwb.* 91 n. 2 [1921]; [D]ERICHSEN, *Dem. Glossar*, 136, 1 [1954].

ⲫⲉⲗ (Crum 514a), 'bean' = L.Eg. (*Wb.* I, 531, 12), *pr*, 'bean', *Vicia faba* L. (Keimer, *BIFAO* 28, 80), from Semitic (cf. Hebrew פּוֹל, Arabic فول).

DÉVAUD, *Études*, 33–4 [1922].

[B]**ⲫⲟⲛⲡⲉⲛ** (Crum 514a), 'overflow', see [S]**ⲡⲟⲙⲡⲉⲙ**.

ⲫⲱⲛϫ (Crum 515a), 'overthrow, destroy' = ?L.Eg. (*Wb.* I, 511, 2), *png*, 'detach?' which is also the origin of [S]**ⲡⲱⲗⲕ**, [B]**ⲫⲱⲗϫ**.

ⲫⲟⲣⲡⲉⲣ (Crum 515b), tr. & intr. 'open, loosen' = (*Wb.* I, 532, 5), *prpr*, 'run to and fro', reduplication of [S]**ⲡⲉⲓⲣⲉ**, [B]**ⲫⲓⲣⲓ**, 'come forth' = , *pry*.

SPIEGELBERG, *Kopt. Handwb.* 94 [1921].

ⲫⲟⲣⲥ (Crum 515b), 'break up?' from Semitic √*prs* (cf. Hebrew פָּרַס).

DÉVAUD's slip.

ⲫⲁⲥⲫⲉⲥ (Crum 515b), pl. 'wiles', from Semitic; cf. فشفش, 'be a great liar'.

STRICKER in *Acta Orientalia* 15, 3 [1937].

Ⲭ

^B^ⲭⲁⲕⲕⲁⲙⲁⲩ, ⲕⲁⲕⲕⲁⲙⲁⲩ (Crum 516b), 'small night owl'. Both ⲭⲁⲕⲕⲁ and ⲙⲁⲩ onomatopoetic, see ⲕⲟⲩⲕⲟⲩ and ⲕⲁⲕⲟⲩⲡⲁⲧ; -ⲙⲁⲩ is probably the absolute form of the first part of ⲙⲟⲩ-ⲗⲁϫ.

^B^ⲭⲉⲗⲙⲓ (Crum 516b, 'meaning unknown'), 'nipple, teat' from Semitic (cf. Arabic حلمة, 'nipple').
CRUM, *JEA* 8, 189 [1922].

^B^ⲭⲗⲟⲙⲗⲉⲙ (Crum 516b), 'to crown', reduplicated verb **klmlm* from ^S^ⲕⲗⲟⲙ, ^B^ⲭⲗⲟⲙ, 'crown, wreath', see this latter.
CRUM, *A Coptic Dict.* 516b [1934].

^B^ⲭⲁⲣⲉⲃ (Crum 516b), 'lowly, abased', prob. connected with Adj. ^S^ⲕⲣⲟϥ, ^B^ⲭⲣⲟϥ, 'guileful, false'.

^B^ⲭⲣⲟⲃⲓ (Crum 516b), 'sickle' = ?  (*Wb.* III, 361, 14), *ḫ3b*, 'sickle'.
BRUGSCH, *Wb.* 1042 [1868].

^B^ⲭⲣⲱϣ (Crum 517a), 'wrinkle', from Arabic كَرِش, 'be pleated, wrinkled (of body's skin)'.
DÉVAUD's slip.

^B^ⲭⲟⲥ (Crum 517b), 'eructation, vomiting' can hardly be dissociated from  (*Wb.* V, 17, 4–6), *ḳis*, 'vomit, vomiting', but the initial ⌂, *ḳ*, of the latter normally requires *ⲕⲟⲥ since in Boh. *ḳ* > ⲭ only before liquids and ⲃ (SETHE, *Verbum*, I, 168, §281). Cf. however ^B^ⲭⲱⲛⲥ < *ḳns*, 'pierce, slay'.
KUENTZ in *Bull. de la Soc. de Ling.* 36, 162 [1935].

Ϣ

[O]ⲱⲉ, ‘become old’, as a gloss in *Dem. Mag. Pap.* 9, 1, explaining (Er. 16, 6) *ỉꜣw*, ‘become old’ < (*Wb.* I, 28, 8), *ỉꜣwy*, ‘become old’.

GRIFFITH in *ZÄS* 46, 127 [1909]; cf. Möller, *Rhind*, glossary, 2*, no. 11 [1913].

ⲱⲱ (Crum 518a), ‘conceive’ child, Qual. ⲉⲉⲧ, ‘be pregnant’ = (*Wb.* I, 56, 1 f.), *ỉwr*, ‘conceive’; (Er. 24, 9), *ỉwr*, ‘conceive’.

[H]CHABAS, *Pap. mag. Harris*, 57 [1860]; [D]HESS, *Stne*, 148 [1888].

ⲱⲃⲧ (Crum 518b), ‘goose’ or other edible bird = (*Wb.* I, 9, 5–8), *ꜣpd*, ‘bird’; (Er. 29, 4), *ỉpt* (*ỉpd*), ‘poultry, goose’.

[H]CHAMPOLLION, *Gr.* 73 [1836] (with doubt); [D]GRIFFITH, *Ryl.* III, 327 [1909].

ⲱⲃϣ (Crum 518b), ‘forget’ = (Er. 4, 3), *ꜣbḫ*, ‘forget’ probably < (*Wb.* I, 8, 9. 10. 14), *ꜣbḫ*, ‘to join, mix with’, the transitional meaning being the confusion caused by mixing.

[D]BRUGSCH, *Wb.* 4 [1867].

ⲱⲕ (Crum 519b), +ϩⲏⲧ, ‘be content’, lit. ‘entering in (the) heart’ = (*Wb.* I, 230, 3 f.), *ꜥḳ*, ‘enter’; (Er. 72, 5), *ꜥḳ*, ‘enter’.

[H]LAUTH, *ZÄS* 6, 91–2 [1868]; BRUGSCH, *Wb.* 701, 1613 [1868]; [D]GRIFFITH–THOMPSON, I, 31 [1904].

[F]ⲁⲕ-, SPIEGELBERG in *Rec. trav.*, 23, 201 [1901].

ⲱⲕ (Crum 519b), ‘go in, sink?’ of sun = (*Wb.* I, 230, 8), *ꜥḳ*, ‘go in, set (of stars)’.

SPIEGELBERG, *Kopt. Etym.* 7 [1920].

ⲱⲕⲙ (Crum 519b), ‘be dark, gloomy, changed (for worse)’ = (*Wb.* I, 34, 5), *ỉꜣkb*, ‘mourn’; (Er. 12, 3), *ꜣkm*, ‘be sad’, also , *ꜣgb*, Erichsen-Schott, *Fragmente memph. Theologie*, p. (41).

[H]BAILLET, *Oeuv. div.* I (= *Bibl. ég.* XV), 35 [1867]; BRUGSCH, *Wb.* 133 [1867]; [D]BRUGSCH, *Wb.* 18 [1867].

ωλ (Crum 520a), 'hold, take, lift up' = (*Wb.* I, 41, 14), *ỉʿr* > , *ʿr*, 'ascend', in Graeco-Roman period also 'lift up'; , *ʿr*, or , *ʿl* (Er. 67, 5), 'ascend, pick up, bring'.

HSPIEGELBERG, *Kopt. Handwb.* 179 [1921]; DBRUGSCH, *De natura*, 23 [1850]. See also **αλε**.

ωλκ (Crum 522a), 'become bent' = (*Wb.* I, 211, 16), *ʿrḳ*, 'bend'; (not in Er.), *ʿlḳ*, 'become bent'.

HSETHE, *Verbum*, I, 89, §145; 145, §244 [1899]; DSPIEGELBERG, *ZÄS* 56, 14 [1920].

ωμс (Crum 523a), 'sink, dip', from Semitic, cf. Arabic غمس, 'set' (of stars), 'dip, plunge (in water)'.

ROSSI, *Etym. aeg.* 250 [1808].

ωμϫ (Crum 524a), 'wean' = ?Late (*Wb.* I, 187, 10), *ʿmḏ*, 'turn away' or sim.

ERMAN–GRAPOW, *Wb.* I, 187, 10 [1926].

ωнε (Crum 524a), 'stone' = (*Wb.* I, 97, 12 f.), *ỉnr*, 'stone'; (Er. 34, 14) *ỉny*, 'stone'.

HCHAMPOLLION, *Gr.* 100 [1836]; DBRUGSCH, *Scriptura Aeg. dem.* 18, §18 [1848].

S**ωнε μμε**, **εнεμμε**, BF**αнαμнι**, 'real, precious stone' = **ωнε** + **με**, 'truth'.

SPIEGELBERG in *Rec. trav.* 28, 163 n. 4 [1906]; see also DÉVAUD, *Muséon* 36, 85 [1923]. Cf. , *ʿꜣt n mꜣʿt*, 'real (precious) stone', lit. 'precious stone of truth' with which Brugsch identified it less satisfactorily (*Wb.* 580 [1868]).

See also **αнιкαμ**, a kind of 'vitriol'.

ωнк (Crum 524b), refl. 'leap' = ? (*Wb.* I, 206, 2. 3), *ʿnḳ*, or , *ỉnḳ*, 'come' (of inundation); 'bring (inundation)'.

ωнϩ (Crum 525a), 'live' = (*Wb.* I, 193, 8 f.), *ʿnḫ*, 'live'; (Er. 63, 6), *ʿnḫ*, 'live'.

HDYOUNG, *Misc. Works*, III, pl. 3, no. 1 (cf. p. 168, no. 108) = *Encycl. Brit.*, Suppl. IV, pl. 76, no. 108 [1819]; cf. HCHAMPOLLION, *Gr.* 61 and 365 [1836] and DBRUGSCH, *Sammlung dem. Urk.* 20–1 and Pl. 4 [1850].

Part. coni. **αнϣ-**, **αн(α)ϩ-** in **αнϣтнυ**, see under **тнυ**, 'wind, breath'.

ⲱⲡ (Crum 526a), 'count, esteem' = (*Wb.* I, 66, 1 ff.), *ỉp*, 'count'; (Er. 28, 8), 'count, examine, think', etc.

^{H}CHABAS, *Oeuv. div.* I (= *Bibl. ég.* IX), 110 n. 4 [1857]; ^{D}BRUGSCH, *Gr. dém.* 38, § 79 [1855].

ⲏⲡⲉ (Crum 527b), 'number' = (*Wb.* I, 66, 22–4), *ỉpt*, 'counting, number'; (Er. 28, 9), *ỉpt*, 'number, counting'.

^{D}BRUGSCH, *Wb.* 48–9 [1867].

ⲱⲣ(ⲉ)ⲃ, ⲱⲣϥ (Crum 528a), 'restrict, surround' = (*Wb.* I, 210, 23 f.), *ʿrf*, 'envelop, tie up'; (Er. 66, 3), *ʿrf*, or (Er. 6, 9), *ꜣrb*, 'enclose, wrap up'.

^{H}CHAMPOLLION, *Gr.* 380 [1836] (**ⲱⲣϥ** and **ⲧⲱⲣ** interchanged through misprint); ^{D}BRUGSCH, *Rhind*, 35 and pl. 35, no. 45 [1865].

(ⲉ)ⲣⲃⲉ (Crum 529a), 'enclosure, pen' esp. for sheep = *rbt* in the toponym: , *Tꜣ-rbt* (Stela Louvre, *PSBA* 14, 238); (Er. 244, 1), *rbt*, 'cavalry camp'.

^{H}YOYOTTE, *Mitt. Kairo*, 16, 416–17 [1958]; ^{D}GRIFFITH in *The Adler Papyri*, 78 [1939]. Cf. also the place-name **ⲉⲣⲏⲃⲉ**, modern Rîfeh.

ⲱⲣⲕ (Crum 529a), 'swear' = (*Wb.* I, 212, 17 f.), *ʿrḳ*, 'swear'; (Er. 66, 6), *ʿrḳ*, 'swear'.

^{H}BAILLET, *Oeuv. div.* I (= *Bibl. ég.* XV), 30 [1867]; cf. BRUGSCH, *Wb.* 210 [1867]; ^{D}SPIEGELBERG, *Petubastis*, 11*, no. 59 [1910].

ⲱⲣϣ (Crum 530a), 'be cold' = (Er. 40, 2), *ỉrš*, 'cold'.

SPIEGELBERG, *Kopt. Handwb.* 9 [1921].

For possible part. coni. ^{B}**ⲁⲣϣ-**, see **ⲁⲣϣⲏⲧ**, 'press upon'.

See also **ⲁⲣⲟϣ**.

ⲱⲣϫ (Crum 530a), 'confirm, fasten, imprison' = (Er. 67, 4), *ʿrḏ*, 'make firm, secure, protect'.

^{D}REVILLOUT, *Pap. mor.* II, 38 n. 2 [1908].

From this probably **ⲁⲣⲏϫ⸗**, 'end, limit'; **ⲧⲁϫⲣⲟ**, however, is caus. of **ϫⲣⲟ**.

ⲱⲥⲕ (Crum 530b), 'delay, continue, be prolonged' = (*Wb.* I, 133, 6 f.), *ỉsḳ*, 'linger, delay'; (Er. 44, 4), *ỉsḳ*, also , *ꜣsḳ*, and , *ʿskỉ*, 'linger'.

[H]REINISCH, *Die aeg. Denkmäler in Miramar*, 276 [1865]; [D]BRUGSCH, *De natura*, 23 [1850].

ωτ (Crum 531 b), 'fat' = (*Wb.* I, 239, 8 f.), *ʿḏ*, 'fat'; (Er. 74, 3), *ʿt*, 'fat'.

[H]LAUTH, *Manetho*, 121 [1865] (but reads the Egn. word *uded, udi*); cf. Pleyte, *Études ég.* I, 9 [1866]; [HD]BRUGSCH, *Rhind*, 35, pl. 35, no. 47 [1865].

ωτπ (Crum 532 a), 'to load' = (*Wb.* I, 23, 16 f.), *ꜣṯp*, 'to load'; (Er. 13, 6), *ꜣtp*, 'to load, carry'.

[H]CHAMPOLLION, *Gr.* 379 [1836]; [D]REVILLOUT, *Poème*, 15 [1885].

ετπω (Crum 532 b), subst. 'burden' = (*Wb.* I, 24, 7–9), *ꜣṯpwt*, subst. 'load, burden'; (Er. 13, 6), *ꜣtpt*, 'load'.

[H]W. MAX MÜLLER, *ZÄS* 26, 79 [1888]; [D]KRALL in Revillout, *Poème*, 194 [1885].

ωτϩ (Crum 532 b), 'tie, sew, weave', see under ουωτϩ.

ωτϩ, ουωτϩ (Crum 498 b, s.v. ουωτϩ adding [A2]ωτϩ Mani Hom. 53, 16), 'draw', especially water = (*Wb.* I, 148, 12 f.), *ìtḥ*, 'draw'; (Er. 14, 2), *ꜣtḥ*, 'draw', and (Er. 14, 4), *ꜣtḥ*, 'draw' a liquid.

[H]STEINDORFF, *Prolegomena*, 4 [1884]; [D]REVILLOUT, *Revue ég.* 4, 75 n. 10 [1885].

[B]αθαϩ (Crum 532 b, s.v. ωτϩ), [A]εταϩ (Crum Corr. to 498 a), [F]ατεϩ, subst. 'burden, load' = (Er. 14, 3), *ꜣtḥ*, 'load'.

MATTHA, *Dem. Ostraka*, 190, note on no. 262, 2 [1945]; cf. Steindorff, *Prologomena*, 4 [1884].

[F]ατεϩ ντωϩ, 'load of straw' = , *ꜣtḥ tḥ*.

LICHTHEIM, *Dem. Ostraca*, 14, no. 13, n. 1 [1957].

ωου (Crum 533 a), 'be long' (in compounds only) = (*Wb.* I, 3, 12 f.), *ꜣwy*, 'be long'; (Er. 57, 1), *ʿw*, 'be wide'.

[H]BRUGSCH, *Wb.* 541 (though he reads the Egn. word *fu*) [1868]; [D]BOESER, *Pap. Insinger*, 6 [1922].

α-, [B]αυ- in ατοοτ⸗, [B]αυτοτ⸗: ειρε νατοοτ⸗ (Crum 426 a), 'to endeavour'. See under τωρε.

Subst. ⲱⲟⲩ, 'length', in ⲱⲟⲩ ⲛⲓⲁⲧ-, 'blessing', lit. 'length, stretch of eye' = (Er. 38, 2; 57, 2), *ꜥw n irt*, 'luck'.

GRIFFITH, *PSBA* 23, 17 [1901]; cf. SPIEGELBERG, *Kopt. Etym.* 28–9 [1920].

ⲱϣ (Crum 533a), 'cry, announce, sound' = (*Wb.* 1, 227, 4 f.) *ꜥš*, 'to call', etc.; (Er. 71, 5), *ꜥš*, 'call'.

[H]CHAMPOLLION, *Gr.* 368 [1836]; [D]BRUGSCH, *Sammlung dem. Urk.* 38 [1850]; *De natura*, 23 [1850].

Part. coni. [A2]ⲁϣ- in ⲁϣ-ⲥⲓⲟⲩ (in [ⲙⲛ]ⲧⲁϣⲥⲓⲟⲩ Mani Hom. 30, 3), 'reader of stars', 'astrologer'.

For ⲁϣϭⲁⲛ, see under ϣϭⲁⲛ.

For ⲱϣⲗⲟⲩⲗⲁⲓ, ⲉϣⲗⲟⲩⲗⲁⲓ, see under ϣⲗⲟⲩⲗⲁⲓ.

[B]ⲱϣⲓ in ⲙⲟⲩ ⲛⲱϣⲓ, 'rain' (Crum 535a) = or (*Wb.* 1, 224, 7), *ꜥḫy*, '(the height of the) sky', ⲙⲟⲩ ⲛⲱϣⲓ therefore = 'water of the sky'. Cf. also (*Wb.* 1, 224, 8), *ꜥḫt nt mw*, 'agglomeration of water (in the eye)'.

SPIEGELBERG, *Kopt. Etym.* 17 and 58 [1920].

ⲱϣⲙ (Crum 535a), 'quench' = (*Wb.* 1, 224, 15 f.), *ꜥḫm*, 'quench'; , *ꜥḫm*, , *ꜥšm* (Er. 70, 3), 'quench'.

[H]CHAMPOLLION, *Gr.* 376, 378 [1836]; [D]BRUGSCH, *De natura*, 23, 35 [1850].

[B]ⲁϣⲙⲓ (Crum 535b), 'wick' = (*Wb.* 1, 225, 1), *ꜥḫm*, some fuel ('wick' acc. to Caminos, *LEM*, 207).

ERMAN–GRAPOW, *Wb.* 1, 225, 1 [1926].

ⲱϥ, ⲱⲃ (Crum 535b), 'lettuce', *Lactuca sativa* L. = (*Wb.* 1, 176, 10), *ꜥbw*, 'lettuce'.

LORET, *Flore*[2], 69, no. 113 (with doubt) [1892]; cf. LORET, *PSBA* 26, 230 [1904].

ⲱϥⲉ (Crum 535b), 'press' = (*Wb.* 1, 41, 3. 4), *iꜥf*, 'press (to extract a liquid)'; (Er. 60, 1), *ꜥfꜥ*, 'be greedy, devour'.

[H]CHAMPOLLION, *Dict.* 85 [1841]; [D]H. THOMPSON's Demotic dictionary.

Part. coni. ⲁϥ-, see ⲁϥϫⲓⲣ, 'greedy of shameful gain'.

ωϥτ (Crum 536a), 'to nail, fix', cf. (*Wb.* I, 183, 14), *ʿfd*, 'the nail?'.

ειϥτ (Crum 536b), 'the nail' = ? (*Wb.* I, 183, 14), *ʿfd*, 'the nail?'.

SPIEGELBERG, *Kopt. Handwb.* 32 [1921].

ωϥτ (Crum 536b), intr. 'wear away' = (*Wb.* I, 72, 1–2), *ỉfd*, 'run away (like wild animals), run over (a place)', orig. 'run on four legs', a denominative from *ỉfdw* > ϥτοοϒ, 'four'. In Love songs Ch. Beatty 23, 9 and 24, 4 heart , *ỉfd*, 'runs away', perhaps already in the sense of 'wears away'.

ᴮωϭτ (Crum 536b), 'drip, trickle' = (*Wb.* I, 236, 13 f.), *ʿṯḫ*, 'pass through sieve'.

ωϩ (Crum 536b), interj. 'woe!' = (*Wb.* I, 12, 4, 5), *ꜣhw*, 'pain, grief'; (Er. 8, 4), *ꜣhw*, 'woe!'.

GLANVILLE's index.

ωϩε (Crum 536b), 'stand' = (*Wb.* I, 218, 3 f.), *ʿḥʿ*, 'stand'; (Er. 68, 10), *ʿḥʿ*, 'stand'.

NB. Fayyûmic Inf. is οϩι; ᶠεϩι is Qual., *JEA* 25, 112.

ᴴDE ROUGÉ, *Oeuv. div.* II (= *Bibl. ég.* XXII), 132 f. [1851]; ᴰBRUGSCH, *Gr. dém.* 37, §77 and 130, §266 [1855].

αϩε (Crum 538b), 'need' with dat. ν- of thing needed = with , *n* or , *ḥr* (*Wb.* I, 220, 4), 'to need'; Dem. *ʿḥʿ n*, 'need' (Er. 68, lower).

ᴴERMAN–GRAPOW, *Wb.* I, 220, 4 [1926].

ωϩc (Crum 538b), 'reap, mow' = (*Wb.* I, 19, 15. 16), *ꜣsḫ*, 'mow (with a sickle)'; (Er. 11, 8), *ꜣsḫ*, 'reap, mow'.

ᴴCHAMPOLLION, *Gr.* 372, 374 [1836]; ᴰGRIFFITH, *Ryl.* III, 332 [1909].

οϩc (Crum 539a), 'sickle' = (*Wb.* I, 19, 18), *ꜣsḫ*, 'sickle'.

CHAMPOLLION, *Gr.* 77 [1836].

ωϫ (Crum 539a), 'thief' = (*Wb.* I, 151, 1), *ỉṯꜣ*, 'thief', (not in Er., exx. Ankhsh. 14, 11; 17, 22; 20, 15), *ꜣḏ*, 'thief'.

ᴴCHABAS, *Oeuv. div.* I (= *Bibl. ég.* IX), 289 [1858]; cf. SETHE, *Verbum* I,

§298, 2; 397, 5 (p. 243) [1899] (both giving the Coptic word the variant form ⲟϫ); [D]STRICKER in *Oudheidkundige Mededelingen*, N.S. 39, 67 n. 73 [1958].

ⲱϫⲛ (Crum 539a), 'cease, make cease, destroy' = (Er. 75, 1), *ʿḏn*, 'destroy, dry up'.

REVILLOUT, *Revue ég.* 14, 9 n. 9 [1914].

ⲱϭⲃ (Crum 540a), 'become cold, frozen' = (Er. 73, 7), *ʿkf*, 'be cold'; connected? with (*Wb.* I, 22, 10 f.), *ꜣgb*, 'flood, inundation', Graeco-Roman , (*Wb.* I, 22, 15), 'to inundate'.

[H]CHAMPOLLION, *Gr.* 376 [1836]; [D]GRIFFITH–THOMPSON, III, 15, no. 139 [1909].

See also **ⲁϭⲃⲉⲥ**, 'moisture' = **ⲱϭⲃ** + **ⲥ** which guarantees also the meaning 'become moist' for **ⲱϭⲃ**.

ⲱϭ(ⲉ)ⲣ (Crum 540a), 'become hard, stiff, freeze', perhaps from Semitic √*ḳrr* (cf. Hebrew קָרַר, Arabic قرّ, Syr. ܩܪ.

DÉVAUD's slip.

ϣ

ϣ-, ⲉϣ- (Crum 541a), impers. verb, 'be able, permitted', lit. 'know' = (*Wb.* II, 442, 7 ff.), *rḫ*, 'recognize'; (*Wb.* II, 444, 13), 'be able'; (Er. 252, 4), *rḫ*, 'know, be able'.

[H]STERN, *Kopt. Gr.* 164, §337; 287, §455 [1880]; [D]REVILLOUT, *Setna*, 83 [1877].

ϣⲁ-, ϣⲁⲣⲟ⸗ (Crum 541b), prep. 'to, toward' = (*Wb.* IV, 408, 9–11), *r-šꜣʿ*, 'as far as'; (Er. 487, 4), *šʿ*, 'as far as'.

[HD]CHAMPOLLION, *Gr.* 517 [1836]; cf. [D]BRUGSCH, *Scriptura Aeg. dem.* 58, v [1848].

NB. The **ⲣ** in **ϣⲁⲣⲟ⸗** which seemed to require a derivation from , *ḥr*, '(go, come) to' (*Wb.* III, 315, 16; cf. Champollion, *Gr.* 474 f.; Spiegelberg in *Rec. trav.* 31 [1909], 157–8) is best explained by influence of the preposition **ⲉⲣⲟ⸗** as in **ϩⲁⲣⲟ⸗** and as in Greek prepositions **ⲕⲁⲧⲁⲣⲟ⸗** and **ⲡⲁⲣⲁⲣⲟ⸗**.

ϣⲁ (Crum 542b), 'begin' = (*Wb.* IV, 406, 4 f.), *šꜣʿ*, 'begin'; (Er. 489, 2), *šʿ* in *ir šʿ*, 'begin'.

[H]CHAMPOLLION, *Dict.* 210. 211 [1841]; [D]BRUGSCH, *Wb.* 1425 [1868].

ϣⲁ (Crum 542b), 'rise' of sun etc. = (*Wb.* III, 239, 4 f.), *ḫʿy*, 'rise, appear'; (Er. 350, 2), *ḫʿ*, 'rise, be resplendent'.

[H]CHAMPOLLION, *Gr.* 304 [1836] (though in *Dict.* 318–19 [1841], he compares the verb *ḫʿ* wrongly with ϣⲱⲓ); cf. Salvolini, *Analyse*, 176–7 [1836]; cf. de Rougé, *Oeuv. div.* VI (= *Bibl. ég.* XXVI), 53 n. 1 [1866]; [D]BRUGSCH, *Scriptura Aeg. dem.* 53 [1848].

ϣⲁ (Crum 543a), 'festival' = (*Wb.* III, 241, 4), *ḫʿ*, 'festival'; (Er. 350, lower), *ḫʿ*, 'festival', lit. 'appearance (of the god in a procession)'.

[H]CHAMPOLLION, *Gr.* 519 [1836]; *Dict.* 318. 319 [1841]; [D]BRUGSCH, *Gr. dém.* 130, §266 [1855].

ϣⲁ ⲱ (Crum 543b), 'great festival' = Gr.-R. (*Wb.* III, 241, 6), *ḫʿ ʿꜣ*, 'public festival', πανήγυρις.

STERN, *Kopt. Gr.* p. 92 [1880].

ⲣ ϣⲁ (Crum 543b), 'make, keep festival' = (*Wb.* III, 241, 5), *irt ḫʿ n*, 'make festival for (a god)'.

ϣⲁ, ϣⲁⲛⲧ⸗ (Crum 543b), 'nose' = (*Wb.* IV, 523, 1 f.), *šrt*, 'nose'; (Er. 484, 12), *šy*, 'nose'.

NB. ⲛ is intrusive as in ϣⲁⲛⲧϥ-ⲥⲱⲧⲙ.

[H]BRUGSCH, *Wb.* 1403 [1868], cf. SCHWARTZE in Bunsen, *Geschichte*, I, 607 [1845]; [D]BRUGSCH, *Rhind*, 48, and pl. 43, no. 385 [1865].

ϭⲱⲃⲉ ⲛϣⲁ, ϭⲃϣⲁ (Crum 544a), 'nostrils', see under ϭⲱⲱⲃⲉ.

[S]ϣⲁⲓ, [O]ϣⲟⲓ (Crum 544a), 'fortune, fate' with ⲡ- as god's name or proper name = (*Wb.* IV, 403, 11 f.), *šꜣw*, 'fate'; (Er. 485, 1), *šy*, 'fate, demon, god Shay'.

SPIEGELBERG, *Eigennamen*, 57*–9* [1901].

See also next entry.

[A2]ϣⲁⲓ (Crum 544b, 'meaning unknown') in ⲃⲁⲛϣⲁⲓ (Mani Ps.) is ϣⲁⲓ, 'fortune, fate' for which see the last entry; therefore ⲃⲁⲛϣⲁⲓ < ⲃⲱⲱⲛ + ϣⲁⲓ, 'evil-fated'. See also ⲃⲁⲛⲉⲓⲣⲉ (under ⲉⲓⲁ, 'eye') and ⲃⲁⲛϩⲟ. Opposite ⲛⲁϥⲣϣⲁⲓ, 'blessed(ness), good fortune', cf. the personal name , *Pꜣ-nfr-šꜣy*, lit. '(Man) of good fortune', Ranke, II, 281, 24.

ALLBERRY, *A Manichean Psalmbook*, II, 4, n. on l. 16 [1938].

ϣe (Crum 544b), 'go' =  (*Wb.* IV, 462, 7 f.), 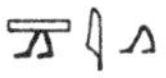 (from XXIst Dyn. onwards), *šm*, 'go';  (Er. 505, 7), *šm*, 'go'.

[H]CHAMPOLLION, *Gr.* 382 [1836]; [D]HESS in *ZÄS* 28, 5–6 [1890]; cf. HESS, *Stne*, 149 [1888]; MASPERO in *ZÄS* 16, 84 and pl. V, no. 163 [1878] (identifies Dem. and hierogl. writing).

Imperative [B]ⲙⲁϣe = * , *ỉmmỉ šm*; 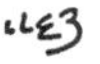 (Er. 506, middle), also , *m-šm*, 'go!'.

[HD]HESS in *ZÄS* 28, 6 [1890]; cf. LEXA, *Dem. Totenbuch*, 51 [1910].

ϣe with dat. eth. ⲛⲁ⸗ =  + suffix (*Wb.* IV, 463, 12), *šm n·* 'go, away, leave'.

ϣe (Crum 546a), 'wood' =  (*Wb.* III, 339, 10f), *ḫt*, 'wood';  (Er. 370, 2), *ḫt*, 'wood, tree'.

[H]CHAMPOLLION, *Gr.* 185 [1836]; [D]BRUGSCH, *Wb.* 1050 [1868]; HESS, *Stne*, 170 [1888].

[B]ϣe ⲛⲛⲟϩ (Crum 546b), a land measure (100 cubits) =  (*Wb.* II, 223, 12; III, 341, 12), *ḫt n nwḥ*, a measure of 100 cubits; 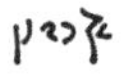 or  (Er. 370, 3), *ḫt-nḥ*, same meaning (Greek σχοῖνος).

[H]LEPSIUS, *ZÄS* 3, 98 [1865]; [D]SPIEGELBERG, *Die demotischen Papyri Hauswaldt*, 14 [1913], cf. SPIEGELBERG, *Kopt. Etym.* 57 [1920].

ϩⲁⲙϣe, 'carpenter', see under ϩⲁⲙ, 'craftsman'.

ϣe (Crum 546b), 'hundred' =  (*Wb.* IV, 497, 9 f.), *šnt*, 'hundred', in L.E. puns with , *šꜣʿ*;  (Er. 701), *š*, 'hundred'.

[H]GOODWIN in *ZÄS* 2, 39 [1864]; cf. SETHE in *ZÄS* 31, 112–13 [1893]; [D]BRUGSCH, *Gr. dém.* 61, § 133 [1855].

Dual ϣⲏⲧ, 'two hundred', = 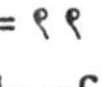 in L.E. puns with 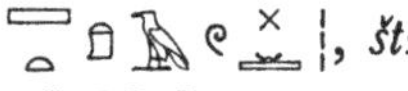, *štꜣ*.

GOODWIN, *ZÄS* 2, 39 [1864]; cf. PLEYTE, *ZÄS* 5, 14 [1867].

ϣe (Crum 547a), 'by' in swearing =  (*Wb.* I, 202, 3), *ʿnḫ*, 'as N.N. lives'; 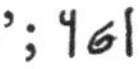 (Er. 64, 1), *ʿnḫ*, same meaning.

GRIFFITH, *Stories*, 93 [1900].

ϣⲉⲉⲓ (Crum 547a), =ϣⲉ+ⲉⲓ, 'go and come', 'be carried to and fro, wander' = (*Wb.* IV, 462, 12), *šm iy*, 'go and come, go to and fro'; , *šm iy*, same meaning.

[HD]SETHE in Spiegelberg, *Kopt. Handwb.* 188 and n. 4 [1921].

ϣⲏⲓ (Crum 547b), 'pit, cistern' = (*Wb.* IV, 397, 1 ff.), *š*, 'pool, lake'; (Er. 484–5), *šy*, 'lake, well'.

[H]CHAMPOLLION, *Gr.* 99 [1836]; [D]BRUGSCH, *Rhind*, 48 and pl. 43, no. 386 [1865].

ϣⲓ (Crum 547b), 'measure, weigh' = (*Wb.* III, 223, 4 f.), *ḫ3y*, 'measure'; (Er. 346, 2), *ḫ(3)y (ḫy)*, 'measure' (verb and subst.).

[H]CHAMPOLLION, *Gr.* 373 [1836]; [D]HESS, *Stne*, 171 [1888].

ϣⲓⲁⲓ (Crum 548b), 'be long' = (*Wb.* III, 237, 7 f.), *ḥy*, 'be high'; (Er. 349, 1), *ḥy*, 'be high'.

[HD]BRUGSCH, *Wb.* 1059 [1868].

ϣⲓⲏ (Crum 549a), 'length' = Gr.-R. (*Wb.* III, 238, 2), *ḥyt*, fem., 'height' (of a statue).

ϣⲱⲓ (Crum 550a), 'what is high, above' = (*Wb.* III, 237, 20), *ḥy*, 'height'; (Er. 349, 1), *ḥy*, 'height'.

[HD]BRUGSCH, *Wb.* 535 and 1058–9 [1868].

ϣⲟ (Crum 549b), 'thousand' = (*Wb.* III, 219, 3 f.), *ḫ3*, 'thousand'; (Er. 702, bottom), *ḫ3*, 'thousand'.

[H]YOUNG, *Misc. Works*, VII, Pl. 4, no. 202 = *Encycl. Brit.*, Suppl. IV, Pl. 77 [1819]; [D]BRUGSCH, *Gr. dém.* 62, § 133 [1855].

ϣⲱ (Crum 549b), 'sand' = (*Wb.* IV, 419, 23 f.), *šꜥy*, 'sand'; (Er. 489, 3), *šꜥ*, 'sand'.

[H]BIRCH in *Archaeologia* 38, 381 [1860]; DE ROUGÉ, *Oeuv. div.* IV (= *Bibl. ég.* XXIV), 134 (with doubt) [1861]; CHABAS, *Oeuv. div.* II (= *Bibl. ég.* X), 240 [1863]; [D]BRUGSCH, *Wb.* 1363 [1868].

ϣⲱ (Crum 550a), pl., a skin disease, read **ⲉϣⲱ**. See under **ⲉϣⲟ**, 'bran'.

ϣⲱⲓ (Crum 550a), 'what is high, above', see under **ϣⲓⲁⲓ**.

ϣⲱⲃ (Crum 550b), 'shave, clip' = (*Wb.* III, 253, 2 f.), *ḫbꜣ* 'hack, chop up' confused with (*Wb.* III, 251, 3 f.), *ḫby*, 'diminish'; (Er. 353, 4), *ḫb*, 'diminish, clip short'.

ERICHSEN, *Dem. Glossar*, 353, 4 [1954].

ᴼ**ϣⲃⲉ, ϣⲃⲏ** (Crum 551a), 'majestic' = (*Wb.* IV, 457, 2 f.), *šfyt*, 'majestic, awe-inspiring appearance'; (Er. 504, 6), *šft*, 'power, awe, esteem'.

ᴴGRIFFITH, *ZÄS* 38, 88 [1900]; ᴰSPIEGELBERG, *Kopt. Handwb.* 189 [1921].

ϣⲏⲃⲉ (Crum 551a), 'rust, verdigris' from Semitic, cf. Syr. ܫܥܘܒܐ (*šaʿubo*), 'rusty'.

DÉVAUD's slip.

ϣⲓⲃⲉ (Crum 551a), 'to change' = (*Wb.* IV, 436, 4 f.), *šby*, 'to mix, change (a message), replace (a person)'; (Er. 497, 1), *šb*, 'mix, change'.

ᴴSTEINDORFF, *ZÄS* 27, 110 [1889]; ᴰGRIFFITH, *PSBA* 31, 52 [1909]; *Ryl.* III, 229 n. 9 [1909].

ϣⲃ(ⲉ)ⲓⲱ (Crum 552b), 'change, exchange, requital' = (*Wb.* IV, 436, 15. 16), 'compensation, payment'; (Er. 497, 2), *šbt*, 'change, exchange, payment'.

ᴴSPIEGELBERG, *ZÄS* 55, 85 [1918]; ᴰSETHE, *Urk.* II, 187, note c [1904]; cf. GRIFFITH in *PSBA* 31, 219 n. 32 [1909].

ϣⲃⲓⲛ (Crum 553a), 'grain' = (Er. 499, 3), *šbn*, 'grain'.

HUGHES, *JNES* 10, 262 [1951].

ϣⲃⲱⲛ (Crum 553a), kind of herb or cereal? = (not in Er, but see Mythus 11, 13), *ḫbn*, a plant.

ϣⲃⲏⲣ (Crum 553a), 'friend, comrade' = (*Wb.* III, 254, 9), *ḫbr*, 'commercial connexion'; (Er. 354, 1), *ḫbr*, 'partner, friend', a loan-word from Semitic (cf. Hebrew חָבֵר, adj., 'united, companion').

ᴴBURCHARDT, *Die altkanaan. Fremdworte*, II, 37, no. 714 [1909]; ᴰHESS, *Gnost. Pap.* 11 [1892]; ˢLACROZE, *Lexicon*, 135 [1775].

ϣⲃⲱⲧ (Crum 554a), 'rod, staff' = (*Wb.* IV, 442, 13. 14), *šbd*, 'stick'; (Er. 499, 5), *šbt*, 'stick'; a loan-word from Semitic, cf. Hebrew שֵׁבֶט, 'rod, staff'.

ᴴCHABAS, *Oeuv. div.* II (= *Bibl. ég.* X), 98 [1860]; ᴰBRUGSCH, *Wb.* 1428 [1868]; ˢLACROZE, *Lexicon*, 123 [1775].

ϣⲟⲃϣⲉⲃ (Crum 554b), 'sharpen, incite', reduplication of ϣⲱⲃ ('shave, clip') = (*Wb.* III, 255, 2 f.), *ḫbḫb*, 'cut to pieces' or sim.; (Er. 354, 2), *ḫbḫb*, 'cut to pieces'.

ᴴBRUGSCH, *Wb.* 1066 [1868]; ᴰSPIEGELBERG, *Mythus*, 223, no. 592 [1917].

ϣⲱⲃϩ, ϣⲱⲟⲩϩ (Crum 554b), 'scorch, wither', see ϣⲱϩⲃ.

ᴮϣⲁⲑⲱⲗ, ᴼϧⲁⲧⲟⲩⲗ (Crum 555a), 'ichneumon' = (*Wb.* III, 236, 10), *ḫꜣtrw*, 'name of a god (with rat-like face)'; (Er. 530, 3), *štl*, or , *ḫtl*, 'ichneumon'. Loan-word from Semitic, cf. Arabic خيطل and Chald. חָתוּל ('cat'). For the meaning *ḫꜣtrw* = 'ichneumon', see Brunner–Traut in *Nachr. Ak. Wiss. Göttingen, phil.-hist. Kl.* 1965, 150 f.

ᴴLEFÉBURE, *PSBA* 7, 194 [1885]; ᴰPARKER, *JEA* 26, 106 [1940]; ˢROSSI, *Etym. aeg.* 253 [1808].

ᴮϣⲑⲉϩ (Crum 555a), 'street', from Semitic, cf. Syr. ܦܠܛܝܐ, 'forum'.

LACROZE, *Lexicon*, 129 [1775].

ˢᴬϣⲓⲕⲉ, ᴬϣⲓⲧⲉ (Crum 555b), 'dig' = (*Wb.* IV, 414, 11 f.), *šꜣd*, > , *šd*, 'dig'; (Er. 528, 1), *šty* (*šdy*), 'dig'.

ᴴSPIEGELBERG, *Kopt. Handwb.* 191 [1921]; DÉVAUD, *Kêmi* 2, 13 (for ᴬϣⲓⲧⲉ) [1929].

ϣⲓⲕ (Crum 556a), 'what is dug, depth' = (Er. 524, 3), *šk*, 'tomb-shaft, grave'.

ERICHSEN, *Dem. Glossar*, 524, 3 [1954]; cf. SPIEGELBERG, *Kopt. Handwb.* 191 [1921].

ϣⲕⲁⲕ (Crum 556a), noun, 'cry, shout', see under ϣϭⲁⲡ.

ϣⲕⲓⲗ (Crum 556b), 'curl' of hair, etymology unknown. For ϣⲕ(ⲉ)ⲗⲕⲓⲗ, 'bell', see under ϣⲕ(ⲉ)ⲗⲕⲓⲗ.

ϣⲕⲓⲗ (Crum 556b), 'curl' (better 'plait') of hair = , *škr*

(not in *Wb.*, only *škr ꜥꜣ* (IV, 550, 8), 'large *škr*'), a basket (exx. O. Cairo Cat. 25619, 5; O. Michaelides 14, 3–4; O. Gardiner 6, 5–6; 36, vo. 1, 8; 123, 8), lit. 'plaited thing'; a derivative of ϣωλκ, 'to plait', see this.

[S]ϣκολ, [B]ϫολ (Crum 556b), 'hole' = [demotic] (Er. 545, 7), *kll*, 'niche, hole'; from Semitic √*ḫll*, cf. Hebrew חלל, 'bore, pierce', Ar. خَلَّة, 'gap'.

[D]GRIFFITH–THOMPSON, III, 88, no. 940 [1909] (comparing [B]ϫολ [Peyron, *Lex.* 383, from Zoëga, *Cat.* 125, 15] which is a misreading for ϫολ); [S]DÉVAUD's slip.

ϣκ(ε)λκιλ (Crum 556b under ϣκιλ), (1) 'plait' of hair. Reduplication of the foregoing ϣκιλ, 'plait' of hair. (2) 'bell' = [demotic] (Er. 524, 7), *šklkl*, 'bell'.

SPIEGELBERG, *Kopt. Handwb.* 191 [1921].

ϣκλκελ (Crum 556b and ϣϭλϭλε 618b), 'gnashing, grinding' (lit. 'ringing') of teeth, of the same onomatopoetic origin as ϣκ(ε)λκιλ, 'bell'. See the preceding entry.

SPIEGELBERG, *Kopt. Handwb.* 191 [1921].

ϣουκρε (Crum 557a), a plant, from Arabic شُكُر, plural of شَكِير, 'shoot, sprout'.

DÉVAUD, *Kêmi* 2, 12 [1929].

ϣωκϩ (Crum 557a), 'dig deep' = ϣωκ (Crum 555a), 'dig'.
ϣικϩ = ϣικ (Crum 556a).

ϣωκϩ (Crum 557a), 'smite' = ? [demotic] (Er. 484, 11), *šꜣkh*, 'pound?'; for the meaning, see Griffith–Thompson, III, 80, no. 827.

[SB]ϣαλ, [A]ϩελ (Crum 557b), 'myrrh' = Late [hieroglyphs] (*Wb.* III, 323, 21), *ḫry*, a kind of myrrh; = [demotic] (Er. 368, 3), *ḫl*, 'myrrh' or sim.

[H]DÜMICHEN, *Geogr. Inschr. Text*, 59 [1866]; [D]BRUGSCH, *De natura*, 35 [1850].

ϣολ (Crum 557b), 'molar tooth, tusk' = [hieroglyphs] (*Wb.* III, 298, 7), 'tooth (of lion)'; [demotic] (Er. 368, 4), *ḫl*, or [demotic] *šꜥl* 'canine tooth', which is a loan-word from Semitic, cf. Hebrew שֵׁן.

[H]GARDINER, *PSBA* 38, 183–4 [1916]; [D]BRUGSCH, *Gr. dém.* 30, §59 [1855]; [S]I. E. S. EDWARDS, letter of 15 September 1961.

ϣⲱⲗ (Crum 557b), 'despoil, spoil, destroy' = (*Wb.* III, 298, 8–14), *ḫnr*, 'disperse', (P. Berlin 10497, 21), 'scatter, destroy'; (Er. 368, 5), *ḫl*, 'rob'.

[H]SPIEGELBERG, *Kopt. Handwb.* 192 [1921]; [D]BRUGSCH, *Wb.* 1132 [1868].

ϣⲱⲗ (Crum 358a), 'flow, loosen, dissolve' = ϣⲱⲗ, 'despoil, spoil, destroy', compare 'poison ϣ. ⲛϩⲏⲧϥ' from Mor. 54, 142, with P. Turin 137, 7, quoted by *Wb.* III, 298, 13.

ϣⲱⲗⲕ (Crum 558b), 'stitch, plait', from Semitic √*śrg*, cf. Hebrew שָׂרַג, 'be intertwined', Arabic شرج, 'set in order, weave'.

DÉVAUD's slip.

Probably a derivative from this is ϣⲕⲓⲗ (Crum 556b), 'plait' of hair, see this.

ϣⲗⲏⲗ (Crum 559a), 'pray' = late (not in *Wb.*; ex. *Urk.* VI, 129, 6), *šrr*, 'shout'; (Er. 519, 4), *šll*, 'pray'. Probably < ⲱϣ, 'cry' + ⲗⲏⲗ, like ϣⲗⲟⲩⲗⲁⲓ < ⲱϣ + ⲗⲟⲩⲗⲁⲓ.

[H]J.-CL. GOYON [letter of 15 April 1969]; [D]BRUGSCH, *De natura*, 38 [1850].

ϣⲗⲟⲗ (Crum 559b), 'folk, people' = (Er. 519, 3), *šll*, 'folk, family'.

VOLTEN, *Das demotische Weisheitsbuch*, 103 [1941].

ϣⲗⲟⲩⲗⲁⲓ (Crum 141b), 'shout aloud' = (Er. 520, 1), *šllwl*, 'jubilate', see ⲗⲟⲩⲗⲁⲓ.

ϣⲱⲗⲙ (Crum 559b), 'smell' = (*Wb.* III, 292, 4 f.), *ḫnm*, 'smell'; (Er. 362, 8), *ḫnm*, 'smell'.

[HD]BRUGSCH, *Wb.* 1101 [1868].

[A2]ϣⲱⲗⲙⲉ, [B]ϣⲉⲗⲉⲙ- (Crum 560a; adding [A2]ϣⲁⲗⲙⲉ- from Mani Ps. 205, 29), 'draw forth' (a sword), from Semitic, cf. Hebrew שָׁלַף, 'draw out', Arabic سلف, the final ⲙ perhaps under influence of ⲧⲱⲕⲙ.

DÉVAUD, *Études*, 51–3 [1923].

NB. It is, however, tempting to assume that the word acquired the wrong meaning 'draw out (a sword)' and that the original sense was 'to place back, sheathe (a sword)', the word deriving from L.E. (*Wb.* IV, 528, 10), *šrm*, 'lay down (arms)', a loan-word from Semitic (cf. Hebrew שָׁלוֹם). This is the etymology proposed by BRUGSCH, *Wb.* 1429 [1868] and accepted by DE ROUGÉ, *Chrest.* 4, 12 [1876].

ϣⲟⲗⲙⲉⲥ (Crum 560a), fem. 'gnat' = (*Wb.* III, 295, 12), masc., *ḫnms*, 'gnat'; (Er. 362, 9), *ḫnms*, masc., 'gnat'; became fem. in Coptic because of -ⲥ which was felt as fem. ending.

HBRUGSCH, *Wb.* 1103 [1868]; DLEXA in *Mél. Maspero*, I, 406 [1935–8].

ϣⲗⲁⲉⲓⲛ (Crum 560a), 'cress, nasturtium' = (Er. 369, 1), *ḫlyn*, 'cress'.

BRUGSCH, *De natura*, 35 [1850].

ϣⲗⲟⲡ (Crum 560a), 'ply, strand' of cord = (Er. 369, 2), *ḫlpi*, or , *ḫlp*, 'tip' of a plant or 'lobe, division of a leaf'. Connected with ϩ(ⲉ)ⲗⲡⲉ, 'navel(-cord)?'; see this latter.

CRUM, *A Coptic Dict.* 560a [1934].

ϣⲉⲗⲉⲉⲧ (Crum 560b), 'bride' = (Er. 520, 7 with doubtful ex.), *šlṱ*, 'bride, new wife'.

GLANVILLE, *'Onkhsheshonqy*, I, 73 n. 169 [1955]; cf. Spiegelberg, *Mythus*, 269, no. 793 [1917].

Sϣⲗⲱⲧ (P. Bodmer XXI in Jos. 7, 24), 'ravine' (φάραγξ), same as ϫⲉⲗⲗⲟⲧ, see this.

KASSER, *Pap. Bodmer XXI*, p. 24 [1963].

ϣⲟⲗϣⲗ (Crum 561b), 'shake' in sieve, 'sift', loan-word from Semitic, cf. Arabic خَلْخَلَ, 'shake'; New Hebrew חלחל, Chald. חַלְחֵל, 'agitate'; Syr. ܚܠܚܠ, 'shake violently'.

ROSSI, *Etym. aeg.* 260 [1808].

ϣⲗⲟϥ (Crum 561b), 'shame, disgrace' = ? (*Wb.* IV, 516, 2. 3), *šnrf*, 'get in disorder' (of cloths, hair); (Er. 518, 11), *šlf*, 'get in disorder' (of hair), and (Er. 518, 12), *šlf*, 'ugly', 'shame'.

HMASPERO, *Ét. de myth et arch.* III (= *Bibl. ég.* VII), 375 n. 8 to p. 374 [1878]; DBRUGSCH, *Gr. dém.* 34, §68 [1855].

NB. Spellings and (Er. 491, 8) suggest that ϣⲗⲟϥ < **šolf*.

ϣⲗϩ (Crum 561b), 'twig, shoot' = Gr.-R. (*Wb.* IV, 528, 12), *šrḥ*, kind of wood; (Er. 520, 4), *šlḥ*, 'shoot, twig'; a loan-word from Semitic, cf. Hebrew שֶׁלַח.

HERICHSEN, *Dem. Glossar*, 520, 4 [1954]; SBONDI in *ZÄS* 33, 68–9 [1895].

ϣⲗⲉϩ, ϣⲗⲏϩ (Crum 561 b), 'use twigs'? in faggots for strengthening canal banks, cf. Gr.-R. (*Wb.* IV, 528, 13), *šrḥ*, 'brook'.

BRUGSCH, *ZÄS* 3, 29 [1865].

ϣⲗⲁϩ (Crum 562 a), 'be afraid' = (Er. 520, 3), *šlḥ*, 'be afraid'.

SPIEGELBERG, *Dem. Denkmäler*, II, 149 n. 5 and Pl. 59 [1908].

ϣⲱⲗϭ (Crum 562 b), 'cut', from Semitic, cf. Ar. شلق, 'split' and شلقاء, 'knife'; Akkadian *šalāqu*.

SDÉVAUD's slip.

SAϣⲗⲓϭ, Bϣⲗⲓⲧ (Crum 563 a and ϭⲗⲓϭ 815 a), 'sharpened thing, spike, forked flame', cf. (Er. 520, 8), *šltt*, in *šltt šbt*, 'forked stick'.

BRUGSCH, *Wb.* 1430 [1868].

ϣⲗϭⲟⲙ, ϣⲗⲧⲁⲙ (Crum 563 a), 'mustard, rape' = (Er. 520, 6), *šlgm*, and , *šltm*, 'rape', like Arabic سلجم from Persian شلغم, 'rape'.

DSPIEGELBERG, *Dem. Denkmäler*, I, 79 [1904]; cf. II, 188 [1908]; ARROSSI, *Etym. aeg.* 259 [1808]; PEREMBER in Sethe, *Dem. Urk.* I, 187 [1920].

ϣⲏⲙ (Crum 563 a), 'small person, thing, quantity', connected with (*Wb.* III, 281, 13), *ḫmꜣꜣ*, 'become thin, meagre' = (Er. 359, 3), *ḫm*, 'small', 'little thing'.

HSTERN in *Pap. Ebers*, II, 60 [1875]; DBRUGSCH, *Sammlung dem. Urk.* Pl. V, l. 35 [1850]; *De natura*, 35 [1850].

ϣⲏⲙ ϣⲏⲙ (Crum 563 b), 'little by little, gradually' = , *ḫm ḫm*, lit. *ḫm sp sn*, 'gradually'.

GRIFFITH–THOMPSON, I, 34, n. on. l. 10 [1904].

ϣⲏⲙ (Crum 564 a), 'sign, omen?', only in ϫⲓϣⲏⲙ, 'take omens, divine'? = , *šm*, or , *šmi* (Er. 508, 2), 'to inspire(?)'.

ϣⲟⲉⲓⲙ (Crum 564 a), 'row, course' (Gk. στίχος) = (Er. 486, 3), *šꜥym*, or , *šym*, 'row' (e.g. of bee-hives, Mythus 7, 5) < (*Wb.* IV, 472, 4), *šmy(t)*, m., 'row (of corn-magazines)' = Gr.-R. (*Wb.* IV, 472, 5. 6), *šmy(t)*, m., 'corridor, passage (round the sanctuary)'.

ϣιμε, ϣοειμε, f., ‘row, course’, cf. (Er. 486, 4), *šymꜣ(t)*, f., a building < or (*Wb.* IV, 481, 15), *šmmt*, ‘street, passage’, and (*Wb.* IV, 466, 13), *šmt*, ‘road’.
All these words are derivatives of , ϣε, ‘go’, as στίχος, ‘row’, is of στείχω, ‘walk, go’.

ϣομ (Crum 564a), ‘father- (or ‘son-’) in-law’ = (*Wb.* IV, 411, 1), *šꜣm*, designation for an in-law relative; (Er. 508, 3), *šm*, ‘father-in-law’. An early loan (?) from Semitic, cf. Hebrew חָם ‘husband’s father’, Arabic حَم.

HGARDINER in N. de Garis Davies, *Five Theban Tombs*, 42 n. 1 [1913]; DBRUGSCH, *Sammlung dem. Urkunden*, 35 and pl. x, col. 3, l. 5 [1850]; SROSSI, *Etym. aeg.* 272 [1808].

fem. ϣωμε, ‘mother- (or ‘daughter-’) in-law = (not in *Wb.*), *šmt*, female in-law relative; (Er. 508, 3), *šmt*, ‘mother-in-law’; pl. ϣμοⲩι = (Ankhsh. 9, 12) (*nꜣ*) *šmw(w)t*, ‘parents-in-law’ in *JEA* 44, 122.

HENGELBACH in *Ann. Serv.* 22, 125 [1922]; DGRIFFITH, *Ryl.* III, 393 [1909]; cf. H. S. SMITH, *JEA* 44, 122 [1958].

ϣωμ (Crum 564b), ‘wash’ clothes, cf. (1) (*Wb.* IV, 411, 4), *šꜣmw*, ‘dirty washings’ and (2) (*Wb.* IV, 411, 5), *šꜣmyt*, ‘dirty water’ of the washerman.

(1) SPIEGELBERG, *OLZ* 8, cols. 65–6 [1905]; (2) ERMAN–GRAPOW, *Wb.* IV, 411, 5 [1930].

ϣωμ (Crum 564b), ‘summer’ = (*Wb.* IV, 480, 5), *šmw*, ‘summer’; (Er. 507, 1), *šm(w)*, ‘summer’, also (Er. 508, 1), *šm*.

HDBRUGSCH, *Nouv. rech.* 10–11; 14; 61–2, and pl. I, nos. 14. 15 [1856]; DBRUGSCH, *Gr. dém.* 30, §61 [1855].

ϣωμ, ‘tribute, tax’ = (*Wb.* IV, 481, 1 f.), *šm*, ‘harvest, harvest tax’; (Er. 507), *šm*, ‘harvest, tax’.

HBRUGSCH, *Nouv. rech.* 12 [1856]; DSPIEGELBERG in Reinach, *Pap. Th. Reinach*, 240 [1905].

ϣω(ω)με (Crum 564b), ‘cliff, precipice’ = (not in Er.), *šmỉ*, ‘cliff (?)’, < ? , *ꜥḫmt*, < (*Wb.* I, 125, 17), ‘shore, border (of river and valley)’.

HDÉVAUD’s slip; DSPIEGELBERG, *Kopt. Handwb.* 195 [1921].

ϣⲙⲁ (Crum 565a), 'be light, fine, subtle, thin' = (*Wb.* IV, 478, 5), 'thin'; (Er. 506, 1), *šm*, 'diminish' or sim.

[H]ERMAN–LANGE, *Pap. Lansing*, 73 [1925]; [D]ERICHSEN, *Dem. Glossar*, 506, bottom [1954].

ϣⲱⲱⲙⲉ, [B]**ϣⲟⲙ** (Crum 565a), 'thin, light' of clothes, cf. (*Wb.* IV, 477, 12 f.), *šmꜥt*, kind of linen, lit. 'fine one'; (Er. 509, 2), *šmꜥṯ*, 'made of fine linen' (verb).

[H]DÉVAUD's slip.

ϣⲙⲟⲩ (Crum 565a), 'peg, stake' = (*Wb.* IV, 467, 12), *šmyt* > Gr.-R. (*Wb.* IV, 467, 11), *šm*, 'stake'; (Er. 510, 4), *šmwt*, 'stake'.

[H]ERMAN–GRAPOW, *Wb.* IV, 467, 12 [1930]; [D]BRUGSCH, *Gr. dém.* 26, §50 [1855].

ϣⲙⲙⲟ (Crum 565b), 'stranger' = (*Wb.* IV, 470, 7 f.), *šmꜣ*, 'stranger, vagabond'; (Er. 510, 1), also (Ankhsh. 16, 19; 20, 5; 22, 14), *šmꜥ*, 'strange, stranger'.

[H]DE ROUGÉ, *Oeuv. div.* III (= *Bibl. ég.* XXIII), 152–3 [1856]; [D]SPIEGELBERG, *Petubastis*, 59*, no. 403 [1910].

ϣⲙⲟⲩⲛ (Crum 566b) = (*Wb.* III, 282, 10), *ḫmnw*, 'eight'.

BRUGSCH, *ZÄS* 12, 145–6 [1874]; cf. Lepsius in *Abhandl. Ak. Wiss. Berlin* 1856, 193–4 [1856].

f. **ϣⲙⲟⲩⲛⲉ** = (*Wb.* III, 282, 10), *ḫmnt*.

-ϣⲙⲏⲛ(ⲉ), 'eight(een etc. with tens)' = (*Wb.* IV, 282, 13), *ḫmnt*, 'eight' (abstract noun).

SETHE, *ZÄS* 47, 9. 12. 16 [1910].

ϩⲙⲉⲛⲉ, 'eighty' = , *ḫmnyw*, 'eighty', alliterating with .

PLEYTE, *ZÄS* 5, 13 [1867] (reading *ssnyw*); BRUGSCH, *Wb.*, Suppl. 921–2 [1881].

ϣⲟⲙⲛⲧ (Crum 566b), 'three' = (*Wb.* III, 283, 8 f.), *ḫmt*, 'three'.

GOODWIN acc. to Brugsch, *ZÄS* 1, 35 [1863]; cf. de Rougé, *ZÄS* 2, 49 [1864].

ϣⲁⲙⲁⲣ (Crum 342b, s.v. **ⲥⲁⲙⲁϩⲏⲣ**), 'fennel' = (Er. 511, 1), *šmr*, 'fennel', from Semitic (cf. New Hebrew שָׁמָר, m., 'fennel, *Anethum foeniculum*').

ϣⲁⲙⲁⲣ ϩⲟⲟⲩⲧ, 'wild fennel', شمار برى = , *šmr ḥwt(y)*, 'wild fennel', cf. Griffith–Thompson, I, 175, n. to l. 11.

[D]BRUGSCH, *Wb.* 1391 [1868]; [S]DÉVAUD's slip.

[B]**ϣⲉⲙⲏⲣ** (Crum 567a), 'leaven', from Semitic, cf. Aram. חֲמִירָא, Arabic خمير, خميره, 'leaven'.

LACROZE, *Lex.* 125 [1775]; cf. Rossi, *Etym. aeg.* 261 [1808].

ϣⲙϣⲉ (Crum 567a), 'serve, worship' = (*Wb.* IV, 482, bottom), *šms*, 'follow, serve'; (Er. 511, 2), *šms*, 'follow, serve'.

[H]YOUNG, *Misc. Works*, III, Pl. 3, no. 19 (cf. p. 171, no. 126) = *Encycl. Brit.*, Suppl. IV, Pl. 76, no. 126 [1819]; cf. CHAMPOLLION, *Gr.* 388 [1836]; cf. DE ROUGÉ, *Oeuvr. div.* II (= *Bibl. ég.* XXII), 188–9 [1851]; [D]YOUNG, *loc. cit.*; cf. BRUGSCH, *Rhind*, 48 and Pl. 43, no. 397 [1865].

[S]**ϣⲙϣⲏϭⲉ**, [B]**ϣⲉⲙϣⲏϫⲓ** (Crum 568a), 'whisper' = (Er. 512, 1), *šmšk*, 'hiss'. From **šemʿsēded*, lit. 'lightness of talk' (**ϣⲙⲁ**, 'become slight' (see this), and (*Wb.* IV, 395, 13), *sḏd*, 'talking', cf. **ϣⲁϫⲉ**.

[D]HESS, *Gnost. Pap.* 14 [1892].

(**ϣⲱⲙϫ**), **ϣⲁⲙϫ⸗** (Crum 568a), 'pierce', from Semitic, cf. Arabic خَزَمَ, 'pierce nostrils of a camel, to pass a ring through them'.

BSCIAI, *ZÄS* 26, 128 [1888].

ϣⲁⲛ (Crum 568b), conj., 'or' = (Kuentz, *La bataille de Kadech*, 243, section 94), *ḫr nꜣ*, 'or'; (Er. 361, 2), *ḫn*, 'or'.

[H]POLOTSKY [1969]; [D]GRIFFITH, *Stories*, 117 (with doubts) [1900]; cf. SPIEGELBERG, *Petubastis*, 46*, no. 303 [1910].

ϣⲏⲛ (Crum 568b), 'tree' = (*Wb.* IV, 498, 6 f.), *šn*, 'tree'; (Er. 513, 2), *šn*, 'tree'.

[H]CHABAS, *Pap. mag. Harris*, 239, no. 681 [1860]; cf. Brugsch, *Geographie*, 196 and Pl. XXXVIII, no. 889 [1857]; [D]BRUGSCH, *Gr. dém.* 25, §44 [1855].

ϣⲛⲏ (Crum 572a), f., 'garden' = (*Wb.* IV, 499, 6), *šnw* (*šny*), 'orchard'; (Er. 513, 3), f., *šn*, 'garden'; probably plural of *šn*, **ϣⲏⲛ**, 'tree'.

[H]BRUGSCH, *Wb.*, Suppl. 1194 [1882]; [D]ERICHSEN, *Dem. Glossar*, 513, 3 [1954].

ϣⲓⲛⲉ (Crum 569a), ‘seek, ask’ = (*Wb.* IV, 495, 8 f.), *šny*, ‘ask (question), say’; (Er. 513, 4), *šn*, ‘ask (question)’.

[H]BRUGSCH, *Wb.*, Suppl. 1190 [1882]; [D]HESS, *Gnost. Pap.* 14 [1892].

ϣⲓⲛⲉ (Crum 569b), ‘inquiry, news, report’, e.g. ϥⲓ ϣⲓⲛⲉ, ‘carry report’ = , *fy*...*n šnt*, ‘carry report’.

VOLTEN, *Ägypter und Amazonen*, 78 [1962].

[S]ϣⲙⲛⲟⲩϥⲉ, [B]ϣⲉⲛⲛⲟⲩϥⲓ (Crum 570a), ‘good news’ = (Er. 514, lower), *šm-nfr*, ‘good news, luck’.

SPIEGELBERG, *Mythus*, 266, no. 773 [1917].

ϣⲱⲛⲉ (Crum 570b), ‘be sick, weak’ = (*Wb.* IV, 494, 15 f.), *šny*, ‘feel pain, suffer’; (Er. 514, 1), *šn*, ‘be sick’.

[H]ERMAN, *Westcar*, I, 59 [1890]; [D]HESS, *Gnost. Pap.* 14 [1892].

ϣⲛ ϩⲏⲧ (Crum 716b, s.v. ϩⲏⲧ), the most correct is [B]ϣⲁⲛ (part. coni.) -ϩⲏⲧ, ‘pitiful of heart’, as verb ‘have pity’ = (*Wb.* IV, 494, 17. 18), *šn ḥ3ty*, ‘suffer of heart, have pity’.

RENOUF, *Egypt. Ess.* I, 126 n. 1 [1862].

ϣⲱⲱⲛⲉ (Crum 571a), ‘exclude, deprive?’ = (*Wb.* IV, 504, 5 f.), *šnʿ*, ‘repel, turn back (trans.)’; (Er. 515, 5), *šnʿ*, ‘repel, keep back’.

[H]BRUGSCH, *Šaï an sinsin*, 39–40 [1851]; [D]SPIEGELBERG, *Dem. Chronik*, 134, no. 553 [1914].

ϣⲛⲉ (Crum 571b), ‘net’ = (*Wb.* IV, 509, 8. 9), *šnw*, ‘net’.

BRUGSCH, *Wb.* 1397–8 [1868].

ϣⲛⲏ (Crum 572a), ‘garden’, see ϣⲏⲛ, ‘tree’.

ϣⲛⲥ (Crum 572a), ‘linen’ of fine flax = (*Wb.* IV, 540, 3–8), *šsr-nsw* < , *sš(r)-nzw* (Firth-Gunn, *Teti Pyramid Cemeteries*, Pl. 6; Text, p. 97), ‘king’s linen’; (Er. 522, 3), *šs-(n)-nsw*, ‘king’s linen’, Greek βύσσος.

[HD]BRUGSCH, *Wb.* 1346 [1868] (but he does not understand the element -ⲛⲥ, see Brugsch, *Dict. géo.* 874 [1879]; cf. SETHE, *ZÄS* 49, 17 [1911] (as to -ⲛⲥ).

ϣⲱⲛⲧ (Crum 572b), ‘to plait’ = L.E. (once, O. IFAO 1395, 11) or (O. IFAO 1000, II, 2; 1017, vo. 1; 1017, vo. 6; etc.), *ḫnd*, ‘plait’ (mats, wreaths).

ϣⲱⲛⲧ (Crum 572b), 'to quarrel' = (*Wb.* IV, 519, 3 f.), *šnṯ*, 'to quarrel'; (Er. 364, 3), *ḫnṯi*, 'quarrel'.

ᴴSPIEGELBERG, *ZÄS* 36, 136 [1898]; ᴰGRIFFITH–THOMPSON, III, 67, no. 665 [1909].

ϣⲁⲛⲧⲉ- + subj. + inf. (Crum 573a), verbal prefix 'until' = Late Aeth. , *šꜣꜥ-mtw*, < L.E. , *šꜣꜥ·t·* + suffix + inf. < , *šꜣꜥ ỉirtw·* + suff. + inf. (*Wb.* IV, 409, 1. 2), 'until'; (Er. 186, middle; 488, 1), *šꜣꜥ-(m)tw*, 'until'.

ᴴGARDINER, *JEA* 16, 231 [1930]; cf. ERMAN, *ZÄS* 38, 6 n. 2; 13 n. 2 [1900]; ᴰBRUGSCH, *Gr. dém.* 194, §397 [1855].

ϣⲟⲛⲧⲉ (Crum 573a), 'thorn tree' (*Acacia nilotica*) = (*Wb.* IV, 521, 1 f.), *šndt*, 'thorn tree'; (Er. 516, 7), *šntt*, 'thorn tree'. As loan-word into Semitic: Hebrew שִׁטָּה, Akkadian *samṭu*, Arabic سُنْط.

ᴴDÜMICHEN, *Bauurkunde*, 42 n. [1865]; ᴰHESS, *Rosette*, 47 (with doubt) [1902]; cf. Griffith–Thompson, III, 82, no. 857 [1909].

ϣⲛⲧⲱ (Crum 573b), 'sheet, robe' of linen = (*Wb.* IV, 522, 2 f.), *šnḏwt*, 'apron'; (Er. 516, 6), *šnt*, 'costume, apron'.

ᴴCHAMPOLLION, *Gr.* 61 [1836]; ᴰBRUGSCH, *Gr. dém.* 40, §84 [1855].

ϣⲛⲁⲩ (Crum 573b), 'market', a loan-word from Semitic √*ḫnw*, cf. Aram. חֲנָוָאָה, 'merchant', חָנוּתָא, 'shop'.

DÉVAUD's slip.

ϣⲛⲟϣ (Crum 573b), 'stink' = (*Wb.* III, 301, 1), *ḫnš*, 'stink'; (*Wb.* IV, 517, 7), *šnš*, 'stink' (of water); (Er. 363, 1), *ḫnš*, 'stink'.

ᴴCHABAS, *Voyage*, 306 [1866]; ᴰREVILLOUT, *Poème*, 8 [1885].

ϣⲱⲛϥ, ϣⲱⲛⲃ (Crum 573b), 'come together, join' = (*Wb.* IV, 440, 5 f.), *šbn*, 'mix'; (Er. 499, 1), *šbn* also , *šnb*, 'unite with, join'.

ᴴBRUGSCH, *Wb.* 1372 [1868]; ᴰBRUGSCH, *Rhind*, 48 and Pl. 43, no. 393 [1865].

ϣ(ⲉ)ⲛϥⲉ (Crum 574a), 'scale' of fish = (*Wb.* IV, 515, 2), *šnft*, 'scale' of fish; (Er. 362, 7), *ḫnfy*, a fish. From Semitic, cf. Arabic سِنْفَة, 'pod'.

[H]GRIFFITH in Davies, *El Amarna*, III, 32 n. 9 [1905]; [D]REVILLOUT, *Revue ég.* I, 159, n. 9 for p. 158 [1880]; [S]STRICKER in *Acta Orientalia* 15, 5 [1937].

ϣⲁⲡ (Crum 574b), prenuptial 'marriage gift' = Gr.-R. (*Wb.* IV, 444, 9), *šp*, 'gift', from (*Wb.* IV, 530, 1 f.), *šsp*, **ϣⲱⲡ**, 'receive', e.g. *šsp*, *ḥswt*, 'receive reward' (*Wb.* IV, 532, 12); (Er. 502, 2), *špi*, or, *šp*, 'gift, reward'.

[H]ERMAN–GRAPOW, IV, 444, 9 [1930]; [D]HESS, *Stne*, 15 [1888].

ϣⲟⲡ (Crum 574b), 'fingerbreadth, palm' = (*Wb.* IV, 535, 3 f.), *šsp*, 'palm'; (not in Er.), *šp* (?), 'palm'.

[H]BRUGSCH, *ZÄS* 2, 43 and 45 [1864]; [D]GRIFFITH–THOMPSON, III, 81, no. 839 [1909].

ϣⲱⲡ (Crum 574b), receive = (*Wb.* IV, 530, 1 f.), *šsp*, 'receive'; (Er. 500), *šp*, 'receive'.

[H]CHAMPOLLION, *Gr.* 380 [1836]; [D]BRUGSCH, *Rhind*, 48 and Pl. 43, no. 395 [1865].

ϣⲱⲡ (Crum 576b), a metal object mostly of silver, necklet, bracelet = ? (*Wb.* IV, 438, 11–13), *šbyw*, 'necklet, armlet?'; (Er. 502, 1), *špi*, a jewel (necklet, armlet or sim.).

[HD]CRUM, *A Coptic Dict.* 576b [1937].

ϣⲱⲡ (Crum 576b), 'moment, instant', only in **ϩⲛⲟⲩϣ(ⲉ)ⲡⲛϣⲱⲡ**, 'suddenly', lit. 'in a passing of moment'; see under **ϣ(ⲉ)ⲡⲛϣⲱⲡ**.

[S]**ϫⲡ-**, [B]**ⲁϫⲡ-** (Crum 777b), 'hour' = ⲧ + **ϣⲱⲡ**.

CHAMPOLLION, *Gr.* 96 [1836] (compares the correct Egn. word, but ignores the presence of ⲧ; only *t* + *š* = ϫ); Chabas, *Mél.* II, 258 n. [1864].

ϣⲓⲡⲉ (Crum 576b), 'be, make ashamed' = or (Er. 503, 3), *špy*, *šyp*, 'be ashamed', probably the old (*Wb.* IV, 453, 10 f.), *špt*, 'be angry, discontent'.

[H]BRUGSCH, *Wb.* 1070 [1868]; [D]BRUGSCH, *Wb.*, Suppl. 1170 [1882] (he does not refer expressly to **ϣⲓⲡⲉ**, but quotes his *Wb.* 1376, where the identification of **ϣⲓⲡⲉ** and *špt* had been quoted from *Wb.* 1070); cf. Revillout, *Setna*, 163 [1877].

ϣⲱⲡⲉ (Crum 577b), 'become, befall' = (*Wb.* III, 260, 7 f.), *ḫpr*, 'become, take origin'; (Er. 355), *ḫpr*, 'become'.

[H]DE ROUGÉ, *Oeuv. div.* II (= *Bibl. ég.* XXII), 53 f. [1851]; [D]BRUGSCH, *Gr. dém.* 127, §260, 3°; 129, §265 [1855].

[S]**ⲉϣⲱⲡⲉ**, [A]**ⲉϩⲱⲡⲉ** (Crum 580b), conjunction, 'if it befall, if, when' < ***ⲉϥϣⲱⲡⲉ** = , *iw·f ḫpr*, 'if it happens that...' < *, *iw·f ḫpr*, same meaning.

, *iw-ḫpr*, is found once in *Dem. mag. Pap.* 3, 19 (Griffith–Thompson, I, 35, n. on l. 19 [1904].

[D]BRUGSCH, *Gr. dém.* 191, §391 [1855].

NB. Sethe's explanation from **iw·s ḫpr* (*ZÄS* 38, 147–8 [1900]) is less satisfactory since *iw·s ḫpr* is not actually attested.

[A]**ⲉϩⲱⲡⲉ** > [A](**ⲉⲓ**)**ϩⲡⲉ**; [A2]**ⲉϣⲡⲉ**; [A](**ⲉⲓ**)**ϩϫⲉ** < ***ⲉϩⲱⲡⲉ + ϫⲉ**, see under [SF]**ⲉϣϫⲉ**, 'if'.

ϣⲱⲡⲉ, **ϣⲱⲃⲉ** (Crum 580b), 'cucumber, gourd' = (*Wb.* IV, 284, 11), *sšpt*, 'cucumber' > (*Wb.* IV, 536, bottom), *š(s)pt*, (*Wb.* IV, 438, 2–4), *šbt*; , *špi*, or , *šwbi* (Er. 503, 2), 'cucumber', *Cucumis Melo* L.

[H]STERN in *Pap. Ebers*, II, 46 (Glossary) [1875]; [D]GRIFFITH–THOMPSON, III, 81, no. 835 [1909].

ⲃⲣⲁ ϣⲱⲡⲉ (Crum 581a), 'cucumber seed' = (*Wb.* IV, 438, 4), *prt šbt*, prob. 'cucumber seed'.

MASSART, *Oudheidk. Meded.*, Suppl. to N.R. 34, 70 [1954].

ϣ(ⲉ)ⲡⲛϣⲱⲡ (Crum 576b under **ϣⲱⲡ**, 'moment'), only in **ϩⲛⲟⲩϣ(ⲉ)ⲡ-ⲛ-ϣⲱⲡ**, 'suddenly', lit. 'in a passing of moment'.

ϣ(ⲉ)ⲡ- = (Er. 501, 3), *ḫp*, in (*n*) *ḫp*, 'suddenly', perhaps the old (*Wb.* III, 258, 3 f.), *ḫpy*, 'walk, pass, pass away'. Cf. Brugsch, *Wb.* 1069 and 1669 [1868] who, however, explains in this way the second part **-ϣⲱⲡ**.

ϣⲱⲡ = (Er. 501, 3), *šp*, 'time, hour, moment' < ? (*Wb.* IV, 283, 10), *sšp*, 'light, daybreak'.

[H]ERICHSEN, *Dem. Glossar*, 501, 3 [1954]; [D]GRIFFITH–THOMPSON, III, [81], no. 838a [1909].

NB. The two Dem. words quoted, *ḫp* and *šp*, are different!

ⳉπηρε (Crum 581 a), 'wonder, amazement' = (*Wb.* III, 263, 2), *ḫprt*, 'that which has happened, event'; (Er. 356, 1), *ḫpry*, 'wonder'.

HERMAN–GRAPOW, *Wb.* III, 263, 2 [1929]; DREVILLOUT, *Revue égyp.* 2, no. IV, 65 [1881].

ϣωπϣ (Crum 582 a), 'arm, foreleg of animals' = (*Wb.* III, 268, 4 ff.), *ḫpš*, 'foreleg'; (Er. 357, 2), *ḫpš*, 'arm, foreleg'.

HCHAMPOLLION in Caillaud, *Voyage à Méroé*, IV, 40 n. 5 [1827]; DHESS, *Gnost. Pap.* 11 [1892].

ϣωπϣ, as constellation name (= 'Αρκτοῦρος) = (*Wb.* III, 268, 9), *ḫpš*; , *ḫpš*, 'Great Bear' (lit. 'the Foreleg').

HCHAMPOLLION, *Gr.* 62 [1836]; DHESS, *Gnost. Pap.* 11 [1892].

ϣⲁπϣι (Crum 582 a), 'noble, distinguished woman' = (*Wb.* IV, 449, 10 f.), *špst*, > Gr.-R. , *špšt*, 'noble lady'; (Er. 504, top), *špšit*, 'noble lady'.

HGRIFFITH, *ZÄS* 38, 92 [1900]; DMÖLLER, *Pap. Rhind*, 55*, no. 379 [1913].

(ϣοπϣπ), ϣ(ε)πϣπ-, ϣπϣωπ- (Crum 582 a), 'take in the arms, nurse', reduplication of ϣωπ, 'receive, take'.

ϣⲁρ- (Crum 582 a), 'being small, short', part. coni. of (*Wb.* IV, 524, bottom), *šrr*, 'be small'. Cf. proper name , *šꜣrt·f*, and , *šꜣrꜣrt·f* (*ϣⲁρ-ρⲁτϥ), 'short-legged' (Spiegelberg, *Äg. und griech. Personennamen*, 35*, no. 240) in Gk. transcription (in Genitive) Σαρα(ρε)χθου.

SETHE, *Verbum*, I, §389; II, §960, 2 [1899].

Sϣⲁⲁρ, Aϩⲁⲁρε (Crum 582 a), 'skin' = L.E., (*Wb.* III, 244, 9 and vol. of references), *ḫꜥr*, 'leather'; (Er. 352, 2), *ḫꜥr*, 'skin, leather'.

HBRUGSCH in *ZÄS* 16, 49 [1878]; DBRUGSCH, *De natura*, 35 [1850].

ϣⲁⲁρ (Crum 582 b), 'price' = (Er. 491, 5), *šꜥr*, 'price', from Semitic, cf. Hebrew and New Hebrew שַׁעַר, 'market price'; Aram. שַׁעֲרָא.

DREVILLOUT, *Pap. moral de Leide*, II, 17 n. 3 [1908] = *Journal as.* série 10, vol. 11, 255 [1908] (but Brugsch must have made the identification by 1868 since in his *Wb.* 1018, he translates the word correctly by 'price'); SSPIEGELBERG, *Kopt. Handwb.* 204 [1921].

ϣⲱⲣ (Crum 583a), 'pile up, make thick, stop up' = (*Wb.* IV, 527, 12 f.), *šrỉ*, 'stop up, block'.

BRUGSCH, *Wb.* 1404 [1868].

ϣⲁⲣⲉ-, ϣⲁ⸗ (Crum 583a), prefix of aorist (i.e. Present of habitude) = * , *ḥr ỉry·f* + Inf. replacing the older + *sḏm·f* (*Wb.* III, 316, 6); (Er. 364, 6), *ḥr*, particle of aorist (Present of habitude) + , *ỉr·*.

[H]SETHE, *ZDMG* 79, 293 and n. 4 [1925]; [D]BRUGSCH, *ZÄS* 26, 18 [1888]; HESS, *Stne*, 93 [1888].

ϣⲁⲁⲣⲉ (Crum 583b), 'smite' = Gr.-R. (*Wb.* III, 244, 8), *ḫʿr*, 'smite (enemy)' < (*Wb.* III, 244, 2–6), *ḫʿr*, 'be furious'; (Er. 352, 1), *ḫʿr*, 'smite', 'become angry' (P. Carlsberg I, 5, 8).

[H]ERMAN–GRAPOW, *Wb.* III, 244, 8 [1929]; SPIEGELBERG, *Sphinx* 5, 200–1 [1902]; [D]BRUGSCH, *Gr. dém.* 35, §70 [1855].

[B]**ϣⲁ(ⲓ)ⲣⲓ** (Crum 584a) in **ⲫⲓⲟⲙ ⲛϣⲁ(ⲓ)ⲣⲓ**, 'Red Sea' = * , *pꜣ yʿm n Ḫꜣrw*, lit. 'the sea of Syria'.

ČERNÝ in *Mélanges Mariette*, 57–62 [1961]. Cf. Champollion, *Gr.* 127 [1836] who transcribes the proper name *Nb-n-ḫꜣrw* as **ⲛⲏⲃⲛϣⲁⲣⲓ**.

ϣⲏⲣⲉ, ϣⲉ- (Crum 584a), 'son, child' = (*Wb.* IV, 526, 9 f.), *šrỉ*, 'child, boy, son'; (Er. 516, 8), *šr*, 'son'.

[H]CHAMPOLLION, *Gr.* 76 [1836] (**ϣⲏⲣⲉ**); STEINDORFF, *ZÄS* 28, 51 [1890] (**ϣⲉ-**); [D]ÅKERBLAD in Young, *Works*, III, 37 [1815].

ϣⲉⲉⲣⲉ, 'daughter' = (*Wb.* IV, 527, 1 f.), *šrỉt*, 'girl, daughter'; (Er. 517, 1), *šrt*, 'daughter'.

[H]SETHE, *Verbum*, I, 137, §236, 2 [1899]; [D]BRUGSCH, *Gr. dém.* 76, §167 [1855].

ϣⲣϩⲟⲟⲩⲧ (Crum 585b), lit. 'male son' = (*Wb.* I, 217, 15; IV, 526, 16), *šrỉ ʿḥꜣwty*, 'male son'.

ϣⲏⲣⲓ (Crum 585b), 'bread' = , *sꜣšrt* > , *sšrt* (*Wb.* IV, 25, 4–5), kind of bread.

DÉVAUD in Spiegelberg, *Kopt. Handwb.* 205 [1921]; cf. KUENTZ, *BIFAO* 30, 879–80 [1931].

ϣⲓⲣⲉ, f. **ϣⲉⲉⲣⲉ** (Crum 585b), 'small' = , *šrr* > , *šr* (*Wb.* IV, 525, 11 f.), 'small'; (Er. 518, 1), *šr*, 'small; deficiency'. Same etymology as for ϣⲏⲣⲉ, 'son', and ϣⲉⲉⲣⲉ, 'daughter'. For fem. ᴮϣⲁⲓⲣⲓ, see STEINDORFF, *Kopt. Gr.* 2nd ed. 53, §105 [1904] and *ZÄS* 27, 107 [1889]. ϩ(ⲉ)ⲣϣⲓⲣⲉ, 'young servant', see under ϩⲁⲗ.

ϣⲁⲣⲃⲁ (Crum 586a), 'scorching heat' from Semitic √*šrb*, cf. Hebrew שָׁרָב, 'burning heat', Aram. שַׁרְבָא.

ROSSI, *Etym. aeg.* 254 [1808].

ϣⲁⲣⲕⲉ (Crum 586b), 'lack of water, drought' = ?*, *šri-kꜣ*, lit. 'small, short of food'. From ϣⲁⲣⲕⲉ the Egn. Arabic شراقى, 'fallow'.

ᴴSPIEGELBERG, *ZÄS* 53, 133 [1917]; ᴬᴿSTERN, *Kopt. Gr.* 5 [1880].

ϣⲱⲣⲡ (Crum 586b), 'be early' = (*Wb.* III, 326, 9 f.), *ḫrp*, 'to lead'; (Er. 366, 2), *ḫrp*, 'come, get up early'.

ᴴBRUGSCH, *Wb.* 1129 [1868]; ᴰBRUGSCH, *Gr. dém.* 179, §348 [1855].

ϣⲟⲣⲡ (Crum 587a), 'earliest, first' = (*Wb.* III, 328, 2 f.), *ḫrp*, 'leader'; (Er. 367, top), *ḫrp*, 'first'.

ᴴDE ROUGÉ, *Oeuv. div.* III (= *Bibl. ég.* XXIII), 176 [1856]; cf. SCHWARTZE in Bunsen, *Geschichte*, I, 603 [1845]; ᴰREVILLOUT, *Pap. mor.* I, 170 n. 6 [1906].

ϣⲟⲣⲧ (Crum 588b), 'awning, veil' = (*Wb.* III, 331, 2), *ḫrd*, kind of fine fabric; (Er. 367, 6), *ḫrṭ*, 'bandage' or sim.

ᴴČERNÝ, *BIFAO* 57, 208–9 [1958]; ᴰBRUGSCH, *Wb.* 1132 [1868].

ˢᶠ**ϣⲣⲁϣ** (not in Crum; see *BIFAO* 64, 50), 'bundle' (translates δέσμη; var. ϣⲟⲗ) = (*Wb.* III, 330, 12), *ḫrš*, 'bundle' (of vegetables); (Er. 367, 3), *ḫrš*, 'bundle'.

ϣⲱⲣϣⲓ (Crum 589a), 'wrinkle, furrow' in skin = (Er. 367, 4), *ḫrš*, 'flaw'.

ERICHSEN, *Dem. Glossar*, 367, 4 [1954].

ϣⲟⲣϣⲣ (Crum 589a), 'upset, overturn' = (*Wb.* III, 330, 7), *ḫrḫr*, 'destroy'; (Er. 367, 2), *ḫrḫr*, 'destroy'.

ᴴSTEINDORFF, *ZÄS* 27, 106 [1889]; ᴰREVILLOUT, *Setna*, 208 [1877]; cf. REVILLOUT, *Nouvelle chrest. dém.* 116 [1878].

ϣⲱⲥ (Crum 589b), 'herd, shepherd' = (*Wb.* IV, 412, 10. 11), *šꜣsw*, Beduin north-east of Egypt and their land.

SALVOLINI, *Campagne de Ramsès-le-Grand*, 15–17 and Pl. I, no. 17 [1835].

ϣⲓⲥⲙⲉ (Crum 589b), 'statue, idol' = (*Wb.* iv, 243, 5 f., especially 244, 12, f.), *sḫm* '(divine) might, figure of a god'; (Er. 454, 8), *sḫm*, and (Er. 463, 10), *sšm*, 'figure of a god'.

D POLOTSKY, *Manich. Homilien*, Index, p. 17* [1934].

Same word as B ϣⲓϣⲉⲙ (Crum 608a), 'phantom, shadow'.

ϣⲥⲛⲉ (Crum 589b), only in ϩⲛⲟⲩϣⲥⲛⲉ, 'on a sudden'. The occurrence of ⲛϣⲥⲣⲟⲧ, 'suddenly', lit. 'in a hard stroke' and of A ϩⲛⲟⲩⲥϩⲉ militates against the traditional deriving of ϣⲥⲛⲉ from Gr.-R. (*Wb.* iii, 469, 19 f.), *sḫn*, 'happen'. ϣⲥⲛⲉ is now more likely to be explained as ϩⲛ-ⲟⲩ-ϣⲥ-ⲛⲉ(ⲓ), 'in a stroke of time' as done by

CRUM, *A Coptic Dict.* 589b [1937].

ϣⲥⲣⲟⲧ (not in Crum; P. Bodmer xxi in Jos. 11, 7) in ⲛϣⲥⲣⲟⲧ, 'suddenly' (ἐξάπινα) = ⲛ-ϣⲥ-ⲣⲟⲧ, lit. 'in (a) hard stroke'; ϣⲥ- (for ⲥϣ-) being the constr. form of ⲥⲁϣ, 'stroke', -ⲣⲟⲧ = Egn. (*Wb.* ii, 410, 13 f., especially 411, 23. 24), *rwḏ*, 'strong, hard', as in ⲃⲁⲣⲟⲧ, a sub-form of ⲃⲁⲣⲱⲧ, 'brass, bronze'.

NB. The existence of ϣⲥⲣⲟⲧ affects the etymology of ϣⲥⲛⲉ, see this latter.

ϣⲥϩⲟⲧ in ⲛϣⲥϩⲟⲧ, 'suddenly', in P. Bodmer xxi = Jos. 11, 7, is—as the photograph suggests—more likely to be read ϣⲥⲣⲟⲧ; see the preceding entry.

ϣⲟⲉⲓⲧ (Crum 590a), in ⲣ, ⲟ ⲛϣⲟⲉⲓⲧ, 'be inspired, possessed' = (*Wb.* iii, 226, 10), *ḫ3wt*, 'be inspired' (cf. also , *ḫ3tyw*, *Wb.* iii, 236, 6–7, > , usually translated 'slaughterers'); (Er. 350, 2), *ḫyṯ*, 'be possessed'.

H W. MAX MÜLLER in *OLZ* 8, col. 245 n. 4 [1905]; cf. W. Max Müller, *Studien für vorderasiatischen Geschichte* (= *Mitteilungen der Vorderasiat. Gesellschaft*, v, 1), 17 n. 3 [1905]; D GRIFFITH, *Stories*, 172 [1900].

ϣⲟⲧ (Crum 590a), 'pillow, cushion, bag(?)' = (*Wb.* iv, 560, 6), *šd*, '(leather) cushion'; ? (not in Er.), *šti*, 'cushion?'.

H VON HALLE in Spiegelberg, *Kopt. Handwb.* 208 [1921]; cf. DÉVAUD, *Études*, 34–5 [1922]; D BOTTI, *Testi demotici*, i, 55 n. 5 [1941].

ϣⲱⲧ, ⲉϣⲱⲧ (Crum 590a), 'trader, merchant' = (*Wb.* iv, 434, 5), *šwyty*, 'merchant'; (Er. 495, bottom), *šwṱ*, 'merchant'.

[H]BRUGSCH, *Wb.* 1369 [1868]; cf. DÉVAUD in *Muséon* 36, 99 [1923].

ⲣ ⲉϣⲱⲧ (Crum 590b), 'be trader, traffic' = (*Wb.* IV, 434, 6), *ỉrt šwyty*, 'be trader, traffic'; (Er. 495, 7), *ỉr šw*, 'traffic'.

[H]BRUGSCH, *Wb.* 1369 [1868]; [D]GLANVILLE, *Cat. of Dem. Papyri*, I, 41 [1939].

ⲓⲉⲡϣⲱⲧ (Crum 81 b, s.v. ⲉⲓⲟⲡⲉ, and 590b), 'trade, merchandise'.

ⲣ ⲉⲓⲉⲡϣⲱⲧ, 'to trade' = , *ỉr wpt šwṯ*, 'to trade'.

LICHTHEIM, *Dem. Ostraca*, 71, no. 159 n. 2 [1957].

[O]ϣⲱⲧ (Crum 590b), in name of planet Jupiter = (*Wb.* IV, 555, 8), *štꜣ*, in [O]ϩⲁⲣ-ⲡϣⲱⲧ (Crum 697b) = Gr.-R. , *Ḥr-p-štꜣ*, < > *Ḥr-wp-štꜣ-tꜣwy*, 'Horus who opens the secret of the Two Lands'; , *Ḥr-pꜣ-št*, or , *Ḥr-št* (Stobart tablets, Brugsch, *Nouvelles recherches sur la division de l'année*, 20 [1856].

ϣⲱⲱⲧ (Crum 590b), 'cut, slay' = (*Wb.* IV, 422, 3 f.), *šꜥd*, 'cut'; (Er. 492, 6), *šꜥṯ*, 'cut, cut off'. Unrelated to ϣⲟⲧϣⲧ, 'carve, hollow'.

[H]CHAMPOLLION, *Gr.* 384 [1836]; [D]BRUGSCH, *Gr. dém.* 40, §86 [1855].

ϣⲁⲁⲧⲥ (Crum 593b), 'cutting, ditch' = (Er. 493, upper), *šꜥṯs*, 'part, portion', also 'cutting' (*JEA* 26, 93).

GRIFFITH–THOMPSON, III, 69, no. 691 [1909].

ϣⲏⲧⲉ (Crum 594a), 'palm fibre', ? whence 'belt, collar' of it = ? (not in Er.), *štỉtw* (pl.), 'fibres?'.

PARKER, *JEA* 26, 94 [1940].

[A]ϣⲓⲧⲉ, 'dig', see under ϣⲓⲕⲉ.

ϣⲓⲧⲉ (Crum 594a), 'demand, extort' = (*Wb.* IV, 560, 8 f.), *šdy*, 'take, exact (taxes)'; (Er. 528, 2), *šty*, 'take (away)'.

[H]BRUGSCH, *Wb.*, Suppl. 1213 [1882]; [D]HESS, *Gnost. Pap.* 14 [1892]; cf. BRUGSCH, *Wb.* 1413 [1868].

ϣⲱⲧⲉ (Crum 595a), 'well, cistern, pit' = (*Wb.* IV, 567, 1. 2), *šdt*, 'water hole, well'; (Er. 529, 4), *šty(t)*, 'ditch, well, canal'.

[H]PLEYTE, *Ét. égypt.* I, 139 [1866]; [D]SPIEGELBERG, *Petubastis*, 60*, no. 412 [1910].

ϣⲱⲧⲉ (Crum 595a), 'flour, dough' = (*Wb.* IV, 569, 5), *šḏt*, 'dough' or sim., > (*Wb.* IV, 567, 3), *šdt*, 'dough'.

STERN in *Pap. Ebers*, II (Glossary), 47 [1875].

ϣⲧⲁ, ϣⲧⲟ (Crum 595a), nn. m., prob. 'cellar' is a result of confusion of two words: (1) (*Wb.* IV, 559, 3 ff.), *štyt* (f.), '(underground) sanctuary, tomb of god Sokar-Osiris; crypt, tomb, underworld', since N.K. , *štꜣ(y)t*, 'cellar' as part of a house (P. Boulaq 10. vo. 10; Turin Lovesongs, vo. II, 2); (2) (*Wb.* IV, 551, 3 ff.), *štꜣ*, 'be hidden' (often of places). Both words are since N.K. sometimes written with as if containing the word , *tꜣ*, 'earth' (Coptic ⲧⲟ). See also ϣⲧⲉⲕⲟ, 'prison'.

[SF]ϣⲧⲁ, [S]ϣⲧⲟ (Crum 595a), 'thicket, wood' = (*Wb.* IV, 555, 9. 10), *štꜣ*, 'tree-grove, copse'; (Er. 527, 7), *štꜣ*, 'wood'.

[H]BUDGE, *An Egyptian Hieroglyphic Dictionary*, 755 [1920]; [D]SPIEGELBERG, *Mythus*, 270, no. 800 [1917].

ϣⲧⲉ (Crum 595a), ship's 'mast' = (*Wb.* III, 342, 7), *ḥt-ṯꜣw*, 'mast', lit. 'wood of the wind'; (Er. 370, middle), *ḥt-tw*, 'mast'.

[H]BRUGSCH, *Wb.* 1052 [1868]; [D]SPIEGELBERG, *Petubastis*, 48*, no. 316 [1910] (with doubt).

ϣⲱⲧⲃ (Crum 595b), 'to muzzle' = (*Wb.* IV, 557, 8. 9), *štb*, 'shut in, muzzle'.

CHABAS, *Pap. mag. Harris*, 238, no. 667 [1860].

ϣⲧⲟⲃ, n., 'muzzle, halter' = (*Wb.* IV, 557, 7), *štb*, 'cage (for birds)'.

SPIEGELBERG, *Kopt. Handwb.* 210 n. 2 [1921].

ϣⲧⲉⲕⲟ (Crum 595b), 'prison' = (Er. 530, 5), *štk*, 'prison' < ϣⲧⲁ 'cellar(?)' + (*Wb.* V, 1, 2), *kꜣ*, 'high'.

[D]GRIFFITH, *Rylands*, III, 395 [1909].

ϣⲱⲧⲙ (Crum 595b), 'to shut', and

ϣⲧⲁⲙ (Crum 596a), 'to shut' = (*Wb.* III, 350, bottom), *ḫtm*, 'to shut in'; (Er. 372, 2), *ḫtm*, 'to shut in'.

[H]CHAMPOLLION, *Gr.* 372 [1836]; [D]BRUGSCH, *De natura*, 35 [1850].

ϣⲧⲟⲙ (Crum 596b), 'thing shutting' or 'shut', 'gate' = (*Wb.* III, 352, 6–10), *ḫtm*, 'shutting, lock, fortress'; (Er. 372, 3), *ḫtm*, 'fence; entrance' or sim., also (Er. 529, 6), *štˁm*, 'fortress' or sim.

[H]SPIEGELBERG, *Kopt. Handwb.* 210 [1921].

ϣⲧⲏⲛ (Crum 597a), f., 'garment, tunic' = ? (Er. 594, 6), *gtn*, 'garment', probably a loan-word from an unidentified language like Hebrew כְּתֹנֶת, 'tunic', Akkadian *kitinnû*, Aram. כתן, Arabic كَتَّان, Greek χιτών, κιτών. Dem. *gtm* seems fem. in Dem. P. Cairo 30799.

HUGHES, *JNES* 16, 57 [1957]; cf. Spiegelberg, *Kopt. Handwb.* 210 [1921].

[B]ϣⲓⲧⲥ, ϭⲓⲧⲥ, [A]ϫⲓⲧ (Crum 598b), 'land tortoise' = (*Wb.* IV, 557, 1 f.), *štw*, 'tortoise'. For -ⲥ, cf. ϯⲃⲥ < *ṯbw*; for ϣ = ϭ, cf. Stern, *Kopt. Gr.* 24, §27.

DÉVAUD in Crum, *A Coptic Dict.* 598b [1937].

ϣϯⲧ (Crum 598b), 'weaver' = (*Wb.* IV, 264, 2), *sḫty*, 'weaver', from (*Wb.* IV, 263, 6), *sḫt*, 'weave' (ⲥⲱϩⲉ); (Er. 457, bottom), *sḫtṱ*, 'weaver'. ϣϯⲧ < **seḫtítey*. See also ϣⲧⲁϯ.

SETHE, *Verbum*, I, 35, §59 [1899].

ϣⲧⲁϯ (Crum 598b), 'edge, border' of garment = (Er. 530, 7), *štt*, 'border' of garment. Originally plural (**seḫtắtyew*) of ϣϯⲧ which also means 'warp' on loom.

HESS, *Gnost. Pap.* 14 [1892].

ϣⲧⲟⲩⲏⲧ (Crum 598b), 'accusation', always in ϯϣⲧⲟⲩⲏⲧ, 'accuse' = (not in Er.), *štwt*, 'claimant of damages(?)'.

MALININE, *Choix de textes juridiques*, I, 48 n. 15 [1953].

ϣⲟⲩϣⲧ (Crum 599a), 'carve, hollow', reduplication of (*Wb.* III, 347, 16), *ḫty*, 'incise'. Cf. the determinative in Gr.-R. period of (*Wb.* III, 353, 13 ff., 354, 4. 5), *ḫtḫt*, 'to retreat, push back'; (Er. 530, 4), *štšt*, 'tear'. Unrelated to ϣⲱⲱⲧ, 'cut, slay'.

[H]DE ROUGÉ, *Oeuv. div.* II (= *Bibl. ég.* XXII), 170 [1851]; [D]SPIEGELBERG, *Mythus*, 270, no. 803 [1917].

ϣⲁⲩ (Crum 599a), 'use, value' = (*Wb.* IV, 404, 13 f.), *šꜣw*, adj. 'worth, suitable' and sim.; (Er. 492, 1), *šw*, 'suitable, useful, worth'.

[H]SETHE, *Verbum*, I, 96, § 161, *a*, *b* [1899]; [D]REVILLOUT, *Poème*, 51–2 [1885].

ⲣ ϣⲁⲩ (Crum 599b), 'be useful, prosperous, virtuous' = , *ir šꜣw*, 'be profitable'.

HESS, *Gnost. Pap.* 14 [1892].

ϣⲟⲩⲙⲉⲣⲓⲧ (Crum 600b), 'lovable' = (Er. 493, bottom), *šw-mr*, 'worthy of love'.

GRIFFITH–THOMPSON, III, 80, no. 831 [1909].

See also **ⲙ(ⲡ)ϣⲁ**, 'be worthy, worth'.

ϣⲁⲩ (Crum 600b), 'trunk, stump, piece' = (Er. 493, 2), *šw*, 'piece, remainder' or sim.

ERICHSEN, *Dem. Glossar*, 493, 2 [1954].

ϣⲟⲩ, ⲥⲟⲩ- (Crum 601a) with preceding **ⲛ-**, 'without' + noun or adjective, perhaps through metathesis from **ⲛⲟⲩⲉϣ** (see this s.v. **ⲟⲩⲱϣ**).

SETHE, *Dem. Urkunden*, 504 [1920].

ϣⲟⲟⲩ (Crum 601a), 'incense, perfume' = Gr.-R. (*Wb.* III, 221, 8–10; XXIInd Dyn. ex. Caminos, *Chronicle*, 144), *ḫꜣw*, a perfumed substance, prob. < (*Wb.* III, 221, 1–7), *ḫꜣw*, 'flowers'; (Er. 353, 2), *ḫwy*, 'incense' or sim.

[H]BRUGSCH, *Wb.* 1025 [1868]; [D]SPIEGELBERG, *Dem. Chronik*, 127, no. 511 [1914].

ϣⲟⲩ- in **ϣⲟⲩϩⲏⲛⲉ** (Crum 688b, s.v. **ϩⲏⲛⲉ**) = **ϣⲟⲟⲩ** + **ϩⲏⲛⲉ**, 'perfume of incense'.

ϣⲏⲩⲉ (Crum 601b adding **ϣⲟⲩ-**, see below), 'altar' = (*Wb.* III, 226, 11 f.), *ḫꜣwt*, 'offering-table'; (Er. 353, 1), *ḫwy*, 'altar'.

[H]CHAMPOLLION, *Gr.* 62 [1836]; [D]CHAMPOLLION, MS. Bibl. Nat. 20313, fols. 140–56, no. 26 [1822] (Sottas, *Lettre à M. Dacier*, p. 52 n.); BRUGSCH, *Rhind*, 46 and Pl. 42, no. 348 [1865].

For **ϣⲟⲩ-** see **ϣⲟⲩⲣⲏ** and **ϣⲟⲩⲧⲁⲗⲗⲟ**, but **ϣⲟⲩ-** in **ϣⲟⲩⲥⲟⲟⲩϣⲉ** and **ϣⲟⲩϩⲏⲛⲉ** different, see respectively **ϣⲟⲩⲥⲟⲟⲩϣⲉ** and **ϣⲟⲟⲩ**, 'incense, perfume'.

ϣⲟⲟⲩⲉ (Crum 601 b), 'be dry' = (*Wb.* IV, 429, 5 f.), *šw*, 'become dry'; (Er. 494, 2), *šw*, 'become dry, dry'.

HBRUGSCH, *ZÄS* 1, 30 [1863]; DBRUGSCH, *Gr. dém.* 39, §82 [1855].

ϣⲟⲩⲓⲉ (Crum 602 a), 'dryness, what is dry' = L.E. (*Wb.* IV, 430, 5), *šwyt*, 'dry place'.

ϣⲟⲩⲟ (Crum 602 a), 'to flow, empty' = (*Wb.* IV, 428, 1. 2), *šw*, 'to empty'? < (*Wb.* IV, 282, 1 f.), *sšwy*, 'to empty'; (Er. 495, 3), *šw*, 'to empty'.

HSPIEGELBERG, *Rechnungen*, 61 [1896]; DERICHSEN, *Dem. Glossar*, 495, 3 [1954].

Qual. **ϣⲟⲩⲉⲓⲧ** (Crum 602 b), 'empty' = (3rd pers. sing. fem. of the Old Perfective), *šwty*, 'being empty'.

SETHE, *Verbum*, II, 37, §91 [1899].

ϣⲟⲩⲏ(ⲏ)ⲃ (Crum 603 a), 'persea tree, lebbakh (لبخة)', *Mimusops Schimperi* = (*Wb.* IV, 435, 10 f.), *šwb*, 'persea tree'; (Er. 496, 3), *šwb*, 'persea tree'.

HBRUGSCH, *Rec. de mon.* I, 49 [1862]; DSPIEGELBERG, *Rec. trav.* 35, 160 [1913].

S**ϣⲟⲩⲱⲃⲉ**: B**ϣⲃⲱⲃⲓ** (Crum 603 a), 'throat' = (*Wb.* IV, 439, 3. 4), *šbb*, > Gr.-R. , *šbbt*, 'wind pipe'.

BRUGSCH, *Wb.* 1372 [1868].

NB. Demotic (Er. 515, 8), *šnbt*, 'wind pipe, throat' is the older (*Wb.* IV, 512, 10 f.), *šnbt*, 'chest, throat', contrary to Brugsch, *Wb.* 1428.

B**ϣⲉⲩⲛⲓ** (Crum 603 b), 'barn' = (*Wb.* IV, 510, 1 ff.), *šnwt*, 'granary'. From Coptic the Eg. Arabic شونة.

BRUGSCH, *Wb.* 1397 [1868]; cf. W. Max Müller, *ZÄS* 32, 32 [1894].

ϣⲟⲩⲣⲏ (Crum 603 b), 'censer, brazier, altar' = or , *ḫ3wt-Rʿ*, 'altar of Rēʿ', **ϣⲟⲩ-** being constr. form of **ϣⲏⲩⲉ**, see this.

SPIEGELBERG, *ZÄS* 66, 38 n. 2 [1931].

ϣⲟⲩⲥⲟⲟⲩϣⲉ (Crum 603 b), 'sacrifice, offering' = * , *sbsb (n) ḫt*, lit. 'disappearing in fire', though only Gk.-R. , *sb-n-ḫt* is attested (*Wb.* III, 218, 6 and 430, 20); (not in Er.; P. BM 10080, iv, 16), *swḫy*, 'offering'. The most correct form is therefore **ⲥⲟⲩⲥⲟⲟⲩϣⲉ**. See also the parallel **ⲥⲃⲛⲥⲉⲧⲉ** under **ⲥⲃ-**.

[H]DÉVAUD's slip; [D]H. THOMPSON's Demotic dictionary.

ϣⲟⲩⲧⲁⲗⲗⲟ (Jos. 9, 2b, in P. Bodmer XXI), 'holocaust', ὁλοκαύτωμα = **ϣⲟⲩ** (constr. state of **ϣⲏⲩⲉ** + **ⲧⲁⲗⲟ**, 'raising up, offering', Crum 409b), 'altar of offering'.

ϣⲟⲩϣⲏⲧ (Crum 603b), herb eaten by sheep = ? (Er. 458, 2), *s(ꜣ)ḫt*, some herb or crop.

GRIFFITH–THOMPSON, III, 72, no. 714 [1909].

ϣⲟⲩϣⲟⲩ (Crum 604a), 'boast', refl. 'pride oneself' = (*Wb.* IV, 54, 13 f.), *sꜥšꜣ*, 'make many, increase the number'; (Er. 492, 2), *šꜥš*, 'make many, praise', also , *šꜥšꜥ*, and , *ššꜥ*.

[H]SPIEGELBERG, *Kopt. Handwb.* 213 [1921]; [D]GRIFFITH–THOMPSON, III, 80, no. 825 [1909].

As noun 'boast, pride' = (plural), *šꜥšꜥ*, 'honour, pride'.

GRIFFITH, *Dem. Graffiti from Dodekaschoinos*, I, 181, no. 325 [1937].

ϣⲁϣ (Crum 604b), part of building = ? (Er. 523, 4), *ššꜣ*, a building.

ϣⲁϣ (Crum 604b), a vessel or liquid measure = (Er. 523, 1), *šš*, a vessel.

GRIFFITH, *Rylands*, III, 270 n. 2; 395 [1909].

See also **ϣⲟϣⲟⲩ**.

ϣⲟⲉⲓϣ (Crum 605a), 'dust' = (Er. 487, 2), *šyḫ*, or , *ḫyḫ*, 'dust', from **ϣⲱϣ**, 'scatter' (see this latter).

[A]**ϩϩ-**in**ϩϩⲧⲱⲣϣ** (Crum 629b), 'rust', lit. 'red dust' (< **ϩⲁⲉⲓϩ** + **ⲧⲱⲣϣ**).

ČERNÝ, *BIFAO*, 57, 211 [1958].

ϣⲟϣ (Crum 605a), a kind of antelope, 'hartebeest', *Bubalis buselaphus* = (*Wb.* IV, 543, 5. 6), *ššꜣw*, 'hartebeest'.

BRUGSCH, *Wb.* 1311 [1868]; cf. LORET, *ZÄS* 30, 28 [1892].

ϣⲱϣ (Crum 605b), 'scatter, spread' esp. of odour and by wind = (*Wb.* III, 233, 17), *ḫꜣḫꜣ*, 'winnow'; (Er. 522, 7), *šš*, and , *ḫḫ*, 'spread, scatter'.

[H]BRUGSCH, *Wb.*, Suppl. 895 [1881]; cf. CHABAS, *ZÄS* 6, 133 [1868]; [D]BRUGSCH, *Gr. dém.* 28, §55 [1855].

ϣⲱϣ (Crum 606a), 'make level, equal, straight' = [hieroglyphs] (*Wb.* III, 331, 12), *ḫḫ*, of an action with the balance.

CHAMPOLLION, *Gr.* 371 [1836].

ϣⲱϣ (Crum 607a), 'twist' rope etc. = L.E. [hieroglyphs] (*Wb.* IV, 413, 12), *š(ꜣ)š(ꜣ)*, 'twist' in [hieroglyphs], *šꜣšꜣ nwḥ*, 'twist rope'; [demotic] (Er. 522, 8), *šš nwḥ*, ϣⲱϣ {ⲛ} ⲛⲟⲩϩ, ϣⲉϣ ⲛⲟⲩϩ, same meaning.

[H]SPIEGELBERG, *OLZ* 27, col. 187 [1924]; [D]MÖLLER in Gressmann, *Vom reichen Mann und armen Lazarus* (*Abhandl. Preuss. Ak.* 1918), 67 n. [1918].

ϣϣⲉ, ⲥϣⲉ (Crum 607b), 'it is fitting, right'? = ⲥ + ϣⲉ ⲉ, lit. 'it goes with respect to' < *[hieroglyphs], *s šm r*, same meaning.

SPIEGELBERG, *Kopt. Handwb.* 187 [1921].

[B]ϣⲓϣⲉⲙ (Crum 608a), 'phantom, shadow' = ϣⲓⲥⲙⲉ, 'statue, idol', see this latter.

ϣⲱϣⲉⲛ (Crum 608a), 'lily' = [hieroglyphs] (*Wb.* III, 485, bottom), *sšn*, 'lotus flower' < [hieroglyphs] (*Wb.* III, 487, 9), *sššn* (*zššn*), same meaning; [demotic] (Er. 464, 5), *sšn*, 'lotus'. Borrowed into Hebrew as שׁוֹשַׁן (cf. Stricker in *Acta Orientalia* 15, 7).

[H]SCHWARTZE in Bunsen, *Geschichte*, I, 588 [1845]; [D]BRUGSCH, *Gr. dém.* 25, §48; 26, §49 [1855].

ϣⲁϣⲛⲓ (Crum 608a), intr., 'reach, obtain' = prob. [hieroglyphs] (*Wb.* IV, 253, 6 f.), *sḫny*, 'alight, rest, dwell'; [demotic] (Er. 455, 4), *sḫn*, or [demotic], *sḫny*, 'reach, meet'.

[D]BRUGSCH, *Wb.* 1294 [1868].

NB. ϣⲁϣⲛⲓ requires a 4 conson. fem. inf. (**saḫnet*); [hieroglyphs] (*Wb.* III, 468, 14 f.), *sḫn*, 'embrace, look for, meet, visit', etc. proposed by Brugsch, *loc. cit.*, and others, would give *ⲥⲱϣⲉⲛ or *ϣⲱϣⲉⲛ. Hieroglyphic texts of Gr.-R. period, however, write *sḫny* with [hieroglyph] as if it were *sḫn*.

[SB]ϣⲟϣⲧ, [B]ϣⲱϣⲧ (Crum 608b), 'hindrance, impediment', so 'key', belongs to ⲥⲱϣⲧ, 'stop, impede', see this.

ϣⲟⲩϣⲧ (Crum 608b), 'window' = [hieroglyphs] (*Wb.* IV, 301, 14 ff.), *sšd*, 'window'; [demotic] (Er. 523, 9), *ššṱ*, 'window'.

[H]BRUGSCH, *Wb.* 1318 [1868]; [D]BRUGSCH, *Wb.* 1430 [1868].

ϣⲟⲩϣⲟⲩ (Crum 609a), 'pot, jar' = [demotic] (Er. 523, 7), *šśw*, 'jar'.
REVILLOUT, *Pap. mor.* II, 37 n. 10 [1908] (= *Journal as.* 1908, 275).
See also **ϣⲁϣ**.

[B]**ϣϣⲏⲟⲩ** (Crum 609a), 'coriander', see **ⲃⲣⲉϣⲏⲩ**.

ϣⲁϥ (Crum 609b), 'waste land(?)' = [hieroglyphs] (*Wb.* III, 271, 13. 14), *ḫfꜣꜣt*, > Gr.-R. [hieroglyphs] and sim., 'bank, field'; [demotic] (not in Er.; Ankhsh. 11, 10), *ḫfꜣ*, 'bank, dyke'.
GLANVILLE's index.

ϣⲱϥ (Crum 609b), 'lay waste, destroy' = [hieroglyphs] (*Wb.* I, 578, 6 ff.), *fḫ*, 'release' > L.E. [hieroglyphs]; [hieroglyphs] and sim., *ḫf*, 'destroy'; [demotic] (Er. 358, 1), *ḫf*, or [demotic], *šf*, 'destroy'.
[H]SETHE, *Verbum*, I, 125, §217, 2 [1899]; [D]GRIFFITH, *Rylands*, III, 378 [1909].
ϣⲱϥ (Crum 610a), 'devastation, destruction' = [demotic] (not in Er., ex. Ankhsh. 24, 17), *ḫf*, 'ruin, destruction'.
GLANVILLE's index.
For **ϣⲁϥⲉ** (Crum 610a), 'desert', see the next entry.

ϣⲁϥⲉ, fem. [B]**ϣⲁϥⲏ** (prob. = [B]**ϭⲁϥⲏ**, Crum 839b), pl. [B]**ϣⲁϥⲉⲩ** (Crum 610a), 'desert' = ?[hieroglyphs] (*Wb.* III, 230, 13), *ḫꜣft*, a kind of land.
BRUGSCH, *Dict. géographique*, 1279 [1879].

[BS]**ϣⲁϥⲉ** (Crum 610a), 'swell' = [hieroglyphs] (*Wb.* IV, 455, 8–11), *šfy*, 'swell'.
STERN in *Pap. Ebers*, II, Glossary, 45 [1875]; cf. BRUGSCH, *Wb.* 1386 [1868].

ϣϥⲱ (Crum 610b), 'tale, fable' = [demotic] (Er. 504, 7), *šfꜣt*, and [demotic] (Er. 454, 5), *sḫfꜣt*, 'tale', perhaps from Gr.-R. [hieroglyphs] (*Wb.* IV, 242, 19), *sḫf*, or [hieroglyphs] (*Wb.* IV, 116, 1), *sfḫ*, 'to write down'.
[H]ERICHSEN, *Dem. Glossar*, 454, 5 [1954]; [D]BRUGSCH, *ZÄS* 26, 35 [1888].

ϣϥⲱ (Crum 611a), measure of length, 'schoenus, parasang' = [demotic] (Er. 454, 4), *sḫf*.
SPIEGELBERG, *Kopt. Etym.* 40–1 [1920]; cf. H. Thompson, *JEA* 11, 151–3 [1925].

ϣⲱϥⲧ (Crum 611 a), 'stumble, err' = (Er. 505, 1), *šft*, 'to sin, err, fall'. Denominative verb from *ẖfty* = ϣⲁϥⲧ (for which see below).

ERICHSEN, *Dem. Lesestücke*, I, 2, 76 [1937]; cf. *Dem. Glossar*, 505, 1 [1954].

ϣⲁϥⲧⲉ (Crum 611 b), 'iniquitous, impious person or thing' = (*Wb.* III, 276, 12 f.), *ẖfty*, 'enemy, adversary'; (Er. 358, 3), *ẖft*, 'enemy'

HCHAMPOLLION, *Gr.* 103 [1836]; cf. SALVOLINI, *Campagne de Ramsès-le-Grand*, 15, and Pl. I, no. 15 [1835]; DHESS, *Gnost. Pap.* 11 [1892].

ⲣ ϣⲁϥⲧⲉ, 'do iniquity' = Aeth. (*Wb.* III, 277, 5), *ỉr ẖfty*, 'be hostile to...', lit. 'act (as) enemy'; , *ỉr šft*, 'to sin'.

HERMAN-GRAPOW, *Wb.* III, 277, 5 [1929]; DREVILLOUT, *Pap. mor.* I, 42 n. 1 [1906].

ϣⲱϥⲧ (Crum 611 b), 'hollow of hand', cf. (*Wb.* IV, 461, 9. 10), *šfd*, 'seize'.

ERMAN–GRAPOW, *Wb.* IV, 461, 9. 10 [1930].

ϣⲟϥϣϥ (Crum 612 a), 'spread, burrow' = Gr.-R. (not in *Wb.*), *šfšf*, 'spread'; ? , *šfšf* (not in Er.), meaning unknown. Cf. also Gr.-R. (*Wb.* III, 273, 16), *ẖfẖf*, 'pour out'. Probably a reduplication of , 'swell', ϣⲁϥⲉ.

HBLACKMAN & FAIRMAN, *JEA* 29, 13, note k [1943]; DPARKER, *JEA* 26, 95 [1940].

ϣⲱϩⲃ (Crum 612 b), > ϣⲱⲃϩ > ϣⲱⲟⲩϩ (Crum 554 b), 'be withered, scorched, scorch, wither', cf. Gr.-R. (*Wb.* IV, 529, 9), *šhb*, name of hot wind, lit. 'scorcher'; (not in Er., ex. Ankhsh. 20, 14), *šhbw*, 'hot winds'; (Er. 496, 5), *šwḥ*, 'dry up'.

HBRUGSCH in *ZÄS* 13, 128 [1875]; DSPIEGELBERG, *Mythus*, 269, no. 794 [1917]; cf. GLANVILLE's index.

ϣⲁϩⲗ (Crum 612 b), something used as fuel, cf. (Er. 520, 9), *šhlꜥlṯ*, 'dried up' (of plants).

ϣⲁϩⲙ (Crum 612 b), ingredient in recipe, prob. = Arab شَحْم, 'fat'.

CHASSINAT, *Pap. méd.* 163 [1921].

ϣⲁϩⲏⲣⲉ (Crum 612b), in recipes = شحيرة, 'substance serving to purify metals, purifier' (Dozy, *Suppl.* I, 732).

CRUM, *A Coptic Dict.* 612b [1937].

ϣⲁϩϣⲉϩ (Crum 612b), 'be harsh, rough, hardy', from Semitic, cf. Arabic شحشح, 'zealous'.

DÉVAUD's slip.

ϣϩⲓϭ, ϣⲓϭ (Crum 612b), 'dust' =  (*Wb.* IV, 529, 10; P. Ch. Beatty IX, vo. B, 18, 10; for meaning cf. Helck, *Die Beziehungen*, 571), *šḥk*, 'dust'; 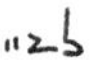 (Er. 397, 1), *ḫkỉ*, 'dust, powder', from Semitic √*šḥq*, cf. Hebrew שַׁחַק, 'dust, cloud', Arabic سحق.

^{S}DÉVAUD, *Études*, 53 [1922].

ϣⲁϫⲉ (612b), 'speak, say' =  (*Wb.* IV, 394, bottom), *sḏd*, 'tell, speak'; 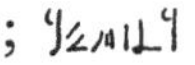 (Er. 482, 6), *sḏy*, 'speak, tell'.

^{H}CHABAS, *Voyage*, 156 [1866]; ^{D}BRUGSCH, *Gr. dém.* 133, §278 [1855].

ϣⲱϫⲉ (Crum 615a), 'contend, wrestle' = 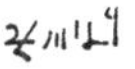 (Er. 482, 7), *sḏy*, 'to fight, beat'.

KRALL in *WZKM* 17, 6 [1903].

ϣϫⲉ (Crum 615a), 'locust' = 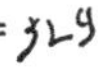 (Er. 482, 3), *sḏ*, 'locust'.

SPIEGELBERG, *Kopt. Handwb.* 135 [1921].

ϣϫⲉ (Crum 615a), 'sprig'? = 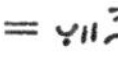 (Er. 524, 8), *škỉ*, 'stalk' or sim.

GRIFFITH, *Rylands*, III, 284 n. 3, 395 [1909].

ϣϫⲓⲗ (Crum 615b), meaning unknown, in **ⲡⲉϣϫⲓⲗ**, perhaps a place name, cf. ? 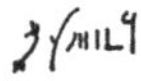 (Er. 483, 1), *sḏyl*, 'lizard' or sim.

^{S}**ϣϫⲏⲛ**, ^{O}**ϭϫⲁⲛ** (Crum 615b), 'garlic' =  (*Wb.* III, 354, 7), *ḫtn*, a vegetable;  (Er. 373, 2), *ḫdn*, a vegetable (garlic). Probably from Hebrew חָצִיר, 'green grass, leek'.

^{HDS}LORET, *Sphinx* 8, 141–4 [1904].

^{S}**ϣⲟϫⲛⲉ**, ^{B}**ⲥⲟϭⲛⲓ** (Crum 615b), 'take counsel, consider' = , *sḏny*, and 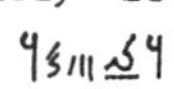 (Er. 480, 3), *sṯny*, 'counsel' < 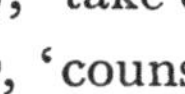 (*Wb.* IV, 358, 3 ff.), *stny*, 'raise up, distinguish'.

^{H}STEINDORFF, *Kopt. Gr.* 1st ed., 112, §245 [1894]; cf. Sethe, *Verbum*, I, 277, §442 [1899]; ^{D}REVILLOUT, *Revue ég.* I, 60 and Pl. I (fasc. 2) [1880]. For construct and pronominal forms, see **ϫⲛⲟⲩ**, 'ask, question, require'.

^S^ϣⲱϫⲡ < ^B^ⲥⲱϫⲡ (Crum 616b), 'be over and above, remain over' = (*Wb.* IV, 380, bottom), *sḏb*, 'remain alive'. Aram. שיזב, Syriac ܫܘܙܒ, Akkadian *šūzubu*, 'leave to remain', are ultimately related.

^S^DÉVAUD's slip.

ϣⲱⲱϭⲉ (Crum 618a), 'smite, wound' = ? (*Wb.* IV, 306, 10 f.), *sḳr*, 'smite'; (Er. 525, 3), *šᶜkᶜ*, 'smite, wound'.

ϣϭⲁ (Crum 618b), 'blow, wound' and constr. Infinitive in ϣϭⲁϭⲓϫ, 'strike, clap hands', cf. ? (pron. Inf.).

^H^BRUGSCH, *Wb.* 1319–20 [1868]; cf. SPIEGELBERG in *Sphinx* 4, 227 [1901]; ^D^BRUGSCH, *Wb.* 1427 [1868].

ϣϭⲉ-, ⲥϭ-, ⲥⲕ- (Crum 618b, adding ⲥⲕⲛⲱϩⲉ ⲛϩⲏⲧ Stefanski-Lichtheim, *Coptic Ostraca*, 11, 2, 9), component of place names = (not in *Wb.* but see Gardiner, *The Wilbour Papyrus*, II, 35), *sgꜣ*, 'hill'.

ČERNÝ, *BIFAO* 57, 209–10 [1958].

ϣϭⲛⲏⲛ (Crum 618b), 'strive, contend', as noun 'strife' = (Er. 526, 4), *šgnn*, 'strife'.

BRUGSCH, *Gr. dém.* 34, §68 [1855].

ϣϭⲁⲡ (Crum 619a) > ϣⲕⲁⲕ (Crum 556a), 'cry, sound' = (*Wb.* IV, 321, 1 f.), *sgb*, 'cry' (verb and subst.); (Er. 469, 6), *sgp*, subst. 'cry'. ⲁϣϭⲁⲡ < ⲁϣϣϭⲁⲡ (= ⲱϣ + ϣϭⲁⲡ) = L.E. (*Wb.* I, 227, 9 and IV, 321, 4. 5), *ᶜš sgb*, 'cry, moan aloud'; , *ᶜš skp*, 'cry aloud'.

^H^STEINDORFF, *Die Apokalypse des Elias*, 37 n. 4 [1899]; ^D^HESS, *Stne*, 176 [1888].

ϣϭⲟⲣ (Crum 619a), 'rent, hire' = (Er. 525, 5), *škr*, 'the tax', from Semitic, cf. Hebrew שָׂכָר, 'hire', Arabic شكر, 'reward, thank'.

^D^BRUGSCH, *Wb.* 1431 [1868]; ^S^ROSSI, *Etym. aeg.* 282 [1808].

Ϥ

-ϥ, Suffix of 3rd pers. masc. sing. =  (*Wb.* I, 572, 1), *f*, same meaning;  (Er. 143, 2), *f*, same meaning.

[H]YOUNG, *Misc. Works*, III, Pl. 2, no. 74 (= *Encycl. Brit.*, Suppl. IV, Pl. 75, no. 74 [1824]; cf. CHAMPOLLION, *Précis*, 1st ed. 82 [1824]; [D]ÅKERBLAD, *Lettre*, 45 [1802].

ϥι (Crum 620 a), 'bear, carry, take' =  (*Wb.* I, 572, 6 f.), *f3y*, 'lift up, carry'; 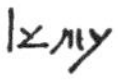 (Er. 143, 5), *f3y*, 'carry'.

[H]CHAMPOLLION, *Gr.* 379, 381 [1836]; [D]BRUGSCH, *Scriptura Aeg. dem.* 3 [1848]; cf. de Saulcy, *Rosette*, 33 [1845].

Part. coni. **ϥⲁⲓ-** (Crum 622 b), 'carrier' = , e.g. in  (*Wb.* I, 574, 6), *f3y-ḥtpt*, 'carrier of offerings'; 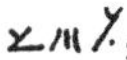, e.g. in 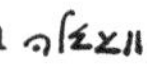, *f3y-tn nb*, 'carrier of golden basket' (fem.), κανηφόρος.

[H]ERMAN–GRAPOW, *Wb.* I, 574, 6 [1926]; [D]YOUNG, *Misc. Works*, III, 24–5, no. 11 = *Museum criticum*, 6, pp. 174–5, no. 11 [1815] (letter to Sacy of 21 October 1814, cf. Sottas, *Lettre à M. Dacier*, p. 50); cf. ÅKERBLAD, *Lettre*, p. 27 [1802].

ⲃⲁⲓⲥⲛⲁⲩ (not in Crum; exx. Kahle, *loc. cit. infra.* and Till, Ostr. 129, 4), a wine-measure, lit. 'carrying two'. Cf. **ⲃⲁⲓⲕⲁϩ**, 'earth carrier, a tool' (Crum 131 b and 622 b).

KAHLE, *Bala'izah*, II, 744 [1954].

ϥⲟ, ⲃⲟ (Crum 623 a), 'canal, water conduit' = ?L.E. 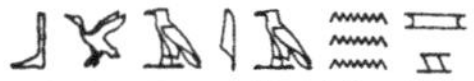 (*Wb.* I, 418, 1), *b3y*, some place with water, identical? with  (*Wb.* I, 417, 15. 16), *b3y*, 'hole, water-hole'; 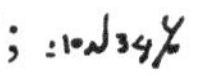 (Er. 144, 3), *fʿ3*, 'canal'.

[H]DÉVAUD's slip; [D]BRUGSCH, *Wb.*, Suppl. 408 [1880].

ϥⲱ (Crum 623 a), 'hair' = L.E.  (not in *Wb.*), *fʿ3*, 'lock (of hair)';  (Er. 144, 4), *fʿy*, 'hair'.

[H]EDWARDS in Černý, *BIFAO* 57, 210–11 [1958]; cf. EDWARDS, *Oracular Amuletic Decrees*, I, 59 n. 42 [1960]; [D]HESS, *Gnost. Pap.* 7 [1892].

[B]**ϥⲟⲩⲕⲁⲥⲓ** (Crum 623 b), nn. f. a fish, cf. ? 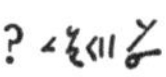 (Er. 145, 4), *fkst*, an insect or sim. Griffith–Thompson, I, 129, however, reject any connexion, and think that *fkst* is possibly an Egyptian rendering of Gk. σφήξ.

ϥⲛⲧ (Crum 623b), 'worm' = (*Wb.* 1, 577, 5–7), *fnṯ*, 'worm, serpent'.
CHAMPOLLION, *Gr.* 74 [1836].

^{B}ϥⲟⲣϥⲉⲣ (Crum 624a), 'fall, rush down' for **ⲃⲟⲣⲃⲉⲣ** is the same word as **ϩⲃⲟⲣⲃⲣ** in its intransitive use (see the latter).

^{B}ϥⲱⲥⲓ (Crum 624a), 'chisel, knife', probably for ***ⲃⲱⲥⲓ, ⲟⲩⲱⲥⲓ**, from **ⲟⲩⲉⲓⲥⲉ**, 'to saw' which latter means also 'to chisel off' (cf. *Wb.* 1, 358, 13).

ϥⲱⲧⲉ (Crum 624a), 'wipe, wipe off, obliterate' = (*Wb.* 1, 580, 14), *ft*(*t*), 'obliterate (writing by licking it off)' < (*Wb.* 1, 581, 16), *fdy*, 'wipe off'; (*Wb.* 1, 582, 1–4), *fdy*, 'eradicate'; (Er. 145, 6), *fty*, 'wipe off, cleanse'.
^{HD}SPIEGELBERG, *Rec. trav.* 17, 97–8 [1895].
Part. coni. **ⲃⲁⲧ-** in **ⲃⲁⲑⲟ, ⲃⲁⲑⲱ**, see the latter.

ϥⲱⲧⲉ (Crum 625a), nn. 'sweat' = (*Wb.* 1, 582, 6–9), *fdt*, 'sweat'; (Er. 145, 7), *fty*, 'sweat'.
^{H}CHABAS, *Oeuv. div.* II (= *Bibl. ég.* X), 178 [1862]; ^{D}GRIFFITH–THOMPSON, I, 131 [1904].

ϥⲧⲟⲟⲩ (Crum 625a), 'four' = (*Wb.* 1, 582, 13), *fdw*, 'four'.
CHAMPOLLION, *Gr.* 210 [1836].
Fem. **ϥⲧⲟ** = , *fdt* (*Wb.* 1, 582, bottom).
-ⲁϥⲧⲉ = (*Wb.* 1, 71, 5), *ỉfdt*, 'fourness'.
CHAMPOLLION, *Gr.* 210 [1836]; cf. SETHE, *ZÄS* 47, 9–10 (§§17, 18). 14, §27 [1910].

ϥⲱϭⲉ (Crum 625b), 'leap, move hastily' = L.E. *fḳꜣ*, Imperat. (not in *Wb.*), *ỉfḳꜣ*, 'out, quickly!'.
MASSART in *Mitt. Kairo* 15, 176 n. 1 [1957].

ϥⲱϭⲉ (Crum 626b), 'pluck, seize' = (*Wb.* 1, 579, 11. 12), *fḳꜣ*, 'tear up by the root (a plant), eradicate'.
GROFF, *Rec. trav.* 24, 130 n. 1 [1902].

ⳉ

[A]ⳉⲟ (Crum 628a), 'road, path' = Gr.-R. [hieroglyphs] (not in *Wb.*, but cf. Brugsch, *Wb.* 1023–4 = Piehl, *Inscr. hiér.* I, Pl. 37), 'path', in [hieroglyphs], *ʿḳ(ꜣ) ḫꜣ*, 'straightforward, correct of path' (cf. *ʿḳꜣ mṯn*, 'straight of road', Ptaḥḥotpe 312 according to Pap. Brit. Mus. 10371/10435).

REVILLOUT, *Rev. ég.* 14, 141 [1914].

[A]ⳉⲓⲧ, ⳉⲓⲉⲓⲧ (Crum 629a), 'threshing floor' = [hieroglyphs] (*Wb.* III, 349, 10), *ḫtyw*, 'threshing-floor'; [demotic] (Er. 371, 4), *ḫtꜣt*, 'threshing-floor'.

[HD]REVILLOUT in *Rev. ég.* 14, 141 [1914]; SPIEGELBERG, *ZÄS* 53, 132 n. 1 [1917].

ⳉ(ⲉ)ⲃⲉⳉⲓⲧ, 'threshing-floor' = ⳉ(ⲉ)ⲃⲉ + ⳉⲓⲧ, the element ⳉ(ⲉ)ⲃⲉ is obscure.

[A]ⳉⲁⲧⲉ (Crum 629a), 'pluck out?' feathers = ?[hieroglyphs] (*Wb.* III, 403, 2), *ḫtt*, 'pluck out' (flax, papyrus or sim.) < ?[hieroglyphs] (*Wb.* III, 236, 11), *ḫꜣd*, 'pluck out feathers'.

RÖSCH, *Vorbemerkungen*, 141–2 (from *ḫtt*) [1909]; DÉVAUD, *Rec. trav.* 38, 200 [1916–17] (from *ḫꜣd*).

[A]ⳉⳉⲧⲱⲣϣ (Crum 629b), 'rust, red blight', see under ϣⲟⲉⲓϣ, 'dust'.

ϧ

[B]ϧⲏⲓ (Crum 630a), 'sun' = [demotic] (Er. 348, 2), *ḫy*, 'light, glare of sun'.

SPIEGELBERG, *Kopt. Etymologien*, 6 [1920].

[B]ϧⲉⲗⲗⲟⲧ (Crum 630a adding [S]ϣⲗⲱⲧ from Jos. 7, 24 in P. Bodmer XXI), 'ravine, wady' including water and rocks = [hieroglyphs] (*sic. l.* [Yoyotte]), *ḫ(ꜣ)rt* (Edwards, *Oracular Amuletic Decrees*, I, 32, n. 16) and Gr.-R. [hieroglyphs] (*Wb.* III, 232, 17), *ḫ(ꜣ)r(w)ṯ*, name of a watercourse; [demotic] (Er. 396, 2), *ḫlṯ* 'canal' or sim. A loan-word from Semitic, cf. Aram. חַלְתָא.

[H]ERMAN–GRAPOW, *Wb.* III, 232, 17 [1929]; [D]REVILLOUT, *Nouvelle Chrest. dém.* p. 83 n. 1 [1878]; [S]ROSSI, *Etym. aeg.* 288 [1808].

^{B}ϧομϧεμ (Crum 630 b and 682 b), 'crush, break, destroy' = reduplication of (*Wb.* III, 281, 1 f.), *ḫm*, 'pull down (a building), crush (enemies)', Gr.-Roman (*Wb.* III, 278, 3), *ḫm*, ingredient of kyphi-incense in powdered state.

NB. On account of its ϧ, ϧομϧεμ must be a different word from ^{B}ϩομϩεμ.

GARDINER, *Eg. Hieratic Texts*, 19*, n. 1 [1911].

^{B}ϧεнι (Crum 630 b), 'to quarrel' = (*Wb.* III, 383, 3 f.), *ḫnn*, 'disturb' or sim.; (Er. 385, 1), *ḫnn*, 'disturb'.

DÉVAUD in Crum, *A Coptic Dict.* 630 b [1937].

^{B}ϧωρ (Crum 631 a), 'destroy', perhaps unreduplicated basis of ϣορϣρ, see this.

^{B}ϧορπc (Crum 631 a), ^{F}ϩαρπc (Crum 703 b), 'outspread hand' > 'handful', from *ϧωρπ + c. *ϧωρπ = (*Wb.* III, 326, 8 f.), *ḫrp*, 'lead', 'be in front' (*Wb.* III, 327, 21. 22), therefore essentially the same as ϣωρπ, 'be early'.

^{B}ϧρο† (Crum 631 a), 'child, young' = (*Wb.* III, 396, bottom), *ḫrd*, 'child'; (Er. 392, 8), *ḫrṱ* '(divine) child'.

^{H}LEPSIUS, *Lettre à M. Rosellini*, 85 n. 14, and Pl. B, no. 85^{c}, 18 [1837]; ^{D}BRUGSCH, *Lettre à M. le Vicomte de Rougé*, 29 and Pl. II, no. 2 [1850].

NB. ϧρο† is a plural form; sing. only ^{O}ρατ in πρατ, i.e. *pꜣ ḫrd*, 'the child', Griffith–Thompson, III, no. 399.

^{B}ϧρω† (Crum 631 b), 'jugular veins' = καρωτίς (i.e. ἀρτηρία), 'carotid artery' (Liddell–Scott).

DÉVAUD's slip.

^{B}ϧαϧ (Crum 631 b), 'neck' = (*Wb.* III, 331, 3 f.), *ḫḫ*, 'neck, throat'; (Er. 396, 4), *ḫḫỉ*, 'neck'.

^{H}CHAMPOLLION, *Gr.* 93 [1836]; ^{D}GRIFFITH, *Rylands*, III, 381 [1909].

NB. The supposed ^{S}ϩαϩ (Chassinat, *Ms. mag. copte*, 13–16) is non-existent; read ϩαc with Drescher in *JEA* 43, 119.

ϩⲁ-, ϩⲁⲣⲟ⸗ (Crum 632a), prep. 'under, in, at' = (*Wb.* III, 386, 1 ff.), *ẖr*, 'under'; (Er. 385, 5), *ẖr*, 'under'.

[H]CHAMPOLLION, *Gr.* 467–70 [1836]; [D]BRUGSCH, *Scriptura Aeg. dem.* 59, IX [1848].

[BS]ϩⲁ-, ϩⲁⲣⲟ⸗ (Crum 634b), 'to, toward' a person = (*Wb.* III, 315, 15–17), 'to, toward' a person.

SPIEGELBERG, *Rec. trav.* 31, 157–8 [1909]; cf. SETHE, *Verbum*, I, 144, §242 [1899].

[S]ϩⲁ, [B]ϧⲁⲓ (Crum 635a), 'winnowing fan' = (Er. 378, 4), *ḫꜥy*, a tool.

[D]REVILLOUT, *Poème*, 13 [1885]; cf. BRUGSCH, *ZÄS* 26, 10 [1888].

ϩⲁ⸗ (Crum 635a), < *ⲟⲩϩⲁ⸗, prefix of Perfect = , *wꜣḥ*, 'to lay down', i.e. 'finish' (doing something); (Er. 77, 1), *wꜣḥ*, auxiliary of perfect.

[H]SPIEGELBERG in *OLZ* 7, col. 199 [1904]; cf. RÖSCH, *Vorbemerkungen*, 162, §144 [1909]; cf. SETHE, *ZÄS* 52, 112–16 [1914]; [D]HESS, *Rosettana*, 51 [1902].

[S]ϩⲁⲉ, [B]ϧⲁⲉ (Crum 635a), 'last thing, end' = Passive Partic. , *ḫꜣꜥ*, 'abandoned, left' = 'last' (not in this meaning in *Wb.* III, 227 ff.; ex. Ramesside graffito at Deir el-Bahari where *ḫꜣꜥ n pr(t)*, 'last in coming out' is contrasted with , *ḥꜣwty n ꜥk*, 'first in coming in'; (Er. 378, 1), *ḫꜥ*, 'last, end'.

[H]STEINDORFF, *ZÄS* 27, 109 [1889]; [D]SPIEGELBERG, *Chronik*, 74, no. 196 [1914].

Fem. [S]ϩⲁⲏ, [B]ϧⲁⲏ = , *ḫꜣt*, or (Volten, *Ägypter und Amazonen*, 108), *ḫꜣꜥt*.

SPIEGELBERG, *Petubastis*, 44*, no. 291 [1910].

[F]ϩⲁⲏ (Crum 636b), an animal = (Er. 290, 1), *ḥꜣl*, an animal.

SPIEGELBERG, *Demotica* I, 25 n. 1 [1925], but Crum, *loc. cit.*, suspects an error for ⲁϩⲏ, 'cow'.

ϩⲁⲓ (Crum 636b), 'husband' = (*Wb.* II, 475, 10. 11), *hꜣy*, 'husband'; (Er. 267, 1), *hy*, 'husband'.

[H]CHAMPOLLION, *Gr.* 80 [1836]; [D]BRUGSCH, *Gr. dém.* 36, §74 [1855].

ϩⲁ(ⲉ)ⲓⲟ, ⲁ(ⲉ)ⲓⲟ (Crum 636b), ϩⲁⲉⲓ (Mani Ps. 142, 21), interj. of entreaty 'yea, verily, come', 'hail!' = ?, *hy*, <, *hꜣ* (*Wb.* II, 471, 1 f., and 482, 12 f.), interjection; (Er. 266, 4), *hy*, 'hail!'.

HSPIEGELBERG, *Kopt. Handwb.* I [1921]; DH. THOMPSON in Allberry, *A Manichaean Psalm-book*, II, note to 142, 21 [1938].

Cf. also Bϩⲉ below.

ϩⲉ (Crum 637a), 'fall' = (*Wb.* II, 472, 3 f.), *hꜣy*, 'descend'; (Er. 266, 6), *hy*, 'fall, perish'.

HCHABAS, *Pap. mag. Harris*, 97 [1860]; DBRUGSCH, *Gr. dém.* 34, §68 [1855].

ϩⲉ (Crum 638b), 'manner' = (Er. 375, 2), *ẖ*, 'manner' < ?, *ẖt*, lit. 'body'; cf. (*Wb.* III, 358, 15), *ẖt*, 'contents, wording' of a document.

DSPIEGELBERG, *Kopt. Handwb.* 221 and n. 11 [1921]; DBRUGSCH, *Gr. dém.* 189–90, §386 [1855]; cf. BRUGSCH, *Wb.* 1043 [1868].

Bϩⲉ (Crum 640a), interj. 'ho!', perhaps Boh. form of ϩⲁ(ⲉ)ⲓⲟ.

Bϩⲉ, BFϩⲏ (Crum 640a), 'hinder part, back' in Bⲥⲁⲙⲉⲛϩⲏ = (*Wb.* III, 10, 1 ff.), *ḥꜣ*, 'hinder part, back'; (Er. 286, 4), (*n*)*ḥꜣ*, 'behind'.

HSTERN, *Kopt. Gr.* 375, §562 [1880]; DSPIEGELBERG, *Der dem. Text der Priesterdekrete*, 159, no. 224 [1922].

ϩⲏ, ϩⲏⲧ⸗ (Crum 640b), 'fore part, beginning' = (*Wb.* III, 19, 2 ff.), *ḥꜣt*, 'fore part, beginning, the best of...'; (Er. 287, 1), *ḥꜣt*, 'fore part, beginning'.

HCHAMPOLLION, *Dict.* 115 [1841]; DBRUGSCH, *Scriptura Aeg. dem.* 61, §46, III [1848].

ϩⲏⲧ⸗ (Crum 640b), go, come, look, etc., 'forward', fear, etc., 'before' = L.E. (*Wb.* III, 24, 10–12), *ḥꜣt*, 'before' (to be understood as ⟨⟩, ⟨*r*⟩*ḥꜣt*.

ϩⲁⲑⲏ (Crum 641b), 'in front of, before', cf. (*Wb.* III, 23, 25 f.), *ḫr-ḥꜣt* (without def. article!), 'in front of, before' = , *ḫr tꜣ ḥꜣt*, 'before'.

HCHAMPOLLION, *Gr.* 491 [1836]; DBRUGSCH, *Wb.* 931 [1868].

ϩⲓⲑⲏ (Crum 642a), 'to, at front, forward' = , *ḫr tꜣ ḥꜣt*, 'before'.

KRALL, *Mitteilungen aus der Sammlung Erzh. Rainer*, VI, 70, no. 208 [1897].

ϩⲓϩⲏ (Crum 642a), 'to, at front, forward' = (*Wb.* III, 23, 14. 15), *ḥr-ḥ3t*, 'before'.

ϩⲏ (Crum 642b), 'belly, womb' = (*Wb.* III, 356, 3 f.), *ẖt*, 'body, belly'; (Er. 373, 4), *ẖ(t)*, 'body'.

[H]DE ROUGÉ, *Oeuv. div.* III (= *Bibl. ég.* XXIII), 146 [1856]; [D]BRUGSCH, *Wb.* 1042–3 [1868].

See also [A]ⲁϩⲧⲛ-, 'against'.

ⲛϩⲏⲧ≈ (Crum 683a, s.v. ϩⲛ-), 'in' = , *n-ẖt*≈ + suffix, 'in the body of, in', replaces since the Demotic of Gr.-R. period the pron. state of ⲛϩⲛ-, cf. Spiegelberg, *Dem. Gr.*, §348c.

GRIFFITH–THOMPSON, I, 186, n. to l. 3 [1904]; III, 63, no. 632 [1909].

ϩⲏ (Crum 643a), 'storey' of house = (*Wb.* III, 358, 9–11), *ẖt*, part of a house; (Er. 374, middle), *ẖ(t)*, 'storey'.

[H]ERMAN–GRAPOW, III, 358, 9–11 [1929]; [D]SPIEGELBERG, *Dem. Pap. Strassburg*, 45 [1902].

ϩⲏ (Crum 643a), 'quarry?' = (*Wb.* III, 360, 11–15), *ẖ3t*, 'mine, quarry'; (Er. 375, 5), *ẖ*, 'quarry'.

[HD]SPIEGELBERG, *ZÄS* 54, 131–2 [1918].

[B]ϩⲏ, ϩⲉ- (Crum 643a), 'season(?)' = (*Wb.* II, 478, 1 f.), *h3w*, 'time'; (Er. 265, 9), *h3*, 'time'.

[H]ERMAN–GRAPOW, *Wb.* II, 478, 3 [1928]; [D]GRIFFITH, *Rylands*, III, 227 n. 10, 368 [1909].

ϩⲉⲃⲱⲱⲛ, 'bad season, famine' = , *h3(w) bin*, 'bad time' (Parker, *A Saite Oracle Papyrus from Thebes*, 52, n. g, and Pl. 19, 2); , *h3 bin*, 'bad time' (Er. 266, top; P. Ryl. IX, 6, 16).

ϩⲉⲛⲟⲩϥⲉ, 'good season, plenty' = , *h3w nfr* (*Wb.* II, 478, 3), 'good time'.

ϩⲓ (Crum 643a), 'thresh, beat, rub' = or (*Wb.* III, 47, 4, 5), *ḥwy*, 'beat', i.e. 'harvest' corn, flax.

CHAMPOLLION, *Gr.* 368, 509 [1836]; cf. Sethe, *Verbum*, II, 301, §683, 6a [1899].

ϩⲓ- (Crum 643b), prep. 'on, at, in' = (*Wb.* III, 131, 3 ff.), *ḥr*, 'on', etc.; (Er. 319, 4), *ḥr*, 'on', etc.

CHAMPOLLION, *Gr.* 456 ff. [1836]; [D]BRUGSCH, *Scriptura Aeg. dem.* 60, XII [1848].

ϩⲗⲉ⸗ (Crum 645 b), archaic pronominal state of ϩⲓ: ϩⲗⲉⲩ = , *ḥr·w*, 'on them'.

TILL, *Kopt. Chrest, f. den fay. Dialekt*, p. 11 n. 10; p. 12 n. 11 [1930]; cf. Polotsky in *OLZ* 34, col. 840 [1931].

ϩⲓⲱⲱ⸗ = * (*Wb.* I, 26, 3. 4), *ḥr ỉȝt*, 'on the back (lit. spine)'; (Er. 12, 12), *ḥr ȝtẖ·*, 'on'.

[HD]BRUGSCH, *Wb.* 21 [1867].

ϩⲓⲉ (Crum 645 b), 'rudder', < ϩⲓⲏⲓⲉ, see this latter.

ϩⲓⲏ (Crum 646 a), ⳉⲓⲏ (P. Bodmer VI), 'road'. The ⳉ of P. Bodmer VI makes now the derivation from (*Wb.* III, 144, 5. 6), *ḥrt*, 'road' (CHABAS, *Pap. mag. Harris*, 246, no. 818 [1860]; cf. Steindorff in *ZÄS* 27, 107 [1899]; MASPERO, *Rec. trav.* 19, 151–2 [1897]) impossible. The etymology of ϩⲓⲏ becomes again unknown.

ϩⲟ, ϩⲣⲁ⸗ (Crum 646 b), 'face' = (*Wb.* III, 125, 7 f.), *ḥr*, 'face'; (Er. 317), *ḥr*, 'face'.

[H]CHAMPOLLION, *Gr.* 91 [1836]; [D]BRUGSCH, *Scriptura Aeg. dem.* 17, §14 [1848]; DE ROUGÉ, *Oeuv. div.* I (= *Bibl. ég.* XXI), 251–4 and Pl. 2, nos. 39–41 [1848].

ϩⲣ- in proper name Ⲫⲣⲣⲏⲣ (i.e. ⲡ + ϩⲣ + ⲣⲏⲣ) = *Pȝ-ḥr-rrỉ*, lit. 'The pig-face', see under ⲣⲓⲣ, 'pig'.

ϯϩⲟ (Crum 647 a), 'turn face, look' = , *ty ḥr*, 'look at'.

HESS, *Stne*, 169 [1888].

ϥⲓ ϩⲟ (Crum 647 b), 'raise face' = Dem. *fȝy ḥr r-ḥry*, 'lift up one's face' (Er. 144, top).

ϫⲓ ϩⲣⲁ⸗ (Crum 648 a), 'disport, amuse, occupy self, converse' = (*Wb.* IV, 378, bottom), *sḏȝy-ḥr* > (since XVIIIth Dyn.) (*Wb.* V, 514, 10–12), *ḏȝy ḥr*, 'amuse self'; (Er. 666, middle), *ṯȝy ḥr*, 'amuse self'.

[H]BRUGSCH, *Wb.* 1357–8 [1868] (*sḏȝy*); RÖSCH, *Vorbem.* 121, §98 (*ḏȝy*) [1909]; [D]HESS, *Stne*, 48, 184 [1888].

ⲉϩⲣⲛ-, ⲉϩⲣⲁ⸗ (Crum 649 a), prep. 'toward face of, to, among' = (*Wb.* III, 129, 12. 13), *r ḥr*, 'before, on'; (Er. 318, 2), *ỉỉr-ḥr*, 'before'.

ⲛⲁϩⲣⲛ-, ⲛⲁϩⲣⲁ⸗ (Crum 649 b), prep. 'in presence of, before' = (Er. 318, bottom), *n-ḥr-ḥr*, 'before'.

ϩⲟ, ϩⲱ, ϩⲁ (Theban) (Crum 650 a), a grain and fodder measure larger than ⲙⲁⲁϫⲉ, perhaps = ᴮϩⲟⲓ, 'heap of grain', see the latter.

ϩⲟⲓ (Crum 650 b), (1) 'field', arable or pasture; (2) 'canal, ditch' = (*Wb.* III, 13, 10. 11), *ḥ3yt*, 'border of a canal or well'.
DÉVAUD's slip.

ϩⲟⲓ (Crum 651 a), f. 'heap of grain' = ?ϩⲟ, ϩⲱ, ϩⲁ (Crum 650 a), m., 'grain and fodder measure' = (*Wb.* I, 220, 10), *ʿḥʿ*, 'heap' (also of corn). It is, therefore, the same word as ⲁϩⲟ, 'treasure', this having the metaphorical meaning, while ϩⲟⲓ kept the original one.
DÉVAUD's slip.

ϩⲱ (Mani Ps. 196, 29), 'sepulchre', ⲛϩⲱ being paraphrased as ⲛⲧⲁⲫⲟⲥ ⲛⲁⲣⲭⲁⲓⲟⲛ 'the ancient tombs', and ⲑⲱ (i.e. ⲧ + ϩⲱ) translating μνῆμα in Kasser, P. Bodmer XXI, p. 24 = (*Wb.* III, 2, 10–14), *ḥwt*, 'tomb'; (Er. 283, 8), *ḥt*, '(larger) tomb (τάφος)'.
H. THOMPSON in Allberry, *A Manichaean Psalm-book*, II, p. 196, n. on 29 (right) [1938].
ᴼϩⲱ (Crum 651), 'mansion, temple' in ⲛⲉⲃⲑⲱ = goddess Nephthys, (*Wb.* II, 233, 6), *Nbt-ḥwt*, lit. 'lady of the mansion'.
ϩⲁⲧ- in ϩⲁⲑⲱⲣ = goddess Ḥatḥōr, (*Wb.* III, 5, 11), *Ḥwt-ḥr*, lit. 'mansion of Horus'.
Also in ⲁⲧⲣⲏⲡⲉ, a place name, see Index of Place names.
ERMAN, *ZÄS* 39, 129 [1901].
ϩⲁ-, in ϧⲁⲛⲉⲓⲏⲥⲉ, a place name, see Index of Place names for this.
ϩ-, in ⲥϩⲃⲱⲛ (< *ϩⲥⲃⲱⲛ), ϩⲛⲏⲥ, ϩⲟⲩⲱⲣ, see Index of Place names for these.
Pl. ϩⲱ, ϩⲟⲩ as place name, see Index of Place names under ϩⲱ.

ϩⲱⲱ- (Crum 651 b), 'self, also, for my, his part' = () + suffix (*Wb.* III, 37, bottom; 38, 19 f.), *ḥʿ·*, 'self' (lit. 'as far as (his) body is concerned'); + suffix (Er. 292, 8), *ḥʿ·*, also , *hw·*, 'self'.
ᴴCHAMPOLLION, *Gr.* 91 [1836]; ᴰBRUGSCH, *Gr. dém.* 94–5, §215 [1855] (); Brugsch, *Wb.* 893 [1868]; REVILLOUT, *Setna*, 39, 41 [1877]; Revillout, *Nouvelle chrest. dém.* 98 [1878].

ϩⲁⲁⲃ (Crum 652 b), 'darkness, depth?' = ?Hebrew **עָב**, 'dark cloud, cloud mass, thicket'.

DÉVAUD in Crum, *A Coptic Dict.* 652 b [1937].

ϩⲓⲉⲓⲃ (Crum 652 b), 'lamb' = (Er. 291, 11), *ḫyb*, < (Er. 268, 6), *hyb*, 'lamb'.

BRUGSCH, *ZÄS* 26, 19 [1888].

Originally perhaps **ϩⲓ** + **ⲉⲓⲃ** < * *ḥry-ꜣb* '(young animal) which is upon the finger nail'; cf. (*Wb.* III, 136, 6), *ḥry-ḏbꜥ* '(young animal) which is upon the finger' and cf. *Revue d'ég.* 11, 159–61. Fem. **ϩⲓⲁⲉⲓⲃⲉ** and sim. is then secondary (on analogy with **ⲣⲓⲣ**, fem. **ⲣⲁⲓⲣⲉ**, 'pig').

ϩⲱⲃ (Crum 652 b), 'send' = (*Wb.* II, 479, 13 f.), *hꜣb*, 'send'; (Er. 271, 7), *hb*, 'send'.

HDE ROUGÉ, *Oeuv. div.* III (= *Bibl. ég.* XXIII), 164 [1856]; cf. SPIEGELBERG, *Rec. trav.* 31, 160 [1909]; DGRIFFITH–THOMPSON, III, 57, no. 559 [1909].

ϩⲱⲃ (Crum 653 a), 'thing, work, matter, event' = (*Wb.* II, 479, 13 f.), *hꜣb*, 'sending' > 'errand' (an early ex. of meaning 'work': P. Sallier II, 4, 7, parallel with , *wpt*, 'message' > 'task'); (Er. 272, middle), *hb*, 'matter'.

DBRUGSCH, *Gr. dém.* 115, §241 [1855].

ϩⲏⲃⲉ (Crum 655 a), 'grief, mourning', cf. (*Wb.* III, 61, 14), *ḥb*, 'mourn'; (Er. 299, 1), *ḥb*, 'mourning'.

HSETHE in Gardiner, *Notes on the Story of Sinuhe*, 159 [1916]; DBRUGSCH, *Wb.* 946 [1868].

ϩⲓⲃⲉ and **ϩⲃⲃⲉ** (Crum 655 b), 'be low, short', cf. (*Wb.* II, 486, 9), *hb*, 'humiliate'? (cf. also its Causative , *shby*, 'dishonour', *Wb.* IV, 207, 11); (Er. 299, 2), *ḥb*, 'humiliate'.

HSPIEGELBERG, *Kopt. Handwb.* 226 [1921]; DGRIFFITH, *Stories*, 191 n. [1900].

See also **ⲑⲃⲃⲓⲟ**.

S**ϩⲓⲃⲱⲓ**, B**ϩⲓⲡ** (Crum 655 b), 'ibis' = *Wb.* II, 487, 1 f.), *hby*, 'ibis'; (Er. 272, 2), *hb*, 'ibis'. The element **-ⲱⲓ** is obscure; the Egn. forms suit the B**ϩⲓⲡ** better (**hîbey*).

[H]CHAMPOLLION, *Gr.* 85 [1836]; cf. LEPSIUS, *Lettre à M. Rosellini*, 38 and Pl. A, VI, 6 [1837]; [D]BRUGSCH, *Rhind*, 44 and Pl. 40, no. 300 [1865] (giving the form ϩⲓⲡⲡⲉⲛ which does not exist).

ϩⲃⲱ (Crum 656a), 'covering, tent' = (*Wb.* III, 60, 17), *ḥbyt*, 'festival hall (in temple); (Er. 299, 3), *ḥbt*, 'tent, baldachin'.
[H]BRUGSCH, *Wb.*, Suppl. 805 [1881]; [D]HESS, *Stne*, 168 [1888].

ϩⲃⲃⲉ (Crum 656b), 'plough' = (*Wb.* II, 485, 10. 11), *hb*, 'plough'.
CHAMPOLLION, *Gr.* 450 [1836].

ϩⲱⲃⲕ (Crum 656b), 'prick, incite', cf. (*Wb.* II, 488, 3. 4), *hbḳ*, 'to pound', Gr.-R. (*Wb.* II, 488, 5), 'crush noisily into...'.
ERMAN–GRAPOW, *Wb.* II, 488, 3–5 [1928].

[SF]ϩⲃⲟⲩⲣ, [A2]ϭⲃⲟⲩⲣ, [A]ϭⲃⲓⲣ (Crum 656b), 'left hand' = (Er. 578, 3), *gbyr*, 'left'.
KRALL, *Mitt. Pap. Erzh. Rainer*, 2–3, 266 [1887].

ϩⲃⲟⲣⲃⲣ (Crum 657a), 'throw down, push' = (*Wb.* III, 64, 1), *ḥbrbr*, or (*Wb.* III, 63, 14), *ḥbnbn*, 'cast oneself on the ground'; (Er. 273, 4), *hbrbr*, 'throw down', a reduplication of (Er., *loc. cit.* ex. Ankhsh. 6, 11), *hbr*, 'be cast down'; [B]ϥⲟⲣϥⲉⲣ (Crum 624a), 'fall, rush down' stands for ⲃⲟⲣⲃⲉⲣ and is the same word as ϩⲃⲟⲣⲃⲣ.
[H]ERMAN, *ZÄS* 34, 57 [1896]; [D]BRUGSCH, *Wb.* 896 [1868]; cf. GLANVILLE'S index.

[S]ϩⲁ(ⲉ)ⲓⲃⲉⲥ, [B]ϧⲏⲓⲃⲓ (Crum 657b), 'shade, shadow' = L.E. (*Wb.* III, 225, 1–6), *ḫ3ybt*, 'shade, shadow'; (Er. 377, 1), *ḫybt*, 'shade'.
[H]DE ROUGÉ, *Oeuv. div.* III (= *Bibl. ég.* XXIII), 88 [1856]; [D]BRUGSCH, *Sammlung dem. Urk.* 41 and Pl. 6, 5 [1850]; *De natura et indole*, 36 [1850]. NB. The -ⲥ of ϩⲁ(ⲉ)ⲓⲃⲉⲥ is attested as early as in of P. Lansing 12, 11, and has its origin in the association with ϩⲏⲃⲥ, 'lamp'.

[S]ϩⲏⲃⲥ, [B]ϧⲏⲃⲥ (Crum 658a), 'lamp' = (*Wb.* III, 230, 3), *ḫbs*, 'wick, lamp'; (Er. 380, 2), *ḫbs*, 'lamp'.
[H]BRUGSCH, *Wb.* 1031 [1868]; [D]BRUGSCH, *De natura*, 36 [1850].

ϩⲱⲃⲥ (Crum 658b), 'cover' = (*Wb.* III, 64, 3 f.), *ḥbs*, 'clothe, cover'; (Er. 300, 5), *ḥbs*, 'clothe, cover'.

[H]CHAMPOLLION, *Gr.* 385 [1836]; [D]BRUGSCH, *Gr. dém.* 39, §84 [1855].

ϩⲱⲃⲥ, [F]**ϩⲁⲃⲥ** (Crum 659a), 'covering, lid' = (*Wb.* III, 66, 18), *ḥbs*, 'lid (of a vase, basket, chest)'.

ERMAN–GRAPOW, *Wb.* III, 66, 18 [1929].

ϩⲃⲟ(ⲟ)ⲥ (Crum 659b), 'covering, garment, linen' = (*Wb.* III, 65, 18 f.), *ḥbs*, 'garment, covering'; (Er. 300, 6), *ḥbs*, 'garment'.

[H]CHAMPOLLION, *Gr.* 81 [1836]; [D]HESS, *Gnost. Pap.* 10 [1892]; cf. BRUGSCH, *Gr. dém.* 39, §84 [1855].

ϩⲃⲥⲱ (Crum 660a), 'garment' = (*Wb.* III, 66, 13–15), *ḥbswt*, 'piece of fabric, covering, garment'.

SETHE, *Verbum*, I, 37, §95b [1899].

ϩⲁⲃⲟⲩⲉⲓ, -ⲓⲟⲩⲓ (Crum 660b), 'wasp'. Though the *scala* equates this with زنبور, 'hornet', the word is probably but a writing of ***ⲁϥⲟⲩⲓ**, the unattested pl. of **ⲁϥ**, 'fly', as **ⲁϥⲟⲩⲓ, ⲁⲃⲟⲩⲓ** is pl. of **ⲁϥ**, 'flesh'. In both P 44, 56 and Tri 424 the word is pl., only **ⲁⲡⲟⲩⲓ** of Mor 54, 104, presumably still another spelling of the word, is sing.

SETHE in *ZÄS* 38, 118 [1892] (as to **ϩⲁⲃ-**).

ϩⲩⲃϣ (Crum 660b, meaning unknown), m., part of pig, 'snout(?)', cf. ? (Er. 379, 9), *ẖbẖy*, f., 'beak (?)' of a bird.

ϩⲁⲕ (Crum 661a), 'cobbling tailor' = (Er. 378, 9), *ẖʿk*, 'cobbling tailor', from **ϩⲱⲱⲕⲉ**.

SPIEGELBERG, *Griffith Studies*, 177 n. 9 [1932]; cf. SPIEGELBERG, *ZÄS* 51, 90 and 93, (3) [1913].

ϩⲓⲕ (Crum 661a), 'magic' (charms, potions, etc.) = (*Wb.* III, 175, bottom), *ḥkꜣ*, 'magic, supernatural power'; (Er. 333, 5), *ḥk*, 'magic'.

[H]BIRCH, 'Observations on an Egyptian Calendar of the reign of Philip Arridaeus', in *Archaeological Journal*, 7, 118 [1850]; [D]GRIFFITH, *Stories*, 174 [1900].

ⲣ ϩⲓⲕ, 'bewitch, enchant' = , *ỉr-ḥyk*, lit. 'make magic' (e.g. Griffith, *loc. cit.*).

See also **ϩⲁⲕⲟ**.

ϩⲱⲱⲕ (Crum 661b), 'gird, brace' with harness, armour = (*Wb.* III,

401, 2–5), *ẖkr*, 'to be adorned';  (Er. 397, 2), *ẖk*, 'to be adorned, armed'.

[H]BRUGSCH, *Wb.* 1048–9 [1868]; [D]KRALL, *Mitt. aus der Sammlung Erzh. Rainer*, VI, 72, no. 243 [1897].

[S]ϩⲁⲕⲟ, [B]ⲁϫⲱ (Crum 662b), 'magician, wizard' =  (*Wb.* III, 177, 10), *ḥḳꜣw*, 'magician'.

DÉVAUD's slip.

ϩⲏⲕⲉ (Crum 662b), a measure of corn = ?  (*Wb.* III, 174, 13. 15), *ḥḳꜣt*, measure of corn and other commodities.

KUENTZ in *Bull. de la Soc. de ling.* 38, 192 [1937].

ϩⲱⲱⲕⲉ (Crum 662b), 'scrape, scratch, shave, shear' =  (*Wb.* III, 365, 1, 2), *ẖꜥk*, 'shave'; 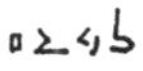 (Er. 378, 8), *ẖꜥk*, 'rub, patch up, shear'.

[H]LEPSIUS, *Lettre à M. Rosellini*, 85 n. 14 and Pl. B, no. 85[c], 19 [1837]; cf. BRUGSCH, *Wb.* 1044 [1868]; [D]ERICHSEN, *Dem. Glossar*, 378, 8 [1954]. See also ϩⲁⲕ, 'cobbling tailor'.

ϩⲕⲟ (Crum 663b), 'be hungry' =  (*Wb.* III, 174, 23 f.), *ḥḳr*, 'be hungry'; 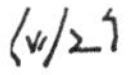 (Er. 334, 2), *ḥḳr*, 'be hungry'.

[H]CHAMPOLLION, *Gr.* 384 [1836]; [D]BRUGSCH, *Gr. dém.* 44, §94; 129, §265 [1855].

ϩⲕⲟ, 'hunger, famine' =  (*Wb.* III, 175, 4–7), *ḥḳr*, 'hunger, famine'; 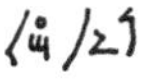 (Er. 334, middle), *ḥḳr*, 'hunger'.

[H]BAILLET, *Oeuv. div.* I (= *Bibl. ég.* XV), 30 [1867]; cf. CHAMPOLLION, *Gr.* 63 [1836]; [D]REVILLOUT, *Pap. mor.* II, 63 n. 4 [1908].

ϩⲏⲕⲉ (Crum 664a), 'poor' =  (*Wb.* III, 175, 2), *ḥḳr*, 'hungry (man)'; 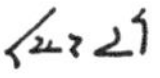 (Er. 334, middle), *ḥḳr*, 'hungry, poor'.

[H]ERMAN, *Äg. Glossar*, 88 [1904]; [D]BRUGSCH, *Rhind*, 46 and Pl. 41, no. 340 [1865].

ϩⲁⲗ (Crum 665a), 'servant, slave' = 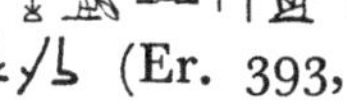 (*Wb.* III, 232, 13–16), *ẖꜣrw(y)*, 'Syrian, Syrian slave'; (Er. 393, 2), *ẖl*, 'young, boy, servant, slave'.

[H]STERN in *ZÄS* 21, 26 [1883]; [D]BRUGSCH, *Lettre à M. le Vicomte Emanuel de Rougé*, 32 and Pl. II, no. 5 [1850]; cf. BRUGSCH, *Sammlung dem. Urk.* Pl. V,

l. 35 [1850]; cf. already ÅKERBLAD, letter to Th. Young of 31 January 1815 (in Young, *Misc. Works*, III, 37) who reads as ϭⲉⲗϣⲓⲣⲓ.

ϩⲙϩⲁⲗ, 'servant, slave' = (Er. 394, lower), *ḥm-ẖl*, 'boy', lit. 'small one, Syrian'.

GRIFFITH, *Stories*, 89 [1900].

ϩ(ⲉ)ⲣϣⲓⲣⲉ (Crum 585b under ϣⲓⲣⲉ), 'young servant, youth' = *, *Ḫ3rw-šry*, lit. 'little (= young) Syrian', attested only as proper name, cf. Ranke, I, 273, 23, and add. p. XXVIII; II, 382; *Ann. Serv.* 28, 10.

BRUGSCH, *Wb.* 1404 [1868] (for -ϣⲓⲣⲉ); SPIEGELBERG, *Eigennamen*, 7* and 17* [1901] (for ϩⲉⲣ).

See also ϩⲗⲗⲟ.

ϩⲱⲗ (Crum 665b), 'fly, go' = Late and Gr.-R. (*Wb.* III, 146, 13), *ḥr(y)*, 'fly (to heaven)'; (Er. 327, 2), *ḥl*, 'fly'; ^{B}ϩⲉⲗϩⲉⲗ (Crum 672a), 'swim, float(?)' is a reduplication of this.

^{H}ERMAN–GRAPOW, *Wb.* III, 146, 13 [1929]; ^{D}REVILLOUT, *Poème*, 140–1 [1885].

ϩⲱⲗ (Crum 666b), 'be hoarse' = (*Wb.* III, 298, 16), *ḫnr*, 'become hoarse' (of voice).

BRUGSCH, *Wb.*, Suppl. 894 [1881].

^{B}ϩⲉⲗⲓ (Crum 667a), nn., 'fear' = (*Wb.* III, 147, 14), *ḥryt*, 'fright, fear'.

CHAMPOLLION, *Gr.* 386 [1836]; cf. Spiegelberg in *ZÄS* 63, 155 [1928].

ϩⲏⲗⲉ (Crum 667a), measure or container of bread = ? (*Wb.* III, 106, 18 f.), *ḥnwt*, 'bowl, pot'.

DÉVAUD's slip.

ϩⲁⲗⲃϣⲉ (Crum 668a), 'breastplate' = (Er. 262, middle), *ḫ-lbš* < *ḫr-lbš*, 'armour, coat of mail'. From ⲗⲱⲃϣ, 'set crown upon < arm, clothe'; see this latter.

KRALL, *Mitt. aus der Sammlung Erzh. Rainer*, VI, 22 and 72, no. 238 [1897]; cf. Spiegelberg, *Petubastis*, 38*, no. 236 [1910].

^{S}ϩⲁⲗⲁⲕ, ^{B}ⲁⲗⲁⲕ (Crum 668a), 'ring' = (Er. 281, 2), *hlk*, also (Spiegelberg, *Dem. Denkmäler* I, 80), *ʿlḳ*, 'ring', a loan-word from Semitic, cf. Arabic حلقة, Pl. حلق.

^D^SPIEGELBERG, *Der Papyrus Libbey*, 9 and Pl. 2, l. 9 [1907]; ^S^ROSSI, *Etym. aeg.* 3 [1808].

ϩⲱⲗⲕ (Crum 668b), 'twist, roll, braid' = **ḥnk*, 'to braid, pleat'; cf. (*Wb.* III, 120, 10), *ḥnkt*, 'plait of hair', (*Wb.* III, 120, 7), *ḥnk*, kind of raft (made of interlaced reeds or branches), etc.; (Er. 280, 4), *hrk*, object made in wicker work, wig (?).

^H^SETHE in Spiegelberg, *Kopt. Handwb.* 231 [1921]; cf. Sethe in *ZÄS* 57, 18 [1922]; ^D^ERICHSEN, *Dem. Glossar*, 280, 4 [1954].

ϩ(ⲉ)ⲗⲕⲟⲩ (Crum 668b), 'sickle', from ⲱⲗⲕ, 'be bent, bend'.

DÉVAUD's slip.

ϩⲗⲟⲗ (Crum 668b), 'darkness', cf. (*Wb.* III, 115, 4), *ḥnr*, also , *ḥnrr*, and , *ḥrr*, 'squint', also as an eye illness; = (Er. 328, 1), *ḥlly*, 'darkness'.

^H^CHASSINAT, *Pap. méd.* 73 [1921]; ^D^SPIEGELBERG, *Dem. Chronik*, 72, no. 183 [1914]. Perhaps also in ^B^ϩⲁⲗⲁⲕⲙⲓ, ϩⲓⲗⲁⲕⲙⲓ (Crum 668b) 'blear-eyed person', =ϩⲁⲗ-ⲁⲕⲙⲓ < *ϩⲁⲗⲗ-ⲁⲕⲙⲓ.

^A^ϩⲁⲗⲓⲗ (Crum 669a; reading confirmed *Crum Mem. Vol.* 385), 'beetle' (κάνθαρος) or 'worm' (σκώληξ); if the latter then cf. ? (*Wb.* III, 150, 1), *ḥr(w)rw*, Pl., '(intestinal) worms' and (*Wb.* III, 150, 2. 3), *ḥrr(t)*, 'worms'.

CRUM, *A Coptic Dict.* 669a [1937].

ϩⲗⲟⲉⲓⲗⲉ (Crum 669a), 'be borne, float' = (Er. 327, 3), *ḥlꜥlꜥ*, 'float'.

SPIEGELBERG, *Petubastis*, 43*, no. 281 [1910] (his form ϩⲗⲟⲟⲗⲉ is not recorded by Crum).

ϩⲗⲟⲟⲗⲉ (Crum 669a), 'nurse, carry' child = (Er. 280, 11), *hll*, 'carry, rock a child, wrap'. Perhaps the L.Eg. (*Wb.* II, 496, 2), *hnhn*, in , *ḥnw n hnhn*, 'cradle songs'.

^H^DÉVAUD's slip; ^D^SPIEGELBERG, *Dem. Texte auf Krügen*, 39, no. 97; 69, no. 136 [1912].

ϩⲗⲗⲟ (Crum 669b), 'old man' = (Er. 55, 2; 394, bottom), *ḫl-ꜥꜣ*, 'old man', lit. 'great (=old) Syrian'. For ϩⲗ-, see under ϩⲁⲗ, 'servant'.

BRUGSCH, *Gr. dém.* 38, §81 [1855].

Fem. ϩⲗⲗⲱ, ‘old woman’ = , *ẖr-ʿȝt*, ‘old woman’.
PARKER, *JEA* 26, 102, and Pl. XIX, 6–7 [1940].
Pl. ϩⲗⲗⲟⲓ, ‘old men’ = , *ẖr-ʿy*, ‘old men, elders’.
SPIEGELBERG, *ZÄS* 45, 100 [1908–9].

ϩⲁⲗⲱⲙ (Crum 670a), ‘cheese’, loan-word from Semitic, cf. Arabic حَالُوم.
ROSSI, *Etym. aeg.* 5 [1808].

ϩⲗⲱⲙ (Crum 670b), ‘louse, flea’, perhaps connected with (Er. 270, 6), *hʿlʿmʿtʿ*, kind of vermin. This latter is referred to in *Dem. Mag. Pap.* 15, 7 as *syb* = ⲥⲓⲃ (see this). *Hʿlʿmʿt* perhaps from Greek ἕλμινς (gen. ἕλμινθος), ‘worm’, cf. Griffith–Thompson, *Dem. Mag. Pap.* I, 105, note on 15, 3.

ϩⲁⲗⲙⲉ (Mani; Crum 670b), ‘spring, fountain’ = [S]ϩⲟⲛⲃⲉ, see this.

ϩⲗⲟⲙⲗⲙ (Crum 671a), ‘become entangled’ = (*Wb.* III, 114, 14), *ḥnmnm*, ‘slip in’.

[S]ϩⲗⲟⲡ, [A]ϩⲗⲁⲡ (Crum 671a), ‘vessel for pouring’ = (Er. 392, 2), *ẖrp*, a vessel for wine.
ČERNÝ, *BIFAO* 57, 211 [1958].

ϩ(ⲉ)ⲗⲡⲉ (Crum 671a), ‘navel’ = (*Wb.* III, 365, 14. 15), *ẖpȝ*, ‘navel’; (not in Er.), *ẖlpy*, ‘navel’. See also ϣⲗⲟⲡ, ‘ply’ of cord.
[H]BRUGSCH, *Wb.* 1045 [1868]; [D]KRALL in *Mitteil. aus der Sammlung Erzh. Rainer*, VI, 72, no. 240 [1897].

ϩⲁⲗⲟⲩⲥ (Crum 671b), ‘spider's web’, a loan-word from Semitic, cf. Arabic هلّوس (W. B. BISHAI, *JNES* 23, 42 [1964]).
SPIEGELBERG, *Kopt. Handwb.* 232 [1921].

ϩⲁⲗⲏⲧ (Crum 671b), ‘flying creature, bird’ = (Er. 270, 5; 327, 2), *hʿlṯ*, ‘bird’; from ϩⲱⲗ, ‘to fly’.
GRIFFITH–THOMPSON, III, 55, no. 543 [1909].

[B]ϩⲉⲗϩⲉⲗ (Crum 672a), ‘swim, float(?)’ is a reduplication of ϩⲱⲗ, ‘fly, go’, see this latter.

ϩⲟⲗϩⲗ (Crum 672a), 'sprinkle, scatter?', cf. (Er. 396, 1), *ẖlẖl*, 'penetrate' or sim. (of a medicament) < (*Wb.* III, 384, 8 f.), *ẖnẖn*, 'approach'.

ᴴᴰERICHSEN, *Dem. Glossar*, 396, 1 [1954].

ϩⲱⲗϭ (Crum 672b), 'embrace' = (Er. 328, 5), *ḥlg*, 'embrace'.

REVILLOUT, *Setna*, 168 [1877].

ϩⲗⲟϭ (Crum 673a), 'be sweet, take delight' = (*Wb.* III, 34, 18–20), *ḥꜣg* > L.Eg. , *ḥnrg*, 'be merry, rejoice'; (Er. 328, 4), *ḥlk*, 'sweet'.

ᴴERMAN, *Sitzber. Preuss. Ak.* XXI, 412–13 [1907]; ᴰBRUGSCH, *Gr. dém.* 121, §244 [1855].

ϩⲁⲙ, ϩⲁⲙ- (Crum 673b), 'craftsman' = (*Wb.* III, 82, 8 f.), *ḥmw*, 'to form, produce'; (Er. 303, 5), *ḥm*, 'produce, form'.

ᴴᴰREVILLOUT, *Poème*, 68, 72 [1885] (reading the Eg. word *ám*); for correct reading cf. W. Max Müller in *Rec. trav.* 9, 164–8 [1887].

ϩⲁⲙⲁⲕⲏ, ϩⲁⲙⲁϭⲏ, see under ⲁⲕⲏ.

ϩⲁⲙⲛⲟⲩⲃ (Crum 221b under ⲛⲟⲩⲃ), 'goldsmith' = (*Wb.* III, 82, 12), *ḥmw-nb*, 'goldsmith'; (Er. 304, upper), *ḥm-nb*, 'goldsmith'.

ϩⲁⲙϣⲉ (Crum 546b, under ϣⲉ), 'carpenter' = , *ḥm-ẖt*, 'carpenter'.

ϩⲁⲙ is part. coni. ϩⲁⲙ- used absolutely.

See also ϩⲟⲙ, 'shoemaker'.

ᴮϩⲟⲙ (Crum 674a), 'shoemaker' = (*Wb.* III, 83, 5), *ḥmww*, 'craftsman' in , *ḥmww, tꜣw(t)* (< *ṯbwy*), 'shoemaker', lit. 'craftsman of sandals'.

NB. Crum's ex. WHatch 762 is now published in *Crum Memorial Vol.*, p. 317.

ČERNÝ, *BIFAO* 57, 211–12 [1958].

ϩⲟⲉⲓⲙ (Crum 674a), 'wave' = (*Wb.* II, 481, 10. 11), *ḥꜣnw*, 'wave'; (Er. 268, 8), *ḥym*, 'wave'.

ᴴSPIEGELBERG, *Rec. trav.* 28, 214 [1906]; ᴰSPIEGELBERG, *ZÄS* 49, 36 n. 1 [1911].

ⲣ ϩⲟⲉⲓⲙ (Crum 674b), 'be covered with waves, be agitated' = L.Eg. (*Wb.* II, 481, 12), *ỉr hꜣnw*, lit. 'make waves'; , *ỉr hym*, same meaning.

HERMAN–GRAPOW, *Wb.* II, 481, 12 [1928]; DSPIEGELBERG, *ZÄS* 49, 36 n. 1 [1911].

ϩⲱⲙ (Crum 674b), 'tread, trample, beat' = (*Wb.* II, 485, 12 f.), *hb*, 'tread, enter (a place)' < (*Wb.* II, 486, 7), *hby*, 'tread, trample', Aeth. , *ḥꜣm*, in , *ḥꜣm ỉrp m ỉꜣrrt*, 'wine is trodden from the vine'; (Er. 275, 2), *hm*, 'trample'.

HSETHE in Vogelsang, *Kommentar zu den Klagen des Bauern*, 49 [1913]; MACADAM, *Kawa*, I, 40 n. 65 [1949]; DGRIFFITH–THOMPSON, III, 58, no. 571 [1909].

ϩⲁⲙⲟⲓ (Crum 675a), interj. 'would, O that' = L.Eg. , *hꜣ my*, or (*Wb.* II, 481, 9), *hꜣnꜣ my*, 'if...were'? < *, *ḥꜣ my*, same meaning; (Er. 275, 6), *ḥmy*, same meaning.

HBRUGSCH, *Wb.*, 1726 [1868] and Suppl. 760 [1881]; cf. Gardiner in *Chronique d'Égypte*, no. 60, 288 f. [1955]; DDE WIT, *Chronique d'Égypte*, no. 59, 15–18 [1955].

ϩⲏⲙⲉ (Crum 675b), 'fare, freight' on ship, camel = (*Wb.* II, 490, 5), *hmt*, 'fare'; (Er. 275, 3), *hm(t)*, or (Er. 275, 4), *hmy*, 'fare'.

HERMAN, *Sitzber. Preuss. Ak.* XXI, 402 [1907]; DSPIEGELBERG, *ZÄS* 37, 32 f. [1899].

ϩⲏⲙⲉ (Crum 676a), vessel as measure = (not in *Wb.*), *hmt*, a vessel.

MACADAM, *Kawa*, I, 13 n. 62 [1949].

B**ϩⲏⲙⲓ** (Crum 676a), 'dower' of divorced wife, is the word **ϩⲏⲙⲉ**, 'fare, freight' (see the last entry) in specialized meaning.

S**ϩⲓⲱⲙⲉ**, A**ϩⲓⲟⲛⲉ** (Crum 676a), 'palm, hollow' of hand = **ḫnt*, 'palm', the existence of which seems to be assured by the phonetic value *ḫn* of Gr.-R. sign in (*Wb.* III, 104, 12), *r-ḫnt*, name of a place, now el-Lâhûn, and in late spellings of the word *ḫnt*, 'swampy lake'. For *n* > **ⲙ**, cf. *hꜣnw*, 'wave' > **ϩⲟⲉⲓⲙ** and *ḫnt*, 'pelican' > **ϩⲙⲏ**.

ϩⲙ-, see **ϩⲙⲛⲧⲱⲣⲉ**, 'token, sign'.

ϩⲓⲙⲉ (Crum 385a under **ⲥϩⲓⲙⲉ**), 'woman' = (*Wb.* III, 76, 16 ff.), *ḥmt*, 'wife, woman'; (Er. 306, 2), *ḥmt*, 'wife'.

ᴴCHAMPOLLION, *Gr.* 61 [1836]; ᴰBRUGSCH, *Gr. dém.* 54, §122 [1855]. See also **ⲥϩⲓⲙⲉ**.

ϩⲙⲉ (Crum 676a), 'forty' = (*Wb.* III, 82, 6), *ḥmw*(?), 'forty'.

GARDINER, *ZÄS* 42, 25 [1905] (pun with , *ḥmw*, 'to fashion'); PIEHL, *PSBA* 13, 199–200 [1891] ('forty-five', **ϩⲙⲉ-ⲧⲏ**, written , *ḥ-mdw*).

ϩⲙⲏ (Crum 676b), 'pelican' = (*Wb.* III, 104, 2), *ḥnt*, 'pelican'. For *n* > **ⲙ**, see **ϩⲟⲉⲓⲙ**, 'wave' and **ϩⲓⲱⲙⲉ**, 'palm' of hand.

DÉVAUD in Spiegelberg, *Kopt. Handwb.* 233 [1921].

ϩⲙⲟⲩ (Crum 676b), 'salt' = (*Wb.* III, 93, 14 f.), *ḥmꜣt*, 'salt'; (Er. 307, 1), *ḥmꜣ*, 'salt'.

ᴴCHABAS, *Oeuv. div.* II (= *Bibl. ég.* X), 178 [1862]; CHABAS, *Mél. égypt.* I, 74 [1862]; ᴰBRUGSCH, *Gr. dém.* 26, §51 [1855].

ϩⲙⲟⲙ (Crum 677a), 'become hot' = (*Wb.* IV, 468, 1 f.), *šmm* (*ẖmm*), 'become hot'; (Er. 380, 6), *ẖmm*, 'hot, become hot'.

ᴴSTERN in *Pap. Ebers*, II, 60 [1875]; cf. BRUGSCH, *Wb.* 1388 [1868] (of Qual. **ϣⲏⲙ** which, however, is not attested by Crum); ᴰBRUGSCH, *Scriptura Aeg. dem.* 19, §22 [1848].

ᴮ**ⲙⲟⲩϧⲏⲙ**, 'hot water', cf. , *pẖrt ẖmt*, 'hot remedy', Pap. Insinger 18, 9. This use of the Qualitative (instead of **ⲉϥϧⲏⲙ**) is probably influenced by the Adjective **ϣⲏⲙ**, 'small'.

ϩⲙⲙⲉ (Crum 677b), 'heat, fever', cf. (*Wb.* IV, 469, 5–7), *šmmt*, 'heat, fever'.

ERMAN–GRAPOW, *Wb.* IV, 469, 5–7 [1930].

ϩⲙⲙⲉ (Crum 677b), 'steersman' in **ⲣ ϩⲙⲙⲉ**, 'to steer, guide', lit. 'to act (as) steersman' = (*Wb.* III, 81, 15), *ỉrt ḥmy*, 'to be (lit. 'make') steersman'; (Er. 308, 4), *ỉr ḥmy*, 'to steer'.

ᴴCHAMPOLLION, *Dict.* 105 [1841]; ᴰSPIEGELBERG, *ZÄS* 44, 100 [1908].

ϩⲟⲙⲛⲧ (Crum 678a), 'copper, bronze' = (*Wb.* III, 99, lower; I, 436–7), *ḥmt*(?) 'copper, ore'; (Er. 309, 2), *ḥmt*, 'copper, copper money'.

[H]LEPSIUS, *Die Metalle in den äg. Inschriften* (*Abh. Preuss. Ak.* 1871), 91 f. [1872] (reading *χmt*); DÜMICHEN in *ZÄS* 10, 107 [1872]; [D]HESS, *Stne*, 42 and 171 [1888] (reading *ẖ°mt*).

ϩⲁⲙⲛⲧ-, see ⲙⲉϩⲧⲱⲡ and ϩⲁⲙⲛⲧⲱⲡ, 'needle', under ⲧⲱⲡ.

ϩⲙⲛⲧⲱⲣⲉ and sim. (Crum 678b), 'token, sign' = ϩⲓⲱⲙⲉ + ⲧⲱⲣⲉ, lit. 'palm of hand' (raised as sign of warning, etc., used only metaphorically while the synonymous ϩⲓⲱⲙⲉ ⲛϭⲓϫ is used literally. In ϩ. the ⲛ is intrusive as in ⲙⲛⲧ-, ⲙⲛⲧⲣⲉ, etc.

ϩⲁⲙⲏⲣ (Crum 679a), 'arms, embrace' = (not in Er.; ex. *Vienna Petubastis* W, 7 and 22), *ḥml*, 'armful' (of grass).

KLASENS in *Bibl. Or.* 13, 223 [1956].

[O]ϩⲙⲏⲣ (not in Crum), 'spell' = (*Wb.* III, 85, 1–2), *ḫmwt-r*, '(magical) spell', lit. 'art of the utterance'.

GARDINER in Crum, *JEA* 28, 11 [1942].

ϩ(ⲉ)ⲙⲥ (Crum 679a), 'ear of corn' = (*Wb.* III, 367, 5. 6), *ḫms*, 'ear of corn'; (Er. 381, 1), *ḫms*, 'ear of corn'.

[H]CHAMPOLLION, *Gr.* 89 [1836]; Salvolini, *Analyse gramm.* 45, no. 191 and Pl. F [1836]; [D]BRUGSCH, *Wb.* 1046 [1868].

ϩⲙⲟⲟⲥ (Crum 679a), 'sit, remain, dwell' = (*Wb.* III, 96, 13 f.), *ḥmsy*, 'to sit'; (Er. 308, 5), *ḥms*, 'sit'.

[H]CHAMPOLLION, *Gr.* 369 [1836]; [D]HESS, *Stne*, 2, 4–6 and 168 [1888].

[F]ϩⲱⲙⲧ (Crum 681a), 'shame, disgrace' = Gr.-R. (*Wb.* III, 80, 12), *ḥmt*, 'disaster, evil' or sim.; cf. the late (*Wb.* III, 80, 8–11), *ḥmty*, a reviling designation of cowards and enemies of gods, therefore 'shameful, disgraceful'; cf. (Er. 304, 1), *ḥm*, 'coward(ice)'.

[O]ϩⲁⲙⲉⲩ (not in Crum), 'sun-folk, mankind' = (*Wb.* III, 114, 6 f.), *ḥnmmt*, > , *hmm(t)* (Gardiner, *Onom.* I, 98*, no. 233), 'sun-folk, mankind'.

GARDINER in Crum in *JEA* 28, 28 [1942].

ϩⲙϩⲙ (Crum 682b), 'roar, neigh' = (*Wb.* II, 491, 2), *hmhm*, 'roar' (of god Mont as bull); (Er. 275, 7), *hmhm*, 'roar'.

Ultimately related to Arabic همهم, '(?) grumble', not borrowed from it as suggested by Stricker in *Acta Orientalia* 15, 3.

HCHAMPOLLION, *Gr.* 378 [1836]; DERICHSEN, *Dem. Glossar*, 275, 7 [1954].

Bϩⲟⲙϩⲉⲙ (Crum 682b), 'tread, trample' = (*Wb.* II, 487, 21 ff.), *hbhb*, 'traverse (a country), trample (a furrow)' and (*Wb.* II, 488, 1. 2), *hbhb*, 'annihilate, destroy'. Reduplication of ϩⲱⲙ, 'tread, trample'.

NB. On account of its ϩ this verb must be different from Bϧⲟⲙϧⲉⲙ.

ϩⲙⲟϫ (Crum 682b), 'become sour', from Semitic √*ḥmz*, cf. Arabic حَمُضَ, Hebrew חָמֵץ, 'be sour, leavened', Syriac ܚܡܰܥ.

DE LAGARDE, *Übersicht über die im Aramäischen, Arabischen u. Hebräischen übliche Bildung der Nomina*, 61 [1889].

ϩⲙⲝ, 'vinegar' = L.Eg. (*Wb.* III, 99, 13), *ḥmḏ*, 'vinegar', a loan-word from Semitic, cf. Hebrew חֹמֶץ, 'vinegar'.

HBURCHARDT, *Die altkanaan. Fremdworte*, II, 35, no. 679 [1910]; SLACROZE, *Lexicon*, 152 [1775].

ϩⲛ- (Crum 683a), prep. 'in, at, on' (constr. state of ϩⲟⲩⲛ) = (*Wb.* III, 370, 16 f.), 'in the interior of, in'; (Er. 381, 2), *ḫn*, 'in the interior of'. The pronominal state lost in Coptic and replaced by Sϩⲏⲧ⸗, Bϧⲏⲧ⸗; in Demotic this substitution is found only in Roman Period (Spiegelberg, *Dem. gr.* §348c).

HRENOUF, *Egypt. Essays*, I, 353 [1865]; DBRUGSCH, *Pap. Rhind*, 46 and Pl. 42, no. 354 [1865].

For the pronominal state ⲛϩⲏⲧ⸗ is used, see ϩⲏ, 'body, womb'.

For ⲉϩⲟⲩⲛ ϩⲛ-, see under ϩⲟⲩⲛ.

ϩⲓⲛ (Crum 685a), a 'vessel, cup', so 'liquid measure' = (*Wb.* II, 493, 2 f.), *hnw*, a vessel, liquid measure (about 0·45 litre); , , etc. (Er. 277, 1), *hn*, a vessel, liquid measure. Hebrew הִין (LXX εἶν) is a loan-word from Egn.

HDGRIFFITH in *ZÄS* 38, 86 [1900]; cf. DGRIFFITH, *Pap. Rylands*, III, 369 [1909]; GRIFFITH–THOMPSON, III, 59, no. 585 [1909].

ϣⲉⲛϩⲓⲛ (Crum 685b), 'divination', lit. 'inquiring of cup' = (Er. 514, lower), *šn-hn*, 'divination'.

GRIFFITH in *ZÄS* 38, 86 [1900].

ϩⲟⲩⲛ (Crum 685b), 'inward part' = (*Wb.* III, 368, 17 f.), *ẖnw*, 'the inside'; (Er. 381, 2), *ẖn*, 'the inside'.

HD BRUGSCH, *Gr. dém.* 161, §317; cf. 132, §273 [1855].

ⲉϩⲟⲩⲛ, 'to inside, inward' = (*Wb.* III, 372, 1 f.), *r ẖnw*, 'to inside'; , *r-ẖn*, 'into'.

D BRUGSCH, *Gr. dém.*, *loc. cit.* [1855].

ⲉϩⲟⲩⲛ (ⲉ)**ϩⲛ-**, **ⲉϩⲟⲩⲛ ⲉϩⲣⲁ⸗** (Crum 684b under **ϩⲛ** and 685a under **ⲉϩ**(ⲉ)**ⲛ**), 'into, toward, at, within' = (Er. 382, middle), *r-ẖn (r-)ḥr*, 'against'.

SETHE in Crum, *JEA* 18, 194 [1932]; cf. POLOTSKY, *JEA* 25, 113 [1939].

ⲛϩⲟⲩⲛ (Crum 686a), 'within' = (*Wb.* III, 371, 25–9), *n ẖnw*, 'within'.

H BRUGSCH, *Wb.* 1094 [1868].

ϩⲓϩⲟⲩⲛ [687a], 'within' = , *ḥr-ẖn*, 'in'.

MÖLLER, *Pap. Rhind*, 48*, no. 312, 4 [1913].

For A2 **ⲁϩⲛ-**, SA2 **ⲁϩⲁⲛ-** (Crum 685a), 'and', see **ⲁϩⲁⲛ-**, 'and'.

S **ϩⲱⲛ**, A **ϩⲛⲁⲛ** (Crum 687a), 'approach, be nigh, comply with' = (*Wb.* III, 373, 9 f.), *ẖn*, 'approach'; (Er. 382, 1), *ẖn*, 'approach, be near'.

H SPIEGELBERG, *Sphinx* 4, 143–4 [1901]; D GRIFFITH–THOMPSON, III, 67, no. 661 [1909].

ϩⲱⲛ (Crum 688a), 'bid, command' = (*Wb.* III, 101, 1 f.), *ḥn*, 'put in order, provide with, command'; (Er. 310, 2), 'command, (subst.) order'.

H ERMAN–GRAPOW, *Äg. Handwb.* 110 [1921]; cf. Brugsch, *Wb.* 962 [1868]; D SPIEGELBERG, *Petubastis*, 42*, no. 272 [1910]; cf. Revillout, *Poème*, 188 [1885].

F **ϩⲁⲁⲛⲓ** (Crum 688b), 'something, anything' = (Er. 312, 3, under *ḥny*, 'spices'), 'something, whatever, anything' (P. Insinger 3, 24; 4, 7; 23, 4, etc.). Hardly identical with **ϩⲏⲛⲉ**, 'spices', but might be A **ϩⲏⲛⲉ**, 'dust'.

ϩⲏⲛⲉ (Crum 688b), 'spice, incense' = (Er. 312, 3), *ḥny*, 'spices, incense'.

SPIEGELBERG, *Petubastis*, 42*, no. 274 [1910].

^Aϩⲏⲛⲉ (Crum 689a), 'lime, dust', see under ^Fϩⲁⲁⲛⲓ, 'something'.

ϩⲏⲛⲉ (Crum 689a, 'meaning unknown, related to clothing'), 'leather (thongs)?' = ? (*Wb.* III, 367, 12 f.), *ḫnt*, 'skin, leather'; (Er. 383, 3), *ḫnt*, and (Ankhsh. 21, 5), *ḫnyt*, 'leather thongs'.

^Sϩⲓⲛⲉ, ^Bϩⲓⲛⲓ (Crum 689a), 'move' by rowing = (*Wb.* III, 374, 1 ff.), *ḫny*, 'row, convey by boat'; (Er. 383, 1), *ḫn*, 'to row'.

^HASMUS, *Über Fragmente*, 52 [1904]; SPIEGELBERG, *Rec. trav.* 26, 40 [1904]; ^DMÖLLER, *Rhind*, 48*, no. 313 [1913].

^Bϩⲓⲛⲓ ⲙⲡⲓⲟⲩⲟⲥⲉⲣ, 'row the rudder', cf. (*Wb.* III, 374, 24), *ḫny wsr*, same meaning.

NB. Boh. ϩ (instead of the expected ϧ) is exceptional and can probably be explained only by confusion with *ϩⲓⲛⲓ of the next entry.

ϩⲓⲛⲓⲉ, ϩⲉⲛⲉⲓⲉ (Crum 689a), 'steering-oar', is unrelated, see ϩⲓⲛⲓⲉ.

(^Sϩⲓⲛⲉ, ^Bϩⲓⲛⲓ), ^Bϩⲉⲛ-, ^Sϩⲛⲧ⸗, ^Bϩⲉⲛ⸗ (Crum 689a), refl. 'move self' = (*Wb.* III, 103, 6–21), *ḥn*, 'run, go, betake oneself'; (not in Er.), *ḥn*, 'betake oneself'.

^HDEVÉRIA, *Mém. et fragments*, 2 (= *Bibl. ég.* V), 240 = *Journal as.* 6e série, vol. 10, 462 [1867]; ^HDBRUGSCH, *Wb.* 961 [1868].

ϩⲓⲛⲓⲉ, ϩⲉⲛⲉⲓⲉ (Crum 689a, under ϩⲓⲛⲉ), 'steering oar, rudder' = (Er. 312, 2), *ḥny*, 'steering oar'.

GRIFFITH, *Stories*, 115 [1900].

ϩⲓⲛⲓⲉ > ϩⲓⲉ, for which see below.

DÉVAUD, *Kêmi*, 2, 9 [1929].

ϩⲓⲉ (Crum 645b), 'rudder' = (not in Er.), *hywt*, 'steering rudder'.

SOTTAS, *Revue ég.* N. Série, 1, 131 [1919].

ϩο(ⲉ)ⲓⲛⲉ (Crum 689b), pl. 'some, certain' = (*Wb.* II, 280, 4 f.), *nhy*, 'something'; (Er. 268, 9), *hyn*, pl. 'some'.

^HSTEINDORFF, *Kopt. Gr.* 1st ed., 65, §122 n. [1894]; ^DBRUGSCH, *Wb.*, Suppl. 746 [1881].

ϩⲉⲛ-, Pl. of indefinite article, is contracted from ϩοⲉⲓⲛⲉ < *nhy*.

^HBRUGSCH, *Gr. hiérogl.* 8 [1872]; cf. Revillout, *Chrest. dém.* 440 [1880]; Steindorff, *Kopt. Gr.* 1st ed., 65, §122 n. [1894]; for actual L.Egn. ex. of *nhy* as Pl. of indef. article, see WOLF, *ZÄS* 69, 108 [1933]; ^DREVILLOUT, *Setna*, 17 and 117 [1877]; Revillout, *Chrest. dém.* 440 [1880].

ϩⲱⲛⲉ (Crum 690a), 'swampy lake' = (*Wb.* III, 105, 1), *ḥnt*, 'swampy lake'; (Er. 311, 9), *ḥny*, 'swampy lake'. For the meaning of the Coptic and Egn. words, see Gardiner, *JEA* 29 (1943), 38 f. and Nims, *JEA* 33 (1947), 92.

[H]Erman–Grapow, *Äg. Handwb.* 110 [1921]; [D]Griffith–Thompson, I, 142 [1904].

[SB]**ϩⲛⲉ-**, [SB]**ϩⲛⲁ⸗**, [A]**ϩⲛⲉ⸗** (Crum 690a), 'will, desire, be willing'. The etymology from + suffix (or noun) (*Wb.* I, 14, 19–24), *ꜣḫ n*, '(it) is useful for...' (Sethe, *ZÄS* 47, 136–41 [1910]) is not satisfactory since the proper meaning of the two expressions is different, and Boh. and Akhm. ϩ cannot derive from , *ḫ*; cf. Vycichl, *Muséon* 68, 235 [1955]; Polotsky, *OLZ* 52, cols. 231–2 [1957]. Still obscure; perhaps = (*Wb.* II, 494, 10 f.), *hnn* > , *hn*; (Er. 276, 1), *hn*, 'approach, agree'.

[H]Brugsch, *Wb.* 902 [1868]; cf. Polotsky, *loc. cit.*

ϩⲓⲛⲏⲃ, [B]**ϩⲓⲛⲓⲙ** (Crum 691a), 'sleep, doze' = ?**ϩⲓ-** (from **ϩⲓⲟⲩⲉ**, 'to beat') + (*Wb.* II, 266, 7), *nmꜥ* > (Brugsch, *Wb.* 792), *nm*, 'sleep'.

Crum, *A Coptic Dict.* 691a and 734b (for **ϩⲓ-**) [1937]; Spiegelberg, *Kopt. Handwb.* 75 (for **-ⲛⲏⲃ**) [1921].

ϩⲟⲛⲃⲉ (Crum 691a), 'spring, well' = (*Wb.* III, 382, 10 f.), *ẖnmt*, 'well'; (not in Er.), *ẖnm*, also (Ankhsh. 23, 23), *ẖnmꜣt*, 'well'.

[H]Brugsch, *ZÄS* 3, 28 [1865]; Lepsius, *ZÄS* 3, 42 [1865]; [D]Lexa, *Beiträge zum demot. Wörterbuch aus dem Papyrus Insinger*, no. 370 (private print) [1916] (*ẖnm*); cf. Glanville's index (for *ẖnmꜣt*).

ϩⲱⲛⲕ (Crum 691a), 'consecrate, appoint' = (*Wb.* III, 117, 5 f.), *ḥnk*, 'present, bestow'; (Er. 315, 1) 'to present'.

[H]Rösch, *OLZ* 14, col. 551–2 [1911]; [D]Shore's communication.

ϩⲛⲕⲉ (Crum 691a), 'beer' = (*Wb.* III, 169, 11 f.), in Gr.-R. period often written , *ḥnḳt*, 'beer'; (Er. 314, 6), *ḥnḳ*, 'beer'.

[HD]Brugsch, *Rec. de mon.* II, 118 [1863]; [D]Brugsch, *Wb.* 976 [1868].

ϩⲟⲛⲧ (Crum 691b), pagan 'priest' = (*Wb.* III, 88, 19 f.), *ḥm-nṯr*, 'god's servant, priest'; (Er. 305, 1), *ḥm-ntr*, 'god's servant, priest'.

[H]Champollion, *Gr.* 104, 167 [1836]; [D]Brugsch, *Wb.* 974 [1868].

Sϩωⲛⲧ, Bϧωⲛⲧ (Crum 691 b), 'approach' = (*Wb.* III, 312, 16 ff.), *ḫnd*, 'step on, step in, enter, go'.

BRUGSCH, *Wb.* 1113–14 [1868].

The meaning of the Coptic verb speaks definitely against connecting it with (*Wb.* III, 309, 3 f.), *ḫnty*, 'sail upstream' as done, for example, by Sethe, *Verbum*, III, 29.

ϩⲉⲛⲉⲉⲧⲉ (Crum 692 a), 'monastery' of monks or nuns = (*Wb.* III, 4, 11 f.), *ḥwt-nṯrt*, 'god's mansion, temple'; (Er. 285, 2), *ḥt-nṯr*, 'temple'. From Coptic the Egn. spoken Arabic هناذة.

HDGRIFFITH, *Stories*, 90 [1900].

ϩ(ⲉ)ⲛⲧⲟⲩ (Crum 692 a), 'Hindu, Indian' = (Gauthier, *Dict. géo*, IV. 6), *Hndwy*, 'India'; (not in Er.), *hntw*, 'India'.

HGAUTHIER, *Dictionnaire des noms géographiques*, IV, 6 [1927]; DKRALL in *Verhandlungen des XIII. Internat. Orientalisten-Kongresses Hamburg September 1902*, 346 [publ. Leiden 1904].

ϩⲛⲁ(ⲁ)ⲩ, ϩⲛⲟ (Crum 692 b), 'vessel, pot, receptacle; thing', any material object = (*Wb.* III, 107, 1 f.), *ḥnw*, 'pot; (pl.) things'; (Er. 313, 3), *ḥnw*, 'pot'.

HCHAMPOLLION, *Gr.* 107 [1836]; DBRUGSCH, *Gr. dém.* 33, §66 [1855].

ϩⲛⲱⲱϩⲉ (Crum 693 a), subst. 'fear' = Late (*Wb.* III, 115, 7), *ḥnḥ*, 'fear' < (*Wb.* III, 130, 23), *ḥr n ḥr*, 'disaster, fear'; (Er. 314, 5), *ḥnḥ*, 'fear' (verb and noun).

HDRÖSCH, *Vorbemerkungen*, 72–5 [1909]; cf. Dévaud in *Sphinx* 13, 100–1 [1910]; DGRIFFITH–THOMPSON, III, 59, no. 588 [1909].

Bϩⲟⲛϩⲉⲛ (Crum 693 a), 'bid', reduplication of ϩωⲛ, 'bid, command'.

ϩⲁⲡ (Crum 693 b), 'judgment, inquest' = (*Wb.* II, 488, 7 f.), *hp*, 'law'; (Er. 274), *hp*, 'law, right, justice'.

HBRUGSCH, *Gr. dém.* 37, §79 [1855]; cf. Schwartze in Bunsen, *Geschichte*, I, 593 [1845]; DSAULCY, *Rosette*, 31 [1845].

ϩⲟⲡ (Crum 695 a), 'feast, marriage feast, bride-chamber' = (*Wb.* III, 57, 5 f.), *ḥb*, 'feast'; (Er. 298, 2), *ḥb*, 'feast'.

HMÖLLER, *Pap. Rhind*, 40*, no. 255 [1913]; DREVILLOUT, *Poème*, 7 [1885].

ϩⲱⲡ (Crum 695a), 'hide' = (*Wb.* III, 30, 6 f.), *ḫꜣp*, 'cover, hide'; (Er. 302, 2), *ḫp*, 'hide'.

[H]BRUGSCH, *Rosettana*, 33 [1851]; cf. Brugsch, *ZÄS* 1, 13 [1863]; [D]BRUGSCH, *Gr. dém.* 121, §244 [1855].

[B]**ϩⲏⲡⲓ** (Crum 696a), 'crypt, underground chamber' = Gr.-R. (*Wb.* III, 31, 4), *ḫꜣpt*, 'hiding place'.

ERMAN–GRAPOW, *Wb.* III, 31, 4 [1929].

[B]**ϩⲱⲡ, ϩⲱⲃ** (Crum 696a), 'horn' = (*Wb.* I, 173, 12 f.), *ꜥb*, 'horn'.

DÉVAUD in Crum, *A Copt. Dict.* 696a [1937].

ϩⲁⲡⲉ (Crum 696a), god 'Apis' = (*Wb.* III, 70, 1 f.), *ḥp*, Apis; (Er. 301, 2), *ḥp*, 'Apis'.

[H]GELL in Young, *Misc. Works*, III, 460 [1828]; SCHÄFER in *Sitzungsber. Preuss. Ak.* 38, 742 n. 2 [1899]; cf. von Lemm, *Kleine koptische Studien*, 110 f. [1900]; [D]GRIFFITH, *Ryl.* III, 436 [1909].

[A2]**ϩⲡⲁⲛ**, Qual. **ϩⲁⲡⲛⲉ** (not in Crum; exx. Mani Hom. 16, 20, and Ps.), 'thrive, prosper; feed' = (*Wb.* III, 366, 12–14), *ẖpn* > , *ẖpn*, 'fat, well fed'; (Er. 380, 4), *ẖpn*, or , *ẖpn*, 'fat'.

ϩⲁⲡⲟⲣⲕ (Crum 696a), 'saddle, saddle-cloth' = **ϩⲁ** (< *ẖ*, as in **ϩⲁⲗⲃϣⲉ**, 'breastplate') + **ⲡⲟⲣⲕ**, 'cloak'.

ϩⲡⲟⲧ (Crum 696b), 'fathom' = (not in *Wb.*), *ḫpt*, a measure of thread.

ČERNÝ in *Festschrift Grapow*, 34–5 [1955].

ϩⲟⲡϩⲡ (Crum 696b), 'disturbance, excitement' or sim. = (Er. 303, 2), *ḥpḥp*, 'be stricken, afflicted' or sim.; prob. not a reduplication of ***ϩⲱⲃ** from which derives **ϩⲏⲃⲉ**, 'mourning', but the old (*Wb.* II, 487, 25), *hbhb*, 'trample (a furrow)' < (*Wb.* II, 487, 21–4), *hbhb*, 'traverse (in all directions)', reduplication of *hb*, **ϩⲱⲙ**, 'tread'.

ϩⲡⲟϭⲡϭ (Crum 743a under **ϩϫⲟⲡϫⲡ**), see under ***ⲡⲟϭⲡϭ**.

ϩⲁⲣ (Crum 696b, meaning unknown), non-existent; read **ϩⲁⲥ**, 'dung, droppings' (not **ϩⲁϩ**, 'neck' = [B]**ϧⲁϧ** as Chassinat, *Ms. mag. copte*, 13–16).

DRESCHER in *JEA* 43, 119 [1957].

Sϩⲣ-, ϩⲣⲉ-, Bϧⲁⲣⲁ (Crum 696b), noun (?) as distributive preposition in ϩⲣⲉⲃⲟⲧ, 'per month', see under ϩⲣⲉ, 'food'.

ϩⲓⲣ (Crum 696b), 'road, street, quarter' = L.Eg. (*Wb.* III, 232, 5, 6), *ḫ(ꜣ)r(w)*, 'street'; (Er. 388, 7), *ẖr(y)*, 'street'.

HBRUGSCH, *Wb.* 1036 [1868]; DBRUGSCH, *Scriptura Aeg. dem.* 16, §XI [1848].

ϩⲓⲣϩⲓⲣⲉ (Crum 697a), 'streets' or sim. = (not in Er.), *ẖyrẖr*, 'streets' or sim.

EDGERTON in Parker, *JEA* 26, 110 [1940].

ϩⲱⲣ (Crum 697b), vb. refl., 'guard (oneself) against, take heed' = (*Wb.* III, 144, bottom), *ḥry*, 'be far, keep away from, avoid'; (Er. 322, 5), *ḥr*, 'take heed'.

HDÉVAUD's slip; DSPIEGELBERG, *Mythus*, 214, no. 553 [1917].

ϩⲣⲧⲏⲩⲧⲛ ⲉⲣⲱⲧⲛ, 'take heed!', cf. (P. Ryl. IX, 12, 7), *ḥrt·k ỉr·k*, the older (Old Perf.) (*Wb.* III, 145, 20), *ḥrty r*, 'beware of... !'.

HERMAN–GRAPOW, *Wb.* III, 145, 20 [1929]; DSPIEGELBERG, *Dem. Pap. Loeb*, 24, (22) [1931].

ϩⲱⲣ (Crum 697b), 'squeeze out' milk, 'milk' = (*Wb.* II, 498, 3), *hr*, 'to milk' (the meaning is certain, cf. Horus & Seth, 10, 7).

GRAPOW, *Über die Wortbildungen mit einem Präfix* m- (*Abh. Preuss. Ak.*), 26 [1914].

ϩⲱⲣ (Crum 697b), god 'Horus' = (*Wb.* III, 122, bottom), *ḥr*, 'Horus'; (Er. 316, 1), *ḥr*, 'Horus'.

HCHAMPOLLION, *Précis*, 128 [1824]; DBRUGSCH, *Scriptura Aeg. dem.* 9 [1848].

For ϩⲁⲣ-ⲡϣⲱⲧ, see under Oϣⲱⲧ.

ϩⲟ(ⲉ)ⲓⲣⲉ (Crum 697b), 'dung' human or animal = (not in *Wb.*), *ḥry*, 'dung'; (Er. 325, 6), *ḥyrt*, 'dung'.

HČERNÝ in Caminos, *LEM* 167 [1954]; cf. Černý in *Festschrift Grapow*, 36–7 [1955]; DBRUGSCH, *Gr. dém.* 44, §94 [1855].

Sϩⲣⲁⲓ, Bϩⲣⲏⲓ (Crum 698a), 'upper part' = (*Wb.* III, 142, 13 f.), *ḥrw* > , *ḥry*, 'upper side, part'; (Er. 323, 1), *ḥry*, 'upper part, above'.

ᴴCHABAS, *Pap. mag. Harris*, 219, no. 309 [1860]; BRUGSCH, *Gr. dém.* 132, §275; 183, §362 [1855].

ⲉϩⲣⲁⲓ, 'to above, upward' = [hieroglyphs] (*Wb.* III, 143, 2–5), *r ḥrw*, 'upward'; [demotic] (Er. 323, middle), *r ḥry*, 'upward'.

ϩⲓϩⲣⲁⲓ (Crum 699b), 'upward' = [hieroglyphs] (*Wb.* III, 143, 7), *ḥr ḥrw*, 'upward'.

ϩⲣⲉ in **ⲥⲁϩⲣⲉ** (Crum 699b), 'upper side' = [hieroglyphs] (*Wb.* III, 133), *ḥry*, 'upper'; [demotic] (Er. 449, 1), *sḥrỉ*, is perhaps unetymological writing of **ⲥⲁϩⲣⲉ**.

ᴴSPIEGELBERG, *Rec. trav.* 31, 158–9 [1909].

ˢ**ϩⲣⲁⲓ**, ᴮ**ϧⲣⲏⲓ** (Crum 700a), 'lower part' = [hieroglyphs] (*Wb.* III, 392, 9 f.), *ẖrw*, 'lower part'; [demotic] (Er. 391, 1), *ẖry*, 'lower part, below'.

ᴴSTERN in *Pap. Ebers*, II, 62 (gl.) [1875]; ᴰBRUGSCH, *De natura*, 36 [1850]; cf. Brugsch, *Scriptura Aeg. dem.* 62 [1848].

ⲉϩⲣⲁⲓ, 'to below, downward' = [hieroglyphs] (*Wb.* III, 393, 1), *r ẖrw*, 'downward'; [demotic] (Er. 391, upper), *r ẖry*, 'downward'.

ⲛϩⲣⲁⲓ (Crum 700b), 'below' = L.Eg. [hieroglyphs] (*Wb.* III, 393, 3), *n ẖrw*, 'downward'.

ᴬ**ϩⲣⲉ** in **ⲥⲉϩⲣⲉ** (Crum 700b), 'downward, below' = [hieroglyphs] (*Wb.* III, 388, 16 f.), *ẖry*, 'lower'.

RÖSCH, *Vorbemerkungen*, 174, §158 [1909].

ϩⲣⲉ (Crum 701a), 'food' of men = [hieroglyphs] (*Wb.* III, 390, 5 f.), *ẖrt*, (a man's) 'due'; [demotic] (Er. 389, 1), *ẖr(t)*, 'due, food'.

ᴴBRUGSCH, *Wb.* 1122 [1868]; cf. Sethe, *ZÄS* 47, 31 [1910]; ᴰBRUGSCH, *De natura*, 36 [1850].

ˢ**ϩⲣⲉⲃⲟⲧ**, ᴮ**ϧⲁⲣⲁⲁⲃⲟⲧ** (Crum 696b, under **ϩⲣ-**) = ([hieroglyph])[hieroglyphs] (*Wb.* III, 391, 17), (*m*) *ẖrt ỉbdw*, '(as) due, need of a month'; [demotic] (Er. 27, middle), *ẖr ỉbt*, same meaning.

ᴴSPIEGELBERG, *Kopt. Etym.* 21–3 [1920]; cf. Spiegelberg in *Rec. trav.* 19, 90 [1897]; ᴰSOTTAS, *Pap. dém. de Lille*, I, 66 [1921].

ϩⲣⲱ (Crum 701b), 'oven, furnace' = [hieroglyphs] (*Wb.* III, 148, 15), *ḥryt*, 'furnace (of a coppersmith)'.

BRUGSCH, *Wb.* 984 [1868].

ˢ**ϩⲣⲃ**, ᴮ**ϧⲉⲣⲉⲃ** (Crum 701b), 'form, likeness', cf. Gr.-R. [hieroglyphs] (*Wb.* III, 396,

8), *ẖrb*, 'change into...'; = (Er. 392, 1), *ẖrb*, 'change into...; (subst.) form'.

[H]BRUGSCH, *Dict. géo.* 96 [1879]; cf. Brugsch, *Wb.*, Suppl. 956 [1881]; [D]BRUGSCH, *Pap. Rhind*, 47 and Pl. 42, no. 366 [1865].

ϩⲣⲉⲃ (Crum 702a), 'chisel' = (not in *Wb.*; exx. O. DM 221, 2; O. Gardiner 180, 3), *ḥry-ỉb*, 'chisel', abbreviation of (O. Gardiner 180, 4), *mdꜣt ḥry-ỉb*, 'middle(-sized) chisel'.

[S]**ϩ(ⲉ)ⲣⲙⲁⲛ**, [B]**ⲉⲣⲙⲁⲛ** (Crum 703a), 'pomegranate' tree or fruit = (*Wb.* I, 98, 14), *ỉnhmn*, 'pomegranate' tree, *Punica granatum* L. (cf. Keimer, *Gartenpflanzen*, I, 47 ff.; 151–2; *BIFAO* 31, 184 n. 3). A loan-word from Semitic, cf. Hebrew רִמּוֹן, Ar. رُمَّان, Akk. (?)*armannu*, 'pomegranate'.

[H]MOLDENKE in *Études...dédiées à Leemans*, 17 [1885]; cf. Loret, *Rec. trav.* 7, 108 f. [1886]; [S]LACROZE, *Lexicon*, 17 [1775].

NB. Demotic (Er. 280, 2), *hrnṯ*, is not this word but L.Eg. (*Wb.* II, 501, 9), *hrnt*, a kind of emmer.

ϩⲱⲣⲡ (Crum 703a), 'sleep, doze' = **ϩⲱⲣⲡ**, 'become wet, drenched', see the next entry. The original meaning of *hrp*, 'sink in water, immerse', also metaphorically 'suppress (a thought)', developed into 'become wet as a consequence of immersion' and into 'sink into sleep, fall asleep, close the eye'. Hence [A2]**ϩⲣⲁⲡ** (for *[S]**ϩⲣⲟⲡ**), 'closing of the eye' in **ϩⲛⲟⲩϩⲣⲁⲡ**, lit. 'in a closing of (the) eye' = 'quickly', and **ϩⲣⲟⲡⲣⲉⲡ** (see this latter).

ϩⲱⲣⲡ (Crum 703b), 'become wet, drenched' = (*Wb.* II, 500, 27 f.), 'sink in water, immerse'; (Er. 282, 4), *hrp*, 'to sink'.

[H]CHAMPOLLION, *Gr.* 376 [1836]; [D]GRIFFITH, *Stories*, 196 [1900]; cf. Klasens, *Bibl. Or.* 13, 223 [1956].

[A2]**ϩⲣⲁⲡ** (Crum 703b), 'closing of the eye', see under **ϩⲱⲣⲡ**, 'sleep, doze'.

ϩⲣⲟⲡⲣⲉⲡ (Crum 703b), 'blink, twinkle with the eyes', is reduplication of **ϩⲱⲣⲡ**, 'sleep, close the eyes'. Also of wings 'flutter' because of similarity of quivering movement.

POLOTSKY in C. Schmidt, *Kephalaia*, note on 71, 33 [1940].

F**ϩⲁⲣⲡⲥ** (Crum 703b), 'outspread hand' = B**ϧⲟⲣⲡⲥ** (Crum 631a), 'handful', see this latter.

KUENTZ in *Bull. de la Soc. ling.* 38, 191 [1937].

S**ϩⲣⲣⲉ**, B**ϩⲉⲣⲓ** (Crum 704a), 'cease, become still' = [hieroglyphs] (*Wb.* II, 496, 6 ff.), *hrw*, 'become content' and sim.; [demotic] (Er. 277, 6), *hr*, 'become content'.

HDE ROUGÉ, *Oeuv. div.* II (= *Bibl. ég.* XXII), 72 [1851]; DBRUGSCH, *Pap. Rhind*, 44 and Pl. 41, no. 302 [1865].

As noun 'delay', cf. [demotic] (Er. 325, 2), *ḥry*, 'delay' or sim. See also **ϩⲣⲟⲩⲣ**.

ERICHSEN, *Dem. Glossar*, 325, 2 [1954].

ϩⲣⲏⲣⲉ (Crum 704a), 'flower' = [hieroglyphs] (*Wb.* III, 149, 8 f.), 'blossom, flower'; [demotic] (Er. 326, 1), *ḥrry*, 'flower'.

HCHAMPOLLION, *Gr.* 77, 89 [1836]; DBRUGSCH, *Scriptura Aeg. dem.* 18, §17 [1848].

ϩⲣⲏⲣⲉ ⲙⲡⲛⲟⲩⲃ (LCypr. 12, a 13–14), 'gold flower' translating ἄνθος χρυσίου, cf. [demotic], *ḥrrt nb*, 'gold flower' interpreting **ⲭⲣⲩⲥⲁⲛⲑⲉⲙⲟⲛ**.

GRIFFITH–THOMPSON, I, 171 [1904].

ⲣ ϩⲣⲏⲣⲉ, 'come to flower, blossom' = [hieroglyphs] (P. Ebers 51, 16), *ỉrt ḥrt*, 'come to flower'.

DÉVAUD's slip.

(**ϩⲱⲣⲧ**), **ϩⲟⲣⲧ⸗** (Crum 704b), 'squeeze, press' (thus Kuentz rightly) is a denominative verb from **ϩⲣⲱⲧ**, 'wine-press, vat'.

KUENTZ in *Bull. de la Soc. ling.* 38, 192 [1937].

ϩⲣⲱⲧ (Crum 704b), 'wine-press, vat' = [demotic] (not in Er.), *ḥrwṯ*, 'vat', connected? with Hebrew *רַהַט, 'trough', Plural רְהָטִים.

DPARKER, *JEA* 26, 108 [1940]; SDÉVAUD's slip.

A2**ϩⲣⲧⲉ** (Crum 704b), f., 'fear' = substantivized imperative of [hieroglyphs] (*Wb.* III, 147, 12), *ḥr*, 'to fear' + **ⲧⲉ**, 'thou' (originally dependent pronoun); see similar cases under **ⲁⲙⲁϩⲧⲉ**. Feminine because of the ending **-ⲉ**.

NB. Spiegelberg's [hieroglyphs], *ZÄS* 63, 154–5, does not exist; the word is *ḥryt*, *Wb.* III, 147, 14 f.).

[S]ϩⲣⲟⲟⲩ, [B]ϧⲣⲱⲟⲩ (Crum 704b), 'voice, sound' = (*Wb.* III, 324, 7 f.), *ḫrw*, 'voice, noise'; (Er. 365, 7), *ḫrw*, 'voice'.

[H]BIRCH acc. to E. de Rougé, *Oeuv. div.* III (= *Bibl. ég.* XXIII), 218 [1856] (de Rougé evidently refers to a passage published only in 1858 in *Mémoires de la Société impériale des Antiquaires de France*, vol. 24, p. 72 of the extract); [D]BRUGSCH, *Wb.* 1119–20 [1868].

ϩⲣⲟⲩⲙⲡⲉ (Crum 705b), 'voice of sky, thunder' = *, *ḫrw n pt*, 'voice of heaven'. Cf. *ḫrw m pt*, Wenamūn 2, 19; Horus and Seth 16, 4.

[S]ϩⲣⲟⲩ(ⲃ)ⲃⲁⲓ, [B]ϧⲁⲣⲁⲃⲁⲓ, 'thunder' = *, *ḫrw bỉꜣ*(?), 'voice of heaven' (, *bỉꜣ*, originally a lake in sky, is used for 'sky, heaven' in Gr.-R. period, *Wb.* I, 439, 9).

PIEHL, *ZÄS* 28, 18 n. 3 [1890].

[S]ϩⲣⲟⲩⲟ, [B]ϧⲉⲣⲟⲩⲱ, 'great voice, boastful talk' = *, *ḫrw ꜥꜣ*, lit. 'great voice'; , *ḫrw ꜥꜣ*, same meaning.

[H]SPIEGELBERG, *Kopt. Handwb.* 88 [1921]; [D]SPIEGELBERG, *Mythus*, 234, no. 614 [1917]; cf. DÉVAUD, *Études*, 35–7 [1922].

[B]ϩⲣⲟⲩⲣ (Crum 705b), 'cease, be quiet' = (Er. 325, 9), *ḥrr*, 'to lag', a reduplication (**hrĕwrĕw*) from , [S]ϩⲣⲣⲉ, [B]ϩⲉⲣⲓ (see the latter).

[H]SETHE, *Verbum*, I, 267, §426 [1899]; [D]BRUGSCH, *Wb.* 335 [1868] (he reads the Dem. word *uarer*, but compares it with ϩⲣⲟⲩⲣ); cf. Revillout, *Setna*, 31, 35 and passim [1880].

[S]ϩⲱⲣϣ (Crum 706a), 'bring into bad state, into difficulty', lit. 'make heavy' (cf. *JEA* 45, 82), Ist Inf. of and having the same etymology as, ϩⲣⲟϣ; 'get into bad state, become heavy, etc.' (IInd Inf.). See also next entry.

[B](ϩⲱⲣϣ), ϩⲉⲣϣ- (Crum 706a), 'run (ship) aground', lit. 'bring (ship) into difficulty', is but a special meaning of the preceding ϩⲱⲣϣ. For etymology see ϩⲣⲟϣ.

ϩⲣⲟϣ (Crum 706a), 'become heavy, slow, difficult, get into bad state' = (Er. 327, 1), *ḥrš*, also (Er. 280, 3), *hrš*, 'heavy, become heavy'.

ϩⲣⲟϣ is IInd Inf. of ϩⲱⲣϣ for which see the last two entries.

BRUGSCH, *Rhind*, 45, no. 326 and Pl. 41 [1865].

^A2^ϩⲟⲩⲣⲉϣⲣⲉϣ [not in Crum; Mani Ps.], see under ⲣⲁϣⲣⲉϣ, 'rejoice'.

ϩⲁⲣⲉϩ (Crum 707b), 'keep, guard' = [demotic] (Er. 326, 2), *ḥrḥ*, 'protect, guard'.

BRUGSCH, *Gr. dém.* 36, §76 [1855].

^A^ⲉⲣⲏϩⲧⲉ, ⲁⲣⲏϩⲧⲉ (Crum 708b) was originally an Imperative of this verb + ⲧⲉ, dependent pronoun of 2nd per. sing., as in ⲁⲙⲁϩⲧⲉ, etc.

SPIEGELBERG, *Rec. trav.* 28, 205 [1908].

^S^ϩⲣϩⲣ, ^B^ϧⲉⲣϧⲉⲣ (Crum 708b), 'snore', from Semitic, cf. Ar. خَرَّ, خَرْخَرَ, 'snore', Syr. ܢܘܚܪܬܐ, 'ronchus (hominis)' (Brockelmann, *Lex.* 122), and Hebrew נָחַר.

ROSSI, *Etym. aeg.* 289 [1808]; cf. Dévaud in *Sphinx*, 12, 122 [1908].

ϩⲣⲟϫⲣ(ⲉ)ϫ (Crum 708b), 'grind' (teeth,) 'rub', reduplication of Semitic √*ḫrk*, cf. Hebrew חָרַק, 'grind (teeth)', Aram. חֲרַק, حَرَقَ, Syr. ܢܘܚܪܩܐ, 'strepitus, stridor (dentium)'.

ROSSI, *Etym. aeg.* 290–1 [1808].

^B^ϧⲣⲓϫ (Crum 709a), '(tooth-)ache' = [demotic] (Er. 368, 1), *hrd*, in *ỉr hrd*, 'grind (teeth)'. From Semitic, see above.

SPIEGELBERG, *Mythus*, 238, no. 630 [1917].

ϩⲱⲣϭ (Crum 709a), 'heap up, set in order', from Semitic √*ʿrk*, cf. עָרַךְ, 'arrange, set in order'.

DÉVAUD, *Kêmi* 2, 13–14 [1929].

ϩⲁⲥ (Crum 709a), 'dung' (of animals, birds) in recipes = [hieroglyphs] (*Wb.* III, 164, 4 f.), *ḥs*, 'excrement'; [demotic] (Er. 328, 8), *ḥs*, 'lime, excrement, dung'.

^H^STERN in *Pap. Ebers*, II (Gloss.), 17 [1875]; ^D^GRIFFITH–THOMPSON, III, 61, no. 608 [1909].

ϩⲱⲥ (Crum 709b), 'sing, make music' = [hieroglyphs] (*Wb.* III, 164, 11 f.), *ḥsy*, 'sing'; [demotic] (Er. 330, 1), *ḥs*, 'sing, song, singer'. Originally different from ϩⲱⲥ, [hieroglyphs] (*Wb.* III, 154, 2 ff.), *ḥsy* (*ḥzy*), 'praise, favour'; [demotic] (Er. 329, 1), *ḥs*, 'praise, reward'.

See SETHE, *Verbum*, I, 157, §264 [1899] for distinction between *ḥsy* and *ḥzy*.

^H^CHAMPOLLION, *Gr.* 378, 382 [1836]; ^D^BRUGSCH, *Wb.* 991 [1868].

ϩⲱⲥ (Crum 710a), ‘block, fill, cover up’ = (*Wb.* III, 159, 4 f.), *ḥsy* (*ḥzy*), ‘betake oneself to..., go against, hamper, cover’.

BRUGSCH, *ZÄS* 14, 95 [1876]; cf. Gardiner, *Hieratic Papyri in the Brit. Museum, Third Series*, II, 39 n. 4 [1935].

ϩⲱⲥ (Crum 710a), ‘thread, cord’ = (*Wb.* III, 166, 4), *ḥsꜣ*, ‘thread, cord’; (not in Er. ex. Vienna Petubastis R22), *ḥs*, in *ẖlꜣ* (*n*) *ḥs*, ‘garment(?) of thread’.

HBRUGSCH, *Wb.* 993–4 [1868] and Suppl. 852 [1881]; DSPIEGELBERG, *Petubastis*, 65 n. 15 [1910].

ϩⲁⲥⲓⲉ (Crum 710a), ‘drowned’, lit. ‘praised person’ = (*Wb.* III, 156, 5 f.), *ḥsy* (*ḥzy*), ‘praised person’, also of deceased people (*Wb.* III, 156, 12–16); (Er. 329, 2), *ḥs*(*y*), ‘praised, drowned person’.

GRIFFITH–THOMPSON, I, 38, n. on l. 31 [1904]; cf. Griffith, *ZÄS* 46, 132 [1909]; cf. Griffith–Thompson, III, 61, no. 612 [1909].

Sϩⲓⲥⲉ, Bϧⲓⲥⲓ (Crum 710b), ‘toil, be troubled, difficult; be wearied, suffering’ = (*Wb.* III, 398, bottom), *ẖsy*, ‘be weak’, etc.; (Er. 396, 6), *ẖsy*, ‘suffer, be weary’.

HHINCKS in *Transaction of the Roy. Irish Academy*, 21, part II, 228 [1848, read in 1846]; cf. Brugsch, *Wb.* 1047 [1868]; DBRUGSCH, *Rhind*, 46 and Pl. 42, no. 346 [1865].

Sϩⲓⲥⲉ, Bϩⲓⲥⲓ (Crum 713a), ‘spin’ = in (*Wb.* III, 159, 2); *ḥst nwt*, ‘spin threads’. Cf. also A O. BM. 50730, 7.

SPIEGELBERG, *OLZ* 27, cols. 568–9 [1924].

ϩⲓⲥⲉ (not in Crum) in ϫⲣⲟ ⲙⲛϩⲓⲥⲉ (Mani Ps. 210, 15), greeting or congratulation ‘greeting and praise(?)’ = (*Wb.* III, 157, 8 f.), *ḥs*(*w*)*t*, ‘favour, reward’; var. (Er. 329, bottom), *ḥst mrt*, ‘praise and love’.

Cf. ALLBERRY, *A Manichaean Psalm-book*, II, 210 n. [1938] (he compares ϩⲱⲥ, ‘praise’, though the verb has no such meaning in Coptic).

ϩⲟⲥⲃ (Crum 713a), ‘market’ = (Er. 332, 4), *ḥsb*, ‘market’, undoubtedly a derivative from the old (*Wb.* III, 166, 11 ff.), *ḥsb*, ‘count, reckon’.

DSPIEGELBERG, *Dem. Pap. Hauswaldt*, 58 n. 1 [1913].

ϩⲟⲥⲙ (Crum 713a), 'natron' (carbonate of soda) = (*Wb.* III, 162, 11 f.), *ḥsmn*, 'natron'; (Er. 332, 5), *ḥsmn*, 'natron'.
[H]CHAMPOLLION, *Gr.* 62, 90 [1836]; [D]BRUGSCH, *Gr. dém.* 26, §51; 39, §84 [1855].

ϩⲁⲧ (Crum 713b, under ϩⲁⲧ, 'silver', c), 'white' = (*Wb.* III, 206, 14 f.), *ḥḏ*, 'white'; (Er. 335, 1), *ḥt*, 'white'.
See also **ϩⲁⲧⲁⲓⲗⲉ** and **ϩⲁⲧⲗⲟⲟⲩⲉ**.

ϩⲁⲧ (Crum 713b), 'silver', 'silver coin, money' = (*Wb.* III, 209, 9 f.), *ḥḏ*, 'silver'; (Er. 335, 2), *ḥt*, 'silver, silver coin, money'.
[H]CHAMPOLLION, *Gr.* 89 [1836]; [D]YOUNG, *Misc. Works*, III, 28–9, no. 75 = *Mus. crit.* VI, 178 [1815] (letter to de Sacy of 21 Oct. 1814); cf. Brugsch, *Scriptura Aeg. dem.* 3, 10 [1848].

ϩⲁⲉⲓⲧ (Crum 713b), 'gateway, porch, forecourt' = (*Wb.* III, 222, 5), *ḥꜣty*, (Pap. Leningrad 1116A, verso 130. 135), *ḥꜣyti*, 'gateway, forecourt'; (Er. 377, 7), *ḥyt*, 'forecourt, entrance'.
[H]SPIEGELBERG, *Kopt. Handwb.* 248 [1921]; cf. Peet, *The Great Tomb-Robberies*, I, 158 n. 1 [1930]; [D]KRALL in Revillout in *Revue ég.* 2, 31 n. 1 [1882]; cf. Spiegelberg, *Kopt. Etym.* 25 [1920].

ϩⲏⲧ (Crum 714a), 'heart, mind' = (*Wb.* III, 26 bottom), *ḥꜣty*, 'heart'; (Er. 289, 2), *ḥꜣṯ*, 'heart'.
[H]CHAMPOLLION, *Gr.* 94 [1836]; [D]BRUGSCH, *Gr. dém.* 29, §56 [1855].
ⲁⲧϩⲏⲧ (Crum 714b), 'without mind, senseless', cf. (*Wb.* III, 27, 15, 16), *iwty ḥꜣty·f*, 'foolish', lit. 'not having his heart'.
ⲥⲱⲕ ϩⲏⲧ (Crum 716a), see under **ⲥⲱⲕ**.

[S]**ϩⲏⲧ**, [B]**ϧⲏⲧ** (Crum 717b), 'north' (lit. 'downstream' on Nile), (*Wb.* III, 354, 9 f.), *ḫdy*, 'travel downstream' (i.e. 'north'); (Er. 397, 4), *ḫt* (*ḫd*), 'travel downstream'.
[HD]GRIFFITH, *Ryl.* III, 225 n. 3; 356 [1909].

ϩⲏⲧ (Crum 718a), 'tip, edge' = (Er. 287, 2), *ḥꜣṯ*, 'point'.
ERICHSEN, *Dem. Glossar*, 287, 2 [1954].

ϩⲓⲉⲓⲧ (Crum 718a), 'pit' = (*Wb.* III, 36, 4), *ḥꜣd*, '(wicker) fish-trap', cf. Lacau in *BIFAO* 54,137 ff.; (Er. 270, 1), *ḥyṯ*, 'pit'.
[H]SPIEGELBERG, *Kopt. Handwb.* 250 [1921]; [D]BRUGSCH in *ZÄS* 16, 49 and Pl. 3, l. 23 [1878].

ϩⲱⲧ (Crum 718b), 'sack, bag' from Semitic, cf. Aram. חת.
ROSSI, *Etym. aeg.* 302 [1808].

ϩⲱⲧ (Crum 718b), in ⲣ ϩⲱⲧ, 'make sail, float' = (*Wb.* III, 182, 16), *ḥtꜣw*, 'the sail'; (Er. 337, 7), *ḥṱ*, 'the sail', also in *ỉr ḥṱ*, 'make sail, travel upstream'.
HSPIEGELBERG, *Petubastis*, 44*, no. 286 [1910]; DGRIFFITH, *Rylands*, III, 231 n. 13; 375 [1909].

Sϩⲁⲧⲉ, Bϧⲁϯ (Crum 719a), 'flow; let flow, pour' = (not in *Wb.*), *ẖdy*, 'flow'.
DÉVAUD, *Études*, 37–9 [1922]; cf. Griffith, *Ryl.* III, 225 n. 3 [1909].

Sϩⲓⲧⲉ, Bϧⲓϯ (Crum 719b), 'move to and fro, rub, whet' = (Er. 377, 8), *ẖyṱ*, 'rub, scrape'.
GRIFFITH–THOMPSON, III, 65, no. 645 [1909].

Sϩⲟ(ⲉ)ⲓⲧⲉ, Aϩⲁ(ⲉ)ⲓⲧⲉ, P. Bodmer VI ⳉⲟϊⲧⲉ (Crum 720b), 'garment' = (not in Er.; ex. P. Petrie (1922), col. E. I. 3, etc., at Oxford, unpubl.), *ḥity*, a garment.
NB. Since ϩ and ⳉ cannot < *ḥ* the derivation from (*Wb.* III, 35, 6, 7), *ḥꜣtyw*, kind of linen; (Er. 337, 2), *ḥt*, a garment (HSETHE in Gardiner, *Admonitions*, 89 [1909]; DHESS, *Stne*, 170 [1888]) must be abandoned.

ϩⲟ(ⲉ)ⲓⲧⲉ (Crum 720b), 'hyena' = (*Wb.* III, 203, 16. 17), *ḥtt*, 'hyena'; (Er. 282, 3), *ḥṱt*, 'hyena'.
HWILKINSON, *Materia hieroglyphica*, autographed text, I [1828]; DHESS, *Gnost. Pap.* 10 [1892].

ϩⲟⲧⲉ (Crum 720b), 'fear' = (*Wb.* III, 182, 6), *ḥty*, 'danger'; (Er. 336, 1), *ḥt* (*ḥṱ*), 'fear' (verb and noun).
HGARDINER, *JEA* 42, 20 [1956]; DBRUGSCH, *Gr. dém.* 35, §70 [1855].
ⲣ ϩⲟⲧⲉ (Crum 720a), 'be afraid' = , *ỉr ḥt*, 'be afraid' (Mythus, 11, 30. 31; 12, 1).
SPIEGELBERG, *Mythus*, 217, no. 565 [1917].

ϩⲟⲧⲉ (Crum 721b), 'hour, moment' = (Er. 338, 3), *ḥṱy*, 'moment, time'.
BRUGSCH, *Gr. dém.* 133, §279; 180, §351 [1855].

For Bⲛ̄ϯϩⲟϯ ⲛ̄ϯϩⲟϯ, 'on a sudden', cf. 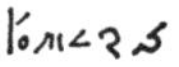 (Vienna Petubastis, L 25), *tꜣy ḥty*, 'immediately'.

STRICKER, *Oudheidkundige Mededelingen*, N.S. 35, 57, no. 48 [1954].

Sϩⲱⲧⲉ, Bϩⲱϯ (Crum 722a), 'rub, bruise' =  (*Wb.* III, 212, bottom), *ḥdy*, 'to damage'; 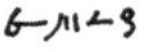 (Er. 338, 2), *ḥty*, 'to damage'.

Sϩⲱⲧⲉ(?), Bϩⲱϯ (Crum 722a), 'tribute' = 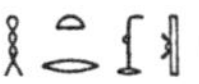 (*Wb.* III, 201, 9 f.), *ḥtr*, 'due, tax, income'; 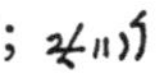 (Er. 343, 2), *ḥtr*, 'tax, due'.

HBRUGSCH, *Wb.* 1012 [1868]; DBRUGSCH, *Gr. dém.* 36, §76 [1855].

Bϩⲱϯ (Crum 722b), 'necessity', as impers. verb 'it is needful' = 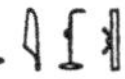 (*Wb.* III, 200, 15 f.), *ḥtr*, 'to tax, assess'; 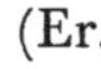 (Er. 343, 1), *ḥtr*, 'to have to, be obliged to; necessity, compulsion'; still also transitive  (Ankhsh. 7, 2), *ḥtỉṯ*, 'compel'.

DSETHE, *Demot. Urkunden*, 32 [1920].

Sϩⲧⲁ(ⲉ)ⲓ, Bϧⲉⲑⲁⲓ (Crum 722b), 'become fat', denominative verb from  (*Wb.* III, 356, 3 f.), *ẖt*, 'body, belly'. Cf. the nisba-adjective from the latter,  as proper name, *ẖty*, 'stout one' (Ranke I, 277, 25. 26), also written 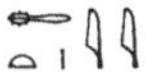 (*Urk.* I, 152, 7).

GUNN's manuscript notes.

ϩⲧⲏ (Crum 723a), 'shaft' of spear, cf.  (*Wb.* III, 181, 16, where the ref. should be P. Turin 132, 4), *ḥtyt*, of a sharp object (needle?).

ERMAN–GRAPOW, *Wb.* III, 181, 16 [1929].

ϩⲧⲟ (Crum 723a), 'horse' =  (*Wb.* III, 199, 11 f.), *ḥtr*, 'team of horses'; 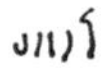 (Er. 342, 2), *ḥtr*, 'team of horses, horse'.

HCHAMPOLLION, *Précis*, 2nd ed., 125 [1828]; DYOUNG, *Misc. Works*, III, 28–9, no. 59 = *Mus. crit.* 6, 178–9, no. 59 [1815] (letter to de Sacy of 21 Oct. 1814); cf. Brugsch, *Gr. dém.* 23, §40 [1855].

ⲣⲱⲙϩⲧⲟ (Crum 723a), 'horseman' = (Selim Hassan, *Le poème dit de Pentaour*, Pl. 29), *rmṯ-ḥtr*, 'horsemen'; 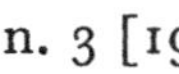 (Er. 342, bottom), *rmt-ḥtr*, 'horseman'.

HDSPIEGELBERG in Reinach, *Pap. Reinach*, 194 and n. 3 [1905].

Bϭⲁⲥⲓϩⲧⲟ (Crum 723a), 'raised on horse, rider', cf. 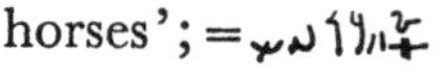 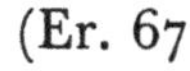 (*Wb.* V, 407, 9), *ṯsy nꜣ ḥtrw*, 'mount the horses'; = (Er. 671, top), *ṯsỉ-ḥtr*, 'rider, knight (as rank)'.

ᴴERMAN–GRAPOW, *Wb.* v, 407, 9 [1931]; ᴰBRUGSCH, *Rhind*, 44 and Pl. 40, no. 289 [1865].

ϩⲱⲧⲃ (Crum 723b), 'kill' = (*Wb.* III, 403, 3 f.), *ḫdb*, 'kill'; (Er. 398, 3), *ḫtb* (*ḫdb*), 'kill'.

ᴴDE ROUGÉ, *Oeuv. div.* I (= *Bibl. ég.* XXI), 192 [1847]; ᴰBRUGSCH, *Wb.* 1050 [1868].

A2ϩⲁϯⲗ (Crum 724a), meaning uncertain ('humble, lowly?'), ?cf. (Er. 344, 1), *ḥtl*, title or epithet. See also the next two entries?

ϩⲁⲧⲁⲓⲗⲉ (Crum 724a), an eye disease. ϩⲁⲧ- is probably ϩⲁⲧ, 'white'; -ⲟⲉⲓⲗⲉ, etc., perhaps = ⲁⲗⲟⲩ or its plural ⲁⲗⲟⲟⲩⲉ, 'pupils' (of eye). ϩ. therefore lit. 'white as to pupils' translates λεύκωμα rather than πτίλος. See also next entry.

HERBERT THOMPSON in Crum, *Copt. Dict.* 713b, s.v. ϩⲁⲧ, c [1937].

ϩⲁⲧⲗⲟⲟⲩⲧ (Crum 724a, 'meaning unknown', reading verified on photo by Shore) is corrupted from ϩⲁⲧⲁⲗⲟⲟⲩⲉ, 'white of pupils', i.e. suffering from leucoma; see the preceding entry. People suffering from ϩ. are said in Mor 51, 36 to eat ⲕⲁⲗⲓⲣⲓⲟⲛ (= κολλύριον, diminutive of κόλλυρα), an eye-salve. For ⲗⲟⲟⲩⲉ cf. ex. from Aeg. 20 quoted by Crum 147b, s.v. ⲗⲟⲟⲩ at end.

ϩⲧⲟⲙⲧⲙ (Crum 724a), 'become darkened' = (*Wb.* v, 309, 9), *tmtm*, in *tmtm* , *ỉrty.f*, of the eyes of an ailing ox.

ERMAN–GRAPOW, *Wb.* v, 309, 9 [1931].

NB. The initial ϩ- through confusion with (*Wb.* III, 199, 5), *ḥtmtm*, which is a reduplication of *ḥtm* (*Wb.* III, 197, 10 f.), 'destroy, wipe out'.

ϩⲱⲧⲡ (Crum 724b), 'attune, be reconciled, sink' = (*Wb.* III, 188, 2 ff.), *ḥtp*, 'be contented, rest, set (of sun and stars)'; (Er. 340, 1), *ḥtp*, 'to rest; peace'.

ᴴDE ROUGÉ, *Oeuv. div.* II (= *Bibl. ég.* XXII), 338 n. 1 [1852]; *Oeuv. div.* III (= *Bibl. ég.* XXIII), 169 [1856]; ᴰBRUGSCH, *Gr. dém.* 128, §262 [1855].

ϩⲱⲧⲡ, 'join' = (*Wb.* III, 71, 16 f.), *ḥpt*, 'embrace, encompass', metathesis *ḥtp* occurring from XXth Dynasty.

CHAMPOLLION, *Gr.* 372 [1836].

[B]ϩⲟⲧⲡ, ϩⲟⲡⲧ (Crum 725b), 'thing joined (?), chain, rim' = sing. of pl. (*Wb.* III, 72, 11), *ḥptw*, crosspieces of the leaves of a door; (Er. 341, 2), *ḥtpw*, same meaning.

[HD]DRIOTON in *BIFAO* 26, 18 [1926].

ϩⲧⲟⲡ (Crum 725b), 'fall, destruction' = (*Wb.* III, 205, 8 f.), *ḥdb*, 'throw, be thrown to ground'; (Er. 341, 1), *ḥtp*, 'fall, destruction', also as verb.

[H]GUNN's manuscript notes; [D]SPIEGELBERG in Reinach, *Pap. Reinach*, 213 [1905].

ϩⲧⲟⲡ (Crum 725b), a measure = (*Wb.* III, 195, 12), *ḥtp*, 'a basket' (also a measure).

CRUM, *A Coptic Dict.*, 725b [1937].

ϩⲁⲧⲏⲣ (Crum 725b), 'hammer', from Semitic, cf. Syriac ܡܚܛܘܪܐ and ܚܛܘܪܐ.

DÉVAUD in *Kêmi* 2, 14–15 [1929].

ϩⲱⲧ(ⲉ)ⲣ (Crum 726a), 'join, double' = (*Wb.* III, 202, 2. 3), *ḥtr*, 'tie together'; (not in Er.), *ḥtr*, 'agree'.

[H]ERMAN–GRAPOW, *Wb.* III, 202, 2. 3 [1929]; [D]SPIEGELBERG, *Dem. Pap. Loeb*, 57(3) [1931].

ϩⲁⲧⲣⲉ (Crum 726b), 'double thing, twin' = Gr.-R. proper name (*Wb.* III, 199, 6), *ḥtr*, 'twin'; (Er. 341, 6), *ḥtr*, 'twin'.

[H]BRUGSCH, *Rec. de mon.* I, 32 [1862]; [D]BRUGSCH, *Wb.* 1011 [1868].

ϩⲧⲟⲣ (Crum 726b adding [O]ⲩⲧⲟ[ⲣ], *OLZ* 7, col. 197), 'necessity, constraint' = (Er. 343, 1), *ḥtr*, 'constraint'.

REVILLOUT, *Nouvelle chrest. dém.* 120 (cf. 107) [1878].

See also ϩⲱϯ, 'necessity'.

ϩⲟⲧⲥ (Crum 727a), vessel or measure = (*Wb.* II, 482, 8. 9), *hꜣṯs*, a jar.

DÉVAUD in *Kêmi* 2, 15–16 [1929].

[S]ϩⲧⲟⲟⲩⲉ, ⲧⲟⲟⲩⲉ, [B]ⲧⲟⲟⲩⲓ (Crum 727b), 'dawn, morning' = (*Wb.* V, 422, 1 f.), *dwꜣw*, 'dawn, morrow'; (Er. 614, 1), *twꜣw* (*dwꜣw*), 'morning'.

[H]CHABAS, *Oeuv. div.* II (=*Bibl. ég.* X), 81 [1860]; cf. BRUGSCH, *Nouvelles recherches sur la division de l'année*, 48–9 [1856] (who, however, explains the initial ϩ- unsatisfactorily); [D]BRUGSCH, *Gr. dém.* 30, §61 and 179, §349 [1855].

The initial ϩ- comes from (*Wb.* III, 207, 27), *ḥd tꜣ*, 'it dawns' (lit. 'the earth becomes bright') > *ϩⲧⲟ.

[B]ϩⲱⲧϥ (Crum 728a), 'to nail' = ⲱϥⲧ, see this latter.

CRUM, *A Coptic Dict.* 728a [1937].

ϩⲁⲑⲱⲣ (Crum 728a), name of 3rd month = (*Wb.* III, 5, 12), *Ḥwt-ḥr*, name of 3rd calendar month after a festival of goddess Hathor.

ERMAN in *ZÄS* 39, 129 [1901]; cf. Lepsius, *Chronologie*, 137 [1848]; Brugsch, *Die Ägyptologie*, 359 [1891].

[S]ϩⲟⲧϩⲧ, [B]ϧⲟⲧϧⲉⲧ (Crum 728a), 'inquire, examine' = (not in *Wb.*; cf. also O. Cairo Cat. 25798, 2), *ẖdẖd*, 'examine'; (Er. 398, 4), *ẖtẖt*, 'examine, investigate'.

[H]GARDINER, *Hieratic Papyri in the Brit. Museum, Third Series*, I, 68 n. 6 [1935]; [D]REVILLOUT in *Rev. égyptol.* 2, 21 [1881].

ϩⲏⲩ (Crum 729a), 'profit, usefulness' = (*Wb.* III, 16, 7 f.), *ḥꜣw*, 'increment, excess'; (Er. 204, 3), *ḥw*, 'increment, profit'.

[H]MASPERO in *Rec. trav.* 25, 19 [1903]; [D]GRIFFITH, *Ryl.* III, 370 [1909]. NB. Gardiner's etymology *ap.* Černý in *Crum Mem. Vol.* 42–4 [1950] must be abandoned.

ϭⲛ ϩⲏⲩ, 'find profit, gain' = , *gm ḥw*, 'find profit'.

LICHTHEIM, *Dem. Ostraca*, 71, no. 159, n. 3 [1957].

ϩⲟⲩ- in ϩⲟⲩⲟ, 'greater part', see this.

ϩⲏⲩ in ⲕⲱⲕⲁϩⲏⲩ (Crum 101a), 'strip, make naked' (for *ⲕⲱⲕϩⲏⲩ) = , *ḥꜣw*, 'naked', Old Perf. of (*Wb.* III, 13, 13 f.), 'uncover'.

SPIEGELBERG, *Kopt. Handwb.* 255 [1921], cf. earlier Champollion, *Dict.* 369 [1841] assuming ⲁϩⲏⲟⲩ, and Brugsch, *Wb.* 919 [1868] who assumes ⲕⲁϩⲏⲟⲩ. Dévaud (*Muséon* 36, 89) also assumes ⲁϩⲏⲩ < **aḥꜣēw* to be the correct form (ⲕⲱⲕ + ⲁϩⲏⲩ), but ϩⲏⲩ < **ḥēꜣew* is far more satisfactory, since *-ḥēw* would thus require long *ē* in closed syllable. The ⲁ is therefore intrusive.

ϩⲟⲟⲩ (Crum 730a), 'day' = (*Wb.* II, 498, bottom), *hrw*, 'day' > (e.g. Wenamūn 1, 51; 2, 8, 58), while the plural (Wenamūn 1, 21) preserves *r* like pl. [A]ϩⲣⲉⲩ; (Er. 278, 2), *hrw*, 'day'.

[HD]YOUNG, *Misc. Works*, III, Pl. 4, no. 178 = *Encycl. Brit.*, Suppl. IV, Pl. 77, no. 178 [1819]; cf. Champollion, *Gr.* 79 [1836] and cf. [H]Lepsius, *Lettre à Rosellini*, 40 and Pl. B, no. 39; 97 [1837]; [D]BRUGSCH, *Scriptura Aeg. dem.* 57 [1848].

[O] **ⲇⲁⲩ-** in **ⲇⲁⲩ ⲉïⲡⲛ**, 'this day', see under **ⲉïⲡⲛ**.

ⲡⲟⲟⲩ (< *ⲡϩⲟⲟⲩ) (Crum 731a), 'the day, today' = (*Wb.* II, 499, 11), *pꜣ hrw*, 'today'; (Er. 278, lower), *pꜣ hrw*, 'today'.

[H]CHABAS, *Pap. mag. Harris*, 228, no. 463 [1860].

[A]**ϥⲧⲉⲩ ⲉⲡⲟⲟⲩ**, 'for last four days', cf. (Horus and Seth 5, 10), *dỉw r pꜣ hrw*, 'for last five days', lit. 'five (days) until today'.

POLOTSKY in *JEA* 25, 112 [1939].

ϩⲟⲟⲩ (Crum 731a), 'be putrid', so 'bad, wicked' is Qual. of ***ϩⲟⲩⲁⲓ**; (*Wb.* III, 50, 6 f.), *ḥwꜣ*, 'be(come) putrid'; (Er. 295, 1), *ḥw*, 'be(come) putrid', 'bad'.

[H]BRUGSCH, *Wb.* 940 [1868]; cf. Renouf, *Aegyptol. Essays*, I, 247 n. 1 [1862]; STEINDORFF, *ZÄS* 74, 69 [1938]; [D]ERICHSEN, *Dem. Glossar*, 295, 1 [1954].

ϩⲱⲟⲩ (Crum 732a), 'to rain', noun 'rain' = (*Wb.* III, 49, 1–3), *ḥwt* 'the rain'; (Er. 295, 2), *ḥw*, 'to rain(?)', noun 'rain'.

[H]ERMAN, *Lebensmüde*, 69 [1896]; [D]GRIFFITH, *Stories*, 197 [1900].

ϩⲟⲩⲙⲡⲉ, 'the rain', cf. (Petrie, *Medum*, Pl. 33, l. 9), *ḥwy pt*, 'the sky beats' and (*LRL* 18, 14), *ḥwy mw tꜣ pt*, 'water of the sky beats' (*ḥwy* is a verb!); (Er. 295, 2), *ḥw m pt*, 'the rain'.

[D]REVILLOUT, *Poème*, 200 [1885].

ϩⲓⲟⲩⲉ (Crum 732b), 'strike, cast, lay' = (*Wb.* III, 46, 1 ff.), *ḥwy*, 'strike'; (Er. 296, 1), *ḥwy*, 'throw, strike, thrash'.

[H]SETHE, *Verbum*, II, 301, §683, 6b [1899]; cf. Champollion, *Dict.* 367–8 [1841]; cf. Brugsch, *Wb.* 914 [1868]; [D]BRUGSCH, *Scriptura Aeg. dem.* 52 [1848].

ϩⲟⲩⲟ (Crum 735b), 'greater part, greatness', cf. (*Wb.* III, 16, 7 f.), *ḥꜣw*, 'increment'; (Er. 294, 3), *ḥw*, 'increment, profit, interest'.

[H]BRUGSCH, *Wb.* 917–18 [1868]; REVILLOUT, *Setna*, 150 [1880].

NB. ϩⲟⲩⲟ cannot be *ḥ3w* itself, but ϩⲏⲩ + ⲟ > ϩⲟⲩ-ⲟ; where ⲟ = 'great', as implied by Sethe, *Verbum*, I, 96, §161α, β [1899] and explicitly stated by Spiegelberg, *Kopt. Handwb.* 254 [1921].

See also ϩⲏⲩ, 'profit'.

ⲛϩⲟⲩⲟ ⲉ- (Crum 736a), 'more than', cf. (*Wb.* III, 18, 3), *m ḥ3w r*, 'more than'; (Er. 294, middle), *n ḥw r*, 'more than'.

[H]DÉVAUD's slip; [D]REVILLOUT, *Setna*, 150 [1880].

(ϩⲟⲟⲩⲣⲉ), ϩⲟⲩⲣⲱ- (Crum 737b), 'deprive' = (*Wb.* III, 56, 8–13), *ḥwrʿ*, 'rob'; (Er. 297, 2), *ḥwrʿ*, 'rob, robbery'.

[H]W. MAX MÜLLER, *ZÄS*, 26, 76 [1888]; [D]BRUGSCH, *Wb.* 941–2 [1868].

ϩⲟⲩⲏⲧ (Crum 738a), 'passenger' on board of ship (?)' = (*Wb.* II, 485, 8), *hwty*, 'sailor' or 'ship's hand' (cf. Gardiner, *Onom.* I, 215*, no. 309); (Er. 269, 3), *hyt*, 'sailor'.

[H]LANGE, *Amenemope*, 133 [1925]; [D]GRIFFITH, *Stories*, 100 [1900].

ϩⲟⲩⲉⲓⲧ (Crum 738a), 'first' = (*Wb.* III, 29, 7 f.), *ḥ3wty*, 'first'; (Er. 288, 3), *ḥ3ṯ*, 'first'.

[H]BRUGSCH, *Wb.* 932 [1868]; [D]BRUGSCH, *Gr. dém.* 65, §139 [1855].

ϩⲟⲟⲩⲧ (Crum 738b), 'male' of men, gods, 'husband'; 'wild' (man or plant) = (*Wb.* I, 217, 8 f.), *ʿḥ3wty*, 'fighter, male god (man or animal)'; (Er. 297, 4), *ḥwt(y)*, 'man, male'.

[H]ERMAN acc. to Brugsch in *ZÄS* 20, 79 [1882]; [D]LEEMANS, *Aeg. Papyrus in demot. Schrift*, 63, no. 68 [1839].

ϩⲟⲟⲩⲧⲛ (Crum 739b), 'road, highway'; cf. ?L.Eg. (*Wb.* III, 75, 18), *ḥfdn*, 'ascend quickly' (mountains).

ϩⲟⲟⲩϣ (Crum 739b), 'abuse, curse' = (Er. 271, 4), *hwš*, 'abuse, hurt' (already in abn. hieratic as 'disrespect', Malinine, *Choix de textes juridiques*, I, 11 n. 9).

[D]GRIFFITH, *Stories*, 82 [1900]; Brugsch, *Wb.* 893 [1868] compares ϩⲱϣ.

[S]ϩⲟⲩϩⲉ, [B]ⲟⲩϫⲉ (Crum 739b), 'untimely birth' = * (*Wb.* I, 339, 16), *why*, 'miss' + (*Wb.* III, 336, 8), *ẖt*, '(mother's) body'.

SPIEGELBERG in *ZÄS* 58, 56 [1923].

ϩⲁⲩϭⲁⲗ (Crum 740a), 'anchor, hook', from Semitic, cf. Ar. هَوْجَل, wooden or iron 'rake'.

STERN, *Kopt. Gr.* 20, §22 [1880].

ϩⲁϣⲏⲧ, ϩⲁⲣϣⲏⲧ (Crum 740b) 'falcon', prob. = taboo word ϩⲁⲣϣ-ϩⲏⲧ, lit. 'slow of heart, patient' (Crum 707b s.v. ϩⲣⲟϣ) or even more probably for ⲁⲣϣ-ϩⲏⲧ, 'cold (ⲱⲣϣ) of heart', i.e. 'merciless' to avoid the bird's real name.

See also ᴮⲁⲣϣⲏⲧ, 'press upon'.

ϩⲟϥ (Crum 740b) 'serpent' = (*Wb.* III, 72, 14–18), *ḥfꜣw*, 'snake'; (Er. 303, 3), *ḥf*, 'snake'.

ᴴCHAMPOLLION, *Précis*, 2nd ed., 126 [1828]; ᴰBRUGSCH, *De natura*, 31 [1850]; fem. ϩϥⲱ, ϩϥⲱ = (*Wb.* III, 72, bottom), *ḥfꜣt*, 'female snake'. W. MAX MÜLLER in *Rec. trav.* 15, 33 [1893]; cf. Brugsch, *Wb.* 954 [1868].

ϩⲁϥⲗⲉ(ⲉ)ⲗⲉ (Crum 741a), 'lizard' = (Er. 303, 4), *ḥflꞽlꜥt*, 'lizard'; cf. late fem. personal name , *ḥfrr* (Ranke II, 305, 15). Ultimately perhaps the same as *ḥfn* (*Wb.* III, 74, 1), 'tadpole'.

ᴰLEEMANS, *Aeg. Papyrus in dem. Schrift*, 62, no. 66 [1839]; cf. Brugsch, *Gr. dém.* 24, §43 [1855].

ϩⲱϥⲧ (Crum 741a), 'steal' = (*Wb.* III, 56, 17 f.), *ḥwtf*, 'rob'.

BRUGSCH, *Wb.*, Suppl. 801 [1881].

ϩⲁϩ (Crum 741b), 'many, much' = (*Wb.* III, 152, 14 f.), *ḥḥ*, 'large number, million'; (Er. 328, 7), *ḥḥ*, or , *hh*, 'multitude, large number'.

ᴴLAUTH in *ZÄS* 4, 36 [1866]; PLEYTE, *Études égypt.* I, 105 [1866]; ᴰBRUGSCH, *Gr. dém.* 184, §367 [1855].

ˢ**ϩⲱϩ**, ᴮ**ϧⲱϧ** (Crum 742a), 'scrape, scratch' = (Er. 396, 5), *ẖẖꞽ*, 'to scratch' or sim.

GRIFFITH–THOMPSON, III, 69, no. 683 [1909].

ϩⲱϩ, 'scratching, itching' = (cursively for), *ḫḫ*, 'itching' as disease.

EDWARDS, *Oracular Amuletic Decrees*, I, 24 n. 17 [1960].

ϩⲱϩϥ (Crum 742b), 'hand' as measure = (*Wb.* III, 272, 16f.), *ḥfʿ*, 'fist, grip', and (*Wb.* III, 273, 7), *ḥfʿ*, 'bundle (lit. handful)' of arrows.

DÉVAUD in Crum, *A Coptic Dict.* 742b [1937].

ϩⲱϫ (Crum 742b), 'press, oppress' = (*Wb.* III, 43, 16. 17), *ḥʿḏꜣ*, 'rob'; (Er. 294, 2), *ḥʿḏ*, 'press' or sim.

HSETHE in *ZÄS* 47, 80 [1910]; DSPIEGELBERG, *Mythus*, 219, no. 574 [1917].

ϩⲱϫ (Crum 742b), 'cold' = (not in *Wb.*), *ḥdy*, 'cold'; (Er. 344, 8), *ḥḏy*, 'be cold'.

HBRUGSCH in *ZÄS* 13, 128 [1875]; DSPIEGELBERG, *Mythus*, 219, no. 575 [1917].

ϩϫⲟⲡϫⲡ (Crum 743a), 'grope, feel' (as blind man), see under ϫⲟⲡϫⲡ.

Sϩⲟϫϩϫ, Bϩⲟϫϩⲉϫ (Crum 743b), 'straighten, compel', reduplication of ϩⲱϫ, 'press'.

Sϩⲁϭⲉ, Bϩⲁϫⲓ (Crum 744a), 'snare' = (Er. 334, 1), *ḥḳy*, 'cord, snare'. Probably **ḥaꜣḳet* from the old verb (*Wb.* III, 32, 14), *ḥꜣḳ*; (Er. 333, 4), *ḥḳ*, 'to capture'.

DKRALL in *WZKM* 17, 6 [1903].

ϩⲱϭⲃ (Crum 744b), 'wither, fade, expire; destroy' = (Er. 273, 6), *ḥbḳ*, 'waste away, fade'.

ERICHSEN, *Dem. Glossar*, 273, 6 [1954].

Sϩⲁϭⲓⲛ, Bⲁϭⲓⲛ (Crum 744b), 'scented herb, mint' = (*Wb.* III, 180, 5–7), *ḥkn*, one of seven sacred oils.

Sϩⲁϭⲓⲛ ⲛⲥⲧⲟⲓ, Bⲁϭⲓⲛ ⲛⲥⲑⲟⲓ, same meaning = *, *ḥkn n sṯy*, lit. 'oil of odour' (*Wb.* IV, 349, 5 f.).

DÉVAUD's slip.

Ϫ

ϫⲁ(ⲉ)ⲓⲉ (Crum 745b), nn., 'desert' and **ϫⲁⲉⲓⲉ** (Crum 746a), Qual. **ϫⲁⲉⲓⲱⲟⲩ** (P. Bodmer XVI), 'become desert' = ? (*Wb.* v, 534, 12), *ḏꜥ*, 'be desert' or sim.

BRUGSCH, *Wb.*, Suppl. 381 [1882].

ϫⲉ- (Crum 746b), conjunction, 'namely', etc. = () (*Wb.* v, 624, 1–6), (*r*)*ḏd*, to introduce direct speech and as conjunction; and sim. (Er. 691, lower), *ḏd*, as conjunction.

^H^DE ROUGÉ, *Chrest. égypt.* III, 78 [1875]; ^D^BRUGSCH, *Gr. dém.* 190, §387 [1855].

ϫⲏ (Crum 747b), 'dish, bowl' for food, incense = (Er. 573, 4), *gꜥ*, 'vessel, censer'.

GRIFFITH, *Rylands*, III, 289 n. 2; 396 [1909].

ϫⲏ (Crum 747b), 'chip, mote' of straw, dust = cf. (*Wb.* II, 377, 7, 8), *nḏꜣ*, 'splinter' or sim.; (not in Er.), *ḏꜥ*, 'chaff'(?).

^H^EDEL, *Altägyptische grammatik*, p. xxxix [1955] = p. lxiv [1964]; ^D^THOMPSON, *Theban Ostraca (Demotic)*, 64 [1913].

ϫⲓⲛϫⲏ, 'emptiness, naught' < **ϫⲏ-ⲛ-ϫⲏ**, 'chip of a chip', i.e. '(practically) nothing'.

SPIEGELBERG, *Kopt. Handwb.* 261 [1921].

ϫⲓ (Crum 747b), 'receive, take' = (*Wb.* v, 346, 1 f.), *ṯꜣy*, 'take'; (Er. 663, 5), *ṯꜣy*, 'take'.

^H^DE ROUGÉ, *Oeuv. div.* III (= *Bibl. ég.* XXIII), 63 [1855] (who distinguishes clearly *ṯꜣy*, **ϫⲓ**, and *ṯꜣwt*, 'steal', **ϫⲓⲟⲩⲉ**); ^D^BRUGSCH, *Gr. dém.* 128, §262 [1855].

Part. coni. **ϫⲁⲓ-** (Crum 751b) = L.Eg. (*Wb.* v, 348, 1 ff.), *ṯꜣy*, 'carrier, holder' of something.

ϫⲓ in **ϫⲓⲟⲟⲣ** (Crum 751b), 'ferry over', different from preceding, see under **ⲉⲓⲟⲟⲣ**.

ϫⲓ (Crum 752a), a (metal) vessel from **ϫⲓ**, 'take' therefore 'container', cf. (*Wb.* v, 349, 5–8), *ṯꜣy*, a (wooden) receptacle, from (*Wb.* v, 346, 1 ff.), *ṯꜣy*, 'take'. See also **ϫⲛⲉϩ**.

DRESCHER's communication.

^{S}ϫⲟ, ^{B}(ⲧ)ϭⲟ (Crum 752 a), ‘sow, plant’ is etymologically identical with the following ^{S}ϫⲟ, ^{B}ϭⲟ, ‘put, send forth’, properly ‘cause to go (into ground)’.

SETHE, *Dem. Urk.* 191–2 [1920].

NB. If Spiegelberg’s etymology from *, *dỉt dgꜣ*, ‘cause [*sic*]t plant’ (*Kopt. Etym.* 16–17) were correct, we should on the contrary expect ^{S}ϭⲟ, ^{B}ϫⲟ. Steindorff (*Lehrbuch*, 129, §279) explains ϫⲟ as the causative of ϫⲓ, ‘take’, which suits excellently the correspondence ^{S}ϫ : ^{B}ϭ, but the meaning ‘cause to take’ is unsatisfactory.

^{S}ϫⲟ, ^{B}ϭⲟ [Crum 752 b], ‘put, send forth, spend’ = (*Wb.* IV, 465, 3. 4), *dỉt šm*, ‘cause to go, send’; (Er. 506, lower), *dỉt šm*, ‘cause to go, send’; phonetically , *tꜣ·f* for *d(ỉt) š(m)·f*, ‘put it’. ^{S}ϫⲟ therefore for *ⲧϣⲟ; ^{B}ϭⲟ- and not the expected ϫⲟ- like in ^{S}ϫⲉⲣⲟ, ^{B}ϭⲉⲣⲟ, ‘blaze, kindle’, ^{S}ϫⲛⲟⲩ, ^{B}ϭⲛⲟⲩ, ‘ask, question’, etc.

^{H}SETHE, *Verbum*, III, 94, s.v. ϫⲟⲟⲩ [1902]; ^{D}GRIFFITH–THOMPSON, I, 136 [1904]; cf. Spiegelberg, *Petubastis*, 59*, no. 402 [1910].

For form with plural suffix ·*w*, -ⲟⲩ, see ϫⲟⲟⲩ, ‘send’.

For ϫⲟ coalesced with ethical Dative *n*·, ⲛⲁ⸗, see the three verbs ϫⲛⲁ⸗.

^{A}ϫⲟ (Crum 753 b), ‘wind, tempest’ = (*Wb.* V, 533, 11 f.), *ḏꜥ*, ‘wind of tempest’.

DÉVAUD in Spiegelberg, *Kopt. Handwb.* 305 [1921].

ϫⲓ- in ϫⲓⲛⲧⲏⲩ, see under ⲧⲏⲩ.

ϫⲟ (Crum 753 b), ‘crook-back’ = (not in *Wb.*), *ḏꜣỉw*, ‘hump’.

DÉVAUD, *Études*, 39–41 [1922].

^{S}ϫⲟ, ^{B}ⲁϭⲟ (Crum 753 b), ‘arm-pit’ = (*Wb.* III, 204, 15. 16), *ẖtt*, ‘arm-pit’ (for the meaning, see Caminos, *Literary Fragments*, 15, note 1).

DÉVAUD, *Rec. trav.* 39, 161–3 [1921].

ϫⲟⲉ, ϫⲟⲓ, ϫⲟ (Crum 753 b), ‘wall’ = Pl. (*Wb.* V, 600, 4), *ḏrỉt*, ‘wall (of wood)’ > , *ḏy* (in the place-name , *Tꜣyw-ḏy*, Spiegelberg, *ZÄS* 53, 2 [1917]; Gauthier, *Dict. géogr.* VI, 7); (Er. 674, 4), *ḏy*, ‘wall’.

Plural ⲉϫⲏ = , *ꜣḏy* (Er. *loc. cit.*).

^{H}SETHE, *Verbum*, III, 92 [1902]; cf. Gardiner, *Admonitions*, 28 [1909]; ^{D}BRUGSCH, *Gr. dém.* 32, §63 [1855].

ϫⲟⲓ (Crum 754a), 'ship, boat' = (*Wb.* v, 515, 6), *ḏꜣy*, 'river-boat'; (Er. 674, 3), *ḏy*, 'ship'.
Plural **ⲉϫⲏⲩ** = , *ỉḏy* (Er. *loc. cit.*).
[H]DE ROUGÉ, *Oeuv. div.* II (= *Bibl. ég.* XXII), 198 [1851]; [D]REVILLOUT, *Pap. mor.* I, 257 n. 3 [1907].

ϫⲱ (Crum 754a), (1) 'say, speak, tell' = (*Wb.* v, 618, 9 ff.), *ḏd*, 'say'; (Er. 689, 1), *ḏd*, 'say'.
[H]CHAMPOLLION, *Dict.* 174 [1841]; [D]ÅKERBLAD in Young, *Works*, III, 37 [1815]; cf. Brugsch, *Scriptura Aeg. dem.* 56 and *passim* [1848].
ⲉϫⲟⲟⲥ ϫⲉ- (Crum 754b), '(as for) saying' = , *ỉḏd·s* < *r ḏd st*, lit. 'to say it'.
THOMPSON, *A Family Archive*, Text, 56 n. 17 [1934].
ϫⲉⲣⲟ-, **ϫⲉⲣⲟ⸗** (Crum 755b), 'mean' < **ϫⲉ ⲉⲣⲟ⸗** < , *ḏd r*, lit. 'say concerning'; Gr.-R. (e.g. Mariette, *Dendérah*, IV, 37, 66), *ḏd r*, 'called'; Demotic (Griffith–Thompson, III, 84, no. 888), *ḏd r*, 'means'. Cf. **ⲛⲁⲣⲟ**, 'observe'.
[H]SPIEGELBERG, *Rec. trav.* 34, 156 [1912]; cf. Steindorff, *Kopt. Gr.* 2nd ed. p. 43*, note *b* [1904]; [D]STRICKER's communication.
(2) 'sing' (Crum 755b) = (*Wb.* v, 621, 17, 18), *ḏd*, 'sing'; (Er. 691, 1), *ḏd*, 'sing, song', different only in writing from *ḏd*, 'say'.
[D]REVILLOUT, *Poème*, p. 13 (verse 35) and passim [1885].
ⲣⲉϥϫⲱ (Crum 756a), 'singer, minstrel' = (Er. 691, bottom), *rmt ỉw·f ḏd*, lit. 'man who sings'.
REVILLOUT, *Chrest. dém.* 430 [1880].

ϫⲱ⸗ (Crum 756a), 'head' = (*Wb.* v, 530, 5 ff.), *ḏꜣḏꜣ*, 'head'; (Er. 673, 3), *ḏ(ꜣ)ḏ(ꜣ)*, 'head'.
[H]DE ROUGÉ, *Oeuv. div.* II (= *Bibl. ég*, XXII), 196 [1851]; cf. CHAMPOLLION, *Gr.* 92 [1836]; [D]BRUGSCH, *Scriptura Aeg. dem.* 60, §XIV [1848].
ϫⲱ⸗ from **ϫⲱϫ**, see this latter.
SETHE, *Verbum*, I, 36, §60 bis [1899].
ⲟⲩⲉϩ ϫⲱ⸗ (Crum 756b), 'bend the head', < *wꜣḥ ḏꜣḏꜣ*, cf. the synonymous (*Wb.* I, 257, 1), *wꜣḥ tp*, 'bend the head'.
ERMAN–GRAPOW, *Wb.* I, 257, 1 [1926].
ⲉϫⲛ- (Crum 757a), 'upon, over', etc. = (*Wb.* v, 531, 8),

r ḏ3ḏ3, 'upon the head of'; [demotic] (Er. 673, bottom), *r-ḏ3ḏ3*, 'upon, to the charge of, for, on account of'.

ᴰBRUGSCH, *Gr. dém.* 172, §333 [1855].

ϩⲁϫⲛ-, ᴮϧⲁϫⲉⲛ- (Crum 758 a), 'beside', lit. 'under the head of' = [demotic], (Er. 673, bottom), *ẖr ḏ3ḏ3*, 'beside'.

GRIFFITH–THOMPSON, III, 99, no. 1094 [1909]; cf. Gunn, *JEA* 27, 144–5 [1941].

ϩⲓϫⲛ- (Crum 758 b), 'on head of', so 'upon, over' = [hieroglyphs] (*Wb.* v, 531, 8), *ḥr ḏ3ḏ3*, 'on head of'; [demotic] (Er. 673, bottom), *ḥr ḏ3ḏ3*, 'upon, after'.

ᴰBRUGSCH, *Gr. dém.* 172, 332 [1855].

ϫⲱ (Crum 759 b), 'cup' = [hieroglyphs] (*Wb.* v, 532, 1 f.), *ḏ3ḏ3w*, 'pot', spelt [hieroglyphs], *ḏ3y*, in unpubl. hierat. O. Berlin 12635; [demotic] (Er. 692, 1), *ḏd*, 'cup'.

ᴴERMAN–GRAPOW, *Wb.* v, 532, 1 [1931]; ᴰBRUGSCH, *Gr. dém.* 33, §66 [1855]; cf. Maspero, *Rec. trav.* 1, 37 n. 56 [1870].

ϫⲃⲃ(ⲉ)ⲥ (Crum 760 a), 'coal' = [hieroglyphs] (*Wb.* v, 536, 8 f.), *ḏʿbt*, 'charcoal'; [demotic] (Er. 677, 3), *ḏbt*, 'charcoal'.

After the loss of final *t* -ⲥ was added under influence of ϩⲏⲃⲥ, 'lamp'.

ᴴBRUGSCH, *Wb.* 1675 [1868]; ᴰGRIFFITH–THOMPSON, III, 98, no. 1074 [1909].

ᴮϫⲁⲃϫⲓⲃ (Crum 760 b), 'small' in stature, see under ˢϭⲉⲃϭⲓⲃ, 'fragments(?)'.

ϫⲱⲕ (Crum 761 a), 'complete, finish' = [demotic] (Er. 687, 3), *ḏk*, 'complete, be completed'.

REVILLOUT, *Poème*, 17 [1885].

ᴮϫⲉⲕ ⲣⲱ⸗ (Crum 289 a), 'fill mouth, satisfy', see ⲣⲟ, 'mouth'.

ϫⲱ(ⲱ)ⲕⲉ (Crum 763 a), 'prick, sting, goad' = [demotic] (Er. 687, 4), *ḏkʿ*, 'hit, engrave'.

GRIFFITH–THOMPSON, III, 99, no. 1090 [1909].

ϫⲱⲕⲙ (Crum 763 a), 'wash, wet' = [demotic] (Er. 687, 5), *ḏkm*, 'wash, bathe'.

BRUGSCH, *De natura*, 38 [1850].

ϫⲓⲕⲣⲓⲥ (Crum 764a), ‘panther, tiger’ is Greek τίγρις, ‘tiger’.
CRUM, *A Coptic Dict.* 764a [1939].

ϫⲉⲕⲁⲁⲥ (Crum 764a), conj. ‘that, in order that’ = *  > **ϫⲉ + ⲕⲁⲁⲥ**, ‘to say: let it (be that)’, pronominal form of **ⲕⲱ** (Crum 95a, under g).
POLOTSKY in *Gött. gel. Anz.* 1934, 59 n. 1 [1934]; cf. STEINDORFF, *Lehrbuch*, 101, §208, note [1951].

^{B}**ϫⲟⲕⲥⲓ** (Crum 765a), ‘crepitus ventris’ = ^{S}**ϭⲁⲧⲥⲉ**; see **ⲥⲁⲣ-ϭⲁⲧⲥⲉ**.

^{B}**ϫⲟⲩⲕϩ** (Crum 765a), ‘prick, bite’ = ^{S}**ϫⲱ(ⲱ)ⲕⲉ** (see this), the ‘ayyin being expressed by **ϩ**.

ϫⲉⲕϫⲓⲕ (Crum 765a), ‘ant’ or other insect. Found as a loan-word in Egn. Arabic as زقزق, species of ant.
STERN in *ZÄS* 21, 22 n. 1 [1883].

ϫⲟⲕϫⲕ (Crum 765a), ‘prick, brand, braid’, reduplication of **ϫ(ⲱ)ⲱⲕⲉ** = **ϫⲟⲩⲕϩ**, see the former.

^{B}**ϫⲁⲗ** (Crum 765b), ‘branch’ = 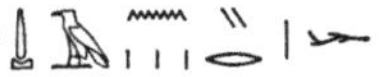 (*Wb.* v, 577, 4), *ḏnr*, ‘branch’; Dem. σγολ (*Actes du Ve congrès intern. de papyrologie*, 79) translating μόσχος.
^{H}CHABAS, *Oeuv. div.* III (= *Bibl. ég.* XI), 465 [1869].

^{BF}**ϫⲟⲗ**, ^{BF}**ϭⲁⲗ** (Crum 765b), ‘wave’; from Semitic, cf. Hebr. גַּל ‘heap, wave’, Aram. גַּלָּא.
ROSSI, *Etym. aeg.* 318 [1808].

^{B}**ϫⲟⲩⲗ** (Crum 765b), ‘fragment’ or sim., from Semitic, cf. Hebrew מְגִלָּה, ‘a roll’ and Aram. מְגִלְּתָא, Eth. ግላ (*gĕlā*), Syriac ܓܠܐ (Brockelmann, p. 54b).
ROSSI, *Etym. aeg.* 321 [1808].
NB. If, however, it were assumed that the meaning of this hapax was ‘veil, web’, it would be possible to explain it as identical with **-ϫⲟⲩⲗ** of **ⲥⲧⲁϫⲟⲩⲗ**, ‘spider’; see this latter.

[S]ϫⲱ(ⲱ)ⲗⲉ, [B]ϭⲱⲗ (Crum 766a), 'gather harvest' (fruit, corn, flowers) = (*Wb.* v, 539, 8 f.), *ḏʿr*, 'seek, collect'; (Er. 684, 9), *ḏlʿ*, or , *ḏʿl*, 'collect'.

[H]ČERNÝ, *Crum Mem. Vol.* 44–5 [1950]; [D]REVILLOUT, *PSBA* 9, 268–9 [1887].

ϫⲗⲁ (Crum 766b), meaning unknown = ?Gr.-R. (*Wb.* v, 387, 2), *ṯrʿ*, kind of field; (Er. 685, 1), *ḏlʿ*, kind of field.

[HD]CRUM, *A Coptic Dict.* 766b [1939].

ϫⲱⲗⲕ (Crum 766b), 'stretch, extend', loan-word from Semitic, cf. דָּרַךְ, 'tread, stretch (a bow)', Ar. أدرك (IVth form), 'reach, overtake'.

DÉVAUD's slip.

ϫⲱⲗϩ (Crum 769a), 'cut, prune', probably the same verb as (ϫⲗⲁϩ), Qual. ϫⲟⲗϩ, 'be smallest, least', see this latter.

[SB]ϫⲱⲗϩ (Crum 769a), 'draw, scoop' water, wine = (Er. 685, 2), *ḏlḥ*, or , *ḏlḥ*, 'draw, scoop', probably from a Semitic √*ṣlḥ* from which Hebrew צַלַּחַת, 'dish', etc. (see ϫⲗⲁϩⲧⲥ); also ?Aram. זלח, 'scoop'.

GRIFFITH–THOMPSON, III, 98, no. 1086 [1909]; cf. BRUGSCH, *Wb.* 1699 [1868] (who compares *ḏlḥ* with ϫⲟⲗϩⲥ (Crum 769b: 'vessel, tube for pouring'), a derivative of ϫⲱⲗϩ); [S]STRICKER in *Acta Orientalia* 15, 4 [1937] (compares זלח).

(ϫⲗⲁϩ), Qual. ϫⲟⲗϩ (Crum 769b), 'become smallest, least', lit. 'be cut down' (see ϫⲱⲗϩ, 'cut') = ? (*Wb.* v, 388, 4), *ṯrḥ*, 'laugh at, disdain' or sim.; (Er. 686, 1), *ḏlḥ*, 'be small, tiny'.

[H]ERICHSEN, *Dem. Glossar*, 686, 1 [1954]; [D]BRUGSCH, *Wb.* 1160 [1868].

ϫⲗⲁϩⲙⲉⲥ (Crum 769b), meaning unknown, perhaps for *ϫⲁⲗ-ϩⲙⲥ 'collector (part. coni. of ϫⲱⲱⲗⲉ) of ears' like (Er. 685, lower), *ḏlꜣ-ḥms*, a word for 'locust', in Vienna Petubastis (ed. Bresciani) 13, 2 with determinative of metal, therefore, like in Coptic, perhaps an object ('rake'?).

ϫⲱⲗϩⲥ (Crum 769b), 'become exhausted?', if correct is secondary formation on ϫ(ⲉ)ⲗϩⲏⲥ. ϫ(ⲉ)ⲗϩⲏⲥ, 'become exhausted, pant' = ϫⲉⲗϩ (from ϫⲱⲗϩ, 'cut down') + ⲗϩⲏⲥ (see under ⲉⲗϩⲏⲥ), 'be cut down as to breath'.

ϫⲗⲁϩⲧⲥ (Crum 770a, emend into ϫⲗⲁϩⲧⲉ?), 'deep pit, vessel' = (not in *Wb.*, ex. O.DM 318, vo. 8), *ḏḥrt*, a vessel, in Akkadian transcription *zilaḫda*, from Semitic, cf. צֵלָחַת, צְלֹחוֹת (Pl.), צְלֹחִית, Syriac etc. (see W. Max Müller, *OLZ* 2 [1899], col. 187).

ϫⲟⲗϫⲗ (Crum 770a), 'surround with hedge', reduplication of ϫⲱ(ⲱ)ⲗⲉ, 'gather harvest', see this latter.

ϫⲟⲗϫ(ⲉ)ⲗ (Crum 770a and 815b, s.v. ϭⲟⲗϭ(ⲉ)ⲗ), 'let drip, drip' = (Er. 686, 4), *ḏlḏl* 'let drip'.
BRUGSCH, *Gr. dém.* 33, §66 [1855].

ϫⲱⲙ (Crum 770b), 'generation' = (*Wb.* v, 523, 4 f.), *ḏ3m*, 'youth, generation'; (Er. 678, 1), *ḏm*, 'generation, descendant'.
HDE ROUGÉ, *Oeuv. div.* II (=*Bibl. ég.* XXII), 198 [1851]; DREVILLOUT in *Journ. as.* 1908, 295 n. 2; *Pap. mor.*, II, 57 n. 2 [1908].

A2**ϫⲱⲙ** (Crum 770b), 'meaning uncertain' (Allberry: 'strive?'), constr. with ⲁ- = (Er. 678, 3), *ḏꜥm*, 'crush, press upon', constr. with , *r*.

ϫⲁⲙⲏ (Crum 770b), 'calm' = (Er. 678, 2), *ḏm*, 'be calm, lazy', 'calm' (of wind).
GRIFFITH, *Stories*, 198 [1900].
See also A2ϫⲁⲙⲏⲧ.

ϫⲱⲱⲙⲉ (Crum 770b), 'sheet, roll of papyrus, written document, book' = (*Wb.* v, 574, 3 f.), *ḏmꜥ*, 'papyrus (sheet or roll)'; (Er. 679, 1), *ḏmꜥ*, 'papyrus (book)'.
HDE HORRACK, *Oeuv. div.* (=*Bibl. ég.* XVII), 11 n. 2 [1862]; DBRUGSCH, *Gr. dém.* 35, § 71 [1855].

ϫ(ⲉ)ⲙⲡⲉϩ (Crum 771b), 'apple' = (*Wb.* v, 568, 10), *ḏpḥ*, 'apple'; (Er. 677, 8), *ḏpḥ*, or , *ḏmpḥ*, 'apple', a loan-word from Semitic, cf. Hebrew תַּפּוּחַ 'apple', Arabic تفّاح.
HLORET, *Rec. trav.* 7, 113 f. [1886]; LORET, *Flore*, 2nd ed., 82–3 [1892]; DBRUGSCH, *Gr. dém.* 25, §44 [1855]; SROSSI, *Etym. aeg.* 314 [1808].

A2ϫⲁⲙⲏⲧ (not in Crum; only in ⲙⲛⲧϫⲁⲙⲏⲧ Mani Ps. 70, 31), 'still, quiet of heart' < *ϫⲁⲙ-ϩⲏⲧ, ϫⲁⲙ- = (Er. 678, 2), *ḏm*, '(be) still'.
See also ϫⲁⲙⲏ, 'calm'.

Bϫⲓⲙⲫⲉϩ (Crum 771 b), 'blight' = *, *dᶜ n pt*, lit. 'storm of sky'. -ϩ added under influence of Sϫ(ⲉ)ⲙⲡⲉϩ, Bϫⲉⲙⲫⲉϩ, 'apple'.
SPIEGELBERG, *Kopt. Handwb.* 271, 305 [1921].

ϫⲓⲛ- (Crum 772 b), prep. '(starting) from', 'since' = AETH or (where stands for) (not in *Wb.*), *tꜣ-n*, '(starting) from'; (Er. 667, 1), *n-ṯ n*, also , *tꜣ*, only, 'from, since'.
HSCHÄFER, *Nastesen*, 59, 82 [1901]; DBRUGSCH, *Gr. dém.* 177, § 343 [1855].

Bϫⲁⲛⲟ (Crum 773 b), 'basket(?)' full of earth = (*Wb.* v, 575, 10; the ref. is now *CT* II, 203 a), *ḏnἰw*, Pl., 'baskets', related to Semitic, cf. Aram. צַנָּא, Hebrew טֶנֶא, unless these are loan-words from Egyptian.
SDÉVAUD in Crum, *A Coptic Dict.* 773 b [1939].

Sϫⲛⲁ⸗, Fϫⲁⲛ⸗ (Crum 773 b), 'strike, deal' blows (ⲥⲏϣⲉ, ϩⲓⲥⲉ and sim.) < ϯ + ϣⲉ + (dat.) ⲛⲁ⸗, 'cause that (blows) should go to...', therefore essentially the same as ϫⲛⲁ⸗, 'send', see the next entry.

Sϫⲛⲁ⸗, Aϫⲉⲛⲉ⸗ (Crum 774 a), 'send' (only person as obj.) = ϯ + ϣⲉ + ⲛⲁ⸗ (ethic dative), 'cause that...should go', Egn. *dἰt šm·f n·f*, 'cause that he should go for himself'. The suffix of the dative was misinterpreted as pronominal object and the true object (originally subject) after ϣⲉ was omitted. Cf. Dem. Mag. Pap. 3, 28: *ἰἰr·k wḫꜣ r dἰt šmἰ* (sic! not *šmἰ·w*) *n·w*, 'if you wish to make them depart' (ex. due to Stricker).
NB. Fϭⲁⲛⲛⲁ-, ϭⲉⲛⲁ⸗, ϭⲁⲛⲛⲁ⸗ listed by Crum as the Fayyûmic equivalent of Sϫⲛⲁ⸗ is a different word, 'compile, make (a list)' [Till, *CPR*, IV, 1, 1.10.13].

Oϫⲛⲁ⸗ (Crum 774 a) from Hor. 84 can be interpreted as the prec. word and the passage translated '(and) send to him a child from year 42... again', see *JEA* 43, 88, l. 152, and n. 152 on p. 93, and cf. what has been said on the origin of Sϫⲛⲁ⸗, 'send'.

^{S}ϫ(ⲉ)ⲛⲁ, ϫⲛⲉ-, ϫⲉⲛⲁ⸗, ^{B}ϭⲉⲛⲟ, ϭⲉⲛⲟ⸗ (Crum 774a), 'be quenched, quench, make cease' is a special case of ϫⲛⲁ⸗, 'send'. E.g. Mor 53, 63 'I am light come ⲉϫⲛⲉ ⲡⲕⲁⲕⲉ to make the darkness depart' is lit. 'to cause that the darkness should go (for itself)'.

ϫⲛⲉ, ϫⲛⲏ (Crum 774a), 'beet' or 'green herbs' generally, cf. ? [hieroglyphs] (*Wb*. v, 575, 5), *d̲nw*, a plant.

ϫⲛⲟⲩ, ^{B}ϭⲛⲟⲩ, ϫⲛⲉ-, ϫⲛⲟⲩ- (Crum 774b), 'ask, question, require' are pronominal and construct infinitives of ϣⲟϫⲛⲉ (see this). ϫⲛⲟⲩ⸗ < **set̲nōy⸗*, ϫⲛⲉ- < **set̲ney-*.

STEINDORFF, *Kopt. Gr.* 1st ed., 112, §245 [1894]; cf. Sethe, *Verbum*, II, 275, §632, 4 [1899].

ϫⲉⲛⲉⲡⲱⲣ (Crum 775a), 'roof' = * [hieroglyphs], *d̲3d̲3 n pr*, lit. 'head of the house', compare [hieroglyphs] (*Wb*. v, 290, 8), *tp-ḥwt*, 'roof', lit. 'head of the mansion'.

MASPERO, *Rec. trav.* 16, 78 [1894] (explains ⲡⲱⲣ differently).

ϫⲱⲛⲧ (Crum 775a), 'try, test' = [demotic] (Er. 682, 5), *d̲nt*, 'test, consider'.

HESS, *Gnost. Pap.* 17 [1892].

^{S}ϫⲛ(ⲁ)ⲁⲩ, ^{B}ϭⲛⲁⲩ (Crum 776a), intr. 'delay' < *ϯ + ϣⲉ + Plural subject + ⲛⲁⲩ, 'cause that...should go away for themselves'. For similar cases, see ϫⲛⲁ⸗, 'strike' blows, ϫⲛⲁ⸗, 'send' and ϫ(ⲉ)ⲛⲁ, 'quench, make cease'.

ϫⲛⲟⲟⲩ (Crum 776b), 'threshing floor', grain 'heaped' there = [hieroglyphs] (*Wb*. v, 575, 6), *d̲nw*, 'threshing area' (see Gardiner, *JEA* 27, 63 for the meaning); [demotic] (Er. 681, 1), *d̲nw*, 'threshing area'.

^{H}BRUGSCH, *Wb*., Suppl. 1384 [1882]; ^{D}ERICHSEN, *Dem. Glossar*, 681, 1 [1954].

ϫⲱⲛϥ (Crum 776b), basic meaning 'correspond, coincide, agree', then 'happen to (do)', 'chance (to be present)', trans. 'meet with, fall upon' = [demotic] (Er. 681, 2), *d̲nf*, 'be even, correct, average, corresponding', etc.

REVILLOUT, *Pap. mor.* I, 21 [1905].

See also ^{B}ϭⲛⲟⲩϥ.

ϫⲛⲟϥ (Crum 777a), 'basket, crate' = (Er. 682, 1), *ḏnf*, 'basket', a loan-word from Semitic, cf. Arabic كنف. The modern Egn. Arabic شنف is a descendant of ϫⲛⲟϥ (cf. Crum, s.v.).

DSPIEGELBERG, *Kopt. Handwb.* 273 [1921]; SROSSI, *Etym. Aeg.* 318 [1808].

ϫⲛⲁϩ (Crum 777a), 'forearm' = (*Wb.* v, 578, 11), *ḏnḥ*, 'upper part of the foreleg, shoulder' (see Gardiner, *Onom.* II, 244*, no. 595, for the meaning), and (*Wb.* v, 578, 13), *ḏnḥ*, 'handle' of a rudder; (Er. 682, 4), *ḏnḥ*, 'arm, forearm'. Ultimately related to Semitic (cf. זְרוֹעַ, ذراع, 'arm'), or borrowed therefrom (cf. Stricker, *Acta Orientalia* 15, 6 [1937]).

HBRUGSCH, *Rhind*, 44 and Pl. 40, no. 292 [1865]; DBRUGSCH, *Gr. dém.* 28, §56 [1855].

Fϫⲛⲉϩ (Crum 777b), container or measure = ϫⲓ, a container + ⲛⲉϩ, 'oil'; in the only ex. known ϫⲛⲉϩ measures or contains ⲃⲁⲣⲛⲉϩ, 'linseed'.

DRESCHER's communication.

Bϫⲁⲛⲏϩⲓ (Crum 777b), part of water-wheel, طارة, rope to which pots oı water-wheel are attached (*ZÄS* 14, 84) or wheel itself (*ZÄS* 76, 47), therefore ?'circuit'; cf. (*Wb.* v, 55, 2), *ḳnḥ*, of gargoyles which '*run round*' under the roof of the temple.

Sϫⲡ-, Bⲁϫⲡ- (Crum 777b), 'hour' followed by fem. (?) numeral, probably < ⲧ-ϣⲡ-, for which see under ϣⲱⲡ, 'moment, instant'. From Boh. form the Arabic plural اجبية, '(canonical) hours' (Mallon in *Mélanges de la Faculté Orientale de l'Université Saint-Joseph* (Beyrouth), 2, 236 n. 2 [1907]). NB. The etymology proposed by Sethe (*Beiträge zur ältesten Geschichte Ägyptens*, 92 [1905] from , 'hour' is untenable, since this latter word is to be read not *ḏbꜥt*, but almost certainly *wnwt* (and is consequently ⲟⲩⲛⲟⲩ), see Spiegelberg, *Petubastis*, Glossary, 15* n. 1 [1910]; Erman-Grapow, *Wb.* v, 567, bottom [1931]; Fairman's letter of 22 Nov. 1964.

ϫⲟⲡ (Crum 778a), 'dish, bowl' = , *ṯꜣb*, , *ṯb* (*Wb.* v, 354, 1 f.), a vessel; (Er. 677, 7), *ḏp*, 'bowl', or sim.

HDÉVAUD's slip; DERICHSEN, *Dem. Glossar*, 677, 7 [1954].

ϫⲡⲓⲟ (Crum 778b), 'blame, upbraid', < *ⲧϣⲡⲓⲟ, causative of ϣⲓⲡⲉ = *, *dỉt špt* (*Wb.* IV, 453, 10 f.), 'cause to be annoyed, ashamed'.

ERMAN, *ZÄS* 22, 30 [1884]; cf. Erman, *Näg. Gr.* 190, §285 [1880] (for *špt*).

ϫⲡⲟ (Crum 778b), 'beget, bring forth', < *ⲧϣⲡⲟ, [A]ⲧϩⲡⲟ, causative of ϣⲱⲡⲉ = (*Wb.* III, 264, 5–15), *dỉt ḫpr·*, 'cause to take origin'; (Griffith–Thompson, III, 65, no. 652), *dỉt ḫpr·*, same meaning.

[H]ERMAN, *ZÄS* 22, 30 [1884]; Bouriant, *Mém. mission arch. franç.* I, 282 [1885]; [D]GRIFFITH–THOMPSON, III, 65, no. 652 [1909].

ϫⲟⲡϫⲡ, ϩϫⲟⲡϫⲡ (Crum 743a under ϩϫⲟⲡϫⲡ), [A2]ϫⲁⲡϫⲡ, ϫⲉⲡϫⲱⲡ≈, 'grope, feel (like a blind man)' = (not in *Wb.*, cf. *JEA* 19, Pl. XXIX, 7), *ḏbḏb*, 'crush by treading', reduplication of ϫⲱⲱⲃⲉ, 'pass by, over'.

(ϩ)ⲡⲟϭⲡϭ, ϩⲡⲟϫⲡϫ is a different word since Mani K 209, 50 uses ϩⲡⲁϭⲡϭ as against [ϫⲁⲡ]ϫⲡ of Mani K 208, 32.

ϫⲓⲣ (Crum 780b), 'brine, small salted fish', from Semitic, cf. صير, 'small salted fish', New Hebr. צִיר, 'fish soup'.

DÉVAUD's slip.

ⲁⲛϫⲓⲣ (Crum 781a), 'lotion, paste of salt', as soap = (Er. 6, 3), *ỉnḏyr*, < **ʿ-n-ḏyr*, 'piece of salt' as soap.

BRUGSCH, *Wb.* 10 [1867].

ϫⲱⲣ (Crum 781a), 'sharpen, whet', from Semitic, cf. Arabic ظَرَّ 'be sharp', Hebrew √צרר.

DÉVAUD in Crum, *A Coptic Dict.* 781a [1939].

ϫⲉⲣⲟ (Crum 781b), 'kindle' = Gr.-R. (*Wb.* V, 595, 14), *ḏr*, 'fire', or sim.; (Er. 669, 1), *ṯꜣy-rꜣ* (*ṯr*), 'kindle', unetymologically for *ty ḫt* (Er. 345, 3) *r*, 'put fire on', L.Eg. (*Wb.* III, 217, 12), *dỉt ḫt r*. The preposition coalesced with the verb as in ϫⲉⲣⲟ-, 'mean' (see under ϫⲱ) and ⲛⲁⲣⲟ.

[D]BRUGSCH, *Gr. dém.* 27, §53; 130, §269 [1855].

ϫⲏⲣⲉ (Crum 782a), 'threshing-floor' = (Er. 683, 3), *ḏryt*, 'threshing-floor'.

REVILLOUT, *Revue ég.* 9, 14 n. 2 [1900]; 13, 14 n. 3 [1911].

ϫωωρε (Crum 782a), 'scatter, disperse' = L.Eg. (*Wb.* v, 603, 4), 'scatter'; (Er. 684, 1), *ḏrʿ*, 'scatter, spread'; probably a loan-word from Semitic, cf. either Hebrew זָרָה, New Hebrew זָרָה, or זָרַע, 'to sow'.

[H]ČERNÝ, *Crum Mem. Vol.* 45 [1950]; [D]KRALL, *Mitt. aus der Sammlung Erzh. Rainer*, VI, 78, no. 357 [1897]; [S]ROSSI, *Etym. aeg.* 315 [1808] (from זרה; STRICKER in *Acta Orientalia* 15, 4 [1937] (from זרע).

[S]**ϫρο**, [B]**ϭρο** (Crum 783a), 'become strong, firm, victorious'; (Crum 783b), 'victory, strength' = (Er. 682, 6), *ḏr*, also , *ḏrꜣ*, 'become strong, victorious; strength; strong'.

ÅKERBLAD in Young, *Works*, III, 37 [1815]; cf. CHAMPOLLION, *Gr.* 357 [1836].

ϫωωρε (Crum 784b), 'strength, (be) strong' = (*Wb.* v, 599, 1 ff.), *ḏrỉ*, 'strong; strongly' in Demotic not distinguishable from *ḏr* = **ϫρο**.

[H]ERMAN-GRAPOW, *Äg. Handwb.* 221 [1921]; cf. DE ROUGÉ, *Revue ég.* 3, 152 n. 6 [1885]; [D]SAULCY, *Anal. gram.*, 34 [1845]; cf. Brugsch, *Gr. dém.* 36, §76; 120, §243 [1855].

[B](**ϫωρεϧ**) (Crum 785a), 'cut open(?)', see under **κωρϥ**, 'bring to naught'.

ϫωρⲙ (Crum 785b), (1) 'make sign, beckon' = (*Wb.* v, 387, 12 f.) *ṯrm*, 'twinkle, blink'; (Vienna Petubastis, N 1), *ḏlm*, 'wink'.

[H]SPIEGELBERG in *ZÄS* 54, 134–5 [1918]; [D]SPIEGELBERG, *Petubastis*, 59, n. 14 [1910].

(2) 'urge, drive, hasten' = (*LRL*, 20, 7), *rṯm* for *ṯrm* (confusion of *rṯ* and *ṯr* not being uncommon in hieratic), 'train (an animal)'; (Er. 684, 4), also *ḏrm*, 'touch, move', and sim.

[H]WENTE, *Late Ramesside Letters*, 41, note *ag* [1967]; [D]SPIEGELBERG, *Mythus*, 19, 33 [1917].

[S]**ϫωρπ**, (*[B]**ϭωρεπ**) (Crum 786a), 'stumble, trip' = (*Wb.* v, 387, 10), *ṯrp*, 'stumble (of a drunk person)'; (not in Er.; exx. Ankhsh. 10, 7 twice; 14, 15), *ḏrp*, 'stumble', also (Er. 584, 11), *grp*, 'offend; offence'.

[H]GARDINER, *PSBA* 38, 184 [1916]; [D]VOLTEN in *Archiv Orientální* 20, 505 [1952]; cf. Spiegelberg, *Mythus*, 284, no. 885 [1917].

[A2] **ϫⲁⲣⲏⲧ** (Natura rerum) = [SBF] **ϫⲁⲣϩⲏⲧ** (Crum 784b, s.v. **ϫⲣⲟ**, **ϫⲱⲱⲣⲉ**), 'strong of heart'.

ϫⲟⲣϫⲣ (Crum 787a), 'overcome', or sim., reduplication of **ϫⲣⲟ**, see this.

ϫⲟⲉⲓⲥ (Crum 787b), 'lord' = (*Wb.* v, 402, 9–19), *ṯsw*, 'commander'; (Er. 671, 1), *ṯs*, 'commander, officer, chief, lord'; fem. . From *ṯsy*, **ϫⲓⲥⲉ**.

[H] Erman, *Äg. Glossar*, 148 [1904]; [D] Brugsch in *ZÄS* 26, 59–61 [1888]; Hess, *Stne*, 185 [1888].

ϫⲱⲥ (Crum 788b), 'pack, load, harden' = (*Wb.* v, 396, 13 f.), *ṯs*, 'to knot, pack'; (Er. 670, 1), *ṯs*, 'to knot, tie'.

[H] Erman, *Äg. Glossar*, 148 [1904]; [D] Möller, *Pap. Rhind*, 61*, no. 434 [1913].

ϫⲓⲥⲉ (Crum 788b), 'exalt' = (*Wb.* v, 405, 1 ff.), *ṯsy*, 'set up(right), lift up', 'ascend'; (Er. 670, 2), *ṯs(y)*, 'ascend, lift up'.

[H] Chabas, *Voyage*, 127–8 [1866]; [D] Brugsch, *Rhind*, 44 and Pl. 40, no. 289 (in **ϭⲁⲥⲓ-ϩⲧⲟ**) [1865]; cf. Brugsch, *Wb.* 1592–3 [1868]. See also **ϫⲟⲉⲓⲥ**, 'lord'.

ϫⲓⲥⲉ (Crum 790b), 'back' = (*Wb.* v, 400, 10–13), *ṯst*, 'vertebra'; (not in Er. cf. Griffith–Thompson, III, 96, no. 1058), *ṯsỉ*, 'back, top'.

[HD] Brugsch, *Wb.* 1596 [1868].

ϫⲁⲥϥⲉ (Crum 790b), 'set in order, repair' = (Er. 687, 2), *ḏsft*, building(?), 'hypothec'.

Brugsch, *ZÄS* 10, 28 [1872].

ϫⲟⲉⲓⲧ (Crum 790b), 'olive tree, its fruit' = (*Wb.* v, 618, 4. 5), *ḏt*, 'olive tree', 'olive'; (Er. 674, 7), *ḏyṯ*, 'olive tree'. From Semitic, cf. Hebrew זַיִת, Arabic زَيْت, 'olive(-tree)'.

[H] Brugsch, *Wb.*, Suppl. 1388 [1882]; [D] Brugsch, *Gr. dém.* 25, §45 [1855].

ϫⲱⲧⲉ (Crum 791b), 'pierce, penetrate' = (*Wb.* v, 636, 1), *ḏdt*(?), 'pierce (with eyes)'.

Dévaud, *Kêmi* 2, 17 [1929].

ϫⲧⲁⲓ (Crum 792a), 'ripen' = Gr.-R. (*Wb.* v, 631, 10 f.), *ḏdꜣ*, 'ripen, let ripen' < (*Wb.* v, 631, 3 f.), *ḏdꜣ*, 'fat'.

ERMAN–GRAPOW, *Äg. Handwb.* 223 [1921]; SPIEGELBERG, *Kopt. Handwb.* 278 [1921].

S**ϫⲧⲟ** (for *ⲧϣⲧⲟ), B**ϣⲧⲟ** (Crum 792a), 'lay down', also 'make sleep' (Till) = ?, *dỉt sḏr·*, 'cause to sleep, lay down'; , also (Er. 480, 5), *štr* (*št*(*r*)), 'lay down, sleep'.

HERMAN, *ZÄS* 22, 30 [1884]; DGRIFFITH, *Ryl.* III, 391 [1909] (doubtfully).

ϫⲁⲧⲙⲉ (Crum 792b), 'heap' of grain = (*Wb.* v, 634, 7–18), *ḏdmt*, 'heap'.

BRUGSCH, *Wb.* 1687 [1868] and Suppl. 1387 [1882].

ϫⲁⲧϥⲉ (Crum 792b), 'reptile' = (*Wb.* v, 633, 6 ff.), *ḏdft*, 'worm, snake'; (Er. 688, 1), *ḏtft*, 'worm'.

HCHAMPOLLION, *Gr.* 86 [1836]; DREVILLOUT, *Setna*, 19, 28 and passim [1877].

O**ϫⲧⲁϩ** (Crum 792b), 'prison' = (*Wb.* v, 635, 13), *ḏdḥw*, 'prison'; (Er. 688, 3), *ḏ*(*d*)*tḥ*, 'arrest' (subst. and noun).

HSPIEGELBERG, *Kopt. Handwb.* 280 [1921]; cf. Griffith, *ZÄS* 38, 78–9 [1900]; DERICHSEN, *Dem. Glossar*, 688, 3 [1954].

ϫⲟⲟⲩ (Crum 793a), 'send' = , *dỉt šm·w*, 'cause that they should go'; (Er. 506, middle), *dỉt š*(*m*)·, 'cause to go'.

HW. MAX MÜLLER, *Rec. trav.* 14, 20 [1893]; DGRIFFITH, *Stories*, 71 ('apparently') [1900]; GRIFFITH–THOMPSON, III, 79, no. 814 [1909]. For form without suffix ·*w*, **-ⲟⲩ**, see **ϫⲟ**, 'put, send forth'.

B**ϫⲱⲟⲩ** (Crum 793b), 'generation' = S**ϫⲱⲙ**, see this latter.

ϫⲓⲟⲩⲉ (Crum 793b), 'steal' = (*Wb.* v, 350, 2 f.), *ṯꜣw*, 'steal'; (Er. 676, 7), *ḏwy*, 'steal'.

HDE ROUGÉ, *Oeuv. div.* III (= *Bibl. ég.* XXIII), 63 [1855]; DBRUGSCH, *Sammlung dem. Urk.* 42 and Pl. 6, 20 [1850].

ⲛϫⲓⲟⲩⲉ (Crum 794a), 'stealthily' = (*Wb.* v, 350, 6–9), *m ṯꜣw*, 'stealthily, secretly', lit. 'through stealing'.

GARDINER, *Hierat. Texts*, 19* n. 17 [1911].

ϫⲟⲟⲩⲧ (Crum 794b), 'base, rejected person' or 'thing' = (not in Er.), *ḏwṯ*, 'impure', or sim.

REVILLOUT, *Poème*, 1 and Pl. 1 [1885]; cf. Parker, *JEA* 26, 102 [1940].

ϫⲟⲩⲱⲧ (Crum 794b), 'twenty' = ∩∩ (*Wb.* v, 552, 8), **ḏwt*, 'twenty', punning with and .

PLEYTE, *ZÄS* 5, 11 [1867].

ϫⲟⲟⲩϥ (Crum 795a), 'papyrus' = (*Wb.* v, 359, 6–10), *ṯwfy*, 'papyrus; papyrus thicket'; (Er. 676, 8), *ḏwf*, 'papyrus'. Hebrew סוּף from Egyptian.

^{H}BRUGSCH, *Wb.* 1580 [1868]; ^{D}BRUGSCH, *Gr. dém.* 25, §44 [1855].

^{A2}**ϫⲟⲩϫⲟⲩ** (Crum 795a, 'fly?', adding Mani P 157, 17; Böhlig-Labib 149, 12, 16, 20), also ⲧⲥⲟⲩⲧⲥⲟⲩ (Crum 437b), 'twitter' (of birds and men), onomatopoetic like ϫⲁϫ, 'sparrow', see this.

^{B}**ϫⲫⲟⲧ**(?), **ϫⲫⲱϯ** (Crum 795a), part of body whereof there are two = dual of = (*Wb.* v, 154, 1–5), *gꜣbt*, 'arm', the masc. (*Wb.* v, 163, 4–12), *gbꜣ*, 'arm', being ^{S}ϭⲃⲟⲓ, ^{B}ϫⲫⲟⲓ; (Er. 577, 3), *gbt* (fem.!), 'arm'.

^{HD}SOTTAS, *Révue ég.* N.S. 1, 130 [1919].

ϫⲟⲩϥ (Crum 795b), 'burn, scorch' = (*Wb.* v, 522, 8–13), *ḏꜣf*, 'burn'; (Er. 677, 10), *ḏf*, 'burn'.

^{H}BRUGSCH, *Wb.* 1694 [1868]; ^{D}BRUGSCH, *Scriptura Aeg. dem.* 19, §22 [1848].

ϫⲟϥⲧⲛ (Crum 796b), in ⲛϫⲟϥⲧⲛ 'headlong, over the edge' = (*Wb.* v, 366, 15; other exx. O. Cairo 25266, 2; P. Turin Cat. 2044, vo. II, 13; O. Cairo 25336, 2, 5), *ṯftn*, '(move) headlong' (see also *JEA* 12, 208 n. 2, for meaning).

LANGE, *Amenemope*, 66 [1925].

ϫⲟϥϫϥ (Crum 796b), 'burn, cook', reduplication of ϫⲟⲩϥ, 'burn' = Gr.-R. (*Wb.* v, 523, 2), *ḏ(ꜣ)fḏ(ꜣ)f*, 'burn'; (Er. 678, upper), *ḏfḏf*, 'burn, cook'.

^{H}ERMAN–GRAPOW, *Wb.* v, 523, 2 [1931]; ^{D}BRUGSCH, *Gr. dém.* 27, §53 [1855].

ϫⲓϩ (Crum 796b), 'spittle' = (Er. 673, 2), ḏ3k, 'spittle', and (Er. 673, 1), ḏ3ẖ, 'foam' (ἀφρός).

ϫⲱϩ (Crum 797a), 'touch' = (*Wb.* v, 389, 4), ṯḥy, 'touch'; (Er. 686, 6), ḏḥ, 'touch'.

HERMAN–GRAPOW, *Wb.* v, 389, 4 [1931]; DBRUGSCH, *Wb.* 1699 [1868].

ϫⲱϩ (Crum 797a), 'smear, anoint', loan-word from Semitic, cf. טוח, 'over-spread, besmear'.

DÉVAUD in Crum, *A Coptic Dict.* 797a [1939].

ϫⲟⲩϩⲉ (Crum 797b), 'limp, halt' = (*Wb.* v, 388, 10), ṯḥ3, 'limp'.

CAMINOS, *LEM*, 53 [1954].

Sϫⲱϩⲙ, Bϭⲱϧⲉⲙ (Crum 797b), 'defile, pollute' = (not in Er.), ḏḥm, 'pollute', probably from Semitic, cf. Hebrew זהם, 'make dirty'.

DPARKER, *JEA* 26, 93 [1940]; SROSSI, *Etym. Aeg.* 323 [1808].

ϫⲁϩϫϩ (Crum 798b), 'strike, gnash' = (*Wb.* v, 67, 6–8), ḳḥḳḥ, 'to hammer, beat'. Different from ⲕⲁϩⲕϩ = Egn. *kḥkḥ*.

BRUGSCH, *Wb.*, Suppl. 1264 [1882]; cf. Dévaud, *Kêmi* 2, 10 n. 1 [1929]; Černý, *Crum Mem. Vol.* 38 [1950].

ϫⲁϫ (Crum 798b), 'sparrow' = (*Wb.* v, 413, 14), ṯṯ, 'sparrow'; , ḏḏ, 'sparrow' (only in a proper name, translating Gk. στρουθός). Onomatopoetic and connected with ϫⲟⲩϫⲟⲩ, 'twitter'.

HCHABAS, *Oeuv. div.* II (= *Bibl. ég.* x), 95 [1860]; cf. Keimer, *OLZ* 30, 80 n. 1 [1927]; DSPIEGELBERG, *Äg. und griech. Eigennamen*, 47*, nos. 320 and 320a, and p. 58 [1901].

ϫⲱϫ (Crum 799a), 'head, capital', see under ϫⲱ≈, 'head'.

HINCKS, *An Attempt* etc. (= *Transactions of the Roy. Irish Ac.* 21, Part II), 94 [1847].

ϫⲁϫⲉ (Crum 799b), 'enemy' = (*Wb.* v, 604, 8–13), ḏrḏr, 'foreign' > Gr.-R. (*Wb.* v, 532, bottom), ḏ(3)ḏ(3), 'hostile, enemy'; (Er. 692, 7), ḏḏy, 'enemy'.

HBRUGSCH, *Wb.* 1692 [1868]; cf. Reinisch, *Äg. Denkm. in Miramar*, 132 n. 2 [1865] (for ḏ(3)ḏ(3)); Gardiner, *The Chester Beatty Papyri, No. I*,

11 n. 3 [1931] (for *ḏrḏr*); cf. Černý, *Crum Mem. Vol.* 46–7 [1950]; ᴰSAULCY, *Analyse de texte dém.* 103–6 [1845] (though he takes the det. for plural ending); cf. Brugsch, *Scriptura Aeg. dem.* 20 [1848].

ϫⲓϫⲱⲓ (Crum 800a), 'single lock' or 'plait of hair' left on head = , *ḏ3ḏ3y* (as proper name, Ranke I, 405, 21), a nisbe-adjective from *ḏ3ḏ3*, 'head'; (Er. 669, 2), *t3y-ḏy* (*tḏ*), 'lock of hair, from which Greek σισόη; also as personal name (Σισοις).

ᴴᴰSPIEGELBERG, *Äg. und griech. Eigennamen*, 45*–6*, no. 316a [1901].

ᴮ**ϫⲁϭⲉ** (Crum 800b), 'bent, maimed person', from ˢ**ϭⲱⲱϫⲉ**, ᴮ**ϫⲱϫⲓ** (Crum 841a), 'to cut'.

SPIEGELBERG, *Kopt. Handwb.* 284 [1921].

ϫⲱ(ⲱ)ϭⲉ (Crum 800b), 'dye, stain' = **ṯk3*, 'dye', from which is derived (Er. 659, 6), *ṯk3*, 'dyer' (βαφεύς).

H. THOMPSON in Glanville, *Griffith Studies*, 159 n. 12 [1932].

ϭ

ϭⲁⲓ (sic l.), **ⲕⲁⲓ** (Crum 802a), a vessel = (*Wb.* V, 150, 5–13), *g3y* > (Amenemope 23, 17), *ḳ3y*, 'bowl, dish'.

SPIEGELBERG, *Kopt. Handwb.* 284 [1921] (*g3y*); LANGE, *Amenemope*, 117 [1925] (*ḳ3y*).

ϭⲁ(ⲉ)ⲓⲉ (Crum 466a, s.v. **ⲧϭⲁ(ⲉ)ⲓⲟ**), 'ugly one, ugliness, disgrace' = (*Wb.* V, 149, 10. 11; further exx. P. BM 10052, 12, 18. 21; 14, 17), *g3*, 'be ugly'; (Er. 570, 5), *g3*, 'ugly, bad'.

ᴰERICHSEN, *Dem. Glossar*, 570, 5 [1954].

ⲧϭⲁ(ⲉ)ⲓⲟ (Crum 465b and probably also Qual. ᴬ²**ϭⲁⲓⲧ** 832b), 'make ugly', hence 'disgrace, condemn' = **ⲧ** + **ϭⲁ(ⲉ)ⲓⲟ**, 'cause to be ugly' (* , *dỉt g3*).

ERMAN in *ZÄS* 22, 30 [1884].

-ϭⲉ (Crum 802a), enclitic particle:

(1) 'then, therefore, but' = (*Wb.* V, 177, bottom), *gr* > (*Wb.* V,

178, 6 ff.), *grt*, L.E. once (*H.O.* xxix, 3, vo. 3), , *g(ꜣ)*, encl. particle 'and, further'; (Er. 583, 1), *gr*, 'also'.

^{H}Champollion, *Gr.* 526, §344 [1836] (from *gr*); ^{D}Spiegelberg, *Dem. Gr.* 188–9, §421 [1925] (from *gr*).

(2) 'again, once more', in neg. phrase 'no longer' = (*Wb.* v, 179, 3–8), *gr*, 'also, no longer'; (Er. 583, 2), *gr*, 'further, yet'.

^{H}Spiegelberg, *Rec. trav.* 30, 142 [1908]; cf. Erman, *Aeg. Gr.* 3, 242, §461 [1911]; Spiegelberg in *Rec. trav.* 32, 154 [1912]; ^{D}Spiegelberg, *Dem. Gr.* 188, §421 [1925].

ϭⲱ (Crum 803b), 'desist, stop' = (*Wb.* v, 179, 9 f.), *gr*, 'be silent'; (Er. 582, 5), *gr*, 'be silent, cease'.

^{H}Griffith, *Rylands*, iii, 251 n. 12 [1909]; ^{D}Revillout, *Journal as.* série 10, vol. 11, 484 n. 8 [1907] = *Pap. mor.* 236 n. 8 [1907].

ϭⲱⲱⲃⲉ (Crum 804b), 'leaf' = (*Wb.* v, 154, 7–9), *gꜣbt*, 'leaf' of a plant; (Er. 578, 1), *gbꜣt*, 'leaf'.

^{H}Brugsch, *Wb.* 1445 [1868]; Pleyte, *Pap. Rollin*, 8 [1868]; ^{D}Brugsch, *Gr. dém.* 25, §44 [1855].

ϭⲱⲃⲉ ⲛϣⲁ, ϭⲃϣⲁ (Crum 544a, s.v. **ϣⲁ**), 'nostril', lit. 'leaf of nose' = (*Wb.* iv, 523, 7; v, 154, 6), *gꜣbt n šrt*, 'nostril'.

^{S}**ϭⲃⲟⲓ**, ^{B}**ϫⲫⲟⲓ** (Crum 805a), 'arm' of man, 'leg' of beast = (*Wb.* v, 163, 4–12), *gbꜣ*, 'arm'; cf. (Er. 577, 3), (fem.!) *gbt*, 'arm'.

^{H}Brugsch, *Geographie*, 7 and Pl. i, no. 23 [1857]; ^{D}Revillout, *Poème*, 2 [1885].

See also ^{B}**ϫⲫⲟⲧ**(?), **ϫⲫⲱϯ**.

ϭⲃⲃⲉ (Crum 805a), 'become feeble, timid' = (*Wb.* v, 161, 8 f.), *gby*, 'become weak, miserable'; (Er. 577, 2), *gb*, 'become weak, weak'.

ϭⲱⲃ (Crum 805b), 'weak (person)', subst. and adj., same etymology.

^{H}Brugsch, *Geographie*, 7 and Pl. i, no. 24 [1857] (**ϭⲱⲃ**); cf. Reinisch, *Aeg. Denkm.* in *Miramar*, 293 [1865] (**ϭⲱⲃ**); Chabas, *Voyage*, 138 [1866] (**ϭⲃⲃⲉ, ϭⲱⲃ**); Baillet, *Oeuv. div.* i (= *Bibl. ég.* xv), 39 [1867]; ^{D}Revillout, *Pap. moral.* 79 n. 2 (subst.) [1907].

ϭⲉⲃϭⲓⲃ (Crum 806a), 'fragments, shreds(?)', ^{B}**ϫⲁⲃϫⲓⲃ** (Crum 760b), 'small' in stature, and perhaps also ϭⲁϫⲓϥ, 'ant' (see this), from (ϭⲟⲃϭⲃ), ϭⲃϭⲱⲃ⸗, 'tread to pieces'. See the following.

SPIEGELBERG, *Kopt. Handwb.* 285 [1921].

[S](ϭⲟⲃϭⲃ), ϭⲃϭⲱⲃ⸗ (Crum 806a), 'tread to pieces', or sim. = (*Wb.* v, 165, 3), *gbgb*, also (P. BM 10083, recto 15–16), *ḳbḳb*, 'throw (enemy) to ground'.

Cf. de Rougé, *Oeuv. div.* II (= *Bibl. ég.* XXII), 148–9 [1851], who compares ϭⲃϭⲱⲃ⸗ with the certainly related = (*Wb.* v, 165, 4–8), *gbgbt*, 'enemies (piled upon ground)'.

ϭⲗ, ϭⲁⲗ (Crum 806a), 'weapon' = (*Wb.* v, 59, 11), *ḳrʿw*, L.Eg. (*JEA* 19, Pl. XXIX, 1), *ḳrʿ*, 'shield'; (Er. 588, 6), *glʿ*, 'shield'. Loan-word from Semitic, cf. Hebrew קֶלַע, 'curtain, hanging'.

[H]BRUGSCH, *Wb.* 1467 [1868]; [D]REVILLOUT, *Rev. ég.* 12, 26, 45 [1907]; [S]DR GROLL's information.

ϭⲟⲗ (Crum 806b), 'lie, liar' = (*Wb.* v, 189, 2 f.), *grg*, 'lie'; (not in Er.), *glk*, 'lie'.

[H]CHAMPOLLION, *Gr.* 102 [1836]; cf. Lacau, *BIFAO* 54, 150 n. 1 [1954]; [D]SOTTAS, *Pap. Lille*, 38, §9 [1921].

[S]ϭⲱⲗ, [B]ϫⲱⲗ (Crum 807a), 'return, roll back, deny' = ? (*Wb.* v, 59, 1), *ḳri*, 'approach, come'; (Er. 588, 7), *glʿ*, 'refute, deceive, deny', from Semitic √*gll*, cf. Hebrew גָּלַל, 'roll'.

[H]DÉVAUD's slip and in Crum, *A Coptic Dict.* 807a [1939]; [D]REVILLOUT, *Pap. mor.* II, 15 n. 4 [1908]; [S]ROSSI, *Etym. aeg.* 83 [1808] (for [B]ϫⲱⲗ); cf. Stricker in *Acta Orientalia* 15, 3 [1937].

ϭⲁⲗⲉ (Crum 807b), 'lame, crippled person' = (Er. 587, 3), *gl*, 'lame, lame person'.

ERICHSEN, *Dem. Glossar*, 587, 3 [1954].

ϭⲟ(ⲉ)ⲓⲗⲉ (Crum 807b):

(1) 'dwell, visit', connected with (*Wb.* v, 59, 8–9), *ḳri* or (*Wb.* v, 7, 4), *ḳi*, 'newcomer, visitor'; = (Er. 572, 5), *gyl*, 'to stay as alien, be alien'.

ᴴERMAN–GRAPOW, *Wb.* V, 59, 8–9 [1931]; ᴰERICHSEN, *Dem. Glossar*, 572, 5 [1954].

(2) 'deposit, entrust' (Crum 808b) = (Er. 589, 2), *glw*, also , *grᶜ*, 'entrust, deposit', or sim. From Semitic, cf. גֵּר, 'sojourner', Arabic جار.

SPIEGELBERG, *Die dem. Pap. Loeb.* 4, (13) [1931]; cf. H. THOMPSON, *A Family Archive*, 26 n. 126 [1934] (for ϭⲁⲗⲟ); ˢVATER in Adelung, *Mithradates*, III, p. 74 [1812].

ϭⲱⲱⲗⲉ (Crum 809a), 'swathe, clothe, cover' = (Er. 589, 1), *glᶜ*, 'swathe, clothe'.

GRIFFITH, *Stories*, 148 [1900].

ϭⲱⲱⲗⲉ, ⲕⲱⲗⲉ (Crum 810a), 'flat cake, loaf', from Semitic, cf. קָלָה, 'roast, parch', Aram. (Targ.) קוֹלְיָא, Gk. κολία, 'bellaria ex melle' (Hesychius).

DÉVAUD's slip.

ᴮϭⲗⲏ (Crum 810a), 'scorpion' = (*Wb.* V, 526, 15 f.), *d̲ꜣrt* (fem.), 'scorpion'; or , etc. (Er. 684, 6), *d̲l*(*t*), 'scorpion' (as constellation and sign in zodiac).

ᴴDE ROUGÉ, *Oeuv. div.* VI (= *Bibl. ég.* XXVI), 382 [1859, but published in 1874]; BRUGSCH, *Wb.* 1697 [1868]; ᴰSPIEGELBERG, *ZÄS* 48, 147 and Pl. IV [1910].

ᴮϭⲗⲟⲓ (Crum 810b), 'ball' = (Er. 567, 2), *klᶜy*, 'ball' (made usually of rags, hence the det.).

BRUGSCH, *Wb.* 1499 [1868].

ᶠϭⲗⲏⲃ (Crum 810b), 'muzzle', from Semitic, cf. Hebrew כְּלוּב, 'basket', in Amarna tablets *kilūbu*.

W. MAX MÜLLER in Gesenius–Buhl, *Hebr. und Aram. Handwörterbuch*, 14th ed., 313 [1905].

ˢϭⲟⲗⲃⲉ, ᴮϣⲟⲗⲃⲓ (Crum 810b), 'garment of wool' = ?Aeth. (Macadam, *Kawa*, I Text, 39 n. 45), *grb*, kind of cloth, from Greek κολόβιον from which also the Egn. Arabic جلابية. Deriving *grb* from Semitic √*klb* seems difficult since , *g*, never expresses Semitic *k*.

ᴳSTERN, *Kopt. Gr.* 69, § 144 [1880].

ᴮϭⲗⲱⲃⲓ (Crum 810b), 'scissors' from Syriac ܟܰܠܒܬܳܐ, 'forceps'.

DÉVAUD in Crum, *A Coptic Dict.* 810b [1939].

ϭⲉⲗⲃⲉⲥⲓ (Crum 810b), 'purple' = [demotic], *krbs*, 'purple', from Greek καρπάσιον (sc. λίνον), 'flax' so named after the town of Carpasia in Cyprus. Also in Syriac as ܟܰܪܦܳܣ, Hebrew כַּרְפַּס, Latin '(*linea*) *carbasea*'.

ᴰVOLTEN, *Ägypter und Amazonen*, 72 and 114 [1962]; ᴳST-PAUL GIRARD in Till, *Orientalia* 7, 103 [1938].

ϭⲁⲗⲓⲗ (Crum 810b), see ⲕⲁⲗⲕⲓⲗ, 'wheel'.

ϭⲗⲓⲗ (Crum 811a), 'burnt-offering' = [hieroglyphs] (*Wb.* v, 61, 11–13), *ḳrr*, 'burnt-offering'; [demotic] (Er. 590, 2), *gll*, 'burnt-offering', a loan-word from Semitic, cf. Hebrew כָּלִיל, 'holocaust'.

ᴴSAULCY, *Rosette*, 29–30 [1845]; cf. Brugsch, *Wb.* 1468 [1868]; ᴰYOUNG, *Misc. Works*, III, 28–9, no. 78 = *Mus. crit.* 6, pp. 178–9 [1815] (letter of 21 Oct. 1814 to de Sacy); ˢROSSI, *Etym. Aeg.* 329 [1808].

ϭ(ⲉ)ⲗⲙ (Crum 811a), 'dry sticks, twigs' = [demotic] (Er. 589, 5), *glm*, 'stalk', probably from Gk. καλάμη.

ᴰGRIFFITH–THOMPSON, III, 87, no. 926 [1909]; ᴳDÉVAUD in Spiegelberg, *Kopt. Handwb.* 287 [1921].

ϭ(ⲉ)ⲗⲙⲁⲓ (Crum 811a), 'jar, vase', loan-word from Semitic, cf. Aram. קלבי, from which also κάλπη, 'urn'.

SPIEGELBERG, *Äg. Sprachgut in den aus Ägypten stammenden aramäischen Urkunden der Perserzeit*, 19 [1906].

ϭⲗⲟⲙⲗⲙ (Crum 811a), 'be twisted, implicated' = [demotic] (Er. 590, 1), *glmlm*, 'wind round, wrap up', probably reduplication of [hieroglyphs] (*Wb.* v, 132, 5), *knm*, 'wrap up, a garment', Egn. *knm* being akin to Semitic *glm*, Hebrew גלם.

ᴴERMAN–GRAPOW, *Wb.* v, 132, 5 [1931]; ᴰGROFF, *Les deux versions dém.* 42 [1888]; ˢEMBER, *ZÄS* 49, 94 [1911].

ϭⲱⲗⲡ (Crum 812a), 'uncover, open, reveal' = [demotic] (Er. 589, 3), *glp*, 'reveal, uncover'.

p.c. ˢϭⲁⲗⲡ-, ᴮⲕⲁⲗⲧ-, see this latter and ϭⲁⲗⲟⲩⲃⲓϩ.

MASPERO, *Rec. trav.* 1, 35 n. 54 [1870].

ϭⲗⲱⲧ, Dual **ϭⲗⲟⲟϭⲉ** < **ϭⲗⲟⲟⲧⲉ** (Crum 813a), 'kidney' = , *grt*, or (*Wb.* v, 190, 11), *grgy(t)*, 'kidney', from Semitic, cf. Hebrew כְּלָיוֹת (Plural), 'kidneys', Syriac ܟܘܠܝܬܐ (Brockelmann, p. 158).
^{H}DÉVAUD's slip (for *grgy*); $^{}$GARDINER, *Onom.* II, 244* n. 1 [1947] (for **ϭⲗⲱⲧ**); ^{S}ROSSI, *Etym. Aeg.* 330 [1808].

ϭⲗⲧⲉ (Crum 813a), 'ring (with a seal)' = (*Wb.* v, 66, 6), *ḳrt*, a precious stone set in gold; (Er. 591, 4), *glṯ*, 'ring (with seal?)'.
^{D}DAUMAS, *Les moyens d'expression*, 221 [1952].

ϭⲁⲗⲓⲧⲉ (Crum 813a), a vessel (prob. also as measure) = (Er. 588, 5), *glyṯt*, a vessel.

^{S}**ϭⲁⲗⲟⲩⲃⲓϩ**, ^{B}**ⲃⲁⲗⲙⲃⲉϩ** (Crum 813a, 'bald-headed person'), distorted from *^{S}**ϭⲁⲗⲡ-ⲃⲟⲩϩⲉ**, 'bare as to eyelids', like **ϭⲁⲗⲡϫⲱϥ**, **ϭⲁⲗⲡϩⲣⲁϥ**. See **ϭⲱⲗⲡ**, 'uncover, open' and **ⲃⲟⲩϩⲉ**. **ϭⲁⲗⲟⲩⲃ-** probably under influence of **ϭⲁⲗⲟⲩⲃⲟⲥ** (= κολοβός), for which see next entry.
LEFORT in *Mélanges Charles Moeller*, I, 231 [1914].

^{B}**ϭ(ⲁ)ⲗⲱⲟⲩϣ**, **ϣⲗⲱⲟⲩϣ** (Crum 813b), 'maimed, paralysed person', from Gk. κολοβός, 'docked, curtailed' (cf. ^{S}**ϭⲁⲗⲟⲩⲃⲟⲥ**, Budge, *Misc. Coptic Texts*, 422).

^{A2}**ϭⲁⲗⲁϣⲓⲣⲉ** (Crum 813b), 'strong man, giant' = (*Wb.* v, 135, 1), *krỉ-šrỉ*, kind of soldier (καλασίριες); (Er. 588, 1), *gl-šr*, also (Er. 574, 1), *gꜥlꜥšyr*, 'warrior'. Cf. Spiegelberg, *Äg. u. griech. Eigennamen*, 17*; *ZÄS* 43, 87–8; *OLZ* 27, cols. 188–9.
^{HD}POLOTSKY, *Manich. Homilien*, Index, p. 20* [1934].
Probably also corrupted into **ⲥⲁⲗⲁϣⲉⲓⲉ**, see this.

ϭⲁⲗⲁϩⲧ (Crum 813b), 'pot', loan-word from Semitic, cf. Hebrew קַלַּחַת, 'cauldron', New Hebr. קַלַּחַת (Dalman), this, however, itself is an old loan-word from or akin to Egn. (*Wb.* v, 62, 12 f.), *ḳrḥt*, 'vessel'.
^{S}ROSSI, *Etym. aeg.* 324 [1808]; cf. de Lagarde, *Übersicht*, 88 n. ** [1889]; cf. Lacau in *Revue d'ég.* 9, 82 n. 1 [1952].

ϭⲱⲗϫ (Crum 814a), 'entangle, ensnare' = (Er. 591, 5), *glḏ*, 'seize', perhaps a loan-word from Semitic (cf. Arabic لزج, لزق).
^{D}GRIFFITH–THOMPSON, III, 87, no. 928 [1909]; ^{S}DÉVAUD in Crum, *A Coptic Dict.* 814a [1939].

ϭⲗⲟϭ (Crum 815a), ‘bed, bier’ = (*Wb.* v, 136, 6), *krkr*, ‘a kind of bed’ > and sim. (not in *Wb.*), *krk*, ‘bed’; (Er. 591, 3), *glg*, ‘bed, bier’.

ᴰBRUGSCH, *Gr. dém.* 162, §318; 197 (corr. of p. 42) [1855].

ϭⲗⲟϭ (Crum 815a), ‘gourd’ from *ⲧⲗⲟϭ (like ϭⲗⲟⲟϭⲉ, ‘ladder’ from ⲧⲗⲟⲟϭⲉ); (*Wb.* v, 470, 4), *dng*, ‘gourd’; (not in Er.; P. Cairo 30982, vo. 11), *glg*, ‘gourd’.

ᴴCRUM, *A Coptic Dict.* 815a [1939]; ᴰSPIEGELBERG, *Dem. Denkmäler*, II, 213 [1908].

ϭⲗⲟ (Crum 815b), ‘colocynth’, prob. mistake for ϭⲗⲟϭ.

ϭⲗⲟⲟϭⲉ < ⲧⲗⲟⲟϭⲉ (Crum 815b), ‘ladder’, loan-word from Semitic, cf. Arabic دَرَجَة, ‘ladder’.

DÉVAUD in *Muséon* 36, 87 [1923].

ϭⲟⲗϭ(ⲉ)ⲗ (Crum 815b), ‘spread to dry’, probably the same as ϫⲟⲗϫ(ⲉ)ⲗ, ‘let drip’, see this latter.

ϭⲁⲙ (Crum 815b), ‘bull(?)’ = L.Eg. (*Wb.* v, 38, 1), *ḳmꜣ*, a kind of sacred young bull; (not in Er., ex. Pap. Berlin 15831, 1) *gm*, ‘young steer’ or sim.

ᴴDÉVAUD in Crum, *A Coptic Dict.* 815b [1939]; ᴰZAUZICH in *MDAIK* 25, 226 n. (g) [1969]; cf. Ray in *JEA* 58, 308–10 [1972].

ϭⲟⲙ (Crum 815b), ‘power, strength’ = (Er. 580, 1), f. *gm*, ‘power, strength’.

GRIFFITH–THOMPSON, III, 85, no. 893 [1909].

ϭⲙ ϭⲟⲙ, ϭⲛ ϭⲟⲙ (Crum 816b), ‘find power, be strong, able’ = ϭⲓⲛⲉ + ϭⲟⲙ, cf. , *gm tꜣ*(?) *gm*, lit. ‘find the power’ = (Er. 580, 1), *gᶜm sp-2*, i.e. *gᶜmgᶜm*, ‘be able’.

GRIFFITH–THOMPSON, I, 121 [1904]; III, 85, no. 894 [1909]; cf. SPIEGELBERG, *Die dem. Pap. Loeb*, 84, (12) [1931].

ϭⲱⲙ (Crum 817b), ‘garden, vineyard, property’ = (*Wb.* v, 106, 4 ff.), *kꜣm*, ‘garden’; (Er. 557, 4), *kꜣm*, ‘garden’.

ᴴDÉVÉRIA, *Mém. et fragm.* I (= *Bibl. ég.* IV), 320 [1862]; ᴰBRUGSCH, *Wb.* 1452 [1868].

ϭⲙⲉ (Crum 817b), 'gardener, vinedresser' = (*Wb.* v, 106, 10), *kꜣmw*, 'gardener, vineyard-keeper'; (Er. 557, 4), *kꜣmy*, 'gardener'.

[H]CHABAS, *Voyage*, 254 [1866]; cf. Brugsch, *Wb.* 1452 [1868]; [D]SPIEGELBERG, *Dem. Chronik*, 84, no. 264 [1914].

ϭⲁⲓⲙⲉ (Crum 818a), 'domestic fowl' = (*Wb.* v, 166, 5), *gmt*, 'black ibis (*Plegadis falcinellus* L.)', cf. Keimer, *ASAE* 30, 20 ff.; (Er. 560, 5), *kymy*, 'hen'; from this Greek diminutive καίμιον, 'chicken' (cf. Karl Fr. W. Schmidt in *Göttingische gelehrte Anzeiger* 184, 104 [1922]; 202, 83 [1940].

[D]SPIEGELBERG, *Dem. Texte auf Krügen*, 75, no. 226 [1912].

ϭⲱⲱⲙⲉ (Crum 818a), 'twist, pervert' = (Er. 580, 3), *gmꜥ*, 'damage, do wrong; fraud'.

[D]BRUGSCH, *Pap. Rhind*, 47 and Pl. 43, no. 380 [1865]; BRUGSCH, *Rosettana*, 95 [1849].

ϭⲁⲙⲟⲩⲗ (Crum 818b), 'camel' = (Er. 581, 1), *gmwl*, 'camel', loan-word from Semitic, cf. גָּמָל, جَمَل, Akkadian *gammalu*.

[D]KRALL, *Mitt. aus der Sammlung Erzh. Rainer*, VI, 51 and 75, no. 308 [1897]; [S]LACROZE, *Lexicon*, 162 [1775].

ϭⲱⲙϩ (Crum 818b, 'meaning unknown'), 'look for, search for' = (*Wb.* v, 171, 5), *gmḥ*, 'look for'.

ϭⲟⲙϭ(ⲉ)ⲙ (Crum 818b), 'touch, grope' = (*Wb.* v, 172, 12), 'touch, try to find', reduplication of , *gmy*, 'find' (*Wb.* v, 166, 6 ff., ϭⲓⲛⲉ); (Er. 564, 2), *kmkm*, 'touch'.

[H]W. MAX MÜLLER, *Liebespoesie*, 15 n. 2 [1899]; cf. Chabas, *Voyage*, 299 [1866]; [D]SPIEGELBERG, *Mythus*, 278, no. 858 [1917].

ϭⲓⲛ- (Crum 819a), prefix forming nouns of action = (*Wb.* v, 15, 5 ff.), *ḳi*, 'form, image' + , *n*, 'of' + Infinitive (cf. *Wb.* v, 16, 4); (Er. 571, 8), *gy*, 'form, kind, intention', etc.

[H]BRUGSCH, *Wb.* 1437 [1868]; [D]BRUGSCH, *Pap. Rhind*, 47 and Pl. 42, no. 376 [1865].

[S]ϭⲓⲛⲉ, [B]ϫⲓⲙⲓ (Crum 820a), 'find' = (*Wb.* v, 166, 6 ff.), *gmy*, 'find'; (Er. 579, 2), *gm*, 'find'. The ⲛ of ϭⲓⲛⲉ comes from the pronominal form **gemtef* > **gentef*.

[H]DE ROUGÉ, *Oeuv. div.* III (= *Bibl. ég.* XXIII), 210–12 [1856]; cf. Mariette, *Oeuv. div.* I (= *Bibl. ég.* XVIII), 196 n. 1 [1856]; [D]HESS, *Stne*, 18, 180 [1888]; cf. Hess in *ZÄS* 28, 3 [1890]; Hess, *Gnost. Pap.* 14 [1892].

[B]ϫⲉⲙ- also in fem. proper name ϫⲉⲙⲙⲁϩⲱⲣ (Heuser, *Die kopt. Personennamen*, 42), lit. 'finder of treasures'.

[O]ϭⲱⲛⲙ (Crum 821a), 'be blinded' = (*Wb.* v, 107, 1), *kmn*, 'be blind, make blind'; (Er. 581, 5), *gnm*, 'become blind.'

[HD]GRIFFITH–THOMPSON, III, 112, nos. 88 and 89 [1909].

ϭⲓⲛⲙⲟⲩⲧ (Crum 821a), 'the Pleiades', cf. (*Wb.* v, 133, 6. 7), *knmty* (also in Plural), a kind of star.

H. THOMPSON in Crum, *A Coptic Dict.* 821a [1939].

ϭⲛⲟⲛ (Crum 821a), 'become soft, smooth, weak' = (*Wb.* v, 172, bottom), *gnn*, 'become weak, soft'; (Er. 581, 7), *gnn*, 'become tender, mild, humid; mildness'.

[H]CHABAS, *Pap. mag. Harris*, Pl. I, no. 17 [1860]; [D]BRUGSCH, *Gr. dém.* 124, §252 [1855].

[B]ϭⲛⲟⲛ, ϭⲛⲉ-, [S]ϫⲛⲉ- (Crum 821b), 'bend, bow' with ϫⲱ⸗ 'head', from Semitic √*kn*ʿ, cf. Hebrew (Niphal) נִכְנַע, 'bow', Aram. כְּנַע, 'bow' (Dalman).

LAGARDE, *Übersicht*, 88 n. ** [1889].

ϭⲟⲛⲥ (Crum 822a), 'might, violence', or sim. = (*Wb.* v, 177, 5), *gns*, 'violence, injustice'; [Er. 541, 5), *ḳns*, 'violence, injustice'.

[H]SPIEGELBERG, *OLZ* 27, col. 185 [1924]; [D]REVILLOUT, *Setna*, 97 and 124 n. 2 [1877].

ⲛϭⲟⲛⲥ, 'violently' = (*Wb.* v, 177, 6), *m gns*, 'unjustly', or sim.

ϭⲱⲛⲧ (Crum 822b), 'become wroth' = (*Wb.* v, 56, 16 f.), *ḳnd*, 'become enraged, angry'; (Er. 565, 6), *knṱ*, 'anger'.

^{H}CHAMPOLLION, *Gr.* 374 [1836]; ^{D}SPIEGELBERG, *Mythus*, 278, no. 859 [1917].

ϭⲛⲟⲩⲧ (Crum 823b), see under ⲙⲁϩⲛϭⲛⲟⲩⲧ.

ϭⲓⲛⲟⲩⲏⲗ (Crum 823b), kind of 'ship' = ? (*Wb.* v, 118, 3–5), *kbnt*, 'Byblos-ship', from ϭⲓⲛⲟⲩⲏⲗ the Arabic شنبر?
CRUM, *BIFAO* 30, 455 [1930].

^{B}ϭⲛⲟⲩϥ (Crum 824a), 'heavy object' = Gr.-R. (*Wb.* v, 381, 6), *ṯnf*, 'weight'; (Griffith–Thompson, III, 98, no. 1080) and sim. (Er. 681, 2), '(average, appropriate) weight, measure' (cf. Pierce in *Journal of Amer. Res. Center in Egypt* 4, 74).
See also ^{S}ϫⲱⲛϥ.

ϭⲱⲛⲁϭ (Crum 824a), a cloak, from Greek καυνάκης, γαυνάκη, this latter from Akkadian *gunakku*, 'frilled and flounced mantle'.
LAGARDE, *Ges. Abh.* 206 [1866]; cf. Liddell-Scott, 932.

ϭⲱⲛϭ (Crum 824a), incomplete reduplication of ϭⲱⲛϭⲛ, 'wring, nip off' = ? (*Wb.* v, 55, 4 ff.), *ḳnḳn*, 'beat, break to pieces'; (Er. 542, lower), *ḳnḳn*, 'beat, fight'.

ϭⲓⲛϭⲗⲱ (Crum 824a), 'bat' = (*Wb.* v, 478, 4), *drgyt*, also (*Wb.* v, 419, 3), *dꜣgy*, and (*Wb.* v, 499, 5. 6), *dgyt*, 'bat'; (Er. 582, 4), *gnglꜣ*, 'bat'.
^{H}STERN in *Pap. Ebers*, II (Glossar), 52 and 53 [1875]; ^{D}SPIEGELBERG, *ZÄS* 37, 34–6 [1899].

^{S}ϭⲛϭⲛ, ^{B}ϫⲉⲛϫⲉⲛ (Crum 824b), 'make music' with instrument or voice = (*Wb.* v, 55, 4 f.), *ḳnḳn*, 'beat', in Gr.-R. period also 'beat (a tambourine)' (*Wb.* v, 55, 7); (Er. 542, 2), *ḳnḳn*, 'beat, fight'.
^{D}LAUTH, *Manetho*, 97 [1865]; NB. Dévaud, *Études*, 53 [1922] derived ϭⲛϭⲛ from Semitic √*qnqn* (cf. Syriac ܩܘܢܩܢ), but this latter is onomatopoetic and has nothing to do with Egn. *ḳnḳn* which is a reduplication of (*Wb.* v, 41, 5 ff.), *ḳny*, 'become strong, defeat'.

ϭⲓⲛϭⲱⲣ (Crum 824b), 'talent', weight or coin = (Er. 566, 7), *krkr*, 'talent', a loan-word from Hebrew כִּכָּר, through Aram. כַּכְּרָא, 'talent'.

ᴰBRUGSCH, *Wb.* 185, 1498 [1867 and 1868]; ˢLACROZE, *Lexicon*, 167 [1775]; cf. Sethe, *Nachr. Gess. Wiss. zu Göttingen, Phil.-hist. Kl.* 1916, 115 n. 5 [1916].

ϭⲛϭⲉϩ (Crum 824b, 'elephantiasis') explained as **ⲕⲓⲗⲫⲓⲁ, ⟨ⲕ⟩ⲉⲗⲩⲫⲁⲓ**, that is κελυφία, 'leprosy', cf. κέλεφος, 'leper' and κελυφοκομῖον, 'lepers' hospital' (Liddell–Scott). **ϭⲉⲛϭⲉϩ** probably < ***ϭⲉⲛϫⲉϩ** < ***ϭⲉⲛϩⲉϫ** = (Er. 582, 1), *gnḥd*, 'cancer (in zodiac)', and undoubtedly also 'cancer (disease)'.

ϭⲟⲡ (Crum 824b), 'sole' of foot, 'foot' = in (*Wb.* v, 119, 1), *kp n rdwy*, 'soles of feet'; (Er. 578, 6), *gp*, 'sole' o foot; from Semitic, cf. כַּף, 'palm' (of hand).

ᴴLEPSIUS, *ZÄS* 5, 72 [1867]; LEPSIUS, *Abh. Preuss. Ak.* 1866, 39 f.; cf. Salvolini, *Analyse gramm.* 22 and Pl. C, no. 69 [1836]; ᴰHESS, *Gnost. Pap.* 14 [1892]; ˢBRUGSCH, *Wb.* 1491 [1868].

ˢᴮ**ϭⲟⲡ** (Crum 825a), cutting instrument; from (Er. 576, 6), *gb*, 'to cut off' which may be the L.Eg. (*Wb.* v, 162, 5), *gb*, 'to damage, injure'.

ᴬ²**ϭⲁⲡⲓ** (Apocr. St John III, 18, 5), 'ape' (var. ˢ**ⲏⲛⲉ**) = (*Wb.* v, 158, 17), *gỉft*, 'female baboon'. Prob. erroneously for **ϭⲁϥⲓ**, cf. Sethe, *Verbum*, I, 124, §216.

ϭⲏⲡⲉ (Crum 825b), 'cloud'; cf. (*Wb.* I, 140, 20), *ỉgp*, 'cloud', and (*Wb.* v, 165, bottom), *gp*, 'cloud'; = (Er. 579, 1), *gpt*, 'cloud'.

ᴴERMAN–GRAPOW, *Wb.* I, 140, 20 [1926]; ᴰREVILLOUT, *Rev. ég.* 12, 37 [1907].

ϭⲟⲡⲉ (Crum 825b), 'small vessel' so 'small quantity', from Semitic, cf. Arabic, Aram. כַּפָּא (Dalman), Syriac (Brockelmann, 'potorium'), all from the same √*kpp* as כַּף, 'palm (of hand)'; see under **ϭⲟⲡ**.

DÉVAUD in Crum, *A Coptic Dict.* 825b [1939].

ϭⲱⲡⲉ (Crum 825b), 'seize, take' = (*Wb.* v, 105, 4), *k(ꜣ)p*, 'catch (birds)?'; (Er. 578, 5), *gp*, 'catch, seize'; cf. (*Wb.* v, 166, 4), *gp*, meaning unknown.

ᴴERICHSEN, *Dem. Glossar*, 578, 5 [1954], (*gp*); ᴰHESS, *Rosette*, 96 [1902].

SBϭⲱⲡⲣⲟ, Bϫⲉϥⲣⲟ (Crum 827a), 'farmstead, hamlet(?)', from Semitic, cf. Hebrew Pl. כְּפָרִים, 'villages', Arabic كَفْر, 'village'. From ϫⲉϥⲣⲟ the Eg. Arabic شُبْرَا.

ÅKERBLAD in *Journal as.* 2e série, vol. 13, 413–14 [1834] (for شبرا); KUENTZ, *Bulletin de l'Institut d'Égypte* 19, 219–21 [1937] (for كفر).

ϭⲁⲡ(ⲉ)ⲓϫⲉ (Crum 827b), a dry measure, a loan-word from Near East, cf. Arabic قفيز, Aramaic קְפִיזָא, Syriac ܩܦܝܙܐ (Brockelmann, 331, 'mensura'), perhaps ultimately Persian, same as καπίθη of Xenophon (*Anab.* I, 5, 6) of 2 Attic choinikes and καπέτις of Polyaenus (IV, 3, 32) containing only one Attic choinix; Hesychius has both καπίθη (of 2 Attic cotyles) and καπέτις (equal to choinix).

LAGARDE, *Übersicht*, 88, n. ** [1889]; cf. Dévaud, *Études*, 54–6 [1922].

ϭⲣⲁ (Crum 828a and 429b s.v. ⲧⲣⲁ), f., 'extremity' of limbs [Crum]; 'leg, foot' [Dévaud] = ? (Er. 583, 6), *grt*, f., 'foot(?)', from Semitic, cf. Hebr. Dual כְּרָעַיִם, 'two legs', Aram. כְּרָעָא f., Arabic كُرَاع, اكارع.

DERICHSEN, *Dem. Glossar*, 583, 6 [1954]; SDÉVAUD's slip.

ϭⲣⲉ (Crum 828a), 'birds'(?) = (*Wb.* V, 181, 1), *gry*, 'birds, fowl'.

W. MAX MÜLLER, *Liebespoesie*, 22 n. 5 [1899].

ϭⲣⲏ (Crum 828a), 'dig', loan-word from Semitic, cf. Hebrew כָּרָה, 'dig', Aram. כְּרָא.

ROSSI, *Etym. aeg.* 332–3 [1808].

Sϭⲉⲣⲱⲃ, Fϭⲁⲣⲱⲙ (Crum 828a), 'staff, rod' = (Er., 584, 12, under *grp*), *grmp*, 'staff'.

HESS, *Stne*, 179 [1888].

ϭⲣⲟⲟⲙⲡⲉ (Crum 828b), 'dove' = (*Wb.* V, 181, 2), *gr-pt*, 'pigeon', lit. 'bird of (the) sky'; (Er. 583, 3), *grmp*, 'pigeon'.

HBIRCH, *ZÄS* 11, 71 n. 2 [1873]; DSPIEGELBERG, *Dem. Texte auf Krügen*, 32 n. 45; 76, no. 230 [1912].

ϭⲣⲏⲡⲉ (Crum 829a), 'diadem' = (Er. 584, 12), *grpt*, 'diadem'.

BRUGSCH, *Gr. dém.* 24, §43 [1855].

ϭⲉⲣⲏⲧ (Crum 829a), ⲕⲉⲣⲏⲧ (Crum 117b), 'dung, dirt' = (Er. 545, 5), *ḳrṭt*, 'dung'.

ϭⲁⲣⲁⲧⲉ (Crum 829a), 'carob pod' = Late (*Wb.* v, 190, 13), *grt*, part of a plant, a loan-word from Greek κεράτιον, 'small horn', as also Arabic قرط and Syriac ܩܪܛܐ, *qirṭ'*, 'siliqua' (Brockelmann 338a).

HMASPERO, *Mémoire sur quelques papyrus*, 33 n. 4 [1875].

ϭⲟⲣⲧⲉ (Crum 829b), 'knife' = (Er. 587, 2), *grṭ*, 'knife'.

BRUGSCH, *Gr. dém.* 40, §86 [1855].

S(**ϭⲱⲣϥ**), B**ϭⲱⲣⲡ** (Crum 829b), 'nip off' = **ⲕⲱⲣϥ**, 'bring to nought, cancel, destroy', see this latter.

ϭⲱⲣϩ (Crum 829b), 'night' = (*Wb.* v, 183, 12 f.), *grḥ*, 'night'; (Er. 585, 6), *grḥ*, 'night'.

HCHAMPOLLION, *Gr. ég.* 62, 79 [1836]; HBRUGSCH, *Rhind*, 47 and Pl. 43, no. 382 [1865].

S**ϭⲣⲱϩ**, B(**ϫⲱⲣϩ**) (Crum 829b), 'be in want, needy', as noun 'want, need' = Gr.-R. (*Wb.* v, 183, 4), *grḥ*, 'arrears in taxes'; (Er. 684, 5), *ḏrḥ*, 'be in want'.

HERMAN–GRAPOW, *Wb.* v, 183, 4 [1931]; DERICHSEN, *Dem. Glossar*, 684, 5 [1954].

S**ϭⲟⲣϫ**(ⲉ), B**ϫⲉⲣϫⲓ** (Crum 830a), 'filth' = ? (not in Er.), *krky*, 'filth'.

SPIEGELBERG, *Die dem. Pap. Loeb*, 49 n. 5 [1931].

ϭⲱⲣϭ (Crum 830a), 'waylay, hunt' = (*Wb.* v, 185, 13 f.), *grg*, 'lay nets, traps' and so 'catch'; (Er. 586, 2), *grg*, 'hunt; catch'.

HBRUGSCH, *Dict. géo.* 521, 854 [1879]; cf. BRUGSCH, *Wb.*, Suppl. 1299 [1882]; DLEXA, *Dem. Totenbuch*, 52, no. 268 [1910]; cf. BRUGSCH, *Wb.* 1301, s.v. *sẖt* [1868].

ϭⲉⲣⲏϭ (Crum 831a), 'hunter' = (Plural; *CT*, VI, 23i), *grgw*, 'trap-catchers, trap-setters' (as divine beings); Gr.-R. (*Wb.* v, 186, 2), *grg*(?), 'trap-catcher, hunter'; (Er. 586, 3), *grg*, 'hunter'.

HGARDINER, *Sinuhe*, 42 [1916]; DGRIFFITH, *Stories*, 200 [1900].

ϭⲱⲣϭ (Crum 831a), 'prepare, provide' = (*Wb.* v, 186, 4 ff.), 'found, equip, settle'; (Er. 586, 4), *grg*, 'found, prepare' and (Er. 567, 9), *klk*, 'equip (with crew)'.

HBRUGSCH, *Wb.*, Suppl. 1300 [1882]; DSPIEGELBERG, *Petubastis*, 62*, no. 435 [1910].

ϭⲱⲣϭ (Crum 831a), noun 'preparation, mixed contents', cf. (*Wb.* v, 187, 22), *grg*, 'prepare (an ointment)'.

ERMAN–GRAPOW, *Wb.* v, 187, 22 [1931].

See also ϭⲣⲏϭⲉ, 'dowry'.

Sϭⲣⲟ(ⲟ)ϭ, Bϫⲣⲟϫ (Crum 831b), 'seed', from Sϭⲱⲣϭ, Bϫⲱⲣϫ (Crum 831a), Egn. *grg* in its specialized meaning 'prepare a field by sowing' (*Wb.* v, 187, 12), therefore lit. 'that which is prepared'.

SAUNERON in *Mélanges Mariette*, 244–5 [1961].

ϭⲣⲏϭⲉ (Crum 832a), 'dowry' = (not in *Wb.*; good exx. in *Revue d'ég.* 20, 171–5), *grgt*, 'dowry'; (not in Er.), *grgt*, 'dowry'. Lit. 'equipment', from ϭⲱⲣϭ, 'prepare, provide'. Cf. also the common masc. (*Wb.* v, 188, 9), *grg*, 'equipment'.

HSTEINDORFF, *Anîba*, II, 28 n. 3 [1937]; DSPIEGELBERG, *Kopt. Handwb.* 292 [1921].

ϭⲁⲣϭⲁⲧⲁⲛⲉ (Crum 832a), 'bread-basket' or sim., from Greek γυργαθός, γυργαθίον, 'wicker-basket, creel'.

CRUM, *A Coptic Dict.* 832a [1939].

ϭⲟⲥ (Crum 832a), 'half' = (*Wb.* v, 196, 1 ff.), *gs*, 'half'; (Er. 592, 1), *gs*, 'half'.

HERMAN, *Die Sprache des Pap. Westcar*, 77 n. 2 [1889]; PIEHL, *PSBA* 12, 114–15 [1889]; DSPIEGELBERG, *Mythus*, 279, no. 867 [1917].

ϭⲓⲥ- = , *gs*, + direct genitive of measure, *Wb.* v, 197, 6. See also ϭⲓⲥⲕⲓⲧⲉ under ⲕⲓⲧⲉ.

ϭⲟⲥⲙ (Crum 832b), 'darkness, tempest' = (*Wb.* v, 206, 12), *gsm*, waters (in the Delta?) with beating waves; (Er. 593, 2), *gsm*, 'tempest, anger'; cf. also (Er. 593, 3), *gsmꜣ* 'land of canals' or sim., χάσμα.

HDREVILLOUT, *Journal as.* v (série 10), 209 [1905]; cf. Revillout, *Pap. moral.* I, 17 n. 6 [1907].

ϭⲁⲥⲧ, ϭⲟⲥⲧ (Crum 832b), measure of length (less than ⲛⲟⲩϩ), prob. = (*Wb.* v, 207, 11 f.), *gsti*, 'palette (of the scribe)' used as measure; (Er. 593, 6), *gst*, 'palette'. Cf. *pꜣ gst Ḫnsw*, 'the palette of Khons' as name of a certain land.

ϭⲟⲥϭ(ⲉ)ⲥ (Crum 832b), 'dance' = (*Wb.* v, 141, bottom), *ksks*, 'dance'; (Er. 593, 5), *gsgs*, 'dance' (verb and noun).

[H]CHAMPOLLION, *Gr. ég.* 365 [1836]; [D]SPIEGELBERG, *Dem. Chronik*, 85, no. 269 [1914].

[A2]ϭⲁⲓⲧ (Crum 832b), probably Qual. of ⲧϭⲁⲉⲓⲟ, see this latter.

ϭⲟⲧ (Crum 833a), 'size, age, form' = (*Wb.* v, 75, 3 ff.), *ḳd*, 'substance, character, form'; (Er. 554, 1), *ḳdy*, same meaning.

[H]GOODWIN in a letter to Renouf (Dawson, *Ch. W. Goodwin*, p. 78) [1862]; cf. BRUGSCH, *Wb.* 1479 [1868]; [B]REVILLOUT, *Poème*, 100–2 [1885].

ϭⲱⲧ (Crum 833a), 'drinking trough' = Late (*Wb.* v, 208, 9), *gt*, designation of a water-course; (Er. 594, 3), *gt*, 'cistern' or sim. Probably a loan-word from Semitic, cf. Hebrew גַּת, 'wine-press'.

[H]BRUGSCH, *Geographie* 166 and Pl. XXXIV, no. 689 [1857]; [D]ERICHSEN, *Dem. Glossar*, 594, 3 [1954]; [S]DÉVAUD in Crum, *A Coptic Dict.* 833a [1939].

[B]ϭⲓⲱϯ (Crum 833a), 'tip (of scorpion's tail)', a lunar station = (Er. 573, 2), *gyṭỉ*, in the expression *rꜣ gyṭỉ* for 'tip, point'.

ϭⲱⲧⲡ (Crum 833b), 'defeat, overcome' = (not in Er.; *JEA* 26, 108), *gꜥtp*, also (Petubastis, P. Krall, v, 6), *[g]tp*, 'defeat'.

PARKER in *JEA* 26, 108 [1940]; cf. Stricker in *Oudheidkundige Mededelingen*, N.S. 35, 62 n. 68 [1954].

ϭⲓⲧⲣⲉ (Crum 834a), 'cedrate', kind of lemon, from κίτρον, unless converse.

PEYRON, *Lexicon*, 419 [1835].

[S]ϭⲱⲧϩ, [B]ϫⲱⲧϩ (Crum 834a), 'wound, pierce' = (Er. 688, 2), *ḏtḥ*, 'pierce, penetrate into', from Semitic, cf. Arabic قدح, 'strike fire', New Hebrew קָדַח, 'kindle, bore', and Aram. קְדַח (Dalman), 'pierce', Syriac ܩܕܚ (Brockelmann, 312).

[D]BRUGSCH, *Gr. dém.* 34, §68 [1855]; [S]EMBER, *ZÄS* 49, 94 [1911].

ϭⲱⲟⲩ (Crum 835a), 'be narrow, narrowness' = (*Wb.* v, 151, 6 ff.), *gꜣw*, 'be narrow'; (Er. 574, 8), *gwꜣ*, 'be narrow; narrowness'.

[H]BRUGSCH, *Dict. géo.*, Suppl. 1340 [1880]; cf. BRUGSCH, *Wb.*, Suppl. 1287 [1882]; [D]GRIFFITH, *Stories*, 118 [1900].

ϭⲱⲟⲩ (Crum 835a), 'push out to sea, sail' = ? (*Wb.* v, 149, 7), *gꜣ*, 'launch (a ship)' or sim.

ERMAN–GRAPOW, *Wb.* v, 149, 7 [1931].

ϭⲟⲟⲩⲛⲉ (Crum 836a), 'hair-cloth, sacking, sack' = (*Wb.* v, 160, 10), pl., *gwn*, 'sack' or sim. From Semitic, cf. Arabic جونة, 'basket'.

[H]SPIEGELBERG, *ZÄS* 34, 15 [1896]; [S]STRICKER in *Acta Orientalia* 15, 5 [1937].

ϭⲟⲟⲩⲣⲉ (Crum 836a), 'slave' or sim. as term of contempt = ? (Er. 575, 3), *gwr*, or , *kwr*, an occupation, 'porter, carrier' or sim.

ϭⲱⲟⲩϭ (Crum 836a), 'twisted, crooked' = (*Wb.* v, 160, 12 f.), *gwš*, 'be crooked, at a slant'.

GARDINER, *JEA* 42, 19 [1956].

ϭⲱϣ (Crum 836b), 'pour forth' = (*Wb.* v, 156, 5), *gꜣš* and Gr.-R. (*Wb.* iv, 142, 6), *kš*, 'pour out'; (Er. 594, 1), *gš*, 'pour out, sprinkle'.

[H]LAUTH in *Sitzber. Bayer. Ak.* 1870, part II, 114 [1870]; [D]SPIEGELBERG, *Dem. Texte auf Krügen*, 38 and 76, no. 233 [1912].

See also **ϭⲟⲩϣϭ(ⲉ)ϣ**.

ϭⲏϣⲉ (Crum 837a), 'goose' or 'large duck' = (*Wb.* v, 208, 2), *gš*, a migrating bird.

CRUM, *A Coptic Dict.* 837a [1939].

ϭⲱϣⲧ (Crum 837a), 'look, see' = (Er. 594, 2), *gšp*, 'see, look'. For ⲡ > ⲧ, cf. [SAA2]ϩⲱϫⲡ > [SAA2]ϩⲱϫⲧ; [B]***ϭⲁⲗⲡ-** > [B]**ⲕⲁⲗⲧ-**.

GRIFFITH, *Stories*, 148 [1900]; cf. Spiegelberg, *Mythus*, 280, no. 870 [1917].

ϭⲟⲩϣϭ(ⲉ)ϣ (Crum 839a), 'sprinkle', reduplication of **ϭⲱϣ** < *gꜣš* (see **ϭⲱϣ**), though [A]**ϫϩϫⲱϩ⸗** seems irreconcilable with **gšgš*).

ϭϩⲟⲥ (Crum 839b), 'gazelle' = [hieroglyphs] (*Wb.* v, 191, 1 f.), *gḥs*, 'gazelle' (*Gazella dorcas* L.).

LEPSIUS in *ZÄS* 5, 72 [1867].

ϭⲟϩⲥⲉ, ϭⲁϩⲥⲉ, fem. of prec. = [hieroglyphs] (*Wb.* v, 191, 9), *gḥst*, 'female gazelle'; [demotic] (Er. 591, 8), *gḥst*, 'gazelle'.

[H]ERMAN, *Äg. Glossar*, 140 [1904], cf. Champollion, *Dict.* 261 [1841] (he compares fem. [B]ϭⲁϩⲥⲓ with masc. *gḥs*); cf. Dévaud in *Kêmi* 1, 144 [1928]; [D]KRALL, *Mitt. aus d. Samml. Erzh. Rainer*, VI, pp. 31 and 55 [1897].

ϭⲓϫ (Crum 839b), 'hand' = [hieroglyphs] (not in *Wb.*), *kḏ(t)*, 'hand'; [demotic] (Er. 595, 4), *g(y)ḏ*, 'hand'.

[H]STEINDORFF in Spiegelberg, *Kopt. Handwb.* 282 n. 12 [1921]; cf. Černý, *BIFAO* 57, 212 [1958]; [D]BRUGSCH, *Gr. dém.* 28, §56; 73, §159 [1855].

ϭⲟⲩϫ (Crum 840b), 'safflower, cardamum', *Carthamus tinctorius* L. = [hieroglyphs] (*Wb.* v, 148, 5–7), *kṯ*, a flower; [demotic] (Er. 595, 6), *gḏ*, a fruit.

[H]BRUGSCH, *Wb.*, Suppl. 1285 [1882], cf., however, W. Max Müller, *ZÄS* 26, 82 [1888]; [D]SPIEGELBERG, *Dem. Denkmäler*, II, 213 [1908].

ϭⲁϫⲉ (Crum 840b), 'earring' = [demotic] (Er. 595, 5), *gḏ*, 'earring'.

ERICHSEN, *Dem. Glossar*, 595, 5 [1954].

[B]ϭⲟϫⲓ (Crum 840b), 'run' = L.E. [hieroglyphs] [[hieroglyph]?] [hieroglyphs] (not in *Wb.*), *kḏ*, 'run'; [demotic] (Er. 693, 1), *ḏḏỉ*, 'run'.

[H]MASSART, *Mitt. Kairo* 15, 179 n. 6 and Pl. XXXI, 8 [1957]; [D]GRIFFITH, *PSBA* 18, 105 [1896].

ϭⲱⲱϫⲉ (Crum 841a), 'cut', a loan-word from Semitic √*qṣṣ*, cf. Hebrew קָצַץ, 'cut off', Aram. קְצַץ, Arabic قصّ ('cut the extremity of ear of an animal'). See also ϭⲟⲩϭ(ⲉ)ϫ and [B]ϫⲁϭⲉ.

EMBER, *ZÄS* 49, 94 [1911].

ϭⲱϫⲃ (Crum 841b), 'be small, less; lessen', from Semitic, cf. קצב, قضب.

STRICKER in *Acta Orientalia* 15, 5 [1937].

ϭⲁϫⲙⲏ (Crum 842b), 'fist, handful' = [hieroglyphs] (*Wb.* v, 82, 12), *kḏm*, 'fistful (as measure of gum)'; [hieratic], *gḏmꜣ* (masc.!), 'handful' (*JEA* 26, Pl. XVIII, B21); [demotic] (Er. 595, 8), *gḏm*, 'hilt' of sword.

Probably a loan-word from Semitic, √*ḳmṣ*, cf. Hebrew קֹמֶץ, Aram. קַמְצָא (Dalman: 'handful'), Syriac ܩܘܡܨܐ. These from verb קָמַץ, 'enclose with the hand' = Gr.-R. (Schott, *Urk.* vi, 106 note *a*), *gḏm*, 'seize'.

[H]SCHOTT, *Urk.* vi, 106 note *a* [1939]; [D]PARKER, *JEA* 26, 99 [1940]; cf. Stricker, *Oudh. Meded.*, N.S. 35, 61 n. 64 [1954].

ϫⲁⲙⲏ, from *ϫⲁϫⲙⲏ = , *ṯ3y-ʿmyt*, or , *ṯ3y-3myt* (Er. 668, 2), 'paw, claw' or sim. as if from , *ṯ3y*, 'seize' (*Wb.* v, 346) + , *3mmt* (*Wb.* i, 11, 1), 'grip, fist'.

[D]SPIEGELBERG, *Mythus*, 305, no. 964 [1917]; cf. Volten in *Archiv Orientální* 20, 505 [1952].

[S]ϭⲁϫⲓϥ, [B]ϫⲁϥϫⲓϥ, ϫⲁⲡϫⲓⲡ, etc. (Crum 842 b), 'ant' = (Er. 536, 5), *ḳpḳp*, 'ant', originally perhaps *ϭⲁⲃϭⲓⲃ, lit. 'tiny piece', see ϭⲉⲃϭⲓⲃ, 'fragments(?)'.

[D]GRIFFITH–THOMPSON, iii, 89, no. 953 [1909].

(ϭⲱϫϩ), ϭⲟϫϩ⸗ (Crum 841 a, s.v. ϭⲱⲱϫⲉ), 'disperse' = (*Wb.* v, 82, 15), *ḳdḥ*, 'disperse'(?), from Semitic, cf. Hebrew קָצַח, 'cut off', Arabic قزح.

[HS]BRUGSCH, *Wb.*, Suppl. 1270 [1882]; cf. Dévaud, *Kêmi* 2, 17–18 [1929].

[S]ϭⲟϫϭ(ⲉ)ϫ, [B]ϭⲟⲧϭⲉⲧ (Crum 842 b), 'cut, smite, slaughter' = (*Wb.* v, 146, 13. 14), *ktkt*, 'slaughter, hit'; (Er. 569, 7), *ḳdḳd*, 'gnaw', from Semitic, cf. Arabic قصقص, 'break to pieces'. Reduplication of ϭⲱⲱϫⲉ, see this.

[H]BRUGSCH, *Wb.* 1503 [1868]; [D]BRUGSCH, *Gr. dém.* 128, §264 [1855]; [S]STRICKER, in *Acta Orientalia* 15, 4 [1937].

[S]ϭⲱϭ, [B]ϫⲱϫ (Crum 843 a), 'roast, bake' = (Er. 568, 9), *kk*, 'roast'.

GRIFFITH–THOMPSON, iii, 88, no. 936 [1909].

ϭⲁⲁϭⲉ, ϭⲁϭⲉ (Crum 843 b), 'baked loaf, cake' = (Er. 561, 4), *kʿkʿ*, or , *gʿgʿ*, or , *ky*, kind of bread, 'loaf of bread'; cf. κακεῖς (Strabo xvii, 824). From Semitic, cf. Arabic كَعْك, Aram. כַּעְכָּא, Syriac ܟܥܟܐ ('placenta').

[D]SPIEGELBERG, *Kopt. Handwb.* 295 [1921]; [S]SPIEGELBERG, *Sethosrechnungen*, 41 [1896].

NB. The identity of ϭⲁⲁϭⲉ with (*Wb.* I, 235, 4), *ʿkk*, a kind of bread, suggested by BRUGSCH, *Wb.*, Suppl. 290 [1880], is doubtful.

[S]ϭⲁϭⲉⲧⲟⲗ (Crum 844a), light ship. The Bohairic form ϫⲁϫⲓⲑⲱⲗ of [S]ϭⲁϭⲓⲧⲱⲛ(ⲉ), 'coarse linen', suggests that ϭⲁϭⲉⲧⲟⲗ is the same word and denotes ships with rigging made of esparto grass (see ϭⲁϭⲓⲧⲱⲛ(ⲉ)).

[S]ϭⲁϭⲓⲧⲱⲛ(ⲉ), [B]ϫⲁϫⲓⲑⲱⲗ (Crum 844a, adding ⲕⲁⲧⲓⲧⲱⲛⲉ, Crum, *Ostraca* 466), 'coarse linen, tow', from *ϭⲁⲧⲓⲧⲱⲛ = (Er. 595, 3), *Gtltn*, i.e. Γαδιτάνη, country round and including the town of Gadeira (modern Cadiz) in Spain, source of coarse cables (see ⲙⲁϣⲣⲧ), '*Hibericus funis*' of Horace (*Epodes*, 4, 3) made of esparto grass (*Stipa tenacissima* L.) eminently suitable for ships' rigging because of its toughness and resistance to sea-water (see Pliny, *Nat. hist.* XIX, 7–8); the , *Ktn*, of Vienna Petubastis L 32 (Spiegelberg, *Petubastis*, 85*, no. 578) is a different word, *ktn*, see ϣⲧⲏⲛ.

APPENDIX: GEOGRAPHICAL NAMES (IN SELECTION)

[O]ⲁⲗⲭⲁⲁ, a sacred place at Abydos = [hieroglyphs] (*Wb.* I, 213, 5), *ʿrḳ-ḥḥ*; [Demotic] (Er. 68, 7), *ʿlk-ḥḥ*, or [Demotic], *ʿlg-hʿh*. Gk. [α]λχαί.

[H]ERMAN, *ZÄS* 21, 104 [1883]; [D]HESS, *Stne*, 149 [1888].

ⲁⲡⲉ, see ⲡⲁⲡⲉ.

[B]ⲁⲧⲃⲱ, see ⲧⲃⲱ.

[B]ⲁⲑⲣⲏⲃⲓ, ⲁⲑⲣⲉⲃⲓ (Am. 66–9) = [hieroglyphs], *Ḥwt-tꜣ-ḥr-ỉb*, later spelt [hieroglyphs], *Ḥwt-ḥr-ỉb* (*Wb.* III, 3, 4; 136, 20; Gauthier IV, 112; 140–1), lit. 'Mansion of the Land of the middle'; [Demotic], *Ḥt-tꜣ-ḥr-(ỉ)b*; Assyrian *Ḫatḫiribi*; Gk. Ἀθρῖβις (Strabo); = اتريب, now تل اتريب, town in the Delta.

[H]BRUGSCH, *Dict. géo.* 527, 1046 [1879]; [D]KRALL in *Mitt. aus der Sammlung Erzh. Rainer*, VI, 30 [1897].

[S]ⲁⲧⲣⲓⲡⲉ, less frequently ⲁⲧⲣⲏⲡⲉ, once ⲁⲧⲣⲉⲡⲉ, [B]ⲁⲑⲣⲏⲃⲓ (Am. 69–70) = [hieroglyphs], *Ḥwt-Rpyt*, 'Mansion of (goddess) Triphis'; ادريب, place near Wannîna, south-west of Sohâg, where Shenūte built the 'White Monastery'.

GARDINER in *JEA* 31, 108–11 [1945]; cf. Brugsch, *Geographie*, 216 [1857] and Maspero in *Rec. trav.* 25, 23 [1903].

NB. The [B]ⲁⲑⲣⲏⲃⲓ is due to a confusion with the Delta town of Athribis, [B]ⲁⲑⲣⲏⲃⲓ, for which see the preceding entry. ⲧⲣⲓⲫⲓⲟⲩ (e.g. Z 567; cf. Am. 529) is the genitive of the Gk. name Τρίφιον.

[S]ⲃⲉⲣϭⲟⲟⲩⲧ, [B]ⲧⲃⲉⲣϭⲱⲧ (Am. 178–9; Crum 44b) = [hieroglyphs] (*Wb.* I, 466, 11), *Brkt*, 'pond', a loan-word from Semitic, cf. בְּרֵכָה, بركة [common as a place-name in New Kingdom, see Gardiner–Faulkner, *Pap. Wilbour*, IV (Index), 76] = برجوط, now فرشوط in the province of Qena. The ⲟⲩ inserted under influence of ⲃⲣϭⲟⲟⲩⲧ, 'chariot', where it represents the *b* of the Semitic original *mrkbt*.

YOYOTTE's communication.

B**ⲃⲟⲩⲥⲓⲣⲓ, ⲡⲟⲩⲥⲓⲣⲓ** (Am. 7–11) = * (Gauthier II, 69), *Pr-Wsỉr*, lit. 'House of Osiris', which is an abbreviation of the full name (*Wb*. I, 514, 1; Gauthier II, 70–1; Gardiner, *Onom*. II, 176* foll.), *Pr-Wsỉr-nb-Ḏdw*, 'House of Osiris, lord of (town) *Djedu*'; , *P-wsỉr*; Assyrian *Pušîru*; Gk. Βούσιρις; Arabic بوصير, now ابو صير بنا, Abû Ṣîr Banâ, in the Delta.

HD BRUGSCH, *Geographie*, 24 and Pl. III, nos. 142 and 143 [1857].

B**ⲃⲟⲩⲧⲟ, ⲡⲟⲩⲧⲟ, ⲡⲟⲩⲧⲱⲟⲩ** (Am. 105–11, 370) = (*Wb*. I, 268, 18; Gauthier II, 65; Gardiner, *Onom*. II, 187*, no. 415), *Pr-Wꜣḏyt*, 'House of (goddess) Wadjōyet'; ; Gk. Βούτω or Βοῦτοι; the modern تل الفراعين, Tell el-Farāʿîn, in the Delta. The ancient name itself preserved in the name of the village إبطو.

H BRUGSCH, *Dict. géo*. 178 [1879] (compares Βούτω but does not quote the Coptic form); D GRIFFITH, *Ryl*. III, 243 n. 5; 422 [1909].

S**ⲡⲃⲟⲟⲩ, ⲡⲃⲁⲩ**, B**ⲫⲃⲱⲟⲩ** (Crum 46b, s.v. **ⲃⲟⲟⲩ**; Am. 331–3) = Definite article **ⲡ** + **ⲃⲟⲟⲩ** 'heap (of stones)', for which see Dict. above; transcribed into Arabic as بافوا, now فاو, Fâw, in the province of Qena, famous for the monastery founded by Pakhomius.

ⲃⲟⲩϣⲏⲙ(ⲓ), ⲃⲟⲩϣⲉⲙ(ⲓ) (Am. 51–4) = * , *Pr-ẖm*, 'House of *ẖm*', the name actually attested being and varr. (*Wb*. III, 280, 15; Gauthier IV, 175; V, 45–6), *ẖm*, lit. 'place of cult, sanctuary' (*Wb*. III, 280, 10–13); Gk. Λητοῦς πόλις; now اوسيم, near Cairo.

BRUGSCH, *Geographie*, 243 and Pl. XLIII, no. 1134 [1857].

(ⲡ)ⲁⲓⲙⲉⲛϩⲱⲣ ⲗⲩⲙⲛⲏ, see under **ϯⲙⲓⲛϩⲱⲣ**.

S**ⲉⲃⲱⲧ** (only Z 551), O**ⲁⲃⲱⲧ** (Am. 154–5) = (*Wb*. I, 9, 1; Gauthier I, 4), *ꜣbḏw*; (Er. 27, 4), *ỉbt*; Gk. Ἄβυδος; modern العرابا المدفونة, El-ʿArâba el-Madfûna.

H CHAMPOLLION, *Gr*. 65 and 133 [1836]; D BRUGSCH, *Scriptura Aeg. dem*. 16 [1848].

B**ⲉⲙⲃⲱ**, see under S**ⲛⲃⲱ**.

ⲉⲣⲏⲃⲉ, also ?**ⲧⲏⲣⲃⲉ** (Am. 165; Crum in Petrie, *Gizeh and Rifeh*, 41) = , *ꜣrb*, lit. 'enclosure, pen, fence' (= **(ⲉ)ⲣⲃⲉ**, for which cf. Dict. s.v. **ⲱⲣ(ⲉ)ⲃ**); Gk. Ἐρέβη, now دير ريفة, a hill to the south of Siût.

D H. THOMPSON, *A Family Archive*, 43 n. 17, and Index, (88) n. 32 [1934].

ⲉⲣⲉⲙⲟⲩⲛ, see **ⲡⲉⲣⲉⲙⲟⲩⲛ**.

[B]**ⲉⲣⲙⲟⲛⲧ**, see under **ⲣⲙⲟⲛⲧ**.

[B]**ⲉⲥⲛⲏ**, see under [S]**ⲥⲛⲏ**.

ⲓⲏⲃ (only once) = (*Wb.* I, 7, 18; Gauthier I, 3), *ꜣbw*; (Er. 49, 8), *yb*; Aramaic יב, Gk. ἰήβ (in Χνουμωνεβιήβ), but commonly Ἐλεφαντίνη, island in the Nile opposite Aswân.
ENGELBACH in *Ann. du Service* 38, 47–9 [1938].

ⲓⲃⲣⲓⲙ, properly [**ⲓⲃ**]**ⲣⲓⲙ**, see under **ⲡⲣⲓⲙ**.

ⲡ-ⲓⲗⲁⲕϩ, see under **ⲡⲓⲗⲁⲕϩ**.

ⲡ-ⲓⲟⲙ, see under **ⲡⲓⲟⲙ**.

[S]**ⲕⲏⲃⲧ, ⲕϥⲧ**, [B]**ⲕⲉϥⲧ, ⲕⲉⲃⲧⲱ, ⲕⲉⲡⲧⲟ** (Am. 213–15) = (*Wb.* V, 163, 1; Gauthier V, 173; Gardiner, *Onom.* II, 28*), *Gbtyw*; (Er. 577, 4), *Gbty*(*w*); Gk. Κόπτος; now قفط in Upper Egypt.
[H]CHAMPOLLION, *Gr.* 153 [1836]; [D]BRUGSCH, *Dict. géo.* 829–30 [1879].

ⲕⲉⲙⲏⲛ, see under **ⲧⲕⲉⲙⲏⲛ**.

[B]**ⲕⲱⲛⲏ** (Am. 393–4) = Καινὴ πόλις of Ptolemy; now قنا in Upper Egypt (Gardiner, *Onom.* II, 29*, no. 342 A).

ⲕⲉⲣⲕⲉ- in place names, see under **ϭⲉⲣϭ-**.

ⲕⲉⲣⲕⲏ, see under **ϭⲉⲣϭⲏ**.

[S]**ⲕⲱⲥ**, [B]**ⲕⲱⲥ ⲃⲉⲣⲃⲓⲣ, ⲕⲟⲟⲥ ⲃⲁⲣⲃⲓⲣ** (Am. 399–400 and 400–1) = (Gauthier V, 178, 220. 221; Gardiner, *Onom.* II, 27*–28*), *Gsꜣ*; later , *Gsy*; Gk. Ἀπόλλωνος πόλις μικρά; Arabic قوص وارویر, now قوص, Qûṣ, in Upper Egypt. The meaning of **ⲃⲁⲣⲃⲓⲣ, ⲃⲉⲣⲃⲓⲣ** is unknown.
PLEYTE, *Les Papyrus Rollin*, 41 [1868].

[S]**ⲕⲱⲥ ⲕⲁⲙ**, [B]**ⲕⲟⲥ ⲕⲁⲙ** (Am. 397–9) = , , etc. (*Wb.* V, 17, 7; Gauthier V, 164–5; Gardiner, *Onom.* II, 77*, no. 374), *Ḳis*; , *Ḳsis* (Er. 550, 2; Spiegelberg, *Mythus*, p. 329, no. 1096); Gk. Κοῦσαι; Arabic قوصقام; now القوصية, El-Qûṣîya in Upper Egypt. The element **ⲕⲁⲙ** is obscure.
[H]BRUGSCH, *Dict. géo.* 868, 1040 [1879].

[B]**ⲕⲁⲓⲥⲓ** (Am. 395–7) =  (*JEA* 38, 45 and 38), *ḳrst*;  (Er. 568, 2), *ks*; now القيس, El-Qês in Upper Egypt.

[H]NIMS in *JEA* 38, 45 [1952]; [D]SPIEGELBERG in *ZÄS* 44, 98 [1907].

[B]**ⲕⲉϥⲧ**, see under [S]**ⲕⲏⲃⲧ, ⲕⲃⲧ**.

[S]**ⲗⲉϩⲱⲛⲉ, ⲗⲓϩⲱⲛⲉ**, [F]**ⲗⲉϩⲱⲛⲓ** (Crum 690a, s.v. **ϩⲱⲛⲉ**; Am. 232) =  (*Wb.* II, 398, 3; III, 105, 3; Gauthier III, 121, 124; Gardiner, *Onom.* II, 116*, no. 392A), *R-ḥnt*, lit. 'mouth of the lake' (namely of that in the oasis of Faiyûm), originally a name for the whole region, later a town; now اللاهون, El-Lâhûn, a large village just at the entrance of the Faiyûm.

[H]KRALL, *Mitteilungen aus der Sammlung Erzh. Rainer*, II/III, 58 [1887].

ⲧⲙⲟⲩⲉⲓ-, ⲧⲙⲟⲩ- alone or as first part of place names (Am. 514–17; Crum 160b, s.v. **ⲙⲟⲩⲉ**) = **ⲙⲟⲩⲉ**, 'island', for which see Dict. above.

BRUGSCH, *Dict. géo.* 246 [1879].

ⲙⲁⲛ- as first element of place names (Am. 237 f.) = **ⲙⲁ** + **ⲛ**, 'place of'. The second part mostly obscure.

ⲙⲁⲛⲃⲁⲗⲟⲧ (Am. 237–8), 'place of fleeces' = now منفلوط, Manfalûṭ (Crum 38b, s.v. **ⲃⲁⲗⲟⲧ**).

ⲙⲁⲛⲕⲁⲡⲱⲧ (Am. 239) = **ⲙⲁⲛ** + [B]**ϭⲁⲃⲱⲧ**, material or instrument used in cleansing sheep (Crum 806a), perhaps some clay since **ⲕⲁⲡⲱⲧ** in **ⲙⲁⲛⲕⲁⲡⲱⲧ** is translated as موضع الكاسات, 'place of earthern pots'; now منقباد (earlier with ض or ط instead of د); but cf. Crum 146, s.v. **ⲁⲡⲟⲧ**.

ⲙⲁⲛⲗⲁⲩ (Am. 239–40), 'place of *lau*' (**ⲗⲁⲁⲩ, ⲗⲁⲩ**, a textile, Crum 145b) = prob. ملّوى, Mallawi in Upper Egypt, as suggested by Amélineau.

[S]**ⲧⲙⲟⲟⲛⲉ, ⲧⲙⲱⲛⲏ**, [B]**ⲑⲙⲟⲛⲏ** (Am. 257–8) = modern المنيه, El-Minya in Upper Egypt = Gk. μονή, '[in IVth cent. A.D.] regularly used...as "monastery", but it also frequently had the sense of *mansio*, i.e. a hostel or lodging for the night, for the use of travellers and hence came to mean "stages" of a journey' (Bell, *Jews and Christians in Egypt*, 64).

CRUM, *A Coptic Dict.* 174a, s.v. **ⲙⲟⲟⲛⲉ** [1930].

[S]**ⲙⲛϥⲉ, ⲙⲉⲛⲃⲉ**, [B]**ⲙⲉϥⲓ, ⲙⲉⲛϥ** (Am. 247–50) = 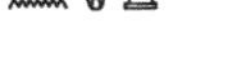 (*Wb.* II, 63,

6; Gauthier III, 38–9; Gardiner, *Onom.* II, 122*, no. 394), *Mn-nfr*, abbreviated from the name of the pyramid of King Phiops I, *Mn-nfr-Ppỉ*, 'The beauty of Pyōpey (= Phiops) is established'; (Er. 161, 6), *Mn-nfr*; Gk. Μέμφις; Assyrian *Mempi*, *Mimpi*; Hebrew מֹף, נֹף; Arabic منف; at the modern village of ميت رهينة, Mît-Rahîna.

[H]CHAMPOLLION, *Gr.* 153 [1836]; cf. ERMAN, *Ägypten und ägyptisches Leben*, 244 [1885] on the origin of the name; [D]BRUGSCH, *Scriptura Aeg. dem.* 16 [1848].

[O]ⲛⲉ, [S]ⲛⲏ (Crum in Winlock and Crum, *Epiphanius*, II, 192, no. 151 n. 2) = (*Wb.* II, 211, 7), *nỉwt*, lit. 'town'; (Er. 210, 5), *Nỉwt*; Assyrian *Ni'*; Hebrew נֹא; Gk; Gk. Θῆβαι or Διὸς πόλις; Thebes.

ERMAN in *ZÄS* 21, 103 [1883]; confirmed by Griffith in *ZÄS* 38, 91 [1900].

[S]ⲛⲃⲱ, ⲛⲃⲟⲩ, [B]ⲉⲙⲃⲱ (Am. 287) = (*Wb.* II, 242, 5; Gauthier III, 83–4; Gardiner, *Onom.* II, 5*, no. 316), *Nb(y)t*; (Er. 30, 8), *'Imbꜣ*; Gk. Ὄμβοι; now كوم امبو, Kôm Ombô, in Upper Egypt.

[H]CHAMPOLLION, *Gr.* 153 [1836]; [D]SPIEGELBERG in Preisigke and Spiegelberg, *Die Prinz-Joachim-Ostraka*, 23 [1914].

[B]ⲛⲓⲕⲉⲛⲧⲱⲣⲓ, see under [S]ⲛⲓⲧⲉⲛⲧⲱⲣⲉ.

[S]ⲛⲙϩⲁⲧⲉ, [B]ⲛⲉⲙϩⲁϯ (Am. 274; Crum, *Wadi Sarga*, 164, no. 213, n. 4) = *, *nꜣ mḥtyw*, lit. 'the Northerners'.

ČERNÝ in *Festschrift Grapow*, 31 [1955].

[S]ⲛⲓⲧⲛⲧⲱⲣⲉ, [B]ⲛⲓⲧⲉⲛⲧⲱⲣⲓ (one MS ⲛⲓⲕⲉⲛⲧⲱⲣⲓ, the scribe must have thought of Κένταυροι) (Am. 140–2) = (*Wb.* II, 362, 7; Gauthier I, 57; Gardiner, *Onom.* II, 30*, no. 343), *'Iwn(t)-tꜣ-nṯrt*, lit. '*ỉwnt* of the goddess (= Hathor)'; , *'Iwnt-tꜣ-ntrt*, also without *ỉwnt* (see the writings in Gauthier, VI, 23), *tꜣ nṯrt*; Gk. Τεντύρα; now دندرة, Dendera, in Upper Egypt. , *'Iwnt*, is the original name of the town; the proper meaning of the word is unknown.

GARDINER, *Onom.* II, 30* [1947] (explains ⲛⲓ-); cf. MARIETTE, *Dendéra*, Text, 77 [1880] (identifies the Egn. name with Gk. Τεντυρίς, but does not quote the Coptic name).

ⲡⲁⲑⲱ (Am. 269–70) = (Gardiner, *Onom.* II, 146* ff.), *N3y-t3-ḥwt*, lit. 'Those of the Mansion (of Ramesses III)'; (Petubastis 4, 11), *N3y-t3-ḥwt*; Assyrian *Nathū*; Gk. Ναθώ; Arabic نتى (prob. mistake for نتو), modern تل اليهودية, Tell el-Yahûdîya, in the Delta.

HD GARDINER, *Onom.* II, 146* ff. [1947].

B ⲡⲟⲩⲃⲁⲥϯ, ⲡⲟⲩⲁⲥϯ, ⲫⲟⲩⲃⲁⲥⲑⲓ (Am. 89, misprinting **ⲡⲟⲩⲣⲁⲥⲧⲓ**) = (*Wb.* I, 423, 8; Gauthier II, 75), *Pr-b3stt*, lit. 'House of (goddess) Bastet'; , *Pr-b3stt*; Hebrew פִּי־בֶסֶת; Gk. Βούβαστις; now تل بسطة, Tell Basta in the Delta.

HD BRUGSCH, *Géographie*, 24 and Pl. III, nos. 144, 145 [1857].

ⲡⲃⲟⲟⲩ, see under **ⲃⲟⲟⲩ**.

S ⲡⲓⲗⲁⲕ, B ⲡⲓⲗⲁⲕϩ (Am. 347; Crum 140b, s.v. **ⲗⲁⲕϩ**) = (*Wb.* I, 47, 9; Gauthier I, 30; II, 52), *P3-ỉw-rḳ*; or , *P-ỉ-lḳ*; Gk. Πιλάκ; Ar. بِلاق, island of Philae, south of Aswân. For the meaning of **ⲡⲓⲗⲁⲕ**, see above p. 71 (s.v. **ⲗⲁⲕϩ**).

H CHAMPOLLION, *Gr.* 154 [1836]; D BRUGSCH, *Gr. dém.* 56, §126 [1855]; cf. BRUGSCH, *Nouvelles recherches*, 2 [1856].

S ⲡⲓⲟⲙ, B ⲫⲓⲟⲙ, F ⲡⲓⲁⲙ (Am. 185–6, 337–40), lit. 'the sea' (**ⲉⲓⲟⲙ**, see in Dictionary), the province of الفيوم, El-Faiyûm, its lake and capital; , *P3-ym* (Er. 50, 1), province (*tš*) and town (*dmy*).

D BRUGSCH in *ZÄS* 31, 24 [1893].

ⲡⲉⲙϫⲉ, ⲡⲙϫⲏ (Am. 90–3) = (Gauthier II, 83), *Pr-mḏ*; or (Er. 134, 2), *P-mḏ*; Gk. Ὀξύρυγχος; modern البهنسا, El-Bahnasâ.

H DE ROUGÉ, *Chrest. ég.* IV, 5 n. 5 [1876]; D BRUGSCH, *Nouvelles recherches*, 2 [1856].

ⲡⲁⲛⲕⲟⲗⲉⲩⲥ (Am. 95–6) < **ⲡⲁ-ⲛⲓⲕⲟⲗⲁⲟⲥ**, lit. 'that (= place) of Nicholas'; Ar. بنكلاوس, Banklâus; near El-Minya (Togo Mina, *Apa Epima*, pp. xxiv–xxv).

B ⲡⲟⲩⲛⲉⲙⲟⲩ (Am. 364–5) = (Gauthier I, 44; Gardiner, *Onom.* II, 180*–1*, no. 413), *P3-ỉw-n-'Imn*, lit. 'The Island of Amūn'; now تل البلامون, Tell el-Balâmûn, in the Delta.

[H]SPIEGELBERG, *Ägyptologische Randglossen zum Alten Testament*, 36 [1904]; cf. Gardiner in *JEA* 30, 41 [1944].

[B]**ⲡⲁⲛⲧⲏⲩ** (Gauthier VI, 111), emended—probably wrongly (cf. Gardiner, *Onom.* II, 46*)—from **ⲡⲁⲛⲉϩⲏⲟⲩ**, see this latter.

ⲡⲁⲛⲁⲩ (Am. 84–5; Gardiner, *Onom.* II, 177*) = ? (Dem. mag. Pap. 19, 6), *Pꜣ-nw*, lit. meaning uncertain; now بنا ابو صير, Banâ Abû Ṣîr, in the Delta.

[D]SPIEGELBERG in *OLZ* 7, col. 198 [1904].

[B]**ⲡⲁⲛⲉϩⲏⲟⲩ** (Am. 299–300), island in the Nile opposite **ϣⲙⲓⲛ**. The name being translated into Arabic as جزيرة السواقى, 'island of the wind', **ⲡⲁⲛⲉϩⲏⲟⲩ** has been emended by some into **ⲡⲁⲛⲧⲏⲟⲩ**, almost certainly wrongly. **-ⲉϩⲏⲟⲩ** is perhaps the plural of **ϩⲟⲓ** (Crum 650 b), 'field', arable or pasture.

CRUM, *A Coptic Dict.* 730 a [1939].

[S]**ⲡⲁⲡⲉ** (BKU I, 35, 2) (Am. 234–5) = prob. **ⲡ** + 𓇋𓊪𓏏𓉐 (*Wb.* I, 68, I. 2), *ἰpt*, lit. 'harem (of god Amūn)', having become masc. in Coptic times. This is an abbreviation of 𓇋𓊪𓏏𓉐𓇔𓏏𓊖 (*Wb.* I, 68, 3; Gauthier I, 68), *'Ipt-rsyt*, 'southern *'Ipt*'; الاقصرين, El-Uqṣurên, now الاقصر, El-Uqṣur, Luxor. The form **ⲁⲡⲉ** without article seems to be the earlier usage, see Crum in Winlock and Crum, *Epiphanius*, I, 105–6.

[H]GOODWIN in *ZÄS* 7, 75 [1869]; cf. Gardiner, *Onom.* II, 25* [1947].

[**ⲡ**]**ⲣⲓⲙ** (**ⲓⲃⲣⲓⲙ** of Gauthier III, 11, is Bouriant's restoration, *Rec. trav.* 7, 218) = 𓊪𓂋𓅓𓏏𓊖 (Gauthier II, 143), *Prm(t)*; (Brugsch, *Dict. géogr.* 1242), *P(r)rmy*; Gk. Πρίμις, Πρῆμ(ν)ις; now قصر ابريم, Qaṣr Ibrîm in Nubia, opposite 'Anîba.

[HD]GAUTHIER, *Dict. géogr.* II, 143 [1925] and III, 11 [1926]; cf. Griffith in *JEA* 20, 8 [1934].

ⲡⲉⲣⲉⲙⲟⲩⲛ (Am. 317–18) = 𓅯𓁹𓇋𓏠𓈖𓊖 (Gauthier II, 36, 58), *Pꜣ-ἰr-ἰmn*, lit. 'That (= town) which Amūn has made'; (Er. 134, 1), *P(r)-ἰr-ἰmn*; Gk. Πηλούσιον; now تل الفرما, Tell Faramâ in the Delta.

[H]GAUTHIER in Gardiner in *JEA* 10, 94 [1924], cf. Gauthier and Sottas, *Un décret trilingue*, 26–7 [1925]; [D]GRIFFITH–THOMPSON, I, 20 [1904]; cf. Spiegelberg in *ZÄS* 57, 69 [1922].

ⲡⲥⲟⲓ (Am. 381–3) = (quoted only by Champollion; but of *Wb.* iv, 65, 14 is in the Delta); compare Gauthier ii, 124 and 150), *Psy Ptrmys*; (Er. 407, 8), *Pꜣ-sy*; Gk. Πτολεμαῒς ἡ Ἑρμείου; Ar. ابصاى, now المنشاة, El-Manshâh in Middle Egypt.

[H]BRUGSCH, *Geographie*, 211 and Pl. xl, no. 973 [1857]; [D]BRUGSCH, *Scriptura Aeg. dem.* 16 [1848].

ⲯⲓⲕⲱ (Grohmann, *Cat. Arab. Pap. Cairo*, iii, no. 167) = ? (Gauthier v, 10, 193), *Sꜣkꜣ*, lit. 'Back of the Bull'; Gk. Κῶ (Ptolemy); prob. modern القيس, El-Qês. Identical with [B]**ⲕⲁⲓⲥⲓ**, see this latter.

GARDINER, *Onom.* ii, 103*–6* [1947].

ⲡⲥⲉⲛⲉⲧⲁⲓ (Am. 378) = ? (Dem. Mag. Pap. 21, 35), *P(ꜣ) snyṯ*; Ar. سنتا; ?modern السنطة, Es-Sinṭa, near Hurbeiṭ in the Delta (cf. Brugsch, *Dict. géogr.* 806 [1879]).

[D]SPIEGELBERG in *OLZ* 7, col. 198 [1904].

[B]**ⲡⲟⲩⲥⲓⲣⲓ**, see [B]**ⲃⲟⲩⲥⲓⲣⲓ**.

[S]**ⲡⲟⲩⲥⲓⲣⲉ**, [F]**ⲡⲟⲩⲥⲓⲣⲓ** (CMSS xxiii, 17, etc.) = (Gauthier ii, 69), *Pr-Wsỉr*, أبو صير الملق, Abûṣîr el-Malaq, at the entrance to the Faiyûm.

[S]**(ⲛ)ⲡⲁⲓⲁⲧ**, [B]**ⲛⲓⲫⲁⲓⲁⲧ**, [F]**ⲛⲉⲡⲁⲓⲉⲧ** (CMSS Appendix, p. 79), Libya and Libyan nome (مريوط, Maryûṭ) and their inhabitants = (Gauthier ii, 44; iii, 68–9), *(nꜣ) pyt*, < and varr. (Edwards, *Hieratic Papyri in the Brit. Mus., Fourth Series*, i, 10 n. 23 and Index, p. 122, s.v. *pwdy*) *Pwd(y)*; (Volten, *Dem. Traumdeutung*, 108); Hebrew פוט; Libyan(s).

[HEBREW]POSENER, *La première domination perse en Égypte*, 186–7 [1936]; [D]KRALL in *WZKM* 18, 122 [1904] (in proper name); cf. SPIEGELBERG, *Demotica*, i, 27 n. 5 [1925].

[B]**ⲡⲟⲩⲧⲟ**, see under [B]**ⲃⲟⲩⲧⲟ**.

ⲡⲉⲧⲉⲙⲟⲩⲧ, a village near Thebes, now المداmود, El-Medâmûd, north of Luxor. **ⲡⲉⲧⲉⲙⲟⲩⲧ** is an Egn. proper name , *Pꜣ-dỉ-mwt*, 'whom (goddess) Mūt has given' (Ranke, *Die äg. Personennamen*, i, 123, 17); the village was called after its owner.

CRUM, *The Monastery of Epiphanius*, ii, 226, no. 278 n. 7 [1926].

[S]ⲡⲓⲑⲱⲙ, [B]ⲡⲉⲑⲱⲙ, [A]ⲡⲉⲓⲑⲱⲙ (Exodus I, 11; Am. 355–7) = (*Wb.* I, 144, 6; Gauthier II, 59–60), *Pr-itm*, lit. 'House of (god) Atūm'; Hebrew פִּיתֹם, Gk. Πάτουμος 'Αραβίας (Herodotus) or 'Ηρώων πόλις (Strabo, Ptolemy); prob. the modern تل الرطابة, Tell er-Raṭâba in the Delta.

BRUGSCH, *Geographie*, 24 and Pl. III, no. 146 [1857].

ⲡⲧⲉⲛⲉⲧⲱ, see under ⲧⲉⲛⲉⲧⲱ.

ⲡⲉⲧⲡⲏϩ, see ⲧⲡⲏϩ.

ⲡⲁⲑⲩⲣⲓⲥ, abbrev. ⲡⲁⲑⲩⲣ (Gauthier VI, 98 from *ZÄS* 22, 51–2) = (Gauthier II, 117), *Pr-Ḥwtḥr*, lit. 'House of (goddess) Hathor' = , *Pr-Ḥwtḥr*; Gk. 'Αφροδίτης πόλις (Strabo), Παθῦρις of Greek papyri (Gardiner, *Onom.* II, 17*), in the nome called Παθυρίτης; modern الجبلين, El-Gebelein.

[HD]BRUGSCH, *Nouvelles recherches*, 2 and Pl. I, no. 1 [1856].

[B]ⲫⲁⲣⲃⲁⲓⲧ (Am. 330–1) = (Gauthier II, 114), *Pr-Ḥr-mrty*, lit. 'House of Horus of the two eyes' = Gk. Φάρβαιθος; now هربيط, Hurbeiṭ in the Delta.

[H]BRUGSCH, *Dict. géogr.* 808 [1879]; cf. SETHE in *ZÄS* 63, 99 [1927].

ⲡϫⲱϫ (Am. 308) = (Gauthier II, 140), *Pr-ḏ3ḏ3*, lit. 'House of the Head'; Ar. بتشت (Btšt) which seems to be a corruption from ابو تشت (Crum 799a, s.v. ϫⲱϫ), Abû Tisht where the town lay, though ⲡϫⲱϫ seems to be preserved in the name of the nearby ابو شوشة, Abû Shûsha, in Upper Egypt.

[H]BRUGSCH, *Nouvelles recherches*, 2–3, and Pl. I, nos. 4 and 5 [1856].

[S]ⲣⲁⲕⲟⲧⲉ, [B]ⲣⲁⲕⲟϯ (Am. 24–44) = (*Wb.* II, 403, 5; Gauthier III, 130); *Rᶜ-ḳdy(t)*; (Er. 242, 6; 551, 4), *Rᶜ-kt*, lit. '(place in the) state of building', name of the village on the site of which Alexandria was later built.

[H]BRUGSCH, *Geographie*, 10 and Pl. V, no. 262 [1857]; [D]Not identified.

[S]ⲣⲙⲟⲛⲧ, [B]ⲉⲣⲙⲟⲛⲧ, ⲉⲣⲙⲱⲛⲧ (Am. 165–7) = (*Wb.* II, 92, 3; Gauthier I, 54–5; cf. II, 86), *'Iwnw-Mnṯw*, lit. ''*Iwnw* of (the god) Mont'; , *'Iwnw-Mnṯ(w)*; Gk. 'Ερμῶνθις (Strabo); now ارمنت, Armant, in Upper Egypt.

[H]BRUGSCH, *Rhind*, 32 and Pl. 34, no. 12 [1865]; cf. Lacau, *Recueil Champollion*, 727 ff. [1922]; [D]BRUGSCH, *Gr. dém.* 56, §126 [1855].

[B]**ⲥⲁⲓ** (Am. 405–7) = (*Wb.* III, 420, 1; Gauthier V, 2), *Sȝw* = (Er. 408, 1), *Sy* = Assyrian *Saja* = Gk. Σαΐς = now صا الحجر, Ṣâ el-Ḥagar. ('Ṣâ, the stones') in the Delta.

[H]CHAMPOLLION, *Gr. ég.* 154 [1836]; [D]BRUGSCH, *Gr. dém.* 56, §126 [1855].

ⲥⲃⲱⲛ, see under **ⲥϩⲃⲱⲛ**.

[F]**ⲡⲥⲁⲃⲉⲧ** (Crum in Petrie, *Medum*, 50 and 54) = **ⲡ** + [S]**ⲥⲟⲃⲧ** (Crum 323a), 'wall' of town, , *sbty*, which in old times is found all over Egypt accompanied by various distinguishing additions (see Gauthier V, 23 ff.), Ar. صفط (spelt also سفط and صفت). The **ⲡⲥⲁⲃⲉⲧ** in question is the Gk. Σωφθις, the modern صفط ميدوم, Ṣafṭ-Maidûm, near Wasta south of Cairo.

ⲥⲃⲉϩⲧ (Am. 463), also **ⲥⲃⲏϩⲧ** (*ZÄS* 68, 67 n. 1) = , *Sbḥt* = Ar. اسفحت, Isfaḥt, now كوم اسفحت, Kôm Isfaḥt in Upper Egypt.

[D]GRIFFITH, *Catalogue of the Demotic Graffiti of the Dodecaschoinos*, I, 82–3, and 312, no. 918 [1937].

[S]**ⲥⲛⲏ**, [B]**ⲉⲥⲛⲏ** (Am. 172–5) = , , and sim. (Gauthier V, 38), *Sn*; Gk. Λάτων πόλις (Ptolemy) or Λατόπολις (Strabo); now اسنا, Esna, in Upper Egypt.

CHAMPOLLION, *Gr. ég.* 153 [1836].

[S]**ⲥⲟⲩⲏⲛ** (CO, p. 41), **ⲥⲟⲩⲁⲁⲛ** (*JEA* 20, 8), [B]**ⲥⲟⲩⲁⲛ** (Am. 467–8) = (*Wb.* IV, 69, 4; Gauthier V, 17–18), *Swnw*; (Er. 414, 2), *Swn*; Hebrew סְוֵנֵה or and סְוֵן ; Aram. סון; Gk. Συήνη; now أسوان, Aswân, at the southern frontier of Egypt.

[H]CHAMPOLLION, *Gr. ég.* 153 [1836]; [D]BRUGSCH, *Gr. dém.* 56, §126; 127, §259 [1855].

[S]**ⲥⲓⲟⲟⲩⲧ**, [B]**ⲥⲓⲱⲟⲩⲧ** (Am. 325 and 464–6) = (*Wb.* III, 420, 2; Gauthier V, 3–4), *Sȝwty*; (Er. 408, 3), *Sywṭ*; Assyrian *Šijâutu*;

Gk. Λυκόπολις (Strabo) and Λύκων πόλις (Ptolemy); now اسيوط, Asyûṭ in Middle Egypt.

ᴴBRUGSCH, *Geographie*, 217 and Pl. XL, no. 1001 [1857]; ᴰH. THOMPSON, *A Family Archive from Siut*, Text, 148 [1934].

ᴮⲥⲁϧⲱⲟⲩ, ⲥⲉϧⲱⲟⲩ (Am. 410; cf. also 335) = [hieroglyphs] (Gauthier IV, 155; Gardiner, *Onom.* II, 181* ff., no. 414), *Ḫ3sww*; Gk. Ξόις; now سخا, Sakha, in the middle of the Delta.

BRUGSCH, *Dict. géogr.* 557, 1044 [1879] (though retracted in the Supplement, pp. vii and 1299 [1880].

ⲥϩⲃⲱⲛ (*Ep.* I, 121, no. 10), ⲥⲃⲱⲛ (*PSBA* 34, 297) = [hieroglyphs] (Gauthier IV, 42 and 126), *Ḥwt-Snfrw*, lit. 'Mansion of (king) Snofru' > [hieroglyphs], and sim., *Ḥsfn*; [demotic], *Ḥsfn* (P.BM 10570A, 3; unpublished); Latin Asfynis, Arabic اصفون, Aṣfûn (see Am. 171), modern اصفون المطاعنة, Aṣfûn el-Maṭâʿna, in Upper Egypt.

ᴴGAUTHIER, *Dict. géogr.* IV, 126 [1927]; cf. Černý in *Rivista degli studi orientali* 38, 89–92 [1963]; ᴰSHORE's communication.

ˢⲦⲂⲞ, ⲦⲂⲰ, ᴮⲐⲂⲰ, ⲀⲦⲂⲰ (Am. 155–7) = [hieroglyphs] (*Wb.* V, 562, 1; Gauthier VI, 126–7), *Db3*; [demotic] (Er. 621, 1), *Tb3*; Gk. 'Απόλλωνος πόλις μεγάλη (Ptolemy); now إدفو, Edfu, in Upper Egypt.

ᴴBRUGSCH, *Geographie*, 94 and Pl. XI, no. 422; 165 and Pl. XXXIV, no. 682 [1857].

ˢⲦⲀⲂⲈⲚⲚⲎⲤⲈ, ᴮⲦⲀⲂⲈⲚⲚⲎⲤⲒ (Am. 469–71) = [demotic] (Pap. Ryl. XVIII, 3; Er. 58, 12), *T3-ʿbt-(n)-'Is*, lit. 'the chapel of (goddess) Isis' (Gk. 'Ισειον), though not the same place; Arabic دفانيس an island in the Nile near Hû in Upper Egypt where Pakhomius built his first monastery.

CRUM, *The Monastery of Epiphanius*, II, p. 196, no. 163 n. 8 [1926] and in Gardiner, *Onom.*, II, 15* n. 1 [1947].

ⲦⲔⲈⲘⲎⲚ (Am. 216–17, s.v. ⲔⲈⲘⲎⲚ, and 308; CMSS Appendix; for Ⲧ- see Togo Mina, *Apa Epima*, XXIX) = [hieroglyphs] (*P. Wilbour*, IV (Index), 68), *T3-i3dt-k3-mn*, 'The Mound The Bull is Established'; a locality near Ihnâsya in Middle Egypt.

ⲦⲀⲔⲒⲚⲀϢ (Am. 121), ⲦⲀⲔⲈⲚⲎϢ (CMSS, p. 66) = [hieroglyphs] (Gauthier, VI, 84) *Tknš*; present دقناش, Diknâsh, at the latitude of Faiyûm.

DE ROUGÉ, *Chrest. ég.* IV, 5 n. 6 [1876].

ⲧⲕⲱⲟⲩ, later **ⲧⲕⲟⲟⲩ**, also (**ⲕⲁϩ**)**ⲕⲱⲟⲩ** (Am. 511–13) = (Gauthier VI, 125), *Ḏw-ḳ3*, lit. 'High Mountain'; = ?, *Ḳww*; Gk. Ἀνταίου πόλις; until recently قاو الكبير, Qâw el-Kebîr, in Middle Egypt, north of Ṭahṭa, but on the east bank.

[H]BRUGSCH, *Dict. géogr.* 1007, 1032, 1039 [1879]; [D]BRUGSCH, *Gr. dém.* 57, § 126 [1855] and *Dict. géogr.* 819–20 [1879], but see Griffith–Thompson, *Dem. Mag. Pap.* I, 184 n. 2 [1904].

ϯⲗⲟϫ (Am. 136–8) = , *T3-i3t-Rṯ* (*Pap. Wilbour*, IV (Index), 68); , *'I(3dt)-Lḏ* (Spiegelberg, *Die dem. Urkunden des Zenon-Archivs*, 6 n. 1, and Pl. 2, a, 2, and b, 2); Gk. Τιλώθις (papyri) or Νειλόπολις (Ptolemy); now دلاص, Dallâṣ, near Beni Suêf in Middle Egypt.

[HD]YOYOTTE's communication; cf. Yoyotte in *Revue d'ég.* 13, 97 [1961].

[B]**ⲑⲙⲟⲩⲓ** (Am. 500–2; Gardiner, *Onom.* II, 151*), lit. 'The Island' (see above, p. 79 (s.v. **ⲙⲟⲩⲉ**, 'island'); Gk. Θμοῦις (Ptolemy), modern village تمى الامديد, Timai el-Amdîd, in the Delta.

[B]**ϯⲙⲓⲛϩⲱⲣ**, (**ⲡ**)**ⲇⲓⲙⲉⲛϩⲱⲣ ⲗⲩⲙⲏⲛ** (=λίμνη, 'lake') (Am. 113–16) = (Gauthier VI, 93–4), *Dmy-n-Ḥr*, lit. 'Town of Horus'; (Brugsch, *Thes.*, 978, inscr. 16; sim. 979, inscr. 19), *P3-dmỉ Ḥr*; Gk. Ἑρμοῦ πόλις ἡ μικρά; Arabic دمنهور الجزيرة, Damanhûr el-Gezîra ('D., the lake'), now دمنهور, Damanhûr, in the Delta.

[H]BRUGSCH, *Dict. géogr.* 87, 521 [1879]; [D]BRUGSCH, *Dict. géogr.* 521 [1879].

ⲡⲧⲓⲙⲉϭⲱⲣϭ, ⲡϭⲓⲙⲉⲛϭⲱⲣϭ (ⲧ > ϭ through assimilation) = **P3-dmy-n-grg*, 'The Town of Hunting'; Gk. Πτεμεγκυρκις, Πτιμινκηρκις, Τεμενκωρκις; a place in the Hermopolite nome.

YOYOTTE, *Rev. d'ég.* 14, 84 [1962].

[B]**ⲧⲁⲙⲓⲁϯ** (Am. 116–17) = ? (*Wb.* V, 456, 10), *Dmytyw*, 'inhabitants of a port' (Pl. of nisbah-adjective formed from Fem. *dmyt*, 'port', *Wb.* V, 456, 8. 9); Gk. Ταμιάθις; now دمياط, Dimyât; Damietta in the Delta.

SETHE, *Die Ächtung feindlicher Fürsten, Völker und Dinge auf altäg. Tongefässscherben des Mittleren Reiches* (=*Abh. Preuss. Ak. d. Wiss.*), 57–8 [1926].

[OS]ⲧⲓⲛ (PGM I, 66, 11; Gardiner, *Onom.* II, 38*, no. 353) = (*Wb.* V, 372, 11. 12; Gauthier VI, 59, 76), *Ṯny*; (Dem. Mag. Pap. 21, 2), *Tny*; Gk. Θίς; somewhere near modern جرجا, Girga, in Upper Egypt.

[H]ERMAN in *ZÄS* 21, 94 [1883] (for Old Coptic); KRALL in *Rec. trav.* 6, 70–1 [1885] (for Sa'îdic); [D]BRUGSCH, *Dict. géogr.* 280–1 [1879].

ⲡⲧⲉⲛⲉⲧⲱ, ⲡⲧⲉⲛⲁⲧⲱ (Z 136, 36) (Am. 385–7) = (Gauthier II, 42), *Pꜣ-tꜣ-n-Wꜣḏyt*, 'The Land of (the goddess) Edjō'; Arabic طنطوا, Ṭanṭwâ, now, كوم الدنطو or كوم الكبير, Kôm ed-Danṭâw or Kôm el-Kebîr in the Delta (Gardiner, *Onom.* II, 192*–4*).

BRUGSCH in *ZÄS* 9, 11 [1871].

[S]ⲡⲉⲧⲡⲏϩ: [B]ⲡⲉⲧⲡⲉϩ (Am. 326) = (*Wb.* I, 120; V, 281; Gauthier VI, 52); (P. Loeb 62, 7), *Tp-iḥw*, lit. 'head of (the) cows'; Gk. Ἀφροδίτης πόλις = modern اطفيح, Aṭfîḥ, on east bank south of Cairo. *Tp-iḥw* was originally an epithet of the local cow-goddess Hathor.

DE ROUGÉ, *Chrest. ég.* IV, 6 n.; 77 n. 1 [1876].

ⲧⲉⲣⲱⲧ (Am. 494–6), name of three localities of which ⲧⲉⲣⲱⲧ(ϣⲙⲟⲩⲛ) = ? (Gauthier VI, 79), *Ṯrti*; present ديروط, *Dêrûṭ*, more precisely ديروط الشريف, Dêrûṭ esh-Sherîf, near Asyût.

DÜMICHEN, *Geschichte des alten Ägyptens*, 190 [1878].

ⲧⲟⲩⲧⲱⲛ, ⲧⲟⲧⲟⲩⲛ (Am. 527–9; Crum, CMSS, 65–6, and in Petrie, *Medum*, 50), town in the Faiyûm = (Er. 627, 1; Gauthier VI, 57, 58, 128), *Tp-tn* = Τεβτῦνις = تطون, Tuṭûn; its ruins at the modern ام البرجات, Umm el-Baragât.

SPIEGELBERG, *Demotische Papyrus* (*CGC*), 21 n. 5 and 6; 574 [1906].

[S]ⲧⲟⲟⲩⲧ, ⲧⲁⲟⲩⲧ, ⲧⲁⲩⲧ (Am. 520–1; Crum, *Ep.* II, 196) = (Gauthier VI, 130–1; Gardiner, *Onom.* II, 22*), *Ḏrti* = الطود, Eṭ-Ṭôd south of Luxor in Upper Egypt.

[S]ⲧⲟⲩϩⲱ, [B]ⲧⲟⲩϩⲟ (Am. 471–2; Crum, *Ryl.* 173 n. 2; Munier in *Bull. Soc. arch. copte*, 5, 241) = (Gardiner, *Onom.* II, 205*), *Tꜣ-wḥt*, lit. 'The settlement' = modern طحا, Ṭaḥâ,

SPIEGELBERG, in *Rec. trav.* 26, 151 [1904].

ⲧⲉϩⲛⲉ, ⲧⲁⲉϩⲛⲉ [Crum 460b] = * (Gauthier VI, 61 and 97–8; and see Gardiner, *Onom.* II, 93*), *Tꜣ-dhnt*, lit. 'The Peak, Crag'; (Er. 651, 1), *Thn*, Gk. Τῆνις = modern طهنا, Ṭihna, in Middle Egypt, on the right bank of the Nile.

[H]DE ROUGÉ, *Chrest. ég.* IV, 23 n. 4 [1876]; [D]SPIEGELBERG in Reinach, *Papyrus grecs et démotiques*, 170, l. 13 with p. 184 n. 16.

[O]**ⲟⲩⲡⲱⲕⲉ** (Crum 286b, s.v. **ⲡⲱϭⲉ**) = (*Wb.* I, 243, 7; 561, 9), *W-pḳr*, lit. 'district of the *pḳr*-tree' (?), holy place at Abydos, see *ZÄS* 41, 107 [1904]; (Er. 141, 4), *w-pḳ*, sacred district at Abydos in which lay the tomb of Osiris.

[HD]MÖLLER in Preisendanz, *Papyri graecae magicae*, I, 74 n. 4 [1928; Möller died in 1921].

NB. **-ⲡⲱⲕⲉ** has therefore nothing to do with **ⲡⲱϭⲉ**, 'fragment'.

[SB]**ⲱⲛ** (Am. 287–8; Gauthier I, 54) = (*Wb.* I, 54, 13; Gardiner, *Onom.* II, 144*–6*), *'Iwnw*; (Er. 24, 5), *'Iwnw*; Babylonian *Ana*, Assyrian *Unu*, Hebrew אֹן, Ων of Septuagint, in Greek usually Ἡλίου πόλις, near the village of El-Matarîya, north of Cairo.

[HD]BRUGSCH, *Dict. géogr.* 40 [1879].

NB. The writing , *Pꜣ-iwnw* (*Ann. Serv.* 51, 441) for the month-name **ⲡⲁⲱⲛⲉ** ('That of the valley') shows that *'Iwnw* and *int*, 'valley' were homonymous and that the name of Heliopolis ought to have been ***ⲱⲛⲉ** if preserved directly; **ⲱⲛ** has been taken over from the Greek form of the Septuagint.

[SB]**ϣⲙⲓⲛ**, [S]**ⲭⲙⲓⲛ** (Am. 18–22) = (Gauthier IV, 177; Gardiner, *Onom.* II, 40*–1*), *Ḫnt-Mn*; (Er. 364, 1), *Ḫnṯ-mn*; Χέμμις of Herodotus II, 91 (back-formation from *Χεμμῖνος, like Θίς from Θινός; now إخميم, Akhmîm.

[H]BRUGSCH, *Geographie*, 213 and Pl. XL, no. 977 [1857]; [D]BRUGSCH, *Gr. dém.* 56, §126 [1855].

[SB]**ϣⲙⲟⲩⲛ** (Am. 167–70), = (*Wb.* III, 283, 2; Gauthier IV, 176; Gardiner, *Onom.* II, 79*, no. 377); (Er. 360, 1), *Ḫmnw*, Greek Ἑρμοῦ πόλις, now الاشمونين, El-Ashmûnein.

[H]BRUGSCH in *ZÄS* 12, 145–6 [1874]; cf. Champollion, *Gr. ég.* 156 [1836]; Brugsch, *Geographie*, 219 and Pl. XLI, no. 1009 [1857]; [D]BRUGSCH, *Gr. dém.* 56, §126 [1855].

SBϣⲉⲛⲉⲥⲏⲧ (Am. 430–2), ϣⲏⲛϫⲏⲑ (Crum, *Coptic MSS from Fayyum*, Appendix, Pap. Bodl. vo. 40) = () (Gauthier III, 69–70; Gardiner, *Onom.* II, 31*, no. 344), *(n3) Šny-n-Stẖ*; Gk. Χηνοβόσκια near Qaṣr wa-'l-Ṣaiyâd; (Cairo 30641, A, 7), *Sny-Stẖ*.

HGAUTHIER, *Dict. géogr.* III, 69–70 [1926]; cf. Daressy in *Rec. trav.* 17, 119 [1895]; DSPIEGELBERG, *Dem. Denkmäler* I, 79 n. 4 [1904].

SBϣⲱⲧⲡ, Bϣⲟⲧⲡ (Am. 423–4) = (*Wb.* IV, 412; Gauthier V, 107–8; Gardiner, *Onom.* II, p. 67*, no. 367), *Š3s-ḥtp*; and , *Šis-ḥtp* = شطب, Shuṭb, in Middle Egypt near Siût.

HLORET in *PSBA* 26, 232 [1904]; cf. Brugsch, *Geographie*, 217 [1857] and Brugsch, *Dict. géogr.* 1040 [1879]; DH. THOMPSON, *A Family Archive*, Index, p. (148), no. 524 [1934].

Bϩⲱ, ϩⲟⲩ (Am. 198–9) = , *Ḥwt*, or , *Ḥwwt* (earliest reference *JEA* 49, Pl. VI, ro. 6) < , *Ḥwt-sḫm* (*Wb.* III, 3, 5; Gauthier IV, 45, 96, 129–30, 226, Gardiner, *Onom.*, II, 33*, no. 346); (Er. 284, 1), *Ḥwt*, once , *Ḥwt-sšmw* (Spiegelberg, *Mythus*, 328, no. 1086) now هو, Hû, in Upper Egypt, near Qena.

HBRUGSCH, *Dict. géogr.* 471–2, 1038 [1879] and Supplément, 1249 [1880], cf. SPIEGELBERG in *Rec. trav.* 35, 38 n. 9 [1913].

SBϩⲛⲏⲥ (Am. 196–8), ϩⲛⲉⲥ (Crum, *Coptic MSS from Fayyum*, LIV, 2) = *Ḥwt-nn-nsw*, earlier , *nn-nsw* (*Wb.* II, 272, 4–6; Gauthier III, 93; IV, 83–4; Gardiner, *Onom.* II, 113*, no. 589); (Er. 285, 1); חָנֵס of the Bible; Assyrian *Ḫininši*; now اهناسية المدينة, Ihnâsya el-Medîna.

HIdentified by de Rougé before 1856 acc. to Lauth, *Manetho*, 65; DKRALL, *Mitt. Erz. Rainer*, VI, 31 [1897] (with doubt).

ϫⲁⲛⲥⲓⲏⲥⲉ (MS. ϫⲁⲛⲉⲓⲏⲥⲉ) = (Gardiner, *Onom.* II, 29*), *Ḥwt-s3-3st* (lit. 'mansion of (the) Son of Isis'), between Koptos and Dendera.
ERMAN in *ZÄS* 21, 95 [1883].

Oϩⲁⲥⲣⲱ = or (*Wb.* III, 168, 12; Gauthier IV, 42–3; Gardiner,

Onom. II, 81*), *Ḥsrt*, name of the necropolis of Hermopolis, i.e. perhaps Tûna el-Gebel, تونة الجبل.

CRUM, *JEA* 28, 23 n. 3 [1942].

Sϩⲟⲩⲱⲣ (Am. 199–200) = , *Ḥ(r)-wr* > , *Ḥ(wt)-wr* (Gauthier IV, 58 and 37; Gardiner, *Onom.* II, 84*–7*) = modern, هور, Hûr, in Middle Egypt, north of El-Ashmûnein.

MASPERO, *PSBA* 13, 511 [1891].

ϩⲁϭⲟⲣ = (Er. 281, 9), *hgr*, 'horse-riding fast messenger', Gk. ἄγγαρος, originally the name of a North Arabian nomad tribe Ἀγάρηνοι or Ἀγραῖοι, Hebr. הַגְרִים.

GRIFFITH, *Ryl.* III, 321 and 421 [1909]; cf. Sethe, *Nachr. Ges. Wiss. Göttingen, Phil.-hist. Klasse*, 1916, 118 ff.

ⲧϫⲕⲱⲟⲩ, less often ϫⲕⲱⲟⲩ, once ⲧϣⲕⲟⲟⲩ and ϫⲉⲕⲟⲟⲩ probably from ⲧϣ-ⲧⲕⲱⲟⲩ (<ⲧⲟϣ-ⲧⲕⲱⲟⲩ), 'nome of Tkou' (see under ⲧⲕⲱⲟⲩ) = إشقاو (كوم), (Kôm) Ishkâw, on the west bank almost opposite Qâw el-Kebîr (Gardiner, *Onom.* II, 59*–60*).

Sϫⲏⲙⲉ, Bϭⲏⲙⲓ (Am. 112–13; 151–3) = (XXth Dyn., Černý, *Late Ramesside Letters*, 29, 5; 31, 7), later , and similarly, *Ḏ3m(t)* (Gauthier VI, 65–6; 105–6; 137; Gardiner, *Onom.* II, 25*–6*); (Er. 678, 4), *Ḏm3*; Arabic شامة in the *Synaxarium*; town built on and around the mortuary temple of Ramesses III at Medînet Habu at Thebes.

HGOODWIN in *ZÄS* 7, 73–5 [1869]; DBRUGSCH, *Dict. géogr.* 988–9 [1879].

Bϫⲉⲙⲛⲟⲩϯ (Am. 411–12) = (*Wb.* V, 361, 1; Gauthier VI, 74), *Ṯb-nṯr*; , *Ṯbn-ntr* (Spiegelberg, *Petubastis*, 86*, no. 581); Assyrian *Ṣabnūti*; Gk. Σεβέννυτος; = سمنّود, Samannûd, in the Delta.

HBRUGSCH in *ZÄS* 9, 12 [1871]; DKRALL in *Mitt. Erz. Rainer*, VI, 29 [1897].

Sϫⲁⲁⲛⲉ, Bϫⲁⲛⲏ, ϫⲁⲛⲓ (Am. 413–14) = (Gauthier VI, 111; Gardiner, *Onom.* II, 199*, no. 417), *Ḏ'nt*; or (Er. 675, 10), *D'ny*; Assyrian *Ṣa'nu*; Hebrew צֹעַן, Gk. Τάνις; now صان الحجر, Ṣân el-Ḥagar, in the eastern Delta.

HROSSI, *Grammatica copto-geroglifica*, 22 [1877]; DKRALL in *Mitt. Erz. Rainer*, VI, 28 and 57 [1897].

INDEXES

1 COPTIC WORDS IN CRUM *A COPTIC DICTIONARY* FOR WHICH NO ETYMOLOGIES ARE GIVEN

ⲕⲁⲡ 113b (cutting tool)
ⲕⲓⲡ 113b
(ⲕⲱⲡϣ) 114b
ⲕⲁⲡⲁϫ[114b
ⲕⲟⲩⲣ 114b (deaf)
ⲕⲟⲩⲣ 114b (blow)
ⲕⲣⲓ 115a
ⲕⲣⲟⲩ 115a
ⲕⲟⲣⲓ 115b
ⲕⲟⲣⲟⲩ 115b
ⲕⲣⲁⲙ 115b
ⲕⲣⲱⲙ 115b
ⲕⲣⲁⲡⲉⲡ 117a
ⲕⲣⲟⲩⲣ 117b
ⲕⲁⲣⲁⲣⲉ 117b
ⲕⲣⲏⲣⲉ 117b
ⲕⲉⲣⲥ 117b
ⲕⲉⲣⲥⲟ 117b
ⲕⲟⲣⲧⲉⲛ 117b
ⲕⲉⲣϩ 119a
ⲕⲣⲁϩ 119a
ⲕⲣⲟϩ 119a
ⲕⲁⲥ 119b (cry)
ⲕⲓⲥⲉ 121a
ⲕⲁⲥⲓⲥⲉ 121b
ⲕⲁⲧⲁⲓ 123a
ⲕⲁϯ 123a
ⲕⲁⲧⲟ 123b
ⲕⲉⲧⲉ 123b
ⲕⲓⲧⲉ 124a (meaning unknown)
ⲕⲓϯ 124a
ⲕⲁⲧⲟⲩⲗⲓ 129a
ⲕⲁⲧⲙⲓⲥ 129a
ⲕⲧⲏⲣ 129a
ⲕⲧⲟⲩ 129a
(ⲕⲱⲧϣ) 129a
ⲕⲁⲧⲁϩ 129b
ⲕⲉⲟⲩⲟⲩ 129b
ⲕⲓⲩⲏ 129b
ⲕⲟⲩⲗⲱⲗ 130a
ⲕⲟⲩⲫⲁⲧ 130a
ⲕⲁⲫⲁϫⲓ 130a
ⲕⲁϣⲉ 130b
ⲕⲁϣⲱ 130b
ⲕⲏϣⲉ(?) 130b
ⲕⲁϣⲟⲩⲗⲓ 131a
ⲕⲁϣⲙⲟⲩ 131a
ⲕⲁϣⲟϣ 131a
ⲕⲱϥ 131a
ⲕⲟⲩϩ 132b
ⲕⲱϩ 132b
ⲕⲱϩⲃ 133b
ⲕⲱϩⲙⲉ 133b
ⲕⲁϫ 134a
ⲕϫⲁ 134b
ⲕⲁϫϩⲉ 134b

ⲗⲓ 135a
ⲗⲉⲃⲁⲛ 137b
ⲗⲁⲃⲁⲥ 137b
ⲗⲓⲃⲟⲥ 137b
ⲗⲏⲃⲧⲉ 137b
ⲗⲓⲕ 138a
ⲗⲟⲩⲕ 138b
ⲗⲟⲩⲕⲗⲁⲕ 139a
ⲗⲟⲕⲙ 139a
(ⲗⲱⲕⲉⲙ) 139b
ⲗⲁⲕⲁⲙⲟⲩ 139b
ⲗⲩⲍ 139b
ⲗⲁⲍⲉ 140a
ⲗⲁⲕⲥⲓ 140a
ⲗⲁⲕⲟⲟⲧⲉ 140a
ⲗⲱⲕϣ 140a
ⲗⲁⲗ 140b
ⲗⲟⲗ 141a
ⲗⲁⲁⲗⲉ 141a
ⲗⲉⲉⲗⲓ 141a
ⲗⲉⲉⲓⲗⲉ 141b
ⲗⲁⲗⲟⲩⲕⲓⲛ 142a
ⲗⲁⲗⲉⲉⲧ 142a
ⲗⲓⲗⲟⲟϩⲉ 142a
ⲗⲁⲙ 142a
ⲗⲟⲙ 142b (meaning unknown)
ⲗⲟⲙ 142b (morsel)
(ⲗⲟⲙⲗⲙ) 143a
ⲗⲓⲙⲏⲛ 143a
ⲗⲁⲙⲣⲏⲧ 143a
ⲗⲉⲙⲁⲥ 143a
ⲗⲁⲙⲧⲓ 143a
ⲗⲁⲙⲱⲟⲩ 143b
ⲗⲉⲛⲧⲏⲛ 142b
ⲗⲁⲡⲛⲓ 144a
ⲗⲁⲡⲥ 144a
ⲗⲉⲯ 144a
ⲗⲱⲡⲥ 144a
ⲗⲉⲡⲁϣⲓ 144b
ⲗⲁⲥ 145a (flax)
ⲗⲏⲥ 145a
ⲗⲱⲱⲥ 145a (fruit)
ⲗⲉⲥⲉ 145a
ⲗⲉⲥⲓ 145a
ⲗⲱⲥⲕ 145b
ⲗⲁⲧ 145b
ⲗⲟⲩⲧ 145b
ⲗⲱⲧⲉ 145b
ⲗⲁⲧⲃⲥ 145b
ⲗⲟⲧϫ 145b
ⲗⲁⲁⲩ 145b
ⲗⲏⲟⲩ 147a
ⲗⲟⲟⲩ 147b
ⲗⲁⲩⲟ 147b
ⲗⲉϣ† 148a
ⲗⲱϣϫ 148a
ⲗⲁϥ 148b
ⲗⲱϥ 148b
ⲗⲁϧⲉⲙ 149a
ⲗⲁϩ 149a
ⲗⲁϩⲏ 149a
ⲗⲟⲓϩⲉ 149a
(ⲗⲁϩⲗϩ) 149b
ⲗⲉϩⲗⲱϩⲉ 149b

(ⲡⲣⲟⲥⲣⲉⲥ) 269b
ⲡⲣⲁϣ 269b
ⲡⲉⲉⲥ 273a
ⲡⲁⲩⲣⲉ 277a
ⲡϫⲱ 285b
ⲡⲓϭⲁ 285b

ⲣⲏⲓ 287b
ⲣⲟ 290a (strand, ply (of cord))
ⲣⲓⲃⲏ 291b
ⲣⲃⲧ 291b
ⲣⲁⲕⲣⲉⲕ 293a
ⲣⲁⲙⲱⲛⲉ 296a
ⲣⲙⲟⲛⲧ 296b
ⲣⲁⲙⲡⲉⲓ 296b
ⲣⲟⲙⲥⲓⲛ 297a
ⲣⲙϩⲛⲉϩ 297b
ⲣⲱⲛ 298b
ⲣⲏⲛⲉ 298b
ⲣⲁⲁⲣ 299a
ⲣⲓⲧⲁ 305b
(ⲣⲱⲧⲃ) 305b
ⲣⲁⲟⲩⲧⲉ 306b
ⲣⲁⲭⲛⲉ 308a
ⲣϩⲉ 310a
ⲣⲱϫⲡ 312b

ⲥⲁ 315a
ⲥⲉⲓ 317a (tree)
ⲥⲟ 317a
ⲥⲱⲓ 318b
ⲥⲃⲉ 321b (meaning unknown)
ⲥⲃⲃⲉ 322a
ⲥⲉⲃⲟⲟⲛ 322b
ⲥⲟⲃⲛ 322b
ⲥⲓϫ 324b
ⲥⲁⲕ 324b
ⲥⲉⲕ 325a
ⲥⲁⲕⲃⲓ 328b
ⲥⲕⲙⲕⲓⲙ 329a
ⲥⲟⲕⲙⲁϫⲓ 329a
ⲥⲕⲟⲣⲕⲉⲣ 330a
ⲥⲉⲕⲥⲓⲕ 330a
ⲥⲓⲕⲏϩⲉ 330a
ⲥⲓⲗⲓ 330b
ⲥⲟⲩⲗⲓ 330b
ⲥⲁⲗⲟⲩⲕⲓ 330b
ⲥⲓⲗⲟⲩⲕⲓ 330b
ⲥⲓⲗⲓⲗ 330b
ⲥⲗⲱⲗ⸗ 330b
ⲥⲱⲗⲁⲗⲉ 330b
ⲥⲉⲗⲓⲗⲉⲛ 330b
ⲥⲱⲗⲙ 330b
ⲥⲗⲉⲡⲗⲓⲡ 331b
ⲥⲗⲟⲡⲗⲉⲡ 331b
ⲥⲗⲁⲁⲧⲉ 332b
ⲥⲗⲁⲧⲗⲉⲧ 333a
ⲥⲟⲗϥ 333a
ⲥⲗⲓϥⲓ 333b
ⲥⲗϩⲟ 333b
ⲥⲗⲓϫ 333b
ⲥⲙⲁ 334b
ⲥⲁⲙⲃⲉϩⲓ 336b
ⲥⲁⲙⲁⲑⲉ 336b
ⲥⲟⲩⲙⲁⲛⲓ 339a
ⲥⲁⲙⲛⲧ 339b
ⲥⲁⲙⲣ⸗ 339b
ⲥⲙⲟⲩⲣ 339b
ⲥⲙⲁⲥ 339b
ⲥⲟⲙⲥ 339b
ⲥⲱⲙⲧ 340b
ⲥⲟⲙⲧⲉ 342a
ⲥⲟⲙϩ 342a
ⲥⲙⲉϩ 342a
ⲥⲉⲙϩⲉⲙ 342a
ⲥⲙⲓϫ 342b
ⲥⲛⲕⲟⲩ 345a
ⲥⲁⲛⲙⲧ 345a
ⲥⲱⲛⲧ 346a (look)
ⲥⲁⲡ 349a
ⲥⲱⲡ 351a (kohl-stick)
ⲥⲟⲡⲉⲧ 353a
ⲥⲓⲣ 353b (jar)
ⲥⲁⲣⲟⲩⲕⲓ 354b
ⲥⲣⲟⲙⲣⲙ 356a (be obscured)
(ⲥⲣⲟⲙⲣⲉⲙ) 356a (enforce)
ⲥⲉⲣⲡ 356a
ⲥⲟⲣⲡ 356b
ⲥⲁⲣⲁⲡⲟⲓ 356b
ⲥⲟⲩⲣⲟⲧ 356b
ⲥⲉⲣⲫⲱⲧ 356b
ⲥⲣⲁϥ 357a
ⲥⲁⲣϥⲉ 357a
ⲥⲣⲁϩ 358a
ⲥⲣⲁϩⲙⲉ 358a
ⲥⲱⲣϫ 358a
ⲥⲓⲱⲥ 358a
ⲥⲁⲥⲉ 358b
ⲥⲓⲥⲉ 358b
ⲥⲁⲥⲉⲗ 358b
ⲥⲓⲥⲙⲏ 358b
ⲥⲁⲧⲉ 360a (fan)
ⲥⲉⲧⲏ 360b
ⲥⲟⲧⲉ 362a
ⲥⲟⲟⲧⲉ 362a
ⲥⲁⲧⲉⲣ 366a
ⲥⲱⲧⲣ 366a
ⲥⲧⲣⲧⲣ 366a
ⲥⲁⲧⲏⲟⲩⲧ 366b
ⲥⲧⲟⲩⲏⲧ 366b
ⲥⲟⲧϩ(?) 367a
ⲥⲁⲓⲟⲩ 367b
ⲥⲛⲟⲩⲓ 369a
(ⲥⲟⲩⲟⲗⲟⲩⲗ) 369a
ⲥⲟⲩⲥⲓⲟⲩ 371a
ⲥⲁⲩϩⲥ 374a
ⲥⲁⲓϣ 374b
ⲥⲟⲉⲓϣ 374b (measure)
ⲥⲱϣⲉ 376b (drag)

ⲫⲱϧⲉⲛ 515b
ⲫⲱϫⲓ 515b

ⲭⲉⲗⲭⲁⲭⲱϥ 516b
ⲭⲁⲛⲥⲣⲱϥ 516b
(ⲭⲱⲣ) 516b
ⲭⲏⲣⲉ 516b
ⲭⲁⲣⲟⲩⲕⲓ 517a
ⲭⲣⲓⲙ 517a
ⲭⲣⲱⲟⲩⲛⲓ 517a
ⲭⲉⲣⲭⲉⲙ 517a
ⲭⲣⲟϣ 517a
ⲭⲁⲣⲱϫⲓ 517a
ⲭⲁⲧⲏⲣ 517b
ⲭⲟⲩⲁⲓⲛ 517b
ⲭⲁϥ 517b
ⲭⲓϥⲧ 517b

ⲱ 517b
ⲱⲗⲓ 522a
ⲱⲗ(ⲉ)ⲙ 522b
ⲱⲙⲕ 523a
ⲱⲛⲧ 525a
ⲱⲛϣ 525a
ⲱⲡⲓϣ 528a
ⲱⲣⲉⲃ 529a
ⲱⲣⲃⲁⲛ 529a
ⲱⲥϭ 531b
(ⲱϣ) 535a
ⲱϣϯ 535b
(ⲱϩ) 536b
ⲱϭⲧ 540b

ϣⲁ 544a
ϣⲁⲓ 544b (new)
ϣⲏⲓ 547b (temples)
ϣⲓ 548b (meaning unknown)
ϣⲓⲱ 549b
ϣⲟ 549b (particle–yea)
ϣⲟⲓ 549b (meaning unknown)
ϣⲟⲓ 549b (arise?)
ϣⲱⲓ 550b
ϣⲁⲁⲃ 550b
ϣⲃⲁ 551a
ϣⲃⲓⲛ 553a (part of sheep's intestine?)
ϣⲓⲃϯ 553b
ϣⲱⲃⲧ 554a
ϣⲉⲃⲟⲓϣ 554b
ϣⲃϣⲓ 554b
ϣⲑⲱⲧ 555a
ϣⲱⲕⲉ 556a
ϣⲱⲕⲁⲥ 557a
ϣⲕⲱϯ 557a
ϣⲟⲕϣⲉⲕ 557a (dig)
ϣⲟⲕϣⲉⲕ 557a (hiss)
ϣⲁⲟⲗ 557b
ϣⲓⲗ 557b
ϣⲟⲗ 557b
ϣⲗⲏ 558b
ϣⲉⲗⲃⲉ 558b
ϣⲁⲗⲟⲩⲕⲓ 558b
ϣⲗⲕⲏⲧ 558b
ϣⲱⲗⲙ 560a (meaning unknown)
ϣⲱⲗⲉⲙ 560a (meaning unknown)
ϣⲗⲉⲙⲗⲉⲙ 560a
ϣⲁⲗⲁⲛⲟⲥ 560a
ϣⲱⲗⲡⲓ 560b
ϣⲗⲟⲡⲗⲡ 560b
ϣⲁⲗⲓⲟⲩ 561a
ϣⲁⲗⲟⲟⲩ 561a
ϣⲁⲗⲁϣⲓⲗ 561a
ϣⲗϣⲓⲗ 561a
ϣⲗϣⲟⲗ 561b
ϣⲟⲗϥ 561b
ϣⲱⲗϩ 562a
ϣⲟⲗϩⲥ 562b
ϣⲗϩⲓⲧ(?) 562b
ϣⲱⲙⲉ 564b
ϣⲙⲟⲩⲗ 565b
ϣⲟⲩⲙⲁⲣⲉ 567a
ϣⲱⲛ 568b
ϣⲏⲛⲉ 569a
ϣⲟⲟⲛⲉ 570b
ϣⲛⲁ 571b (profligate)
ϣⲛⲁ 571b (waste land, same as last?)
ϣⲛⲁ 571b (meaning unknown)
ϣⲟⲩⲛⲓⲥ 572a
ϣⲉⲛⲏⲧ 572b
ϣⲉⲛⲧⲱⲗⲓ 573b
ϣⲉⲛⲧⲏⲥ 573b
ϣⲛⲧⲁⲉⲥⲉ 573b
ϣⲛϣⲱⲧⲉ 573b
ϣⲛⲟⲩϥ 574a
(ϣⲱⲛϩ) 574b
ϣⲏⲡ 574b
ϣⲓⲡⲁ 576b
ϣⲡⲟⲛⲟⲩ 581a
ϣⲉⲡⲁϣ 582a
ϣⲟⲡϣⲟⲡ 582a
ϣⲏⲣ 583a
ϣⲁⲓⲣⲉ 584a
ϣⲁⲣⲟ 584a
ϣⲓⲣⲉ 586a
ϣⲣⲱ 586a (cast forth?)
ϣⲣⲱ 586a (menstruation, same as last?)
ϣⲱⲣⲧ 588b
ϣⲁⲣⲱⲧ 588b
ϣⲣⲱⲧ 588b
(ϣⲱⲣϣ) 588b
ϣⲣϣⲉ 588b
ϣⲉⲣϣⲓ 588b
ϣⲱⲣϫ 589b
ϣⲱⲥⲙ 589b
ϣⲟⲥⲙⲉⲥ 589b

ϩⲁⲗⲉ 667a

ϩⲁⲗⲏ 667a

ϩⲁⲗⲱ 667a

ϩⲟⲟⲗⲉ 667a

ϩⲱⲗⲉ 667b

ϩⲱⲱⲗⲉ 667b (pluck)

ϩⲱⲱⲗⲉ 667b (meaning unknown)

ϩⲗⲓ 667b

ϩⲁⲗⲃ- 668a

ϩⲁⲗⲓⲃ 668a

ϩⲟⲗⲕⲓ 668b

ϩⲗⲟⲩⲗ 669a

ϩⲱⲗⲉⲙ 670a (seize)

(ϩⲱⲗⲉⲙ) 670b (meaning unknown)

ϩⲁⲗⲙⲏ 670b

ϩⲁⲗⲙⲓ 670b

ϩⲉⲗⲙⲏ 670b

ϩⲉⲗⲙⲓⲥ 671a

ϩⲁⲗⲙⲏϩⲉ 671a

ϩⲗⲟⲡⲗ(ⲉ)ⲡ 671a

ϩⲗⲟⲥⲧ(ⲉ)ⲛ 671b

ϩⲁⲗⲁⲧⲏⲩ 672a

ϩⲗⲟⲩⲗⲱⲟⲩ 672a

ϩⲁⲗ̣ϣⲏⲩ 672a

ϩⲱⲗϥ 672a

ϩⲟⲗϩⲗ 672a (slay)

ϩⲉⲗϩⲉⲗⲉⲓ 672b

ϩⲉⲗϩⲓⲗⲉ 672b

ϩⲁⲗⲁϩⲱⲗ̣[672b

ϩⲁⲗⲁϩⲱⲙ 672b

ϩⲗⲟϫⲗⲉϫ̣ 672b

ϩⲁⲗϭⲓⲥ 673b

ϩⲁⲙ 674a

ϩⲏⲙ 674a

ϩⲟⲙ 674a (implement)

ϩⲟⲩⲙ 674b

ϩⲁⲙⲉ 675a

ϩⲁⲙⲏⲓ 675a

ϩⲟⲙⲉ 676a

ϩⲱⲱⲙⲉ 676a

ϩⲙⲓ 676b

ϩⲙⲛ 678a

ϩⲁⲙⲁⲛⲉⲓ 678a

ϩⲟ(ⲟ)ⲙⲉⲥ 679a

ϩⲙⲟⲧ 681a

ϩⲁⲛ- 683a (necessity?)

ϩⲁⲛ 683a (meaning unknown)

ϩⲁⲉⲓⲛ(?) 683a

ϩⲱⲛ 688a (go aground)

ϩⲱⲛ 688b (destroy?)

ϩⲱⲛ 688b (gift at betrothal)

ϩⲏⲛⲉ 689a (body of cart)

ϩⲛⲉ 690b (meaning unknown)

ϩⲛⲁⲩ 693a

ϩⲱⲛϫ 693b

ϩⲁⲡⲥ 696a

ϩⲱⲡϣ 696b

ϩⲏⲣ 697b (meaning unknown)

ϩⲏⲣ† 696b (meaning doubtful)

ϩⲓⲣ† 697a

ϩⲟⲣ 697a

ϩⲱⲣⲁ 697b

ϩⲉⲣⲉ 697b

ϩⲉⲉⲣⲉ 697b

ϩⲏⲣⲉ 697b

ϩⲣⲁ 697b

ϩⲣⲁ⸗ 698a

ϩⲣⲓ 701b

ϩⲣⲟⲉⲓ 701b

ϩⲣⲃ 702a

ϩⲱⲣⲃ 702a

ϩⲣⲏⲃⲉ 702a

ϩ(ⲉ)ⲣⲃⲱⲧ 702a

ϩⲱⲣⲕ 702a

ϩⲣⲟⲕ 702b

ϩⲣⲓⲙ 703a (pelican)

ϩⲣⲓⲙ 703a (artemisia)

ϩⲣⲏⲣ 704a

ϩⲣⲉⲥⲓⲛ 704b

ϩⲟⲣⲧϥ 704b

ϩⲣⲟⲩϫ(ⲉ)ⲃ 706a

ϩⲣⲟⲩⲟⲩϫϥ 706a

ϩⲱⲣϣ 706a (break?)

ϩⲣⲟϩ 708b

ϩⲟⲣϩ(ⲉ)ⲣ 708b

ϩⲁⲣⲁϫ 708b

ϩⲣⲱϫⲉ 708b

ϩⲁⲉⲓⲥ 709b

ϩⲱⲥ 710a (weakling)

ϩⲏⲥⲉ 710b

ϩⲱⲥⲉ 713a

ϩⲁⲧ 713b (meaning doubtful)

ϩⲟⲧ 718b

ϩⲱⲧ 719a

ϩⲧⲁⲓ 722a (deceive)

ϩⲧⲟⲓ 723a

ϩⲟⲧⲛ 724b

ϩϯⲧ 727a

ϩⲁⲩ 728b

ϩⲁⲟⲩⲉ 732a

ϩⲟⲩⲣⲓⲧ 738a

ϩⲟⲩⲱⲣⲧ 738a

ϩⲟⲩⲧ 738a

ϩⲟⲩⲧⲉⲛ 739b

ϩⲟⲩⲏⲟⲩ 739b

ϩⲁⲩϣ 739b

ϩⲟⲓϣ 740a

ϩⲱϣ 740a

ϩⲱϣϥ 740b

ϩⲁϣϩϣ 740b

ϩⲟⲩϥ 741a

ϩϥⲟⲩⲣ 741a

(ϩⲱϥⲧ) 741b

ϫⲏϥ† 795b
ϫⲏϥ 795b (meaning unknown)
ϫⲓϥ 795b
ϫⲟⲩϥ 796a
ϫⲱϥⲓ 796b
ϫϩⲟⲩ 796b
ϫⲁϩ 796b
ϫⲁϩⲗⲉ 797b
ϫϩⲓⲙ 797b
ϫⲁϩⲛⲓ 798b
ϫⲁϩⲁⲟⲩϫⲉⲓ 798b
ϫϩⲁⲁϩ 798b
ϫⲁϫ 799a
ϫⲉϫ 799a
ϫⲱϫ 799a (needle)
ϫⲁ(ⲁ)ϫⲉ 799a
ϫⲁⲁϫⲉ 799b
ϫⲁϫⲱ 800a
ϫⲓϫⲓ 800a
ϫⲉϫⲣⲉ 800b
ϫⲉϫⲥ 800b
ϫⲁϭⲏ 800b

ϭⲁ 802a
ϭⲏ 803a
ϭⲓⲉ 803a
ϭⲓⲏ 803a
ϭⲱ 804b (meaning unknown)
ϭⲱⲃⲉ 805a
ϭⲃⲓⲉ 805a
ϭⲁⲃⲱⲧ 806a
ϭⲁⲃϭⲁⲃ 806a
ϭⲃϭⲱⲃⲉ 806a
ϭⲓⲕⲥ 806a
ϭⲏⲗ 806a
ϭⲱⲗ 806b
ϭⲉⲗⲓ 807b
ϭⲱⲱⲗⲉ 809b (burst, split?)
ϭⲗⲁ 810a
ϭⲗⲏ 810a (strengthen?)
ϭⲗⲟ 810a (vanity)
ϭⲗⲟ 810a (surround)
ϭⲗⲱ 810b (twig)
ϭⲗⲃⲟⲟⲩ 810b (a fish)
ϭⲉⲗⲃⲟⲟⲩ 810b (a plant?)
ϭⲁⲗⲟⲩⲕⲥ 810b
ϭⲗⲓⲗ 811a (axe)
ϭⲗⲁⲙ 811a (kindle)
ϭⲗⲁⲙϭⲗ[ⲙ] 812a
ϭⲱⲗⲡ 812b (create)
ϭⲱⲗⲡ 812b (faggot)
ϭⲱⲗⲡ 813a (projecting roof)
ϭⲗⲁⲡ 813a
ϭⲁⲗⲉⲥ 813a
ϭⲟⲟⲗⲉⲥ 813a
ϭ(ⲉ)ⲗϩ 813b
ϭⲁⲗⲟϫ 814a
ϭⲗⲓϭ 815a
ϭⲗⲟϭ 815b
ϭⲟⲙ 817b
ϭⲓⲙⲉ 818a
ϭⲟⲛ 819b
ϭⲓⲛⲉ 821a
ϭⲛⲟ 821a
ϭⲁⲛⲛⲁⲥ 822a
ϭⲁⲛⲁϩ 824a
ϭⲓⲛϭⲉ 824a
ϭⲓⲛϭⲓⲛ 824b
ϭⲱⲡ 825a (meaning unknown)
ϭⲉⲡⲏ 825a
ϭⲁⲡⲗⲏⲩⲉ 827a
ϭⲓⲡⲥ 827a
ϭⲟⲩⲯ 827a
ϭⲁⲡⲁⲧ 827b
ϭⲁⲡⲉⲧ 827b
ϭⲁⲡϭⲉⲡ 827b
ϭⲁⲣ- 827b
ϭⲱⲣ 827b
ϭⲓⲣⲁ⸗ 827b
ϭⲱⲣⲉ 828a
ϭⲣⲉ 828a (ladle)
ϭⲣⲱ 828a
ϭⲱⲣⲙ 828b
ϭⲣⲓⲙ 828b
ϭⲣⲱⲡ 829a
ϭⲣⲉⲡⲣⲉⲡ 829a
ϭⲣⲏϩⲓ 830a
ϭⲉⲥ 832a (epithet of iron)
ϭⲉⲥ 832a (epithet in Grk. corn assessment)
(ϭⲱⲥ) 832b
ϭⲱⲥ 832b
ϭⲏⲥⲉ 832b
ϭⲟⲥⲧ 832b
ϭⲱⲧⲥ 834a
ϭⲁⲩ 835a (meaning unknown)
ϭⲛⲟⲩ 835a
ϭⲟⲩ 835a
ϭⲱⲟⲩ 835a (be narrow)
ϭⲟⲩⲏⲗ 835b (locust)

2 HIEROGLYPHIC WORDS NOT GIVEN IN ERMAN–GRAPOW *WÖRTERBUCH DER ÄGYPTISCHEN SPRACHE*

ꜣrr 5
ꜣrkt 5
ỉrr 46
ỉsy 122
ỉsp(t) 13
ꜥwꜣw 209
ꜥšꜣ 16
wꜣḏḥ 220
wbꜣ 210
wr 98
wḏḥ (*wdḥ*) 220
wšꜣw 40
bꜣsꜣ 27
brgt 2
prṯ, *prḏ* 129
pš 131
fꜥꜣ 265
fḳꜣ 266
mnty 86
mrynt 88
mḫtr 97
mssbt 91
mšdd 97
mk 80
mtbr 183
nb 106
ngy 119
rwš 142
rfrf 75
rḫt 142
rsyt 139
ḥmt 282
ḥpt 290
ḥry 291
ḥry-ỉb 293
ḫꜣ 267
ḫnd 246
ḫḫ 306
ḫr nꜣ 245
ḫdy 299
ẖdẖd 303
s(ꜣ)ḥ 172
sꜣsꜣ 163
sꜣk ḥꜣty 149
swn 168
sbn 167
sbḥ 148
sp 158
snṯ 156
sḥmy 173
sḥsḥ 175
sḫn 174
sḳrḳr 150
sgꜣ 264
sgrgr 150
stw 165
sḏꜣw 164
šfšf 262
šmt 243
šrr 240
škr 238
ḳs 64
ḳḏ 340
ḳḏ(t) 340
knḥ 60
knḥ 60
krk 330
kḥkḥ 68
ksks 64
ksksty 64
grb 327
grgt 337
tp 191
thm 204
ṯꜣ-n 315
ṯfṯf 44
dhr 196
ḏꜣỉw 309
ḏbḏb 318
ḏḥrt 314

3 DEMOTIC WORDS NOT GIVEN IN ERICHSEN *DEMOTISCHES GLOSSAR*

ꜣwšw 221
ꜣmys 35
ꜣmwnyꜥk 6
ꜣnḏr 10
ꜣḏ 232
ỉwy 45
ỉnbꜣn 80
ỉkr 17
ym 46
ꜥlk 228
ꜥlk 278
ꜥkn 19
ꜥklṯꜣ 19
wꜣḥ sy 145
whyṯ 223
wsr 216
wšyp 221
wgyt pꜣ rꜣ 224
wtby 219
bynt 25
byṯt 27
b[ꜥr]ḥ 26
bkt 21
pynꜥks 25
pꜥy 124
pꜥr 127
pn 126
pr-nfr 128
pḥs 132
pẖ 131
pgy 133
pts 130
mwy 79
mbꜥ 86
mm 82
mnṯ 86
mšḥtỉ 97
mḏꜣl 101
nyn 109
nꜥwḏ 118
nbt 107
nḥb 117
nšyt 115
nt 110
nḏhy 119
rht 143
rḥt 143
rḥṯw 143
lꜣn 74
lbs 75
lms 73
lhs 34
lks 71
lḏlḏ 76
hywt 287
hntw 289
ḥml 284
ḥn 287
ḥrwṯ 294
ḥs 297
ḥtr 302
ḫbn 237
ḫf 261
ḫfꜣ 261
ẖꜣt, *ẖꜣꜥt* 269
ḫty 299
ḫyrḫr 291
ḫnm, *ḫnmꜣt* 288
ḫlpy 280
swḫy 258
sbt 166
spy, *sby* 159
spy 159
splỉlyn 159
smwỉ(t) 154
smḥ 154
snfỉ 157
snsn 156
srf{s}rf 162
slꜣt 151
sḥm 173
sksk 150
st 164
stbḫf 165
stf 166
šp (?) 248
šfšf 262

4 GREEK

5 LATIN

6 AKKADIAN

7 ARABIC

أَثْل 122

أَجَبِيَّة 317

إِجْر 50

إِرْدَب 141

إِشْو 50

أَعْقَد 3

إِيَّل 46

بَدِنْجَان 129

بَرَاءَة 127

بِرْبَة 138

بَرْسِيم 26

بَرْق 33

بُرْنُوف 128

بَشَرُوش 196

بَصَل 101

بَلَح 30

بُورِيّ 25

بُوم 23

تِبْن 203

تُرْمُس 194

تُفَّاح 314

تَلّ 185

تَلَم 186

تَنّ 190

تِنّ 190

جَرَف 63

جِرَان 61

جَفْن 161

جَلَّابِيَّة 327

جَمَل 331

جَار 327

جُونَة 339

حَرَق 296

حُفْنَة 161

(حُفَن pl.)

حَلَقَة 278

(حَلَق pl.)

حَلَمَة 226

حَالُوم 280

حَم 243

حُمُّص 2, 38

حَمُض 285

خَرّ 296

خَرْخَر 296

خَزَم 245

خَيْطَل 238

خَلَّة 239

خَلْخَل 241

خَمِير 245

خَمِيرَة 245

خُنْفُس 37

دَرَجَة 330

دَرَك 313

ذِرَاع 317

رَحَض 90

رَكّ 70

رَكْرَك 71

رَمّ 73

رُمَّان 293

رُمْح 90

رِيش 53

زَحَم 173

فْت 73, 74

زِقْزِق 312

زُنْبُور 276

زَيْت 320

لَبَاءَة 69
لَبَخَة 258
لَبِس 70
لُبُوس 70
لَبْلَب 70
لَبُؤَة 69
لَزّ 76
لَزِج 76, 329
لَزِق 329
لَعِب 73
لَفْت 74
لَفْلَف 75
لَقَّم 71
لُقْمَة 71

لَهَب 75
لُوبِيَه 215
لَاج 76
مَزَج 101
مِسْحَل 92
مُشْط 97
(مِشَاط pl.)
مِلْح 81
مَلَط 81
مِلَاط 81
مِنْجَل 86
مِنْشَار 29
مُوَبَّالَة 183

نَسْر 115
نَضَخ 119
نَهَم 76
هُدْهُد 54
هَلُّوس 280
هَمْهَم 285
هَنَاذَة 289
هَوْجَل 306
وَاح 222
وَحْوَح 30
وَرْد 215
وَلْوَل 211

8 ARAMAIC AND NEW HEBREW

אַרְדַּב 141
אָשְׁפִּין 15
בְּעְבֵּעַ 20
בִּצָּא 31
בַּרְקָא 33
בַּשָּׁשׁ 29
בַּשָּׁשָׁא 29
גוּץ 69
גַּלָּא 312
גָּלָל 56
גְּרִיץ 63
וְרָד 215

זְלַח 313
זָרָה 319
זָרַע 319
חַלְחַל 241
חִלְתָּא 267
חֲמִירָא 245
חֲנָוָאה 247
חִפּוּשִׁית 37
חֲרַק 296
חת 299
חָתוּל 238
טְפְטֵף 44

יַוְנָאִין 213
כּוּזָא 69
כּוֹזָא 69
כּוֹר 61
כַּכְּרָא 334
כְּלְבָּא 55
כְּנַע 332
כַּעְכָּא 341
כַּפָּא 334
כְּרָא 335
כְּרָעָא 335
כִּתָּן 256
לָגֵינְתָא 71

9 HEBREW

כָּלִיל 328
כָּנַע 332
כַּף 334
כֹּפֶר 61
כָּרָה 335
כְּרָעַיִם 335
כַּרְפַּס 328
כְּתֹּנֶת 256

לָבִיא 69
לְבִיָּא 69
לָבַשׁ 70
לֹג 70
לַהַב 75
לֶהָבָה 75
לָחַךְ 76
לָחַם 81
לָחַץ 76
לָעַב 73

מִגְדָּל 102
מַגָּל 86
מְגִלָּה 312
מֵזַח 101
מֶלַח 81
מֶלֶט 81
מֹלֶךְ 81
מָסַךְ 101
מֶסֶךְ 101
מֶרְכָּבָה 27
מַשּׂוֹר 29

נֶבֶל 22
נֵבֶל 118
נָבַע 20
נָזָה 119

נָחַר 296
נָטַף 34
נָקַר 107
נֶשֶׁר 115

סוּף 322
סִרְפַּד 162

עָב 274
עָגִיל 19
עֲגָלָה 19
עֲדָשִׁים 19
עוּל 4
עֲטִישָׁה 10
עָקָר 19
עֲקָרָה 19
עֲרָבָה 11
עֵרָבוֹן 11
עָרַךְ 296

פּוּל 225
פָּלַג 125
פָּצַע 132
פָּרַח 128
פָּרַס 225
פָּרַץ 129
פָּרַק 128
פָּתַח 130

צְלֹחִית 314
צַלַּחַת (pl. צֵלָחוֹת) 313, 314
צָרַר 318

קוּר 61
קוּרֵי עַכָּבִישׁ 116
קָטַף 66
קָלָה 327
קַלַּחַת 329

קֶלַע 326
קָמַץ 341
קֹמֶץ 341
קָצַב 340
קָצַח 341
קָצַץ 340
קֵרֵחַ 63
קָרַע 62
קָרַץ 63
קָרַר 233
קֶשֶׁר 64

רַהַט (pl. רְהָטִים) 294
רָחַץ 90
רַךְ 70
רִמּוֹן 293
רֹמַח 90
רָצַח 76
רָצַץ 76

שְׂאֹר 160
שָׂכַר 264
שַׂעֲרָה 162
שָׂפָה 159
שַׂק 149
שָׂרַג 240
שַׂרַפַּת 162

שֵׁבֶט 238
שׁוּשַׁן 260
שַׁחַק 263
שִׁטָּה 247
שָׁלוֹם 240
שֶׁלַח 241
שָׁלַף 240
שָׁמֵן 153

10 SYRIAC

11 PERSIAN

12 MISCELLANEOUS

13 PLACE NAMES
A. GREEK

Παθῦρις 351
Παθυρίτης 351
Πάτουμος ᾿Αραβίας 351
Πηλούσιον 349
Πιλάκ 348
Πρίμις, Πρῆμ(ν)ις 349
Πτεμεγκυρκις 354
Πτιμινκηρκις 354
Πτολεμαὶς ἡ ῾Ερμείου 350

Σαΐς 352
Σαμαχήρ, -ρε, Σαμαήρ 154
Σεβέννυτος 358
Συήνη 352
Σωφθις 352

Ταμιάθις 354
Τάνις 358
Τεβτῦνις 355
Τεμενκωρκις 354
Τεντύρα, Τεντυρίς 347
Τῆνις 356
Τιλώθις 354
Τρίφιον 343

Φάρβαιθος 351

*Χεμμῖνος 356
Χέμμις 356
Χηνοβοσκία 163, 357
Χνουμωνεβιήβ 345

Ων 356

B. LATIN

Asfynis 353

C. ARABIC

أبصاع 350
إبطو 344
أبو تشت 351
أبو شوشة 351
أبو صِير بنا 344
أبو صير الملق 350
أتريب 343
إخميم 356
أدريب 343
إدفو 353
أرمنت 351
إسفحت 352
إسنا 352
أسوان 352
أسيوط 353
الأشمونين 356
أصفون 353
أصفون المطاعنة 353
أطفيح 355
الأقصر 349
الأقصرين 349
أم البرجات 355
أهناسية المدينة 357
أوسيم 344

بتشت 351
برجوط 343
بركة 343
بلاق 348
بنا أبو صير 349
بنكلاوس 348
البهنسا 348
بوصير 344

تطون 355
تل أتريب 343
تل بسطة 348
تل البلامون 348
تل الرطابة 351
تل فراعين 344
تل الفرما 349
تل اليهودية 348
تمى الأمديد 354
تونة الجبل 358

الجبلين 351
جرجا 355
جزيرة السواقى 349

دفانيس 353
دقناش 353
دلّاص 354
دمنهور 354
دمنهور الجزيرة 354
دمياط 354
دير ريفة 344
ديروط 355

D. ARAMAIC AND HEBREW

E. FROM CUNEIFORM SOURCES

Lightning Source UK Ltd.
Milton Keynes UK
UKHW04f2111220718
326118UK00001B/5/P

9 781108 013994